DATA NETWORKS
Concepts, Theory, and Practice

Uyless Black

PRENTICE HALL, Englewood Cliffs, New Jersey 07632

Library of Congress Cataloging-in-Publication Data
Black, Uyless D.
  Data networks.

  Includes bibliographies and index.
  1. Computer networks.   2. Data transmission systems.
I. Title.
TK5105.5.B565   1989   004.6   88-25385
ISBN 0-13-198466-7

Editorial/production supervision: Evalyn Schoppet
Interior design: Meryl Poweski
Interior artwork: Asterisk Group
Cover design: Meryl Poweski
Manufacturing buyer: Mary Noonan

©1989 by Prentice-Hall, Inc.
A Division of Simon & Schuster
Englewood Cliffs, New Jersey 07632

Printed in the United States of America

10 9 8 7 6 5 4 3 2 1

ISBN 0-13-198466-7

Prentice-Hall International (UK) Limited, *London*
Prentice-Hall of Australia Pty. Limited, *Sydney*
Prentice-Hall Canada Inc., *Toronto*
Prentice-Hall Hispanoamericana, S.A., *Mexico*
Prentice-Hall of India Private Limited, *New Delhi*
Prentice-Hall of Japan, Inc., *Tokyo*
Simon & Schuster Asia Pte. Ltd., *Singapore*
Editora Prentice-Hall do Brasil, Ltda., *Rio de Janeiro*

This book is dedicated to Holly J.

Contents

PART II THE LAYERS OF A DATA NETWORK

Preface

This book is intended to provide the reader with a detailed explanation of data communications systems and computer networks. It is the product of almost two years of research, writing, editing, and rewriting. I hope the book will be as satisfying for you to read as it was for me to write.

The book is intended for use by data communications professionals and students. It is designed as an introductory text and is also suited for mid-level college courses. It can serve as a textbook for a two-semester class. It is also intended to be a reference and has extensive explanations of the more widely used standards and products in the industry.

ORGANIZATION AND NOTATIONS

The book is organized into three parts. Part I, Concepts and Theory, describes the basics of communications theory and concepts, with emphasis on both analog and digital systems. Part II, The Layers of a Data Network, is organized around the OSI (Open Systems Interconnection) seven-layer model. Each chapter in Part II is organized as follows:

Introduction to the services provided in the layer.

A more detailed examination of these services.

Discussions on the more prevalent CCITT, ISO, IEEE, EIA, and ANSI specifications used in the layer.

Examples of the IBM and DEC protocols that reside in the layer.

Description of the more widely used U.S. Department of Defense protocal that reside in the layer.

Part III, Networks for Special Applications, is devoted to specialized systems and networks. Although several of the topics in Part III could have been placed in the first two parts, they span several topics and layers. Moreover, their breadth, importance, and specialized nature necessitate separate treatment.

I have attempted to partition the subjects into individual chapters, but in some instances a standard or a vendor's product does not always fit neatly into one chapter or layer. For example, the X.400 recommendations span the applications and presentation layers. The same holds true for several vendors' systems. In recognition of this situation, these standards and products are explained in the chapters that most closely match their functions and the vendor's or standards group's interpretation of where they reside.

It is impossible to include all the specifications from all the standards organizations in one book. To lend continuity to the book, the major CCITT/ISO recommendations are explained for each layer. The 1988 CCITT Blue Book recommendations have been included where appropriate. Other standards are also covered in the layers where they are prevalent (as an example, EIA-232 at the physical layer).

IBM and DEC protocols are described in each layer due to the positions these companies hold in the data communications and network industries. The Department of Defense systems are also explained due to their influence on vendors' products and international standards. The reader may choose to skip this material without any loss of continuity.

The data link and network layers are each divided into two chapters in Part II. This division is required because of the scope of the subjects. Moreover, many vendors and standards groups now divide these layers into sublayers.

Several of the chapters contain appendices which are useful for the reader who wishes to know more about the details of certain subjects. However, the appendices do not have to be read to comprehend the other material in the chapter. Each appendix is referred to at the appropriate point in the chapter.

Questions following each chapter include true/false, multiple choice, and short essay questions. Suggested answers are provided for many of them. The remaining answers are found in the Instructor's Manual.

References are identifed with the first four letters of the person's name (or book, etc.), followed by the last two digits of the year of publication (or the letters "ND" if a date is unavailable). A bibliography for these references is provided at the end of the book. The CCITT, EIA, ISO, IEEE, and ANSI standards are cited with the specific number of the recommendation.

No agreement exists in the industry on how to depict the format of data units. Some organizations draw the unit with the most significant digit on the left, and others draw it on the right. No attempt was made to change them to a common format. This book follows the conventions of each organization so that material agrees with the original specification document.

Acknowledgments

Many people have contributed to this book, and I wish space were available to acknowledge and thank all of them. I certainly owe special thanks to the standards organizations. The individuals in these organizations and the people participating in the many standards development committees deserve a credit line on the cover of this book as much as the author. I can only commend the selfless work of these individuals and thank them for their contributions to our industry.

I am indebted to the following publishers for permission to use their material:

Figures 2-17, 3-1, 3-2, and 3-6, and Table 3-6 from HeathKit/Zenith Educational Systems.

Figures 3-34, 3-35, and 3-36 from *Digital Telephony* by John Bellamy, © 1982 by John Wiley & Sons, Inc.

Figures 3-22, 4-10, and 5-4 form *Engineering & Operations in the Bell System*, 2d ed., prepared by members of Bell Telephone Laboratories, Inc., © 1983 by Bell Telephone Laboratories, Inc.

Table 6-1 from *Data Compression* by Gilbert Held, © 1983 by John Wiley & Sons, Ltd.

Figures 10-16 and 10-18 from "Automatic-Repeat-Request, Error-Control Schemes," by Shu Lin, Daniel J. Costello, Jr., and Michael J. Miller, *IEEE Communications Magazine*, Vol. 22, No. 12, December 1984. © 1984 by IEEE.

Figures 3-15 and 3-16 from "Modulation Techniques for Microwave Digital Radio" by T. Naguchi, Y. Dardo, and J. A. Nossek, *IEEE Communications Magazine*, Vol. 24, No. 10, October 1986. © 1986 by IEEE.

Figure 6-8 from *An Introduction to Information Theory* by John R. Pierce, © 1980 by Dover Publications, Inc.

Figure 18-15 from "Distributed SNA," *Data Communications*, February 1987. © 1987 by McGraw Hill, Inc. All rights reserved.

Figures 4-6, 7-13, 20-18, and 20-19 from *Data and Computer Communications* by William Stallings. © 1985 by MacMillan Publishing Company.

Figure 20-14 from "Flow Control" by Werner Bux, *Data Communications*, February 1986. © 1986 by McGraw Hill, Inc. All rights reserved.

Excerpts from CCITT recommendations X.25, X.224, and X.225 contained in Chapters 13, 15, and 16 respectively were authorized by the ITU/CCITT organizations, the copyright holders. The choice of these excerpts is that of the author and does not affect ITU/CCITT in any way. Full text may be obtained from ITU Sales Section, Place des Nations, Geneva, Switzerland.

Valerie Ashton, my editor at Prentice Hall, was a very positive and important contributer to this book, and I thank her for her patience and faith in the ideas that led to its production. Evalyn Schoppet was my production editor, and I was fortunate to have her in my corner. I certainly am grateful to her for all her efforts. I would also like to extend my thanks to Richard Lutzke for his superior artwork.

My "extended family" has provided me support and friendship, some for many years. Their presence in my life, however short or long, has been a source of joy. The families of Boose, DeRose, DiTullio, Dietz, Fitzpatrick, Hammock, Hughes, Lombardi, Malin, Nold, Mahoney, Santamauro, Schleicher, Stum, Vistins, and Waters have my thanks and my love.

My son, parents, brothers and sisters-in-law have supported me in all my efforts. To Ed, Ross and Cherrill, Tom and Kaky, thank you. To my nephew Ronnie, thanks for giving me the impetus to read something each weekend besides technical journals: the sports page.

CHAPTER 1

Introduction

INTRODUCTION

What was once extraordinary is now commonplace. Twenty years ago, the computer was considered by most people to be a mysterious, esoteric machine. Very few people understood even the most rudimentary aspects of the computer and most individuals viewed it with mistrust and suspicion. On countless occasions, the computer was blamed for problems that were actually the fault of humans. Those who used computers were said to be associated with a *priesthood*, a term that was used in a derogatory sense to connote a profession that operated in a world largely unknown to the general public.

In less than two decades, the computer has entered the mainstream of our personal and professional lives and has dramatically reshaped our society. The computer has literally created a technological revolution.

Today, the computer is accepted as simply another tool for doing work. Indeed, many younger people take the computer for granted. They are not aware of the B.C. period (before computers). They view a computer commercial on television with the same nonchalance as an automobile advertisement. Discussions at parties often revolve around the latest software package for a personal computer. These now mundane events were simply unthinkable twenty years ago.

As the power and speed of the computer increase, its impact will be even more profound in the future than it is today. As humans become more computer literate, computers will become more people literate. The application of artificial intelligence (AI) will provide services to our society that will even surpass the imagination of writers of today's most far-fetched science fiction.

A vital factor in this information revolution is the use of communications systems to connect computers together. Facilities we take for granted today, such as automated teller machines, personal computer information services, automated factories, and space programs are all dependent upon communications facilities to support the transfer of information between computers' files and data bases. The information revolution also is dependent on communications systems.

Like the computer industry, the communications industry is growing and changing at a fantastic pace. Both computers and communications are being driven by the continuing progress in the development of integrated circuits, lightwave technology, and in the not too distant future, superconductors will bring about more change. It is difficult to think of other technologies that have changed at such a rapid rate. Consider the following:

- Twenty years ago, the maximum transfer rate on a communications line was 1.5 million bits per second. Today, optical fiber is capable of a transfer rate of over 600 million bits per second.
- Today, a small personal computer has the processing power of a room-size mainframe of the 1960s.
- Twenty years ago, a printer could produce a few hundred lines of print per minute. Today, laser printers produce output at the rate of over 20,000 lines per minute.
- Twenty years ago, a few hundred logic elements could be placed onto a single hardware chip. Today, several thousand elements are on one chip, and it is predicted that 100 million elements per chip is attainable by 1990.
- Optical switches are now being manufactured that are one fourth the size of the head of a dwarf ant. These switches process data at a rate of 20 billion bits per second. To relate this figure to something more meaningful, this switch can process (examine, switch, etc.) over 10,000 copies of the book you are currently reading—in one second.

Both technical and social scientists believe these trends will continue. The items in the list above will probably be commonplace in a few short years. The rate of change seems to be increasing exponentially.

Our goal in this book is to examine one aspect of this revolution: the role of communications in the use of computers. To meet this goal, we will have to go into considerable detail. It will require some patience and fortitude on the part of the reader. However, as Goethe wrote, "What we do not understand, we do not possess." In no way can we hope to cope with the revolution under way, if we do not understand its foundations. Indeed, we can paraphrase Goethe's remark and apply it to computers and communications: "What we do not understand, we do not process"; or worse still, "we process erroneously."

This book is a modest attempt to help the reader to gain an understanding of how communications systems fulfill the vital role of linking computers together. With the introduction behind us, let us now examine some rather fascinating similarities between the communications of humans and the communications of machines.

Communications: Humans and Machines

Humans have been using symbols to communicate for many years. As early as 15 B.C., the Seirites (in the Red Sea area) developed a system of using letters which were strung together to form sentences. This was one of the first times in recorded history when symbols were put together to form both written and oral communications.

Computers and terminals also communicate with each other through symbols. These symbols are called codes. The codes provide instructions to the machines and direct their actions and interactions. The codes are similar to human languages. Indeed, communications between humans are similar in many ways to communications between machines.

For example, assume a dialogue is to take place between two computers. The computers perform the interaction by sending several signals (codes): (a) an indication that data is forthcoming (as in a human's "code" of hello); (b) codes that represent data (like a human's conversation); (c) an indication that the machine has completed its transmission (as in the human's good-bye). Like humans, the machine may repeat the "conversation" (some humans repeat conversations over and over again).

Each computer transmits and receives data, until one machine conveys a "good-bye" with the use of a special code. The dialogue is then completed. The two machines have finished the communications process.

Machines and people communicate on two levels. One level is physical and the other is logical. The physical level is a means to an end: to enable logical communications to take place. Physical communications entail:

- *Humans*: Getting the listener's attention by providing sufficient speech of good quality (loudness, pitch, and enunciation) to allow recognition.
- *Machines*: Alerting the receiver to the incoming signal by providing a signal with minimal distortion (sufficient amplitude, proper frequency, and accurate symbol representation) to allow detection and recognition of the codes.

If a physical connection is achieved, machines and people can then communicate logically. However, the physical level must always be operable if logical communication is to take place.

Table 1-1 provides a comparison of the various logical interactions that take place in both human and machine communications. The table contains some new terms that are explained later in the book.

While Table 1-1 is a somewhat facetious example of human and machine communications, it is quite accurate in showing similarities. How-

TABLE 1-1. Human and Machine Signals

Functions of Signals	Human Signals	Equivalent Machine Signals
Gaining receiver's attention (beginning communications)	Greeting, such as "hello"	Special synchronization codes, called syn (SYN), flag or start
Identification of communicator	"This is Mr. Smith..."	Codes to depict the name or address of the machine
Ongoing communications	A conversation	Codes representing symbols and letters of a language
Controlling communications	"Talk to me"	A code representing a poll signal
Controlling communications	"I want to talk to you"	A code representing a select signal
Controlling communications	"You are talking too fast" or "Go away, I'm busy"	Receive not ready code (RNR) or acknowledgment but wait code (WACK)
Controlling communications	"You are talking too slowly" or "I'm ready to listen"	Receive ready code (RR) or enquire code (ENQ)
Comprehensible communications	"I understand"	Positive acknowledgment code (ACK)
Incomprehensible communications	"I do not understand; please say again"	Negative acknowledgment code (NAK)
Incomprehensible communications: cannot be made comprehensible (and may never be)	"I do not understand; you will have to talk to my boss" or "Let's form a committee"	Abort code or execution of a higher level instruction in the machine
Relay of communications	"Would you tell Mr. Smith that I ...."	Use of switches
Protection of communications	"Don't tell anyone about this, but...."	Use of encryption/decryption methods
Ceasing communications	"Good-bye"	End-of-transmission codes (EOT) or stop bits

ever, communication between machines is quite primitive in comparison to communication between humans. The vast difference between the "intelligence" of the machine and that of the human mind is due to the fantastic (and largely unexplained) inferential power of the human brain.

As an example, humans often infer accurate meaning in speech, even though some individual words in the speech are not heard and are "lost" (due to noise, inattention, etc.). Machines cannot reconstruct lost transmissions (unless they are in the small minority of machines that use artificial intelligence [AI], and even these machines pale in comparison to the inferential power of the human mind). The communications process that humans take for granted and use almost unconsciously (such as the "signals" in Table 1-1) must be implemented in a machine with exacting and laborious instructions and codes.

Fortunately, because the machine is quite limited in its intelligence, its instructions and codes can be implemented with well-ordered, step-by-step logic (and a limited set of codes). Consequently, the process of machine communications can be understood—if one takes the time and effort to study it.

Our simple comparison must also emphasize that a machine designed properly and instructed accurately will seldom misconstrue a code or symbol received from another machine. The very limits of its intelligence set a limit on its inferential power. In contrast (and alas) humans often misconstrue their signals to each other because of the vast and complex sets of values, motives, and prejudices that every person possesses. Moreover, the humans' codes are numerous and complex—just consider the diversity of languages as an example.

Thus, we can conclude that computers do not communicate easily due to their limited "intelligence." Yet computers usually communicate without ambiguity if (a) they are instructed (programmed) correctly and (b) the communications signals between them are not distorted. In contrast, humans communicate with each other with relative ease because of their vast intelligence, but their intelligence often creates ambiguities that can lead to many misunderstandings between them.

Fortunately, our task in this book is to examine machine communications—a much simpler job than examining communications between humans. First, we examine some basic terms and components used in communications between computers and terminals. Our goal in the remainder of this chapter is to develop an understanding of several basic concepts in data communications.

BASIC COMPONENTS OF A
DATA COMMUNICATIONS SYSTEM

The purpose of a data communications system is to transport data between users' computers, terminals, and applications programs. While the concept is simple, the actual effort involves many steps. We hope to describe and clarify these steps in this book, and Figure 1-1 will get us started. It shows the basic components of a data communications system.

The user application resides in the data terminal equipment or DTE. DTE is a general term used to describe the end-user machine, which is usually a computer or terminal. The DTE could be a large computer or a small machine such as a terminal or personal computer. The term user station (or station) is also used in this book to describe the DTE. The end-user applica-

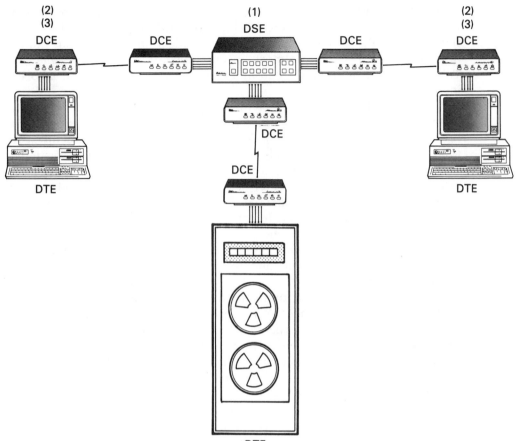

DTE: Data Terminal Equipment (User Station)
DCE: Data Circuit Terminating Equipment (2)
DSE: Data Switching Equipment (Switch)
⌐⌐: Communications Link

Notes: (1) Not used in some systems
       (2) DCE not present in some systems (short connections)
       (3) DCE may be placed inside the DTE

FIGURE 1-1. Basic Components of a Data Communications System

tions process (AP) and data files reside at the DTE. The AP is another name for a user program.

The function of a data communications system is to interconnect the DTEs so that they can share resources, exchange data, and provide back-up for each other.

The path between the DTEs is called a line, link, circuit, or channel. It may consist of wires, radio signals, or light transmissions. A telephone company often provides this link between the user devices.

Figure 1-1 also shows the data circuit-terminating equipment (DCE). Its function is to connect the DTEs into the communication line. The DCEs designed in the 1960s and 1970s were strictly communication devices. However, in the last few years, the machines have incorporated more user functions, and today some DCEs contain a portion of a user application process. Nonetheless, the primary function of the DCE is to provide an interface of the DTE into the communication link.

The DCE may be located inside the DTE or stand alone as a separate unit. Wherever it is located, it is used primarily to convert the signals representing user data to a form acceptable to the receiving channel. As a simple example, it might convert an electrical signal from a terminal to a light signal for an optical fiber link. As we shall see, the DCE performs many other important tasks for the data communications link.

The DTEs and DCEs communicate with protocols. Protocols are agreements on how the machines "converse" with each other. They may include the logic and codes which stipulate a required or recommended convention or technique. Typically, several levels of protocols are required to support an end-user application, and may be implemented in both software and hardware. The lower level protocols are usually found in hardware, and the upper levels use software.

The link is often connected by another component, the DSE (data switching equipment), or switch. As Figure 1-1 shows, the switch allows the DTEs to use different channels at different times to communicate with different user stations. This arrangement is known as networking. The DSE provides other important functions such as routing around failed or busy devices and channels. The DSE may also route data to the final destination through other switches.

Many computers and terminals can be interconnected to form networks. This arrangement may or may not use a switch. In Figure 1-1, a switch performs the interconnections that move the data through the network. This type of network is called a switched network.

Another approach is the broadcast network. All stations share a common channel, and a station transmits its signal to all other stations. The stations "copy" the signal if it is destined for them. Radio systems, such as CB, are examples of broadcast networks. Television and commercial radio are other examples.

CODES

Codes are the symbols used by the machines to direct their actions. The codes are based on binary numbers. Most of us are familiar with the decimal number system, consisting of the numbers 0-9. However, machines and the interconnecting channels are designed to support only two signal states: 0 or 1. For example, the binary equivalent of 394 is 110001010. Its decimal value can be established through positional notation:

Bit Positions (4 3 2 1) →	0000	0001	0010	0011	0100	0101	0110	0111	1000	1001	1010	1011	1100	1101	1110	1111
(8 7 6 5) ↓																
0000	NUL	DLE	DS		SP	&	-									0
0001	SOH	DC1	SOS				/		a	j			A	J		1
0010	STX	DC2	FS	SYN					b	k	s		B	K	S	2
0011	ETX	DC3							c	l	t		C	L	T	3
0100	PF	RES	BYP	PN					d	m	u		D	M	U	4
0101	HT	NL	LF	RS					e	n	v		E	N	V	5
0110	LC	BS	EOB	UC					f	o	w		F	O	W	6
0111	DEL	IL	PRE	EOT					g	p	x		G	P	X	7
1000		CAN							h	q	y		H	Q	Y	8
1001		EM							i	r	z		I	R	Z	9
1010	SMM	CC	SM		¢	!	|	:								
1011	VT				.	$	,	#								
1100	FF	IFS		DC4	<	*	%	@								
1101	CR	IGS	ENQ	NAK	(	)	_	'								
1110	SO	IRS	ACK		+	;	>	=								
1111	SI	IUS	BEL	SUB	|	¬	?	"								□

FIGURE 1-2. EBCDIC CODE

$$1 \times 2^8 + 1 \times 2^7 + 0 \times 2^6 + 0 \times 2^5 + 0 \times 2^4 + 1 \times 2^3 + 0 \times 2^2 + 1 \times 2^1 + 0 \times 2^0$$

or $\quad 1 \quad + \quad 1 \quad + \quad 0 \quad + \quad 0 \quad + \quad 0 \quad + \quad 1 \quad + \quad 0 \quad + \quad 1 \quad + \quad 0$

or $\quad 256 \quad + \quad 128 \quad + \quad 0 \quad + \quad 0 \quad + \quad 0 \quad + \quad 8 \quad + \quad 0 \quad + \quad 2 \quad + \quad 0$

or $\quad 394_{10}$

Each binary digit is called a bit. A group of eight bits makes up a byte or octet (although in some systems seven bits comprise a byte).

Binary numbers and codes are represented by several signalling techniques. The data can be represented by simply switching a current on or off; by changing the direction of current flow, or by measuring a current and its associated electromagnetic field. It is also possible to measure the voltage state of the line (such as on/off voltage, or positive or negative voltage) to represent binary 1s and 0s. Increasingly, optical fiber systems are used to transmit light pulses to represent binary 1s and 0s.

In addition to number representations, data communications systems must also represent other symbols, such as the letters of the alphabet or special characters (like the question mark, ?).

The early codes used in data communications were designed for telegraphic transmission. For example, the antiquated Morse code consists of dots and dashes in a particular sequence to represent characters, numbers, and special characters. The dots and dashes represent how long the telegraph operator presses the key on the transmitter to produce an electrical current.

Figures 1-2 and 1-3 are examples of two codes in wide use today: the

Bit Positions			7	0	0	0	0	1	1	1	1
			6	0	0	1	1	0	0	1	1
4	3	2	1	5	0	1	0	1	0	1	0	1
0	0	0	0	NUL	DLE	SP	0	@	P	\	p
0	0	0	1	SOH	DC1	!	1	A	Q	a	q
0	0	1	0	STX	DC2	''	2	B	R	b	r
0	0	1	1	ETX	DC3	#	3	C	S	c	s
0	1	0	0	EOT	DC4	$	4	D	T	d	t
0	1	0	1	ENQ	NAK	%	5	E	U	e	u
0	1	1	0	ACK	SYN	&	6	F	V	f	v
0	1	1	1	BEL	ETB	'	7	G	W	g	w
1	0	0	0	BS	CAN	(	8	H	X	h	x
1	0	0	1	HT	EM	)	9	I	Y	i	y
1	0	1	0	LF	SUB	*	:	J	Z	j	z
1	0	1	1	VT	ESC	+	;	K	[	k	{
1	1	0	0	FF	FS	'	<	L	\	l	:
1	1	0	1	CR	GS	–	=	M	]	m	}
1	1	1	0	SO	RS	·	>	N	∧	n	~
1	1	1	1	SI	US	/	?	0	–	o	DEL

FIGURE 1-3. ASCII/IA5 Code

EBCDIC code, developed and sponsored by IBM, and the ASCII code, published by the American National Standards Institute (ANSI). The ASCII code is an international standard, in that it is in conformance with the International Alphabet 5 or IA5. The EBCDIC is widely used primarily because of IBM's position in the industry. EBCDIC is an eight-bit code. The bit positions in Figure 1-2 are arranged to show the first four bits at the top of the table with the remaining four bits to the side of the table. The ASCII code is a seven-bit code, although many vendors add an eighth bit for error-checking purposes. This bit, called a parity bit, is explained in Chapter 7 of this book. (The reader should examine Table 1-1 to locate the ACK, NAK, EOT and SYN codes in Figures 1-2 and 1-3.)

The codes perform several important functions, and we will refer to them throughout this book.

TRANSMISSION SPEEDS

Data are transmitted between machines using bit sequences to represent codes. The speed of the data transmission is described in bits per second (or bit/s). Typical speeds of data communications systems are shown in Table 1-2. Later chapters discuss the reasons (and trade-offs) for the channel bit rates. Table 1-3 is also provided to explain commonly used terms. For example 9600 bit/s is often shortened to 9.6 Kbit/s (that is, 9.6 kilobit/s).

The data communications world is fairly slow relative to the computer world. For example, a conventional data processing system with disk files attached to computers operates at 10 megabits per second (Mbit/s) and up. The slow speeds stem from the fact that computers usually communicate through the telephone line, which was the most convenient and readily available path when the industry developed computers and began to interface them with terminals and other computers in the 1960s. The telephone channel is not designed for fast transmission between high-speed computers,

TABLE 1-2. Link Speeds and Uses

Typical Speed in Bit/s	Typical Uses
0-600	Telegraph, older terminals; telemetry
600-2400	Human-operated terminals; personal computers
2400-19,200	Applications requiring fast response and/or throughput; some batch and file transfer applications
32,000-64,000	Digital voice; high-speed applications; some video
64,000-1,544,000	Very high speed for multiple users; computer-to-computer traffic; backbone links for networks; video
greater than 1,544,000	Backbone links for networks; high-quality video; multiple digital voice

TABLE 1-3. Base Ten Numbering System and Terms

Multiplication Factor	Prefix	Symbol	Meaning
1 000 000 000 000 000 000 $= 10^{18}$	exa	E	Quintillion
1 000 000 000 000 000 $= 10^{15}$	peta	P	Quadrillion
1 000 000 000 000 $= 10^{12}$	tera	T	Trillion
1 000 000 000 $= 10^{9}$	giga	G	Billion
1 000 000 $= 10^{6}$	mega	M	Million
1 000 $= 10^{3}$	kilo	K	Thousand
100 $= 10^{2}$	hecto	h	Hundred
10 $= 10^{1}$	deka	da	Ten
0.1 $= 10^{-1}$	deci	d	Tenth
0.01 $= 10^{-2}$	centi	c	Hundredth
0.001 $= 10^{-3}$	milli	m	Thousandth
0.000 001 $= 10^{-6}$	micro	μ	Millionth
0.000 000 001 $= 10^{-9}$	nano	n	Billionth
0.000 000 000 001 $= 10^{-12}$	pico	p	Trillionth
0.000 000 000 000 001 $= 10^{-15}$	femto	f	Quadrillionth
0.000 000 000 000 000 001 $= 10^{-18}$	atto	a	Quintillionth

but for voice transmission between people, which does not require the speed associated with data transmission. The point is explained in considerable detail in later chapters.

THE ERROR-LADEN CHANNEL

In previous discussions, we learned that computers (DTEs) can be programmed to communicate with very little ambiguity. (Without question, the task is difficult because machines are relatively "unintelligent.") Yet, data transmitted correctly from the source DTE often arrive incorrectly at the destination (sink) DTE. Due to a myriad of factors, the data can be damaged on the channel en route, such that the binary 1s and 0s representing codes and symbols are misinterpreted by the receiver.

To gain an understanding of the magnitude of the problem, consider some performance measurements of a dial-up connection between two user stations on long-distance carriers in the United States [MICR86]. A 1.2 Kbit/s speed transmission experiences a bit error rate (BER) of 1 in 10^5 (moderate quality) to $1:10^3$ (very poor). In other words, we may expect one bit to be damaged in every 1000 to 100,000 bits transmitted. It takes little imagination to recognize that bit errors are frequent.

Bit errors are also often random; they cannot be predicted. Even though an error may or may not occur in a block of data, studies reveal that a dial-up telephone line experiences an incidence of 0.7 to 142.6 errors in every one thousand blocks sent (each block consisting of 1000 bits).

Is this a problem? It depends on the needs of the user. The transmission of certain textual data may not require extensive error-detection efforts, since an occasional corrupted character can be ignored as no more serious than a typing error. On the other hand, an electronic funds transfer system can ill afford an error. The distortion of a decimal place or zero could have either disastrous or serendipitous consequences: disastrous for the individual losing the decimal place, and serendipitous for the individual gaining it.

One solution to the problem is the use of a circuit that is as error-free as possible, and substantial relief results from the use of conditioned, dedicated circuits and other high-quality media. Moreover, circuits using optical fiber offer superior performance over conventional media. Nonetheless, errors will occur, and some method must be used to deal with them—regardless of how frequent or infrequent they are. After the preventive maintenance efforts of using high-quality circuits, and well-designed hardware and software, the next line of defense is to (a) check for transmission errors at the receiver, (b) attempt to correct the error at the receiver, and (c) request the sender to retransmit the damaged data.

The specific component in a data communications system that performs this vital function is called a data link control or a line protocol. It is introduced here and discussed in more detail in Chapters 10, 11, and 20.

DATA LINK CONTROL—AN OVERVIEW

Data link controls (DLCs) are so named because they control the data flow between stations on one physical communications link. All traffic on the link is controlled by the link protocol. For example, if a communications link has several users accessing it, the DLC is responsible for the data to be transported error-free to the receiving user station on the channel (or at least as error-free as possible). Data link controls follow well-ordered steps in managing a communications channel.

- *Link establishment.* Once the DCE has a physical connection to the remote DCE, the DLC (residing usually in the DTE) "handshakes" with the remote DLC logic to ensure that both systems are ready to exchange user data.
- *Information transfer.* User data is exchanged across the link between the two machines. The DLC checks the data for possible transmission errors and sends acknowledgments back to the transmitting machine. In the event an error is detected, the receiver requests the transmitter to retransmit the data.
- *Link termination.* The DLC relinquishes control of the link (channel), which means no data can be transferred until the link is reestablished. Typically, a DLC keeps a link active as long as the user community wishes to send data to the other stations.

SYNCHRONIZING DATA COMMUNICATIONS COMPONENTS

The data link control (DLC) assumes the devices on the link are already physically connected and communicating with each other. As we learned earlier, this means the physical level is operating properly, in order for the logical communications to take place.

It is a good idea to pause here and consider what is meant by physical communications, because the topic is fundamental to the subject of data communications.

In order for computers and terminals to communicate, they must first notify each other that they are about to transmit data. Second, once they have begun the communications process, they must provide a method to keep both devices aware of the ongoing transmissions. Let us address the first point. A transmitter, such as a terminal or a computer, must transmit its signal so the receiving device knows when to search for and recognize the data as it arrives. In essence, the receiver must know the exact time each binary 1 and 0 is propagating through the communication channel. This requirement means that a mutual time base, or a common clock, is necessary between the receiving and transmitting devices.

The transmitting machine first forwards to the receiving machine an indication that it is sending data—something like a human saying "hello." If the transmitter sends the bits across the channel without prior notice, the receiver will likely not have sufficient time to adjust itself to the incoming bit stream. In such an event, the first few bits of the transmission would be lost, perhaps rendering the entire transmission useless. Moreover, the receiver may not be able to "train" itself onto the transmission if it does not detect the first part of the signal.

This process is part of a communications protocol and is generally referred to as synchronization. Connections of short distances between machines often use a separate channel to provide the synchronization. This line transmits a signal that is turned on and off or varied in accordance with pre-established conventions. As the clocking signal on this line changes, it notifies the receiving device that it is to examine the data line at a specific time. It may also adjust the receiver's sampling clock to enable the receiver to stay accurately aligned on each incoming data bit. Thus, clocking signals perform two valuable functions: (1) They synchronize the receiver onto the transmission before the data actually arrives; and (2) they keep the receiver synchronized with the incoming data bits.

In summary, the clock provides a reference for the individual binary 1s and 0s. The idea is to use a code with frequent signal level transitions on the channel. The transitions delineate the binary data cells (1s and 0s) at the receiver, and sampling logic continuously examines the state of the transmissions in order to detect the bits. Receiver sampling usually occurs at a higher rate than the data rate in order to define the bit cells more precisely.

ASYNCHRONOUS AND SYNCHRONOUS TRANSMISSION

We now know that clocking is a major consideration in data communications. Two data formatting conventions are used to help achieve synchronization. These two methods are illustrated in Figure 1-4. The first approach is called asynchronous formatting. With this approach, each data character has start and stop bits (i.e., synchronizing signals) placed around it. The purposes of these signals are to (a) alert the receiver that data is arriving and (b) give the receiver sufficient time to perform certain timing functions before the next character arrives. The start and stop bits are really nothing more than unique and specific signals which are recognized by the receiving device.

Asynchronous transmission is widely used because the interfaces in the DTEs and DCEs are relatively inexpensive. For example, most personal computers use asynchronous interfaces. Since the synchronization occurs between the transmitting and receiving devices on a character-by-character basis, some allowance can be made for inaccuracies, because the inaccuracy can be corrected with the next arriving character. In other words, a looser timing tolerance is allowed, which translates to lower component costs.

A more sophisticated process is synchronous transmission. It uses separate clocking channels or a self-clocking code. Synchronous formats eliminate the intermittent start/stop signals around each character and provide signals which precede and sometimes follow the user data stream. The preliminary signals are usually called synchronization (sync) bytes, flags or preambles (see Table 1-1.) Their principal function is to alert the receiver of incoming user data. This process is called framing.

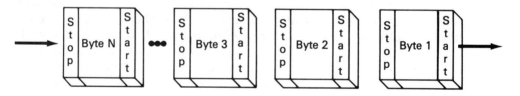

(a) Asynchronous Format

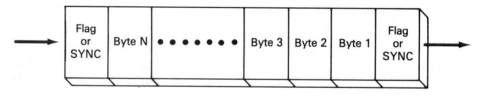

(b) Synchronous Format

FIGURE 1-4. Asynchronous and Synchronous Transmissions

NETWORK ARCHITECTURES
AND LAYERED PROTOCOLS

Earlier in this chapter, we learned how machines communicate through established conventions called protocols. Since computer systems provide many functions to users, more than one protocol is required for this support. A convention is also needed to define how the different protocols of the systems interact with each other to support the end user. This convention is referred to by several names: network architecture, communications architecture, or computer-communications architecture. Whatever term we use, most systems are implemented with layered protocols, wherein each layer performs a specific function.

Layered protocols are used to meet the following objectives:

- Provide a logical decomposition of a complex system into smaller, more understandable parts (layers).

- Provide for standard interfaces between systems; for example, provide standard interfaces between the software or hardware modules that comprise the layers.

- Provide for symmetry in functions performed at each site in the network. Each layer performs the same functions as its counterpart in other machines in the network. This approach greatly simplifies the interfaces between the layers of the network.

- Provide a means to predict and control the consequences of any changes made to the network system's logic (software or microcode); the logical decomposition aids in making these changes.

- Provide a standard language to clarify communications between and among network designers, managers, vendors, and users when discussing the logic of network systems.

The OSI Model

The Open Systems Interconnection (OSI) model was developed by several standards organizations and is now a widely used layered functional model. It warrants serious study, because it is becoming a pervasive approach to implementing layered data communications systems.

The stated purpose of the model is to:

- Establish a common basis for standards development
- Qualify products as open by their use of these standards
- Provide a common reference for standards

From the author's perspective, the model also:

- Provides standards for communications between systems
- Removes any technical impediment to communication between systems

- Eliminates the need to describe the internal operation of a single system
- Defines the points of interconnection for the exchange of information between systems
- Narrows the options in order to increase the ability to communicate between systems without expensive conversions and translations. This means different vendors' products can communicate with each other more easily.

In summary, OSI is intended to diminish the effects of the vendor-specific mentality that has resulted in each vendor system operating with unique protocols. The OSI approach has relieved end users of the need to purchase expensive and complex protocol converters in order to interconnect and interface various systems.

Due to the wide use of OSI layers, several chapters in this book are devoted to explaining their attributes and characteristics. (The organizations responsible for developing OSI are discussed next.) The following material offers a brief explanation of the layers, and Part II of this book explains the layers in more detail.

The OSI Layers

The seven OSI layers are depicted in Figure 1-5. The lowest layer in the model is called the *physical layer*. The functions within that layer are responsible for activating, maintaining, and deactivating a physical circuit between a DTE and a DCE and providing the clocking signals discussed earlier. There are many standards published for the physical layer; for example EIA-232, V.22 bis, and V.35 are physical level protocols. Physical level protocols are more frequently called physical level interfaces (refer to Chapters 9 and 12).

As discussed earlier, the *data link layer* is responsible for the transfer of data across the link. It delimits the flow of bits from the physical layer. It also provides for the identity of the bits. It usually ensures that the data arrives safely at the receiving DTE. It often provides for flow control to ensure that the DTE does not become overburdened with too much data at any one time. One of its most important functions is to provide for the detection of transmission errors and provide mechanisms to recover from lost, duplicated, or erroneous data (refer to Chapters 10, 11, and 12).

The *network layer* specifies the interface of the user into a network, as well as the interface of two DTEs with each other through a network. It also defines network switching/routing and the communications between networks (internetworking) (refer to Chapters 13 and 14).

The *transport layer* provides the interface between the data communications network and the upper three layers (generally part of the user's system). It is the layer that gives the user options in obtaining certain levels of quality (and cost) from the network itself (i.e., the network layer). It is

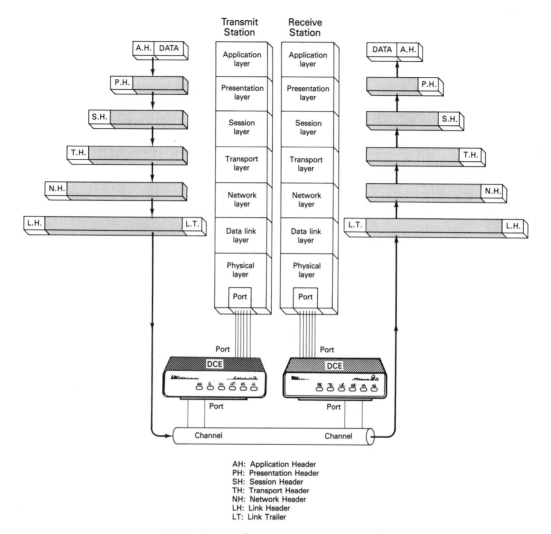

AH: Application Header
PH: Presentation Header
SH: Session Header
TH: Transport Header
NH: Network Header
LH: Link Header
LT: Link Trailer

FIGURE 1-5. The OSI Seven-Layer Model

designed to keep the user isolated from some of the physical and functional aspects of the network. It also is the first layer to provide for end-to-end accountability across more than one link (refer to Chapter 15).

The *session layer* serves as a user interface into the transport layer. This layer provides for an organized means to exchange data between users, such as simultaneous transmission, alternate transmission, checkpoint procedures, and resynchronization of user data flow between user applications. The users can select the type of synchronization and control needed from the layer (refer to Chapter 16).

The *presentation layer* provides for the syntax of data; that is, the representation of data. It is not concerned with the meaning or semantics of the data. Its principal role, for example, is to accept data types (character, integer) from the application layer and then negotiate with its peer layer as to the syntax representation (such as ASCII). Thereafter, its functions are limited. The layer consists of many tables of syntax (teletype, ASCII, Videotex, etc.; refer to Chapter 17).

The *application layer* is concerned with the support of the end-user application process. Unlike the presentation layer, this layer is concerned with the semantics of data. The layer contains service elements to support application processes such as job management, financial data exchange, programming languages, electronic mail, and data base management (refer to Chapter 18).

ENCAPSULATION AND DECAPSULATION

Figure 1-5 depicts how the layers of a network communicate. The vast majority of networks use this approach, so the reader is encouraged to review this section carefully (Part II provides more explanation of these concepts).

At a transmitting station, user data are presented by a user application to the upper layer (application). This layer adds its protocol control information (PCI) to the user data and usually performs some type of support service to the user. (A more common term for the PCI is *header.*) It then passes its PCI and the user data to the next lower layer, which repeats the process. With the exception of the physical layer, each layer adds a PCI/header. A combination of the PCI and user data is called the protocol data unit (PDU). This concept is somewhat inaccurately called encapsulation (the data from the upper layers are only encapsulated at one end). The only layer that completely encapsulates the data is the data link layer, which adds both a header PCI and a trailer PCI.

The fully encapsulated data are transported across the communications circuit to a receiving station. Here the process is reversed: the data go from the lower layers to the upper layers, and the header created by the transmitting peer layer is used by the receiving peer layer to invoke a service function for (a) the transmitting site and/or (b) the upper layers of the receiving site. As the data go up through the layers, the headers are stripped away after they have been used to invoke the services. This process is called decapsulation.

Insofar as possible, the internal operations of the layers are independent of each other. The idea is to reduce complexity and to allow changes to be made in one layer without affecting others. For example, a change to a routing algorithm in one layer should not affect the functions of, say, sequencing, that are located in another layer in the architecture.

Layered network protocols allow interaction between functionally paired layers in different locations. This concept aids in permitting the distribution of functions to remote sites. In the majority of layered protocols, the data unit passed from one layer to another is not altered. The data unit contents may be examined and used to append (i.e., encapsulate) additional PCIs (trailers/headers) to the existing unit. These concepts are key to the OSI model. Chapter 8 and Part II provide considerably more detail on OSI and layered protocols.

STANDARDS ORGANIZATION

The growing acceptance of common conventions and protocols is the result of the efforts of several standards organizations. An overview of these groups is provided here (see Table 1-4 for their addresses). A more thorough description is provided by other sources [OMNI85].

The American National Standards Institute (ANSI)

The American National Standards Institute (ANSI) is a national clearing house and coordinating agency for standards implemented in the United States on a voluntary basis. It is a member of the International Organization for Standardization (ISO) and also develops and coordinates standards in data communications for the OSI. It develops standards for encryption activities and office systems. ANSI tries to adopt the ISO standards, but its specifications may differ due to unique aspects of North American systems.

In 1960, ANSI formed X3, a committee to establish standards for data communications, programming languages, magnetic storage media, and the OSI model. It parallels the work of the ISO technical committee (TC) 97.

The Electronic Industries Association (EIA)

The Electronic Industries Association is a national trade association that has been active for many years in the development of standards. Its best-known standard is EIA-232. The EIA publishes its own standards and also submits proposals to ANSI for accreditation.

The EIA's work is hardware-oriented. The TR-30 Technical Committee, Data Transmission, is responsible for EIA-232 (first issued in 1962). TR-30 meets with ANSI X3S3 to ensure that work of the two groups is cohesive. TR-30 is responsible for the physical layer part of the OSI Reference Model; X3S3 deals with the data link and network layers.

The European Computer Manufacturers Association (ECMA)

The European Computer Manufacturers Association is dedicated to the development of standards applicable to computer and communications technology. It is not a trade organization, as the name might imply, but a standards and technical review group. It was formed in 1961 as a non-com-

TABLE 1-4. Standards Organizations

ANSI	American National Standards Institute 1430 Broadway, New York, NY 10018 Telephone: (212) 354-3300
EIA	Electronic Industries Association 2001 Eye Street, Washington DC 20006 Telephone: (202) 457-4966
FED-STD	General Services Administration Specification Distribution Branch Building 197, Washington Navy Yard Washington, DC 20407 Telephone: (202) 472-1082
FIPS	U.S. Department of Commerce National Technical Information Service 5285 Port Royal Road, Springfield, VA 22161 Telephone: (703) 487-4650
CCITT	*Outside the United States:* General Secretariat International Telecommunications Union Place des Nations, 1121 Geneva 20, Switzerland Telephone: +41 22 99-51-11 *In the United States:* U.S. Department of Commerce National Technical Information Service 5285 Port Royal Road, Springfield, VA 22161 Telephone: (703) 487-4650
ISO	*Outside the United States:* International Organization for Standardization Central Secretariat 1 rue de Varembe, CH-1211 Geneva, Switzerland Telephone: +41 22 34-12-40 *In the United States:* American National Standards Institute (address above)
ECMA	European Computer Manufacturers Association 114 rue du Rhone, CH-1204 Geneva, Switzerland Telephone: +41 22 35-36-34
IEEE	Institute of Electrical and Electronic Engineers 345 East 47 Street, New York, NY 10017 Telephone: (212) 705-7900
NBS	National Bureau of Standards Institute for Computer Sciences and Technology Technology Building Gaithersburg, MD 20899 Telephone: (301) 921-2731
CBEMA	Computer & Business Equipment Manufacturer's Association 311 First Street NW, Suite 300 Washington, DC 20001 Telephone: (202) 737-8888

mercial organization to promulgate standards for data processing and communications systems. The ECMA works in close coordination with many of the ISO and the CCITT technical committees and study groups. Initially organized by Compagnie des Machines Bull, the IBM World Trade Europe Corporation, and International Computers and Tabulators Limited, it now includes all European computer manufacturers.

The Institute of Electrical and Electronic Engineers (IEEE)

The Institute of Electrical and Electronic Engineers has been involved for many years in standards activities. It is a well-known professional society with chapters located throughout the world. Its recent efforts in local area networks have received much attention. The IEEE activity addresses local area networks and many other standards as well. The 802 structure; is as follows:

- *IEEE 802.1* Higher Layer Interface Standard (HILI)
- *IEEE 802.2* Logical Link Control Standard (LLC)
- *IEEE 802.3* Carrier Sense Multiple Access with Collision Detection (CSMA/CD)
- *IEEE 802.4* Token Bus
- *IEEE 802.5* Token Ring
- *IEEE 802.6* Metropolitan Area Network (MAN)
- *IEEE 802.7* Broadband Technical Advisory Group
- *IEEE 802.8* Fiber-Optics Technical Advisory Group

The International Organization for Standardization (ISO)

The International Organization for Standardization (ISO) is a voluntary body. It consists of national standardization organizations from each member country. The activities of ISO are principally from the user committees and manufacturers in contrast to the carriers that are represented in CCITT. The American National Standards Institute (ANSI) is the primary U.S. representative to the ISO.

Technical committee 97 (TC97) deals with information technology. As such, its activities affect many of the products and systems that are used in the industry. The ISO documents are designated as IS (International Standard), DIS (Draft International Standard), and DP (Draft Proposal). Table 1-5 summarizes the ISO Subcommittees (SC) and Working Groups (WG).

International Telegraph & Telephone Consultative Committee (CCITT)

The International Telegraph & Telephone Consultative Committee is a member of the International Telecommunications Union (ITU), a treaty

TABLE 1-5. Subcommittees (SC) and Working Groups (WG)

SC 2: Character Sets and Information Coding
  WG 1: Code extension techniques
  WG 2: 2-bit graphic character set
  WG 4: Coded character sets for text communication
  WG 6: Additional control functions
  WG 7: 8-bit coded character set
  WG 8: Coded representation of pictures

SC 6: Telecommunications and Information Exchange Between Systems
  WG 1: Data link layer
  WG 2: Network layer
  WG 3: Physical interface characteristics
  WG 4: Transport layer
  WG 5: Architecture and coordination of layers 1–4

SC 18: Text and Office Systems
  WG 1: User requirements
  WG 2: Symbols and terminology
  WG 3: Text structure
  WG 4: Procedures for text interchange
  WG 5: Text preparation and presentation
  WG 6: Text preparation and interchange equipment
  WG 7: Keyboards for office machines and data processing equipment
  WG 8: Text

SC 20: Data Cryptographic Techniques
  WG 1: Secret key algorithms and applications
  WG 2: Public key cryptosystems and use
  WG 3: Use of encryption techniques in communications

SC 21: Information Retrieval, Transfer, and Management of OSI
  WG 1: OSI architecture
  WG 2: Computer graphics
  WG 3: Data bases
  WG 4: OSI management
  WG 5: Specific application services and protocols
  WG 6: Session, presentation, common application service elements

organization formed in 1865. The ITU is now a specialized body within the United Nations. CCITT sponsors a number of recommendations dealing primarily with data communications networks, telephone switching standards, digital systems, and terminals. The State Department is the voting member on CCITT from the United States, although several levels of membership are permitted. For example, the recognized private operating agencies (RPOA) are allowed to participate at one level (such as the regional Bell Operation Companies).

The CCITT's recommendations (also known as Standards) are very widely used. Its specifications are republished every four years in a series of books that take more than two feet on a bookshelf. The books covering each four-year period can be identified by the color of their covers. The 1960

TABLE 1-6. CCITT Study Groups

Number	Name
I	Definition, operation, and quality of service aspects of telegraph, data transmission, and telematic services (facsimile, Teletext, Videotex, etc.)
II	Operation of telephone network and ISDN
III	General tariff principles, including accounting
IV	Transmission maintenance of international lines, circuits, and chains of circuits; maintenance of automatic and semi-automatic networks
V	Protection against dangers and disturbances of electromagnetic origin
VI	Outside plant
VII	Data communications networks
VIII	Terminal equipment for telematic services (facsimile, Teletext, Videotex, etc.)
IX	Telegraph networks and terminal equipment
X	Languages and methods for telecommunications applications
XI	ISDN and telephone network switching and signalling
XII	Transmission performance of telephone networks and terminals
XV	Transmission system
XVII	Data transmission over the telephone network
XVIII	Digital networks, including ISDN

books were red; 1964, blue; 1968, white; 1972, green; 1976, orange; 1980, yellow; and, in 1984, once again red. The 1988 blue books use about four feet of shelf space! The CCITT Study Groups are summarized in Table 1-6.

U.S. National Committee (to CCITT)

In the United States, the State Department is the principal member of CCITT, and a National Committee is the coordinating group for U.S. participation in CCITT. Moreover, advisory committees coordinate contributions to CCITT Study Groups. These U.S. CCITT Study Groups prepare actions for CCITT consideration:

Study Group A: U.S. Government of Regulatory Policies
Study Group B: Telegraph Operations
Study Group C: Worldwide Telephone Network
Study Group D: Data Transmissions

Several government organizations have important roles in developing international standards. As mentioned earlier, the State Department is the United States voting member of CCITT. The National Communications System (NCS) is a consortium of federal agencies that have large telecommunications capabilities. The NCS works very closely with other organizations such as the EIA, ISO, and CCITT. One of its jobs is to develop federal input to the international standards organizations, and NCS is using the OSI architecture for its work. Indeed, the majority of government organizations are using OSI.

The National Bureau of Standards

The National Bureau of Standards (NBS) is also very active in international standards committees. Currently, it is working on the upper layers of the OSI standard. It is also responsible for the Federal Information Processing Standards (FIPS). A large number of ANSI documents are incorporated into the FIPS standards.

NBS is also responsible for the publications of GOSIP (U.S. Government Open Systems Interconnection Protocols), a specification that defines the specific protocols to be used by U.S. Government agencies. GOSIP is explained in Chapter 8.

QUESTIONS

TRUE/FALSE

1. Computers usually communicate without ambiguity if they are programmed correctly.
2. The basic purpose of a data communications system is to transport data between DCEs.
3. In a telephone system, switching offices are connected by local loops.
4. A group of either seven or eight bits comprise either a byte or octet.
5. Most user devices such as terminals and personal computers use a non-return-to-zero code (NRZ).
6. Match the function to the appropriate component:

   Function

   a) Manages traffic on the link
   b) End-user device name
   c) Manages routing between links
   d) Interfaces user station onto link
   e) A convention or agreement in data communications
   f) Interconnection of computers and terminals

   Component

   1. Protocol
   2. DSE
   3. Data Link Control
   4. DTE

5. Network
6. DCE

7. Match the function to the appropriate component:

Function

a) An international voluntary standards organization
b) Represents a consortium of U.S. federal agencies
c) U.S. national clearinghouse and coordinating body
d) Noted for local area network standards
e) Part of the U.N. structure.
f) A prominent North American trade association; developed RS-232-C and EIA-232-D.

Organization

1. IEEE
2. The National Communications System
3. The ISO (International Standards Organization)
4. The International Telegraph & Telephone Consultative Committee (CCITT)
5. The Electronic Industries Association (EIA)
6. The American National Standards Institute (ANSI)

8. Under the Open Systems Interconnection (OSI) concept, a convention describes how the layers communicate with each other. This text describes the convention for layer communications with the term _____

9. Which layer is tasked with end-to-end accountability on one link? _____

10. Which layer is tasked with the end-to-end accountability through a network? _____

11. The _____ protocol data unit (PDU) is created at the network level and the _____ protocol data unit (PDU) is created at the data link level.

12. Why must a machine, such as a computer, be programmed with exacting and detailed instructions?

13. What is the primary purpose of a data communications system?

14. Compare a switched network with a broadcast network.

15. Name three of five functions provided by data communications codes.

16. Synchronization between components can be achieved by two techniques. Describe them.

17. What is the principal function of data link control?

18. Describe the differences between encapsulation and decapsulation.

19. Describe some benefits of the encapsulation/decapsulation concept.

SELECTED ANSWERS

1. True, if the signals are not distorted on the communications channel.

2. False. The communication between DCEs is the means to an end: communication between DTEs.

3. False. Local loops connect the user instrument (telephone, etc.) to the end office. The switching offices are connected by trunk circuits.

4. False. Seven bits do not comprise an octet.

5. True, because EIA-232 is an NRZ code.

6.

Function	Component
a	3
b	4
c	2
d	6
e	1
f	5

7.

Function	Organization
a	3
b	2
c	6
d	1
e	4
f	5

9. Data link control layer

10. Transport layer

11. packet, frame

16. One approach is to use a separate clocking channel in which case the receiver derives its timing from the signals on this channel. The other approach is to embed the clocking signal in the data stream. This is accomplished by (a) start/stop bits in an asynchronous transmission or (b) the use of a self-clocking code in a synchronous transmission.

18. Encapsulation is invoked at the transmitting station. It adds protocol control information (headers/trailers) to the data unit in each layer as the unit is passed down through each layer. Decapsulation is invoked at a receiving station. It strips away the protocol control information from the data unit as the unit is passed up through each layer.

CHAPTER 2

Concepts and Theory

INTRODUCTION

Most data communications systems use the voice-oriented telephone network for transmission and reception of data. Therefore, the reader should have an understanding of the characteristics of voice signals and human speech, and how data are transmitted over communications lines that are designed for voice. This knowledge is also needed to understand digital networks and certain aspects of the rapidly growing integrated services digital networks (ISDN) in which voice and data signals are integrated and transported across the same line. Equally important, an examination of this subject provides a means to explore several other concepts and theories in the fields of voice and data communications. For the reader who is unfamiliar with certain mathematical and algebraic symbols, Appendix I (at the end of the book) should be read before delving into this chapter.

THE VOICE SIGNAL

When we speak, our lungs and diaphragm force air past our vocal cords to produce sounds. The other speech-supporting organs, such as the tongue, soft palate, nose, lips, and teeth, modify the sounds to produce a unique speech pattern for each person.

Speech is actually a physical disturbance of the air; in effect, it is slight movements of air molecules that are produced by the human voice. In its essential physical nature, speech is nothing more than a pressure change in the air. Air molecules in close proximity to the mouth push against air molecules in front of them and, in turn, these molecules push on other molecules further from the mouth. The sound propagates through the air, and gradually diminishes in intensity as the disturbance moves further away from the speaking person. The various pressure fluctuations are received by the ear, converted into nerve impulses, and interpreted by the brain as, one hopes, some form of intelligent utterance.

The speech pattern produces various levels of air pressure. Certain utterances create more air pressure than others. Periods of high-pressure sound signals are called condensations (the air is compressed), and periods of low sound levels are called rarefactions (the air is less dense). Human speech is a continuous train of these sound waves as shown in Figure 2-1.

The changes in air pressure are not as abrupt as might be inferred from Figure 2-1. Rather, the sound changes gradually (and continuously if the speech is sustained) from high to low pressure. Figure 2-2 shows this relationship. The shape of the signal resembles a wave and is actually called a sound wave.

Figure 2-3 plots air pressure as a function of distance from the speaker and measures the distance between any two successive points. This distance is called the wavelength and is designated by the Greek letter lambda (λ). Talking or singing creates a complex set of waveforms that change in pressure several hundred to several thousand times per second.

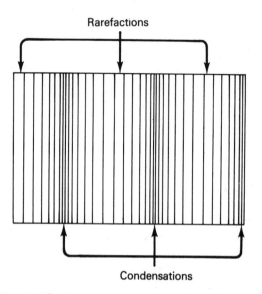

FIGURE 2-1. The Transmission of Sounds and Air Pressure

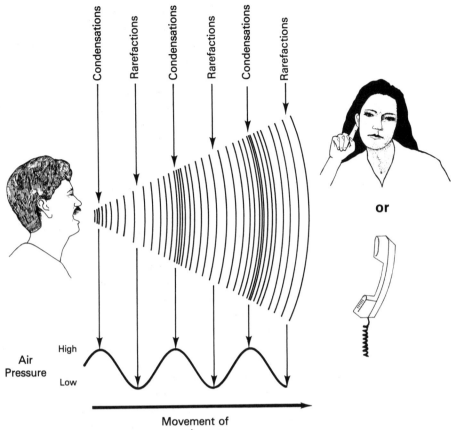

FIGURE 2-2. Propagation of Sound Waves

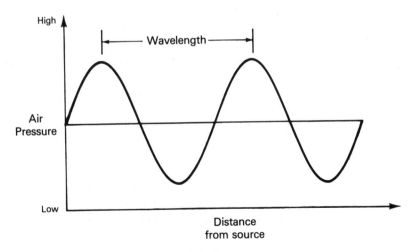

FIGURE 2-3. Sound Waves

When we speak into a telephone, the telephone handset transforms the physical speech waveform into an electrical waveform. Both waves have very similar characteristics. For example, the various heights of the sound waves are translated by the telephone into signals of continuously variable electrical voltages, or currents.

Before discussing the characteristics of the waveform, let us examine the basic characteristics of electrical signals (optical and other signals are explained in Chapter 4). The reader who is familiar with these concepts may wish to skip to the next section, "The Waveform."

CHARACTERISTICS OF COMMUNICATIONS SIGNALS

Electricity provides the basis for storing and conveying information in a communications system. It is an invisible force that can produce many physical effects such as digital and analog signals. All electrical systems have something in common: the existence of particles of electric charge, which are described as electrons and protons. The electron is the smallest amount of electrical charge that concerns most engineers in the data communications world. The electron has negative polarity and the proton is the basic particle that has positive polarity. The negative and positive polarities indicate two opposite characteristics that, for our purposes, are fundamental in almost all physical applications.

An analogy to electricity is that of the north/south poles in magnets. Opposite poles of a magnet attract each other, and like poles repel. In electricity, electrons and protons attract each other, and like charges repel, that is, electrons repel other electrons. It is the arrangement of the electrons and protons that determines the electrical characteristics of the many parts of the communications network.

The movement of electrons provides current in a conductor, such as the copper wire. The electron movement creates an electrical current, which can be used to convey information across the communications channel. Due to its electrical instability, copper wire is a very good conductor of electrical signals, and consequently it is widely used in many communications systems.

Communications and electrical components provide a means to excite electrons in a wire and hence create a communications signal. This excitation is accomplished through a concept called the unit of potential difference. Simply stated, when one charge is different from another charge between two components, a difference in potential exists. Potential actually refers to the possibility of moving electrical particles such as the electrons.

Current (and thereby the ability to carry information through current) occurs when the potential difference between two charges forces electrons to move through a conductor. The difference in charge is measured in a unit called the volt. A volt is really nothing more than what it takes in an applied charge to create a potential difference to get the free electrons moving through the conductor.

In data communications, the conductor is called a circuit, line, link, or channel. Generally, all metals are good conductors. Silver is best and copper is second because the atomic structure of both materials allows free movement of electrons. Of course, silver is quite expensive, and therefore copper is used for most metal conductors due to its conductivity and relatively low cost. Later chapters discuss transmission circuits, the use of the atmosphere as a conductor, as well as optical fiber circuits.

A battery has positive and negative charges on the terminals to create energy within the battery by repulsing electrons at the negative terminal and moving current through the wires connected to the poles of the battery. The higher the voltage (or stated another way, the greater the difference in potential between the terminals on the circuit), the greater the current flow will be. This means a greater intensity of electrons moves through the circuit. We will see shortly how either current flow or voltage levels can be made to represent data and data communications signals.

In the early configurations of communications circuits, the return circuit for the current was earth. This technique provided one wire for the signal and the earth medium for the return circuit, also called the ground (or ground electrode). The grounding occurred against some piece of metal, such as a pipe. It resulted in terminating the connection into the earth, the actual ground itself. In such a system, the earth or ground replaced the wire as the return path for the current flow, and the earth became the return conductor. In electronic equipment, the ground merely indicates a metal chassis which is used as a common return. In printed wiring, a conducting path around the board is used as a common return for chassis ground.

The signals on a communications link can be measured by their voltages or currents. A voltmeter measures voltage and an ammeter measures current flow. For example, a positive voltage is often used to signify a binary 0 and a negative voltage is used to signify a binary 1. The direction or intensity of the current flow is also used to represent binary numbers, codes, and symbols.

THE WAVEFORM

The voice waveform spoken into a telephone creates an electrical alternating current (ac): the voltage alternating reverses its polarity, which produces current that reverses its direction. Figure 2-4 shows one simple method to create the ac waveform [GROB71]. The rotary generator (an alternator) consists of a conductor loop that rotates through a magnetic field. The rotation generates an induced voltage by varying the relative polarity of the loop in the magnetic field.

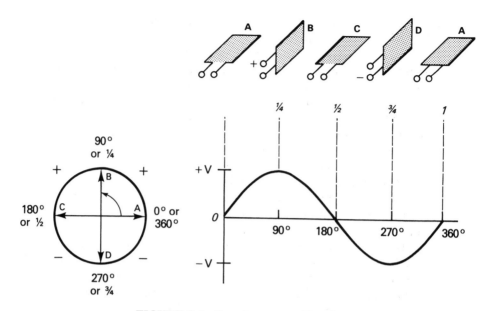

FIGURE 2-4. Creating an ac Waveform

The amount of voltage depends on the position of the loop conductors in the magnetic field. As the conductor rotates counterclockwise through the field, it produces (a) at ¼ turn, maximum positive voltage; (b) at ½ turn, zero voltage; (c) at ¾ turn, maximum negative voltage; and (d) at the completion of one turn, zero voltage.

Note the relationship in Figure 2-4 to the conductor's rotations and the accompanying 360° circle. The relationships are shown as:

    A: 0° = 0 turn
    B: 90° = ¼ turn
    C: 180° = ½ turn
    D: 270° = ¾ turn

The full revolution creates an electrical waveform of varying voltages and alternate directions in current flow (i.e., an alternating current). The wavelength is shown as the variations between two successive points having the same voltage value and varying in the same direction of current flow.

Alternating current (ac) can be fed to a transformer which changes its voltage levels up or down to represent the waveform. This technique allows large amounts of power to be transmitted over high capacity lines, yet transformed down for use in homes and offices. This characteristic is the reason ac is used in many power systems and communications systems.

Direct current (dc) is the type of current created by batteries. It produces a steady voltage which, of course, produces a steady current in one direction only. Even though it cannot be stepped up or down with transformers, it is a voltage source for many communications systems.

CYCLES, FREQUENCY, AND PERIOD

Several terms are now introduced to compare the voice signal to (a) its electrical counterpart and (b) the digital signal stored and used in a computer. The key terms are cycle, frequency, and period.

The wavelength measures the cycle of the wave; that is, the interval of space or time in which the waveform reaches a successive point. The cycle describes a complete oscillation of the wave. The number of oscillations of the acoustical or electrical wave in a given period (usually a second) is called the frequency (f). Frequency is expressed in cycles per second, or more commonly hertz (Hz). Frequency describes the number of cycles that pass a given point in one second (for example, our ear, a telephone mouthpiece, or a receiver in a computer). The signal travels one wavelength during the time of one cycle.

The time required for the signal to be transmitted over a distance of one wavelength is called the period (T). The period describes the duration of the cycle and is a function of the frequency:

$$T = 1/f$$

Also, frequency is the reciprocal of the period:

$$f = 1/T$$

Sound waves (as well as other waveforms such as electrical and light waves) propagate through the air or other media at a certain speed. The velocity (V) of a sound wave is about 1090 feet (332 meters) per second, measured at 0 degrees Celsius. The propagation speed of any waveform is calculated as:

$$V = f * (\lambda)$$

Since velocity (V), frequency (f) and wavelength (λ) are interrelated, if any two of the values are known, the third can be calculated:

$$V = f * \lambda; \quad \lambda = V/f; \quad f = V/\lambda$$

The transmission medium also determines the propagation velocity. For example, sound travels about four times faster in water than in air and about 15 times faster in metal. Sound propagation velocity also increases with each degree of increase in temperature (about 2 feet or 0.6 meter per second).

Voice signals move away from our mouths at about 1090 feet per second in a circular expanding pattern. The train of compressions and rarefactions create the waveform as depicted in Figure 2-3 with gradually changing patterns of high and low air pressure.

THE SINE WAVE

The waveform is often described in terms of (a) circular motion and (b) trigonometric functions. If we understand the basic relationships between the waveform and certain trigonometric functions, we will also be able to gain an understanding of the relationships of analog signals to digital data signals. To that end, let us examine the trigonometric aspects of the waveform.

A convenient method of measurement in trigonometry is a Cartesian coordinate system. With this method, a grid is used to represent vertical and horizontal positions on a plane. Figure 2-5 shows the plane as four quadrants with positive or negative ordinates in the planes. A plot (point) on the grid is positive if it is above the x axis and negative if below.

If a line is drawn from the origin (O) to a point on the grid (P), a triangle is formed with OP, PM, and MO representing the three sides of the triangle. The sides are labeled r, y, and x. From the lengths of r, y, and x, the following ratios can be obtained (four other ratios are possible but not relevant to our discussion): y/r and x/r. The relationships of r, y, and x are determined with the value of the angle θ at 0. The values of the ratios depend upon the size of θ. Two ratios are defined and labeled as:

sine θ = y/r; abbreviated as sin θ
cosine θ = x/r; abbreviated as cos θ

Sin θ and cos θ are called trigonometric functions because the values of the ratios depend on the value of θ. This idea is illustrated by comparing Figure 2-5 with Figure 2-6 (a). As θ increases, y increases, and therefore y/r increases.

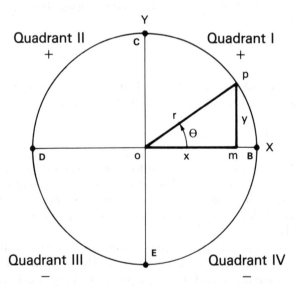

FIGURE 2-5. Angles and Their Trigonometric Functions

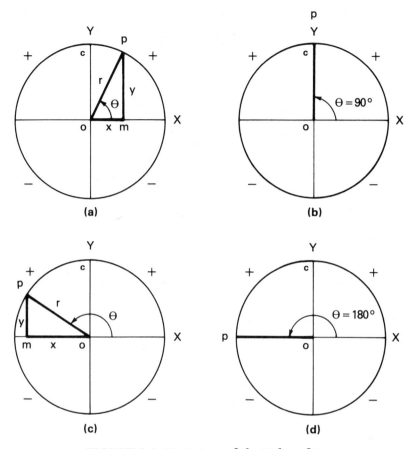

FIGURE 2-6. Variations of the Value of θ

However, the continuing increase of θ does not create a continuing increase in y/r. Notice in Figure 2-6 (b) that θ is a 90° angle, P coincides with y, and y = OC = r. Yet, in Figure 2-6 (c), as θ goes from 90° to 180°, y becomes smaller, and in Figure 2-6 (d) sine θ decreases in value to 0.

The rotation of the line OP into the negative quadrants creates the same (but negative) values of sine θ as we found in the positive quadrants.

In order to construct a graph of sine θ, let Y = sine θ. From tables readily available in math books, Figure 2-7 (a) is drawn. Each value of sine θ can be plotted and the curve drawn through the plotted points. The plotted curve is called a sine wave because its shape is proportional to sine θ and the position within the quadrants. The curve can be smoothed by plotting more points. However, these points are sufficient for our discussion.

As θ increases beyond 360°, the curve repeats its behavior. This characteristic is known as a periodic function. The graph of Y = sin θ demonstrates that the sine wave oscillates about the x axis with a maximum distance of 1 from the axis.

θ	0°	90°	180°	270°	360°
Y (sin θ)	0	1	0	−1	0

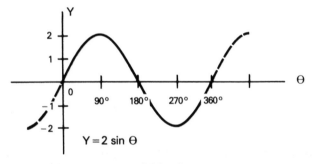

(a) Y = sin θ

θ	0°	90°	180°	270°	360°
sin θ	0	1	0	−1	0
Y (2 sin θ)	0	2	0	−2	0

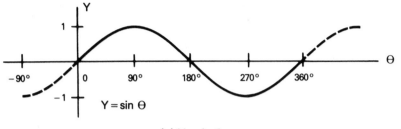

(b) Y = 2 sin θ

FIGURE 2-7. Graph of the Sine Curve

The Amplitude Factor and the Cosine Curve

Another curve can be plotted as $Y = a \sin \theta$ with each value of $\sin \theta$ multiplied by the value a to determine the corresponding value of Y. The a value is called the amplitude factor because it determines the curve's swing about the x axis. An amplitude factor 2 ($Y = 2 \sin \theta$) is plotted in Figure 2-7(b).

The cosine curve resembles the sine curve, but differs by 90°. The cosine curve can be plotted with $y = \cos \theta$ as depicted in Figure 2-8. Like the sine curve, the cosine curve is repetitive and rotates about the θ axis. The cosine

Θ	0°	90°	180°	270°	360°
Y cos Θ	1	0	−1	0	+1

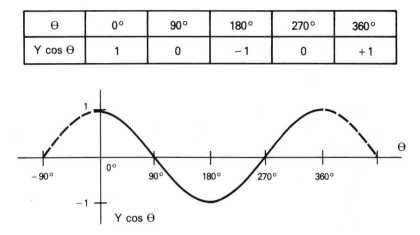

FIGURE 2-8. Graph of the Cosine Curve

wave shows a shift of ¼ of a period [Y = cos (θ − 90°)]. The cosine curve is merely moving ¼ of one period to the left of the origin. This curve is the cosine curve with respect to the original axis.

The relationships we have just discussed are summarized in Figure 2-9. A vector starts at position zero and rotates counterclockwise around a circle. The end of the rotating vector can be marked off by a horizontal scale (the dotted lines in Figure 2-9) at any point in the rotation. The complete rotation of the vector around the circle is plotted as a sine wave. We have learned it is so named because the amplitude (a) is proportional to the sine of the angle of rotation of the vector. The circle on the left side of Figure 2-9 is called a phase diagram.

The angles of vectors are expressed in radians (rad = 57.3°). The radian is a convenient term because it describes the angular part of the vector rotation that includes an arc equal to the radius of the circle. The circumfer-

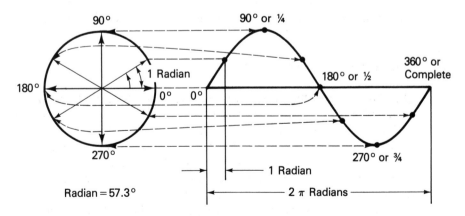

FIGURE 2-9. Rotating Vector Plotted as a Sine Wave

ence around the circle equals 2 π rad. As Figure 2-9 demonstrates, the vector goes through 2 π radians during one complete revolution. Thus, the length of one cycle is 2 π radians, because 2 π rad = 360° (2 * 3.141592 * 57.3 = 360).

Angular Velocity

The sound or electrical waveform is subject to varying frequencies. From the context of Figure 2-9, a rapidly rotating vector produces more cycles per second. This rate of vector rotation is called the angular velocity (AV). A rotation rate of 2 π radians per second produces 1 cycle per second; 4 π radians per second produces 2 cycles per second, and so on. Angular velocity is a function of the frequency of the waveform:

$$AV = 2 \pi * f$$

Where: AV = radians per second; 2 π = radians per cycle; and f = cycles per second.

Figure 2-9 also shows another important component of the waveform, the phase. It represents the relative position of time within the period of a signal. The phase is usually measured in degree markings, which depict the position in the waveform. For example, a 90° phase describes the vector angle and the point in the waveform of a relative position of ¼ t; that is, a position of one fourth through the wave.

A single waveform is represented by the equation:

$$a = A \sin (2\pi \, ft) + \theta$$

Where: a = instantaneous amplitude; A = maximum amplitude; f = frequency; t = time; and, θ = phase.

Figure 2-10 shows two sine waves of the same frequency but out of phase with each other. One wave is described as a = A sin (2 π ft) and the other by a = A sin (2 π ft + θ), where θ represents the phase difference.

From previous discussions, we now know that we can also plot one of these curves as a sine curve and the other as a cosine curve.

ANALOG AND DIGITAL SIGNALS

The data communications systems that use the telephone line must cope with the fact that the majority of telephone local lines (loops) to our homes and offices are designed and constructed around human speech. Those signals exhibit the analog waveform characteristics discussed in the previous section. Analog means a periodic signal gradually changes its amplitude levels or current strength. Periodic means the sine wave variation from crest to crest is just like the other preceding waves.

However, computers, printers, terminals, and other data communications devices are digital devices: numbers and other symbols are represent-

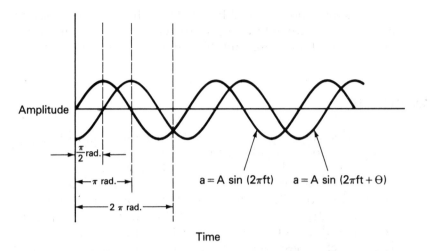

FIGURE 2-10. Phase Differences of Waveforms

ed by discrete signals. Typically, these symbols take the form of binary (1 and 0) values by abrupt changes in voltage levels or current flow (see Figure 2-11).

The earliest computational machines (e.g., Leibniz's calculator in 1673; Hollerith's tabulator in 1890) were discrete signalling devices. Today's computers employ solid state technology to represent letters and numbers as a code of discrete, digital signals. As we shall see in Chapter 3, a data communications system can modify certain characteristics of the analog waveform (its amplitude, frequency, or phase) to represent the digital data of computers.

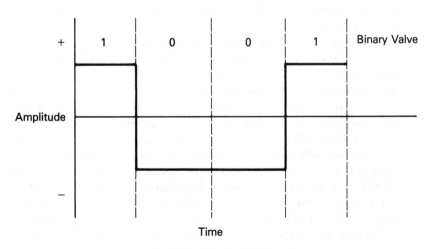

FIGURE 2-11. Digital Signals

It should now be readily apparent why we must understand the nature and characteristics of the analog waveform: it is used to carry data across an analog communications link to/from computers and terminals.

BANDWIDTH

The analog voice signal is not made up of one unique frequency. Rather, the voice signal on a communications line consists of waveforms of many different frequencies. The particular mix of these frequencies is what determines the sound of a person's voice. Many phenomena manifest themselves as a combination of different frequencies. The colors in the rainbow, for instance, are combinations of many different lightwave frequencies; musical sounds consist of different acoustic frequencies that are interpreted as higher or lower pitch. These phenomena consist of a range or band of frequencies called the bandwidth, stated as:

$$BW = f_1 - f_2$$

Where: BW = bandwidth; f_1 = highest frequency; f_2 = lowest frequency.

As examples, a piano can produce a wide range of frequencies ranging from about 30 Hz (low notes) to over 4200 Hz (high notes). Its bandwidth is from 30 Hz to 4200 Hz. The human ear can detect sounds over a range of frequencies from around 40 to 18,000 Hz, but the telephone system does not transmit this band of frequencies. The full range is not needed to interpret the voice signal at the receiver, because most of the energy is concentrated between 300 and 3100 Hz, as shown by Figure 2-12. In fact, the vowels in speech occupy mostly the lower portion of the frequency band and the consonants, which actually contain most of the information in speech, use much less power, and generally occupy the higher frequencies. Due to economics, only the frequency band of approximately 200 to 3500 Hz is transmitted across the path.

It is not necessary to reproduce the speech signals with complete accuracy on the channel, because the human ear is not sensitive to precise frequency differences, and the human brain possesses great inferential powers to reconstruct the intelligence of the speech. Even with the frequency cutoffs, 98% of the speech energy and 85% of the intelligence are still present in a transmission. Nonetheless, the band-limited channel is one reason why voices sound different on a telephone line.

The so-called voiceband (or voice-grade) channel is defined as a band of 4000 Hz. This means the channel consists of frequencies ranging from 0 to 4000 Hz. The speech signal is bandlimited to between 200 and 3500 Hz [REY83]. For purposes of convenience and brevity, this book uses the value 3 KHz as the bandwidth for a voiceband channel. The other frequencies on both sides of the speech signal allow for guardbands, which lessen interfer-

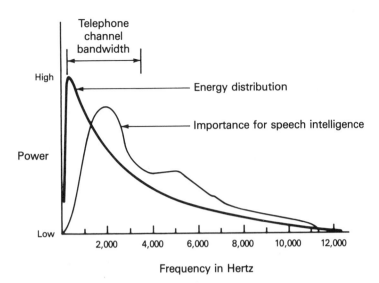

FIGURE 2-12. Energy Distribution and Speech Intelligence

ence between the channels that are placed on the same physical media such as a wire or cable. The relationship of human hearing, speech, and the voiceband channel are shown in Figure 2-13.

We have learned that speech signals on a voiceband channel are made up of many frequencies. This also holds true for other communications circuits such as radio and television channels. The spectrum of the signal describes the range of frequencies of the signal, or its bandwidth.

Bandwidth is a very important concept in communications because the capacity (stated in bits per second) of a communications channel is partially dependent on its bandwidth. If the telephone channel were increased from a bandwidth of 3 kilohertz (KHz) to 20 KHz, it could carry all the characteristics of the voice. The same is true for transmitting data; a higher data transmission rate can be achieved with a greater bandwidth.

The greater the bandwidth, the greater the capacity. This statement is explained by Table 2-1. The frequency spectrum ranges from the relatively limited ranges of the audio frequencies through the radio ranges, the infrared (red light) ranges, the visible light frequencies, and up to the X-ray and cosmic ray band. The capacity of the higher frequencies can readily be seen by an examination of the bandwidth of the audio-frequency spectrum and that of radio. The bandwidth between 10^3 and 10^4 is 9000 Hz $(10,000 - 100 = 9000)$, which is roughly equivalent to three voice-grade bands. The bandwidth between 10^7 and 10^8 (the HF and VHF spectrum) is 90,000,000 Hz $(100,000,000 - 10,000,000 = 90,000,000)$, which could support several thousand voiceband circuits.

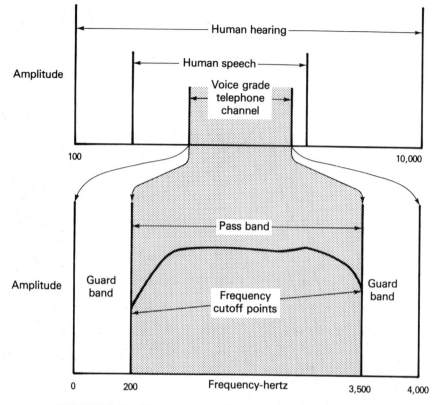

FIGURE 2-13. Hearing, Speech, and Voiceband Channels

SQUARE WAVES AND HARMONICS

A periodic signal such as acoustic speech or an electrical signal conveying speech is made up of a number of waveforms. The exact multiples of the fundamental frequency are called harmonic frequencies (or just harmonics). Typical audio waveforms exhibit odd harmonics (odd multiples of the fundamental frequency) and even harmonics (even multiples of the fundamental frequency). A person's voice is distinguished from someone else's voice because the harmonic components differ.

Earlier material demonstrated that a periodic waveform has the same shape with each cycle. Figure 2-14 shows some examples of signals that are periodic waveforms. These square wave and sawtooth wave signals can be shaped by superimposing a number of waves onto each other, each with specific phase, frequency, and amplitude attributes.

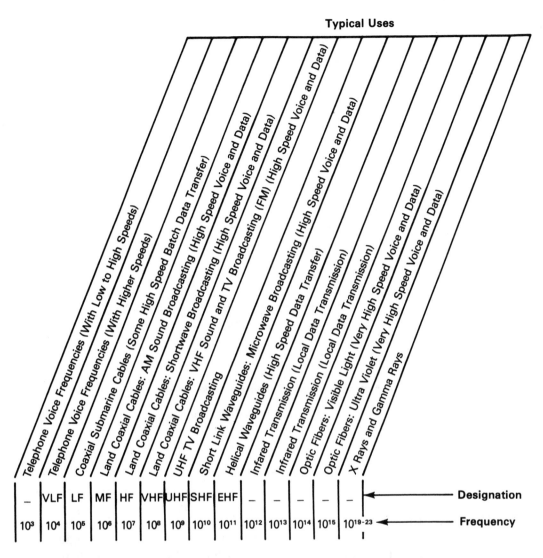

Typical Uses

	VLF	LF	MF	HF	VHF	UHF	SHF	EHF	–	–	–	–	–			**Designation**
10^3	10^4	10^5	10^6	10^7	10^8	10^9	10^{10}	10^{11}	10^{12}	10^{13}	10^{14}	10^{15}	10^{19-23}			**Frequency**

Note: Applications may "overlap" the frequency designations or not use the entire frequency spectrum. For example, the highest UHF TV Channel (83) is 8.84 – 8.90 $* 10^8$ Hertz.

TABLE 2-1. The Frequency Spectrum

Any periodic signal can be shown to be a sum of its components, where each component is a sinusoid:

$$x(t) = \sum_{n=0}^{\infty} a_n \cos(2\pi nf_0t) + \sum_{n=1}^{\infty} b_n \sin(2\pi nf_0t)$$

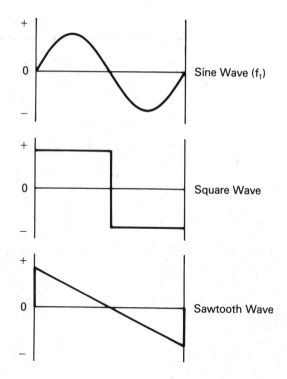

Note: Frequency is 1 KHz and period is 1ms

FIGURE 2-14. Periodic Waveforms

Where: f_0 = the inverse of the period of the signal (f_0 = 1/T).

The sine wave in Figure 2-14 also appears on a spectrum analyzer as in Figure 2-15, which graphs the signal's frequency versus its amplitude. As you can see, the frequency domain is a bar graph showing all the frequency components that exist within a wave. A pure sine wave (in Figure 2-15) contains only one frequency component (in this illustration a period of 1 ms and a frequency of 1 KHz).

The superimposition of an odd multiple of wave harmonics onto each other creates a different type of signal called a square wave (see Figure 2-16 [a]) [HEAT81]. In fact, the perfect square wave is made up of an infinite number of odd harmonics. With each addition of an odd harmonic, the resultant waveform approaches the shape of a square wave. The frequency domain of the square wave is depicted in Figure 2-16 (b). The signal is composed of odd order harmonics, and an infinite number of harmonics creates a perfect square wave. Yet another waveform (the sawtooth) is depicted in Figure 2-16 (c). The resultant signal is created from both odd and even harmonics. The frequency domain of the sawtooth wave is shown in Figure 2-16(d).

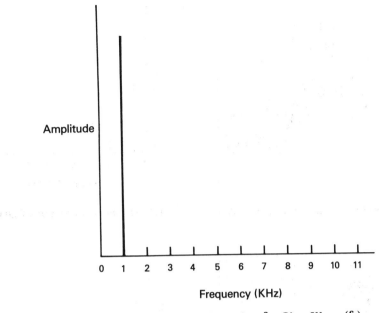

FIGURE 2-15. Frequency Domain of a Sine Wave (f_1)

Two important points of this discussion to remember are: (1) waveforms and signals can be created from many varieties of frequencies, and (2) a signal can be broken down into its constituent, individual sine waves.

Figures 2-16 (e) and 2-16 (f) show the signal with a dc component, which is a unidirectional flow of the signal on the channel of a fixed voltage polarity. The signals explained thus far have exhibited ac components that periodically alternate in polarity. Notice the ac component signal has an average amplitude of zero. The dc component signal has a nonzero average voltage value (in this case, positive voltage). We examine dc and ac components later in discussions on data encoding.

The spectrum of the square wave in Figure 2-16 (b) extends from f_1 to $5f_1$. Its bandwidth is the total number of frequencies it contains, stated as:

$$W = hf - lf$$

Where: W = bandwidth; hf = highest frequency in the signal; lf = lowest frequency in the signal. In Figure 2-17 (a), the bandwidth is $4f_1$ ($5f_1$ − $1f_1$). If f = 1000 Hz, then W = 4000 Hz.

BROADBAND AND BASEBAND SIGNALS

Signals are usually categorized as either broadband or baseband. A broadband signal is identified by the following characteristics:

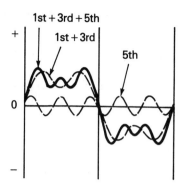

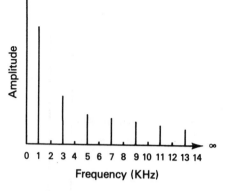

(a) Components of a Square Wave

(b) Frequency Domain of a Square Wave

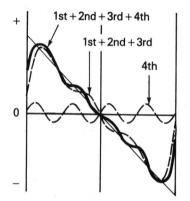

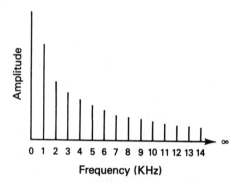

(c) Components of a Sawtooth Wave

(d) Frequency Domain of a Sawtooth Wave

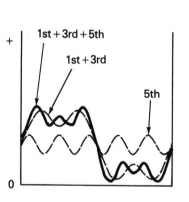

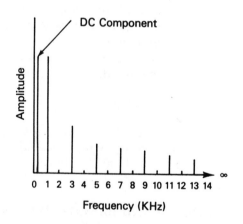

(e) DC Component in Square Wave

(f) Square Wave With DC Component

FIGURE 2-16. Frequency Domain Analysis [HEAT81]

- uses analog waveforms
- has a large bandwidth (typically in the megahertz to gigahertz range)
- uses analog modulation
- often uses frequency division multiplexing for channel sharing

A baseband signal is identified by the following characteristics:

- uses digital signals (voltage shifts)
- bandwidth is limited
- does not use modulation
- may use time-division multiplexing for channel sharing

The reader should be aware that some people use the term baseband to describe an unmodulated signal. A baseband signal may be used to modulate an analog carrier signal, but the carrier need not be a broadband carrier; it may be a voiceband carrier, which is not considered a broadband signal.

FILTERS

It is often quite desirable to be able to separate the frequencies that operate on a circuit. To emphasize the importance of frequency separation, consider these examples. The lower and higher frequencies on a voice-grade channel are separated and blocked for purposes of economics and performance. Radio signals also require channel separation and many signals are separated from each other through guardbands to prevent signal interference. Moreover, signal separation plays a vital part in the process of analog-to-digital (A/D) and digital-to-analog (D/A) conversion systems.

The most common approach is the use of a filter to select or reject a frequency or a group of frequencies. For example, Figure 2-17 shows a high-pass filter that passes a 10 KHz input signal but blocks a 100 Hz signal. Conversely, the low-pass filter performs the opposite service.

Generally, data communications systems make use of four kinds of filters (see Figure 2-17 [b]):

- *High-pass filter:* attenuates lower frequency signals and passes higher frequency signals
- *Low-pass filter:* passes lower frequency signals and attenuates higher frequency signals
- *Band-pass filter:* attenuates frequencies above and below a specific level and passes the signals within the band
- *Band-stop filter:* passes signals above and below a specific band and attenuates the signals within the specified frequency band

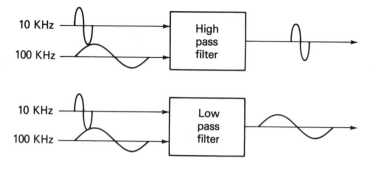

(a)

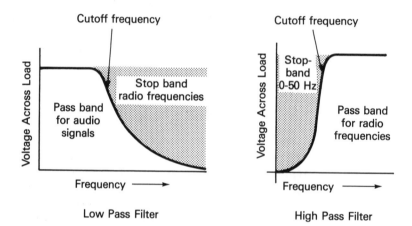

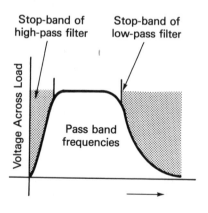

(b)

FIGURE 2-17. Filters [GROB71]

THE DECIBEL

The engineers who design and maintain communications systems must be concerned with the quality and strength of the signals in the system. Typically, a communications link consists of a number of different components such as amplifiers, communications lines, and switches. Each component will introduce signal loss or gain into the signal.

These losses and gains are described as a ratio of power into and out of the component:

$$\text{Power ratio} = \frac{\text{Power Out}}{\text{Power In}}$$

A tandem link (in which several components connect the two communicating devices) necessitates a calculation of loss/gain at each component and the multiplication of these ratios together. For example, assume five components introduce the following losses or gains:

$$\tfrac{1}{2} * \tfrac{1}{10} * \tfrac{1}{50} * \tfrac{1}{50} * \tfrac{10000}{1} = 2$$

Thus, the signal is twice as strong at the end of the tandem link as it was at the beginning.

This multiplication process can be tedious and the numbers can be very small or very large. Instead of multiplying the numbers together, the same result can be obtained by adding the logarithms of the numbers. Today, the standard practice is to use the logarithms of the ratios, rather than the ratios themselves.

The term decibel (dB) (named after the inventor of the telephone, Alexander Graham Bell) is used in communications to express the ratio of two values. The values can represent power, voltage, current, or sound levels. It should be emphasized that the decibel is (1) a ratio and not an absolute value, (2) expresses a logarithmic relationship and not a linear one, and (3) can be used to indicate either a gain or a loss. The logarithm is useful because a signal's strength falls off logarithmically as it passes through a cable.

A decibel is 10 times the logarithm (in base 10) of the ratio:

$$dB = 10 \log_{10} P_1/P_2$$

Where: dB = number of decibels; $\log_{10}$ = logarithm to the base 10; P_1 = one value of the power; P_2 = comparison of value of the power.

Decibels are often used to measure the gain or loss of a communications signal. These measurements are quite valuable for testing the quality of lines and determining noise and signal losses, all of which must be known in order to design communications systems. It is a very useful unit because it can be added or subtracted as a signal is cascaded through a communications link. For example, if a line introduces 1 dB of loss in a span of one mile, a three-mile length will produce a loss of 3 dB. If the line is connected to an amplifier with a gain of 10 dB, then the total gain is 7 dB.

Suppose a communications line is tested at the sending and receiving ends. The P1/P2 ratio yields a reduction of the signal power from the sending to receiving end by a ratio of 200:1. The signal experiences a 23 dB loss ($23 = 10 \log_{10} 200$). The log calculations are readily available from tables published in math books.

The decibel is often used to describe the level of noise on the circuit by a signal-to-noise ratio. As Table 2-2 shows, 0 dB is equivalent to a 1:1 ratio of the signal to noise.

Since the decibel is a ratio and not an absolute unit, it is meaningless if we have no reference level by which to apply the ratio. For example, a 30 dB increase of 1 watt of power is considerably different from a 30 dB increase of 1 milliwatt of power. It is common practice to use a reference level of a watt or a milliwatt.

The dBW (decibel-watt) is employed for microwave systems. The measurement is made to a reference and expressed as:

$$\text{Power (dBW)} = 10 \log \frac{\text{Power (W)}}{1W}$$

The dBm is used as a relative power measurement in which the reference power is 1 milliwatt (0.001 watt):

$$\text{dBm} = 10 \log_{10} P/001$$

TABLE 2-2. Decibels and Signal-to-Noise Ratios

Decibels (dB)	Signal-to-Noise Ratios
0	2:1
+ 3	2:1
+ 6	4:1
+ 9	8:1
+10	10:1
+13	20:1
+16	40:1
+19	80:1
+20	100:1
+23	200:1
+26	400:1
+29	800:1
+30	1000:1
+33	2000:1
+36	4000:1
+39	8000:1
+40	10000:1

Where: P = signal power in milliwatts (mW).

This approach allows measurements to be taken in relation to a standard. A signal of a known power level is inserted at one end and measured at the other. A 0 dBm reading means 1 mW.

Carriers (such as telephone companies) use a 1004 Hz tone (referred to as a 1 KHz test tone) to test a line. The 1 KHz tone is used as a reference to other test tones of a different level. The test tone is used to establish a zero transmission level point (TLP). The TLP is a convenient concept for relating signal or noise levels at various points in the communications system. It is common practice to consider the outgoing 2 wire class 5 system as the 0 dB TLP reference point and all gains/losses are compared to this value.

CHANNEL (LINK) CAPACITY

Channel capacity is determined by, dependent upon, or related to several factors that will be explained at appropriate sections in this book:

Bandwidth

Data rate

Amount of noise on the channel

Modulation techniques

Encoding techniques

Let us examine the relationship of bandwidth to data rate (later we will add the other factors, but the bandwidth analysis is sufficient for the present). The greater the bandwidth of a channel, the greater the data rate (in bits per second) can be. Conversely, the greater the data rate, the greater the bandwidth must be to support the data rate. For example, if a positive voltage represents a binary 0 and a negative voltage represents a binary 1, then a channel can support two voltage changes per cycle. The periodic waveforms in Figure 2-16 can represent a 1 or 0 in each half of the cycle.

It is instructive to note that each period (t) contains a bit value of 0 or 1, so the data rate in bits per second is $2f_1$. If f_1 is 1000 Hz$_1$, the bit rate is 2000 bit/s. Figure 2-16 (a) shows that a fifth harmonic is needed to adequately shape the signal on the channel. Consequently, the bandwidth (W) requirement for 2000 bit/s is: $5f_1 - f_1 = 4$ KHz. A bandwidth of twice the data rate provides an accurate representation of the binary 1 or 0, but later discussions demonstrate that the signal can be recovered with less bandwidth.

The discussions thus far have focused on data rate as a function of bandwidth. Several other critical factors are also involved, and are discussed in the next section.

THE FOUNDATIONS OF COMMUNICATIONS THEORY

The early communications devices (and many devices today) did not use analog signalling. The use of dc signals was preferred because the systems were inexpensive and simple. The technique is still a widely used technology.

The dc signals are sent over a channel at their originating frequencies; they are not modified but are transmitted as voltage pulses or current changes, as shown in Figure 2-11. This type of transmission is called a baseband signal.

The telegraph is an example of baseband dc signalling. Although the telegraph is not used much today, baseband signalling is quite prevalent in modern systems such as EIA-232 connectors and many local area networks, (as examples, the IBM token ring and the baseband version of Ethernet).

We now examine the early development of the telegraph and the attributes of baseband signalling. Both subjects are important steps to gaining an understanding of a data communications system.

The Telegraph

In 1832, Samuel F. B. Morse began work on the first successful telegraph. After several attempts, he and Alfred Vail designed a code in 1838 to represent the letters of the alphabet with spaces (absence of an electric current); dots (an electric current of short duration), and dashes (an electric current of longer duration—three times longer than a dot).

This code is the Morse code. It was cleverly designed. The most frequently occurring characters were assigned short code symbols. For example, the letter E was assigned the symbol value of one dot, and a Z was assigned successive dash, dash, dot, dot symbols. (The reader should remember that one symbol was represented by one signal in this early system.) This variable-length code reduced the number of strokes the operator had to make and also decreased the number of signals transmitted across the circuit.

Amazingly, Morse and Vail determined the code structure by counting the number of letters in each bin of a printer's type box. Modern information theory tells us the code could only be improved by some 15 percent!

The endeavors and intuition of these men are still relevant today, for, as we shall see, it matters greatly how data is encoded and changed into the symbols suitable for the communications channel.

One of the major problems encountered by the pioneers was intersymbol interference. The dc current does not build up or decay on the line in an abrupt and clean manner. Consequently, the current takes time to be detected at the receiver. When the telegraph sent a space (no current), the decay of the signal also took time. Intersymbol interference occurred when the dots and dashes followed each other so closely that they ran together at the receiving end, thus becoming indistinguishable. Although we are discussing historical events to provide a background for more complex topics, intersymbol interference remains a problem today.

The main causes of this signal distortion are resistance (R) and capacitance (C); they apply to ac and dc systems. Resistance is the opposition of the conductor to the current flow on the circuit. Capacitance is the tendency of conductors to store energy, i.e., to collect a charge. The buildup and decay of a signal take time. This time factor is called the time constant (RC) and is a function of the resistance (R) and capacitance (C) of the circuit.

The earlier telegraphers devised several methods to ameliorate the undesirable effects of intersymbol interference and signal distortion. One approach had unfortunate consequences. In order to overcome the effects of noise on the first trans-Atlantic cable, and to increase the intelligibility of the code, unduly high voltages were placed on the line, which eventually destroyed the insulation and rendered the cable useless.

Other approaches were more successful. Since a dash takes three times longer to send than a dot, double-current telegraphy was implemented to reduce the longer dash time period. A current in one direction represented a dash and a current in the other direction represented a dot. No current represented a space. Double-current telegraphy improved the speed of the transmission considerably.

Thomas Edison also contributed to the field of communications. In 1874, he developed the novel idea of the quadraplex telegraph. It represented more than one symbol per signal. This idea is known today as multiple level signalling and is an integral part of modern communications.

The quadraplex telegraph used two intensities of current and two directions of current. The two states were independent of each other and thus provided four different conditions of current flow. This technique further increased the speed of transmissions because more information could be transmitted in a given time.

Even though these early efforts were quite valuable to the development of modern data communications systems, a French mathematician and physicist, Jean Baptiste Fourier, laid the foundations for practically all communications theory. Perhaps the reader is unaware of it, but our previous discussions on harmonics, spectral analysis, frequency domains, and filters are all based on Fourier's theory.

Fourier developed his theory based on his observations of the flow of heat and the sine wave. Its relevance to communication theory is (as we know from earlier discussions) that any periodic function F(t) is represented by the sum of a number of sinusoidal variations of different amplitudes, frequencies, and phases. The simplest algorithmic explanation of Fourier's theorem is written as follows:

$$F(t) = A_0 + A_1 \sin(2 \pi \, ft + \theta_1)$$
$$+ A_2 \sin(2 \pi * 2ft + \theta_2)$$
$$\cdot$$
$$\cdot$$
$$\cdot$$
$$+ A_n \sin(2 \pi * nft + \theta_n)$$

Fourier's contemporaries were taken aback by the simplicity, elegance, and significance of his theorem. It applies to the composition of many physical phenomena such as the color of light, the vibration and resulting sounds of a musical instrument, the temperature of an electric heater, as well as the signals in a communications system.

The implication of Fourier to data communications can be seen in Figure 2-18 [TANE81]. Let us assume an 8-bit ASCII/IA5 character is transmitted (the letter b: 01100010, with odd parity). We have learned previously that a low bandwidth prevents the transmission of multiple harmonics. As Figures 2-18(b), 2-18(c), and 2-18(d) show, the limited bandwidth and resulting harmonics restrict the accurate shaping of the transmitted letter. In contrast, Figure 2-18(e) shows that sufficient bandwidth and harmonics allow the signal to be shaped quite accurately.

Assume for the time being that each bit is represented by one signal change (or cycle in this case) on the line. Recall from earlier discussions that $t = 1/f$; therefore, a 2400 bit/s transmission has a t value of .000416 second. It then takes 3.33 mseconds (.000416 * 8 bits = .00333) to send the letter b through the channel. (Stated another way, t for the letter b is 8/2400 = .00333).

Since a voiceband telephone line is bandlimited to around 3000 Hz, the highest number of harmonics that can be passed is approximately: bandwidth / first harmonic transmitted. This limit is determined by not only the bandwidth but the frequency of the first harmonic. These relationships are shown in Table 2-3.

Our analysis reveals that sending a high data rate (such as 9.6 Kbit/s) over a conventional voice grade line (without error correction or clever encoding schemes) is likely to make accurate reception very difficult. Since only two harmonics can be transmitted, the received waveform resembles Figure 2-18(c).

Thomas Edison, The Quadraplex Telegraph, and Multilevel Signalling

How do the modern systems actually transmit data rates of 9.6 Kbit/s and even 19.2 Kbit/s over a low bandwidth channel? Today, these high data rates can be obtained on a relatively low-quality, voiceband-limited dial-up telephone line. We are not defying Fourier; we have simply borrowed some ideas from the pioneers in this field. The earlier introduction of Edison's quadraplex telegraph provides the first clue.

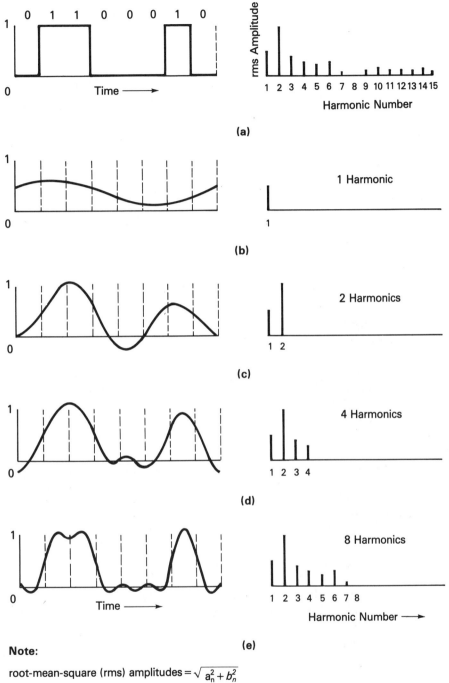

Note:

root-mean-square (rms) amplitudes $= \sqrt{a_n^2 + b_n^2}$

rms is used to measure a current or voltage: rms $= .0707 * $ peak value

which is a value of $45°$.

FIGURE 2-18. Transmission of the Letter b [TANE81]

TABLE 2-3. Data Rate and Harmonics

Bit Rate (in bit/s[1])	Time Required to Transmit 8-bit Character (bits in character/bit rate)	First Harmonic Transmitted	Number of Harmonics Sent (bandwidth/first harmonic)
300	26.67	37.5	80
600	13.33	75	40
1200	6.67	150	20
2400	3.33	300	10
4800	1.67	600	5
9600	0.83	1200	2
19200	0.42	2400	1
38400	0.21	4800	0

[1]Data assumes *one-to-one* relationship between bit rate and signed change.

Edison's machine represented multiple symbols per current state. As discussed previously, this design permitted each signal to represent (a) current direction and (b) current intensity; each was independent of the other. In modern terms, this means two symbols (1 or 0) can be sent with each signal change. Today we describe the rate of signalling change by the term baud. Baud describes the number of signalling changes per second. Edison's primitive machine was a multilevel device: sending multiple symbols (two) per baud.

Table 2-3 shows a system wherein 1 bit/s equals a baud. This single-level scheme restricts the bit throughput due to the limited bandwidth. Multilevel transmission offers the opportunity to increase the bit rate across the line. To understand this concept more fully, we must examine the classical work performed by Harry Nyquist in the 1920s concerning the capacity of a noiseless channel [NYQU24].

Noiseless Channels and Harry Nyquist

Nyquist showed that a channel with bandwidth W can carry 2W symbols per second. However, if a signal change takes the form of more than two states (for example, four voltage levels), then the channel capacity is 4W symbols per second. Four symbols can represent any combination of 0 and 1:

00   first symbol possibility
01   second symbol possibility
10   third symbol possibility
11   fourth symbol possibility

Eight alternative voltages per signal change (i.e., baud) can be used to provide any possible combination of 3 bits ($2^3 = 8$). Sixteen voltages per baud represent any combination of 4 bits ($2^4 = 16$) and so on.

From the above discussion, it follows that in the absence of noise, channel capacity (C) is stated as:

$$C = 2W \log_2 L$$

Generally speaking, n bits can be transmitted by 2n possible signalling levels. A signal with a signalling rate of 2nW bit/s can be sent through a channel with W Hz of bandwidth. The following relationship exists:

$2n = L$, therefore
$n = \log_2 L$

Where: L is the number of signalling levels (for example, multiple amplitude levels or multiple combinations of phase changes). An 8-level transmitter (for example, a typical modem) yielding 3 bits per baud provides a C of 18,300 bit/s on a noiseless channel.

We now know how modern systems achieve such a high bit rate across a seemingly low capacity voiceband telephone line: by multilevel signalling.

The inquiring reader might wonder if this equation restricts the volume of L. Indeed, why not make L very large and achieve a very high data rate? Several factors restrict the magnitude of L value. First, the electrical properties of the line (resistance, capacitance, attenuation, etc.) restrict L. Second, the larger the value of L, the smaller the increments must be between the levels within the signal. If a signal is restricted to five volts, a large L value means the signal voltage differences are quite small. As a result, the receiver must be very sophisticated (and expensive) to discern the small differences between the small voltages. Moreover, any slight distortion on the channel makes the voltage differences indistinguishable. Third, the channel is not noiseless; the signal must manifest itself in the presence of noise which limits C rather dramatically.

Noisy Channels

With this in mind, we must examine the characteristics of one type of noise (others are explained in Chapter 7). Then we can understand the profound implications of the work of Shannon and Hartley, as well as the concepts of entropy and data encoding.

The noise to which we refer is the thermal noise, and all communications conductors and electronic circuitry possess it. It cannot be eliminated. Thermal noise is called Gaussian noise because its amplitude varies randomly around a certain level. It is also called white noise because the noise is distributed uniformly (i.e., averaged) across the frequency spectrum, just as white light is an average of all the color frequencies.

In a conductor, such as a wire or cable, the nonrandom movement of electrons creates an electric current that is used for the transmission signal. Along with these signals, all electrical components also experience the vibrations of the random movement of electrons. These vibrations cause the emission of electromagnetic waves of all frequencies. Other kinds of noise exist that can affect transmission quality. For example, space noise results from the sun and other stars radiating energy over a broad frequency spectrum. Atmospheric noise comes from electrical disturbances in the earth's atmosphere.

The thermal noise (N) present in an electrical conductor can be calculated as:

$$N = k\,TW$$

Where: k is Boltzmann's constant ($1.37 * 10^{-23}$ joules per degree); T is temperature in degrees (Kelvin); and W is bandwidth (note that bandwidth [W] is one determinant of thermal noise).

Some twenty years after the work of Nyquist, Claude Shannon developed a set of theories that have become known as Shannon's Law. Its best-known concept is that the capacity of a channel (in bit/s) is determined by its bandwidth (W) and the ratio of the power in the signal to the power in the noise [SHAN48]:

$$C = W \log_2 (1 + S/N)$$

Where: S is the power in the signal and N is the power in the thermal noise.

The law is not refutable. We can certainly achieve faster data rates by increasing the bandwidth, increasing the signal power, or both. Nonetheless, Shannon's Law sets the absolute data transmission rate that can be achieved.

The Signal-to-Noise Ratio

A typical voice-grade line yields a S/N ratio of 1000 to 1. Given a bandwidth of 3100 Hz, the channel could theoretically support a data transmission rate of 30.8 Kbit/s (C = 3100 $\log_2$ (1 + 1000/1) = 38,894). (Many user devices do not utilize the full voiceband spectrum and are much slower.) This theoretical rate is further constrained by other factors such as signal decay (attenuation) and other types of noise. Consequently, modern powerful high-speed modems operate at lesser speeds, generally from 9.6 Kbit/s to 19.2 Kbit/s.

The signal-to-noise ratio is often used to determine an effective data rate and a permissible S/N value. This determination rests on the ratio of energy level per bit (E_b) to the energy level per hertz (N_0), or E_b/N_0. At a given bit rate, the increase of N_0 also requires an increase in E_b. Moreover, at a given E_b/N_0, an increase in the data transmission rate increases the number of bits that will be distorted. Consequently, the ratio is important because the power level must be increased relative to noise to support an increased bit rate.

Entropy

Shannon's work went beyond his famous law. Prior to his work on this formula, he was concerned with what kind of signal would give the fastest transmission over the noisy channel. Stated another way, how could data be represented or encoded to attain a faster transmission? Samuel Morse approached this topic by empirical observation; Shannon used the concept of entropy.

Entropy is a measure of uncertainty or randomness. An increase in entropy means a decrease in order. Recent research has lead to a startling discovery about randomness: (1) It is fundamental to almost all events; a very simple deterministic system can generate random behavior; and (2) gathering more data about certain phenomena will not make them more predictable. This aspect of randomness is called chaos [CRUT86].

We will have more to say about randomness, chaos, and entropy in later discussions on data compression, error control, and artificial intelligence. For the present analysis, the relevance of entropy to information theory and data communications can be summarized from [HART28].

The entropy of received data in a communications system is a measure of the uncertainty of the contents in the data stream. The entropy associated with an 8-bit character can vary from 0 to 8 bits. For example, in Figure 2-18, if we do not know what is transmitted (the letter b), the entropy is 8 bits per character and can have $2^8 = 256$ possible different states, since each bit can be 0 or 1.

The entropy (H) of the 8-bit symbol is:

$$H = -(P_1 \log_2 P_1 + P_2 \log_2 P_2 \ldots + P_{256} \log_2 P_{256})$$

Or, more simply:

$$H = - \sum_{i=1}^{n} P_i \log_2 P_i$$

Where: n = possible states. That is, entropy (H) is the negative of the sum of each probability multiplied by the logarithm of each probability.

Yet we know (as did Morse) that certain characters are transmitted more frequently than others. For example, the letter E is transmitted more frequently than the letter Z. If we know for certain what the symbol will be, then one of the P values is 1, all the others must be 0 and:

$$H = - \log_2 1 = 0$$

Therefore, entropy equals zero when we are certain of the contents of the data.

If the character consists of 8 bits, each of which could be 0 or 1, the entropy can range from 0 to 8:

$$H = -256 * \frac{1}{256} \log_2 \frac{1}{256}$$
$$-256 * \frac{1}{256} * \text{-8}$$
$$- 1 * \text{-8} = 8$$

To expand the discussion, let us pick a smaller number of possible states (although we return to the coding of characters shortly because it is the essence of this discussion). Suppose we observe the tendencies of a football team in first down situations; it runs $\frac{3}{4}$ of the time and passes $\frac{1}{4}$ of the time. Then:

$$H = - (\frac{1}{4} \log_2 \frac{1}{4} + \frac{3}{4} \log_2 \frac{3}{4}) = .811$$

which is less random than the value 1.

A football scout knows more about what to expect from this team, at least on first down situations. (With some teams I have observed, entropy equals 0 on most of their plays.) In the same manner, if data transmissions contain some degree of (a) predictability or (b) redundancy, then the entropy value will be less than if they were purely random. This being the case, it is possible to develop a variable coding scheme for an alphabet that uses the fewest number of bits per transmitted character.

Shannon approached this topic by describing entropy (H) as the number of bits per symbol and stated it was possible to transmit across a channel of bandwidth C at a rate of C/H. In less elegant terms, we mean that if H is less than or equal to C we can transmit the traffic over the channel; otherwise, don't bother.

This work of Shannon had profound implications for modern communications. It established engineering limits and targets for transmission equipment and media. It set about other efforts to devise coding schemes to maximize throughout and it led to the establishment of data compression techniques.

The reader should now have sufficient background to read Chapter 3, which explains how signals (voice, data, video, etc.) are coded and transmitted across a communications channel.

SUGGESTED READINGS

For the reader who wishes to examine the original references on communications theory, [SHAN48] should be obtained. In addition, [NYQU24] and [HART28] are detailed discussions of the material in this chapter. [TANE81] provides a succinct presentation of the subject. One of the most interesting discourses on communications theory is from [PIER80]. [MART76] remains one of the better references.

QUESTIONS

TRUE/FALSE
1. A signal travels one wavelength during the time of one cycle.
2. The time required for a signal to be transmitted over a distance of one wavelength is called the frequency (f).
3. Exact multiples of a frequency are called harmonics.
4. The superimposition of an odd multiple of wave harmonics onto each other creates a sawtooth wave.
5. The decibel is a ratio that can express either a linear gain or linear loss.
6. Given a sine wave in which 40 cycles are generated in 200 seconds, the sine wave has a period of 20 seconds.
7. Given a sine wave with a period of .0250, its frequency is 40 hertz.
8. When voltages are out-of-phase, the total voltage can be found by adding:
     a) arithmetically
     b) vectorially
     c) peak values
     d) average values
9. The term "angular velocity" as applied to electricity refers to the number of:
     a) radians per second a voltage vector rotates
     b) degrees averaged together
     c) degrees subtracted from the radians
10. Two voltages with 120 Hz have their maximum values displaced by 90°. What is the time difference between the phases?
11. The value(s) associated with sine waves of voltage are:
     a) average
     b) maximum
     c) instantaneous
     d) all of the above
12. From the discussions on sine waves, cycles, and radians, it can be concluded that a radian is always equal to:
     a) the radius of the circle
     b) the circumference of the circle
13. The number of radians per second transversed by an alternating voltage vector is closely related to its:
     a) current sine wave
     b) voltage sine wave
     c) frequency
     d) none of the above

14. Match the term to the appropriate definition:

    Definition

    a) The range of frequencies present in a signal.
    b) Any periodic function is represented by the sum of a number of sinusoidal variations of different amplitudes, frequencies, and phases.
    c) Channel capacity is a function of bandwidth and the signal-to-noise ratio.
    d) The maximum signalling rate is equal to twice the bandwidth.

    Term

    1. Fourier's Theorem
    2. Nyquist Theorem
    3. Bandwidth
    4. Shannon's Law

15. Explain how sound propagates through the air. Include in your description the terms condensations and rarefactions.

16. The interval of space or time in which a waveform reaches a successive point is called a:

    a) cycle
    b) hertz
    c) frequency

    Explain why the two choices you did not select are inappropriate answers.

17. Calculate the period (t) for the following frequencies:

    a) 1800 Hz
    b) 750 KHz

18. Draw a vector around a circle at 45°, 135°, 225°, and 315°. Plot the vector across a horizontal scale to create a sinewave.

19. Write the formula that states: Angular velocity is a function of the radians per second and frequency.

20. To expand on Figure 2-7, fill in the following values:

θ	0°	30°	90°	120°	180°	210°	270°	300°	360°
Sin θ	0		1		0		−1		0
2 sin θ	0		2		0		−2		0

21. Summarize the differences between broadband and baseband signals.

22. Discuss the determinants of channel capacity.

23. If a line loss of two decibels per mile occurs, how much loss occurs on this line, if it extends to 25 miles?

24. Determine the decibels of attenuation from these amounts of surviving power:

Surviving Power	*Decibels of Attenuation*
0.1	
0.001	
0.0001	

25. Given the following information about a sinusoidal signal:

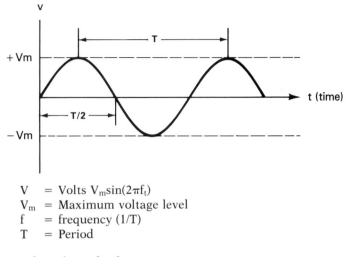

V   = Volts $V_m \sin(2\pi f_t)$
V_m = Maximum voltage level
f   = frequency (1/T)
T   = Period

State the values of V for:
   a) t = 0
   b) t = T/4
   c) t = T/2
   d) t = 3T/4

26. Given the information in the figure in question 25, describe the following terms and concepts:
   a) T
   b) Sinusoid period
   c) frequency
   d) angle in radians
   e) $+V_m$ and $-V_m$

27. Contrast a low-pass filter with a band-pass filter.

28. Compute the decibel loss for an amplifier that has an input of 10 watts and an output of 40 watts.

29. Compute the decibel loss for an amplifier that has an input of 20 watts and an output of 80 watts.

SELECTED ANSWERS

1. True, see Figure 2-3.
2. False. The correct answer is the period (t). It describes the duration of the wavelength and is a function of the frequency.
3. True.
4. False. A square wave is created.
5. False. It experiences a logarithmic gain or logarithmic loss, not linear.
6. False. Since the period is the time required to produce one cycle, the period is: 200/40 = 5 seconds.

7. True. The frequency is equal to 1 divided by the period or:
   1/.0250 = 40

8. b)

9. a)

10. .00416 seconds

11. d)

14.

Definition	Term
a)	3
b)	1
c)	4
d)	2

20.

θ	0°	30°	90°	120°	180°	210°	270°	300°	360°
Sin θ	0	0.5	1	0.9	0	−0.5	−1	−0.9	0
2 sin θ	0	1	2	1.8	0	−1	−2	−1.8	0

24.

Surviving Power	Decibels of Attenuation
0.1	10
0.001	30
0.0001	40

27. A low pass filter rejects signals with high frequencies. In contrast, a band-pass filter attenuates frequencies above and below a specific level (band) and passes (amplifies) the frequencies within the band.

28. $dB = 10 \log_{10} {}^{40}/_{10}$
    $dB = 10 \log_{10} 4$
    $dB = 6.021$ dB of gain

CHAPTER 3

Encoding and Modulation

INTRODUCTION

We know digital signals are used in computer systems to represent binary numbers and we know analog signals are found in most voice-oriented systems. It is common practice today to convert analog to digital signals and vice versa. Four possible conversions are:

1. *Digital-to-analog*: Conversion of digital computer-oriented signals to analog signals in order to use analog-oriented facilities (for example, telephone loops and radio systems).
2. *Analog-to-digital*: Conversion of analog video and voice signals to represent digital signals in order to use more efficient, less expensive and less complex equipment, and to provide one technology (digital) for all forms of transmission.

On the other hand, the initial analog and digital signals may be converted to the same type of signal, but with different characteristics.

3. *Analog-to-analog*: Conversion of analog voice frequency band signals to a different portion of the analog frequency spectrum to share the bandwidth and to take advantage of the capacity of the higher band spectrum.
4. *Digital-to-digital*: Conversion of digital signals to another form of digital signal to use a more efficient encoding structure.

Presently, the industry uses all four techniques to support communication systems. For the immediate future, all will continue to be used. However, digital-to-analog conversion will most certainly decline in use as more telephone systems are converted to digital schemes.

Several systems described in this chapter use a combination of the conversions. For example, digital microwave systems can transmit a voice signal that has been converted to a digital representation through analog-to-digital conversion. The digital microwave system then uses digital-to-analog schemes to modulate the digital signal onto an analog carrier frequency. At the receiving end, the signal is converted to digital signals with analog-to-digital conversion schemes. These digital values are then converted to a close resemblance of the original voice signal with digital-to-analog techniques. This example is one of several systems described in this chapter.

Our task is to examine each of the four conversions. This information is valuable in itself, but it is also needed to understand subject matter in later chapters, because signal conversion is the foundation of many data communications systems.

The reader should keep in mind that several similar modulation techniques are employed in these conversions. For example, similar techniques are used for the analog-to-analog and digital-to-analog schemes. They are explained separately in this chapter because they are used with different applications.

ANALOG-TO-ANALOG CONVERSION

In many situations, such as telephone voice networks and wideband radio systems, the analog voice signal is converted to yet another analog signal. This process may appear redundant, but it is quite useful for the following reasons:

1. Multiple voiceband transmissions cannot occupy the same frequency spectrum on a single medium because the same frequencies cannot be recovered and separated at the receiver. Yet several to many lower bandwidth channels can be supported through one high bandwidth channel. If they are placed onto different frequencies, they can be separated at the receiver by band-pass filters and converted to the original frequencies.

2. Low frequency (e.g., voiceband) signals require very large radio antenna. A direct relationship exists between the wavelength of signals and the size of the antenna. The antenna should be $\frac{1}{4}$ to $\frac{1}{2}$ wavelength in size. A 3 KHz signal would require an immense antenna.

3. Analog signals can be frequency division multiplexed, a technique that permits multiple signals to occupy one transmission medium (thus overcoming the problem cited in point 1).

Amplitude Modulation

A basic amplitude modulation (AM) system is shown in Figure 3-1. A frequency carrier (cos 2 π f$_c$t) and an input signal (a modulating signal or x[t]) are mixed in a modulator, such as a diode or transistor, to produce the resultant signal (s[t]). The output waveform corresponds exactly to the modulating signal waveform. The AM process can be shown as:

$$s(t) = [1 + n_a \, x(t)] \cos 2 \, \pi \, f_c t$$

Chapter 2 explains all the variables to the equation except the modulation index (n$_a$). Its description follows shortly. (The value 1 is a dc component used to prevent loss of information in the signal.)

The Modulation Envelope. AM waveforms exhibit a modulation envelope. The envelope is an expression of the amplitude and frequency of the modulating signal. As Figure 3-2 shows, a high amplitude, low frequency signal produces a different envelope than a low amplitude, high frequency carrier [HEAT81]. The two resultant waveforms have different degrees of modulation, also known as the modulation factor or modulation index n$_a$ (which must range from 0 to 1). The value n$_a$ is calculated as:

$$n_a = \frac{Amax - Amin}{Amax + Amin}$$

Where: Amax = maximum amplitude; Amin = minimum amplitude.

In Figure 3-2, we assume a maximum amplitude of 45 volts and a minimum amplitude of 15 volts. The ratio is:

$$n_a = \frac{45 - 15}{45 + 15} = .5$$

As a general rule, a high modulation index produces a better signal since a receiver only recovers the modulation envelope and not the original

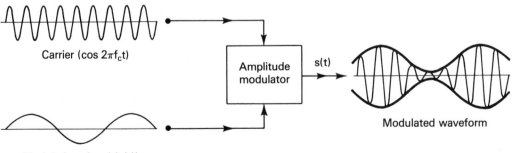

Carrier (cos 2πf$_c$t)

Amplitude modulator

s(t)

Modulated waveform

Modulating signal (x(t))

FIGURE 3-1. Basic Amplitude Modulation

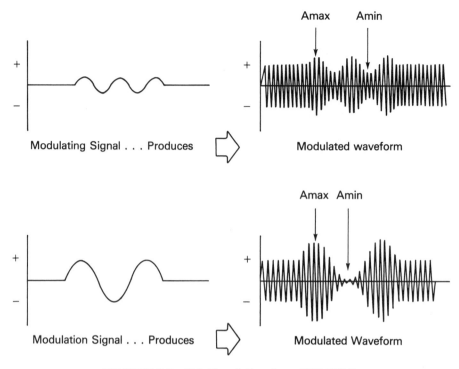

FIGURE 3-2. AM Signal Envelope [HEAT81]

signal (more on this point later). In essence, a higher modulated waveform produces a stronger signal at the receiver, as depicted in Figure 3-3(a) and 3-3 (b). Figure 3-3(b) exhibits a higher modulated waveform. However, whenever the ratio of the input signal to the carrier is too high (as seen in Figure 3-3[c]), the carrier will cut off a portion of the envelope and distort the received waveform. In this example, the minimum amplitude of the carrier is 0 volts. The envelope crosses the time axis and signal information is lost. A portion of each cycle appears to be cut off.

Notwithstanding this overmodulation problem, the following expression demonstrates that n_a should be as close to 1 as possible (although it must remain below 1), in order for the signal power to carry most of the information:

$$P_s(t) = P_c (1 + n_a^2/2)$$

Where: $P_s(t)$ = total transmitted power of the signal; P_c = transmitted power in the carrier.

An interesting situation occurs when the AM signal is applied to a band-pass filter: the original modulating signal is not present. For example, assume a 100 KHz carrier is modulated by a 3 KHz signal. A tuneable band-pass filter on a spectrum analyzer would find the following signals:

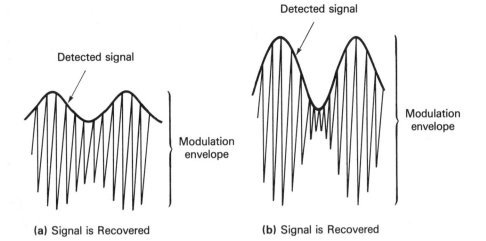

(a) Signal is Recovered

(b) Signal is Recovered

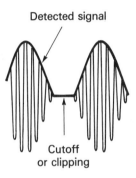

(c) Signal is Not Recovered

FIGURE 3-3. Signal Recovery

—97 KHz

—103 KHz

Sidebands

The two signals 97 KHz and 103 KHz are called sidebands and are an inevitable result of amplitude modulation. The sidebands are calculated as:

$$LSB = f_c - f_m$$
$$USB = f_c + f_m$$

Where: LSB = lower sideband; USB = upper sideband; f_c = carrier frequency; f_m = modulating frequency.

It is instructive to note that both the upper and lower sidebands are replicas of the modulating signal, but the latter signal does not exist. A careful analysis of filter outputs shows how AM actually works. The sidebands constitute different frequencies and consequently are periodically in-phase or out-of-phase with each other. As Figure 3-4 illustrates, when the sidebands are in-phase with each other and the carrier, the modulated envelope displays a high amplitude (point 1). When the sidebands are in-phase

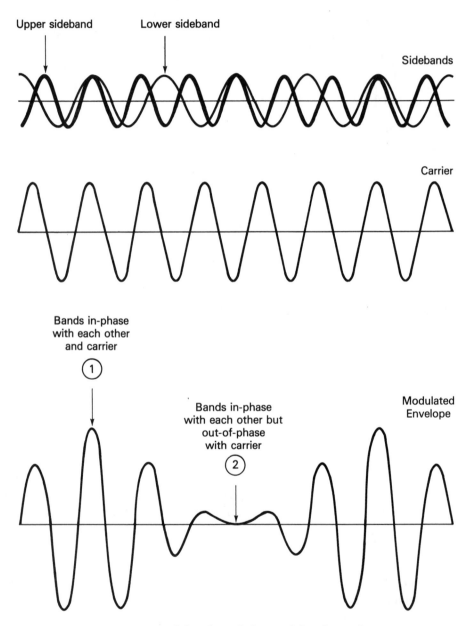

FIGURE 3-4. Sidebands and the Modulated Envelope

with each other but out-of-phase with the carrier, the modulated waveform displays a low amplitude (point 2).

In summary, an analog-modulated waveform is characterized by the following attributes:

- The modulating signal determines the sidebands.
- The sidebands determine the shape of the modulation envelope.
- The envelope's amplitude is determined by the sideband amplitude (percent of modulation).
- Intelligence is contained only in the sidebands.
- The two sidebands contain the same information; their intelligence is redundant.
- The bandwidth of the AM signal encompasses the lowest to the highest sideband frequency. So, the AM channel bandwidth is twice the highest modulating frequency ($BW = 2f_m$).

The AM process discussed thus far in this chapter is called standard AM or more precisely, double sideband transmitter carrier (DSBTC). We now know that the carrier and both sidebands are carried on the channel. It is a relatively simple and inexpensive process and is used by AM broadcast radio stations and most citizens-band radio systems. However it suffers from three disadvantages:

1. The bandwidth requirement is twice that of the intelligence in the waveform since the sidebands contain the same information.
2. The carrier signal does not contribute to the intelligence of the waveform (it is only a reference frequency) yet it contains most of the power in the signal. Consequently, this power is wasted. The problem is more pronounced when the modulation index is less than 1.
3. The envelope requires the carrier and the sidebands to maintain precise amplitude and phase relationships. However, different frequencies have different attenuation and propagation properties. Noisy channels, poor weather conditions, etc. can cause signal distortion and create errors at the receiver when the carrier and sideband frequencies arrive out-of-phase or are severely attenuated.

The disadvantage of wasted power can be eliminated by removing the carrier before the signal is transmitted by a process called double sideband suppressed carrier (DSBSC). This technique is more efficient than double sideband transmitted carrier (DSBTC), but it is an expensive and complex undertaking because the carrier, which acts as a reference, must be recreated and inserted at the receiver in order to demodulate the signal accurately. This process requires very precise timing, because the inserted carrier must be the same frequency as the original and it must also be exactly in phase with the original. DSBSC is used in FM stereo broadcasts and also is used as part of color television transmission, but it has not seen much use in less elegant systems.

The three disadvantages of DSBTC can be overcome by yet another technique: sideband suppressed carrier (SSB). This approach transmits only one sideband; the carrier and the other sideband are suppressed at the transmitter. While SSB is more complex and expensive than standard AM, the reinserted carrier need not be precisely the same as the original carrier. Consequently, SSB is less expensive and less complex than DSBSC. Single sideband has other advantages:

1. The bandwidth requirement is reduced by one half of the bandwidth for double sideband, which doubles the capacity of any frequency range.
2. All transmitted power contains intelligence. Consequently, an SSB transmitter can produce the same signal quality at $1/3$ the power required for a DSBTC transmitter.
3. SSB performs better on poor-quality channels primarily because of the reduced power/bandwidth requirements and removal of the precise phase/frequency relationships required for double sideband systems.

An SSB signal is usually generated at a very low power level. A level of less than 1 watt is common, although amplifiers are needed to boost the power of the signal. Care must be taken to amplify the SSB signal linearly, i.e., without introducing spurious signals and harmonics.

SSB is not without its problems. For example, the suppressed carrier could be used for synchronization purposes, which is impossible if it is suppressed. Some systems offer a compromise arrangement: vestigial sideband (VSB), which carries one sideband and a reduced power carrier.

Sideband Filters

Filters are used to generate the SSB signal. (The reader might wish to review the material on filters in Chapter 2.) Figure 3-5 shows a block diagram of a SSB transmitter and its pass band. In Figure 3-5 (a), a voice signal is amplified and applied to a modulator. The output of the modulation is a double sideband suppressed carrier, which is applied to a sideband filter. Figure 3-5 (b) depicts the SSB filter pass band. Since one sideband is attenuated, the filter must change from 0 dB attenuation to approximately 50 dB within the frequency range that separates the sidebands.

Angle Modulation

Analog-to-analog conversions are also accomplished through the process of frequency modulation (FM) and phase modulation (PM), which are collectively called angle modulation. The techniques are illustrated in Figure 3-6.

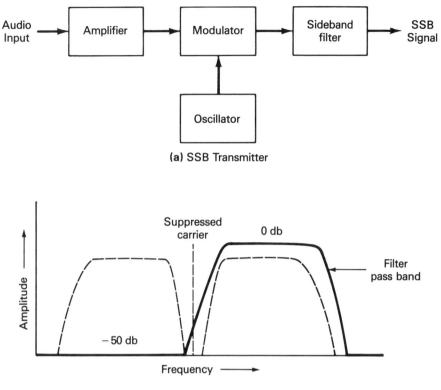

(a) SSB Transmitter

(b) SSB Filter

FIGURE 3-5. Single Sideband (SSB) [HEAT81]

It is obvious that FM and PM are almost identical, but a closer comparison reveals one subtle difference:

Characteristics of Modulated Waveform

Frequency Modulation (FM)	Phase Modulation (PM)
Carrier frequency change (deviation) is proportional to the amplitude of the modulating signal.	Carrier frequency change (deviation) is proportional to the amplitude and the frequency of the modulating signal.

Frequency Modulation (FM)

Figure 3-6 shows the difference. First, to illustrate frequency modulation, examine Figure 3-6 (c). The modulated signal reaches its maximum or minimum frequency change (frequency deviation) when the modulating signal

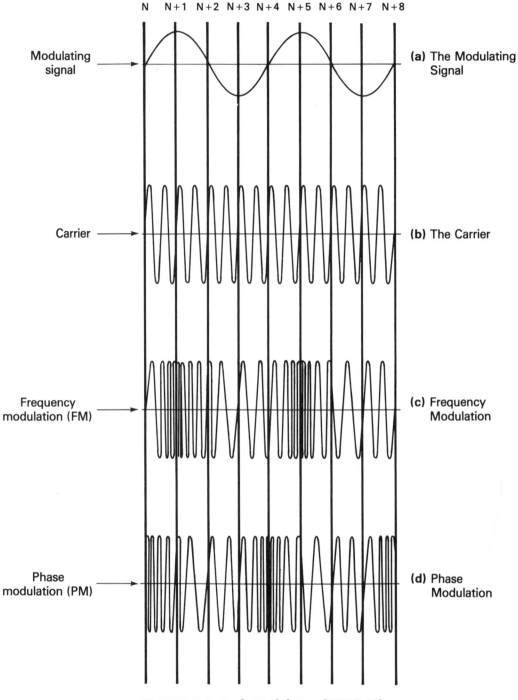

N N+1 N+2 N+3 N+4 N+5 N+6 N+7 N+8

Modulating signal → **(a)** The Modulating Signal

Carrier → **(b)** The Carrier

Frequency modulation (FM) → **(c)** Frequency Modulation

Phase modulation (PM) → **(d)** Phase Modulation

FIGURE 3-6. Angle Modulation [HEAT 81]

reaches its maximum amplitude—either negative or positive. The reader should notice that the frequency of the modulating signal determines the rate of frequency deviation but not the amount of deviation.

Phase Modulation (PM)

To illustrate phase modulation, Figure 3-6 (d) shows that maximum frequency deviation occurs when the modulating signal crosses the zero voltage axis. Since the zero axis is crossed in each cycle, increasing the frequency of the modulating signal increases the number of zero axis crossings per second. As a consequence, the carrier's deviation increases in proportion to the increase of the modulating frequency.

Phase modulation is sometimes called indirect FM because the modulating signal (1) phase-modulates the carrier and (2) indirectly frequency-modulates it.

Modulation Index

We have learned that AM is measured by the modulation factor index and varies from 0 to 1. Angle modulation also uses a modulation index, which is calculated as:

$$MI = \frac{f_d}{f_m}$$

Where: MI = modulation index; f_d = frequency deviation; f_m = modulating frequency.

The modulation index for angle modulation can be high. For example, an FM broadcast exhibiting a frequency deviation of 75 KHz with a 1 KHz modulating audio frequency yields a modulation index of 75.

For angle modulation, the following formula is applicable:

$$s(t) = A_c \cos (2 \pi f_c t + MI\ m(t))$$

Angle Modulation Sidebands and Bandwidth

Amplitude modulation has only two sidebands, the upper and lower. The number of angle modulation sidebands is theoretically infinite because the frequency changes caused by the modulating signal generate many sidebands. However, most can be disregarded, since they contain an insignificant amount of power.

The modulation index plays an important role in the sidebands of angle modulation. Remember that the amplitude remains constant for angle modulation. As a consequence, as the distribution and amplitude of the individual sidebands change, the carrier must also change to maintain a constant waveform amplitude. The modulation index maintains this relationship by

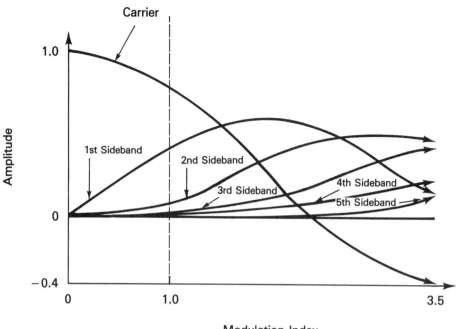

FIGURE 3-7. Relationship of Carrier to Sidebands [MART76], [HEAT81]

determining (a) the carrier's amplitude, (b) the number of significant sidebands, and (c) the sideband's amplitude.

The relationship of the modulation index to the carrier and the sidebands is shown in Figure 3-7 [HEAT81], [MART76]. A modulation index of 0 means the carrier amplitude is 1 and no sidebands exist. The increase of the modulation index creates more sidebands, and also necessitates a reduction in the carrier's amplitude. The addition of more sidebands further reduces the carrier until the carrier disappears completely. Eventually, a high modulation index places the carrier 180° out-of-phase with the sideband components.

With angle modulation, the bandwidth depends on the number of sidebands in the wave. In turn, the number of sidebands is determined by the (a) modulation index and (b) the modulating frequency. (Remember, the formula for the modulation index includes the frequency deviation and the modulating frequency.) Consequently, if the modulation frequency and the frequency deviation are known, the bandwidth can be determined.

Table 3-1 shows the relationships between the modulation index and the carrier and sideband amplitudes. (Sidebands of less than 1% of the original carrier are not shown, since they are considered insignificant.) To illustrate, a modulation index of 1.0 has a carrier amplitude of 0.77 and three significant sidebands with amplitudes of 0.44, 0.11, and 0.02.

TABLE 3-1. Relationship of Modulation Index and Sidebands

Carrier	Modulation Index	1st	2nd	3rd	4th	5th	6th	7th	8th	9th	10th	11th	12th	13th	14th	15th	16th
−0.01	15.0	.21	.04	.1	−.12	.13	.21	.03	−.17	−.22	−.09	.10	.24	.28	.25	.18	.12
−0.15	12.0	.22	.08	.2	−.18	−.07	.24	.17	.05	.23	.30	.27	.20	.12	.07	.03	.01
−0.25	10.0	.04	.25	.06	−.22	−.23	.01	.22	.31	.29	.20	.12	.06	.03	.01	—	—
−0.09	9.0	.24	.14	.18	−.27	−.06	.20	.33	.30	.21	.12	.06	.03	.01	—	—	—
0.17	8.0	.23	.11	.19	−.10	.19	.34	.32	.22	.13	.06	.03	—	—	—	—	—
0.30	7.0	.00	.30	.17	.16	.35	.34	.23	.13	.06	.02	—	—	—	—	—	—
0.15	6.0	.28	.24	.11	.36	.36	.25	.13	.06	.02	—	—	—	—	—	—	—
−0.18	5.0	.33	.05	.36	.39	.26	.13	.05	.02	—	—	—	—	—	—	—	—
−0.40	4.0	.07	.36	.43	.28	.13	.05	.02	—	—	—	—	—	—	—	—	—
−0.26	3.0	.34	.49	.31	.13	.04	.01	—	—	—	—	—	—	—	—	—	—
−0.05	2.5	.50	.45	.22	.07	.02	—	—	—	—	—	—	—	—	—	—	—
0.22	2.0	.58	.35	.13	.03	—	—	—	—	—	—	—	—	—	—	—	—
0.51	1.5	.56	.23	.06	.01	—	—	—	—	—	—	—	—	—	—	—	—
0.77	1.0	.44	.11	.02	—	—	—	—	—	—	—	—	—	—	—	—	—
0.94	0.5	.24	.03	—	—	—	—	—	—	—	—	—	—	—	—	—	—
0.98	0.25	.12	—	—	—	—	—	—	—	—	—	—	—	—	—	—	—
1.00	0.0	—	—	—	—	—	—	—	—	—	—	—	—	—	—	—	—

Let us use Table 3-1 to determine the bandwidth of a signal with angle modulation. Given a modulating frequency of 6 KHz and a maximum deviation of 36 KHz, the modulation index is:

$$\frac{f_d}{f_m} = \frac{36 \text{ KHz}}{6} = 6$$

Table 3-1 reveals a modulation index of 6 has 9 significant sidebands.

Calculating Bandwidth. In angle modulation, the bandwidth (W) is calculated as:

$$W = f_m * SB * 2$$

Where: f_m = the modulating frequency, SB = the number of significant sidebands. Thus:

$$W = 6 \text{ KHz} * 9 * 2 = 108 \text{ KHz}$$

DIGITAL-TO-ANALOG CONVERSION

Since the subject matter of this book is data communications, the reader is likely to be very interested in the conversion of digital-to-analog signals. The

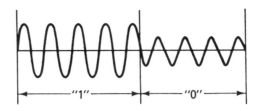

(a) Amplitude Modulation

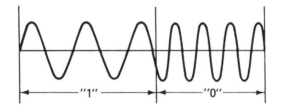

(b) Frequency Modulation

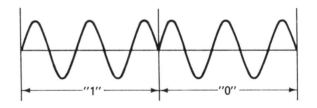

(c) Phase Modulation

FIGURE 3-8. Modulation Techniques

technique is most often used when a user device such as a terminal or computer transmits and receives data through the public switched telephone network (PSTN). The device used to support this type of communications, the familiar modem, is explained in considerable detail in Chapter 9.

Three basic methods of digital-to-analog modulation exist. Some modems use more than one of the methods. Each method impresses the data on a carrier signal, which is altered to carry the properties of the digital data stream. The three methods are called amplitude modulation, frequency modulation, and phase modulation (see Figure 3-8).

Modulation Rate (baud) and Bit Rate (bits per second, or bit/s)

The carrier signal is typically changed as often as possible since each change represents binary data and frequent changes increase the bit transmission rate. The change rate is called the signalling rate, or modulation rate, or baud(s).

The terms baud and bit/s are often used incorrectly to convey the same meaning. In this section, the two terms will be defined. It will be evident that they are indeed different, except when applied to low-speed devices. (The term *bit rate* is an informal and widely used term to describe the transfer rate of a system, in bits per second.)

Multilevel Modulation

Baud(s) and bit rate are only equal if one bit is represented with each signal change (also called the signalling interval). Such is the case with lower-speed modems, typically in the range of 1200 bit/s and less. Higher-speed modems use multilevel modulation in which more than one bit is represented with each baud. The baud(s) is calculated as:

$$B = 1/T$$

Where: B = baud(s); T = length of signalling interval (in time).

A signal can be modulated over a voice-grade line with the multilevel technique based on the following general definition:

$$R = D/N$$

Where: R = signalling or modulation rate, in bauds; D = data rate in bit/s; N = number of bits per signalling element.

Table 3-2 shows the relationship of baud(s), bit rate, and signalling interval for several of the widely used CCITT V Series modems (explained in more detail in Chapter 9). The V.21 and V.26 bis modems are single-level DCEs; they employ a modulation technique of one bit per baud. The other modems are multilevel devices; the modulation schemes carry more than one bit per baud.

The multilevel modems permit a higher bit rate on the communications link, which of course achieves more throughput across a given

TABLE 3-2. Comparison of Bit Rate, Baud, and Signalling Interval

CCITT Specification	Modulation Rate (baud or B)	Signalling Interval (1/B)	Bits per Baud	Bit Rate (bit/s)
V.21	300	.003333	1	300
V.22 bis	600	.00166	4	2400
V.26 bis	1200	.000833	1	1200
V.26 ter	1200	.000833	2	2400
V.27 ter	1600	.000625	3	4800
V.29	2400	.000416	3	7200
V.32	2400	.000416	4	9600

bandwidth. However, a limit exists on the number of bits represented by each signalling interval since multilevel transmission is more expensive and more subject to error. The closer differences between the signal levels are more difficult to detect and more easily distorted. As Table 3-2 shows, the higher-speed modems encode 4 bits per baud.

If a limit exists on the number of bits per signalling interval, why not increase the modulation rate? For example, if the V.32 modulation rate of 2400 bauds were increased to 4800 bauds, the transmission rate could be increased to 19,200 bit/s. Such rates are now possible, but it is instructive to examine the column labeled "Signalling Interval" in Table 3-2. The higher-speed modem uses a signalling interval that is shorter than that used by lower-speed modems. For example, the V.21 interval is .003333 second and the V.29 interval is only .000416 second. The shorter signalling intervals are less rugged; they are more easily distorted on the communications link than the low-baud modems. Moreover, the higher signalling rates introduce more harmonics and thus require more bandwidth.

For bandwidth-limited channels, multilevel transmission is achieved by applying the following formula:

$$R = \log_2 L(1/T)$$

Where: R = the data rate in bit/s; L = number of encoding levels (bits per baud); T = length of signalling interval.

The reader is also encouraged to review Chapter 2, which explains the relationship of the bit transfer rate to the channel's bandwidth.

Amplitude Modulation (AM)

AM modems alter the carrier signal amplitude in accordance with the modulating digital bit stream (see Figure 3-8 [a]). The frequency and phase of the carrier are held constant and the amplitude is raised or lowered to represent a binary value of 0 or 1. In its simplest form, the carrier signal can be switched on or off to represent the binary state.

AM modulation is not often used by itself due to its sensitivity to distortion and transmission power problems. However, it is commonly used with phase modulation to yield a method superior to either FM or PM.

The AM signal is represented as:

$$S(t) = A \cos (2 \pi f_c t + \theta_c) \quad \text{for binary 1}$$
$$S(t) = 0 \quad \text{for binary 0}$$

Where: $S(t)$ = value of carrier at time t; A = maximum amplitude of carrier voltage; f_c = carrier frequency; and θ_c = carrier phase.

This approach also shows a binary 0 represented by no carrier, which is called off/on keying, or amplitude shift keying (ASK).

The ASK signal is classified as linear modulation. In the section on analog-to-analog conversion, we learned of this technique with the examples

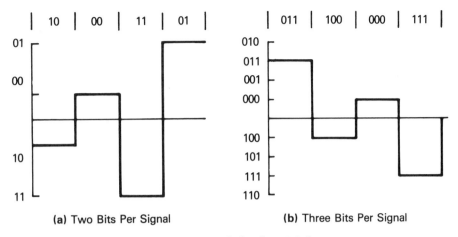

(a) Two Bits Per Signal   (b) Three Bits Per Signal

FIGURE 3-9. Multilevel AM Schemes

of double sideband, single sideband and vestigial sideband modulation. With digital-to-analog conversion, the 0 and 1 signal levels are converted to the carrier frequency f_c.

The conventional AM data signals are detected at the receiver by envelope detection. The signal is rectified at the receiver, and smoothed to obtain its envelope. This approach does not require the use of a reference carrier. Consequently, ASK is a relatively inexpensive process (the use of a carrier reference is a more complex and expensive undertaking). However, envelope detection does require both sidebands for accurate detection.

The use of AM for data communications has decreased because a multilevel scheme requires the use of several to many signal levels. As the number of signal levels increases, the distance between them decreases. As Figure 3-9 illustrates, the signal levels' distance between the single and multiple level systems are quite close. AM transmitters often "saturate" these narrow distances, and in some systems they must be used at less than maximum power to diminish the saturation problem.

Thus, AM modems must be designed: (a) with sufficiently long signalling intervals (low baud) to keep the signal on the channel long enough to withstand noise and to be detected at the receiver; and (b) with sufficient distances between the AM levels to allow accurate detection and to diminish saturation.

Frequency Modulation (FM)

Figure 3-8 (b) illustrates frequency modulation. This method changes the frequency of the carrier in accordance with the digital bit stream. The amplitude is held constant. In its simplest form, a binary 1 is represented by one frequency and a binary 0 by another frequency.

Several variations of FM modems are available. The most common FM modem is the frequency shift key (FSK) modem, using four frequencies within the 3 KHz telephone line bandwidth. The FSK modem transmits 1070 and 1270 Hz signals to represent a binary 0 (space) and binary 1 (mark), respectively. It receives 2025 and 2225 Hz signals as a binary 0 (space) and binary 1 (mark). This approach allows full duplex transmission over a two-wire voice-grade telephone line. Frequency shift keying is expressed as:

$$s(t) = A \cos (2 \pi f_1 t + \theta_c) \quad \text{binary 1}$$
$$s(t) = A \cos (2 \pi f_2 t + \theta_c) \quad \text{binary 0}$$

FSK is used for low-speed modems (up to 1200 bit/s) because it is relatively inexpensive and simple. Many of the personal computers use FSK for communications over the telephone network. FSK is also used for radio transmission in the high-frequency ranges (3 to 30 mHz) and some local area networks (LANs) employ FSK on broadband coaxial cables. However, its use on voice-grade lines is decreasing as more manufacturers implement DCEs with phase modulation techniques. Moreover, phase modulation techniques are almost exclusively used today on high-speed digital radio systems.

Phase Modulation (PM)

Previous discussions of the sine wave (in Chapter 2) describe how a cycle is represented with phase markings to indicate the point to which the oscillating wave has advanced in its cycle. PM modems alter the phase of the signal to represent a 1 or 0 (see Figure 3-8 [c]).

The phase modulation method is also called phase shift key (PSK). A common approach to PSK is to compare the phase of the current signal state to the previous signal state, which is known as differential PSK (DPSK). This technique uses bandwidth more efficiently than FSK because it puts more information into each signal, but it requires more elaborate equipment for signal generation and detection. The PSK signal is represented as:

$$S(t) = A \cos (2 \pi f_c t + \pi) \quad 1$$
$$S(t) = A \cos (2 \pi f_c t) \quad 0$$

Phase shift key is used to provide multilevel modulation. The technique is called quadrature signal modulation. For example, a dibit modem (2 bits per baud) typically encodes the binary data stream as follows:

11: = 45°
10: = 135°
01: = 225°
00: = 315°

Quadrature Signal Representation

As an introduction to quadrature signalling, please examine Figure 3-10. A common technique to determine impairments and/or signal quality is the use of a ternary "eye" diagram. These diagrams are shown on an oscillo-

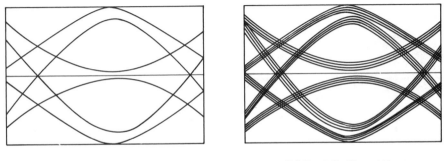

(a) Open Eye   **(b)** Partially Closed Eye

FIGURE 3-10. Eye Diagram

scope by synchronizing the clock frequency to a time base and then superimposing and displaying the states of a long sequence of digits. The eye diagram is so named because a nondistorted signal shows a wide-open eye and a degraded signal shows a closing eye. The smaller the eye opening, the greater the signal degradation and the higher the probability of errors occurring. (The eye diagram is also used to show the effects of multilevel signalling with the quadrature and quadrature amplitude modulation methods.)

The quadrature signal representations are provided by the following function:

$$\cos (2\pi f_c t + \theta) = \cos \theta \, (\cos 2\pi f_c t - \sin \theta) \sin 2\pi f_c t$$

The phase diagram (also called a constellation pattern) is used to represent quadrature modulation. The $\cos 2\pi f_c t$ signal is referred to as the in-phase or I signal; the $\sin 2\pi f_c t$ signal is referred to as the out-of-phase or Q signal. This relationship is depicted in Figure 3-11.

Another PSK modem is a tribit device (3 bits per signalling interval) which employs 8-PSK modulation. The phase diagram for the 8-PSK modem is also shown in Figure 3-11. The quadrature coefficients for 4-PSK and 8-PSK are depicted in Table 3-3.

Distance Between Points. The calculation for the distance between adjacent points in a PSK system is:

$$d = 2 \sin (\pi/N)$$

Where: N = number of phases.

As the value of N increases, an increase in the bit rate results, but it is more difficult for the receiver to distinguish close points from each other.

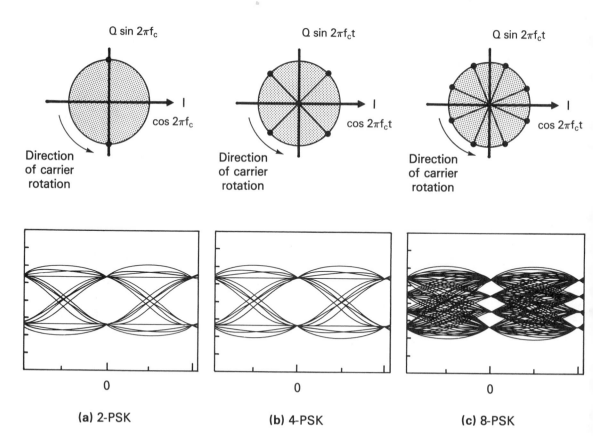

FIGURE 3-11. Phase Shift Key Constellations and Eye Diagrams [NAGU86]

TABLE 3-3. Quadrature Signal Coefficients

Data Bits	Quadrature $\sin 2\pi f_c$	Coefficients $\cos 2\pi f_c$
4 PSK:		
01	−0.707	0.707
00	−0.707	−0.707
10	0.707	−0.707
11	0.707	0.707
8 PSK:		
011	−0.383	0.924
010	−0.924	0.383
000	−0.924	−0.383
001	−0.383	−0.924
101	0.383	−0.924
100	0.924	−0.383
110	0.924	0.383
111	0.383	0.924

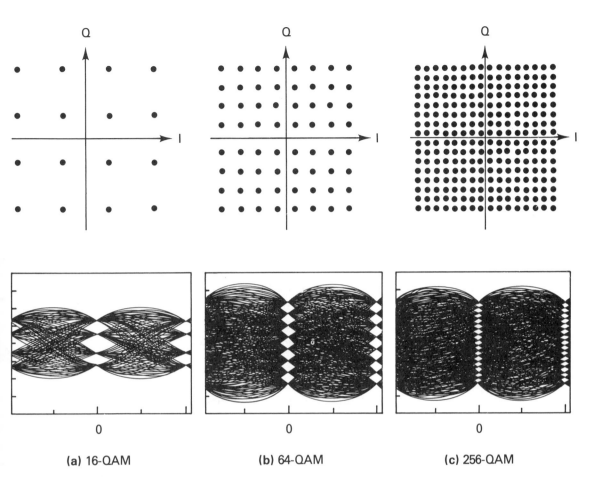

(a) 16-QAM   **(b)** 64-QAM   **(c)** 256-QAM

FIGURE 3-12. QAM Constellations and Eye Patterns [NAGU86]

Quadrature Amplitude Modulation

A special extension of multiphase PSK modulation is quadrature amplitude modulation (QAM) (see Figure 3-12) [NOGU86]. The dots in the figure represent composite signal points and the lattice markings represent amplitude levels in each quadrature channel.

The QAM and PSK spectrum shapes are identical. For example a 16-PSK spectrum shape is the same as a 16-QAM spectrum shape. However, a QAM system exhibits considerably better error performance than its PSK counterpart. The distances between points are smaller in a PSK system. Moreover, the following expression for QAM distances between adjacent points than an n-ary QAM system performs better than an n-ary PSK system:

$$I = \frac{\sqrt{2}}{(L-1)}$$

Where: L = power levels on each axis.

QAM systems are widely used and are evident in several implementations of the CCITT V Series modems, the Bell modems and the Hayes modems for personal computers. Chapter 9 describes these systems in more detail.

Bandwidth Considerations

An important factor in the analysis of digital-to-analog modulation is bandwidth efficiency: the efficiency of the bandwidth used for modulating data onto analog signals. It is expressed in the ratio of the data rate to the bandwidth [COUC83A] [STAL85].

For ASK and PSK, the following formula applies:

$$B_T = (1 + r)\,R$$

Where: B_T = transmission bandwidth; R = the bit rate; r = the filtering technique to establish the bandwidth (usually 0 ‹ r ‹ 1). For FSK, the bandwidth is:

$$B_T = 2\Delta F + (1 + r)\,R$$

Where: $\Delta F = f_2 - f_c = f_c - f_1$, which is the offset of the modulated frequency from the carrier frequency. It can be seen that ΔF is quite significant with high carrier frequencies.

For multilevel signalling, the bandwidth is:

$$B_T = \left(\frac{1 + r}{\log_2 L}\right) R$$

Where: l = the number of bits that are encoded per signalling element; L = the number of signalling elements.

ANALOG-TO-DIGITAL CONVERSION

Advantages of Analog-to-Digital Conversion

Since the early 1960s, telephone companies, specialized carriers, and network vendors have increasingly implemented systems with digital technology. Today, many transmission components use digital transmission schemes, including such diverse devices as PBXs, multiplexers, and switches.

The process of digitization was developed at Bell Laboratories in the 1960s to overcome some of the limitations of analog transmission and analog image recording. An analog signal experiences a continuous variance of amplitude over time. When an individual speaks into a telephone, the physical oscillations of the air (high and low air pressure) are transformed into an electrical signal with similar waveform characteristics. The telephone acts as a transducer to change a signal from one form of energy (sound) to another (electrical). As the signal is transmitted through the communications channel, it must be amplified periodically to prevent excessive signal decay.

Several problems arise regarding the analog signal and how it is transmitted across the channel. First, the signal is relayed through amplifiers and other transducers. These devices are designed to perform the relaying function in a linear fashion; i.e., the waveform representing the signal maintains its characteristics from one end of the channel to the other. A deviation from this linearity creates a distortion of the waveform. All analog signals exhibit some form of nonlinearity. Unfortunately, the intervening components, such as amplifiers, increase the nonlinearity of the signal.

The second problem pertains to noise on the channel. An electrical signal on a wire or cable is created by the nonrandom movement of electrons. Thermal noise is also created on a wire or cable channel by the random variations of the electrons in the channel or transducer. Moreover, noise is introduced in non-wire transmissions (radio, satellite) by electrical disturbances in the earth's atmosphere and radiation from the sun and stars.

Third, all signals are weakened (or attenuated) during transmission through the medium. The decay can make the signal so weak that it is unintelligible at the receiver. A high-quality wire cable with a large diameter certainly mitigates decay, but it cannot be eliminated.

Fourth, voice and data systems have evolved using different signalling and control systems. The older telephone signalling systems do not interface with data systems very well.

Digital systems overcome many of these problems by representing the transmitted data with digital and binary images. The analog signal is converted to a series of digital numbers and transmitted through the communications channel as binary data. The digital numbers represent samples of the waveform.

Of course, digital signals are subject to the same kinds of imperfections and problems as analog signals—decay and noise. However, the digital signal is discrete: the binary samples of the analog waveform are represented by specific levels of voltages, in contrast to the nondiscrete levels of an analog signal. Indeed, an analog signal has almost infinite variability. As the digital signal traverses the channel, it is only necessary to sample the absence or presence of a digital binary pulse, not its degree, as in the analog signal.

The mere absence or presence of a signal pulse can be more easily recognized than the magnitude or degree of an analog signal. If the digital signals are sampled at an acceptable rate and at an acceptable voltage level, the signals can then be completely reconstituted before they deteriorate below a minimum threshold. Consequently, noise and attenuation can be completely eliminated from the reconstructed signal. Thus, the digital signal can tolerate the problems of noise and attenuation much better than the analog signal.

Signal Conversion

Several methods are used to change an analog signal into a representative string of digital binary images. The first notable approach was developed in 1939 by A. H. Reeves of Bell Laboratories. Even though the Bell technique entails many processes, it is generally described in three steps: sampling, quantizing, and encoding. These concepts are explained in this section, as are other more efficient techniques.

The devices performing the digitizing process are called channel banks, or primary multiplexers. They have two basic functions: (1) converting analog signals to digital form (and vice versa at the other end) and (2) combining the digital signals into a single time division multiplexed (TDM) data stream (and demultiplexing them at the other end). This conversion can be done in a single integrated circuit chip called the codec (coder/decoder).

The Nyquist Criterion

Analog-to-digital conversion is based on Nyquist sampling theory. If a signal f(t) is sampled instantaneously at regular intervals and at a rate at least twice the highest frequency in the channel, the samples will contain sufficient information to allow an accurate reconstruction of the signal.

The signal f(t) can be reconstructed from the samples by a low-pass filter. Theoretically and ideally, the sampling provides an amplitude value at a specific time and the continuous signal is reconstructed by applying the samples to the low-pass filter. Practically speaking, sampling is done over a finite time and the reconstruction filters are not ideal. Nonetheless, the process is sufficient to provide adequate reproduction at the receiver.

In 1933, Harry Nyquist defined the minimum sampling frequency needed to convey all information in an analog waveform:

$$f_s > 2BW$$

Where: f_s = sampling frequency; BW = bandwidth of the input signal.

Figure 3-13 shows the results of the Nyquist relation. The sampling process is concerned with a narrow train of pulses which contains the fundamental sampling frequency plus a multitude of harmonics. The original signal must first be passed through a band-limiting filter for two reasons: (a) to limit the frequencies to ensure the sampling rate is at least double the highest frequency component being sampled and (b) to remove frequency components greater than $f_2/2$ to prevent output signals from occurring that do not come from the source.

To address point (b), in Figure 3-14, a 5.5 KHz waveform contains the same sample values as a 2.5 KHz signal [BELL82]. This presents a problem

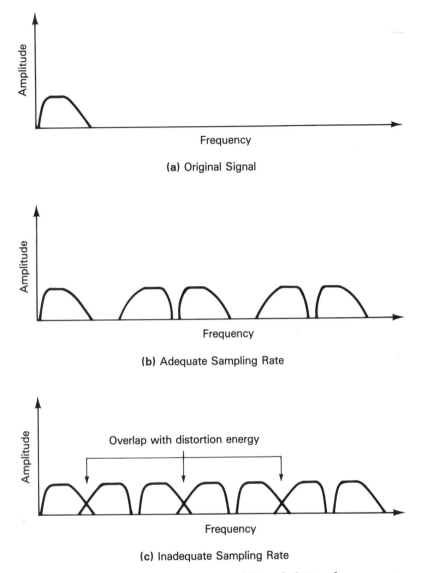

(a) Original Signal

(b) Adequate Sampling Rate

Overlap with distortion energy

(c) Inadequate Sampling Rate

FIGURE 3-13. Spectrum of Sampled Signals

because the 5.5 KHz input signal would be interpreted as 2.5 KHz output after passing through a 4 KHz low-pass output filter. By bandlimiting the original input signal, the problem is avoided.

Figure 3-13(b) shows a double sideband spectrum produced from the sampling. In this figure, the signal is sampled at an adequate rate. However, Figure 3-13(c) shows an inadequate sampling rate. In this case, the original spectrum is overlapped by the sidebands, and the original input signal cannot be separated by a filter. This problem is known as foldover distortion.

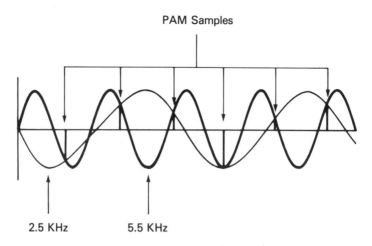

FIGURE 3-14. Signal Aliasing

Foldover distortion is also called aliasing. The reader has probably seen an example of aliasing or foldover distortion in some old movies in which an automobile tire or a wagon wheel appears to be rotating backward while the vehicle is moving forward. This effect is simply an example of inadequate sampling. For example, if the camera produces a picture frame every 350° of the wheel rotation, the wheel will appear to be moving backwards.

The accepted sampling rate in the industry is 8000 samples per second. Based on Nyquist sampling theory, this rate allows the accurate reproduction of a 4 KHz channel (and filters prevent signals above 4000 Hz). The 8000 samples are more than sufficient to capture the signals in a telephone line if certain techniques (discussed shortly) are used. In Figure 3-14, the 5.5 KHz signal must be filtered to prevent aliasing.

A signal bandlimited to f_m Hz is completely described by the amplitude of its samples spaced in time (T). The value T represents the period between the samples. The following formula demonstrates that T yields .000125 for the 4 KHz channel:

$$T = 1/(2f_m)$$

As discussed in Chapter 2, most of the speech energy and speech intelligence are contained in the frequency components between 200 and 3500 Hz. Therefore, the 4 KHz voice channel is maintained for the digital environment.

Pulse Amplitude Modulation (PAM)

The samples are stored and collected at the predetermined rate of 8000 times per second. The idea of the sampling process is to modulate a pulse

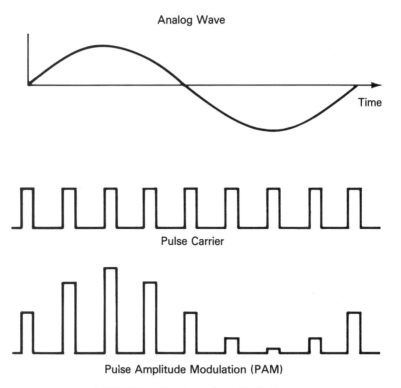

Analog Wave

Time

Pulse Carrier

Pulse Amplitude Modulation (PAM)

FIGURE 3-15. Sampling Techniques

carrier (see Figure 3-15) with the sample of the analog signal. The pulse carrier is the sampling pulse clock, and can be modulated with pulse amplitude modulation (PAM).

With PAM, the pulse carrier amplitude is varied with the value of the analog waveform. As Figure 3-15 shows, the pulses are fixed with respect to duration and position. PAM is classified as a modulation technique because each instantaneous sample of the wave is used to modulate the amplitude of the sampling pulse.

The 8 KHz sampling rate results in a sample pulse train of signals with a 125 microsecond time period between the pulses (1 second/8000 = .000125). Each pulse occupies 5.2 microseconds of this time period. Consequently, it is possible to interleave sampled pulses from other signals within the 125 microsecond period. The most common approach in North America utilizes 24 interleaved channels, which effectively fill the 125 microsecond time period (.0000052 * 24 = .000125). The samples are time division multiplexed (TDM) into a digital TDM as shown in Figure 3-16 [REY83]. TDM provides an efficient and economical means of combining multiple signals for transmission on a common facility.

The PAM signals are rarely transmitted over long distances because they are vulnerable to noise and crosstalk. Instead, the PAM signals are

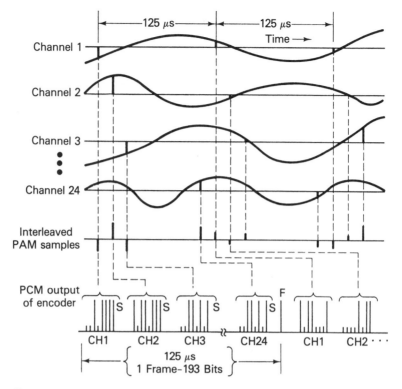

Notes:

1. Framing bit is 193rd bit (F).

2. Signaling bit is 8th bit in each channel in one frame out of six (S).

3. The output pulse rate shown is 1.544 Mbps, the DS1 level in the TDM heirarchy.

FIGURE 3-16. Time-Division Multiplexing [REY83]

converted to digital signals, which are periodically sent through regenerative repeaters to remove distortion and reshape the signals.

The End-to-End A/D and D/A Process

The complete analog-to-digital (A/D) and digital-to-analog (D/A) process is shown in Figure 3-17. The waveform (1) is bandlimited (2) and (3), and sampled (4) to produce PAM signals. These signals are encoded into a digital value (5) (each sample is represented by an 8-bit value) and sent to the receiver. The receiver divides the digital values into 8-bit words, and every 1/8000 of a second establishes the height of an analog output pulse [FLAN86]. This process creates a staircase effect (6), which closely resembles the original PAM pulses. A low-pass reconstruction filter smooths the output

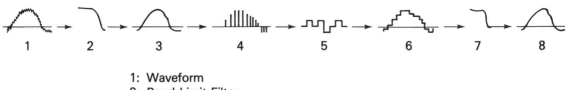

1: Waveform
2: Band Limit Filter
3: Output from Filter
4: Samples (PAM)
5: Digital Representation of PAM Signals
6: Analog Output Pulse (Staircase Effect)
7: Reconstructive Filter
8: Resultant Waveform

FIGURE 3-17. End-to-End Code Modulation

pulses (7) to create the resultant waveform that is quite similar to the original input waveform (8).

Pulse Code Modulation

The PAM signals are still considered analog because of their varying amplitudes. As stated earlier, this characteristic is changed by coding the signals with numbers to represent the amplitudes. The codes are then treated as binary pulses (1s and 0s) as shown in Figure 3-18. This technique is known as pulse code modulation (PCM), and the specific process of assigning a value

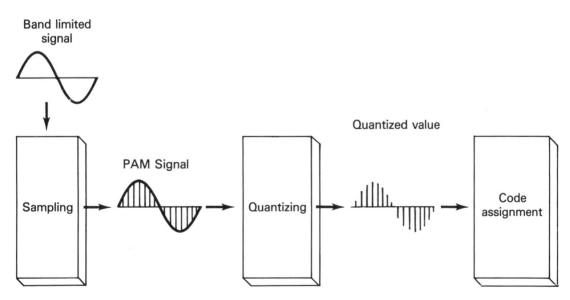

FIGURE 3-18. Pulse Code Modulation

to each sample is called quantizing (i.e., restricting something to a specific value). Each PAM pulse is approximated by an n-bit value.

Quantizing inherently introduces an error because only discrete values representing the sample size are allowed. However, once quantized, the signal can be relayed for any distance without further distortion if the added noise does not prevent correct detection and regeneration of the signal. In this regard, analog and digital systems vary significantly: (a) analog noise is controlled by repeater spacing and medium characteristics; (b) digital noise is controlled by the number of discrete quantizing steps (n).

The magnitude of n is quite important. As shown in Figure 3-19(a), (assuming a linear relationship between the PAM sample and the PCM n value) an n value of 1 (i.e., 1 or 0) would only allow a system to distinguish in which half of the amplitude range the PAM signal resided. On the other hand, an n-bit code value divides the coding range into 2n segments. (These segments are referred to as quantization levels.) As seen in Figure 3-19(b), an 8-bit n code provides more accurate quantization.

The older PCM systems used an n of 7 bits; the newer systems use n = 8. If the quantizer assigns one of 128 values to the signal, 7 bits are required for each sample ($2^7 = 128$). If the quantizer uses 256 possible values, 8 bits are required for each sample ($2^8 = 256$). The 128-quantum-step quantizer requires a 56,000 bit/s rate (8000 x 7 = 56,000). The 256-quantum-step quantizer requires a bit rate of 64,000 bit/s (8000 x 8 = 64,000). This bit transfer rate is required for each signal (channel) of the PCM system, but the more modern systems have reduced the bit rate substantially (more about these systems later).

Sampling and Quantizing Errors

Digital transmission is not without its problems. A digital signal can be distorted in a number of ways. First, as discussed earlier, inadequate sampling can create a distortion in the signal. The problem can be solved by more frequent sampling, but it also requires more expensive components and greater bandwidths (higher bit rates) to support the increased data transfer rates. No technique that completely eliminates sampling distortions exists because of the analog nature of the waveform. The fundamental anomaly results from applying discrete (digital) samples to a nondiscrete (analog) signal.

The second problem arises through quantizing errors (quantizing noise). The quantizing process does not represent precisely the amplitude of the PAM signal; it is an approximation. Consequently, the reconstructed signal is not exactly the same as its original signal. The signal-to-noise ratio for quantizing noise is [BELL82]:

$$S/N = 6n + 1.8 \text{ dB}$$

This formula demonstrates that each additional bit increases the S/N ratio by 6 dB.

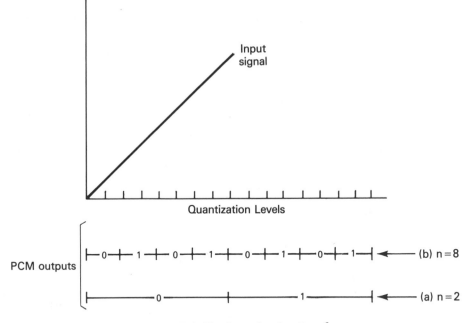

FIGURE 3-19. Quantization Levels

Fortunately, the PCM quantization errors are generally distributed randomly and are not correlated to each other. So the errors can be treated as additive noise if the signal has time to change by several quantizing intervals between successive samples. Because of this situation, if a signal is sampled beyond the Nyquist rate, the successive samples may occur within the same quantization interval and lose the randomness in the distribution.

Since the signal distortion is proportional to the step size, one earlier approach to solve the quantizing noise problem was to increase the number of quantizing steps available to represent the signal. Even though the increased levels of quantizing increased the costs of the components and the number of bits required to represent the signal, the 128-step quantizer has been replaced by the 256-step quantizer.

Earlier systems exhibited a linear relationship between PAM signals and PCM code called linear coding in which quantization levels were equally spaced between the two. As a consequence, equal changes in the signal amplitude produced equal changes in the PCM codes, and the error for each sample was the same. This effect created significant quantization distortion in lower amplitude signals. Even worse, due to the nature of analog speech patterns, the large signals do not occur as frequently as the small signals.

Companding

Newer techniques compress the higher amplitude signals to a smaller amplitude range for a given number of quantization levels. In other words, the smaller amplitude signals are expanded. On input, more gain is imparted to weak signals than to strong signals, which increases the number of available quantization levels, and decreases the overall quantization distortion. After the signal is decoded, it is restored to its original amplitude level. The combination of compressing and expanding is called companding. In effect, large quantization intervals are assigned to large samples and small quantization intervals are assigned to small samples (see Figure 3-20).

The distortion in the quantization is a function of the differences between the quantized steps. Since the voice signals in a telephone system can span 30 dB of variation, it makes sense to vary the distribution of the quantization steps. The variable quantizing levels reduce the quantizing noise.

This technique represents small amplitude PAM signals by larger coding variations than similar changes in large amplitude PAM signals; that is,

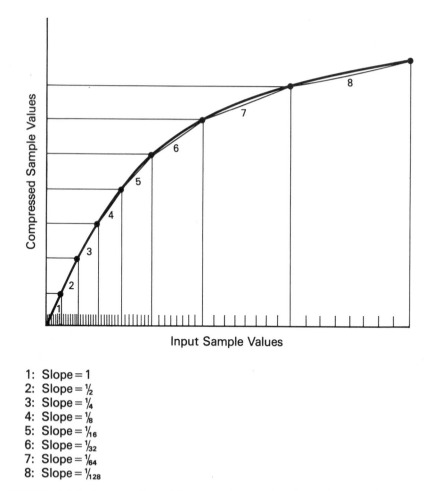

1: Slope = 1
2: Slope = ½
3: Slope = ¼
4: Slope = ⅛
5: Slope = 1/16
6: Slope = 1/32
7: Slope = 1/64
8: Slope = 1/128

FIGURE 3-20. Companding (8-Segment Approximation of μ = 255) [BELL82]

more quantizing steps are used for low amplitude signals. The quantization error is reduced as the PAM signal level is reduced. As a consequence, a constant signal-to-distortion (S/D) ratio is maintained over a wide range of PAM signals.

However, if an acceptable S/D performance of the signal distribution is to be maintained, a logarithmic compression law must be used. Two common methods of modifying a true logarithmic law are described herein.

The A Law and the μ Law

The coding process to modify companding to make it nearly linear for low sound levels is defined by a relationship in the form of the μ law (used in North America and Japan) and the A law (used in Europe). The laws are quite similar except that the A law uses a truly linear relationship in the small-amplitude range. The minimum step size is 2/4096 for the A law and 2/8159 for the μ law. Thus, the A law is inferior to the μ law in the context of signal quality.

The laws are defined as [BELL82]:

μ *law:*

$$F\mu^{-1}(y) = \text{sgn}(y) \; \frac{1}{\mu} \; [(1 + \mu)|y| - 1]$$

Where: y = the compressed value = $F\mu(x)$ $(-1 \le x \le 1)$; sgn (y) = the polarity of y; μ = the companding parameter.

A *law:*

$$F_A(x) = \text{sgn}(x) \; \frac{A\,|x|}{1 + \ln(A)} \qquad 0 \le x \le 1/A$$

$$F_A(x) = \text{sgn}(x) \; \frac{1 + \ln|A\,x|}{1 + \ln(A)} \qquad 1/A \le x \le 1$$

The nonlinear companding is actually implemented in a stepwise linear process. For the μ law, the μ = 255 is used and the companding value is coded by a set of eight straight-line segments that cut across the compression curve (actually eight for negative segments and eight for positive segments; since the two center segments are colinear, they are considered one).

Figure 3-20 shows the segment approximation. With this approach, each segment is double the amplitude range of its preceding segment and each segment is also one-half the slope of the preceding segment. In this manner, the segments representing the low range of PAM signals are more accurately encoded than the segments pertaining to the high range of PAM signals.

The A law functions similarly to the μ law characteristic. Eight positive and eight negative segments exist as in the μ law characteristic, but it is described as the 13-segment law.

TABLE 3-4. PCM Code Format for μ 255

Quantization Code (Q)		Segment(s) 000	001	010	011	100	101	110	111
		0	31	95	223	479	991	2015	4063
0000	0								
		1	35	103	239	511	1055	2143	4319
0001	1								
		3	39	111	255	543	1119	2271	4575
0010	2								
		5	43	119	271	575	1183	2399	4831
0011	3								
		7	47	127	287	607	1247	2527	5087
0100	4								
		9	51	135	303	639	1311	2655	5343
0101	5								
		11	55	143	319	671	1375	2783	5599
0110	6								
		13	59	151	335	703	1439	2911	5855
0111	7								
		15	63	159	351	735	1503	3039	6111
1000	8								
		17	67	167	367	767	1567	3167	6367
1001	9								
		19	71	175	383	799	1631	3295	6623
1010	10								
		21	75	183	399	831	1695	3423	6879
1011	11								
		23	79	191	415	863	1759	3551	7135
1100	12								
		25	83	199	431	895	1823	3679	7391
1101	13								
		27	87	207	447	927	1887	3807	7647
1110	14								
		29	91	215	463	959	1951	3935	7903
1111	15								
		31	95	223	479	991	2015	4063	8159

The code of μ 255 PCM consists of (a) a 1-bit polarity, where 0 = positive sample value and 1 = negative sample value; (b) a 3-bit segment identifier(s); and (c) a 4-bit quantizing step identifier.

The code format is shown in Table 3-4 [BELL82]. The first step in the process is to determine the polarity. Next, the segment identifier S is determined by identifying the smallest end point that is greater than the sample value. Next, the quantization interval within each segment is determined. As shown in Table 3-4, the polarity bit, the S and Q values are coded into the 8-bit code word. As Table 3-4 demonstrates, the S and Q values can be concatenated to produce a 7-bit code to represent one of 128 quantization levels of the compressed signal. The A law works in a similar fashion to the μ law. Tables 3-5 and 3-6 show the structure for the μ 255 and the A law encoding/decoding process [BELL82].

Conversion Between the Companding Laws

Since countries have implemented either the μ law or the A law, a need exists to interface the two digital systems. While the laws are similar to each

TABLE 3-5. PCM μ255 Encoding/Decoding Table

Range of Amplitude Input	Segment(s) Code	Step Size	Quantization (Q) Code	Code Value
0-1	—	1	0000	0
1-3 ↓ 29-31	000	2	0001 ↓ 1111	1 ↓ 15
31-35 ↓ 91-95	001	4	0000 ↓ 1111	16 ↓ 31
95-103 ↓ 215-223	010	8	0000 ↓ 1111	32 ↓ 47
223-239 ↓ 463-479	011	16	0000 ↓ 1111	48 ↓ 63
479-511 ↓ 959-991	100	32	0000 ↓ 1111	64 ↓ 79
991-1055 ↓ 1951-2015	101	64	0000 ↓ 1111	80 ↓ 95
2015-2143 ↓ 3935-4063	110	128	0000 ↓ 1111	96 ↓ 111
4063-4319 ↓ 7903-8159	111	256	0000 ↓ 1111	112 ↓ 127

[BELL82]

other, conversion facilities are employed to allow interconnections of different systems.

Both laws exceed the minimum requirements in reducing lower signal level distances, as demonstrated in Figure 3-21. The straight line shows the result of no companding in relation to the signal-to-distortion (S/D) ratio. By using either the A or μ laws, the lower signal levels are more accurately encoded, which results in less quantization distortion. Thus the S/D ratio can be maintained at a constant value over almost all the range of speech. This approach does cause some degradation of the higher-level signals, but it is indistinguishable to the human ear.

The systems discussed thus far perform instantaneous companding in that they encompass instantly the entire range of the signal with each sam-

TABLE 3-6. A-Law Encoding/Decoding Table

Range of Amplitude Input	Segment(s) Code	Step Size	Quantization (Q) Code	Code Value
0-2			0000	0
2-4			0001	1
↓	000	2	↓	↓
30-32			1111	15
32-34			0000	16
↓	001		↓	↓
62-64			1111	31
64-68			0000	66
↓	010	4	↓	↓
124-128			1111	126
128-136			0000	132
↓	011	8	↓	↓
248-256			1111	252
256-272			0000	264
↓	100	16	↓	↓
496-512			1111	504
512-544			0000	528
↓	101	32	↓	↓
992-1024			1111	1008
1024-1088			0000	1056
↓	110	64	↓	↓
1984-2048			1111	2016
2048-2176			0000	2112
↓	111	128	↓	↓
3968-4096			1111	4032

[BELL82]

ple. The μ law and A law companding systems use this technique. However, the speech signals exhibit considerable power level redundancy in the sampling process. For example, it is not unusual for the power levels to remain fairly constant over 100 or more samples. Other techniques take advantage of the power redundancy to produce high-quality signals at a reduced bit rate.

Differential Pulse Code Modulation (DPCM)

Today's systems have more sophisticated approaches than the conventional PCM technique. One widely used system is differential pulse code modulation (DPCM). This technique encodes the differences between samples of the signal instead of the actual samples (see Figure 3-22[a]). Since an analog

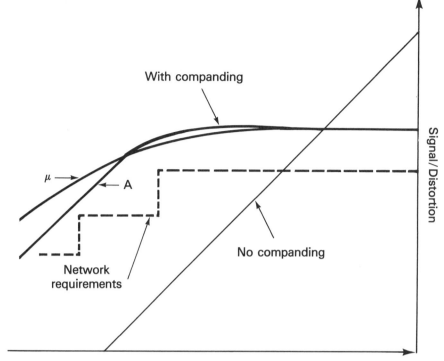

With companding

μ →

← A

Network
requirements

No companding

Range of Speech

Signal/Distortion

FIGURE 3-21. Performance of μ and A Laws

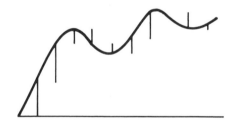

(a) Measurement of Change Between Samples

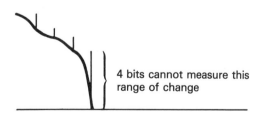

4 bits cannot measure this
range of change

(b) Distortion Caused by Sharp Changes

FIGURE 3-22. Differential PCM (DPCM)

waveform's samples are closely correlated with each other (almost sample-to-sample redundant), the range of sample differences requires fewer bits to represent the signal. Studies reveal that the predictability between adjacent 8-KHz samples is 85% or higher [FLAN79]. This redundancy in the PCM codes can be exploited to reduce the bit rate.

However, DPCM is subject to errors when an input signal changes significantly between samples. The DPCM equipment is not able to code the change accurately, which results in large quantizing errors and signal distortion (see Figure 3-22 [b]).

Adaptive DPCM

DPCM can be improved by assigning the 4-bit signals to represent different ranges of the signal. For example, in Figure 3-22(b), the 4 bits can be coded to represent a change between samples. This technique is called adaptive DPCM (ADPCM) because the systems increase or decrease the volume range covered by each 4-bit sample value.

ADPCM uses a differential quantizer to store the previous sample in a sample-and-hold circuit. The circuit measures the change between the two samples and encodes the change. Differential PCM achieves a smaller voice digitization rate (VDR) than do the conventional PCM techniques (32 Kbit/s, for example). These systems have seen extensive use in digital telephony.

Adaptive-Predictive DPCM

Some DPCM systems use a feedback signal (based on previous samples) to estimate the input signal. These systems are called adaptive-predictive DPCM. The technique is quite useful if the feedback signal varies from the input (due to quantization problems) and the next encoding sample automatically adjusts for the drift. Thus, the quantization errors do not accumulate over a prolonged period.

Many systems store more than one past sample value, with the last three sample values commonly used. The previous samples are then used to produce a more accurate estimate of the next input sample. The predictor values are typically recalculated every 10 to 20 ms. These methods are broadly classified as higher-order prediction systems.

Since DPCM and ADPCM do not send the signal but the representation of the change from the previous sample, the receiver must have some method to know where the current level is. Due to noise, the level may vary drastically or during periods of speech silence (no talking), several samples may be zero. Periodically, the sender and receiver may be returned (referenced) to the same levels by adjusting them to zero [FLAN86].

DPCM conversion can be linear or companded and some systems use adaptive quantization steps which vary with the power level of the input signal. A typical system provides high-quality signals at 48 Kbit/s. However, they have not been used much because the industry has settled on the converted 64 Kbit/s PCM and 32 Kbit/s ADPCM. Moreover, the delta modulation process discussed in the next section provides comparable quality at a reduced cost.

Delta Modulation

Another widely used A/D, D/A technique is delta modulation (DM). It uses only 1 bit for each sample, and follows the same concepts of DPCM by exploiting the sample-to-sample redundancy of the speech signal (see Figure 3-23).

Delta modulation measures the polarity of difference of successive samples and uses a 1 bit to indicate if the polarity is rising and a 0 bit to indicate if the signal is decreasing. A pulse train supplies pulses to a modulator, which adjusts the polarity of the pulses to coincide with the amplitude changes of the analog signal.

The technique actually approximates the derivative of the analog signal and not its amplitude. The signal is encoded as a "staircase" of up and down sequences at each sampling time (see Figure 3-23 [a]). The digital code can later be used to reconstruct the analog signal (analog-to-digital [A/D] process) by "smoothing" the staircase back to the original signal.

Delta modulation is simple to implement. However, it requires a higher sampling rate than PCM or DPCM because each sample does not carry much information. Many systems use 32,000 samples a second to derive a 32 Kbit/s digital signal.

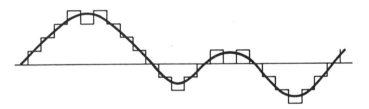

(a) Delta Modulation (Nondistortion)

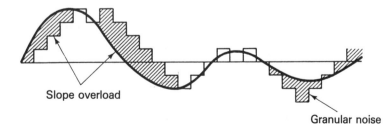

Slope overload

Granular noise

(b) Distortion

FIGURE 3-23. Delta Modulation

Delta modulation assumes the encoded waveform is no more than one step away from the sampled signal. However, a signal may change more rapidly than the staircase modulator can reflect, producing a problem called slope overload. In contrast, a slow-changing signal also creates distortions, called granular noise (see Figure 3-23 [b]). The effect of inaccurate representation of the waveform is called quantization noise (it also occurs with PCM systems) and can be mitigated by CVSD.

Continuously Variable Slope Delta Modulation (CVSD)

One widely used variation of delta modulation is continuously variable slope delta modulation (CVSD). (Another term for this technique is adaptive delta modulation [CROC83].) CVSD transmits the difference between two successive samples and employs a quantizer to change the actual quantum steps based on a sudden increase or decrease of the signal. CVSD increases the staircase step size when it detects that the waveform's slope is increasing and reduces the step size upon detecting a decrease in the slope.

CVSD does not send any information about the height of the curve (PCM) or the change in the height of the curve (ADPCM). It sends information about the changes in the shape of the curve.

A CVSD transmitter compares the input signal (its voltage) to a controlled reference signal. It increases or decreases the reference (bends up or bends down) if the input is greater or smaller than the reference (see Figure 3-24 [a]). In effect, CVSD steers the reference signal to follow the input.

A CVSD receiver reconstructs the original signal by increasing the slope of the curve when a 1 is received and decreasing the slope when a 0 is received. A filter is then used to smooth the curve (waveform).

CVSD monitors the input signal for the occurrence of successive 1s (1111) or 0s (0000). The former indicates the signal is rising too fast for the reference; the latter indicates the signal is falling too slowly for the reference. In other words, slope overload is occurring. These signals are used to produce increased step-size voltage as depicted in Figure 3-24(b).

While CVSD systems exhibit some fidelity problems at the beginning of words and very strong syllables (slope overload), the technique generally produces high-quality signals. Some CVSD systems operate at rates less than 32 Kbit/s with adequate (but poor quality) fidelity and crispness.

Vocoders

In addition to the waveform analysis techniques just discussed, the industry has devoted considerable research to a technique called parameter coding (also, vocoding). Vocoders are not used on the telephone network because

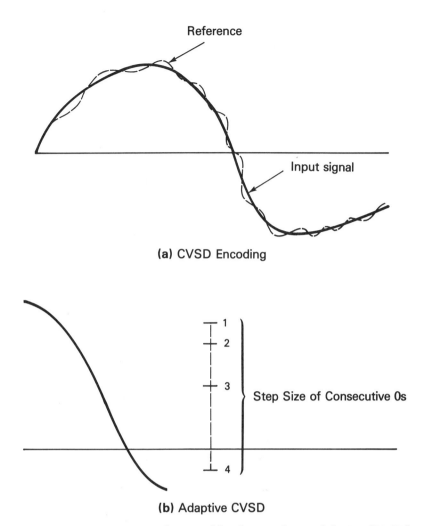

(a) CVSD Encoding

(b) Adaptive CVSD

Step Size of Consecutive 0s

FIGURE 3-24. Continuously Variable Slope Delta Modulation (CVSD)

they are designed to encode speech signals only and cannot accommodate other analog signals, such as modem transmissions. In contrast, PCM can convey data or voice.

Vocoders do not preserve the character of the waveform; rather, the input waveform is processed into parameters that measure vocal characteristics. The speech is analyzed to produce a varying model of the waveform. Parameter coding then computes a signal that most closely resembles the original speech. These parameters are transmitted through the channel (or stored on disk) for later reproduction of the speech signal. Vocoders are commonly used for recorded announcements (e.g., weather information), personal computers, voice output, and electronic video games.

DIGITAL-TO-DIGITAL CONVERSION

The last conversion scheme is digital-to-digital conversion. It is used in many systems to improve the synchronization of the signals (on the channel) between machines. It is also used to decrease the number of bits that must be transmitted.

In Chapter 1 we discussed the concept of coding structures, clocking codes, and self-clocking transmission systems. Clocking is a vital part of a data communications system, and is discussed in several parts of this book. This section explains the use of certain coding schemes to enhance clocking. Chapters 6, 9, and 19 then expand this discussion with more detail on multiplexing synchronization, physical level clocking connections, and digital network synchronization, respectively.

All digital systems must have a "clock" to keep the receiving device synchronized to the transmitting device. Regardless of the accuracy and stability of the clocks, a certain amount of error and instability occur due to a myriad of problems. The term to describe these instabilities in timing is jitter. It is associated with the receiver's sampling logic. This logic is often implemented with a phase-locked loop.

A phase-locked loop (PLL) is a common method of maintaining synchronization. An oscillator is connected to the PLL and operates at a rate considerably faster than the bit rate (16 or 32 clock periods per sample, for example). A phase detector measures the difference between a local clock and one derived from the signal. If the incoming signal and the local clock "drift" from each other, the frequent clock periods usually still provide an accurate indication of the line transitions. Moreover, the PLL readjusts if line transitions occur more or less often than the total clock periods per bit cell. The time periods between pulses are shortened or lengthened to keep the sampling close to the "clock" in the signal.

The receiver maintains a desired average clock frequency, but some error is inevitably introduced into the process as the local interface "hunts" for the source frequency. This error is called phase jitter. If the received clock is used to control the clock for the outgoing link (as is the case with regenerative repeaters), the jitter finds its way into the next link. The jitter then accumulates and cascades through each repeater and may accumulate to the point of causing sampling errors and loss of synchronization.

In order for the devices to stay synchronized, it is of paramount importance that the receiver be able to detect transitions in the incoming signal. The best signal for "deriving the clock" is one in which line transitions occur very often. One approach used for digital systems is the insertion of signal transitions in the code to ensure that line transitions occur frequently. One common approach is the T1 system which forces a state change in the event 15 zero bits occur in succession (wherein no line transition occurs).

Another approach is to provide synchronization in a specific slot for each system or transmission component. This idea uses the eighth bit of each slot of each channel for timing considerations. Another common approach is to provide bit stuffing which ensures that sufficient timing is provided in a data signal. This technique is used with data link controls such as SDLC, LAPB, and HDLC.

Yet another approach is to randomly scramble the data patterns to ensure that repetitive data patterns do not exist. Many modems use this technique to scramble the signal traffic. Some of the higher speed T1 carrier systems use scrambling as well.

Regardless of which technique is used, some kind of digital-to-digital conversion mode is necessary, because DTEs normally operate with TTL logic, which for various reasons is unacceptable on a communications channel. In this section, we provide more detail on digital-to-digital encoding, known as line coding. While digital-to-digital encoding is common to baseband transmission systems, it is also used on some broadband systems: The codes are modulated onto an analog carrier.

DTE/DCE Interface

A DTE typically uses a 3-volt signal to represent a binary 1 and a near-0-volt signal for a binary 0. This unbalanced signal works well enough for a computer, but a more efficient scheme for a communications link is to balance the voltages around 0 volt to reduce the power requirements. When the signal is to be transmitted onto a communications channel, the physical level interface converts the TTL logic signal to signals/codes acceptable to the DTE/DCE interface (EIA-232, V.28, etc.).

CODING

Figure 3-25 provides an illustration of several common binary coding schemes used in the industry. We will discuss each of them and describe their advantages and disadvantages. These signals exhibit one or several of the following four characteristics:

- *Unipolar or unbalanced code.* No signal below zero voltage or no signal above (i.e., algebraic sign does not change: 0 volts for 1; 3 volts for 0).
- *Polar or balanced code.* Signal is above and below zero voltage (opposite algebraic signs identify logic states: +3 volts and −3 volts).
- *Bipolar code.* The signal varies between three levels.
- *Alternate mark inversion (AMI) code.* Uses alternate polarity pulses to encode binary 1s.

Figure 3-25 (a) shows the non-return-to-zero code (NRZ). Notice the signal level remains stable throughout the bit cell. In this case, the signal level remains low for a bit 1 and goes to a high voltage for a bit 0. (Opposite voltages are also used in many devices.) NRZ is a widely used data commu-

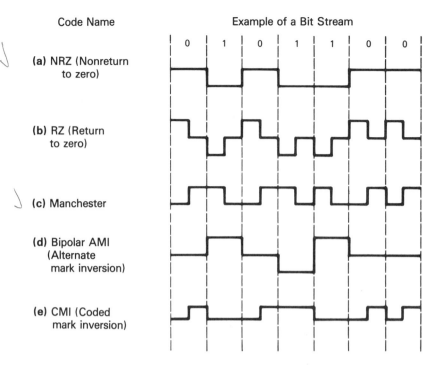

Code Name   Example of a Bit Stream

(a) NRZ (Nonreturn to zero)

(b) RZ (Return to zero)

(c) Manchester

(d) Bipolar AMI (Alternate mark inversion)

(e) CMI (Coded mark inversion)

FIGURE 3-25. Digital Codes

nications coding scheme, because of its relative simplicity and low cost. The NRZ code also makes very efficient use of bandwidth, since it can represent a bit with each baud (signal change). However, it suffers from the lack of self-clocking capabilities, since a long series of continuous 1s or 0s do not create a signal state transition on the channel. As a consequence, the receiver's clock could possibly drift from the incoming signal. The line sample would not occur at the right time, and the transmitter and the receiver might actually lose synchronization with each other. NRZ balanced is widely used in communications because it requires simple encoding or decoding and it uses a channel's bandwidth very effectively.

Another disadvantage of NRZ is the presence of a direct current (dc) component. A long series of 0s or 1s can create dc wander which is a common source of errors. Moreover, most transmission links (telephone lines) do not pass dc signals, and many systems also use alternating current (ac) for coupling with transformers. The dc signal requires direct physical attachment.

Some NRZ systems use a technique called differential encoding. The signals are decoded by companding the polarity of adjacent signal elements. Absolute values are not used. An advantage to this approach is that it is more reliable to detect the signal elements in the presence of noise.

The return-to-zero code (RZ) usually entails the changing of the signal state at least once in every bit cell. This scheme is illustrated in Figure 3-25 (b). As a bipolar code, since RZ code provides a transition in every bit cell, it has very good synchronization characteristics. Moreover, the dc wander problem is eliminated with bipolar schemes since three levels are used to encode the data. The average voltage level is maintained at 0. The RZ code's primary disadvantage is that it requires two signal transitions for each bit. Consequently, an RZ code requires twice the baud of a conventional NRZ code. This type of code is found in some of the more sophisticated systems dealing with local area networks, lightwave technologies, and optical fibers.

Figure 3-25 (c) illustrates a code found in many communications systems today, the Manchester code (or diphase code). This code provides a signal state change in every bit cell. Consequently, it is a good clocking code, and dc wander is nonexistent. The interface devices used to achieve this higher baud are more expensive than the NRZ interfaces. It should also be noted that biphase Manchester code does not have any means of monitoring the performance of the signal. It contains no bipolar violation capabilities, for example. Manchester code is commonly found in magnetic tape recording, optical fiber links, coaxial links, and local area networks.

Figure 3-25 (d) shows a code used by AT&T, the Bell Operating Companies, and other carriers. This was originally called the Bell System PCM code. This signalling structure is an example of bipolar AMI (alternate mark inversion) where alternate polarity pulses are used to encode logic 1 (mark). This particular code presents some problems when a long series of 0s are located in a transmission. The components in the system have no way to synchronize with 0-bit cells because there are no changes in the state of the line.

The bipolar AMI scheme has an advantage in that it can detect polarity violations. For example, if the detection of two successive pulses indicates they are the same polarity, an error has occurred known as bipolar violation. In other words, no single bit error can occur without the notation of a bipolar violation. Many systems, such as the T1 carrier, were designed to monitor bipolar violations and to provide alarm measures in the event thresholds are exceeded. The T1 line repeaters maintain timing as long as no string greater than fifteen 0s is allowed to occur.

It is possible to use the bipolar violations scheme to provide not only error detection, but also error correction. By storing a sequence of pulses and by examining the successive sample values, the forward error correction logic can determine where an error was most likely to have occurred. This is a technique described generally as maximum likelihood or viterbi [SPIL77].

Figure 3-25 (e) shows a variation of the AMI scheme called coded mark inversion (CMI). It is used on CCITT high-level multiplexers (139.264 Mbit/s). This code is a two-level NRZ. It uses the following coding rules:

- *Binary 0*: Always a positive transition at the midway point of the binary unit time interval (the bit cell).

- *Binary 1*: 0 does not change state within a bit cell.

- Positive transition at the start of the bit cell if preceding level was high.
- Negative transition at start of bit cell if last binary 1 was encoded at low level.

CMI provides many signal transitions and, unlike other codes, no ambiguity exists in interpreting 1s or 0s. However, because one-half of a 0-bit cell looks like a 1-bit cell, it does suffer in performance when compared to the diphase code.

The BNZS Codes

Bipolar coding requires a minimum density of binary 1s in the data stream to maintain timing at the repeaters. Even though a long string of 0s is precluded, a low density of pulses increases timing problems (called timing jitter). To solve this difficulty, most of the newer digital transmission systems perform some kind of substitution of the data by replacing strings of 0s with special codes to increase pulse density. In fact, these systems replace N zeros with a special N-length code, that purposely produces bipolar violations. Hence, they are called binary N zero substitution (BNZS) codes.

The B3ZS Code. Several BNZS techniques are employed to increase pulse density. This example is called binary 3 zero substitution (B3ZS) and is used in several systems in North America. Europe and CCITT specify it for high-speed coaxial systems. Each string of three 0s in the data stream is encoded with one of two codes:

00V: Two bit intervals with no pulses (00), followed by a bipolar violation pulse (V)

B0V: A pulse with a bipolar alteration (B), followed by no pulse (0), followed by a bipolar violation pulse (V).

Notice that the last bit position contains the bipolar violation. This approach makes it easy to identify the position of the substitution.

The choice of 00V or B0V is based on keeping the number of unviolated pulses (B pulses) between violation (V) at an odd increment. If an odd number of 1s have been transmitted since the last substitution, 00V is coded. If an even number of 1s have been transmitted, the B0V is coded.

Table 3-7 summarizes the B3ZS substitution rules. The reader should attempt to apply the table to encode the data stream shown in Figure 3-25.

The B6ZS Code. The AT&T/Bell Systems (T2, 6.312 Mbit/s carriers) employ the bipolar with 6 zeros substitution (B6ZS). CCITT specifies B6ZS for its 6.312 Kbit/s digital pair cable. In this format, a code is substituted when 6 0s in succession occur in the original signal. The code actually

TABLE 3-7. B3ZS Encoding Rules

Polarity of Preceding Pulse	Number of 1 Pulses Since Last Substitution	
	Odd	Even
−	00−	+0+
+	00+	−0−

TABLE 3-8. B6ZS Encoding Rules

Polarity of Preceding Pulse	Six Bit Substitution
−	0−+0+−
+	0+−0−+

TABLE 3-9. B8ZS Encoding Rules

Polarity of Preceding Pulse	Eight Bit Substitution
−	000−+0+−
+	000+−0−+

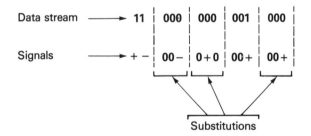

FIGURE 3-26. B3ZS Substitution Example

substituted for the 6 0s depends on the polarity of the pulse immediately preceding the 0s. Table 3-8 defines the rules for B6ZS.

The B8ZS Code. Another coding scheme used on several of the newer T1 systems is known as binary 8 zeros supression, or B8ZS. The code is also specified for the T1 (1.544 Mbit/s carrier by CCITT). B8ZS is another modified AMI code. Eight consecutive 0s are replaced with 000+−0−+ if the preceding pulse is +. If the preceding pulse is −, the substitution is 000−+0+−. Table 3-9 summarizes the B8ZS rules, and Figure 3-27 shows an example of the substitution logic.

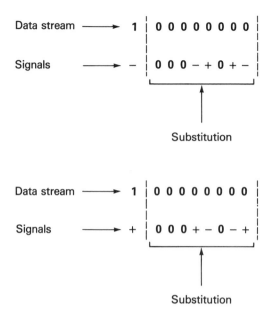

Data stream ⟶ 1 | 0 0 0 0 0 0 0 0 |

Signals ⟶ − | 0 0 0 − + 0 + − |

Substitution

Data stream ⟶ 1 | 0 0 0 0 0 0 0 0 |

Signals ⟶ + | 0 0 0 + − 0 − + |

Substitution

FIGURE 3-27. B8ZS Substitution Example

The HDB3 Code (High Density Bipolar Three).   HDB3 replaces strings of four 0s with a substitution code. It does not allow more than three consecutive 0s—hence its name, HDB3. It is identical to B3ZS except that it substitutes four consecutive 0s, whereas B3ZS substitutes three consecutive 0s. HDB3 adheres to the following rules (also see Table 3-10):

TABLE 3-10.   HDB3 Encoding Rules

Polarity of Preceding Pulse	Number of 1 Pulses Since Last Substitution	
	Odd	*Even*
−	000 −	+ 00 +
+	000 +	− 00 −

- 1s alternate in polarity.
- Strings of four 0s are substituted as follows:
  - The first bit of the 4-bit code is coded as a 0 if the preceding 1 of the HDB3 signal has a polarity opposite to the polarity of the preceding violation and is not a violation by itself; otherwise, it is coded as a 1.
  - The second and third bits are always coded as 0s.
  - The last bit is coded as a 1, and the polarity must violate the AMI rule (therefore, successive substitutions produce successive violations).

ISDN Line Codes

The ISDN (and code) is explained in considerable detail in Chapter 19, but a brief description of its digital code is appropriate for this chapter. The current CCITT specification uses pseudo-ternary coding with 100% pulse width. The ISDN pseudo-ternary code adheres to the following rules:

- Binary 1 is represented with no line signal.
- Binary 0 is represented with a positive or negative pulse.
- The first 0 following a framing balance bit is the same polarity as the balance bit.
- Subsequent 0s must alternate in polarity.
- A balance bit is 0 if the number of binary 0s following the previous balance bit is odd.
- A balance bit is a 1 if the number of binary 0s following the previous balance bit is even.

SUGGESTED READINGS

The material on encoding and modulation is vast. One of the best books on the subject is [BELL82], a lucid and detailed account of digital systems. [MART76] is somewhat aged but is still excellent. [AKGU74] provides an analysis of the digital local loop. [HEAT81] is one of the best tutorials on analog modulation, and several concepts in this chapter were derived from this document. Other valuable sources are [FLAN86], [MCNA82], [CROC83], [ABT67], and [RAI78]. A comprehensive list of references is available in [BELL82].

QUESTIONS

TRUE/FALSE:

1. The quantization distortion of a signal is a function of the differences between the quantized steps.
2. The bandwidth in angle modulation depends on the number of sidebands.
3. Through the use of filters, it is possible to separate multiple voice transmissions occupying the same frequency spectrum.
4. With amplitude modulation (AM), the modulation envelope is an expression of the amplitude and frequency of the modulation signal.
5. One disadvantage of non-return-to-zero (NRZ) signalling is the presence of a direct current (dc) component.
6. Pulse amplitude modulation describes a pulse amplitude that varies in accordance with the modulating signal.
7. Modern digital systems use a low-pass filter to demodulate a PAM signal.

8. Channel separation on a frequency division multiplexed system is accomplished by band-pass filters.

9. In a PCM system, quantizing noise can be reduced by either increasing the pulse width or using limiters at the receiver.

10. What is the Nyquist rate for a 30 KHz signal? *twice*

11. A 75 MHz carrier with an amplitude of 50 V is modulated by a 3 KHz audio signal with an amplitude of 20V. What is the modulation factor? What frequencies comprise the modulated wave?

12. A 4 KHz signal modulates a 107.6 KHz carrier. The resultant FM signal has a frequency derivation of 50 KHz. What are the highest and lowest frequencies of the resultant signal?

13. Match the term to the appropriate definition:

Definition

a) The signal varies between three levels.
b) Uses alternate polarity pulses to encode binary 1s.
c) No signal below zero voltage or no signal above (i.e., algebraic sign does not change: 0 volts for 1, 3 volts for 0).
d) Signal is above and below zero voltage (opposite algebraic signs identify logic states: $+3$ volts and -3 volts).

Term

1. Unipolar or unbalanced code
2. Bipolar code
3. Polar or balanced code
4. Alternate mark inversion (AMI)

14. Match the term to the appropriate definition:

Definition

a) Digital technique that encodes the differences between the samples of the signal.
b) Digital technique that uses a feedback signal.
c) Digital technique that uses one bit per sample.
d) Digital technique that "reconstructs" analog signal by increasing or decreasing the shape of the curve.

Term

1. Adaptive predictive DPCM
2. Delta modulation
3. Differential pulse code modulation (DPCM)
4. Continuously variable slope delta modulation (CVSD)

15. Analog-to-analog conversion is useful for a number of reasons. Summarize these reasons.

16. Given the following definitions:
    lower sideband = fc − fm
    upper sideband = fc + fm

where: fc = carrier frequency; fm = modulating frequency, what is the modulator output for a double sideband transmitter carrier (DSBTC) of 50 KHz with a modulating signal of 10 KHz?

17. What is the required bandwidth of the AM system described in question 16?

18. Describe some disadvantages of double sideband modulation.

19. State the frequency of a sinusoidal signal with the following periods:
    a) .001 second
    b) .0001 second
    c) .00001 second

20. The following waveform and pulse carrier shows the effect of a high sampling rate:

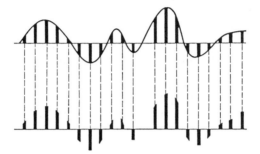

Draw the resultant PAM signals for the following lower sampling rate:

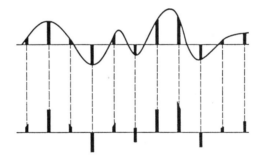

21. A widely used modulation technique is multilevel signalling. Describe it and include in the description the concepts of bauds and length of signalling interval.

22. Describe problems associated with analog signalling and the practice of using analog and digital signals in one system.

SELECTED ANSWERS

1. True. Consequently, to reduce quantizing errors, the distribution of the quantization steps are varied.

2. True. In addition, the number of sidebands is determined by the modulating index and the modulating frequency.

3. False. The same frequencies cannot be separated by a conventional filter. Therefore, voice frequencies are multiplexed onto different carrier frequencies.

4. True. See Figure 3-1 for a visual explanation.

5. True. The dc component can create "dc wander." Also, dc signals are not coupled with transformers, but require a direct physical attachment.

6. True.

7. True.

8. True.

9. False. The preferred technique is to increase the number of quantums in the system.

10. The Nyquist rate is 60 KHz.

11. The modulation factor is calculated as 20V/50 = 0.4. The frequency content of the AM signal consists of the carrier and the sidebands:

$$f_c = 75 \text{ MHz}$$
$$f_c + f_a = 75 \text{ KHz} + 3 \text{ KHz} = 75003 \text{ KHz}$$
$$f_c - f_a = 75 \text{ KHz} - 3 \text{ KHz} = 74997 \text{ KHz}$$

13.

Definition	Term
a	2
b	4
c	1
d	3

18. The main disadvantages of double sideband modulation are:

The bandwidth requirement is twice that of the intelligence in the waveform since the sidebands contain the same information. The carrier signal does not contribute to the intelligence of the waveform (it is only a reference frequency), yet it contains most of the power in the signal. The envelope requires the carrier and the sidebands to maintain precise amplitude and phase relationships.

20.

21. The change rate of a modulated signal is called the signalling rate, modulation rate or bauds. This rate is defined as:

   B = 1/T

Where: B = baud(s); T = length of signalling interval in time.

Multilevel signalling permits more than one bit to be represented with each baud. It is a function of:

   R = D/N

Where: R = signalling or modulation rate in bauds; D = data rate in bit/s; N = number of bits per signalling element.

CHAPTER 4

Communications Media

INTRODUCTION

The movement of data between computers and terminals can take place along several different media paths. This chapter describes the media most commonly used today, as well as their transmission characteristics. Several of these media are also described in other chapters in connection with their unique attributes and/or their relationship to other aspects of data communications.

In many instances the data communications user has no option in choosing a medium. For example, when a user dials a computer, the user does not instruct the phone company to use microwave, coaxial cable, or optical fiber. Ideally, the user does not care. The medium type should remain transparent to the communications process, and it usually does.

However, it is useful to have an understanding of transmission media for the following reasons:

- Transmission impairments occurring on a medium often affect the data—the impairments may even destroy portions of the data stream.
- Response time and throughput are partially dependent on the type of medium.
- The type of path may be selected by communications personnel in an organization, especially if the medium is privately owned, such as a local area network within an office building.
- Media vary greatly in their costs; their installation and maintenance can significantly affect the organization's budget.

This chapter describes the physical and operational characteristics of the following communications media:

Hardwire Systems

Wire pairs
Coaxial cable
Submarine cable
Optical fiber

Softwire Systems

Microwave
Satellite channels
Waveguide
Cellular systems
Infrared

HARDWIRE SYSTEMS

Wire Pairs

The telegraph was one of the first systems to use wire transmission. After its development in the 1840s, it became a major factor in the business and personal lives of many people. The first transcontinental telegraph line was completed October 25, 1861. The system was developed by Western Union and spanned the 2000-mile distance between St. Joseph, Missouri, and Sacramento, California. It dramatically changed the way people communicated.

The telephone followed the telegraph and rapidly grew in use beyond anyone's predictions. Indeed, the popularity of the telephone in its first few years caught nearly everyone by surprise. As the telephone's use increased, the provision for telephone circuits became a major problem, because the embryonic industry was not positioned for rapid growth.

During the early days of telephony, the circuits used only one wire for transmission and a ground return (some systems in remote locations still use this technique). Signal quality on the lines was very poor due to signal noise and decay. Often, the system was useless due to the imperfections of ground return. Consequently, in 1883, telephone companies began to install a second wire to provide a non-ground return. Today, this is known as a two-wire circuit. These early efforts improved the circuits but required double the amount of wire. The increased need for wiring almost destroyed the industry, which at that time was financially unstable and had little capital.

Open-Wire Pairs

The early communications systems used open-wire pairs. They consisted of uninsulated pairs of wires strung on poles about 125 feet apart (see Figure 4-1). The air space between the wires insulated (isolated) them from each other. With the early systems, a limited number of wires could be accommodated on a pole and the wires were very susceptible to corrosion, storm damage, and interference from power lines.

Open-wire systems have largely disappeared. They proved inadequate in large urban areas, and they were unattractive as well as cumbersome to install and maintain. In large cities in the 1890s, some poles were 90 feet high in order to support crossarms supporting 300 wires. Certain parts of cities were literally covered by wires.

In 1883, the first underground cables were laid (in Brooklyn and Boston). Two years later, lead sheathing was placed around cables to provide protection. Prior to the use of the lead sheath, oil was used to insulate the

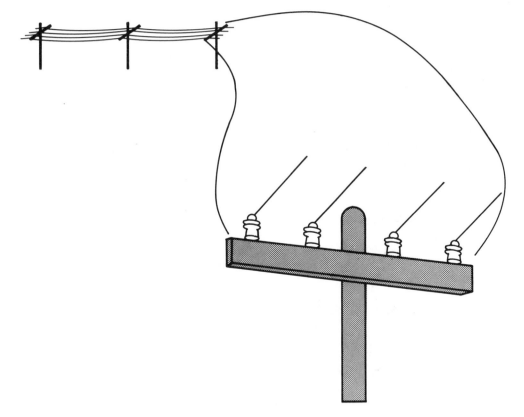

FIGURE 4-1. Open-Wire Pairs

wires. It now was possible to use dry paper for insulation and it rapidly became the industry standard.

The wire pair improved the signal quality but the two wires experienced mutual interference (crosstalk). Later, the pairs were twisted around each other to compensate for (and cancel) the effects of pair interference. These circuits are pervasive today and are called twisted-pair cable (see Figure 4-2). They can be used to support both analog and digital signals.

Balanced and Unbalanced Twisted Pairs

The two-wire system often insulates the conductors from each other in a cable. In addition to this insulation, the system has an outer insulation cable. At one time, the outer insulation was made of compositions such as lead. Today the insulation is comprised of various kinds of plastic or similar substances.

The twisting of each pair (in a multipair cable) is staggered (see Figure 4-2). Radiated energy from the current flowing in one wire of the pair is largely cancelled by the radiated energy of the current flowing back in the return wire of the same pair. This approach greatly reduces the effect of crosstalk. Moreover, each pair in the cable is less susceptible to external noise; the pair cancels out much of the noise because noise is coupled almost equally in each wire of the pair. This technique is often called TTP (for telephone twisted pair).

These characteristics describe a balanced line. Both wires carry current; the current in one wire is 180° out-of-phase with the current in the other wire. Both wires are above ground potential. In contrast, an unbalanced line carries the current on one wire and the other wire is at ground potential. The reader may wish to review the material in Box 4-1 for information on grounding.

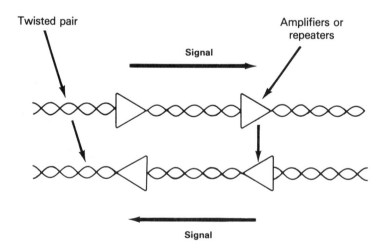

FIGURE 4-2. Twisted-Pair Cable

BOX 4-1. A Brief Discourse on Grounding

Grounding is defined as a conducting circuit through which equipment is connected to earth or to a conducting body that is at earth potential [MILL79]. Potential is a term to describe the differences of charge between two points on a circuit. Anything that is at ground potential has the same electrical charge as the earth. Ground potential describes anything that has the same charge (zero) as the earth ground.

The term ground electrode or grounding medium describes a connection mode to ground by the conductor. In residential systems, the ac power line is usually grounded to earth, usually by a connection to a pipe.

Electronic equipment may provide grounding on a metal chassis, which is used as a common return for the connection.

With a non-metal chassis (a plastic printed board), a connection around the board is used as a common return for chassis ground.

When the ground return was used for a telephone circuit the system had near-0 resistance (measured in ohms). As a consequence, considerable disturbance was introduced into the circuit by the unbalanced nature of the system and stray currents. Moreover, actual soil conditions and the moisture content of the soil determined the nature of ground return.

Earlier telephone systems also used a common return, although this practice is not used much today With this approach the return conductor to the central office is used for several circuits. This arrangement is better than a grounded return, but not nearly as good as a fully metalized circuit. A metalized circuit means the currents are carried entirely on the two wires between the devices.

The idea of a common return often creates confusion because many people are under the impression that a wire will not carry two currents in opposite directions. Yet, it can be demonstrated that a wire can carry currents in different directions at the same time, but the electrical energy is partially cancelled.

Wire Sizes.   Wires are described by their size. The sizing system in the United States is called the American wire gauge (AWG) system. The AWG system specifies the diameter of the wire. Interestingly, the higher-gauge numbers indicate thinner wire sizes.

The smaller the diameter of the wire, the greater its resistance to the propagation of a signal. This means the increased resistance results in a decreased bit transfer rate across the communications path. A smaller wire produces less total surface for the radiating signal, resulting in an increased signal loss. A larger wire with a greater cross-sectional area will allow for an increased signal intensity. The local telephone loops are usually 22 to 26 gauge, with the bulk of telephone twisted pairs (TTP) using 24 gauge. Long-

TABLE 4-1. Copper Wires

Gauge	Area in Circular Mils	Ohms per 1000 Ft. at 20° C.
10	10,381	0.997
11	8,234	1.257
12	6,580	1.586
13	5,178	1.999
14	4,107	2.521
15	3,257	3.179
16	2,583	4.009
17	2,048	5.055
18*	1,624	6.374
19*	1,288	8.038
20	1,021	10.14
21	810.1	12.78
22*	642.4	16.12
23	509.4	20.32
24*	404.0	25.63
25	320.4	32.31
26*	254.1	40.75
27	201.5	51.38
28	159.8	64.79
29	126.7	81.70
30	100.5	103.0
36	25.0	414.2

*Indicates wire sizes commonly used in the telephone plant.

distance lines typically employ 19 gauge wires. The gauges, wire sizes, and resistances of copper wire are shown in Table 4-1 [LEE73].

The transmission distances obtainable on wires depend upon the gauge, line condition, operating environment, and speed of transmission. Table 4-2 provides speed, distance, and gauge comparisons for unloaded

TABLE 4-2. Laboratory Performance of Wire Pairs

Kbit	#19 mi	#19 km	#22 mi	#22 km	#24 mi	#24 km	#26 mi	#26 km
1.2	32	51	22.5	36	17.5	28.5	14	22.5
2.4	28	45	19.5	31.5	15.5	25	12	19.5
4.8	24	38	16	26	12.5	20	10	16
9.6	14	22.5	9	15	7	11.5	5.5	9
19.2	12.5	20	7.5	12	5.6	9	4.3	7
48.0	11	18	6.2	10	4.4	7.1	3.2	5.2
56.0	10.5	17	6	9.5	4.2	6.7	3	4.8
64.0	10	16	5.8	9.3	4.0	6.5	2.9	4.6

wires under laboratory conditions (unloaded means certain equipment is removed from the line). Actual operations performance could be considerably less, with ranges from 30% to 50% less than the laboratory performance.

Table 4-3 provides further information on pair characteristics [REY83]. It can be seen that the frequency and characteristic impedance influence the performance of the gauges.

The longer a wire, the higher its resistance because more work is required for the electrons to drift from one end of the wire to the other. The larger the wire, the less its resistance since more free electrons are available in the larger cross-sectional area of the wire:

$$R = P * L/A$$

Where: R = total resistance; L = length of wire; A = cross-sectional area; P = specific resistance or resistivity.

Shielded and Unshielded Pairs. The bulk of TTP cable is unshielded 24 AWG copper wire. Unshielded wire has no metallic cover around it. These wires are inexpensive and offer reasonable performance over a long distance. However, they are quite susceptible to crosstalk and interference from external power sources.

Shielded twisted pairs (also called data-grade media) improve the resistance to crosstalk and external noise. The shield surrounds the wire with a metallic sheathing or braid. Several analyses reveal that a shielded pair system improves resistance to crosstalk and noise by a factor of 1000 or more [BATE86]. Attenuation of TTP is about 2.3 times more severe than shielded pairs. (It is suggested that each copper conductor be made from the

TABLE 4-3. Actual Performance of Wire Pairs

Gauge	Frequency (Hz)	Characteristics Impedance (ohms)	dB/Mile
19	1000	297–j278	1.26
	2000	217–j190	1.72
	3000	183–j150	2.04
22	1000	414–j401	1.82
	2000	297–j279	2.53
	3000	247–j224	3.05
24	1000	518–j507	2.30
	2000	370–j355	3.21
	3000	306–j286	3.89
26	1000	654–j645	2.92
	2000	466–j453	4.10
	3000	383–j367	4.99

same production run to ensure the pair is balanced. Also, the insulation must be carefully crafted and a low dielectric-constant material must be used.)

One might think that unshielded cable is not a good choice for a media. However, TTP is quite effective for data communications links of relatively short distances of a few hundred feet in an electrically benign environment. By limiting the high-frequency signal components with a filter (also, to stay within FCC regulations), a TTP can support transmission speeds of up to 10 Mbit/s.

Many wire pairs can be placed into one tough protective sheath. Some systems have hundreds of wires in the cable. The cable is quite heavy and requires substantial resources to install. A foot-long section of 22-gauge 600-pair cables weighs over 10 pounds!

Coaxial Cables

Coaxial cables (coax) have been in existence since the early 1940s and are another very widely used medium. They are employed extensively in long-distance telephone toll trunks, urban areas, and local networks. The coax

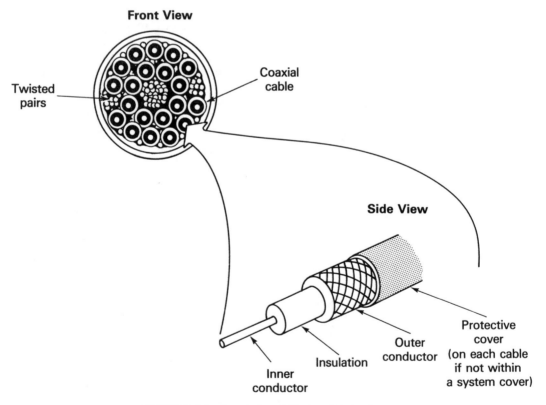

FIGURE 4-3. Coaxial and Twisted-Pair Systems

consists of an inner copper conductor held in position by circular spacers (insulating disks) (see Figure 4-3). The inner wire and disks are surrounded by an outer conductor which forms a cylinder around the inner conductor and disks. The covering acts as a shield to protect the conductor and prevent interference from signals from other media. The center copper conductor ranges from 10 AWG, used on long-distance transmission, to very small sizes of only .1 inch.

Generally, coaxial cables carry signals in only one direction. Consequently, they are often used in pairs. Coaxial cable systems usually include 8, 12, 20, and 22 coaxials with two cables dedicated as standbys in case of problems.

Coaxial cables provide for greater bandwidth and faster bit rates than wire cables. Typical coaxial cable systems can carry as many as 10,800 voice-grade channels. As stated earlier, the use the higher frequencies on a wire pair is limited because higher frequencies tend to produce a current flow on the outside portion of the wire. This phenomenon (the "skin effect") creates significant attenuation and crosstalk problems on uninsulated wires. The same holds true for coaxial cables: The current flows more on the outside of the wire at higher frequencies. However, since the wire is encased in the shell, the current is actually flowing inside the outer shell, and outside the inner wire. This approach allows for a system above the 60-megahertz (MHz) bandwidth (and 10,800 voice-grade circuits). The technology is somewhat limited due to repeater design and signal loss at higher frequencies. In fact, the attenuation of coaxial cable increases as the square root of frequency.

Figure 4-3 also shows a typical coaxial composite cable. Several coaxial tubes are placed into a protective sheathing along with signal wires and twisted-wire pairs. The composite cable can have many combinations and sizes of wire and coaxial cable. Finally Table 4-4 summarizes the North American Coaxial L-Carrier System [REY83]. The table is self-descriptive except for the term *protection switching*. This refers to the number of spare cables per working cable: *1 by 10* means 1 spare for 10 working cables.

TABLE 4-4. Coaxial L-Carrier System

Characteristic	L1	L3	L4	L5	L5E
Service date	1946	1953	1967	1974	1978
VF capacity/tube pair	600	1860	3600	10,800	13,200
Cable size (tubes)	8	12	20	22	22
Protection switching	1 by 3	1 by 5	1 by 9	1 by 10	1 by 10
Working VF channels	1800	9300	32,400	108,000	132,000
Top frequency (MHz)	2.8	8.3	17.5	60.6	64.8
Bandwidth (MHz)	2.7	8	17	57.5	61.5
Repeater spacing (miles)	8	4	2	1	1
Technology	Vacuum tubes	Vacuum tubes	Solid state	Solid state	Solid state

Submarine Cable

Submarine copper-core cable was introduced for transmission under bodies of water to replace or augment high-frequency radio schemes. The technology has been around since 1850, when a cable was laid across the English Channel. The first submarine cable in North America was laid in 1852 between New Brunswick and Prince Edward Island. Cables with telegraph lines were installed in 1858 between New Foundland and Ireland. But until 1956, when the first voice cable was laid, radio was the only means of transmitting telephone calls across the ocean. This system, TAT-1, connected New Foundland to Scotland and carried only 52 calls.

Since the 1950s, and until 1983, new systems were installed every six or seven years to meet the increased traffic demand. The newer systems employ one cable, with 3-KHz channels separated by single sideband (SSB) AM multiplexing.

Land-based coaxial cable differs from undersea coaxial. The undersea cable consists of only one cable with a solid dialectic to withstand the tremendous sea pressure. Since maintenance is quite expensive and sometimes

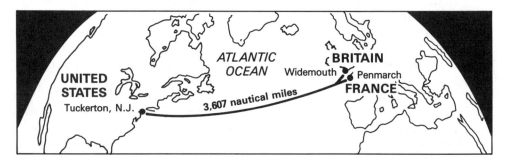

(a) Transatlantic System

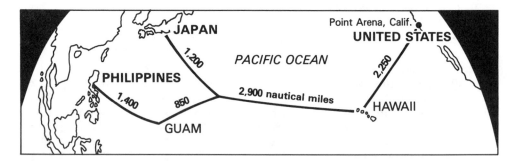

(b) Transpacific System

FIGURE 4-4. Submarine Optical Fiber Systems

impossible, submarine coaxial cable must be very reliable. Its operating goals are to be 100 times more reliable than land cable and to experience no more than four service interruptions within a 20-year period. Once the cable is laid, some ongoing control functions are exercised from the shore. For example, some of the equalizers on the cable are periodically adjusted to compensate for changing cable characteristics due to the aging process.

The last submarine copper cable was TAT-7, installed in 1983 at a cost of $191 million. TAT-7 carries up to 9000 voice calls (or multilevel data and video signals within this capacity).

The submarine cables today are optical fiber systems. Two major systems are in various stage of implementation; the trans-Pacific and the trans-Atlantic (see Figure 4-4). The trans-Atlantic system handles the equivalent of 40,000 voiceband transmissions. The cable spans 3607 nautical miles and terminates at Tuckerton, New Jersey, Widemouth, England, and Penmarch, France. The trans-Pacific system spans 8000 nautical miles from an area just north of San Francisco to points in Hawaii, Guam, Japan, and the Philippines.

Near the shoreline, the cable is buried in a shallow trench. Further out to sea, the cable is laid directly on the seabed in regions generally devoid of sharp peaks and mountains.

The system provides much better quality than the other copper cables, and avoids the delay of the satellite systems. It is expected to lead to reduced costs as well.

Comparison of Wire Pairs and Coaxial Cable

Twisted-pair cable is usually balanced: The two wires have the same "electrical references" to ground potential, and the current in each conductor is usually 180° out-of-phase with that in the other. This latter feature is attractive if other signals interfere, since radiated fields that are 180° out-of-phase tend to cancel each other. Twisted pairs exhibit relatively low signal loss (attenuation).

A coaxial cable is an unbalanced circuit. The center conductor carries the current and the sleeve acts as another conductor operating at ground potential (or ground return). The sleeve (also called a shield) prevents energy from radiating into the surrounding area. An unbalanced coaxial line experiences greater attenuation than balanced wire pairs, but it is easier to install and maintain.

A balanced transmission line must not collect moisture, which will change the electrical properties between the two lines, resulting in signal reflections and additional line losses. The line must also be kept clear of other conductors such as downspouts, rain gutters, and metal towers.

In contrast, coaxial line has an outside shield at ground potential, so it can be mounted anywhere. A balanced line offers the lowest attenuation, but coaxial cable is still widely used because it is easy to install. The greater bandwidth gives it greater transmission capacity.

The initial commitment of ISDN to twisted pair ensures the immediate future of this medium, but today optical fiber is often being installed in place of twisted pair or coaxial cable.

Optical Fibers

Light has been used for sending messages for hundreds of years. As early as 30 B.C. the Romans used a "torch telegraph" system in which torches were positioned on a wall to represent a code. Smoke signals were used by the American Indians as early as 800 A.D., and the French in 1791 used optical telegraphs. The French system consisted of a pointer that was rotated against a dial to present a graphic visible image. The image was viewed by a long-distance "spy glass" from another position. All these efforts had limited success because light signals attenuate rapidly in the atmosphere.

Today, the use of light for transmitting data, voice, and video has become pervasive. However, cables (optical fibers) rather than the atmosphere are used for the transmission.

Without question, optical media have a bright future (no pun intended) for several reasons:

- Optical transmission has a very large information capacity. As Table 2-1 indicates, the frequencies encompassing lightwave transmission are very high in the spectrum. The reader may recall that bandwidth is largely dependent on the frequency range. Optical fiber bandwidths in the range of 500 MHz are not unusual today, and Bell Laboratories has successfully placed 30,000 simultaneous telephone calls on one optical fiber. Figure 4-5 compares the performance/attenuation of optical fiber, coaxial cable, and wire pairs [STAL85].
- Optical fibers have electrically nonconducting photons instead of the electrons found in metallic cables such as wires or coaxial cables. This is attractive for applications in which the transmission path traverses environments that are subject to fire and gaseous combustion from electricity. Optical cables are not subject to electrical sparks or interference from electrical components in a building or computer machine room.
- Optical fibers have less loss of signal strength than copper wire and coaxial cables. The strength of a light signal is reduced only slightly after propagation through several miles of cable. Repeaters can be spaced as far as 20 to 30 miles apart (32 to 48 Km). In contrast, North American standards on existing copper cables stipulate repeaters every 2.8 miles (4.48 Km) (a T1 carrier operating at 1.544 Mbit/s).
- Optical fibers are more secure than copper cable transmission methods. Transmission of light does not yield residual intelligence that is

found in electrical transmission. Moreover, it is quite difficult to tap an optical cable.

- Optical cables are very small (roughly the size of a hair) and weigh very little. For example, 900 copper wire pairs pulled through 1000 feet in a building would weigh approximately 4800 pounds. Two optical fibers pulled the same distance with protective covers (and greater capacity) weigh only 80 pounds.
- Optical fibers are relatively easy to install and operate in high and low temperatures.
- Due to the low signal loss, the error rate for optical fibers is very low. For example, a typical error rate on an optical fiber is 10^{-9} versus 10^{-6} in metallic cables.
- Semiconductor technology has been refined to provide transmitting and receiving devices for the system. The rapidly decreasing costs of solid state chips have further spurred the optical fiber industry.

Methods of Transmission. Typically, the light signal is transmitted down the optical fiber in the form of on/off pulses representing a digital bit stream (see Figure 4-6). The fiber consists of three concentric cylinders of dielectric material, the jacket, the cladding, and the core. The core and cladding are made up of transparent glass (some systems use plastic) which guide the light within the core and reflect it as it travels between the core and the cladding.

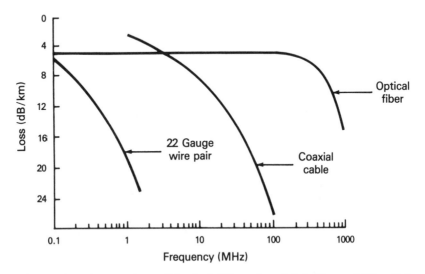

FIGURE 4-5. Comparison of Optical Fiber, Coaxial Cable, and Wire Pairs [STAL85]

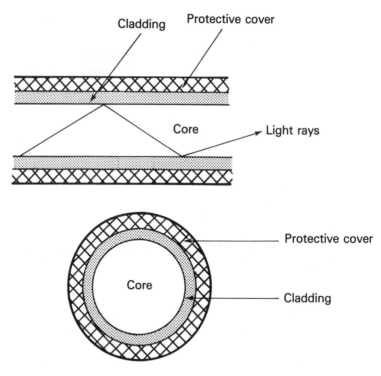

FIGURE 4-6. Optical Fiber

The core and the cladding have different refractive indices (refraction is the ratio of the velocity of a lightwave in free space to its velocity in a medium, such as core and cladding). Since the refractive index of the two differ, light propagates faster in the cladding than it does in the core. As the light moves toward the cladding (a region of higher velocity) it is bent back toward the core and guided along the fiber (hence, another name of optical fiber is lightguide cable).

LEDs and Lasers. The light signal source is usually a laser or a light-emitting diode (LED). The lasers provide for greater bandwidth and yield significantly greater capacity than other methods. For example, a wire-pair cable has a bandwidth distance parameter of 1 MHz/Km; a coaxial cable has a 20 MHz/Km parameter; and an optical fiber has a 400 MHz/Km distance parameter. The signal is emitted from microchips composed of semi-conducting materials that transmit near-infrared-wavelength signals. Silicon photodetectors are used to receive the signals and convert the light ray to the original off/on electrical pulse for interface into the terminal, computer, or modem. Both the laser and LED emit a beam of light into the fiber when a voltage is applied. The advantages and disadvantages of LEDs and lasers are summarized in Box 4-2.

LEDs

Advantages	low cost
	long life
	less sensitive to temperature changes
Disadvantages	low power output
	relatively low data rate
	couples only to multimode fiber (see later discussions)
	wide beam of light creates dispersion and affects quality

Lasers

Advantages	high power output
	high data rate
	couples to multimode or single mode fiber
	narrow beam of light
Disadvantages	high cost (but dropping)
	short life (but improving)
	sensitive to temperature changes

Single-Mode and Multimode Fiber. The methods of transmission depend on the size of the core diameter and are broadly classified as single mode and multimode. In a step-index multimode fiber (Figure 4-7 [a]), the core and cladding interface is sharply defined. The light rays bounce off the interfaces into the core at different angles, resulting in different path lengths (modes) for the signal. This causes the signal to spread out along the fiber and limits the step-index cable to approximately 35 MHz/Km. This spreading phenomenon is called modal dispersion.

A better approach, called graded-index multimode, alters the cladding/core interface to provide different refractive indexes within the core and cladding (Figure 4-7[b]). Light rays traveling down the axis of the cable encounter the greatest refraction and their velocity is the lowest in the transmitted signal. Rays traveling off axis encounter a lower refractive index and thus propagate faster. The aim is to have all modes of the signal attain the same net velocity through the fiber in order to reduce modular dispersion.

A step-index single-mode fiber is yet another improvement (see Figure 4-7[c]). The core size, only 7–9 microns in diameter, and core/cladding index allow for only one mode to propagate down the fiber because only one path is available through the cable. Single-mode cable is more difficult to couple, but it does eliminate modal dispersion.

Optical transmission is also subject to spectral or chromatic dispersion. The light passing through the fiber is made up of different frequencies

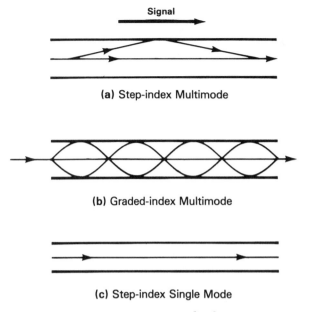

(a) Step-index Multimode

(b) Graded-index Multimode

(c) Step-index Single Mode

FIGURE 4-7. Optical Fiber

and wavelengths. The refractive index differs for each wavelength and allows the waves to travel at different net speeds. LEDs, with a wide wavelength spread, are subject to considerable spectral dispersion. Lasers exhibit a nearly monochromatic light (limited number of wavelengths) and do not suffer any significant chromatic dispersion.

Optical signal wavelengths near 1.33 μm all travel at about the same speed. However, shorter wavelengths result in the "red" part of the light traveling slightly faster than the "blue" part of the light. The opposite effect is found in wavelengths longer than 1.33 μm.

Optical signal loss can also occur. The cable itself can absorb or scatter light due to impurities that are introduced into the cable during manufacturing. An optimum wavelength to avoid chromatic dispersion is 1.33 μm. To avoid optical loss, a wavelength of 1.55 μm is preferable. A completely monochromatic laser (at 1.33 μm) would largely solve the problem, but a technically feasible and economically viable laser will still exhibit some speed in wavelength.

While ANSI and other groups have been fostering standards on optical fiber mode and wavelength, divergence still exists in the industry. Table 4-5 summarizes several contending specifications [MIER86].

Waveguides

Prior to the advent of optical fibers, waveguides were considered to be the upcoming technology for short-haul transmissions. The technology entails

TABLE 4-5. Specifications for Optical Fibers

	ANSI X3T9.5	LOCAL AREA NETWORKS SPONSORING ORGANIZATION AT&T Information Systems	IBM Corp.
Specification	Fiber Distributed Interface (FDDI)	Premises Distribution System (PDS)	Cabling System Type 5 Fiber
Fiber Type	Multimode	Multimode	Multimode
Core/Cladding Diameters (in microns)	50/125 62.5/125 or 85/125	62.5/125	100/140 (said to be moving to 62.5/125)
Light Source	Designed for LED	LED Currently	LED Initially, Laser Eventually
Nominal Distance Without Repeaters	2 Km	2.2 Km	to 2 Km (at up to 40 Mbit/s)
Light Wavelength (in nanometers)	Optimized for 1,300		850 (LED, initially) 1,300 (eventually)
Transmission Data Rate/Bandwidth	100 Mbit/s	Current product operates at 8.64 Mbit/s. Manchester encoded; higher rates likely	Unspecified; to 150 MHz-Km using 850-NM light; to 500 MHz-Km using 1,300-NM light

	Bellcore and ECSA T1 × 1.2/.4	LONG HAUL APPLICATIONS SPONSORING ORGANIZATION AT&T Network Systems	EIA FO6.6
Specification	Synchronous Optical Network (Sonet)	Metrobus	Class 4A Fiber Nondispersion-Shifted
Fiber Type	Single Mode	Single Mode	Single Mode
Core/Cladding Diameters (in microns)	8-9/125 (per EIA)	8/125	8-9/125
Light Source	Designed for Laser	Laser	Primarily for Laser
Nominal Distance Without Repeaters	Around 30 Km	to 52 Km (at 146 Mbit/s) to 42 Km (at 878 Mbit/s)	Unspecified
Light Wavelength (in nanometers)	1,310, Initially	1310; 1550	1100-1700 (1300 Is Optimum)
Transmission Rate	49.92 Mbit/s	1.544 and 4.736 Mbit/s Initially; 146.432, 878.592 Mbit/s	Unspecified

the transmission of radio waves through a tube. The tubes are designed to transmit waves of very high frequency and provide for very high data transfer rates. Until recently the tubes could not be sharply bent and were expensive to build. Waveguide tubes are used in certain limited situations, for example, as a feeder between a microwave antenna and the equipment on the ground. The technology is sound, fast, and reliable, but it cannot match the performance and flexibility of the optical fiber.

SOFTWIRE SYSTEMS

Principal examples of softwire media are microwave and satellite systems. Both use radio signals for transmitting and receiving traffic. (Note: The term *softwire* is relatively new to the industry. Some venders use it to describe any medium that does not use a hardwire.)

While we take radio systems for granted today, it was only a generation ago that the first radio station was completed. This claim was made in 1920 by a radio station in San Jose, California. That station was the world's first example of "Muzak." A Victrola record player was used to play popular music of that day. The records were borrowed from a local San Jose music store. Fortunately, commercial radio became a great success. Unfortunately, Muzak spear-headed "sound pollution" and found its way into office buildings, elevators, hallways, telephone systems, department stores—even doctors' waiting rooms.

Electromagnetic radiation was predicted by James Clark Maxwell as early as 1873, and in 1887, Heinrich Hertz actually produced radio waves. These waves are fields of force. They are similar to light (both are radiations of electromagnetic energy), but radio waves are longer and more coherent in phase. The signals can be modulated to carry information in the form of binary bits.

Electromagnetic radiation is created by inducing a current of sufficient amplitude into an antenna whose dimensions are approximately the same as the wavelength of the generated signal. The signal can be generated uniformly (like a light bulb) or can be directed as a beam of energy (like a spotlight).

Radio signals are radiant waves of energy transmitted into space. The signals are similar to those of heat or light. In a vacuum, they travel at the speed of light (186,000 miles per second or 297,000 kilometers per second). As we discussed in earlier chapters, due to the resistance of media (such as cable, air, and water) waves travel at a rate less than the theoretical maximum. The radio frequency spectrum is divided and classified by frequency bands. Table 4-6 explains the frequencies and their associated identifiers.

Radio signals are sent from transmitting antennas in one of two ways: sky waves and ground waves.

Sky Waves

The reader may recall from earlier school days that the earth is surrounded by several layers of gases, principally oxygen and nitrogen. The sun's ultraviolet radiation ionizes these gases at the higher altitudes, which removes some electrons from the parent atoms. These gases are formed in different layers. The density of the layers (and even their existence) depends on the time of day and night. The term ionization comes from the fact that the atoms have a positive charge and free electrons exist in the atmosphere.

The ionosphere acts as a medium of conductivity for radio waves. Some

TABLE 4-6. Radio Frequency Bands

Classification Band	Initials	Frequency Range
Extremely low	ELF	Below 300 Hz
Infra low	ILF	300 Hz–3 KHz
Very low	VLF	3 KHz–30 KHz
Low	LF	30 KHz–300 KHz
Medium	MF	300 KHz–3 MHz
High	HF	3 MHz–30 MHz
Very high	VHF	30 MHz–300 MHz
Ultra high	UHF	300 MHz–3 GHz
Super high	SHF	3 GHz–30 GHz
Extremely high	EHF	30 GHz–300 GHz
Tremendously high	THF	300 GHZ–3000 GHz

frequencies reflect off the ionosphere with very little loss, and others incur considerable attenuation. For example, low frequency (LF) and very low frequency (VLF) signals reflect off the lower edge of the ionosphere with very little loss. These signals also reflect off the earth and can be used in a multi-hop transmission. The received signal's strength is inversely proportional to the distance travelled.

Medium frequency (MF) waves suffer considerable loss during the day-time, but certain levels of the ionosphere disappear at night. These levels would attenuate the MF signals, but at night the MF frequencies are used for multihop transmissions.

Higher frequencies (VHF and SHF) usually pass straight through the ionosphere layers. The ionosphere does not provide much refraction of these signals.

Some low frequency signals never reflect back to the earth. The actual reflection of the signal depends on two factors, the critical angle and the critical frequency. If the signal is radiated out at an angle greater than the critical angle, it is not bent back to earth but travels out into space. The critical frequency is also a factor. Reflection normally occurs with frequencies from the 2 megahertz to the 30 megahertz range (commonly called short waves).

The density and height of the layers varies depending on the sun's radiation. And as just mentioned, a significant difference exists in the performance of radio systems between night and day transmission.

Ground Waves

As the name suggests, ground waves travel close to the ground between the transmitter and the transceiver. The earth curvature and elements between the transmitter and receiver are critical features in ground waves' connectivity to the transceiver. Ground waves are also affected by surface features such as water and moisture conditions in the waves. Ground waves are found in many systems. One of the most prevalent systems is microwave.

Microwave

Microwave is a directed line-of-sight radio transmission. It is used for radar and wideband communications systems and is quite common in the telephone system. In fact, well over half of the toll and long-distance telephone trunks use microwave transmission. The first commercial microwave system was used across the English Channel. In 1931 in Dover, England, the International Telephone Company implemented this microwave system.

Microwave covers a wide range of the frequency spectrum. Typically, frequencies range from 2 to 40 GHz, although most systems operate in the range of 2 to 18 GHz. The data rate is greater at the higher frequencies. For example, a data rate of 12 Mbit/s can be obtained on a 2 GHz band microwave system, yet a data rate of 274 Mbit/s is possible on an 18 GHz band system [PICK83].

Television transmission also utilizes microwave transmission, because microwave provides the capacity required for video transmission. The high bandwidth gives a small wavelength and the smaller the wavelength, the smaller one can design the microwave antenna. Microwave is very effective for transmission to remote locations. For example, Canada has one of the most extensive systems in the world, and the Soviet Union has placed microwave systems in such remote areas as Siberia. Several U. S. carriers' primary product line is the offering of voice-grade channels on their microwave facilities.

Transmission Characteristics. The microwave transmitting and receiving towers can be spaced many miles apart. The actual distance is determined by:

$$d = 7.14 \sqrt{Kh}$$

Where: d = distance between antennas; h = height of antenna; K = factor to compensate for the slight bending of the signal with the curvature of the earth, usually the value of 4/3 (distances are in meters).

For example, two microwave antennas at a height of 50 meters could be 58 Km (35 miles) apart (7.14 $*$ $\sqrt{66.65}$ = 58). If the antennas were placed at a height of 100 meters, they could be placed 83 Km (50 miles) apart. As we shall see shortly, other factors must also be taken into account such as clearances for the beam path over obstructions, predicted windfall, and the actual frequency spectrum utilized.

Of course, the distance between antennas also depends on the signal attenuation. All transmission systems experience signal loss. Microwave loss (L) is defined as:

$$L = 10 \log (4 \pi d/\lambda)^2 \text{ dB}$$

Where: λ = the wavelength of the signal; d = the distance transmitted. It can be seen that the loss varies as the square of the distance.

The transmitted radio beam is focused narrowly to the receiving antenna. (These towers must be quite sturdy to prevent wind deflection.) They can be seen throughout cities and the countryside, and have become a familiar landmark to the motorist. The antennas are also frequently placed on the rooftops of buildings.

Some microwave antennas are designed for signal polarization, which describes the direction of a signal's magnetic field. The system's capacity can be doubled by using two signals at the same frequency but perpendicular to each other. Typically, this system uses just one antenna for each route direction. Adjacent channels in the microwave band are transmitted with alternate polarizations.

Microwave systems employ protection switching. This technique keeps a spare RF channel on standby. If an ongoing channel fails, the spare RF channel is switched into service. For example, the terminology to describe protective switching is 1 by 10: one spare channel is available for every working channel.

Microwave Systems

Table 4-7 lists the major features of several common microwave systems used in the United States [REY83]. The TM-2A short haul operates in the 6 GHz carrier band; 16 radio frequency (RF) assignments (each 29.65 MHz wide) are used within the band. The system length is about 250 miles.

The TN-1 is an example of an 11 GHz short-haul radio system. Its band is 1000 MHz wide, with each band ranging from 10.7 to 11.7 GHz. TN-1 is configured in one of two plans: (a) up to 12 two-way RF channels with one antenna, using alternate polarizations on adjacent channels; (b) two antennas for each direction, with the voice frequency (VF) load per RF channel reduced from 1800 to 1200 VF channels (but up to 23 two-way RF channels are supported).

Long-haul microwave radio systems have come into common use in the last two decades. They generally operate in the 4- and 6-GHz range. They now constitute a sizeable portion of the total circuit miles in North America.

A simplified depiction of a 4-GHz station is shown in Figure 4-8 [REY83]. The stations are placed between 20 and 30 miles apart, depending on clearances, fading, and interference. A station consists of four antennas, two for receiving and two for sending in each direction. To the right in Figure 4-8 is an intermediate repeater station. The signal is received at the antenna. Next, the RF channels are separated by radio waveguide networks, applied to radio receivers and transmitters and transmitted to the next station.

To the left in Figure 4-8 is a main station. It accepts voice, data, or video signals and modulates them onto frequencies for transmission. The opposite and complementary functions are performed by the receivers.

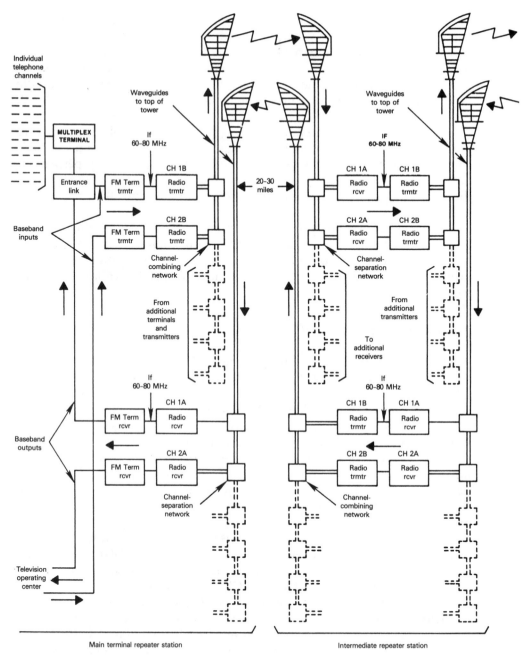

FIGURE 4-8. A Microwave System [REY83]

These systems generally employ frequency modulation (FM), single-side-band amplitude modulation (SSBAM) or some form of phase modulation for digital transmissions. Table 4-8 also depicts the characteristics of 4- and 6-GHz long-haul systems. (The older systems are not shown.)

TABLE 4-7. Microwave Systems

| Characteristics | SHORT HAUL | | | |
| | (5.925–6.426 GHz) | | (10.7–11.7 GHz) | |
	TM-2	TM-2A	TL-A2	TN-1
VF Channels per RF Channel	1200	1800	1200	1800/1200
Radio Channel Assignments	16	16	24	24/46
Total 2-Way RF Channels	8	8	6	12/23
Protection Switching	1 by 7	1 by 7	1 by 5	1 by 11/2 by 21
Working VF Channels	8400	12,600	6000	19,800/25,200
System Length (miles)	250	250	250	250
Transmit Power (watts)	1.0	1.6	1.0	3.0
Repeater Type	Baseband	Baseband + intermediate frequency	Baseband	Heterodyne or baseband
Repeater Spacing (miles)	5 to 35	5 to 35	5 to 35	5 to 35

TABLE 4-8. Microwave Systems

Characteristic	3.7 to 4.2 GHZ	
Service Date	1973	1979
VF Channels per RF Channel	1500	1800
Radio Channel Assignments	24	24
Total 2-Way RF Channels	12	12
Protection Switching	1 by 11	1 by 11
Working VF Channels	16,500	19,800
Transmit Power (watts)	2.0/5.0	5.0

Characteristic	5.925 to 6.425 GHZ	
Service Date	1970	1981
VF Channels per RF Channel	1800	6000
Radio Channel Assignments	16	16
Total 2-Way RF Channels	8	8
Protection Switching	1 by 7	1 by 7
Working VF Channels	12,600	42,000
Baseband Modulation	FM	SSBAM

QAM in Digital Radio. The microwave digital radio systems make extensive use of QAM methods. Just ten years ago, digital radio used low-level schemes such as 2-PSK and 4-PSK. Now, 64 QAM is common and efforts are directed toward the use of 256 QAM and 1024 QAM. Table 4-9 summarizes the systems implemented or planned in Europe and North America [NOGU86].

Satellites

Characteristics of Communications Satellites. As compared to other media, satellite communications are unique for several reasons:

- The technology provides for a large communications capacity. Through the use of the microwave frequency bands, several thousand voice-grade channels can be placed on a satellite station.
- The satellite has the capacity for a broadcast transmission. The transmitting antenna can send signals to a wide geographical area. Applications such as electronic mail and distributed systems find the broadcast capability quite useful.
- Transmission cost is independent of distance between the earth sites. For example, it is immaterial if two sites are 100 or 1000 miles apart as long as they are serviced by the same communications satellite. The signals transmitted from the satellite can be received by all stations, regardless of their distance from each other.
- The stations experience a significant signal propagation delay. Since satellites are positioned 22,300 miles above the earth, the transmission has to travel into space and return. A round-trip transmission

TABLE 4-9. Digital Microwave Systems

Bit Rate Mbit/s	CHANNEL BW		
	20 MHz	30 MHz	40 MHz
EUROPE			
34	4 PSK	4 PSK	4 PSK
68	16 QAM	8 PSK	4 PSK
140	256 QAM	64 QAM	16 QAM
280	—	1024 QAM	256 QAM
NORTH AMERICA			
45	*	*	*
90	64 QAM	16 QAM	8 PSK
135	256 QAM	64 QAM	16 QAM
180	1024 QAM	256 QAM	64 QAM
270	—	1024 QAM	256 QAM

*FCC requires a minimum of 78 Mbit/s for common carriers.
[NOGU86]

requires a minimum of about 240 milliseconds (ms), and could be greater as the signal travels through other components. This may affect certain applications or software systems.

• The broadcast aspect of satellite communications may present security problems, since all stations under the satellite antenna can receive the broadcasts. Consequently, transmissions are often changed (encrypted) for satellite channels.

A Brief History. Although satellite communications concepts have existed for many years, the ideas could only be implemented after the advent of space age technology and solid state electronics. The United States and the Soviet Union lead in the development of the technology. The Soviet Union was first off the launching pad with its Sputnik I on October 4, 1957, and the United States followed shortly with Explorer I on January 1, 1958. Neither of these rockets carried communications satellites. The United States Army is credited with the first communications satellite (SCORE), which was launched December 18, 1958. The world's first commercial satellite, Early Bird, was orbited from Cape Kennedy on April 6, 1965. The WESTAR satellite launched by Western Union in 1974 was the first U. S. domestic satellite. COMSAT was credited with the first satellite communications system for ships at sea with the 1976 Marisat System.

The earlier satellites were still not commercially viable. The limited rocket power could boost the satellite into orbits no greater than 6000 miles above the earth. The low orbit resulted in the satellite moving faster than the earth's rotation and, as the satellite moved across the horizon, the earth station had to rotate its antennas. Eventually, the satellite would disappear and tracking would be passed to another earth station or satellite. The North Atlantic region would have required about 50 satellites for continuous coverage, a very expensive arrangement.

Geosynchronous Systems. Many satellites are in a geosynchronous orbit. They rotate around the earth at 6900 (11,040 Km) miles/hour and remain positioned over the same point above the equator. Thus, the earth stations' antennas can remain in one position since the satellite's motion relative to the earth's position is fixed. Furthermore, a single geosynchronous satellite with nondirectional antennas can cover about 30% of the earth's surface. The geosynchronous orbit requires a rocket launch of 22,300 miles (35,680 Km) into space. Geosynchronous satellites can achieve worldwide coverage (some limited areas in the polar regions are not covered) with three satellites spaced at 120° intervals from each other (see Figure 4-9).

Today, the typical satellite operates in the 6- and 4-GHz bands (the C band) for the up link and down link, respectively. The bandwidth can be divided in a variety of ways. The Western Union satellites have 12 channels, each using a bandwidth of 36 MHz, with a 4 MHz spacing between the channels. These channels are further divided into lower speed circuits such

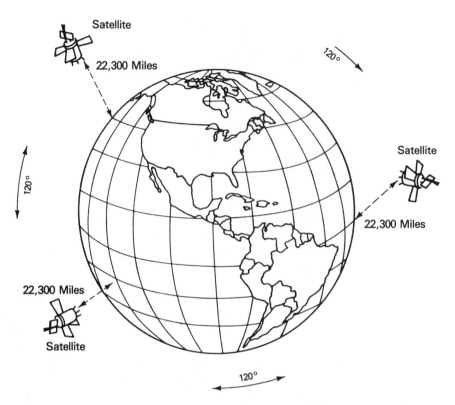

FIGURE 4-9. Geosynchronous Satellites

as voice-grade channels. The voice-grade channels may be further divided to operate subchannels at speeds such as 1200, 2400, 4800, or 9600 bps.

Increasingly, satellites are using frequencies in the 11/12/14 GHz range (Ku band). The 30/20 GHz (K band) range will also be used. The 6/4 GHz bandwidths are also assigned to terrestrial microwave systems, and the use of the higher frequency spectrums will eliminate what are now serious interference and signal congestion problems between microwave and satellite systems.

The 30- and 20-GHz satellites are also very attractive due to the spectrum/orbit problem. While ample space exists 22,300 miles above the earth for all the satellites, the satellites must be spaced apart in order to prevent radio interference from adjacent satellites. The 6/4 GHz requires about 4° (450 miles/720 Km) of separation. The wavelengths of the 30/20 GHz satellites are more narrow and thus the satellites can be placed more closely together, about 1° of arc apart. This is an important consideration because the 6/4 slots over the United States and Puerto Rico are already overcommitted. Satellites are now carrying antennas that operate both in the 6/4 and 16/12 GHz bands, because these signals will not interfere with each other. The 14/12 and 30/20 bands also require smaller antennas because the wavelengths are shorter.

The 14/12 and 30/20 GHz bands are not without problems. The major obstacle to their use is their susceptibility to rain. The water and oxygen molecules in the rain absorb the electromagnetic energy. Attenuation of the higher frequencies with the shorter wavelengths is particularly severe. In contrast, the 6/4 GHz bands are relatively immune to rain. The problem is more severe for earth stations that are located farther away around the globe from the satellite stations since these stations experience a greater "look angle," requiring the signal to travel through more atmosphere. The rain loss problem could be solved by boosting power in the satellites and in the earth stations, but this has not been cost effective.

Satellite communication certainly represents one of the more powerful technologies in data, voice, and video communications today. The advances made in the use of higher frequencies will result in smaller and cheaper earth station antennas. The potential applications for satellite use will increase dramatically as smaller antennas are made available. Individual homeowners are now able to install small antennas (about 3 feet in diameter) for direct television communication with satellites.

The impact on the telephone companies, their local loops, and on distributed processing are enormous. Specialized common carriers are now able to bypass the telephone company facilities completely to service large corporations, small businesses, and even private citizens. With just over 1400 satellites in orbit, the earth is indeed "shrinking" as worldwide communications become commonplace. A notable example is the teleport, now used throughout the world. The teleport consists of earth stations shared by multiple users. For example, the users may be tenants in an office building within an industrial complex. The users of the teleport are linked to the satellite through cable, optical fibers, or microwave. The idea is to share the high-capacity satellite channels in order to reduce users' overall communications costs. The teleport transmits all types of images (voice, data, facsimile, and video) with a wide diversity of data rates. The digital transmission speeds range from low speeds to 1.544 Mbit/s.

Cellular Radio

Cellular radio was conceived as a terrestrial voice telephone network. Its purpose is to upgrade the existing mobile radio-telephone system. The idea goes back to 1972 when the FCC recognized that the demand for mobile telephones was exceeding the frequencies available.

The FCC then opened up frequencies initially in the 800–900 MHz band, and schemes were developed to reuse the same frequencies in the same geographical vicinity. In 1979, a prototype network was built in Chicago by AT&T. In a few short years, cellular radio has grown to reach all metropolitan areas, and systems are being developed for nationwide service.

It seems that having a cellular phone is a mark of prestige. A company in southern California sells a phony clip-on antenna for attachment to an automobile. No radio is sold with the antenna; it is just for show. It is the only example known to the author of a connectionless physical level interface.

A cellular radio network is structured around the concept of "cells" (see Figure 4-10). Each cell is a geographical area with a low-power transmitter. The mobile telephone in the automobile, truck, etc. communicates with the transmitter, which in turn communicates with the Mobile Telephone Switching Office (MTSO). The MTSO is an extension of the telephone central office, and the mobile channel appears to be the same as a wire line to the stored program control logic (SPC) at the telephone office.

As the mobile unit passes through the network, the user is assigned a frequency for use during transit through each cell. Since each cell has its own low-power transmitter, the signals for nonadjacent cells do not interfere with each other. As a consequence, the non-contiguous cells can use the same frequencies.

Cellular Radio and Data Transmission. Cellular radio technology was designed for voice communications. Two major problems must be addressed for data communications.

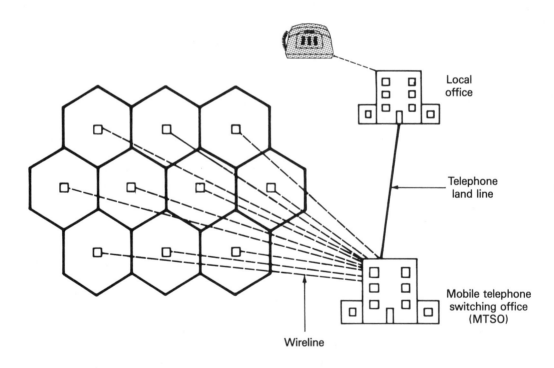

□ Cell site with radio transmitter/receiver

Note: Local office and MTSO may be in same location

FIGURE 4-10. Cellular Radio

- Radio fading causes the loss of several characters of data.
- The handing-off to another cell entails a "blanked-out" period of 300 to 900 ms. This period is insignificant for voice but causes the loss of data.

Several systems now are available to deal with the loss of data in mobile systems. They are designed around the Hayes modem specification. All systems entail some type of error correction scheme and a retransmission occurs if the error correction effort does not repair the corrupted data.

Infrared

The use of infrared frequencies for short-haul transmission is another option that has proved quite successful for some applications. The system is built around optical transceivers that transmit and receive at relatively short distances (approximately one mile maximum).

Infrared has several attractive features. First, the signals are not subject to microwave interference, and the FCC does not require the users to obtain permission to use the frequency spectrum. Second, unlike hardwire systems, infrared requires no cable-pulling, and consequently, the user may not have to obtain rights of way for infrared installation. Third, the systems are relatively inexpensive and easy to install. Fourth, the systems operate at relatively high data rates, typically in the Mbit/s range.

However, the distance is limited to about 1 mile due to a myriad of factors. The signal experiences scattering due to fog, smog, and dust. It can also experience shimmer due to air temperature variations which changes the reflective index of the air. Rain will also cause a distortion of the signal. Notwithstanding, infrared works quite well for special, short-distance applications.

SUGGESTED READINGS

A good description of transmission media can be found in [MART76]. [RILE76] is an instructive tutorial on telephone transmission systems. [CLEMND] discusses the basic concepts of transmission. [NELS75] is an excellent, non-mathematical description of transmission media and carriers. [REY83] is highly recommended as well.

QUESTIONS

TRUE/FALSE

1. An FM commercial broadcast system has a higher bandwidth requirement than does an AM commercial broadcast system.
2. The antenna diameter for VHF and above decreases with frequency.

3. A balanced line is above ground potential.

4. A metallized circuit uses a grounded return.

5. The total resistance of a wire conductor is a function of wire length rather than wire diameter, and specific resistance.

6. Match the term to the appropriate description:

   Description

   a) Line of sight with superhigh frequencies
   b) Uses ionosphere reflection
   c) Line of sight with ultrahigh frequencies
   d) Uses optical transceivers

   Term

   1. Sky waves
   2. Cellular radio
   3. Microwave
   4. Infrared

7. Skin effect describes the tendency of:

   a) dc conductors to carry the circuit current on their surface
   b) ac conductors to carry the circuit current on their surface
   c) both a and b
   d) neither a nor b

8. In the early days of telephony, the circuits consisted of only one wire. How was return provided?

9. Cite the advantages and disadvantages of using hardwire and softwire systems.

10. What are the advantages of optical fibers over metallic media?

11. Compare the LED and laser mode of optical transmission.

12. A wire conductor experiences the following characteristics:

    a) Resistance increases with wire length
    b) Resistance increases with the decrease in wire diameter
    c) a and b
    d) none of the above

13. The ionosphere:

    a) reflects high-frequency radio waves
    b) reflects microwave signals
    c) a and b
    d) none of the above

14. Describe the unique characteristics of satellite communications.

15. What are some typical applications that could be placed on a satellite circuit.

16. When using wire-pair cable, crosstalk can be diminished by:

    a) Using cables for the two directions of transmission.
    b) Selecting pairs in different cables.
    c) Both a and b
    d) Neither a or b

17. Describe some advantages of coaxial cable over wire-pair cable.

18. Describe the functions of (a) optical fiber core, (b) cladding, and (c) the jacket cover.

19. Discuss the differences between single-mode and multi-mode optical fibers.

20. Does the industry favor one type of transmission media over another? What will be the preferred media in the 1990s?

SELECTED ANSWERS

1. True

2. False

3. True

4. False, the current is carried entirely on the wires.

5. False. $R = P * L/A$. Where: R = total resistance; P = specific resistance; L = wire length; A = wire diameter.

6.

Description	Term
a	3
b	1
c	2
d	4

7. b)

8. A ground return was used.

11. No predominant media exists in the industry at the present time. There is extensive installation of twisted pair, coaxial cable, shortwave radio, microwave, satellite transmission, optical fibers. In the 1990s, the preferred media will increasingly be the use of optical fibers (and perhaps super conductors). Twisted pair is not "going away" in the near future. Telephone companies and building owners have too big an investment in this media to move away from it any time soon. Moreover, long distance transmissions with microwave and the use of satellites will be a cost-effective transmission scheme for many years to come. It can be stated that optical fiber will supplant much of the metallic cable.

CHAPTER 5

The Telephone System

INTRODUCTION

The telephone facilities that many of us take for granted are truly an amazing engineering feat. Practically every residence and office has a telephone with communications capabilities to other telephones located almost everywhere in the world.

Many people are familiar with the famous sentence, "Mr. Watson, come here, I want you." It was the first known spoken communication between humans on a telephone, and was spoken by Alexander Graham Bell in his Boston laboratory on March 10, 1876. The invention making the transmission of that momentous sentence possible has forever altered the way humans communicate. In slightly over one hundred years, the societal relationships among humans have undergone extraordinary changes—many of them due to the telephone. Try to imagine the impact of this machine; or better yet, try to imagine our lives without it.

The telephone is a fairly recent invention and the first transcontinental telephone line in the United States was only completed January 25, 1915. The system ran between San Francisco, New York, and Washington. It consisted of four copper wires which were strung on 130,000 poles! The system provided a capacity for three telephone and four telegraph circuits.

This chapter explores the major characteristics of the telephone and the interrelationships of data communications systems and telephone systems. The literature on the subject is vast, and suggested readings are provided at the end of the chapter. More detail is provided on Common Channel Interoffice Signalling (CCIS) and particular emphasis is placed on Signalling System No. 7 (SS7), since the pedagogical literature on these important systems is rather sparse. Moreover, with the inevitable integration of voice and data networks, the reader should become familiar with voice signalling. The chapter is organized around the following sections:

- General characteristics of telephones and telephone systems
- Local loops and the long haul network
- Telephone switching systems
- Signalling systems (with CCIS and SS7 emphasized)
- Traffic engineering

GENERAL CHARACTERISTICS OF TELEPHONES AND TELEPHONE SYSTEMS

The telephone is an elegantly simple instrument. When you look at the telephone mouthpiece, all you see is a plastic cover with holes in it, but behind the cover are two components that convert your audio signals to electrical signals: a diaphragm and a carbon chamber. (Newer telephone sets use more advanced approaches, but this example explains the most widely used technique.) These two devices are transducers: they convert one form of energy to another form. Figures 5-1 and 5-2 illustrate the conversion process [BELLND].

The telephone transmits voice signals through a rheostat concept (a rheostat is an electrical device that controls a current by varying the resistance in the circuit). The diaphragm in the telephone is a circular piece of very thin aluminum and is sensitive to physical sound waves (Figure 5-1). The outer edge of the diaphragm is fixed to the mouthpiece, but the rest of the surface is free to vibrate in response to sound waves.

The chamber inside the diaphragm is filled with carbon granules. The underside of the diaphragm has an attached dome which vibrates inside the carbon chamber. When a voice signal (air pressure wave) moves toward the diaphragm, it forces the diaphragm inward (Figure 5-2[a]). This movement forces the dome into the chamber, which compresses the carbon granules more closely together within the diaphragm's chamber. Consequently, the resistance is lowered (i.e., the conductivity is increased), and more current flows through the transmitter.

When a person stops talking, the sound wave pressure on the diaphragm is released (Figure 5-2[b]). The diaphragm moves to its original position, which creates less pressure on the carbon granules and thus increases the resistance of the transmitter. The diaphragm continues to move in and out in response to the strength of the utterances of the voice signal.

The receiver in the telephone handset also has a diaphragm that moves in coordination with the transmitting diaphragm. However, the receiver diaphragm is attached to a circular frame of permanently magnetized iron.

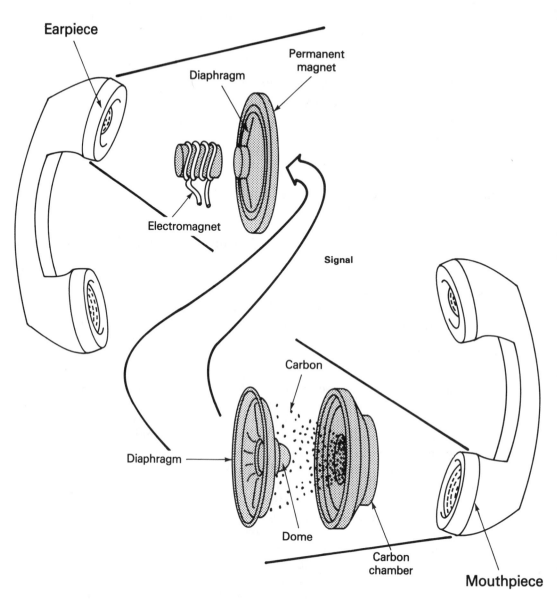

FIGURE 5-1. The Telephone Handset [BELLND]

Behind the diaphragm is an electromagnet (a cylinder of soft metal with wire wrapped around it). The magnet provides a push/pull force on the diaphragm which moves in and out at the same rate as the force of the magnetic field. This movement pushes and pulls the air and vibrates it at the same rate. The air vibration becomes a reproduction of the voice signal.

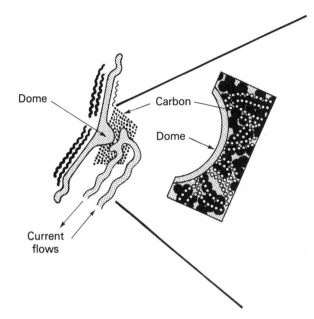

(a) Waveforms Vibrate Diaphragm and Compress Carbon Modules

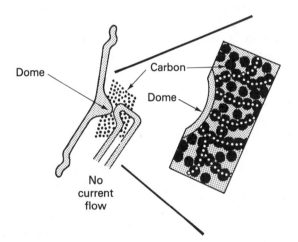

(b) Absence of Waveforms Release Pressure on Carbon Modules

FIGURE 5-2. The Telephone as a Transducer [BELLND]

Early Telephone Systems

During the early days of telephony (in the 1880s), all customers had private lines. Later, calls were placed between subscribers with the assistance of a human operator. The operator would perform the connection operations after receiving instructions from the subscriber. In effect, the operator was a human switch. In those days the operators were dubbed "hello girls," because they replaced male operators who greeted callers with "Ahoy." The reason for this greeting is lost in history.

The operator, after requesting and receiving the number from the caller, plugged the proper cords and jacks into the switchboard to provide the direct connection. If the call was destined for a location outside the plugboard, it would be routed to another switchboard operator. In this manner, the call would be switched through the system to the final destination.

The manual switchboard was replaced by the automatic exchange, a step-by-step switch called the Strowger switch. Almon P. Strowger (a Kansas City undertaker) suspected that calls meant for him were being diverted to a competitor by the human operator. Necessity is the mother of invention, so Strowger set to work to eliminate the human element in the telephone call. In 1892, his first automatic exchange opened in LaPorte, Indiana.

The Strowger switch operated on each dialed number by adjusting an electromechanical device to connect an incoming line to an outgoing line. The dialed number positioned a contact to an interface (of 100 contacts) to outgoing circuits. Each number moved the switch in a step-by-step fashion until the desired outgoing line was found. If the line was free, the caller was connected; if not, a busy signal was returned to the caller.

The Strowger switch was quite slow and subject to considerable electrical noise. The next major improvement was the crossbar switch (which is still found in some systems today). This switch also connects input line to output lines but uses electromagnets to open or close vertical and horizontal bars to establish the physical connection.

Telephone "Dialing."   The early systems did not use the rotary dial or push buttons that we use today. Instead, the telephone consisted of several buttons; one button was labeled hundreds, one was labeled tens, and so forth. These buttons were directly connected with many wires to the telephone office. The telephone subscriber was left to pick out the proper number and press the correct buttons. This system was undesirable because it required more than a pair of wires for each telephone, and the subscriber often pushed the wrong button when making a call.

The telephone rotary dial (which is still used in many parts of the world) was first installed in 1896 in Albion, New York, and Milwaukee, Wisconsin. This dial sets up a series of pulses in the current of the telephone circuit to the telephone office.

The telephone dial in reality moves an additional position when the dial is rotated. For example, when the number 1 is dialed, the rotary actually moves two positions. The additional position is never used within the dial number itself. The purpose of this step is to give the central office a little extra time. The central office, by sensing this delay, would know that one digit was completed and the next digit was about to be sent.

Interestingly, we have gone full circle from the push buttons to the rotary back to the push button, but today's push buttons are a considerable improvement over the old system.

The system today employs the concept of multi-frequency keying. Each button depressed produces two frequencies. Both frequencies operate within the voice bandwidth. The frequencies range from 697 hertz to 1477 hertz.

The tones generated must be detected at the central office and delineated from the user voice or background sounds in the speaker's room. The receiving office provides this function by series of timing circuits and parity checking. It is possible to subtract out the frequencies in the transmission, other than the proper multi-frequency tones, if they are involved in the total content of the transmitted signal.

The telephones in our homes and offices carry the voice or data images to and from the telephone network in the format of analog signals. Increasingly, digital techniques are being used both within the telephone network and at the local interfaces. Since the telephone system plays a key role in data communications, we examine its major features.

LOCAL LOOPS AND THE LONG HAUL NETWORK

Figure 5-3 illustrates the existing telephone network (which will eventually be replaced with a less rigid structure). The components are arranged in a hierarchy starting with the customer location at the bottom of the hierarchy. The customers, either in homes or offices, connect through the telephone system into the class 5 office, which is also called the central office (CO), local exchange, or end office. Thousands of these offices may be installed around a country. Connection is provided to the CO through a pair of wires (or four wires) called the local loop or subscriber loop.

Connections between COs are also provided by a facility called a tandem center (also called a tandem switch or toll center). The tandem center interconnects COs that do not have direct connections with each other. Four classes of tandem centers exist in the United States and Canada: toll centers, primary centers, sectional centers, and regional centers. The regional center (10 in the United States) has the largest area to serve, with each lesser class serving a smaller area.

The system is designed for each switching center to be connected to an office of a higher level, except at the highest level. The top-level offices are the shortest path and/or the fewest number of switches. This design approach reduces the delay of establishing the connection with the other telephone set, and the fewer number of intermediate switches reduces the expense to the telephone company. As the tandem path becomes longer, it must go through more components, incurring more delay and additional expense.

The system is built around high-usage trunks (or high-volume trunks),

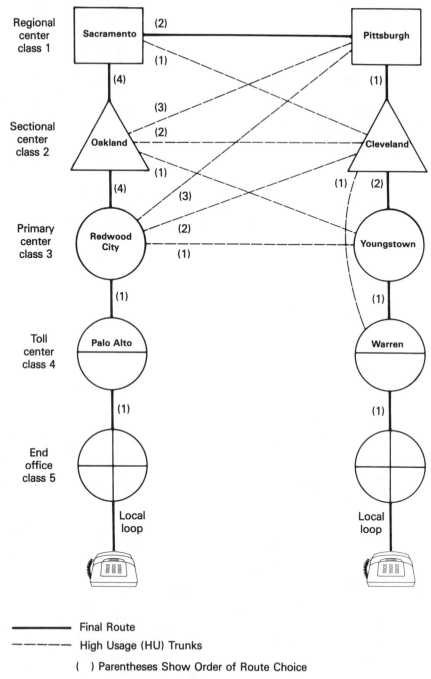

which carry the bulk of the traffic. High-usage trunks are established when the volume of calls warrants the installation of high-capacity channels between two offices. Consequently, trunk configurations vary depending on traffic volume between centers. The system attempts to switch the call down into the hierarchy, across the hierarchy, or, as a last resort, up into the hierarchy. Routing the call up usually entails more intermediate switching, thereby increasing the connection delay and the telephone company's cost to obtain the connection.

Figure 5-3 provides an example of the routing. Assume a connection is desired from a terminal in Palo Alto, California, to a computer in Warren, Ohio. The connection would be made from the Palo Alto central office to its tandem office (the center in Redwood City). If high-usage trunks did not exist, the path would follow the final trunk route. However, a high-usage trunk connects Redwood City to Warren's toll center in Youngstown. If a trunk (channel) is free, the route follows this path. If all trunks were busy on the Redwood City-Youngstown group, the next choice would be to the sectional center serving Warren, which is Cleveland, Ohio. If all possible routes are occupied, the call is blocked, resulting in a busy signal.

Nonhierarchical Routing

Many telephone companies have begun the implementation of a new routing concept, nonhierarchical routing (NHR). This new technology is not constrained by a fixed hierarchical structure, but allows a choice of path based on heavy overflow traffic from the fixed topology. Major portions of NHR will have replaced much of the hierarchical network by the early 1990s. NHR will mean fewer busy signals and faster connections to the end user. It has been demonstrated that nonhierarchical routing can provide up to a 15% cost reduction over the traditional routing schemes of the telephone system.

The telephone companies are using a variety of approaches in their nonhierarchical schemes. In the United States, AT&T uses a decentralized approach; each node involved in the route stores a predetermined series of alternate paths. The sequence of these paths and their number will vary depending on the time of day and the day of the week. Bell Canada uses a centralized dynamic technique. The routes through the Bell Canada network change as the traffic conditions change. This set-up is similar to the adaptive scheme discussed in Chapter 13 with packet switching. Bell Canada maintains a central routing processor that receives switching information. The information contains the load on the units and descriptions of idle trunks that are available. The processor then selects the routes and sends this information back to the distributed switches. Many of the European systems do source routing. With this technique, the originating office chooses the routes.

Switched and Nonswitched Options

A telephone customer may choose to acquire a leased or private line, through which the customer has a permanent connection in the telephone network from one site to another. (Private lines can also be switched through private switches.)

A private, nonswitched line is often very useful when users cannot afford the delay of a connection or the actual blockage of a call when all circuits are busy. Moreover, users that have traffic with several hours of connection time per day can save money by using a leased line. The major tradeoffs between switched, dial-up and nonswitched, leased circuits are:

Switched Advantages
Flexible
Inexpensive for low volume

Disadvantages
Slow response
Blocking possible (busy signals)
Low quality
Expensive for high volume

Nonswitched Advantages
Supports higher volume
Higher quality possible
No blockage (busy signals)

Disadvantages
Expensive for low volume
Lack of flexibility when line is inoperable

Local Loops and Facilities

The telephones in our homes and offices are connected through the local loops to a local facilities network. This network consists of switching gear located at office centers. The actual building is called a wire center. It services a wire center area. The customers in a wire center area can communicate with each other through the wire center by direct links or tandem links.

A more detailed depiction of a local facilities network is given in Figure 5-4 [REY83]. This picture shows a wire center is generally divided into geographical areas (a typical division is four). These areas are referred to as feeder route areas. In turn, the feeder route areas are further divided into allocation areas. The allocation areas are divided into distribution areas (generally one to five distribution areas are used).

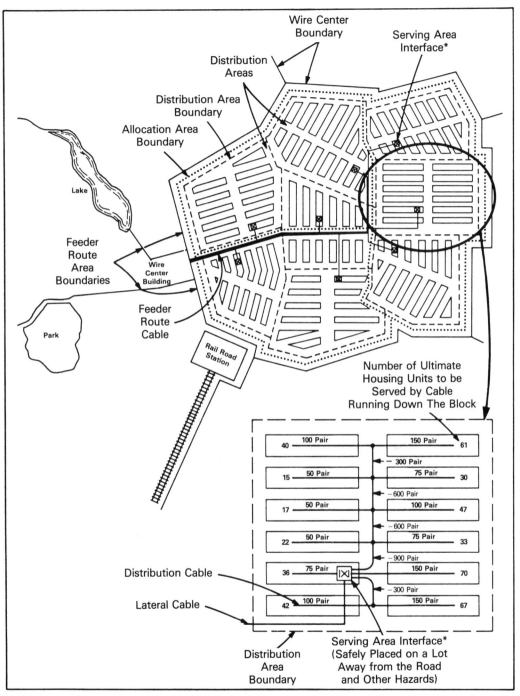

*A rearrangeable cross-connect point between feeder and distribution cables in the loop plant.

FIGURE 5-4. Local Facilities in a Telephone System [REY83]

Figure 5-4 depicts the local facilities network as a tree-like structure. The wire center uses feeder routes consisting of large paired cables which are placed at various points along the route. Distribution cables are then joined to the cables for further branches, and at the end of the tree the customers' equipment is connected to the distribution cable. The wire cable emanating from the wire center is generally very large wire pair systems. Of course, at each cable splice, the feeder cables become smaller as the tree branches out to the customer premises equipment. The connections to the smaller cables are done through hybrid taps. This is an extension of the distribution cable beyond the customer. Bridged taps are not used for most trunk cables, which are directly joined.

The majority of local loops use two wires to save copper wire and to be compatible with the two-wire interface systems. Due to numerous problems with two-wire facilities, longer distance voice frequency (VF) circuits employ four wires. A separate transmission path is used for each direction.

The interfaces between the wires is provided by a device called a hybrid. It is used to interface between the two-wire and four-wire circuits. The hybrid acts as a transformer. It is quite useful in providing efficient coupling between circuits having different electrical characteristics.

TELEPHONE SWITCHING SYSTEMS

The telephone switching systems today are classified as either electro-mechanical or stored program control (SPC). Electromechanical systems are controlled by wired circuits. The electromechanical switches are motor driven, electromechanically operated, or driven by electrical impulses. In wired logic systems, routing logic is designed into the hardware. To change the operations of one of these devices, it is often necessary to rewire circuits or redesign them.

Stored program control (SPC) systems use software for the switching logic. The program controls the sequencing of operations to establish the telephone call. Changes are considerably easier, because they can be done by changing software. SPC systems are rapidly replacing electromechanical switches.

The following switching systems have been the most widely used. Readers wishing to examine each switch in more detail may refer to [REY83].

Electromechanical

Switchboard
Step-by-step
No. 1 and No. 1A crossbar
Crossbar tandem

4A crossbar
No. 5 crossbar

Stored Program Control (SPC)

No. 1ESS and 1AESS
No. 2ESS and 2AESS
No. 3ESS
No. 4ESS
No. 5ESS
DMS-10
DMS-100/200

TELEPHONE SIGNALLING SYSTEMS

Telephone signalling is defined as the transfer of information between two parts of a telephone network for the control of connection establishment, management, and disconnection. This section describes the following types of signalling:

Customer line signalling
Interoffice trunk signalling
Special services signalling

Customer Line Signalling

As discussed earlier, the customer facility is connected to the central office through two or four wires. The signalling between the customer device and the central office is performed by a current sensing system at the central office to detect the customer's off-hook and on-hook status.

The customer loops may consist of (a) a pair of wires between its equipment and the central office or (b) a pair of wires connected to a nearby carrier system. In the latter case, the customer station equipment is connected to a remote terminal carrier rather than the central office. Whatever the system may be, the customer equipment and the telephone equipment have a standard format of signalling called metallic loop signalling. This means that a continuous dc voltage is applied toward the station at the same time a current sensing device is used to recognize the supervisory status. Normal operations at the telephone system use a dc voltage of 48 volts (generally called battery voltage or battery).

The purpose of the metallic loop signalling is to detect off-hook, on-hook conditions. No current flow (or an idle) is sensed as an on-hook condition. An off-hook condition (or seizure) is provided with the flow of current.

We have discussed in previous sections of this chapter how the on-hook and off-hook signals are used to provide a call connection, so we will not repeat the procedure in this section.

The terms ring and tip were named from the parts of the telephone plug (in the "old days"). The tip was the end of the plug; the ring was one of the inner parts. In the modern telephone system, the negative battery minus 48 volts is provided with the ring and the tip is set to ground. The off-hook, on-hook sensing signalling is provided through what is called the switch hook operations.

Obviously the customer must send a dial number (address) of the called party to the end office. The old systems used a rotary dial to provide the addresses. With these systems, the pulses were conveyed with short on-hook signals occurring as interruptions in the off-hook signals. The signals were transmitted at the rate of 10 pulses per second. In most telephone systems today, the address is provided through the touch tone buttons on the telephone instrument. Each touch tone button produces a pair of tones; for example, if the number 8 button is pressed, the 1336 Hz and 852 Hz frequencies are generated. The central office receivers then recognize this number as an 8. After all the numbers have been assembled in the class 5 office, they can then be utilized for interoffice trunk signalling.

Interoffice Trunk Signalling

Historically, the telephone system has used interoffice trunk signalling in a manner required the call set-up between the stations to follow the same path as the actual connected call. This approach was deemed reasonable to avoid separate transmission channels for signalling control and the call. This technique is still used and is called per-trunk signalling.

The per-trunk system is clearly inefficient for several reasons. First, the call is initiated without a priori knowledge of a probable successful connection. During periods of heavy traffic, calls originating from the external users seize resources inside the network. Even though a telephone user has not received a connection, the user is reserving resources on a piecemeal basis from the network. Theoretically, a network would eventually support less traffic than it does under lighter loads. In essence, partially completed calls satisfy no one, but still consume network resources.

COMMON CHANNEL INTEROFFICE SIGNALLING (CCIS)

A better technique which has seen pervasive use in the last few years is common channel interoffice signalling (CCIS). It has grown to become the largest private data network in the world [DONO86].

Several years ago, telephone companies recognized the inefficiency of integrating control signals on the same channel with voice traffic. Consequently, they devised the common channel interoffice signalling (CCIS) system, which transmits the signalling information for a group of trunks over a separate channel from the user communications channel, a technique also known as clear channel signalling.

CCIS is based on the CCITT Signalling System No. 6 (SS6), [Q.251] through [Q.300]. In the CCIS discussions, the Q-Series are referenced where appropriate. AT&T/Bell designed the present CCIS protocol to be consistent with CCITT signalling system No. 6 (with this exception: the CCIS version uses a 4.8 Kbit/s rate, in contrast to the international system of 2.4 Kbit/s). Newer systems utilize the digital-oriented Signalling System No. 7 (discussed next).

CCIS also interfaces with a telephone caller for long-distance calls. For example, at most coin-operated telephones, the dial of a 0 plus the destination number is accepted by CCIS, which routes the call to a data base. CCIS provides a prompt to the telephone user, such as asking (through digitized voice) the telephone user to dial a credit-card number. The number is also sent via CCIS to the data base for further validation. CCIS then initiates the call and stores accounting information for later billing of the call to the respective telephone user. This process is completely automated—no operator is involved and the voice has been stored digitally to simulate a human operator.

CCIS offers several notable advantages over the inband techniques [AT&T80]:

1. Since CCIS passes signals faster than conventional systems, call set-up and take-down are performed faster.
2. This speed reduces a customer's post-dialing delay.
3. The holding time for equipment and trunks is reduced.
4. CCIS has more capacity than the inband system.
5. CCIS uses full duplex signalling, and it allows control signals to be passed during a conversation.
6. Inband tone signals (dialing signals) are eliminated from trunk signalling, and obtaining free calls by mimicking dial tones is a thing of the past. (This may not be cited as an advantage by some people; where one stands on a subject depends on where one sits—in a telephone office or in a telephone booth.)
7. CCIS is designed for flexibility; the control messages and software can be changed to include new services.

CCIS is organized around packet switching network concepts. CCIS was the first major packet-switching system implemented by AT&T/Bell. The packets are used for call set-up and take-down. Sets of information are called signal units (SU), which consist of 28 bits (8 bits are used for error detection). CCIS places 12 signal units in a packet for transmission. Eleven SUs contain signalling information, and the twelfth SU is an acknowledge

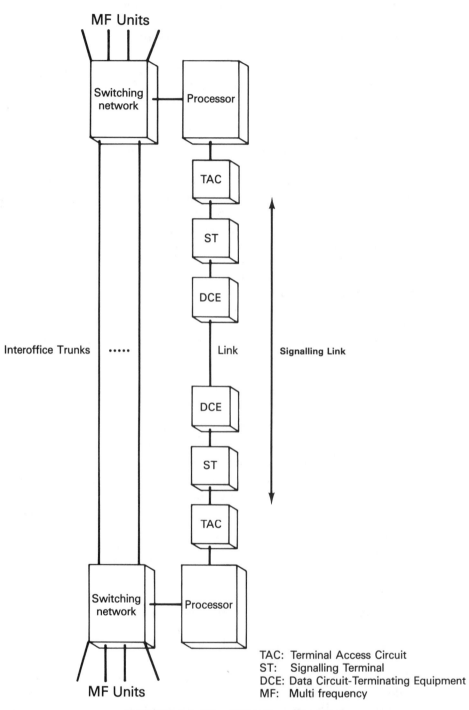

FIGURE 5-5. The CCIS Signalling Link

SU (ASU). The signal units within the packet have the same destination.

Figure 5-5 shows a block diagram of the CCIS signalling link. The functions of the components are:

- DCEs: Modems or digital service units that perform signal-to-signal conversion.
- Signalling terminals (STs): Store incoming and outgoing messages; perform error detection and retransmission; monitor data carriers for link outage; transmit on the alternate link in event of problems.
- Link: A four-wire link; a dedicated conditioned line.
- Terminal access circuit (TAC): Provides the processor access to the signalling links; chooses link based on processor instructions.
- Processor: Acts as CCIS link controller; generates and receives CCIS messages (SUs); chooses link; switches reserve links on line, if necessary.

CCIS Messages

As discussed earlier, the CCIS signal unit is 28 bits in length. It conforms to the SS6 format [Q.257]. The last 8 bits are used for error detection by a data link protocol based on the polynomial $X^8 + X^2 + X + 1$. The remaining 20 bits contain the signalling information, which is summarized in Box 5-1. It is recommended that the reader study the contents of Box 5-1, because they illustrate the CCIS services. An example of the CCIS message is provided in Figure 5-6.

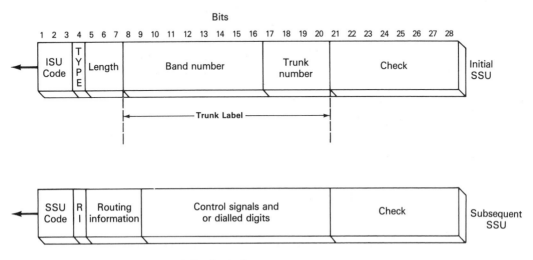

FIGURE 5-6. A CCIS Multi-unit Message (MUM)

Bits 1–7 contain the heading. It identifies the type of SU, an indication if multiple SUs are associated together (MUM for multiple message units), and a length indicator. This indicator provides a count of how many subsequent SUs are to be expected. The trunk label identifies a band number and a trunk number. The number identifies the specific trunk in a group, and the band number is used to determine the routing in the network. The routing information field is used to transmit unique information associated with the call. The other fields contain signalling information, such as the dialed dig-

---

BOX 5-1. Examples of CCIS Signals

ADN   **Address-Complete Signal, No Charge:** A signal sent in the backward direction indicating that all the address signals required for routing the call to the called party have been received, and that the call should not be charged on answer.

ADI   **Address-Incomplete Signal**: A signal sent in the backward direction indicating that the number of address signals received is not sufficient for setting up the call.

ANC   **Answer Signal, Charge**: A signal sent in the backward direction indicating that the call is answered and subject to charge.

BLO   **Blocking Signal**: A signal sent for maintenance purposes to the office at the other end of a trunk to cause that trunk to appear busy to subsequent calls outgoing from that office.

CFL   **Call-Failure Signal**: A signal sent in the backward direction indicating the failure of a call set-up attempt.

CB   **Clear-Back (Hang-Up) Signals**: Signals sent in the backward direction, the first of which indicates that the called party has hung up.

CLF   **Clear-Forward (Disconnect) Signal**: A signal sent in the forward direction to terminate the call or call attempt and release the trunk concerned. It is normally sent at the end of a call when the calling party hangs up.

COT   **Continuity Signal**: A signal sent in the forward direction to indicate continuity of the preceding CCIS trunk(s) and a successful check of the selected trunk to the following office.

SSB   **Customer-Busy Signal**: A signal sent in the backward direction indicating that the line connecting the called party with the office is busy.

FDT   **Forward-Transfer (Ring-Forward) Signal**: On operator-to-operator calls, sent in the forward direction when the outgoing office operator wants to recall the distant operator.

MVT   **Manual-Voice-Frequency-Link-Transfer Signal**: A signal sent in either direction as an indication that the active link should be interchanged with the inactive link.

TSV   **Test-Voice-Frequency-Link Signal**: A signal sent in either direction indicating that the sending end is prepared to test the standby link and requesting the other end to prepare for the test.

its, call failure, clear call, and other signals, some of which are shown in Box 5-1.

An initial address message (IAM) contains all fields just described as well as the dialed digits of the called party.

Signal Sequence for a Telephone Call

Figure 5-7 illustrates the message signals associated with a 10-digit call. This depiction shows a routine call with no problems encountered. The figure is self-explanatory, except for one new term: the continuity check. This check ensures the selected trunk is operating within acceptable limits. The originating processor places a signal on the selected trunk concurrent with sending the initial address message (IAM) on the CCIS link. Upon receiving the IAM, the terminating office returns a signal. The originating office checks this returning signal to verify that it is within acceptable limits. If not, another trunk is selected and the trunk is unblocked (made available), if it passes the continuity check.

The continuity check is considered to have failed if the receiver has not responded by a set time (by two seconds, at least). The time-out period of the check always exceeds the continuity recognition time (T_{CR}) as defined by [Q.271]:

$$T_{CR} = 2T_P + T_{IAM} + T_{TC} + T_L + T_R + T_T$$

Where: T_P = one-way propagation time of the speech circuit; T_{IAM} = emission time of the longest initial address message (IAM); T_{TC} = TASI clip time (if not used, $TTC = 0$); T_L = maximum loop connecting time; T_R = receiver response time; T_T = maximum transceiver connecting time.

If retransmission of the IAM is included in the T_{CR}, the following formula is used:

$$T_{CR} = 4T_P + 2T_{IAM} + T_{ACU} + T_X + T_Y + T_L + T_R - T_T$$

Where: T_{ACU} = emission time of an ACU; T_X = time between receiving an IAM and sending an ACU; T_Y = time between receiving an ACU and sending an IAM.

SIGNALLING SYSTEM NO. 7 (SS7)

We now turn our attention to SS7, a clear channel signalling system specification published by the CCITT and now being implemented throughout the world. SS7 will become the most widely used signalling system because (a) it is designed to operate with the integrated services digital network (ISDN), and (b) it is a widely accepted specification unto itself.

CCIS and SS6 have performed well enough, but the data line speeds of 2.4 and 4.8 Kbit/s and the limited size of the service unit (SU) limit their

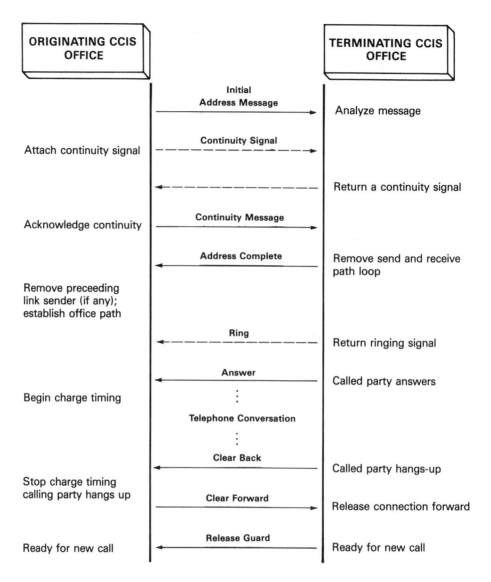

ORIGINATING CCIS OFFICE		TERMINATING CCIS OFFICE
	Initial Address Message →	Analyze message
Attach continuity signal	- - **Continuity Signal** - →	
	← - - - - - - - - - - - - -	Return a continuity signal
Acknowledge continuity	**Continuity Message** →	
	← **Address Complete**	Remove send and receive path loop
Remove preceeding link sender (if any); establish office path		
	← - - **Ring** - - -	Return ringing signal
	← **Answer**	Called party answers
Begin charge timing	⋮	
	Telephone Conversation	
	⋮	
	← **Clear Back**	Called party hangs-up
Stop charge timing calling party hangs up	**Clear Forward** →	Release connection forward
Ready for new call	← **Release Guard**	Ready for new call

Note: Inband signals are depicted with dotted line.

FIGURE 5-7. Signal Sequence for a Telephone 10-Digit Call

capabilities. Also, the band-based routing is awkward to manage. Many telephone companies and administrations have now moved to SS7. AT&T and Telecom Canada are implementing a Message Transfer Part (MTP), an Integrated Service Digital Network User Part (ISDN UP), and a Signalling Connection Control Part (SCCP) [AT&T84]. The system is called CCITT Signalling System No. 7 or CCS7.

CCS7 uses digital 56 Kbit/s trunks. The topology of the network remains about the same as CCIS but the signalling transfer points (STPs) are configured around only seven regions. The STPs handle both CCIS and CCS7 protocols.

Signalling System No. 7 consists of the following major parts. Our focus in this section is the signalling specifications relating directly to telephone systems.

Message Transfer Part (MTP) (Q.701–Q.709)
PABX application (Q.710)
Signalling Connection Control Part (SCCP) (Q.711–Q.714)
Integrated Services Digital Network User Part (ISDN UP)(Q.761–Q.766)
MTP Monitoring and Measuring (Q.791)
Operations and Maintenance Application Part (OMAP)(Q.795)

SS7 can also be applied to call control for a telephone service (Q.7 and Q.110), and to circuit switched data transmission systems (X.60). Its use in international systems is specified in X.87.

SS7 defines the procedures for the set-up and clearing of a call between telephone users. It performs these functions by exchanging telephone control messages and signals between the SS7 telephone exchange and SS7 signalling transfer points (STPs). At the broadest level, the SS7 telephone signalling messages are made up of (a) telephone signalling message types and within the types, (b) the identification of specific components relevant to the telephone call. Q.722 describes these components and they are summarized in Box 5-2.

Summary of Principal SS7 Recommendations

This section describes the functions of the principal recommendations. The reader can also refer to [SCHL86] for a summary of SS7.

Message Transfer Part (MTP)

SS7 divides the functions described in the Q recommendations into (a) the Message Transfer Part (MTP) and (b) User Parts. The idea is shown in Figure 5-8. The MTP serves as a transport system for the users. It transfers signalling messages between the user locations. It is responsible for (a) providing the physical link(s), (b) providing data link control functions, and (c) routing messages between user locations. The primary functions of MTP are described in the following material.

SS7 Level 1 (Q.702). The SS7 signalling data link is a full duplex, digital transmission channel operating at 64 Kbit/s. Optionally, an analog link can be used with either 4 or 3 KHz spacing. The SS7 link operates on both terrestrial and satellite links. The actual digital signals on the link are

BOX 5-2. General Functions of SS7 Messages and Signals

Message Components

- Identifiers of: circuit signalling points, called and calling parties, incoming trunks, and transit exchanges
- Control codes to set up and clear down a call
- Called party's number
- Indicator that called party's line is out of service
- Indication of national, international, or other subscriber
- Indication that called party has cleared
- Nature of circuit (satellite/terrestrial)
- Indication that called party cleared, then went off-hook again
- Use of echo suppression
- Notification to reset a faulty circuit
- Language of assistance operators
- Status identifiers (calling line identity incomplete; all addresses complete; use of coin station; network congestion; no digital path available; number not in use; blocking signals for certain conditions)
- Circuit continuity check
- Call forwarding (and previous routes of the call)
- Provision for an all-digital path
- Security access calls (called closed user group [CUG])
- Malicious call identification
- Request to hold the connection
- Charging information
- Indication that a called party's line is free
- Call set-up failure
- Subscriber busy signal

derived from pulse code modulation multiplexing equipment (see Chapter 3) or from equipment that employs a frame structure (see Chapter 11).

The link must be dedicated to SS7. In accordance with the idea of clear channel signalling, no other transmission can be transferred with the signalling messages. Extraneous equipment must be disabled or removed from an SS7 link. For example, the A and μ law conversions discussed in Chapter 3 must be removed. Also, equipment such as echo suppressors must be disabled.

SS7 permits data transfer rates greater or less than the 64 Kbit/s rate. The minimum data rate is 4.8 Kbit/s. The standard 2.048 Mbit/s, and 8.448

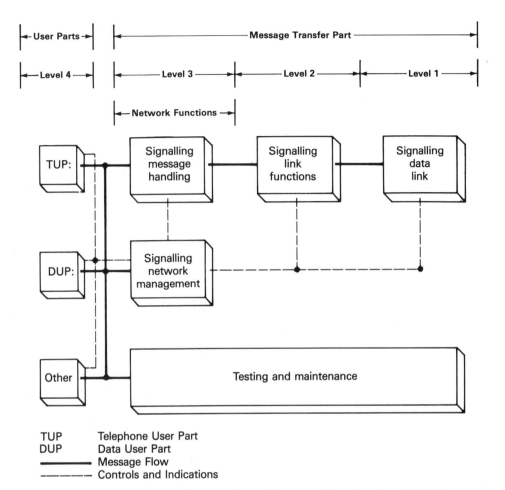

FIGURE 5-8. A General View of SS7 (Message Transfer Part [MTP])

Mbit/s (in North America 1.544 Mbit/s) rates are all permitted if used within the appropriate CCITT recommendations. AT&T and Telecom Canada use 56 Kbit/s.

The use of analog signals is supported through several of the V Series recommendations. While SS7 provides leeway in the bit transfer rates for an analog connection, it stipulates the use of V.27 or V.27 bis for a 4.8 Kbit/s link.

SS7 Level 2 (Q.703). Q.703 describes the procedures for transferring SS7 signalling messages across one link. It performs the operations that are typical of level 2 protocols. Since these operations are explained in considerable detail in Chapters 10, 11, and 20, they are not repeated here.

Q.703 has many similarities to the HDLC protocol (high level data link control). For example, both protocols use flags, error checks, and sending/receiving sequence members. The messages are transferred in variable length signal units (SUs), and the primary task of this level is to ensure their error-free delivery. The SUs are of three types (see Figure 5-9):

Message signal unit (MSU)
Link status signal unit (LSSU)
Fill-in signal unit (FISU)

The MSU carries the actual signalling message forward to the user parts (UP). Q.703 transfers the MSU across the link and determines if the message is uncorrupted. If the message is damaged during the transfer it is retransmitted. The LSSU and FISU do not transport user part (UP) signals;

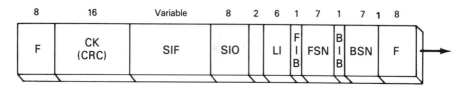

(a) Message Signal Unit (MSU)

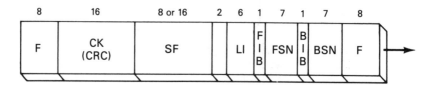

(b) Link Status Signal Unit (LSSU)

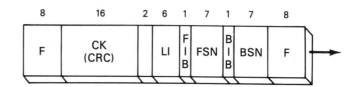

(c) Fill-in Signal Unit (FISU)

CK = Check bits
F = Flag
LI = Length indicator
BSN = Backward sequence number
FSN = Forward sequence number
BIB = Backward indicator bit

FIB = Forward indicator bit
SF = Status field
SIF = Signalling information field
SIO = Service information octet
CRC = Cycle redundancy check

Note: Numbers over each field signify the number of bits for that field.

FIGURE 5-9. SS7 Signal Units

they are used to provide level 2 control and status signal units between the level 2 Q.703 protocols at each end of the link.

All SUs begin and end with the 8-bit flag, and all SUs use a $X^{16} + X^{12} + X^5 + 1$ cyclic redundancy check (CRC). Two sequence numbers are used to provide flow control and user message accountability. The backward sequence number (BSN) acknowledges messages and the forward sequence number (FSN) identifies the service unit in which it resides. The BSN and FSN perform the same functions as the N(R) and N(S) fields that are used in many other level 2 protocols (HDLC, SDLC, LAPB, etc.). They are used with the forward indicator bit (FIB) and the backward indicator bit (BIB) to perform sequencing and acknowledging functions. The FSN/FIB are associated with the BSN/BIB in one direction. They are independent of the FSN/FIB and BSN/BIB in the other direction. This concept permits independent flow across both directions of the full duplex link.

The length indicator (LI) field specifies the number of octets that follow up to the CK (CRC) field (see Figure 5-9).

The service information octet (SIO) is divided into two fields. The service indicator is used by level 3 to perform message distribution and routing functions. The values identify the type of message. For example, the user parts (UP) are identified, such as ISDN user part, telephone user part, etc. The subservice field also contains 4 bits and is used by signalling message handling functions to distinguish between international and national messages.

The signalling information field (SIF) contents depend on which user part is contained in the service unit. It is used by level 3 for routing control. Its contents are explained in the section devoted to SS7 level 3.

The status field (SF) is an 8-bit field, in which 3 bits are used to activate and restore the link and to ensure link alignment; that is, proper recognition and delineation of the flags and the service units' contents.

SS7 Level 3 (Q.704). The SS7 level 3 functions are called signalling network functions and fall into two categories:

- Signalling message handling functions: Direct the message transfer to the proper link or user part.
- Signalling network management functions: Control the message routing and the configuration of the SS7 network.

Figure 5-10 depicts an SS7 signalling network. The switching nodes in the network are referred to as signalling transfer points, which are connected by the level 2 signalling links. If multiple parallel links connect the signalling points, they are called a signalling link set. A group of links with identical characteristics is referred to as a link group.

A message is generated at a user part function, known as the originating point and is sent to another user part function, known as the destination point. The intermediate nodes are signalling transfer points (STP).

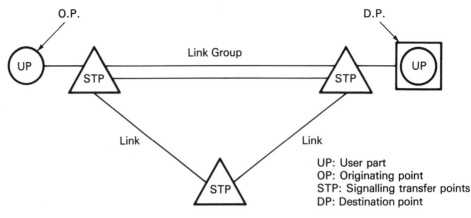

FIGURE 5-10. SS7 Level 3 (Q.704)

The STPs use information in the message to determine its routing. A routing label contains the identification of the originating and destination points. A code is also used to manage load sharing within the network. The routing label is used by the STP in combination with predetermined routing data to make the routing decisions. The route is fixed unless failures occur in the network. In this situation, the routing is modified by level 3 functions. The load-sharing logic (and code in the label) permit the distribution of the traffic to a particular destination to be distributed to two or more output signalling links.

Figure 5-11 shows the modules of SS7 level 3. Their functions are:

- Message routing: Selects the link to be used for each message.
- Message distribution: Selects the user part at the destination point (by checking the service indicator code).
- Message discrimination: Determines at each signalling point if the message is to be forwarded to message routing or message distribution.
- Signalling traffic management: Controls the message routing functions of flow control, rerouting, changeover to a less faulty link, and recovery from link failure.
- Signalling link management: Manages the activity of the level 2 function. Provides logical interface between level 2 and level 3.
- Signalling route management: Transfers status information about signalling routes to remote signalling points.

We now turn our attention to the primary reason SS7 exists: to support call control signalling between telephone systems.

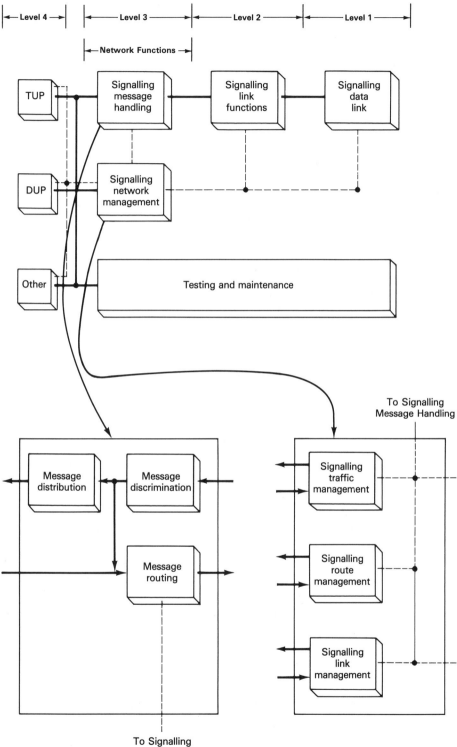

FIGURE 5-11. Layer 3 Modules of SS7

SS7 Telephone User Part (TUP) (Q.723) and Signalling Procedures (Q.724)

The TUP defines the telephone signalling functions for Signalling System No. 7. Its use is suitable for national and international calls on semiautomatic and automatic equipment. The most efficient approach to learning about SS7 TUP is to examine the contents and functions of the telephone user messages. These messages reside in the signalling information field (SIF) of

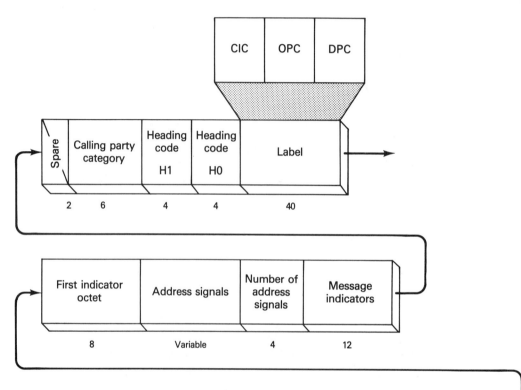

DPC: Destination point code
OPC: Originating point code
CIC: Circuit identification code
Note: Numbers under each field signify the number of bits in that field.

FIGURE 5-12. SS7 Initial Address Message (IAM) in an SIF

the signal units (see Figure 5-9). The contents of the SIF vary, depending on the particular type of user (telephone, data, ISDN, others). Figure 5-12 shows one example of the TUP signalling information field (SIF).

The TUP Message (Q.723)

The first 40 octets of the TUP message is called the label. It consists of three fields:

- Destination point code (DPC): The destination signalling point—the destination for the TUP message.
- Originating point code (OPC): The originating signalling point for the message.
- Circuit identification code (CIC): The identification of a specific speech circuit that is connected to the destination and origination points.

The DPC and OPC codes must permit the unique identification of signalling points. The codes can be established for either national or international networks. The CIC is used to identify the specific time division multiplexed (TDM) digital time slot or frequency division multiplexed (FDM) frequency channel for the speech circuit. The values in the CIC field identify either (a) a time slot in a digital carrier (further defined in Q.732, Q.734, Q.744, and Q.746) or (b) FDM systems using a pulse code modulation (PCM) standard.

The next fields of the TUP are the heading codes H1 and H0. These fields provide the identification of the type of message. As many as 256 possible message codes can be used. Examples of the messages codes are explained below (the reader should read Q.722 if all the messages must be known):

- *Charging message* (CHG): H0 = 0100; H1 = 0010. A message that contains charging information.
- *Call failure signal* (CFL): H0 = 0101; H1 = 0101. A message that indicates the failure of a call set-up attempt.
- *Reset-circuit signal* (RSC): H0 = 0111; H1 = 0111. A message used to release a circuit due to faulty conditions.
- *Reanswer signal* (RAN): H0 = 0110; H1 = 0101. A message to indicate the called party (after clearing the call) lifts the telephone's receiver or in some way reproduces an answer condition.
- *Answer signal, charge* (ANC): H0 = 0110; H1 = 0001. A message to indicate that a call is answered, the calling subscriber is to be charged, and the calling meter begins running.

- *Closed user group validations check message* (CVM): H0 = 1001; H1 = 0101. A message sent from the originating or redirecting exchange to a closed user group (CUG) data base to validate a CUG connection request (CUGs may be set up for privacy or security purposes).
- *Subscriber busy signal* (SSB): H0 = 0101; H1 = 1001. A message to indicate the line(s) connecting the called party to the exchange are busy.

SS7 stipulates the coding for H0/H1 in an initial call set-up to also be used with the calling party category field to identify the calling party's language and other categories. Currently, codes are reserved for French, English, German, Russian, and Spanish, with other codes available to telephone administrations to use as they wish.

The 12-bit message indicators field is used for several purposes: (a) identification of a national or international number; (b) indication of the use of a satellite circuit; (c) requirement for a circuit-continuity check; (d) use of echo suppression ; (e) indication of a redirected call; (f) requirement for an all-digital circuit; (g) a spare bit which can be used for providing μ/A law conversion.

The number of address signals field and the address signals contain information about the addresses in an initial address message. The coded addresses are half-octet binary numbers.

The first indicator octet performs several functions. The bits are coded to indicate (a) the use of a specific network capability or user facility information, (b) an indication if a closed user group information is included, (c) indication of additional calling party information, (d) indication of additional routing information, (e) indication of calling line identity, (f) indication of original called address being included, and (g) indication of charging information being included.

The following fields are coded (if present) to convey this information:

- *Network capability or user facility information:* This field indicates if a called line is requested.
- *Closed user group information:* This field indicates if the call is an ordinary call or if outgoing access is allowed.
- *Additional calling party information and additional routing information:* This field is not yet defined by CCITT.
- *Calling line identity:* This field indicates if the calling identity is a subscriber, national or international number, and if the identity of the calling line is restricted.
- *Original called address:* This field identifies the original called address.
- *Charging information:* This field is not yet defined by CCITT.

Example of an SS7 Call

In this section we piece together some of the information explained earlier by providing an example of how the SS7 signalling procedures and call set-up occur (refer to Figure 5-13). It will be evident that SS7, while different from CCIS and SS6, uses many similar procedures. For examples, compare Figure 5-13 with Figure 5-7.

A call set-up begins when an initial address message is sent to an exchange. This message contains all the information required to set-up and route the call. All codes and digits required for the call routing through the national and international network will be sent in this message. Other signals may also be sent in certain situations. For example, the end of pulsing (ST) signal is sent to indicate the final digit has been sent of the digits in the national or international numbers. Also, since the SS7 network does not pass over the speech path, it must provide facilities to provide a continuity check of the speech circuit to be used. It also makes cross-office checks to ensure the reliability of the connection through the various digital exchanges.

A call is processed by the outgoing exchange analyzing the address signals in the message. Based on these address messages, an appropriate outgoing circuit is seized and an initial address message (IAM) is forwarded to the next exchange.

This exchange analyzes the address message to determine (a) the circuit to be seized, (b) routing through another country, if necessary, (c) the nature of the circuit (terrestrial or satellite), (d) if echo control is needed, (e) the calling party's category (discussed earlier), and (f) the need for continuity checks. The exchanges will disable any echo suppressors (if necessary) at this time.

If all the checks are completed successfully, the network begins the call establishment (when enough address signals are received to determine routing). The address messages are analyzed to determine if all the required signals have been received, at which time the speech path set-up is completed. The destination exchange provides a ringing tone back to the originator, and upon the receiving telephone user answering the call, the answer signals are returned by the originating exchange to the user.

Eventually the call subscriber hangs up, which activates a clear back message to the originating exchange. After a certain period of waiting, if no other signals emanate from the end user, additional supervisory signals are exchanged between the two exchanges to make the circuit available for new traffic.

Signalling Connection Control Part (SCCP)

The SCCP is situated between the user layers (with the exception of the Telephone User Part and the Message Transfer Part) and the MTP (see Figure 5-14). Its purpose is to provide additional functions to the MTP and to sup-

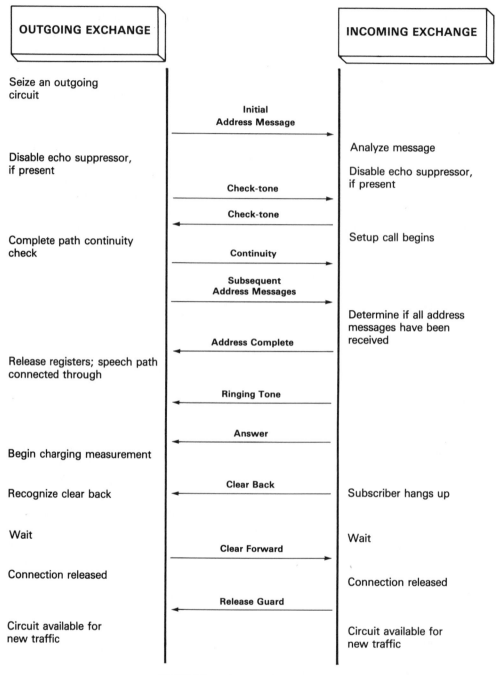

OUTGOING EXCHANGE

INCOMING EXCHANGE

Seize an outgoing
circuit

Initial
Address Message

Analyze message

Disable echo suppressor,
if present

Disable echo suppressor,
if present

Check-tone

Check-tone

Complete path continuity
check

Setup call begins

Continuity

Subsequent
Address Messages

Determine if all address
messages have been
received

Address Complete

Release registers; speech path
connected through

Ringing Tone

Answer

Begin charging measurement

Clear Back

Recognize clear back

Subscriber hangs up

Wait

Wait

Clear Forward

Connection released

Connection released

Release Guard

Circuit available for
new traffic

Circuit available for
new traffic

FIGURE 5-13. An SS7 Operation

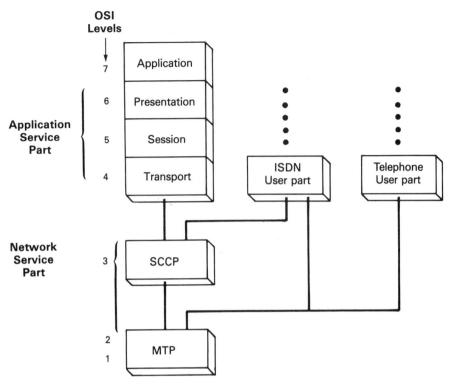

OSI Levels

7	Application
6	Presentation
5	Session
4	Transport

Application Service Part

3	SCCP

Network Service Part

ISDN User part

Telephone User part

2	MTP
1	

Note: An identical structure exists at a remote user node.

FIGURE 5-14. SCCP in SS7 Architecture [SCHL86]

port both connectionless and connection-oriented network services between SS7 nodes. (These terms are explained in Chapter 8, but briefly, connection-oriented services require a session to be set up end-to-end and data units associated with the session are kept in sequence and related to each other. Connectionless services use no set-up and data units are treated as independent entities.)

The combination of the MTP and SCCP is called the "Network Services Part" and adheres to the OSI Reference Model X.200. For example, primitives, protocol data units, connectionless and connection-oriented services, and service access points (SAPs) are defined in Q.711.

The primary value of SCCP is that it provides a means to use the OSI protocols in the upper layers to communicate with SS7. This important concept is illustrated in Figure 5-14 [SCHL86].

SCCP Protocol Classes. SCCP provides five classes of network service, which are categorized as protocol classes. (The reader may wish to compare these classes to the transport layer protocol classes in Chapter 15):

- *Protocol class 0, basic connectionless service:* Data units are passed to SCCP from upper layers without prior set-up and are transported independently of each other. They may be delivered out of sequence. This protocol class is a connectionless service.
- *Protocol class 1, sequenced (MTP) connectionless service:* Enhances class 0 by performing sequencing of the data units. Basically, class 1 is a sequenced connectionless service.
- *Protocol class 2, basic connection-oriented class:* Supports a temporary or permanent signalling connection between nodes. It also supports the multiplexing of a number of SS7 connections onto one MTP network connection. Flow control and sequencing are not provided. It is a simple connection-oriented service.
- *Protocol class 3, flow control connection-oriented class:* Supports classes 0 and 1 and provides enhanced features: expedited data transfer, message loss detection, and sequence checks. This class is connection-oriented with flow control.
- *Protocol class 4, error recovery and flow control connection-oriented class:* Supports class 3 and includes a capability for recovering from lost, mis-sequenced, or corrupted SS7 messages.

Functions of SCCP Messages. The messages are carried within the signal units (SUs) in the sequence information field (SIF) (see Figure 5-9). Their purpose is to provide a peer-to-peer session between two SCCPs. The messages are created by SCCP as a result of receiving OSI primitives from an upper layer. In turn, SCCP exchanges primitives with MTP with the goal of transferring the message unit to the remote SCCP.

Appendix 5A is provided for the reader who wishes to examine the SCCP messages in more detail.

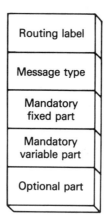

FIGURE 5-15. SCCP Message Format

TABLE 5-1. SCCP Message Types and Protocol Classes

SCCP Message	Classes of Protocol				
	0	1	2	3	4
CR connection request			X	X	X
CC connection confirm			X	X	X
CREF connection refused			X	X	X
RLSD released			X	X	X
RLC release complete			X	X	X
DT1 data form 1			X		
DT2 data form 2				X	X
AK data acknowledgment				X	X
UDT unitdata	X	X			
UDTS unitdata service	X	X			
ED expedited data				X	X
EA expedited data acknowledgment				X	X
RSR reset request				X	X
RSC reset confirmation				X	X
ERR error			X	X	X
IT inactivity test			X	X	X

Format of the SCCP Message. The format of the SCCP message is shown in Figure 5-15. It contains five major fields:

- *Routing label*: This field is the standard routing label explained in previous material.
- *Message type*: This field identifies the types of SCCP message (e.g., connection request [CR], data form 1 [DT1], etc.).
- *Mandatory fixed part*: This field contains the mandatory parameters for a particular message type (addresses, cause codes, etc.).
- *Mandatory variable part*: Some messages use a variable number of parameters. They are contained in this field.
- *Optional part*: Certain messages are used only with specific protocol classes.

Table 5-1 shows the message type (explained in Appendix 5a) used for each protocol class.

Monitoring and Measurements for the MTP (Q.791)

Q.791 defines the parameters for measuring the performance of an SS7 network. This specification contains 57 measurements grouped into the following categories for the MTP:

- *Signalling link performance:* Measures errors, failures, and delay on the link.
- *Signalling link availability:* Measures unavailability blocking, signalling inhibition, and link changeovers.
- *Signalling link utilization:* Measures throughput and congestion.
- *Signalling linkset and route set availability:* Measures failures, recoveries, and duration of unavailability.
- *Signalling point status:* Measures status of adjacent signalling points (SP).
- *Signalling traffic distribution:* Measures number of SIF and SIO octets transmitted and received.

Operations and Maintenance Applications Part (Q.795)

This brief recommendation discusses recommendation and protocols for the operation and maintenance of (a) controlled signalling points and (b) controlling signal points. We do not examine this material since some of it is still to be defined.

Other Thoughts on Telephone Signalling Systems

The reader should now realize that the new telephone control networks are data communications networks. Indeed, in today's systems, voice networks are controlled by data networks. As digital systems and data networks evolve, they will incorporate more of the voice telephone systems into their architectures. In the not too distant future, they will be integrated. We pick up this theme in Chapter 19.

TRAFFIC ENGINEERING

In providing service to its customers, the telephone system has a problem similar to that of organizations such as grocery stores, banks, and department stores: how to provide efficient service to customers yet provide it in a cost-effective manner. (The organizations' stockholders are also interested in this problem.) For example, we often experience a wait in a bank because an insufficient number of tellers are available to process deposits and withdrawals. If the bank adds more tellers and service windows, the lines become shorter and the wait times decrease. However, each additional teller and teller equipment is an added expense to the bank. Bank management constantly faces the question of cost versus quality of service. In simplest terms the problem comes down to: how many resources are needed to meet the customer needs, and at the same time, keep costs at an acceptable level? For both banks and telephone systems, the primary consideration is to develop a system of optimum capacity, with consideration given to costs, and then implement the system based on the expected demand.

This technique is called traffic engineering. A considerable amount of traffic engineering is based on probability theory and queuing theory. In this section, we delve into these subjects and explore the approach used by the telephone companies in designing telephone networks.

Traffic engineering is distinguished by how a system treats a traffic overload. Two methods are used. A loss system discards the traffic without providing service. This method is also called a block-call-cleared (BCC) system. A delay system queues the traffic and provides service when resources become available. This method is also called block calls-delay (BCD). The conventional telephone circuit-switching network uses the loss system concept. For example, a congested telephone network rejects a call with a busy signal. In contrast many data networks operate with delay systems. Almost all message switching and many packet switches queue the overload traffic and service it on a delay basis.

However, the distinction is not clear-cut. In later chapters, we shall see that many packet switches also discard overload traffic and electronic circuit-switching systems provide some delay features for call control. We shall also see that integrated voice/data systems (Chapter 19) must deal with both delay and loss systems. Interestingly, most of the evolving voice/data networks discard overload voice signals and queue overload data signals. The discussions in this section emphasize the telephone loss system, but it should be remembered that it is possible to use a mix of loss and delay systems.

In any situation where waiting for a service is a part of the process, the common feature is demand on the system. This is called the offered load (or subscriber demand) and it could be in the form of telephone calls or customers waiting in a queue in a bank. Whatever the type of load that exists in a service system, offered load is defined by two random processes: (a) the average arrival rate of the customers who are requesting the service (average arrival) λ; (b) the average length of time the customer requires the service (average holding time) T.

The system cannot always service the customer immediately. For example, a customer experiences a wait when the telephone system is servicing other calls. In some systems, the customer waits for the service by joining a line or queue. The queue length is somewhat unpredictable because the customers ask for service on a random basis.

A perfect system with respect to time entails no delay. If n subscribers are connected to a network, a "no delay" system would require $n(n-1)/2$ direct connections—clearly an impossible task. Consequently, the telephone system is designed to provide a reasonable delay during normal traffic conditions, yet refuse (block) calls during periods of heavy traffic. Naturally, what is reasonable and normal is quite subjective.

For any service system with enough servers to service customers immediately upon their request, the average number of busy servers is always the product of λ and T. This relationship is independent of the patterns of arrivals and variations of holding time [COOP81]. As a result of this supposition, the offered load (a) is defined as:

$$a = λ * T$$

For example, if 300 customers need to be serviced per minute during an hour, and each customer requires 2 minutes of service, then offered load a = 600. However, this does not tell the whole story. If peak periods exist beyond the average (which certainly is the case in most service systems), then we must accommodate the additional traffic by having additional service facilities.

The offered load expressed in an hour of calls is called traffic intensity. In the previous paragraph, the traffic intensity is 300/60 minutes = 5 hour calls. Traffic intensity represents the average number of simultaneous calls.

Traffic intensity is not the same as traffic density. This latter term refers to the number of simultaneous calls in a given instant. Traffic intensity describes the average traffic density during a length of time (typically a one-hour period). Also, the offered load is usually different from the carried load since the system does not carry (service) all requests.

Average arrival rates and average holding times are generally expressed in the same unit of time. This means a is a dimensionless quantity. Its values are expressed as erlangs (after the Danish mathematician A. K. Erlang, one of the founders of traffic theory). One erlang represents a service facility occupied for one hour.

As an example, assume 200 callers generate 60 requests during a busy hour [KLEI86]. The average holding time for the calls is 240 seconds. The arrival rate is:

$$60/3600 = 1 \text{ request/second}$$

The erlang is calculated as:

$$\frac{60 \text{ calls}}{3600 \text{ seconds}} * \frac{240 \text{ seconds}}{\text{call}} = 4 \text{ erlangs}$$

In addition to the erlang, telephone systems measure the load in one hundred call seconds (CCS) per hour. CCS is calculated as:

$$CCS = NCBH * HT/100$$

Where: NCBH = number of calls during a busy hour; HT = holding time.

One hour consists of 3600 seconds. Therefore, a continuous traffic load of 1 hour represents 36 CCS or 1 erlang. The CCS unit is a common, widely used term of measurement for telephone system traffic engineering. To continue our example, the number of 100 call seconds is:

$$(60 * 240)/100 = 144 \text{ CCS}$$

The traffic per caller is:

4 erlang/200 customers = 0.02 erlang/caller

or

144/200 = .72 CCS/caller

A single server has a capacity of 1 erlang. This means the server is always busy. The maximum capacity (in erlangs) is equal to the number of servers. However, the actual activity must be less than the maximum server capacity because a telephone loss system experiences infinite blocking probability when the traffic intensity is equal to the server capacity. In our example, more than four links are required to adequately serve the callers.

It is instructive to note that the development of a system to accommodate variable loads to the satisfaction of the customer and to the satisfaction of the telephone stockholder would be an impossible task. However, even though loads vary from hour to hour, historically they vary in predictable and recognizable patterns. As a consequence, the telephone system can utilize measures to more effectively accommodate peak periods.

Of course, the system does not always service customers to their satisfaction. During Mother's Day and other notable events, the traffic is simply too much for the telephone system to handle, and we experience the familiar busy signal during such holidays. During most times, even though the exact number of calls that must be serviced is not known, it can be determined (historically and statistically) that there will be some number of them. The probability that a call will be serviced and leave the system can also be estimated.

AT&T/Bell uses the busy season, busy hour (BSBH) to define its engineering period for peak load. This criterion is the busiest hour of the busiest weeks of the year. The average busy season busy hour (ABSBH) is the average value of 20 ABSH throughout the busy season. They are selected from the actual business days.

The trunk groups between switches are measured by the average of 20 BSBH. The design criteria for the trunks are stated in terms of a percent of blocking during the period, because the trunk groups are engineered as loss, BCC (block calls cleared) systems.

The concepts involved in the design of the telephone network are founded on a common assumption that the probability of an arrival of a call at an exchange during some small internal (T, T+t) is proportional to the length of this small interval; that is, t. Furthermore, the proportionality constant is average arrival rate (λ); therefore:

$P (T, T+t) = \lambda * t$

This important yet simple assumption has been used to develop many traffic theory techniques.

Poisson Distribution Process

One of the most widely used equations for studying practically any kind of user service situation is the Poisson distribution process. This equation describes a large independent number of potential users such that the community of users may have only a small number requesting service at any one time. It is defined as:

$$P(k,t) = \frac{(\lambda t)^k}{k!} e^{-\lambda t}$$

Where: p (k,t) = probability that k calls arrive in any interval of fixed length t.

(This famous formula is said to have been published by Simeon Denis Poisson in 1887 but others believe it was discovered by Abraham de Moivre in 1718 [BECK68].)

The Poisson process is used also in evaluating the performance of queuing systems such as packet networks (see Chapter 13) and many other applications, such as semiconductor design (predicting the load on junctions).

It should also be noted that the arrivals of the calls are memoryless: they are independent of each other. The probability of the event at time (T, T + t) depends on the probability of time only—which is one case of a Markov process [PAPO84].

In any service system such as bank or telephone network, traffic engineering must also consider that the customer will eventually leave the system (in a bank, walking out the door, and in a telephone system, hanging up the telephone). Consequently, we can make the assumption that during the interval length (t) each customer or call will terminate with probability "μt" where "μ" is the departure rate. The following formula describes the probability that a given arrival requires service for t seconds or less.

$$H(t) = 1 - e^{-\mu t}$$

Where: H(t) = probability that a given arrival requires service in t seconds or less.

This equation is one of the well-known formulas in traffic engineering. It is called the negative exponential distribution. One of the surprising aspects of the formula is that it describes the calls' remaining time in the system, regardless of how long the calls have been in progress. This equation may seem unrealistic, or inaccurate (or both), but it has been verified empirically. In essence, it describes the distribution of calls quite well.

In summary, even though calls within a telephone system can be predicted based on time of day and holiday factors, etc., generally the telephone system engineers assume the calls are random for purposes of analysis. Random traffic means that arrivals follow a Poisson process and the holding times follow a negative exponential distribution. Based on these factors, our next discussion will focus on some methods to analyze traffic.

Erlang C and Erlang B

Two widely used equations for telephone traffic engineering are Erlang C and Erlang B. (References are provided at the end of this chapter on their derivations.) Erlang C (Erlang's delay formula) is defined as:

$$C(c,a) = \frac{a^c}{(c-1)!(c-2)} \left[\frac{a^c}{(c-1)!(c-a)} + \sum_{K=0}^{c-1} \frac{a^K}{K!} \right]^{-1}$$

Where: C(c,a) = probability of an arriving call being delayed with a load and c servers [REY83].

Since Erlang C describes a blocked-calls-delayed system (all calls are eventually serviced), it is not suitable for telephone systems design. We also need to consider a system that blocks (or reroutes) traffic. To do so, we describe the probability that an arriving call is blocked as [KLEI86]:

$$F(C) = (A^C/C!) * 1/ (\sum_{N=1}^{c} A^N/N!)$$

Where: C = number of trunks in a group; A = erlangs.

This is the Erlang B formula (or Erlang's loss formula). It is a block-calls-cleared (BCC) model; it allows calls to be lost or rerouted when servers are busy.

Returning to our original bank teller problem of quality vs. cost, the Erlang B formula can be applied to determine an optimum mix of servers vs. offered load. Moreover, the Erlang B distribution matches the telephone systems' practice of alternate routing where a call is first offered to a high-usage trunk group and if busy, routed to an alternate trunk group. The final group is usually engineered on a Poisson basis [KLEI86].

Telephone system designers also find a BCC model very useful because it allows them to make objective and rational trade-offs on networks performance and network costs. As depicted in Figure 5-16, to maintain a set blocking (B) value, as a load increases, the number of additional servers needed to keep B stable actually decreases [REY83].

As an example of Erlang B, assume a group of telephone subscribers originate 25 calls with an average holding time of 288 seconds (4.8 minutes). Two trunks are used in the high usage group. If these trunks are busy, calls are routed to an alternate trunk group. First, we determine how many calls must be rerouted:

$$C = 2$$
$$A = 25 * 288/3600 = 2 \text{ Erlangs}$$
$$F(C) = (A^c/C!) * 1/ (\sum_{N=1}^{c} A^N/N!)$$

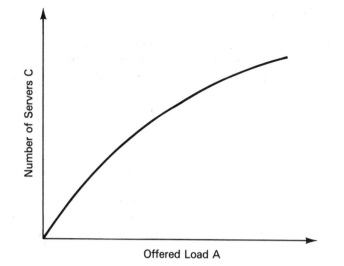

FIGURE 5-16. Servers Needed for Offered Load

F(C) = $2^2/2!$ * $1/(2^0/0! + 2^1/1! + 2^2/2!)$
    = $4/2 * 1/(1 + 2 + 2)$
    = $2 * 1/(5)$
    = 0.4

Therefore, the proportion of rerouted calls is 0.4. The number of calls actually rerouted is $0.4 * 25 = 10$.

The efficiency of this set-up can be easily calculated as:

$$\text{Efficiency} = \text{Total traffic handled/ traffic capacity}$$
$$\text{or}$$
$$= \frac{(\text{erlangs} * \text{proportion of non-routed traffic})}{\text{number of trunks}}$$
$$= [2 * (1 - 0.4)]/2$$
$$= 0.60$$

Then, from Poisson tables readily available from traffic engineering texts, it is possible to determine how many trunks will be required to handle the overflow traffic and the efficiency of that trunk group. We leave this task to a more advanced treatise of telephone traffic engineering.

Poisson Blocking Formula

Figure 5-3 shows two types of telephone trunk groups: high usage (HU) and final groups. The final groups are designed to provide an average blocking of 0.01 during the busy season. However, the average blocking for the average busy hour is less than the average blocking during the busy season. Therefore, Erlang B underestimates the capacity needed for the trunk groups. As a consequence of this situation, the Poisson blocking formula is used by the telephone companies to build the trunk group tables.

$$P(c, \overline{a}) = e^{-\overline{a}} \sum_{k=c}^{\infty} \overline{a}^k/k!$$

Where: c = number of servers; $\overline{a}$ = load during the average busy season, busy hour (ABSBH); k = an index of the number of arriving calls.

This formula offers a reasonable compromise to Erlang C (calls wait indefinitely) and Erlang B (calls do not wait). It predicts a smaller number of servers than C and a greater number than B. These day-to-day variations tables are now used by the Bell Operating Companies (BOCs) for network design and have largely replaced the Poisson tables. The interested reader should obtain the Neal-Wilkinson $\overline{B}$ tables, named after the people who developed them [NEAL76][WILK56].

ECCS Engineering

We have assumed that the trunk groups are behaving independently. However, as Figure 5-3 shows, the trunks are linked together to form a network. Consequently, we need some additional refinements to develop a scheme to provide for alternate routing within the network, because an alternate routing network provides better service at lower costs than either alternate routes only or direct routes only.

Figure 5-17 shows the model used to determine the number of HU trunks. The incremental cost (C) of putting n trunks in the Central Office A to Central Office B HU group is [REY83]:

$$C(n) = nC_D + \frac{\alpha(n)}{\lambda A} C_A$$

Where: C_A = a known cost per alternate route trunk; C_D = cost per direct trunk; λA marginal capacity of group (both the same); $\alpha(n)$ = overflow from n-trunk HU group to an alternate route.

The well-known function Bell cost function graph in Figure 5-18 depicts the previous equation and the fact that C(n) has a minimum that occurs at the value n such that:

$$C(n) = \frac{\lambda A}{C_R}$$

Where: $C_R = C_A/C_D$.

The quantity $\lambda A/C_R$ is the most economical load on the last trunk and the optimal is when the last trunk's group carries a $\lambda A/C_R$ load. We learned earlier that the telephone companies measure load in CCS. They refer to

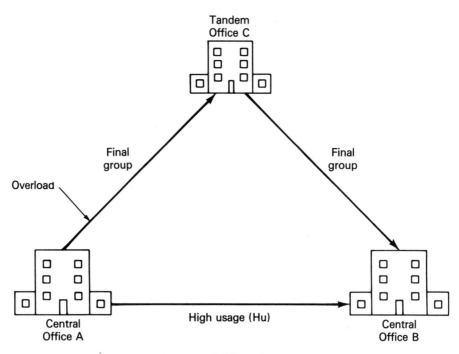

FIGURE 5-17. Model for Alternate Routing

$\lambda A/C_R$ as the economic CCS (ECCS) and the sizing of the trunk group is called ECCS engineering. With some modifications, the ECCS model is now used for sizing telephone trunks.

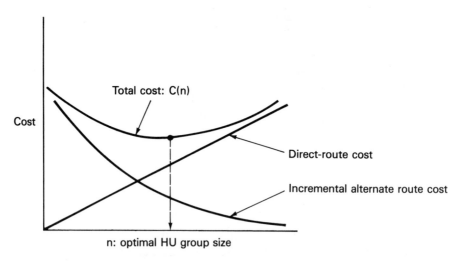

FIGURE 5-18. Alternate Routing Costs

SUGGESTED READINGS

A complete and well-written description of the telephone system can be found in [REY83]. [REY83] does not explain much about emerging digital technology, but [AT&T80] covers the basics of this area quite well. [BELL82A] is another book by Bell Labs that offers detailed descriptions of the telephone system. [BECK68] provides a thorough analysis of traffic engineering. [TALL87] contains a very good general reference on telephone switching systems. Many of the IEEE publications provide excellent information as well. The reader is encouraged to obtain the *IEEE Communications* magazine. Several of the issues are devoted to telephone systems. *Telephony* magazine also provides topical articles on the telephone industry. Other references are contained in the bibliography.

APPENDIX 5A
SS7 SIGNALLING CONNECTION CONTROL PART (SCCP) MESSAGES

Connection Request (CR). On request from the upper layers, SCCP initiates the set-up of a signalling connection. A calling SCCP sends a connection request message to the called SCCP to indicate a request for signalling connection set-up with characteristics defined in the parameters of the CR messages. This message must contain a local reference number for identification purposes, a proposed protocol class, and the address of the called party.

Connection Confirm (CC). The called SCCP indicates to the calling SCCP that it has performed the set-up of the signalling connection. A connection confirm message must contain the following information: the destination local reference number, the source local reference number, and the selected protocol class.

Connection Refusal (CREF). The called SCCP or an intermediate node indicates to the calling SCCP that it has refused the set-up by sending this message. A message must contain the destination local reference number and a refusal cause.

Released (RLSD). This message is sent to indicate that the resources associated with the released connection at the sending node have been brought into the disconnect pending condition and that the receiving node should also release that connection and any other resources associated with it. The message must contain the destination local reference number, the source local reference number, and a release cause.

Release Complete (RLC). This message is sent to indicate the concerned node has released the associated resources, and that the released message has been received. A release complete message must contain the destination local reference number and the source local reference number.

Data Form 1 (DT1). The function of this message, sent by either end of a signalling connection, is to send transparently information from upper layers from one SCCP to another SCCP. This is used only with protocol class 2.

Data Form 2 (DT2). This message passes user data transparently from the upper layers of one SCCP to the upper layers of the SCCP at the other end. It can acknowledge messages flowing in the other direction. This is used only in protocol classes supporting flow control (classes 3, 4).

Data Acknowledgment (AK). This message is used for flow control and window control. The message must contain the destination local reference number, the receive sequence number, and a credit (a credit value determines how many messages can be sent in a given period).

Expedited Data (ED). With flow control in operation, either end of the signalling connection can send this message which has the ability to bypass the flow control mechanism.

Expedited Data Acknowledgment (EA). This message is used to acknowledge an EA message (before another ED message may be sent).

Reset Request (RSR). This message is used only with protocol classes permitting flow control. The message is sent by a SCCP to indicate it is requesting re-initialization procedures.

Reset Confirmation (RSC). This message is sent by the requesting SCCP when it completes the reset procedure.

Protocol Data Unit Error (ERR). This message is sent on detection of any protocol errors. It must contain the destination local reference number and an error cause. It may contain the diagnostic information.

Reject (RJ). This message is used only with protocol class 4 and it is not yet fully defined by CCITT. It is sent by a SCCP to ask for a retransmission starting at the last message plus one, taking into account a credit value.

Restart Request (RTR). This message is subject to further study by CCITT.

Restart Confirmation (RTC). This message is subject for further study by CCITT.

Inactivity Test (IT). This message may be sent by either end to determine if the signalling connection is active at both ends.

Unitdata (UDT). A SCCP sends data in a connectionless mode with this message. The message must contain the called party address field, the calling party address field, the protocol class, and user data.

Unitdata Service (UDTS). Whenever it is not possible to route a unitdata message and a message return option is used, this message is sent back to the originator. The message contains the called party address, the calling party address field, a diagnostic cause code, and the user data.

QUESTIONS

TRUE/FALSE

1. The Strowger switch is electromechanical and the crossbar switch is electrical.
2. The interface between 2-wire and 4-wire circuits is provided by a hybrid, which acts as a transformer.
3. In a telephone system, the "ring" is a negative charge and the "tip" is set to ground.
4. Packet-switched systems support both voice and data networks.
5. CCIS links are fully redundant.
6. Match the following CCIS terms to their appropriate function:

   Function

   a) Provides link access
   b) Stores messages
   c) CCIS processor

   Term

   1. A CCIS link controller
   2. Signalling terminal
   3. Terminal access circuit

7. What are the disadvantages of a per-trunk signalling system?
8. Explain the principal concept behind common channel interoffice signalling (CCIS).
9. What are the advantages of CCIS over inband signalling?
10. Cite disadvantages of CCIS and SS6.

11. SS7 provides many functions to the telephone network. These functions are provided by the SS7 messages. List some of the SS7 message components.

12. Explain the major features of a SS7 physical level link.

13. Explain the major features of a SS7 level 2 link, by an examination of the SS7 message signal unit (MSU).

14. SS7 provides five classes of network service (0-4). Each higher number provides more support functions to the network and user. What are the principal differences between class 0 and class 4?

15. What is the difference between a loss system and delay system in handling traffic overload? Which approach is used by a telephone system?

16. A telephone system services 100 users that create 60 calls during a busy hour. The average holding time is 90 seconds.
   a) What is the average occupancy of the system, stated in erlangs?
   b) What is the number of hundred call seconds (CCS)?
   c) What is the traffic per customer in erlangs?
   d) What is the traffic per customer in hundred call seconds (CCS)?

SELECTED ANSWERS

1. False. Both switches are electromechanical.

2. True. The hybrid contains inductive windings.

3. True.

4. True. Indeed, packet networks are an integral part of telephone system signalling.

5. True. The STPs are so connected to provide reliability.

6.

Function	Term
a	3
b	2
c	1

8. The Common Channel Interoffice Signalling (CCIS) system transmits the signalling information for a group of trunks over a separate channel from the user channel, a technique also known as clear channel signalling.

9. Since CCIS passes signals faster than inband systems, call set-up and take-down are performed faster. This speed reduces a customer's post-dialing delay and the holding time for equipment and trunks is reduced. CCIS has more capacity than the inband system, and since CCIS uses full-duplex signalling, control signals can be passed during a conversation. CCIS is flexible; the control messages and software can be changed to include new services.

14. Class 0 requires no call set-up. All message units are independent of each other and may be delivered out of sequence. It is a connectionless service. Class 4 is connection-oriented. It has options for flow-control, retransmission, error-checking, multiplexing, and expedited transfer.

CHAPTER 6

Compression and Multiplexing

INTRODUCTION

One could reasonably ask why the subjects of compression and multiplexing are placed into the same chapter. They are included in Chapter 6 because they both attempt to make better use of a valuable and expensive resource: the communications channel. Interestingly, to perform multiplexing, we are faced with a problem which is the exact opposite of the problem of compression. Multiplexing attempts to make better use of a potentially underused resource. Compression attempts to make better use of a potentially overused resource. Thus, they have the same goal, but they achieve the goal with different methods. This point will become clear when we examine them. The first section of this chapter examines data compression. The second section is devoted to multiplexing.

DATA COMPRESSION

Practically all symbols generated and used by computers are comprised of a fixed number of bits coded to represent a character. The codes (principally EBCDIC and ASCII) have been designed as fixed length because computers require a fixed number of bits in a code to efficiently process data. Most machines use octet (8-bit) alignment. The fixed-length format means all characters are of equal length, even though the characters are not transmitted with equal frequency (Figure 6-1[a]). For example, characters such as vowels, blanks, and numbers are used more often than consonants and char-

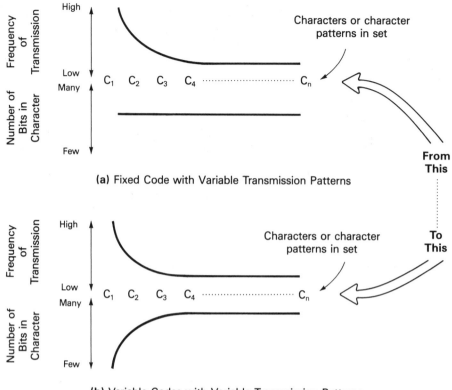

(a) Fixed Code with Variable Transmission Patterns

(b) Variable Codes with Variable Transmission Patterns

FIGURE 6-1. Data Compression

acters such as a question mark. This practice can lead to considerable link inefficiency, a practice, as we learned in Chapter 2, that Morse avoided with the variable-length Morse code.

One widely used solution to code inefficiency is adapting a variable-length code to represent the fixed-length codes. The most frequently transmitted characters are compressed: represented by a unique bit set smaller than the conventional bit code (Figure 6-1[b]). This data compression technique can result in substantial savings in communications costs. Systems today can easily compress data to one-half its original length (2:1 ratio), and many systems achieve compression ratios of 20 or 30 to 1. Several time division multiplexers use data compression techniques to further increase channel throughput.

Data compression also provides two other significant benefits. First, let us suppose an application requires a 9.6 Kbit/s transfer rate, which entails expensive modems and a high-quality (more expensive) channel. If the data can be compressed by 50%, the application now only needs a 4.8 Kbit/s link, which is less expensive and less subject to errors. Second, if the application is using a service (i.e., a public packet network) that charges on traffic volume transmitted, the compression can reduce the volume of data and charges to the user.

Data compression techniques are classified as reversible and nonreversible; reversible techniques are further divided into semantic independent and semantic dependent procedures [REGH81]. Nonreversible techniques (often called data compaction) permanently eliminate the irrelevant portions of the data. Obviously, what is relevant or irrelevant depends on the data. Typically, data items with leading blanks or trailing zeros are eliminated with data compaction. The discussion in this chapter concentrates on reversible techniques.

Our goal in this section is to provide an overview of data compression. In so doing, the following methods are described:

- Bit mapping and half byte (packed decimal) compression
- Character suppression
- Run length encoding
- Diatomic encoding and pattern substitution
- Relative encoding
- Statistical encoding

The reader is encouraged to review the material in Chapter 2 in the section titled "The Foundations of Communications Theory." The material on multilevel signalling and entropy will be useful in understanding several concepts pertaining to the subject of compression.

Bit Mapping and Half Byte (Packed Decimal) Compression

Bit mapping is used in a number of applications besides data communications (data storage for example). It is often used on data that exhibit a large number of specific character types such as zeros and blanks [HELD84]. A simple implementation of bit mapping uses one octet to describe the absence or presence of character types. Figure 6-2 shows bit mapping with blanks compressed. Figure 6-2 (a) is a string of uncompressed data and Figure 6-2 (b) shows the data after it is compressed. The leading octet indicates which of the following 8 bytes of the specific character have been compressed. Binary 1s show the positions of data and binary 0s show the position of blanks.

This system only compresses one particular character. If a data stream contains a high incidence of more than one character, other variations of bit mapping can be employed that use more than one control octet, or other compression techniques can be used.

A classic variation of bit mapping called half byte or packed decimal compression is based on a transmission stream that contains numeric EBCDIC or ASCII code. As Figure 1-2 (in Chapter 1) indicates, the high order

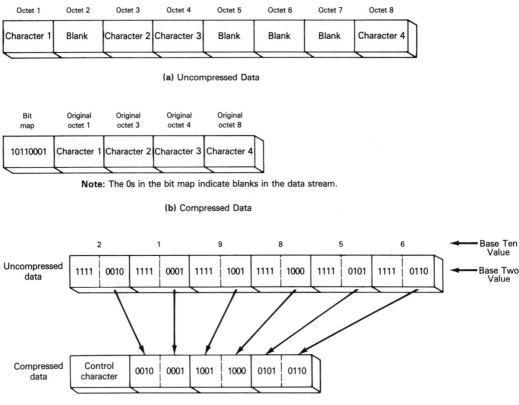

(a) Uncompressed Data

Note: The 0s in the bit map indicate blanks in the data stream.

(b) Compressed Data

(c) Half-Byte or Packed Decimal Compression

FIGURE 6-2. Bit Mapping

4 bits of EBCDIC numerics are 1111s, which convey no intelligence. For ASCII numeric data, Figure 1-3 reveals that the high order 3 bits are 011. ASCII code can be further compressed, because the comma, asterisk, dollar sign, and period use 010 in the high order bit positions. Figure 6-2 (c) shows an uncompressed and compressed EBCIDC numeric data stream.

Character Suppression

Several communications data link protocols employ character suppression. The IBM 3780 Bisync protocol is an example of a protocol that suppresses blanks. With this approach, a data stream is examined before it is transmitted onto the link. When three or more of the specific characters are successively encountered in the data, a count field is retained and incremented to indicate how many successive characters have occurred in the data stream. The system must indicate that the compression count field has been placed in the data stream to allow the receiver to decompress (reconstruct) the sequence of characters that were inserted in the original data.

Character suppression can be quite powerful if used with some imagination. The 3780 Bisync protocol only suppresses blanks. However, logic could be used to suppress more than just blanks if it is known that other character types occur frequently in the data stream.

Character suppression is a variation of bit mapping but it allows compression of more than one character type—assuming the frequency of the types can be approximated to allow the compression routines to be programmed to look for the relevant characters.

Run Length Encoding

Run length encoding is a variation of character suppression, but requires three characters to convey the intelligence. Consequently, it should be used in data streams in which the characters occur frequently and continuously. It is counterproductive if used with recurring short strings of repeating characters. It has proved to be an effective approach for compressing graphic images.

The repeated characters are compressed as shown in Figure 6-3. The first character indicates the next two characters are compression codes. The second character is the code of the repeated character, and the third character is the count field indicating the number of consecutive, uninterrupted occurrences of the characters in the data stream.

A well-known personal computer protocol, Kermit, uses this compression technique. The transmitting Kermit module precedes the repeating character with (a) a control character, (b) the repeat count, and (c) the character that is needed.

The IBM 3780 data communications system provides blank (space) compression as one of its features. If the 3780 is operating in non-transparent mode and the compression feature is enabled, space characters will be automatically compressed when loading the data and expanded with input from the line. This is accomplished by sending an IGS (EBCDIC) or GS (ASCII) character and a count character in place of the deleted spaces. The count character indicates that 2 to 63 spaces were removed.

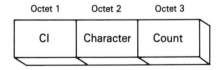

CI: Character indicating compression follows
Character: The compressed, repeated data character
Count: The number of time the character is repeated

FIGURE 6-3. Run Length Encoding

Diatomic Encoding and Pattern Substitution

Diatomic encoding codes a pair of characters with one special character. This approach works if one knows (a) the characteristics of the data stream (such as the most commonly occurring pairs) and (b) that the special characters that will be used for the compression codes will not occur in the data stream. Since diatomic encoding substitutes one character for two, it achieves a 2:1 compression ratio. Certain files (in which character types are predictable) lend themselves quite well to diatomic encoding. This includes program listings, numeric data files and all character files. In Table 6-1 [JEWE76] and [ARON77] have shown the 25 most frequently occurring character pairs in a 12,198 character English text file. The character combinations are substituted by another special character at the transmitting station. At the receiving station, the special character is decoded to the original two characters.

TABLE 6-1. JEWELL Character Pairing

Rank	Combination*	Occurrences	Occurrences per Thousand
1	Eb	328	26.89
2	bT	292	23.94
3	TH	249	20.41
4	bA	244	20.00
5	Sb	217	17.79
6	RE	200	16.40
7	IN	197	16.15
8	HE	183	15.00
9	ER	171	14.02
10	bI	156	12.79
11	b0	153	12.54
12	Nb	152	12.46
13	ES	148	12.13
14	bB	141	11.56
15	ON	140	11.48
16	Tb	137	11.23
17	TI	137	11.23
18	AN	133	10.90
19	Db	133	10.90
20	AT	119	9.76
21	TE	114	9.35
22	bC	113	9.26
23	bS	113	9.26
24	OR	112	9.18
25	Rb	109	8.94

*b = a blank or space

Data Compression by Gilbert Held © 1983 Reprinted by permission of John Wiley and Sons, Ltd.

Pattern substitution is an extended form of diatomic encoding but uses special characters to represent a longer pattern of characters. The process has long been utilized in data base and file compression algorithms, and in program source-code library management systems. We use the latter as an example. This example is also called adaptive scanning.

The technique uses a dictionary to store frequently occurring strings of characters. The common character string is substituted by a shorter code. For example, program source code is often transmitted across a link or stored in a program library. Thus, the character string PERFORM might appear often in a program written for a COBOL compiler. Adaptive scanning examines the text and substitutes a code (e.g., @) in place of each PER-FORM. The result is fewer bits transmitted.

Relative Encoding

Relative encoding is a widely used and simple technique. It is generally employed on a data stream that exhibits symbols or symbol strings that vary slightly relative to each other. Process control and telemetry data often exhibit this attribute.

Let us assume the measurements at a pressure valve in a factory yield 6300, 6302, 6301, 6300, 6299, 6298. To compress this data, each measurement except for the first is coded as a relative difference between it and the preceding measurement. The compressed data stream would appear as: 6300, 2, −1, −1, −1, −1.

Relative encoding does not perform well if the fluctuations between successive values require numbers longer than the original values. It is quite effective for small fluctuations and on data with similar or redundant patterns within the stream. The reader may recognize some similarities of relative encoding with the analog-to-digital encoding techniques, explained in Chapter 3 (e.g., sample-to-sample redundancy of the analog PAM signals).

Statistical Encoding

In Chapter 2, the concept of entropy was introduced. We repeat it here to provide background on statistical encoding:

$$H = - \sum_{i=1}^{n} P_i \log_2 P_i$$

Where: H = entropy (0 is certainty or nonrandomness); P = each probability; n = number of all probabilities.

The concepts of entropy are employed in data compression. The equation is used to determine the average bits per symbol and is applied to determine the most effective encoding scheme for the data compression. In effect, entropy requires short codes to be assigned to the more frequently occurring symbols and vice versa. Of course, this is the main thrust of data compression as illustrated in Figure 6-1(b).

Huffman Code

The Huffman code is a widely used compression method that relies on the concept of entropy. It has been proved that the code will always require less than one binary digit per symbol more than entropy [PIER80].

With Huffman code, the most commonly used characters contain the fewest bits and the less commonly used characters contain the most bits. For example, assume the characters A, B, C, and D comprise the complete character set. An analysis reveals that A accounts for 50% of the total transmitted traffic, B accounts for 25%, C for 15% and D for 10% (average figures). A code and tree to take advantage of the skewed character distribution can appear as in Figure 6-4. The rules to develop the tree are:

- Arrange the character set in a column with the most frequently occurring character first in the list on down to the least frequently occurring character.
- From the bottom of the column, draw lines out horizontally and merge the two lowest frequencies to obtain a new summation of the two frequencies. Draw a line from this line with the new summed frequency entered.
- Continue this process, until all lines are merged.
- Place a 0 and 1 at the end of each nodal line.
- Trace the tree back to origin to obtain the code for the character.

The following transmitted message is interpreted by the decision chart (Figure 6-5). The data are examined and decoded by reading the bit stream left to right, and following the decision chart down the proper logic path:

```
A :  D  : B :  C
0 : 111 : 10 : 110
```

It might appear at first glance that the 0 acts as a delimiter for the code. While it could perform this function for a very short code set, Huffman coding is considerably more flexible and versatile. Consider a character set consisting of seven characters in Figure 6-6. This assignment tree code for characters C_1 through C_7 allows the development of the decision chart in Figure 6-7. The figure illustrates how the binary stream of 10110000111010010 is decoded to C_5, C_4, C_1, C_7, C_2, C_2.

Notice that a 0 is not necessary for the character delimiter. Indeed, if the algorithm were designed to use a 0 as a delimiter, the least frequently occurring character in the 26-letter alphabet would require 25 1s and the trailing 0.

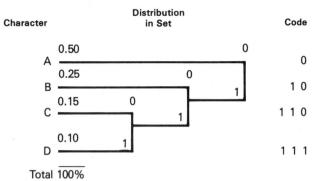

FIGURE 6-4. Huffman Code Tree

The decision chart in Figure 6-7 points to an attractive feature of Huffman coding: it can be decoded as the individual bits arrive at the receiver, without waiting for the complete user data stream to arrive.

The average bits per symbol is determined by adding all the code lengths (multiplied by their probability of occurrence). For Figure 6-4, average bits per symbol is:

$$1 * .50 + 2 * .25 + 3 * .15 + 3 * .10 = .5 + .5 + .45 + .3 = 1.75 \text{ bits/symbol}$$

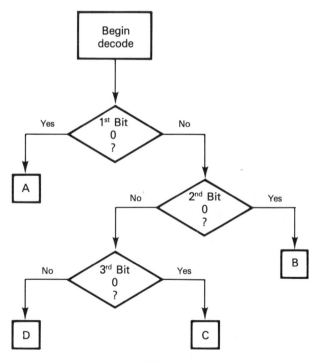

FIGURE 6-5. Huffman Decision Chart

Code Character

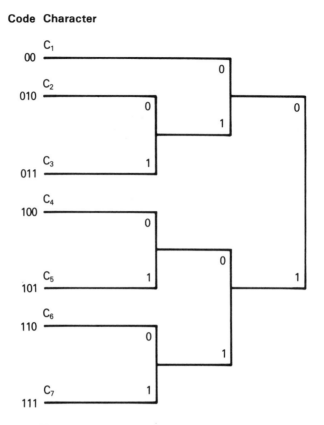

Note: Follow tree from right to left to build code.

FIGURE 6-6. Seven-Character Code Set

To determine the number of bits needed to encode a character using the Huffman scheme, the following formula applies [HELD84]:

$$B = INT \, (- \, \log_2 P)$$

Where: B = number of bits required; INT = function rounded up to nearest integer; P = probability of the occurrence of the letter in the character set.

To illustrate the use of this equation, the letter E has a probability of occurrence of .13 in the typical English text. Our formula reveals that B = 2.94, and 3 bits are required to represent it [PETE78].

The Prefix Property. Huffman codes also have a rather astonishing feature called a prefix property. This means no short code group will be interpreted as the beginning of a larger group. For example, if the bit stream 100 is a code for a symbol, then 10001 cannot be a code for another symbol since a left to right scan would detect a 100 symbol, followed by a 01 symbol [HELD84].

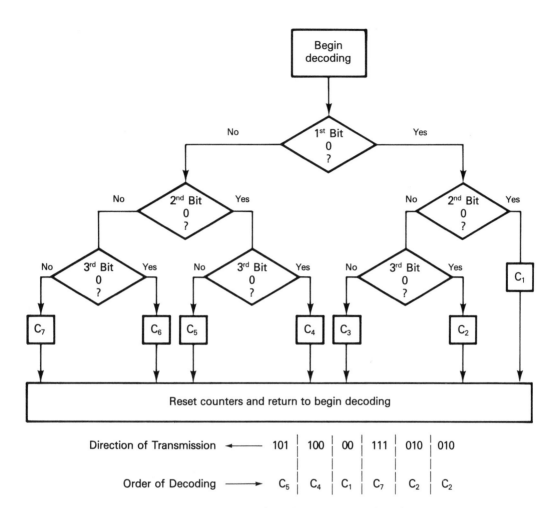

FIGURE 6-7. Decoding the Compressed Code

This property also means that it is not necessary to know where a message starts to actually decode it. The only requirement is to begin the decoding by searching for the shortest sequence of bits that constitute a known symbol.

For example, let us consider the set of symbols in Table 6-2 [PIER80]. The tree has been constructed previously to reveal the codes for the words in the left column. Assume a message is coded as "the man sells the house to the man the horse runs to the man." The message is encoded as depicted in Figure 6-8 (a). We see in Figure 6-8 (b) that the message is decoded beginning with the 7th bit in the message. In a few sequences of decoding, the decoding logic aligns the words correctly!

Of course, the first several bits are not decoded and part of the message is lost. However, if the message is repeated, the Huffman technique will eventually find the full message.

TABLE 6-2. Example of the Huffman Prefix Property

Word	Probability	Code
the	.50	1
man	.15	001
to	.12	011
runs	.10	010
house	.04	00011
likes	.04	00010
horse	.03	00001
sells	.02	00000

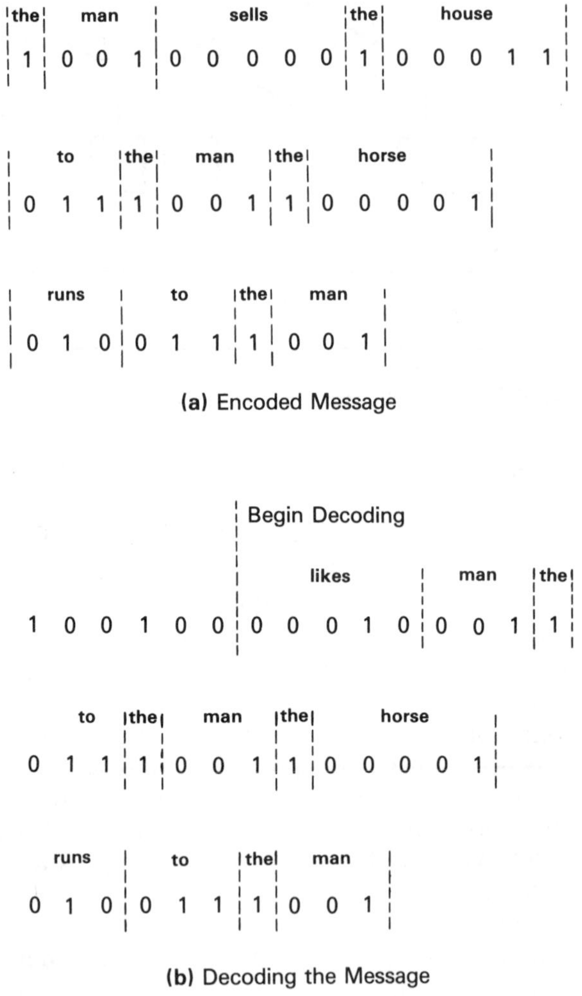

(a) Encoded Message

(b) Decoding the Message

FIGURE 6-8. Example of Huffman Prefix Property [PIER80]

The prefix property can be applied to many applications such as variable length message transmissions, and some forms of forward error correction (FEC). One of its widest uses is in data compression and facsimile systems (discussed next).

The prefix property requires the message to be encoded in blocks, not on a symbol-by-symbol basis. One reason for block encoding is to make the code with negligibly more bits than entropy. In other words, we must account for the influence of the preceding characters or the probability that a given character will be the next symbol. By using larger blocks and applying the following equation, our goals are attained:

$$H = - (1/N) \sum_i P(B_i) \log P(B_i)$$

Where: H = entropy; N = number of symbols; $P(B_i)$ = probability of a specific block of one of many blocks.

Facsimile Compression

One of the most useful applications for data compression is the transmission of documents or graphics, commonly known as facsimile transmission (FAX). Documents lend themselves to compression because their contents have many recurring redundant patterns of space (white patterns) or print patterns (black patterns). The CCITT publishes several recommended standards relating to facsimile transmission. These classes are described as Group 1, Group 2, Group 3, and Group 4 and are labeled as CCITT recommendations T.2, T.3, T.4, and T.5, respectively. Their basic characteristics are shown in Table 6-3 [RYAN86] and Table 6-4 [T.5].

Facsimile use is growing very rapidly. The price for a machine is approaching the point of costing less than a low-end personal computer. The speed of transferring one page (10 seconds) makes the use of FAX machines a

TABLE 6-3. CCITT Facsimile Recommendations

Group Number	Transmission Signal	Compression Used	Page Transfer Time
1	Analog (AM), (PM)	None	6 minutes
2	Analog (AM), (PM)	Some	3 minutes
3	Digital (with V.27 ter modulation)	Extensive	less than 1 minute
4	Digital	Extensive	less than 10 seconds

TABLE 6-4. CCITT Facsimile Group 4

Attribute	Circuit Switched Network	Packet Switched Network	Telephone Network
Interface	X.21	X.25 (levels 1, 2, 3)	Not defined
Link Procedure	LAPB of X.75	LAPB of X.25	T.71
Bit Rates	Classes of Service 4-7 of X.1	Classes of Service 8-11 or X.1	Not defined

very attractive alternative to express mail. If the trend continues, most businesses and many private citizens will have their own FAX machines.

Facsimile compression treats each facsimile line as a series of white and black runs. A scanner examines a document left to right and top to bottom and creates an electronic image of the runs. The runs are coded based on their length, and the code is transmitted instead of the full "bit picture" of the document.

The facsimile scanner creates a bit map of the page image. The bit map describes the black or white regions of the document. Each bit map contains the blackness of each dot as the document is read. A typical document would require approximately 3.5 to 4 million dots to represent an 8½ x 11-inch page, if one bit were represented per dot. It is easy to see that an excessively long transmission time would be required to process a one-page letter. However, over 80% of copy consists of white picture elements. Consequently, it is possible through compression to reduce the number of bits needed to represent the document. Moreover, successive scan lines are often similar. This permits further compression by describing only how a succeeding row differs from the preceding row. This technique is known as two-dimensional coding.

Generally, 100 scan lines per inch produce sufficient clarity in the decompression and reproduction process. Since each line uses 1728 picture elements (PELs or pixels), a sheet of paper requires 850 scan lines * 1728 PELs, or well over a million bits that must be transmitted across the communications channel. However, facsimile compression can reduce these bits by a factor of 20 or 30 to 1. Modified Huffman codes are employed for this job. They do not approach the ideal encoding scheme but they do permit the use of cost-effective equipment (FAX machines).

The document image is conveyed through codes representing the picture element (PEL). These codes were established by a study performed by the CCITT. The PEL defines the length of recurring white and black images. Each PEL is given a unique bit code. The end of line code (EOL) follows each line of data. Its format is: 000000000001. The end of document transmission is indicated by six consecutive EOLs.

Table 6-5 shows the codes for the modified Huffman code technique. Table 6-5 (a) contains codes for PELs with white or black run lengths up to

White Run Length	Code Word	Base 64 Rep	Black Run Length	Code Word
0	00110101	0	0	0000110111
1	000111	1	1	010
2	0111	2	2	11
3	1000	3	3	10
4	1011	4	4	011
5	1100	5	5	0011
6	1110	6	6	0010
7	1111	7	7	00011
8	10011	8	8	000101
9	10100	9	9	000100
10	00111	a	10	0000100
11	01000	b	11	0000101
12	001000	c	12	0000111
13	000011	d	13	00000100
14	110100	e	14	00000111
15	110101	f	15	000011000
16	101010	g	16	0000010111
17	101011	h	17	0000011000
18	0100111	i	18	0000001000
19	0001100	j	19	00001100111
20	0001000	k	20	00001101000
21	0010111	l	21	00001101100
22	0000011	m	22	00000110111
23	0000100	n	23	00000101000
24	0101000	o	24	00000010111
25	0101011	p	25	00000011000
26	0010011	q	26	000011001010
27	0100100	r	27	000011001011
28	0011000	s	28	000011001100
29	00000010	t	29	000011001101
30	00000011	u	30	000001101000
31	00011010	v	31	000001101001
32	00011011	w	32	000001101010
33	00010010	x	33	000001101011
34	00010011	y	34	000011010010
35	00010100	z	35	000011010011
36	00010101	A	36	000011010100
37	00010110	B	37	000011010101
38	00010111	C	38	000011010110
39	00101000	D	39	000011010111
40	00101001	E	40	000001101100
41	00101010	F	41	000001101101
42	00101011	G	42	000011011010
43	00101100	H	43	000011011011
44	00101101	I	44	000001010100
45	00000100	J	45	000001010101
46	00000101	K	46	000001010110
47	00001010	L	47	000001010111
48	00001011	M	48	000001100100
49	01010010	N	49	000001100101
50	01010011	O	50	000001010010
51	01010100	P	51	000001010011
52	01010101	Q	52	000000100100
53	00100100	R	53	000000110111
54	00100101	S	54	000000111000
55	01011000	T	55	000000100111
56	01011001	U	56	000000101000
57	01011010	V	57	000001011000
58	01011011	W	58	000001011001
59	01001010	X	59	000000101011
60	01001011	Y	60	000000101100
61	00110010	Z	61	000001011010
62	00110011	•	62	000001100110
63	00110100	=	63	000001100111

(a) Least Significant Digit Table (LSD)

White Run Length	Code Word	Base 64 Rep	Black Run Length	Code Word
64	11011	1	64	0000001111
128	10010	2	128	000011001000
192	010111	3	192	000011001001
256	0110111	4	256	000001011011
320	00110110	5	320	000000110011
384	00110111	6	384	000000110100
448	01100100	7	448	000000110101
512	01100101	8	512	0000001101100
576	01101000	9	576	0000001101101
640	01100111	a	640	0000001001010
704	011001100	b	704	0000001001011
768	011001101	c	768	0000001001100
832	011010010	d	832	0000001001101
896	011010011	e	896	0000001110010
960	011010100	f	960	0000001110011
1024	011010101	g	1024	0000001110100
1088	011010110	h	1088	0000001110101
1152	011010111	i	1152	0000001110110
1216	011011000	j	1216	0000001110111
1280	011011001	k	1280	0000001010010
1344	011011010	l	1344	0000001010011
1408	011011011	m	1408	0000001010100
1472	010011000	n	1472	0000001010101
1536	010011001	o	1536	0000001011010
1600	010011010	p	1600	0000001011011
1664	011000	q	1664	0000001100100
1728	010011011	r	1728	0000001100101
EOL	00000000001		EOL	000000000001

(b) Most Significant Digit Table (MSD)

TABLE 6-5. CCITT Groups 3 and 4 Codes

63; Table 6-5 (b) provides for encoding of PELs greater than 63. The two tables are used together to establish the exact code for longer PELs. The use of the two tables reduces table sizes and look-up delays.

The 0-63 table establishes the least significant digit (LSD) in the code word. The 64-1728 table (if used) represents the most significant digit (MSD) in the code word. During a scan, if a run of PELs greater than 63 is encountered, the MSD table is used to select a code word for an integer N such that N * 64 does not exceed the run length entry. The difference of the PEL length and the run length chosen from the MSD table is then applied as a key into the LSD table. Then, the remainder of the code is selected. The approach requires that (a) the first run must be a white run, and (b) the runs must alternate between black and white PELs.

Let us assume that the following PELs shown in Figure 6-9 have been encoded from a document scan through a facsimile device. Using the prefix property concept, the receiving device decodes the PELs to the original scan values.

The original scan established an overall run length of 1010 bits and the compression resulted in an encoded line of 54 bits. This results in a 19:1 compression ratio, which is a conservative achievement. Far better ratios are possible.

An Observation of the Prefix Property

Before leaving the subject of compression, let us show an example of the prefix property principle. To simplify matters, assume that a facsimile device receives the following black run bit stream: 0000111.

The receiver decodes the data on a bit-by-bit basis. The first bit is checked against a table of values (for example, the black PEL column in Table 6-5). If it matches a value in the table, the bit stream is considered to be decoded. If not, the next bit and the preceding non-decoded bits are com-

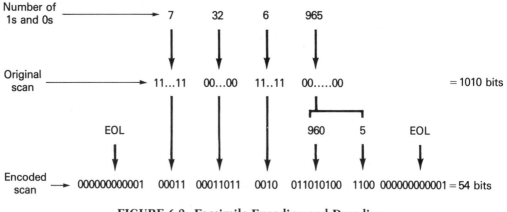

FIGURE 6-9. Facsimile Encoding and Decoding

pared to the next value in the table for a match. The process continues until a code in the table is found that matches the bit stream. The data stream of 0000111 is decoded with the procedures defined in Figure 6-10.

Just a few years ago, a standard 8½ x 11-inch document took over six minutes for transmission over a 4.8 Kbit/s line. The Huffman technique reduced this time significantly to approximately one minute. Recent improvements in compression techniques and modem speeds have further improved the process. As we learned earlier, today's systems perform the task in about 10 seconds. It is now possible to compress a television transmission of about 80 Mbit/s into a 56 Kbit/s channel (although the fidelity and resolution are not very high in quality). In the not too distant future, we will be transmitting letters, charts, and photographs with a FAX board located inside a low-cost personal computer. The possibilities are enormous.

MULTIPLEXING

A medium-speed communications line is capable of a 9.6 Kbit/s rate using multilevel modems. Theoretically, this type of line can transmit 17,280,000 bits in 30 minutes (1800 seconds * 9600 bits = 17,280,000). Yet many devices use only a small fraction of this line capacity. A keyboard terminal

Task: Decode the value 0000111 (Black Run)
Access Black Run Table and perform the following search (see Table 6-5)

Black Run Length	Search & Compare	Black Run Length Code	No Match at Bit:
0	⟶	0000110111	7
1	⟶	010	2
2	⟶	11	1
3	⟶	10	1
4	⟶	011	2
5	⟶	0011	3
6	⟶	0010	3
7	⟶	00011	4
8	⟶	000101	4
9	⟶	000100	4
10	⟶	0000100	6
11	⟶	0000101	6
12	⟶	0000111	Match

Note: The bold bits indicate where the system detects a match/no match in the data stream.

FIGURE 6-10. Observation of the Prefix Property

operated by a human typically sends and receives only a few thousand bits during a 30-minute session with the computer. Many applications by their nature do not use the link continuously. Assuming 4000 eight-bit characters were exchanged during a 30-minute period, the efficiency ratio of the total capacity of the 9.6 Kbit/s line would be 0.0018 [(4000 bytes * bits per byte)/17,280,000 bit capacity = 0.0018]. This is a very poor use of an expensive component in the data communications system. Moreover, with the increasing use of faster lines, the ratio is worse.

The solution is to provide more traffic for the path. Since many applications use low-speed keyboard terminals as input into the network, the high-speed lines can be given more traffic by placing more than one terminal device or user application on the line. The increased traffic provides better line utilization.

Multiplexers (MUXs) accept lower-speed voice or data signals from terminals, telephones, and user applications and combine them into one high-speed stream for transmission onto a link. A receiving multiplexer demultiplexes and converts the combined stream into the original multiple lower-speed signals. Since several separate transmissions are sent over the same line, the efficiency ratio of the path is improved.

Frequency-Division Multiplexing

In the previous decade, the most widely used multiplexing technique was frequency-division multiplexing (FDM). While it has largely disappeared from end-user equipment, it is still widely used in telephone, microwave, and satellite carrier systems. This approach divides the transmission frequency range (the bandwidth) into narrower bands (called subchannels). The subchannels are lower-frequency bands and each band is capable of carrying a separate voice or data signal. Consequently, FDM is used in a variety of applications such as telephone systems, radio systems, and the familiar cable television (CATV) that many people have installed in their homes. CATV provides a separate FDM band for each TV channel. Figure 6-11(a) depicts the FDM scheme.

FDM decreases the total bandwidth available to each user, but the narrower bandwidth is usually sufficient for the low-speed devices. The transmissions from the multiple users are sent simultaneously across the path. Each user is allocated a fixed portion of the frequency spectrum.

The carriers' communications channels (for example, a telephone system) are grouped together to take advantage of the greater bandwidths of coaxial cable, microwave, and satellite transmission schemes. The channels are subdivided by using frequency modulation techniques. With a carrier frequency generated for each channel. Each carrier channel is assigned a different frequency to prevent interference from other channels, and each channel is separated with unused portions of the spectrum, called guardbands.

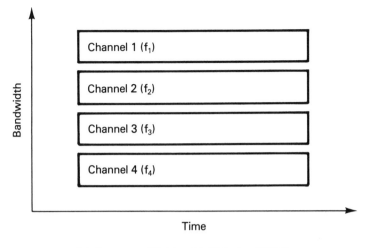

(a) Frequency Division Multiplexing (FDM)

(b) Time Division Multiplexing (TDM)

FIGURE 6-11. Multiplexing

The FDM plan in the United States uses several different modulation and multiplexing steps in the FDM hierarchy. At the lowest level, 12 voice frequency (VF) channels are combined to occupy the frequency spectrum from 60 to 108 KHz. This forms the output of the FDM channel bank. At the second level, each of the group signals modulates one of five carriers, spaced 48 KHz apart between 42 KHz and 612 KHz. The process continues until the L5E carrier system is reached, which carries 13,200 VF channels.

To gain a better understanding of FDM carrier systems, let us examine the FDM VF (voice frequency) channel bank in more detail, since it is the first frequency translation performed in the hierarchy. As Figure 6-12 depicts, 12 VF channels are modulated into the 60 to 108 KHz bandwidth as single sideband AM (SSBAM) signals at 4 KHz apart. The double sideband

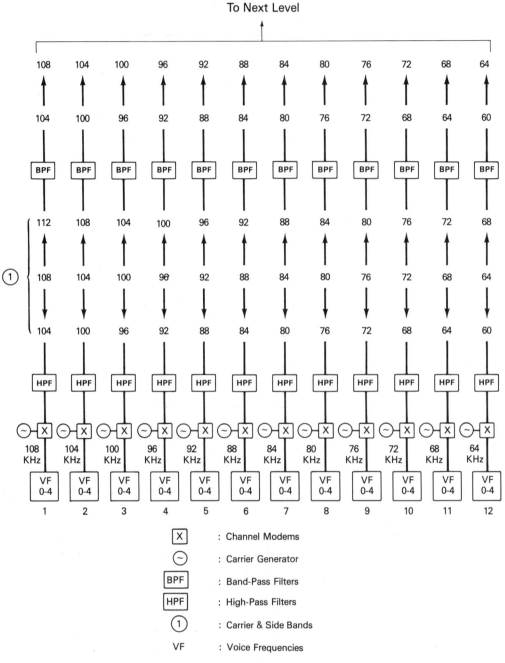

FIGURE 6-12. Creating the Basic FDM Group

signal from the modulator output is passed through a high-pass filter to filter VF energy and through a band-pass filter to suppress the upper side-band. The 12 signals are then combined to form a composite group signal. At the other end, the same types of filters select the proper channels and the demodulators translate the signals to VF.

Time-Division Multiplexing

Time-division multiplexing (TDM) provides a user the full channel capacity but divides the channel usage into time slots. Each user is given a slot and the slots are rotated among the attached users (Figure 6-11[b]). The time-division multiplexer cyclically scans the input signals (incoming data) from the multiple incoming points. Bits, bytes, or blocks of data are separated and interleaved together into frames on a single high-speed communications line. TDMs are discrete signal devices and will not accept analog data.

Figure 6-13 illustrates the structure of a typical TDM system. (For simplicity, only one direction of the full duplex operation is shown.) The TDM

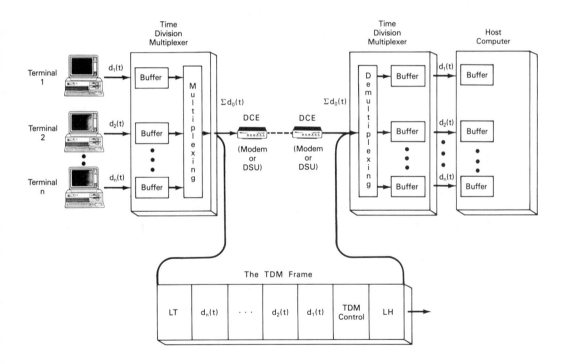

LT: Link Trailer
LH: Link Header
TDM Control: Identification of specific TDM controls (may not exist on some TDMS)
$d_n(t)$: Fixed, predetermined slots for each device.

FIGURE 6-13. A Time-Division Multiplexer (TDM)

scans each device and organizes the data into a frame. The slots in the frame are fixed such that:

$$\sum_{i=m}^{N} d_i(t) = d_0(t)$$

input lines = output line

Where: $d_i(t)$ = capacity of each device in bit/s; $d_0(t)$ = capacity of output line in bit/s; N = number of input devices.

The buffers in the multiplexer are emptied before the next data stream arrives and is placed into a reserved slot in the frame. If a device has no traffic, its slot is empty, because the slots are preassigned to the devices. Obviously, this approach (as well as FDM) leads to some wasted capacity, but it yields some benefits:

- It is simple to implement.

- It is quite effective for devices that transmit continuously or almost continuously (remote job entry station [RJE], for example).

- Many TDMs handle varying device speeds and accommodate the faster devices with more preassigned slots.

Unlike FDM, TDM is employed extensively in end-user multiplexers. It is also very widely used in carrier transmission systems. Both uses are described in this chapter.

Bit vs. Byte (Character) Multiplexing

Time-division multiplexers operate in one of two modes. The first, bit multiplexing, assigns a bit from a channel to each time slot, and the second, byte multiplexing, assigns a longer slot to a channel. These techniques are also called bit interleaving and character interleaving, respectively.

The method used depends on the type of traffic. Digitized voice systems use character interleaving because each sample is an 8-bit value. It makes sense to transmit the complete sample value in one slot. User DTEs such as terminals and computers also use character multiplexing because these systems operate on the concept of character-by-character transmission. On the other hand, systems using one-bit samples are used in systems that do not benefit from an accumulation of multiple bits. For example, we learned in Chapter 3 that delta modulation uses 1 bit per sample. Consequently it makes no sense to accumulate the samples into a word because (a) it introduces delay and (b) the accumulated samples provide no additional information.

TDM Carrier Systems

The TDM carrier hierarchy is changing as carriers implement newer systems with optical fiber and adaptive differential pulse code modulation (ADPCM) schemes. Chapter 19 describes these new systems, as well as the M44 multiplexer.

Statistical Multiplexing

The conventional TDM wastes the bandwidth of the communications line for certain applications because the time slots are often unused. Vacant slots occur when an idle terminal has nothing to transmit in its slot. Statistical TDM multiplexers (STDMs) dynamically allocate the time slots among active terminals. Figure 6-14 shows how the STDM "compresses" the empty slots out of the signal. Notice the control field in the STDM frame. It is used to identify the owners of the slots. The demultiplexer uses this control field to reassemble each channel's traffic at the receiving node and pass it to the proper recipient.

Dedicated subchannels (FDMs) and dedicated time slots (TDMs) are not provided for each port on a STDM. Consequently, idle terminal time does not waste the line's capacity. It is not unusual for two to five times as much traffic to be accommodated on lines using STDMs in comparison to a TDM.

However, it must be emphasized that statistical multiplexing performs well with "bursty" input streams. This term describes a system in which transmissions are sporadic, occurring at irregular intervals. The STDM takes advantage of this characteristic and assigns slots to devices that need the slots. Statistical multiplexers will not improve a system such as digitized voice, or remote job entry (RJE), which exhibit continuous, nonbursty characteristics.

In many statistical multiplexers, the length of the slots varies in accordance with the input data streams. These streams usually come from asyn-

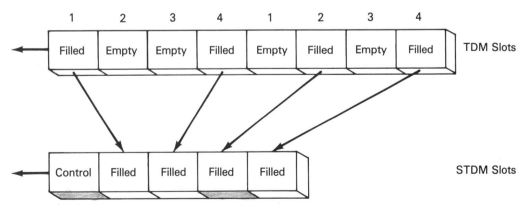

FIGURE 6-14. Statistical Time Division Multiplexing (STDM)

chronous start/stop terminals. The majority of statistical multiplexers support synchronous devices as well. Isochronous transmission is accepted on some vendor's models. The frames must contain information on which channels have transmitted data within the frame. Typically, each frame provides "mapping" (MAP) that tells which devices have data and the number of data bits or bytes in each frame. The frames also have headers, sequence numbers, and error-checking fields for purposes of identification and control.

Statistical multiplexers have evolved in a short time to become very powerful and flexible machines. Today, vendors sell machines that overlap the functions found in PBXs, message/packet switches, front ends, concentrators, and even satellite delay compensation units. STDMs have virtually taken over the FDM market and now offer serious competition to the TDMs. Statistical multiplexers also provide extensive error-checking techniques and buffer management, as well as data flow control. Some STDMs provide modulation circuitry for interfacing into analog networks. Otherwise, separate modems are required. Flow control is used to prevent the transmitting devices from sending data too fast into the multiplexer's buffers.

An STDM technique is often used with elastic buffers to manage traffic. It is called pulse stuffing. If the input lines do not create enough data to fill this fixed-length, variable-slot frame, the MUX (multiplexer) stuffs dummy bits (pulses) into fixed locations. They are identified and removed by the demultiplexer.

Figure 6-15 depicts a typical STDM configuration and an STDM frame. The MUX is configured by the number of "ports" it supports. Connections to the port and the attached devices (usually terminal work stations) is through an EIA-232 cable or some other physical level interface. The MUX may use an external modem for an interface to an analog circuit or a digital service unit (DSU) for an interface to an analog link. It may also place the modem or DSU inside the MUX cabinet.

Figure 6-15(b) illustrates the STDM frame. This frame format is identical to the frame discussed in detail in Chapter 10. The information field (I) contains the slots of data taken from the stations and a control field to identify the owners of the slots. Typically, a short address and a length indicator (LI) is sufficient to decode the slots in the I field.

Concentrators

The term concentrator is often used to describe a statistical multiplexer. This is certainly understandable since the functions of the two components overlap. Strictly speaking, a concentrator has n input lines, which, if all input devices are active, would exceed the capacity of the m output line. Consequently, in the event excessive input traffic is beginning to saturate the concentrator, some terminals are ordered to reduce transmission or are not allowed to transmit at all. We find this type of function in STDMs. Many

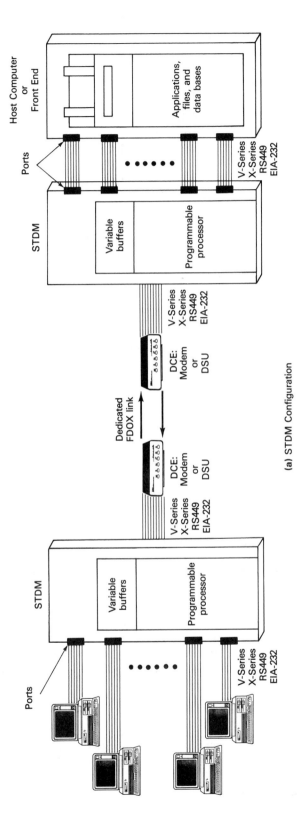

(a) STDM Configuration

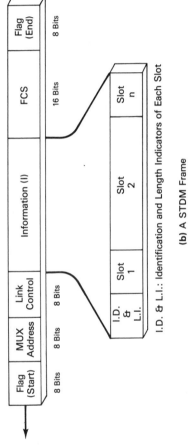

I.D. & L.I.: Identification and Length Indicators of Each Slot

(b) A STDM Frame

FIGURE 6-15. A STDM Configuration and Frame

219

people now use the terms concentrator and statistical multiplexer to mean the same thing.

Multiplexer Capacity

Calculating the load for a FDM system is a relatively simple process since the input is fixed. The TDM system requires additional considerations since queuing is utilized in the multiplexer. One approach is defined as:

$$AC = PF \sum_{I=1}^{K} (C_i L_i)$$

Where: AC = aggregate capacity of multiplexer (and output link) in bit/s; PF = processing factor to account for queuing delays and processing delays in the multiplexer; K = number of input channels; C = capacity of input channel (in bit/s); L = length of character set (in bits).

STDMs require a more detailed analysis in order to obtain proper performance and sizing. The statistical multiplexer operates as a delay system: it services requests on a demand basis and queues excess traffic in buffers and services this traffic as resources and link capacity become available. If the input demand exceeds the capacity of the MUX and/or its output line, the MUX typically issues flow control commands to the attached stations.

Statistical multiplexing requires the use of queuing analysis if the system is to properly service the traffic. Several approaches can be used to size the multiplexer. [MART72] will be used to illustrate the process. If this material is of interest to you, read the section in Chapter 5 titled "Traffic Engineering," which introduces queuing theory and the Poisson distribution.

For the reader's convenience, Box 6-1 contains the definitions of the parameters used in the equations in the remainder of this chapter. Each parameter is also explained within the context of the equation.

A multiplexer is considered a "single server" facility. The users wait to be serviced by one facility. The facility is utilized in various degrees, depending upon the demand on the facility. The facility utilization is an important factor in sizing a multiplexer. If it is too high, poor service will result and queues may become quite large.

Facility utilization can be depicted as the ratio of (a) the actual traffic on a facility to the traffic capacity of the facility or (b) the time the facility is used to the total time available at the facility. Our discussions will focus on both ratios.

Facility utilization of the multiplexer is defined as:

$$p = E(n) E(t_s)$$

Where: p = facility utilization of one serving facility; E(n) = average number of arrivals per second; $E(t_s)$ = average service time for all items.

p	Facility utilization (one server)
$E(n)$	Average number of arrivals per second
$E(t_s)$	Average service time for all items
$E(w)$	Average number of items waiting for service
σ	Standard deviation
t_s	Service time for one item
q	Number of items in the system
$E(q)$	Average number of items in the system
tq	Time an item spends in the system
$E(tq)$	Average time an item spends in the system
N	Queue size
$P(q \geqq N)$	Probability that q is greater than or equal to the stated queue size N
$P(tq \rangle T)$	Probability that tq is greater than a stated time T

In other words, p describes the fraction of time the facility (server) is busy. The facility utilization is usually compared to the average number of items waiting and being served (in the system) to estimate queue sizes.

Before calculating queue sizes, we need some more equations. The basic equation for the single server is stated as

$$E(w) = \frac{p^2}{2(1-p)} \{1 + [\sigma t_s/Et_s]^2\}$$

Where: $E(w)$ = average number of items waiting for service; σt_s = standard deviation of t_s font call (the standard deviation is the root-mean-square deviation of the values).

This formula applies to random arrival times and any distribution in the times to service the items. It holds as long as the item is not selected based on service time needed. It may be selected based on other criteria. For example, it may choose higher priority items first. However, it may be necessary to substitute this formula in situations where the system strives to lower mean service time by servicing certain items before others.

Using several substitutions, we can obtain for constant service times:

$$E(q) = p + p^2/2(1-p)$$

and for service times that are exponentially distributed:

$$E(q) = p + (p^2/1-p) = p/1-p$$

Where: $E(q)$ = average number of items in the system.

The average time an item spends in the system, $E(tq)$, is defined as:

$$E(tq) = E(t_s) [1 + (p/2(1-p))] \text{ for constant service times.}$$

and

$$E(tq) = E(t_s) [1 + (p/1-p)] = E(t_s)/1-p \text{ for exponential service times.}$$

If designers recognize that service time is not usually constant in a system, then the exponentially distributed service time formula is used.

To show the effects of these calculations, let us examine some situations where the facility utilization of a statistical multiplexer increases.

Figure 6-16 plots mean queue sizes (number of items) for a single server facility with a Poisson arrival rate and different values of σt_s. A few observations can be made regarding this plot. As the mean number of items in the queue increases, the p also increases. Moreover, as utilization reaches 80% and beyond, the queues grow very fast. (Some designers refer to this problem as exponential growth with linear input.) A small number of items may cause severe congestion, queuing overflow, and decreased performance. The same effects can be shown to exist on queuing delay as well. Figure 6-17 plots the effect on queuing delay.

The Amplification Factor

The consequence of queuing on facility utilization can be severe. In effect, it is like a rabbit hutch that is half full of rabbits. The rabbits are reproducing

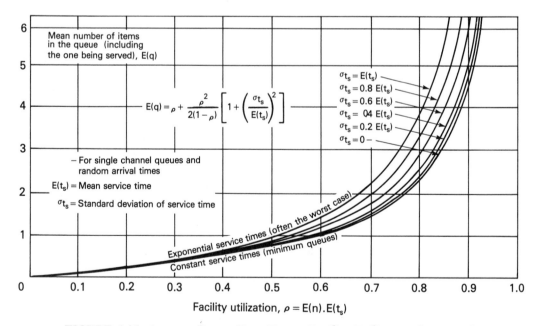

FIGURE 6-16. Average Queue Sizes Versus Facility Utilization [MART72]

Compression and Multiplexing

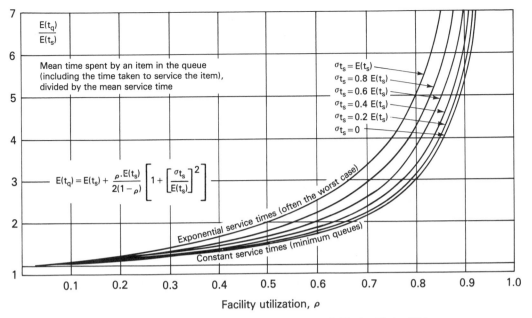

Note: Mean waiting time before being served, $E(t_w) = E(t_q) - E(t_s)$.

FIGURE 6-17. Average Queue Times Versus Facility Utilization [MART72]

at an exponential rate, so one day the hutch is half full and the next day it is full.

The same kind of effect can be seen with the Poisson process. It is known as the amplification factor. A small increase of δx in input will cause an increase in the queue size by:

$$(E(t_s) + (E(t_s) p(2-p) / 2(1-p)^2) \{1 + [\sigma_{ts} / E(t_s)]^2\}) \delta x$$

A small increase in traffic in a facility operating at 90% utilization causes an effect on queue sizes 25 times greater than if the same input traffic were applied to a facility operating at 50% utilization!

The amplification factor affects all queuing systems. Host computers perform many functions through the use of queues. Their utilization must be carefully monitored by the systems personnel.

The amplification factor is a fact of life for any system that uses delay. We will have more to say on this subject when we discuss packet switching in Chapter 13.

To provide some examples of using these figures, assume 20 customers are using a queuing system (for example, an automated teller machine [ATM] during a peak hour). On an average, it takes 2.25 minutes to service each ATM customer. The ATM is 75% utilized:

$$p = (2.25 * 20)/60 = .75$$

Upon a quick review of Figure 6-16, a facility utilization value of .75 reveals a queue length at the ATM of about 1.8 to 3.0 people, depending upon the standard deviation.

By consulting Figure 6-17 or by using E(q) = E(n) E(tq), the length of time the customer stands in the ATM queue can be determined by cross-checking the p value (x axis) to the σ curve and the mean time scale (y axis): about 2.5 to 4 minutes.

Calculating Queue Size and Waiting Time

Now that we have a general idea of how to calculate queue sizes and waiting time, it should prove useful to know how to estimate when a queue size or a waiting time is exceeded. If we do not have an understanding of these estimates, it will be very difficult to make any rational decision about sizing the multiplexer. After all, there is a great deal of difference between a multiplexer that has the "power" to keep the maximum queue size to an acceptable level 90% of the time, compared to another multiplexer that keeps the queue size to an acceptable level only 70% of the time.

As with the previous analysis, we define the probability (p) that the number of items in the system (q) is greater than the number of arrivals (N), and the probability that queuing time (tq) is greater than a specified time (T). In both equations, we assume the worst case: exponential service time.

The probability that q is greater than or equal to N is:

$$P(q \geq N) = \sum_{q=N}^{\infty} (1-p) p^q$$

The probability that tq is greater than T is:

$$P(tq > T) = e^{-(1-p) T/E(t_s)}$$

The results of these equations are plotted in Figures 6-18 and 6-19.

Sizing the Multiplexer

The reader should not assume that an organization will purchase or lease a multiplexer that ensures the desired performance goals will always be met. It may be too expensive. Therefore, cost/performance factors must be considered, and the following questions must be answered:

- What are the consequences (delayed response time, degraded throughput) to the user community if the multiplexer's capacity is exceeded?
- What is the cost to the company to provide multiplexers that always accommodate the peak load?

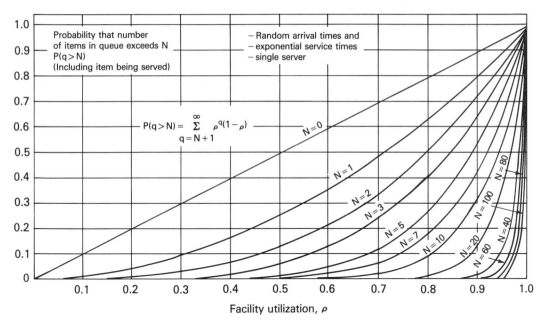

FIGURE 6-18. **Probability of Exceeding a Queue Size** [MART72]

Within the figure:

Probability that number of items in queue exceeds N
P(q > N)
(Including item being served)

— Random arrival times and
— exponential service times
— single server

$$P(q > N) = \sum_{q=N+1}^{\infty} \rho^q(1-\rho)$$

N = 0, N = 1, N = 2, N = 3, N = 5, N = 7, N = 10, N = 20, N = 40, N = 60, N = 80, N = 100

Facility utilization, ρ

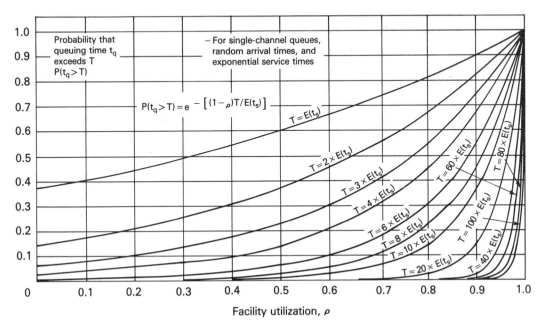

FIGURE 6-19. **Probability of Exceeding Certain Queuing Times** [MART72]

Within the figure:

Probability that queuing time t_q exceeds T
$P(t_q > T)$

— For single-channel queues, random arrival times, and exponential service times

$$P(t_q > T) = e^{-\left[(1-\rho)T/E(t_s)\right]}$$

$T = E(t_s)$, $T = 2 \times E(t_s)$, $T = 3 \times E(t_s)$, $T = 4 \times E(t_s)$, $T = 6 \times E(t_s)$, $T = 8 \times E(t_s)$, $T = 10 \times E(t_s)$, $T = 20 \times E(t_s)$, $T = 40 \times E(t_s)$, $T = 60 \times E(t_s)$, $T = 80 \times E(t_s)$, $T = 100 \times E(t_s)$

Facility utilization, ρ

• Is it possible to devise a compromise between the cost and performance issues?

The next formula can be used to assist in reaching decisions on multiplexer sizing. It is based on the following assumptions: (a) The number of devices that will use the multiplexer are known; (b) it is possible to estimate the probability of a device being busy (i.e., using the multiplexer) during a specific time (a peak hour, for example). These assumptions should be known, usually through observation of the use of the current system.

$$P(N) = N^cM * P(ON)^N * [1 - P(ON)]^{M-N}$$

Where: $P(N)$ = probability of N devices being active at the same time; $P(ON)$ = probabilty of N devices having data to send; N = number of devices with data to send; M = total number of devices; N^cM = number of possible combinations, taken N at a time. Note: N^cM represents the total number of combinations in which N devices of M total could be active at a time. This figure is calculated from the formula: $N^cM = M!/N!(M - N)!$.

Box 6-2 contains a program written in MS-DOS BASIC that executes this equation [BLAC87B]. One possible output of the program is shown in Table 6-6. The following assumptions were made for this specific execution: (a) 16 devices are to use the multiplexer (not all at once); (b) when a device is logged on to the multiplexer, it transmits data 20% of the time. The remainder of the time it is idle while the operator pauses to think, drink coffee, etc. Table 6-6 yields the following information.

Sixty-three percent of the time, four or fewer devices will have data to send. If work stations are operating at 2400 bit/s, and sharing a multiplexed line of 9600 bit/s, then queuing occurs when five or more devices have data to transmit. The queuing occurs approximately 37% of the time, and during these periods the work stations will notice decreased throughput and longer response time.

Each active device beyond three will further degrade the throughput of each device. To illustrate:

Five: 9600/5 = 1920 bit/s
Six: 9600/6 = 1600 bit/s
Seven: 9600/7 = 1371 bit/s

If the P(ON) can be reduced, then fewer devices will have data to send and queuing would occur less frequently. Of course, reducing P(ON) means reducing the activity on the devices.

In conclusion, it must be emphasized that a quantitative evaluation of queuing and response time is only as accurate as the data on which the equations operate. The parameters describing arrival rates and service times are often quite difficult to quantify. Nonetheless, Figures 6-16 through 6-19 and the related equations provide a rather simple and straightforward

BOX 6-2. Calculating STDM Loading

```
500   REM PROGRAM IS FOR STAT MUX LOADING AND QUEUING
      ESTIMATIONS
510   INPUT "TOTAL NUMBER OF DEVICES AT THIS MUX"; M
520   INPUT "PROBABILITY OF AN ACTIVE DEVICE HAVING DATA TO SEND";
      PON
530   INPUT "TOTAL WITH DATA TO SEND, IF FINISHED ENTER − 1"; N
560   IF N = − 1 THEN GOTO 720
580   FAC = M
590   GOSUB 740
600   MFAC = TOT
610   FAC = N
620   GOSUB 740
630   NFAC = TOT
640   FAC = M − N
650   GOSUB 740
660   MNFAC = TOT
670   NOM = MFAC / (NFAC * MNFAC)
680   PROB = NOM * (PON ^ N) * ((1 − PON)^(M − N))
690   LPRINT "PROBABILITY FOR "M" DEVICES WITH "N" OF THEM WITH
      DATA & BUSY "PROB
700   TOTPROB = TOTPROB + PROB: LPRINT "RUNNING TOTAL
      PROBABILITY = "TOTPROB
710   GOTO 530
720   LPRINT "SUM OF P (0) THROUGH P(N) = "TOTPROB
730   STOP
740   TOT = 1
750   FOR I = 2 TO FAC
760   TOT = TOT * I
770   NEXT I
780   RETURN
```

means to develop a general assessment of the problem. The reader is encouraged to pursue references in the "Suggested Readings" for more information.

SUGGESTED READINGS

Several sources provide descriptions of data compression techniques. [HELD84] and [REGH81] are excellent surveys of the field, and [HELD86] is highly recommended. [RUBI76] describes techniques for text compression. [RUTH72] explains compression of business files. CCITT publishes recommended standards for facsimile compression.

TABLE 6-6. Output of Program, Assuming 16 Devices with P(ON) = .2

Devices with Data To Send		Percentage of Time	Cumulative Percentage of Time (Rounded)
P(1)	=	0.053	0.063
P(2)	=	0.133	0.197
P(3)	=	0.207	0.404
P(4)	=	0.225	0.630
P(5)	=	0.180	0.810
P(6)	=	0.110	0.920
P(7)	=	0.052	0.972
P(8)	=	0.019	0.992
P(9)	=	0.005	0.998
P(10)	=	0.001	0.9997
P(11)	=	0.0002	0.9999
P(12)	=	0.00003	0.9999
P(13)	=	0.000003	0.9999
P(14)	=	0.0000002	0.9999
P(15)	=	0.00000001	0.9999
P(16)	=	0.0000000002	0.9999

Almost all books on networks contain chapters on multiplexers. [DOLL78] and [SHER85] present good overall views of the subject. For the mathematical analysis, [MART72] is somewhat old, but contains very valuable tables and charts. [CHU73] also provides detailed analysis and description of multiplexing systems. [SCHW87] is an excellent book for the more advanced reader.

QUESTIONS

TRUE/FALSE

F 1. Compression with bit mapping is rarely used for data that contain a large number of specific character types.

T 2. Bit mapping is often implemented with packed decimal compression.

T 3. Run length encoding is utilized with recurring long strings of repeating characters.

F 4. Time-division multiplexing (TDM) is utilized for analog transmission systems.

5. Statistical time-division multiplexing and concentrators operate under the same concept: the dynamic assignment of channel usage.

6. Match the description to the appropriate term:

Description

a) Based on representing most commonly used characters with the fewest number of bits.

b) Based on slight differences between values.

c) Based on the occurrence of one special character.

d) Based on the data streams in which the same characters occur frequently.

Term

1. Run length encoding
2. Huffman encoding
3. Diatomic encoding
4. Relative encoding

7. To review the principle of the prefix property, the following facsimile white run value is to be decoded: 0010111. Using Table 6-5, analyze this white code run and create a notation to show how the run is decoded (use Figure 6-10 for guidance).

8. What is the difference between multiplexing and compression?

9. Assume a frequency division multiplexed system operates with carriers spaced four KHz apart. The FDM modulators are double sideband transmitter carriers (DSBTC). Describe the signals in this system.

10. The statistical multiplexer often uses a standard frame format for transporting the user data across the communications link. Describe the contents of the frame's information (I) field.

11. A single-server statistical time-division multiplexer is utilized at $-.70$. What is the mean queue time of a unit if the multiplexer operates with a constant service time (use Figure 6-17)?

12. Referring to Question 11, if the communications system designer is tasked by management with keeping the average queue size to one, what actions must be taken?

SELECTED ANSWERS

1. False. For a description of this point, see Figure 6-2.
2. True.
3. True.
4. False. Due to the discrete time-slot requirements for time-division multiplexing, it is unsuitable for analog systems.

5. True.

6.

Description	Term
a	2
b	4
c	3
d	1

8. Multiplexing makes a better use of a potentially underused resource. Compression makes a better use of a potentially overused resource.

CHAPTER 7

Transmission Impairments, Error Detection, and Error Correction

INTRODUCTION

This chapter is divided into three sections. The first section is a description of the major causes of transmission errors. After major problems are discussed, the second section describes measures that can be taken to reduce or eliminate the presence of errors. If the problem cannot be eliminated, we then examine in the third section some techniques to detect and correct the erroneous data.

Data does not always arrive correctly at the receiving site. For numerous reasons, a bit or several bits often become distorted or garbled during transmission. A typical dial-up, voice-grade, low-speed line experiences a rate of 1 erroneous bit in every 10,000 bits transmitted (or $1:10^4$). (Unfortunately, most of the errors occur randomly.) Some user applications find this error rate acceptable and might choose to ignore an infrequent error. However, certain applications cannot tolerate any errors. For example, the loss of 1 bit in a transmission of financial data could have severe consequences for a funds transfer system. For these applications, the transmission must be made as error-free as possible.

Treating errors in a data communications system is a more difficult task than one might imagine. Four factors contribute to this situation:

1. Distance between components
2. Transmission over hostile environments
3. Number of components involved in transmission
4. Lack of control over the process

231

Distance Between Components

Computers and terminals connected by communications links may be located hundreds of miles from each other. The transmission speed of the signals between the sites can be very fast, as in a radio transmission (186 miles per 1 ms), or considerably slower, as in certain wire pairs (10 miles per 1 ms). Whatever the propagation speed may be, the distance introduces a delay.

Error analysis is made more difficult due to the distances involved and the inherent delays in receiving an indication of a problem. It is not unusual for an error condition on a transmission path to disappear after a few fractions of a second without a trace to its origin. Such an error would usually be identified in a centralized mainframe environment. The longer the delay in error analysis, the more difficult it is to identify and resolve the error.

Transmission Over Hostile Environments

When we consider the differences between the data communications and centralized mainframe environments, it becomes clear that data communications systems are more subject to error because the transmissions take place through a "hostile" environment. A microwave signal is illustrative. During transmission, it may encounter varying temperatures, fog, rain, and snow, as well as other microwave signals that tend to distort the signal.

On the other hand, the flow of data inside a computer room is subject to strict temperature, humidity, and electromagnetic radiation controls. It is not surprising that the error rate on a channel inside a computer room is several orders of magnitude better than that of a voice-grade communications line.

Number of Components Involved in Transmission

A transmission through a communications system travels through several components, and each component introduces an added probability of errors. For example, as a signal moves through a network, it must pass through switches, modems, multiplexers, and other instruments. If the interfaces among these components are not established properly, an error is likely to occur, and the components themselves often introduce errors. For instance, some of the older circuit switches can create considerable interference on the line. Moreover, line segments connected in tandem (to form an end-to-end channel) are more error-prone than one stand-alone link.

Lack of Control Over the Process

The centralized mainframe operating system (OS) exercises considerable control over its resources. Events do not usually occur without the permission of the OS. In the event an error occurs, the operating system interrupts the work in progress, suspends the problem program, stores its registers and buffers, and executes the requisite analysis to uncover the problem. In a sense, the error and problem are "frozen" to simplify the analysis.

A data communications system may not allow for this type of control. First, it is often impractical to suspend and freeze resources because they may be used by other components. Second, their condition may have changed by the time a network control component receives the error indication. Third, networks do not always operate under the tight centralized manner found in the centralized mainframe. For example, one computer in a network may not be allowed to control and analyze errors that affect it because they occur in other parts of the system. This problem is especially evident if networks are internetworked together.

MAJOR IMPAIRMENTS

Transmission impairments can be broadly defined as random or nonrandom events. The random events cannot be predicted. Nonrandom impairments are predictable and, therefore, are subject to preventive maintenance efforts. The following list contains the major kinds of transmission impairments often found on communications circuits.

Thermal noise
Electrical noise
Transients
Crosstalk
Echoes
Intermodulation noise
Phase jitter
Timing jitter
Radio signal fading
Attenuation
Delay
Harmonic distortion
Spacing and marking distortion

Thermal Noise

The nonrandom movement of electrons creates an electric current on a hardwire that is used for the transmission signal. Along with these signals, all electrical components also experience the vibrations of the random movement of electrons. These vibrations create thermal energy and cause the emission of electromagnetic waves of many frequencies. The phenomenon is also called white noise because it contains an average of all the spectral frequencies equally, just as white light does. Other names are Gaussian and random noise. Figure 7-1 shows an example of thermal noise [MART76].

FIGURE 7-1. Thermal Noise [MART76]

The power of noise is proportional to temperature, as demonstrated by:

N = k TW

Where: N = power of noise; k = Boltzman's constant: $1.37 * 10^{-23}$ joules per degree; T = temperature in degrees kelvin; W = bandwidth.

Practically speaking, this equation is of little value for earth circuits but is important to deep-space communications, because the system can operate with reduced power while in low-temperature space conditions. This equation also demonstrates that channel capacity is not exactly proportional to bandwidth, because bandwidth is only part of the equation. The doubling of bandwidth does not double the capacity. Figure 7-2 depicts the relationship [MART76].

One partial solution to the noise problem for voice communications is the use of a compandor. This device prevents strong (high amplitude) signals from overloading an amplifier. It reduces the volume range by compressing these signals before they are transmitted. The low amplitude or weak signals are also raised above the probable noise level for transmission across the line. Since the noise is not yet detected by the transmitter, the noise level is not amplified by the compandor. The process is changed at the receiver. The compandor restores the signal to its original range, and the noise is lowered to a level below the level that existed on the channel. The expander reverses the effect of the compressor by adding a loss which is equal to the compressor gain. Generally, the use of compandors improves the signal-to-noise ratio by about 20 dB.

Electrical Noise

This impairment includes aspects of background noise but warrants further discussion. Electrical noise stems from high-voltage, high-frequency inter-

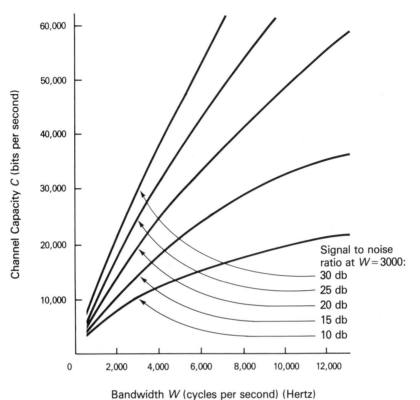

FIGURE 7-2. Noise, Bandwidth, and Channel Capability [MART76]

ference on a line. Two basic types of electrical noise exist: common mode (electrical interference between line and ground) and transverse mode (interference across lines).

Electrical noise stems primarily from two sources. First, radio frequency interference (RFI) originates from television, radio, microwave, and radar transmissions. Distant lightning can create electrical noise, and machinery such as arc welders is also a source. Second, electromagnetic interference (EMI) originates from equipment such as motor drive devices and heating and cooling units. Even seemingly innocuous devices such as electric pencil sharpeners and electric typewriters are a source of EMI.

Transients

This impairment is a major cause of errors in a data transmission. The sources of transients are many. All unwanted electronic effects, such as voltage changes, dialing noise, dirty electrical contacts, and movement of poorly connected electrical joints are contributing factors to transients. The telephone system's older step-by-step switches and the electric power companies' power supplies are also a major source of transients, and of course, electrical storms create serious transients.

A short transient may last only a few milliseconds. In these instances, it can be easily detected with simple and inexpensive logic at the receiver. Some transients last 10-20 ms. Consequently, a 4800 bps transmission would have about 50 bits affected by the 10 ms impairment; a 9600 bps line would lose about 100 bits. In either case, simple checks may not work and error correction would be more difficult. The message is usually retransmitted.

Crosstalk

Most of us who use the public telephone network have experienced the interference of another party's faint voice on our line. This is crosstalk (or intelligible crosstalk), the interference of signals from another channel. One source of crosstalk is in physical circuits that run parallel to each other in building ducts and telephone facilities. The electromagnetic radiation of the signals on the circuits creates an inductance and capacitance effect on the nearby circuits. Crosstalk can also occur with the coupling of a transmitter and receiver at the same location, which is called near-end crosstalk, or NEXT. The coupling of a transmitter to an incorrect remote receiver is called far-end crosstalk, or FEXT. Near-end and far-end crosstalk travel in different directions.

Echoes

Almost everyone using a telephone has also experienced echoes during a conversation. The effect is similar to being in an echo chamber; the talker's voice is actually echoed back to the telephone handset. Echoes are caused by the changes in impedances in communications circuits. (Impedance is the combined effect of inductance, resistance, and capacitance of a signal at a particular frequency.) For example, connecting two wires of different gauges could create an impedance mismatch. Echoes are also caused by circuit junctions that erroneously allow a portion of the signal to find its way into the return side of a four-wire circuit.

An echo is often not noticed. The feedback on a short-distance circuit happens so quickly that it is not perceptible. Generally, an echo with a delay of greater than 45 ms (0.045 sec) presents problems. For this reason, long-distance lines and satellite links employ techniques to reduce the strength of the echo or eliminate it completely. The techniques are called (a) via net loss, (b) echo suppression, and (c) echo cancellation. They are discussed later in this chapter.

Intermodulation Noise

Chapter 6 describes the common carrier's frequency multiplexed systems wherein many voice-grade circuits are modulated onto a high-capacity link, such as coaxial cable and microwave. These channels can interfere with each other if the equipment is slightly unlinear. Typically, two signals from two separate circuits combine (intermodulate) to form a frequency band reserved for another circuit. The reader has likely heard intermodulation noise during a telephone call; it sounds like a jumble of low speaking voices, none clearly perceptible.

Intermodulation noise can occur in the transmission of data when a modem uses a single frequency to keep the line synchronized when data are not being sent. The single frequency may actually modulate a signal on another channel. This problem can be avoided by transmitting either a variable-frequency signal or a signal of low amplitude. Intermodulation noise can also stem from the data within the transmission. A repetitive code in the transmission could create the problem. In Chapter 3, coding schemes are described that eliminate a repetitive code transmission. We also discuss this topic later in this chapter.

Phase Jitter

Occasionally, a signal's phase will jitter, causing an ill-defined crossing of the signal through the receiver. The signal appears to be frequency or phase modulated. Noise-laden signals resemble jitter but are caused by different impairments. Jitter is usually created by a multiplexed carrier system that creates a forward and backward movement of the individual frequency, and a ringing current (of 20 Hz) can cause phase jitter on an adjacent channel. Most phase jitter measurements are made below 300 Hz.

Timing Jitter

The synchronizing clocks introduced in Chapter 3 are subject to instabilities due to noise and other factors. For example, high-frequency components of the signal undergo more attenuation than low-frequency components. This effect spreads the signal out in time. The term used to describe this problem is timing jitter. Since a device often derives its outgoing clock from the incoming signal, the jitter builds up at each clock recovery point on the link (like a repeater) in the system. Excessive buildup causes the actual loss of the clock.

Radio Signal Fading

Microwave transmissions are particularly subject to fading. This impairment occurs in two ways. The first, selective fading, occurs when the atmospheric conditions bend a transmission to an extent that signals reach the receiver in slightly different paths. The merging paths can cause interference and create data errors. Other channels in the microwave transmission are not affected by a selective fade. Therefore, backup channels are usually provided to allow for protection against this problem.

Flat fading is a more serious problem because it can last several hours and alternate channels will not provide relief. Flat fading occurs during fog and when the surrounding ground is very moist. These conditions change the electrical characteristics of the atmosphere. A portion of the transmitted signal is refracted and does not reach the receiving antenna.

Attenuation

The strength of a signal attenuates (decays) as it travels through a transmission path. The amount of attenuation depends on the frequency of the signal, the transmission medium, and the length of the circuit. Unfortunately, signal attenuation is not the same for all frequencies. The nonuniform loss across the bandwidth can create amplitude distortion (which is also referred to as attenuation distortion) on a voice channel.

To combat the loss on the line, inductive loading is utilized. The use of inductive loading provides a means of reducing the natural loss in the cable. By placing loading coils at regular intervals in the subscriber loop, the electrical loss throughout a specific range of frequencies can be better managed. Since the natural loss of a cable increases rapidly with frequency and distance, the loading systems can be used to create a consistent performance across the bandwidth in the channel. The characteristics of loaded and non-loaded loops are shown in Figure 7-3. They permit the wire to be extended up to three times the length of non-loaded circuits.

However, loaded cables act like a low-pass filter and severely attenuate frequencies above 3000 Hz. Figure 7-3 shows this effect on loaded and non-loaded cable. Loaded cable reduces the signal propagation by as much as a factor of three, which increases transmission delay. Loading also introduces significant delay distortion (which requires equalization on longer lines). Also, VF repeaters are required to obtain additional range, due to the attenuation.

Delay

A signal consists of many frequencies. These frequencies do not travel at the same speed, and they arrive at the receiver at different times. Excessive delays create errors known as delay distortion, or envelope delay. The problem is not serious for voice transmissions because a human ear is not very

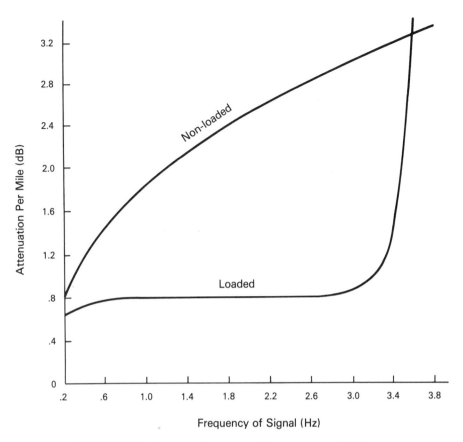

FIGURE 7-3. Attenuation versus Frequency and Distance

sensitive to phase. However, delay distortion creates problems for data transmissions.

The variation of propagation is equivalent to a phase shift and is also called phase distortion. The problem is depicted in Figure 7-4, which shows the effect of the delay of a wave from the 1- and 3-KHz frequency components. Contrast this figure with Figure 2-16 (a) in which all harmonics are in perfect alignment. The higher frequency experiences 0.135 ms more delay, which significantly changes the resultant shape of the wave at the receiver.

Harmonic Distortion

Certain electronic components generate signal components that are not present in the original transmitted signal. Amplifiers, modulators, and demodulators may produce these added signals. They are called harmonics because they are integer multiples of the original signal. The effect is also called nonlinear distortion. The amplitude of the output of the device is nonlinearly proportional to the output.

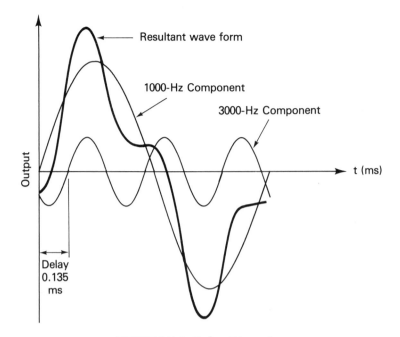

FIGURE 7-4. Delay Distortion

Spacing and Marking Distortion

This error occurs when the receiving component samples the incoming signal at the wrong interval or threshold, and/or the signal takes too long to build up and decay on the channel. This problem can occur in interfaces such as EIA-232 (V.28) if the EIA standard is not followed. EIA specifies that the capacitance of the cable and the terminator shall be less than 2500 picofarads (a measure of capacitance). If this specification is violated, the transition from a 1 (mark) to a 0 (space), and vice versa, may exceed the EIA-232 standard stated as "time required to pass through the -3 V to $+3$ V or $+3$ V to -3 V transition region shall not exceed 1 millisecond or 4% of a bit time, whichever is smaller."

The net effect of this impairment is that the signal takes too long to complete the transitions from (or to) marks and spaces. Spacing distortion results when the receiver produces space bits longer than the mark bits. Marking distortion occurs when the mark bits are elongated.

These problems may cause data errors, especially if the sampling clock is inaccurate and noise exists on the line. As we learned earlier, the spreading of a pulse signal can affect timing and lead to accumulated timing jitter.

ERROR-CONTROL METHODS

In this section we examine several options and choices that can reduce the number of data errors that result from the transmission distortions.

The primary objective in devising error-control methods is to provide perceived availability to the user. This means that an error or malfunction in the network remains invisible; the user perceives that the system is fully operational. From the user's point of view, perceived availability is achieved by the network providing optimum performance in:

Mean time between failure (MTBF)

Mean time to recover (MTTREC)

Mean time to repair (MTTREP)

MTBF should be increased to the greatest extent possible. This is accomplished in two ways. First, failures are reduced to the maximum extent possible and second, the scope of effect of the failures is kept as isolated as possible.

MTTREC is kept as low as possible. In the event of a failure, the recovery should be fast. For example, redundant components should assume network functions without perceptible delay. In the event a component fails, MTTREP requires rapid diagnosis of the problem and facilities that provide rapid corrective action.

The MTBF, MTTREC, and MTTREP performance factors should be continuously monitored. The installation should establish performance thresholds against which the system is measured. The statistics should provide for both trend analysis and identification of potential trouble areas for preventive maintenance.

Mitigating the Effects of Distortions

Combating noise. The first task in dealing with a noise problem is to determine the type and extent of the noise. As a start, noise power should be measured. Since noise usually manifests itself within a predominant frequency component, weighting filters are often used to identify the noise source. Several techniques are used to measure noise, and one of the most common is the use of the C-message filter and the notch filter.

The C-message filter (Figure 7-5 [a]) measures typical noise levels that exist in a telephone voice transmission. It is not really relevant to data transmissions, but it is widely used for noise measurements. The notch filter is used with the C-message filter because noise is generated by the communications device. The notch filter (Figure 7-5 [b]) removes the signal (tone)

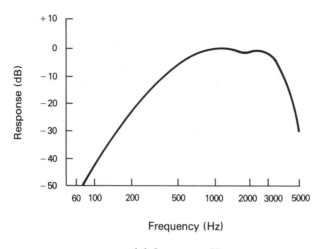

(a) C-message Filter

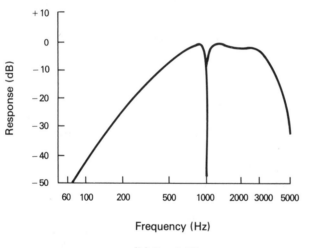

(b) Notch Filter

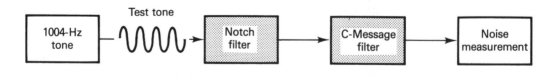

(c) Using Both Devices

FIGURE 7-5. The C-Message and Notch Filters

before the noise is measured. Typically, a 1004-Hz test tone is transmitted and notched out so the resultant noise can be measured (Figure 7-5 [c]).

The signal-to-noise (S/N) ratio can be computed by comparing the level of the test tone with the noise. An acceptable channel limits the S/N ratio to 28 dB minimum. This check is a quick and easy method to determine the quality of a channel, but unlike the notched filter, it does not isolate the source of the noise.

Power line noise can also be diminished by the installation of power protection devices. Some of the more commonly used are the following:

Passive filter. Attenuates noise in a specific band of frequencies.

Surge suppressor. Clips high-voltage transients.

Ultraisolation transformer. Limits current to protect against overloads and short circuits.

Uninterrupted power supply (UPS). Provides power in case of brownouts or blackouts.

Several of these functions can be acquired in one device.

Combating crosstalk and intermodulation noise. Shielding can diminish the effect of crosstalk on cable pairs, and filters are often employed on frequency-division multiplexing (FDM) systems to avoid channel overlap. Most carrier systems also place guardbands between channels to reduce channel interference.

Telephone companies are quite zealous in dealing with crosstalk for voice systems, since intelligible crosstalk means a loss of privacy. Therefore, carriers establish a crosstalk index which is a value representing the probability of hearing an intelligible signal from another channel. The index varies from 0.1% to 1.0%. The variance depends on the type of trunk/loop used for the connection.

Dealing with echoes. Echo suppressors are used to filter out the unwanted signals that are sent back to the transmitter. A suppressor can be placed on the return circuit to suppress the echoes. The suppressor determines which signal is on the line from a talker and inserts a very high loss (35 dB or more) in the opposite direction of the speaker.

Echo suppressors cannot be used for data transmission over a voice line. The speech detector is designed to detect speech signals. Moreover, the delay in reversing the activation of the suppressors at each end often causes the clipping of the first part of a signal. Clipping also occurs when two persons talk at the same time. The clipping effect is probably familiar to the reader. It does not usually present serious problems in a voice transmission, but can cause distortions in a data transmission.

Since the telephone network is a primary facility in a data communications network, the echo suppressors must be disabled for data transmissions.

This is accomplished by the transmission of a 2000- to 2250-Hz signal for approximately 400 ms. In the event the transmission of messages is not continuous, a signal must be placed on the line to keep the suppressors disabled. Carrier signals can accomplish this purpose.

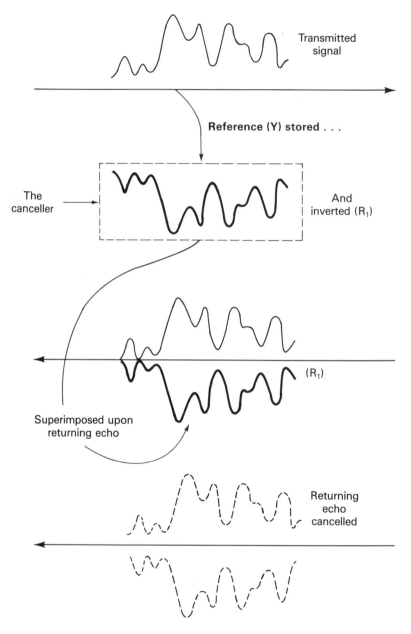

FIGURE 7-6. Echo Cancellation [BLAC87a]

Echo cancellation is another technique for handling echoes. As Figure 7-6 illustrates, a canceller is placed near the origin of the echo [BLAC87A]. A reference signal (Y) is sent to the canceller. In effect, this is a replica of the transmitted signal. The replica is inverted and stored as R_1. The echo (R) is returned along with the near-end talker signal. The canceller then uses the R_1 signal to subtract from the signal. As Figure 7-6 shows, the (R) is an inverted replica of the transmitted voice pattern. By superimposing it onto the returning signal, the echo is cancelled.

Echo cancellation is used in both voice and data transmission. The Y reference signal for a data echo canceller is the sequence of transmitted data signals. Full duplex data channels have no echo problem since there is no receiver on the transmitting end to be affected by the echo.

Another technique to deal with echo is called the via net loss plan (VNL). This plan introduces a loss in the path to the listener and in the return path to the talker. The actual loss depends upon the length and type of circuit. Echo exceeding 45 ms and/or a toll trunk greater than 185 miles requires the use of an echo suppressor or an echo canceller.

Phase jitter. Phase jitter presents few problems for voice transmission since the ear is insensitive to phase, but phase modulation modems are particularly sensitive to phase jitter. Timing problems often result and the modems can lose synchronization for several seconds.

Phase jitter can be measured by sending a test tone (usually 1004 Hz) to a receiver that establishes a reference phase to measure the jitter (based on the phase reference). Most carrier standards permit no more than 10° or 15° jitter on their systems.

Removing timing jitter. As we learned in previous discussions, timing jitter can accumulate to the point a message (frame) loses synchronization. Ironically, one approach to deal with jitter is to ensure that the timing "slip" causes the deletion of an entire frame. The frame is recovered by layer 2 protocols and the link remains synchronized.

Controlled frame deletion is accomplished by using an elastic buffer which is increased or decreased by one full frame as the slip occurs (see Figure 7-7). The process works by the system writing the data into memory. The output logic fetches the data from the memory location in the same sequential order as it was written. The system is structured with the following rules:

- The read times occur midway between the write times, permitting timing variations of $\frac{1}{2}$ a frame size.
- The memory "writes" use alternate memory locations.
- The memory "reads" use the same alternating scheme after being given the correct address (or automatically flip-flopping to the alternate locations).

In Figure 7-7, we assume the output clock (OC) is faster than the input clock (IC). Eventually, the memory reads will access the same frame twice. Due to the lower IC, the write logic has not received directions to access memory address 2. (A more typical system automatically reads the alternate location and accesses the same data from a previous read.) Therefore, it performs a double read.

However, it is easy to program the write logic with a counter so that it knows it has read from the same location or data twice. It discards the frame and as Figure 7-7 shows, the read logic then accesses the correct memory location.

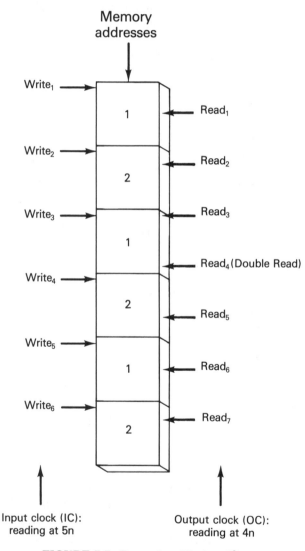

FIGURE 7-7. Removing Timing Slips

The time between slips ΔT is defined as:

$$\Delta T = N/\Delta R$$

Where: N = number of bits that are dropped or repeated due to a slip; ΔR = difference between input and output data rates.

Other methods are used to remove timing jitter. The frame deletion method we just examined is used on several AT&T/Bell digital switches. Discussion of the other methods, notably pulse stuffing, must be deferred until we examine digital frames in more detail (Chapter 19).

Diminishing the effects of attenuation and delay distortion. A user has two options in reducing the effects of attenuation and delay distortion. Line "conditioning" can be purchased from the telephone company for leased lines. The carrier adds special equipment to the circuit, such as amplifiers, attenuation equalizers, and delay equalizers.

Conditioning provides measures to diminish the problems of attenuation and delay but it does not remove the impairments. Rather, it provides for more consistency across the bandwidth. For attenuation, the common carrier introduces equipment that attenuates those signals in the bandwidth that tend to remain at a higher level than others. Thus, attenuation still occurs but is more evenly distributed across the channel. The same idea is used in delay. The faster frequencies are slowed so that the signal is more consistent across the band.

An attenuation equalizer adds a loss to the lower frequencies of the signal, since these frequencies decay less than the higher frequencies in the band. The result is that the signal loss is consistent throughout the transmitted band. After equalization is applied, amplifiers restore the signal back to its original level.

A delay equalizer compensates for envelope delay. The higher frequencies reach the receiver ahead of the lower frequencies. Consequently, the equalizer introduces more delay to these frequencies to make the entire signal propagate to the receiver at the same time.

The second option is to use modems that are equipped with equalizers. Conditioning is not available over the switched telephone network, so these modems may be required, especially for high rates of data transmission.

Reducing the effects of harmonics and noise. The telephone company also provides a service called D conditioning to address harmonic distortion and noise. It is an option that was developed primarily for 9600 bit/s operation. The standard specification requires a signal-to-noise ratio of not less than 24 dB, a second harmonic distortion of not more than -25 dB, and a third harmonic distortion of not more than -30 dB. With the conditioning service, the carrier gives a S/N ratio specification of 28 dB, a signal-to-second-harmonic distortion ratio of 35 dB, and a signal-to-third-harmonic distortion of 40 dB.

Testing and Monitoring

The majority of communications networks have a network management center (NMC). The NMC is responsible for the reliable and efficient operation of the network. It monitors and tests the communications systems and repairs or replaces failed components. The NMC is also responsible for day-to-day preventive maintenance operations in the network. It uses a wide variety of tools and techniques to keep the network running smoothly and to provide perceived availability to the user. The NMC may use the following equipment. (All equipment described in the following section may have overlapping functions.)

Typical Diagnostic Equipment

Testing and monitoring communications channels and networks are very important in achieving perceived availability to the user. Without question, a high positive correlation exists between problem resolution/system availability and the use of diagnostics and monitoring. The use of test equipment allows a facility to isolate and identify the majority of problems and to furnish the carrier with credible data. If the carrier has test results from which to begin the troubleshooting analysis, hours of downtime are often saved.

Pattern generators and analyzers introduce a signal into the channel. A typical product transmits specific bit patterns and analyzes the return signal in order to detect errors at specific points in the channel. These devices pinpoint error locations and measure bit error rates.

Pattern generators need not interrupt main channel data flow. A technique known as side-channel testing provides simultaneous data and test signal transmission. To implement side-channel diagnosis, a modem divides the channel into two subchannels, one for data and one for testing.

A breakout box plugs into the two cables connecting two devices by using an interface such as a V.24/EIA-232. The breakout box acts like a tap and enables the testing of signal timing, voltage levels, and data quality. Breakout boxes are also used to test the DTE circuitry (i.e., logic) for the V.24/EIA-232 or V- and X-series interface.

A protocol tester simulates the system host and terminal ends of the link to verify that the line protocol, usually stored in the DTEs, is functioning properly. Most of the numerous protocol testers available test the following commonly used protocols:

IBM binary synchronous communications (BSC)
IBM synchronous data link control (SDLC)
ISO high-level data link control (HDLC)
CCITT X.25
Various asynchronous protocols

Protocol testers verify such functions as polling, device select, the proper sending and receiving of status messages (e.g., from a device coming on line for the first time), correct user data transmission, and the DTE message error-checking capability.

A transmission monitor passively monitors a circuit to analyze the quality of a signal. A typical monitor performs the following tests:

Marking and spacing distortion
Gain hits
Background noise
Delay
Carrier signal dropouts
Harmonic distortion
Clock slip (loss of synchronization)
Jitter

Bit and Block Error Rates

Channel quality is often measured by the number of erroneous bits received during a given period. This bit error rate (BER) is derived by dividing the number of bits received in error by the number of bits transmitted. A typical error rate on a high-quality leased telephone line is as low as $1:10^6$. In most cases, the errors occur in bursts and cannot be predicted precisely. The BER is a useful measure for determining the quality of the channel, calibrating it, and pinpointing its problems.

BER should be measured over a finite time interval, and the time measurement should be included in the description of the error rate. The following equation calculates BER:

$$BER = B_e/RT_m$$

Where: R = channel speed in bits per second; B_e = number of bits in error; T_m = measurement period in seconds.

The actual bit sequences are important to BER. Pseudorandom bit sequences have all the appearance of random digital data. These sequences, generated in repeating lengths of $2^n - 1$ bits, will generate all but one possible word combination of bit length n. The most common sequences (defined by CCITT) are 511 and 2047 bits long, representing $n = 9$ and $n = 11$, respectively.

The block error rate (BLER) is a ratio of the number of blocks received that contain at least one erroneous bit to the total blocks received. BLER is thus calculated by dividing the number of blocks (also called frames) received in error by the number of blocks transmitted. The BLER is an effective calculation for determining overall throughput on the channel and is often used by network designers to perform line loading and network topology configuration.

Another useful calculation is to determine the percentage of seconds during a stated period in which no errors occur. Error-free seconds (EFS) are calculated by:

$$\% \text{ EFS} = [S - S_e/S] \times 100\%$$

Where: S = measurement period in seconds; S_e = number of 1-second intervals during which one bit error occurred.

The parameter S is important since, like T_m in BER, it is necessary to specify a measuring interval. The period tested may be hours or even days.

EFS is a valuable measure of performance on channels where data are transmitted in blocks (e.g., an HDLC/SDLC channel). BER is not a very good measure of performance of throughput, but it is widely used to evaluate the performance of modems and other DCEs.

Loopbacks

A problem communications link is tested by placing the modems in a loopback mode. Practically all modems can be put into loopback tests with a switch on the modem (see Figure 7-8; note: the loop numbers conform to CCITT V.54). The loopback signals are analyzed to determine their quality and the bit error rate resulting from the tests. The loopbacks can be sent through the local modem to test its analog and digital circuits; this test is called a local loopback (or loop 3). The DTE interface logic can be tested with an internal loopback (loop 1). If the bit error rate is not beyond a specified level, the next step is likely to be a remote line loopback that tests the carrier signal and the analog circuitry of the remote modem (loop 4). The remote modem must be placed in the loopback mode in order for this test to be completed. Care should be taken in drawing conclusions from the remote analog loopback tests since the looped signal may be tested at twice its specification. Due to this problem, it is often advisable to send the signal through the remote modem digital circuitry in order to boost the signal power. This test is called a remote digital loopback (loop 2).

ERROR DETECTION

Since errors are inevitable in a data communications system, some method of detecting the errors is required. While the methods vary, they all have one goal: detect the corrupted bits.

Parity Checking

Vertical redundancy check (VRC). VRC is a simple parity technique. It consists of adding a single bit (a parity bit) to each string of bits that comprise a character. The bit is set to 1 or 0 to give the character bits an odd

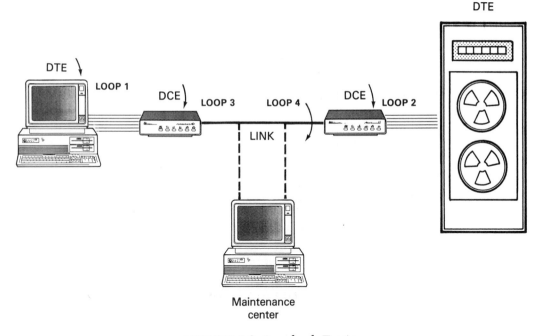

FIGURE 7-8. Loopback Testing

or even number of bits that are (a) 1s for a 1-parity protocol or (b) 0s for a 0-parity protocol. This parity bit is inserted at the transmitting station, sent with each character in the message, and checked at the receiver to determine if each character is the correct parity. If a transmission impairment caused a "bit flip" of 1 to 0 or 0 to 1, the parity check would so indicate. Figure 7-9 shows the single parity check logic. The second bit of the third character is distorted due to noise, etc. Since the VRC bit was set to a 1 to give the third character an odd number of 1 bits (in this case, five 1 bits), the detection of an even number of 1 bits serves as an indicator of error. The protocol may then ask for a retransmission or ignore the error if it is of no consequence.

The single parity check works well enough for a single bit error, but errors also occur in "clusters." Figure 7-9 (b) shows this type of error will not be detected. The problem is illustrated in Figure 7-10 [STAL85]. At a transmission rate of 1200 bit/s, the probability of more than one erroneous bit occurring within seven bits is almost 50 percent. Fortunately, the multiple bit errors may not occur within one character in the data stream, but may fall between two successive characters. Nonetheless, the problem is serious enough to apply to other methods. A common solution to the single parity check problem is the use of additional parity checks.

Longitudinal Redundancy Check (LRC). LRC is a refinement of the VRC approach. In addition to a parity bit on each character, LRC places a

Characters

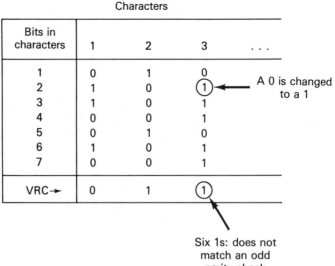

Bits in characters	1	2	3	. . .
1	0	1	0	
2	1	0	① ← A 0 is changed to a 1	
3	1	0	1	
4	0	0	1	
5	0	1	0	
6	1	0	1	
7	0	0	1	
VRC→	0	1	①	

Six 1s: does not
match an odd
parity check

(a) Error is detected

Characters

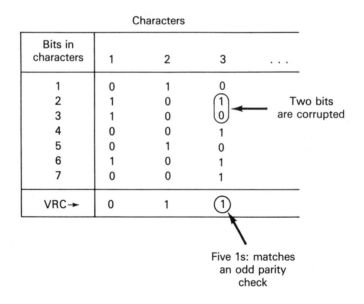

Bits in characters	1	2	3	. . .
1	0	1	0	
2	1	0	1 ← Two bits are corrupted	
3	1	0	0	
4	0	0	1	
5	0	1	0	
6	1	0	1	
7	0	0	1	
VRC→	0	1	①	

Five 1s: matches
an odd parity
check

(b) Error is undetected

FIGURE 7-9. A Single Bit Error Detection Scheme

parity (odd or even) on a block of characters. The block check provides a
better method to detect errors across characters. LRC is usually
implemented with VRC and is then called a two-dimensional parity check

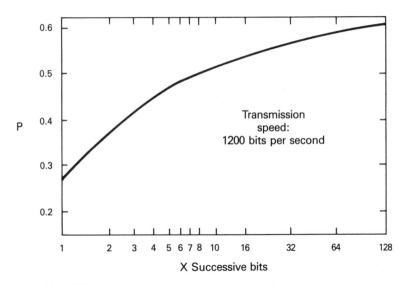

P = Probability of another erroneous bit following an initial erroneous bit within X bits

FIGURE 7-10. Successive Bit Error Probability [STAL85]

code (see Figure 7-11). The VRC-LRC combination provides a substantial improvement over a single method. A typical telephone line with an error rate of $1:10^5$ can be improved to a range of $1:10^7$ and $1:10^9$ with the two-dimensional check.

The parity check is expressed mathematically by the use of the EXCLUSIVE OR $\oplus$ operation. The EXCLUSIVE OR of two binary digits is 1 if the digits differ; if they are the same (both 0s or both 1s), the EXCLUSIVE OR result is 0.

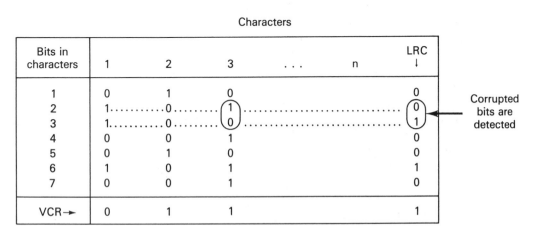

FIGURE 7-11. A Two-Dimensional Parity Check

The following equation demonstrates the use of parity:

$$P_j = b_{ij} \oplus b_{ij} \ldots \oplus b_{nj}$$

Where: P_j = parity bit of jth character; b_{ij} = ith bit in the jth character; n = number of bits in the character.

Echoplex

This rather primitive technique is used in many asynchronous devices, notably personal computers. Each character is transmitted to the receiver, where it is sent back or echoed to the original station. The echoed character is compared with a copy of the transmitted character. If they are the same, a high probability exists that the transmission is correct.

Echoplex requires the use of full duplex facilities. In the event a full duplex configuration is not available, a device is usually switched to local echo, which sends the echo through the local modem back to the user device. Local echo permits the system to operate as if it were echoplex, but be aware that local echo does not check for errors across the link.

Error Checking Codes

Any discussion of error control must include two widely used error checking codes: block codes and convolutional codes. This general discussion is derived from [LIN83]. The purpose of these codes is to detect errors that have corrupted the signals. (With some codes, the errors are also corrected.)

Block Codes. A block code consists of an information sequence. This sequence is called a block or blocks. The block is also called a message. Each block contains k information bits. For binary-based codes, a total of 2^k possible messages exists. In Chapter 3, we learned that an encoder transforms the bits in the message into a code, and 2^k code words are possible from the output of the encoder. The term block code (or [n,k] block codes) is associated with the set of 2^k code words of length n.

Another term important to this discussion is the code rate (R) defined as R = k/n. It is the ratio of the number of information bits per transmitted symbol.

For a different code word to be assigned to each symbol, k ‹ n or R ‹ 1. Redundant bits can be added to a message to form a code word if k ‹ n. The number of redundant bits can be n − k. It is these redundant bits that enable a communications system to deal with transmission impairments.

The encoder "outputs" the code based only on the input value of the k-bit message. Therefore, the encoder is said to be memoryless, and can be implemented with combinational logic.

A block code contains an important attribute called the minimum distance [HAMM50]. It determines its error-detecting and error-correcting capabilities and is described as the Hamming weight or Hamming distance. As an example, the Hamming distance between the binary n-tuples of $X = (11010001)$ and $y = (01000101)$, written as $d(x,y)$, is 4. Reading left to right, they differ in the first, third, fourth, and sixth positions.

It is possible to compute the Hamming distance between any two code words. The minimum distance is defined as:

$$d_{min} = \min \{d(x,y) : x, y \in C, x \neq W\}$$

Where: C = a code block; x and y = code vectors.

When a code vector v is transmitted over a channel, a number of L errors will result in the received vector r which is different from vector v in L places. Hamming theory states that, for code C, no error of $d_{min} - 1$ (or fewer) can change one code into another. It follows that any code word received with an error pattern of $d_{min} - 1$ or fewer errors will be detected as an error. In other words, the received code word is not a code word of C.

The Hamming code detects all errors of $d_{min} - 1$ or fewer errors and it can also detect a large number of errors with d_{min} or more errors.

It is preferable to develop a block code with the Hamming distance to be as large as possible. A large minimum distance increases the likelihood of detecting errors.

Convolutional Codes. The convolutional encoder has a memory. It too accepts blocks of k-bit information and produces an encoded value of n-symbol blocks. However, in contrast to block coding, the code word value depends on the current k-bit message and on m previous message blocks. The encoded value is called a (n,k,m) convolutional code, and is implemented with sequential logic.

The sequential aspect of convolutional codes allows us to describe their operation with a state diagram (see Figure 7-12). Each branch on the state

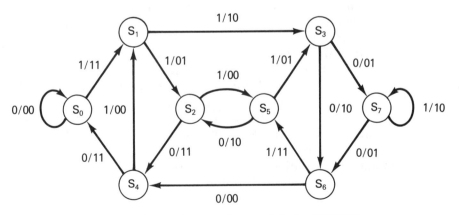

FIGURE 7-12. Convolutional Codes [LIN83]

diagram is labeled with the k inputs causing the transition and its corresponding n inputs. Starting at S_0 the path is followed through the state diagram according to the k bits input [u(1) ... u(k)]. The output label is the resulting code symbol [v(1) ... v(n)]. After the last non-0 bit, the path is followed back to S_0 with all 0s appended to the code.

For example, a bit stream of 11101 produces the code word: 11, 10, 01, 01, 11, 10, 11, 11. The path through the state diagram is:

$$S_0 \rightarrow S_1 \rightarrow S_3 \rightarrow S_7 \rightarrow S_6 \rightarrow S_5 \rightarrow S_2 \rightarrow S_4 \rightarrow S_0$$

Convolutional codes are also evaluated in relation to their distance properties. This is achieved by several analyses but the simplest is the minimum free distance, d_{free}:

$$d_{free} \stackrel{\Delta}{=} \min\{d(v^1, v^{11}): u^1 = u^{11}\}$$

Where: v^1 and v^{11} = code words corresponding to information u^1 and u^{11}, respectively.

This discussion on block and convolutional codes only touches the surface of error-control coding. However, it provides us with enough background to understand two error-control techniques used widely today in data communications: (a) cyclic coding using block coding concepts and (b) trellis coding using convolutional coding techniques.

Cyclic Redundancy Check (CRC)

Many error-detection codes for data transmission use logic based on the cyclic redundancy check (CRC). It is so named because the bits in a message $v = (v_0, v_1 ... v_{n-1})$ are cyclically shifted through a register one place at a time: v (one place) = $(v_{n-1}, v_0 ... v_{n-2})$. The CRC method is derived from the concepts of block coding. So the CRC technique is memoryless and can be implemented with combinational logic. Moreover, cyclic codes possess algebraic properties that lend themselves to relatively simple error-detection implementations.

With this technique, the transmitter generates a bit pattern called a frame check sequence (FCS) (also called a block check count [BCC]), based on the contents of the frame. The combined contents of the FCS and the frame (F) is exactly divisible by some predetermined number with no remainder, or as an alternative, divisible by the number with a known remainder. If the contents of the frame are damaged during transmission, the receiver's division will yield a non-zero or a value other than a known remainder as an indication of an error.

CRC detects all of the following errors:

- All single-bit errors
- All double-bit errors if the divisor is at least three terms

- Any odd number of errors, if the divisor contains a factor $(x + 1)$
- Any error in which the length of the error (an error burst) is less than the length of the FCS
- Most errors with larger bursts

If the reader wishes more information on these assertions, [PETE61] provides the rationale for them and a more detailed discussion.

An algebraic notation is used to describe the FCS generation and checking process. The modulo 2 divisor is called a generator polynomial (a polynomial is an algebraic expression consisting of two or more terms). The divisor is actually one bit longer than the FCS. Both high-order and low-order bits of the divisor must be 1s. For example, a bit sequence of 11001001 is represented by the polynomial:

$$f(x) = x^7 + x^6 + x^3 + 1$$

The leading bits in the left-hand side correspond to the higher-order coefficients of the polynomial.

In general terms, the following rules apply to the CRC operations, and later examples show these rules implemented with EXCLUSIVE OR cyclic shift registers.

- The frame contents are appended by a set of 0s equal in number to the length of the FCS.
- This value is divided modulo 2 by the generator polynomial (which contains one more digit than the FCS and must have high- and low-order bits of 1s). The divisor "can be divided" into the dividend, if the dividend has as many significant bits as the divisor.
- Each division is carried out in the conventional manner, except the next step (subtraction) is done modulo 2. Subtraction and addition are identical to EXCLUSIVE OR $\oplus$ (no borrows or carries):

$$\begin{array}{cccc} 1 & 1 & 0 & 0 \\ -\,1 & -\,0 & -\,1 & -\,0 \\ \hline 0 & 1 & 1 & 0 \end{array}$$

and

$$\begin{array}{cccc} 1 & 1 & 0 & 0 \\ +\,1 & +\,0 & +\,1 & +\,0 \\ \hline 0 & 1 & 1 & 0 \end{array}$$

- The answer provides a quotient, which is discarded, and a remainder, which becomes the FCS field.
- The FCS is placed at the back of the frame contents and sent to the receiver.
- The receiver performs the same division on the frame contents *and* the FCS field. The FCS replaces the appended 0s used at the transmitter.

- If the result equals the expected number (a 0 or the predetermined number) the transmission is considered error-free.

To illustrate CRC let us assume the following:

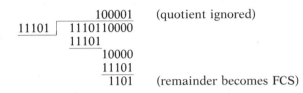

Frame contents: 111011
Polynomial: 11101 $(x^4 + x^3 + x^2 + 1)$
Frame contents and appended 0s: 1110110000

The transmitter performs the following calculation:

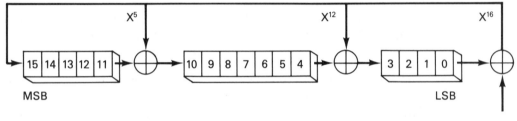

```
           100001    (quotient ignored)
    11101 ) 1110110000
            11101
            10000
            11101
             1101    (remainder becomes FCS)
```

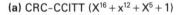

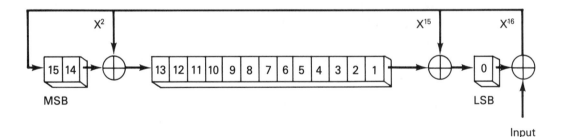

(a) CRC–CCITT $(X^{16} + x^{12} + X^5 + 1)$

(b) CRC–16 $(X^{16} + X^{15} + X^2 + 1)$

⊕ –Exclusive-Or gate

MSB–Most significant bit

LSB–Least significant bit

FIGURE 7-13. CRC-CCITT and CRC-16 Polynomials

At the receiver, the frame contents and the FCS are divided by the same polynomial. As this example shows, if the remainder equals 0, the transmission is accepted as having no errors:

$$
\begin{array}{r}
100001 \\
11101 \overline{)\,1110111101} \quad \text{(FCS)} \\
11101 \\
\hline
11101 \\
11101 \\
\hline
00000 \quad \text{(remainder: no errors)}
\end{array}
$$

The division operation is equivalent to performing an EXCLUSIVE OR operation. The CRC calculations are actually performed in a cyclic shift register that uses EXCLUSIVE OR gates. EXCLUSIVE OR logic outputs 0 for inputs of 1 or 0; it outputs 1 if the inputs differ. The setup of the register depends on the type of generator polynomial.

Figure 7-13 shows the registers for CRC-CCITT ($X^{16} + X^{12} + X^5 + 1$) and CRC-16 ($X^{16} + X^{15} + X^2 + 1$). The former detects errors of bursts up to 16 bits in length. It detects more than 99% of error bursts greater than 12 bits. The CRC-16 detects more than 99% of error bursts greater than 16 bits.

It is evident from a study of Figure 7-13 that the feedback logic means that the register contents at a given instant are dependent upon the past transmission of bits. Consequently, the chances of a multiple bit burst creating an undetected error (a 0 remainder) is very unlikely.

For the reader who wishes more detail on the frame check sequence, Box 7-1 explains the technique used for HDLC [ECMA79].

DETECTING AND CORRECTING ERRORS

Trellis Coding.   In Chapters 10 and 11, we discuss methods that detect errors and request a retransmission of the erroneous data. Retransmission is a time-honored compromise to the error laden channel and it has served the industry well. Nonetheless, other techniques have emerged that not only detect an error but, in many cases, correct the error without requesting a retransmission. One of these techniques, trellis coding, is highlighted here to give the reader an idea of the value of newer forward error correction (FEC) techniques. We discuss the concepts first, followed by an examination of the CCITT V.32 modem that uses trellis coded modulation (TCM).

Earlier discussions explained that the greater the Hamming distance of a code the better it can correct a corrupted message. A larger Hamming distance is possible by making the code more complex or changing the code rate (ratio of FEC bits to user bits). However, the greater the number of extra (redundant) bits, the lower the user data throughput.

This creates a dilemma on how to use the existing band-limited link and still produce a greater number of bits per symbol. Moreover, the redundant bits require a denser constellation pattern which reduces the transmission signal's immunity to noise.

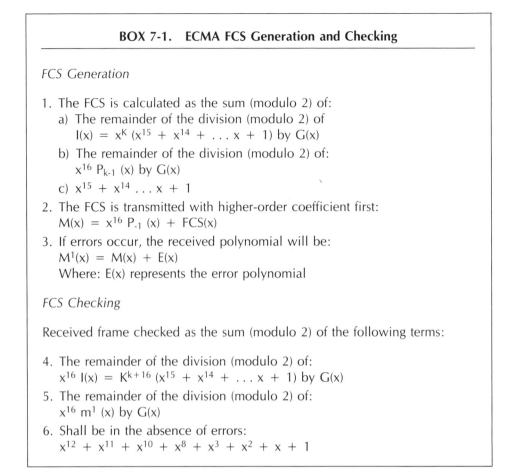

BOX 7-1. ECMA FCS Generation and Checking

FCS Generation

1. The FCS is calculated as the sum (modulo 2) of:
   a) The remainder of the division (modulo 2) of
      $I(x) = x^K (x^{15} + x^{14} + \ldots x + 1)$ by $G(x)$
   b) The remainder of the division (modulo 2) of:
      $x^{16} P_{k-1} (x)$ by $G(x)$
   c) $x^{15} + x^{14} \ldots x + 1$
2. The FCS is transmitted with higher-order coefficient first:
   $M(x) = x^{16} P_{-1} (x) + FCS(x)$
3. If errors occur, the received polynomial will be:
   $M^1(x) = M(x) + E(x)$
   Where: $E(x)$ represents the error polynomial

FCS Checking

Received frame checked as the sum (modulo 2) of the following terms:

4. The remainder of the division (modulo 2) of:
   $x^{16} I(x) = K^{k+16} (x^{15} + x^{14} + \ldots x + 1)$ by $G(x)$
5. The remainder of the division (modulo 2) of:
   $x^{16} m^1 (x)$ by $G(x)$
6. Shall be in the absence of errors:
   $x^{12} + x^{11} + x^{10} + x^8 + x^3 + x^2 + x + 1$

However, we can reasonably pose the following scenario. Granted, the many elements involved in a data transmission will often create errors. Yet the transmission/signal always starts at a known value and the value is confined within certain limits. Suppose a method is devised whereby the signal (derived and coded from the user data bit stream) is allowed to assume only certain characteristics (states) on the line. Furthermore, suppose the user bits are interpreted such that only certain of the states are allowed to exist from prior states.

This means the transmitting device accepts a series of user bits and develops additional yet restricted bit patterns from these bits. Moreover, the previous user bit pattern (called a state) is only allowed to assume certain other bit patterns (states). Other states are invalid and are never transmitted.

The transmitter and receiver are programmed to understand the allowable states and the permissible state transitions. If the receiver receives states and state transitions (because of channel impairments) that differ from predefined conventions, it is assumed an error has occurred on the circuit.

But trellis coding goes further. Since, by convention, the transmitter and the receiver know the transmission states and the permissible state transitions, the receiver analyzes the received signal and makes a "best guess" as to what state the signal should assume. It analyzes current states, compares them to previous states, and makes decisions as to the most relevant state. In effect, it uses a path history to reconstruct damaged bits.

It is obvious that trellis coding is a convolutional code. Its encoded values depend on the corresponding k-bit message and also on m previous message blocks. As discussed earlier with convolutional codes, the trellis encoding has a memory order of m.

The process is illustrated in Figure 7-14 [PAYT85]. The original signal in Figure 7-14(a) is transmitted to allow the four states depicted in the four circles. Each circle represents a signal point (a signalling interval). The points in the figure represent various combinations of phase modulation.

Due to transmission impairments, the signal is interpreted as depicted in Figure 7-14(b). A conventional receiver would interpret the signal in an entirely different constellation pattern and misconstrue 1s for 0s, and vice versa.

Figure 7-14(c) shows that the received signal, while certainly erroneous, is not entirely invalid. Received signals at signal points 1 and 3 are close enough approximations of the original signal such that the predefined state transition rules based on prior states can be used to make a best guess on the signal and essentially forward error correct the errors in Figure 7-14(d).

CCITT V.32 Trellis Coded Modulation (TCM). This recommendation has created considerable interest because V.32 DCEs can operate at rates up to 9600 bit/s at full duplex on a dial-up, 2-wire line. Many manufacturers now offer a V.32 modem and several modems are available which use TCM on 19.2 Kbit/s links. The principal characteristics of V.32 are:

- Provides duplex mode of operation on switched and 2-wire, point-to-point leased circuits.
- Any combination of the following data signalling rates may be implemented in the modems:
    - 9600 bit/s synchronous
    - 4800 bit/s synchronous
    - 2400 bit/s synchronous (for further study)

Figure 7-15 shows the functional logic of V.32 trellis coding. The user data stream is divided into 4 bit groups. The bits are designated $Q1_n$, $Q2_n$, $Q3_n$, and $Q4_n$, where n designates the sequence number of the group. Bits $Q1_n$ and $Q2_n$ are encoded as $Y1_n$ and $Y2_n$. The rules for encoding these bits are shown in Table 7-1. The table shows that the values of the previous

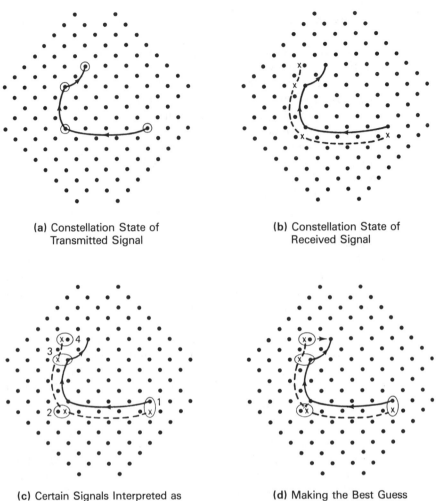

(a) Constellation State of
Transmitted Signal

(b) Constellation State of
Received Signal

(c) Certain Signals Interpreted as
Correct or Incorrect

(d) Making the Best Guess

FIGURE 7-14. Trellis Coded Modulation (TCM) [PAYT85]

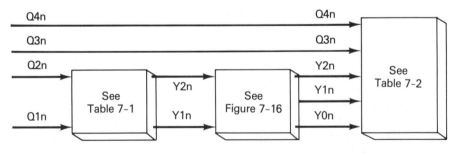

FIGURE 7-15. Trellis Coded Modulation (TCM) for V.32 (9600 Bit/s)

TABLE 7-1. Rules for Encoding Bits Q1ₙ and Q2ₙ

Inputs		Previous Outputs		Outputs	
$Q1_n$	$Q2_n$	$Y1_{n-1}$	$Y2_{n-1}$	$Y1_n$	$Y2_n$
0	0	0	0	0	0
0	0	0	1	0	1
0	0	1	0	1	0
0	0	1	1	1	1
0	1	0	0	0	1
0	1	0	1	0	0
0	1	1	0	1	1
0	1	1	1	1	0
1	0	0	0	1	0
1	0	0	1	1	1
1	0	1	0	0	1
1	0	1	1	0	0
1	1	0	0	1	1
1	1	0	1	1	0
1	1	1	0	0	0
1	1	1	1	0	1

outputs $Y1_{n-1}$ and $Y2_{n-1}$ are used to determine the current output of the encoding process.

Bits $Y1_n$ and $Y2_n$ are input to another encoder. This logic generates a redundant bit $Y0_n$ based on the rules and logic shown in Figure 7-16. Finally, the 5 bits $Y0_n$, $Y1_n$, $Y2_n$, $Q3_n$, and $Q4_n$ are encoded according to the rules shown in Table 7-2. The resulting constellation pattern is depicted in Figure 7-17. It has a 32-point signal structure since 5 bits are used to convey the information ($2^5 = 32$).

As we learned earlier, the receiving DCE uses the redundant coding to determine the closest permissible signal point in the constellation. In effect, the tables are used to decode the signal point.

What does FEC hold for data communications systems and networks? It has the potential to redo much of our software and hardware that concerns itself with the transmission and reception of data in our currently existing systems. For example, TCM reduces the error rate by three orders of magnitude [PAYT85]. TCM is becoming pervasive, and data link controls (line protocols) will undergo significant changes due to this form of FEC.

SUGGESTED READINGS

For the reader who wishes a detailed examination of error control coding, [LIN83] is highly recommended. [VITE67] discusses some of the earlier

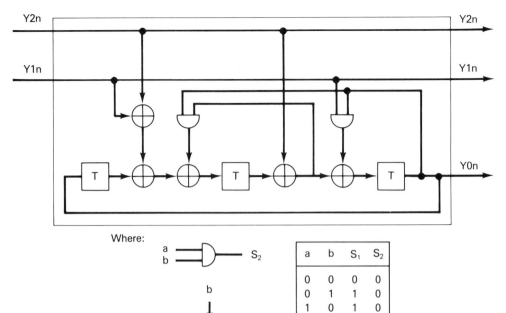

Where:

a	b	S_1	S_2
0	0	0	0
0	1	1	0
1	0	1	0
1	1	0	1

FIGURE 7-16. V.32 Convolutional Coder

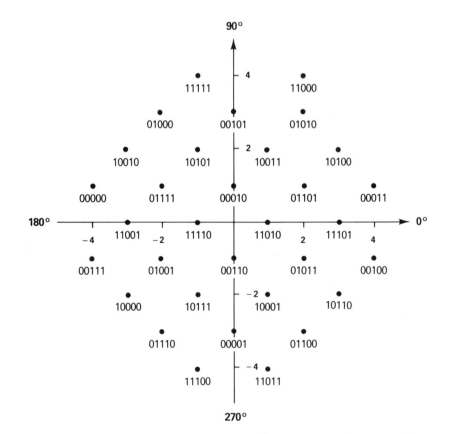

FIGURE 7-17. 32-Point V.32 Constellation Pattern (9600 Bit/s)

TABLE 7-2. Trellis Rules for Coding Y0, Y1, Y2, Q3, and Q4 Bits

| | Coded Inputs | | | | Trellis Coding | |
(Y0)	Y1	Y2	Q3	Q4	Re	Im
0	0	0	0	0	−4	1
	0	0	0	1	0	−3
	0	0	1	0	0	1
	0	0	1	1	4	1
	0	1	0	0	4	−1
	0	1	0	1	0	3
	0	1	1	0	0	−1
	0	1	1	1	−4	−1
	1	0	0	0	−2	3
	1	0	0	1	−2	−1
	1	0	1	0	2	3
	1	0	1	1	2	−1
	1	1	0	0	2	−3
	1	1	0	1	2	1
	1	1	1	0	−2	−3
	1	1	1	1	−2	1
1	0	0	0	0	−3	−2
	0	0	0	1	1	−2
	0	0	1	0	−3	2
	0	0	1	1	1	2
	0	1	0	0	3	2
	0	1	0	1	−1	2
	0	1	1	0	3	−2
	0	1	1	1	−1	−2
	1	0	0	0	1	4
	1	0	0	1	−3	0
	1	0	1	0	1	0
	1	0	1	1	1	−4
	1	1	0	0	−1	−4
	1	1	0	1	3	0
	1	1	1	0	−1	0
	1	1	1	1	−1	4

work on trellis coding and [VITE79] explains the use of trellis to deal with intersymbol interference. [PAYT85] explains some practical applications of trellis coding. [SHER85] provides a good nonmathematical look at transmission impairments and diagnostic tools. [PIER80] is a very good explanation of noise and entropy. [REY83] describes impairments from the telephone network perspective. Other references are contained in the bibliography.

TRUE/FALSE

1. Treating data communications errors is difficult due to the number of components in the system and the error-prone nature of the links.
2. One of the principal disadvantages of a mainframe operating system is the lack of control over program execution.
3. Channel capacity in bits per second is a function of the thermal noise-to-signal ratio as well as bandwidth.
4. If noise has less entropy than a Gaussian distribution, a higher data rate can be obtained.
5. Trellis coding uses convolutional coding techniques.
6. Match the term to the appropriate definition:

   Definition

   a) Noise often found in multiplexed signals.
   b) Increased voltage level that does not exceed 12 dB.
   c) Noise lasting longer than 4 ms and greater than 12 dB.
   d) Ongoing noise.
   e) Transmitter and receiver coupling.

   Term

   1. Dropouts
   2. White noise
   3. Gain hits
   4. Intermodulation noise
   5. Crosstalk

7. Describe the major sources of thermal noise.
8. Describe how a compandor reduces the effects of noise.
9. What are the differences between selective fading and flat fading?
10. Summarize at least three problems with the use of loaded lines.
11. You must interface two protocols. One protocol uses ASCII code, odd parity with 1s. The other protocol uses ASCII code, even parity with 0s. Is the error detection logic of these protocols acceptable for a compatible interface? Why or why not?
12. What is the principal difference between block codes and convolutional codes?
13. A bit stream of value 1001 is to be encoded based on the state diagram in Figure 7-12. What is the resulting code word? Show the path through the state diagram.
14. Perform the EXCLUSIVE OR operations on the following binary bit stream:

$$0110101$$
$$\oplus \underline{1010111}$$

15. You have had a request from your technical staff to acquire a protocol analyzer at a cost of several thousand dollars. You have no funds in your budget for such an item. How would you justify the purchase of this expensive item to your boss?

SELECTED ANSWERS

1. True

2. False. Indeed, the centralized operating system exercises considerable control over the process.

3. True. For a review see Figure 7-2.

4. True.

5. True.

6.

Definition	Term
a)	4
b)	3
c)	1
d)	2
e)	5

10. Loading cables: (1) severely attenuate higher frequency signals, (2) reduce signal propagation, (3) introduce delay distortion.

11. The protocols are not compatible. To understand why, consider the following examples:

Example 1

7 Bit Code:	001100
8th bit, odd parity with 1s:	0011000 **1**
8th bit, even parity with 0s:	0011000 **0**

One protocol would use a 1 as the parity bit and the other protocol would use a 0.

Example 2

7 Bit Code:	0000001
8th bit, odd parity with 1s:	0000001 **0**
8th bit, even parity with 0s:	0000001 **1**

13. 11, 01, 11, 00, 01, 11, 11
$$S_1 \rightarrow S_2 \rightarrow S_4 \rightarrow S_1 \rightarrow S_2 \rightarrow S_4 \rightarrow S_0$$

15. The use of a protocol analyzer can often lead to reduced downtime of the communications facilities. It is found to be most useful for organizations

which depend upon themselves (and not vendors or consultants) for their systems operations. Most experienced managers believe the use of diagnostic equipment, such as the protocol analyzer, will reduce the time that is required for a telephone company or other communications support vendor to find the problem in the communications system. The best justification to a boss for the purchase of this expensive item would be more efficient communications, less downtime and better productivity of the individuals using the communications systems.

CHAPTER 8

Layered Protocols, Network Architectures, and the OSI

INTRODUCTION

In Part II, we discuss the concepts of network architectures and layered protocols. The major recommended standards used in layered protocols are examined, and we focus on the recent work of the CCITT, ISO, IEEE, EIA, and ANSI. We also examine the protocols of IBM (SNA) and DEC (DECnet). We selected IBM and DEC because of their prominence in the data communications network industry. Several other vendors' systems and products use the concepts described in this chapter. The Department of Defense (DOD) has implemented several communications protocols which are now used worldwide. These systems are also examined in this part of the book.

It has become painfully clear that the vendor-specialized, one-at-a-time approach to product development has created a multitude of heterogeneous systems that are (at best) difficult to connect together or (in many cases) simply incompatible. Consequently, in 1977 the International Organization for Standardization (ISO) established committees to develop a common architecture to be used to connect (interface) heterogeneous computers and other devices. In 1984, ISO published this specification in the document ISO 7498 and called it Open Systems Interconnection (OSI). The CCITT publishes a comparable recommendation as X.200. Part II of this book is structured around ISO 7498, X.200, and their related and complementary protocols.

The CCITT meets every four years in a Plenary Assembly to revise and update their "recommendations," which most people call "standards." The chapters in Part II of this book that deal with the X Series reflect the latest changes made at the 1988 Plenary Assembly. The published standards are known as the "Blue Books" because of the color of their covers. The entire set of Blue Books contain several thousand pages! Our goal in this part is to summarize and clarify those Blue Book recommendations that pertain to data networks.

Those readers who may have finally mastered the CCITT X.200 1984 release (the Red Books) will be relieved to know that the 1984 and 1988 X.200 versions are almost identical, with only some minor changes in wording, grammar, and definitions. However, other X Series have been added or revised since 1984, and they will be noted in the appropriate chapters of this book.

To begin our analysis of network architectures and protocols, let us define the terms architecture, protocol, and topology. The term architecture is commonly used today to describe networks. Paraphrasing the dictionary definition, an architecture is a formation of a structure. A network architecture describes what things exist, how they operate, and what form they take. An architecture encompasses hardware, software, data link controls, standards, topologies, and protocols.

Like architecture, the term protocol is borrowed from other disciplines and professions. Basically, a protocol defines conventions on how network components establish communications, exchange data, and terminate communications.

The term topology is used to describe the form of a network. A network topology is the shape (or the physical connectivity) of the network.

LAYERED PROTOCOLS

The majority of protocols that make up the OSI "suite" of protocols are founded upon the concept of layered protocols, and no explanation of OSI can be fully understood unless this subject is also known. So, before discussing OSI, we will take a brief excursion into the basic concepts of layered protocols.

The software and hardware of the stations operating on these networks typically consist of a wide range of functions to support the communications activities. Without question, the network designer is faced with an enormous task in dealing with the number and complexity of these functions. To address these problems, many systems are designed by a well-ordered and structured "layering" of the functions. The term used today to describe the technique is layered protocols. The term is used so often it is almost a cliché, but it identifies some very worthy concepts. As we shall see in this section, a well-designed layered protocol system can provide:

- A logical decomposition of a complex system into smaller, more comprehensible parts (layers)

- Standard (and limited) interfaces between the layered functions
- Symmetry in functions performed at each layer in a system: each layer in a station performs the same function(s) as its counterpart in other stations
- A means to predict and control any changes made to logic (software or microcode)

Ideally, layered protocols that use common conventions permit different systems to communicate openly with each other without changing the logic of the communicating layers. Therefore, heretofore "closed" systems that were unable to communicate with each other should be able to communicate with relatively little change to the software and hardware.

Realistically, the task is formidable. It is somewhat analogous (actually it is far simpler) to that of asking people to use a common language when speaking with each other.

The name associated with open communications is, logically enough, Open Systems Interconnection (OSI). The layers of OSI are used as the structure for Part II of this book. They serve as a foundation for many standards and products in the industry today. (The reader may wish to review Chapter 1 for an introduction to OSI and its sponsoring organizations.)

Communications Between Layers

In layered protocols and the OSI model (Open Systems Interconnection), a system consists of layers. Figure 8-1 depicts a layer providing a service or a set of services to users A and B. The users communicate with the service provider through an address or identifier commonly known as the service

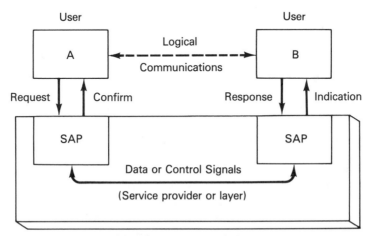

SAP: Service Access Point

FIGURE 8-1. OSI Layer and Service Provider

access point (SAP). The SAP is allowed to take several forms, just as long as it provides a unique and unambiguous identification of the specific object (person, computer, layer service, etc.). Through the use of four types of transactions [Request, Indication, Response, and Confirm (called primitives)], the service provider coordinates and manages the communications process between the users. The other terms shown in Figure 8-1 are explained shortly.

A layer is a service provider and may consist of several services. For example, one layer could provide a service for code conversion such as International Alphabet #5 (IA5) to/from EBCDIC. Each layer is considered a subsystem and may also be made up of entities. An entity is a specialized module within the layer. For example, a layer could contain a data compression entity, an encryption entity, a multiplexing entity, etc.

The entities within a layer are called peer entities. It is not necessary that all entities in a layer communicate with each other. Indeed, they may not be allowed to communicate. For example, they may not support the same subsets within the layers and therefore they would have no logical relationship to each other. In our example, a data compression entity would not be associated with an encryption entity.

A layer can also be divided into smaller logical substructures called sublayers. Entities can also exist within the sublayers.

The basic idea of layered protocols is for a lower layer to add a value to the services provided by the layers above it. Consequently, the top layer, which interfaces directly with an end-user application, is provided with the full range of services offered by all the lower layers. The actual services invoked are dictated by the upper layers to the lower layers, but it is the responsibility of the lower layers to perform the service. The upper layers are generally unaware of how the service is performed. As long as the service meets the requirements established by the upper layers, the detail of the service activities is transparent to the upper layer service user.

In most systems, layers, sublayers, and entities are made up of software programs. Consequently, within the context of OSI, software programs invoke the service of other software programs through the use of the primitives, which may be implemented with program subroutine calls. Increasingly, certain sublayers and entities are being placed into hardware, but the OSI principles discussed here remain the same.

Design Principles of Layered Systems

In this section, we examine the principles behind the OSI reference model and compare them to some well-accepted concepts in system design. For purposes of continuity, the concepts of layered protocols explained in Chapter 1 are reiterated here with additional detail.

Early networks that provided communications services were relatively simple (and did not use layers). In a typical configuration, terminals were connected to a computer, in which several software programs controlled the communications process by transmitting and receiving data to/from a telephone line. The line was usually attached to an interface unit within or connected to the computer. The unit provided signalling and synchronization services.

As organizations became larger, more complex, and more geographically dispersed, the supporting communications software and hardware assumed more tasks and grew in size and function. Many of these components grew haphazardly. The system often became unwieldy and difficult to maintain. In some instances, telecommunications programs became quite complex. When these systems were changed, the resulting output sometimes had unpredictable results.

Moreover, the earlier networks often used several different protocols that had been added in a somewhat evolutionary and unplanned manner. (Many systems today still suffer from these deficiencies.) The protocols in the networks often had poorly defined interfaces. It was not uncommon for a change in the network software at one site to adversely affect a seemingly unrelated component at another site. In many instances, the components in a network were simply incompatible.

The concept of layered protocols developed largely as a result of the situation described above. The basic purpose of layered protocols is to eliminate or diminish the interface problems by (a) reducing complexity, (b) providing for peer-to-peer layer interaction across nodes, and (c) allowing changes to be made in one layer without affecting others. For example, a change to a routing algorithm in a network control program should not affect the functions of message sequencing, which is located in another layer in the protocol.

Layered protocols also permit the partitioning of the design and development of the many network components. Since each layer is relatively self-contained, different design teams (perhaps located at different sites) can work on different layers.

Binding, Coupling, and Atomic Actions. Layered functions also owe their origin to several concepts generally called structured techniques. These ideas provide an impetus to design hardware or software systems that have clearly defined interfaces. The systems contain modules that perform one function or closely related functions (sometimes called the cohesiveness of functions or the binding of related functions together). These techniques can also produce a system in which a change to a module does not affect any component in a system that the changed module does not control. This approach is called loose coupling. For computing resources to function efficiently and logically, they must adhere to the following atomic action principles [RAND79].

- An action is atomic if X process is not aware of the existence of other active processes, and other processes are not aware of process X, during the time that process X is performing the action.

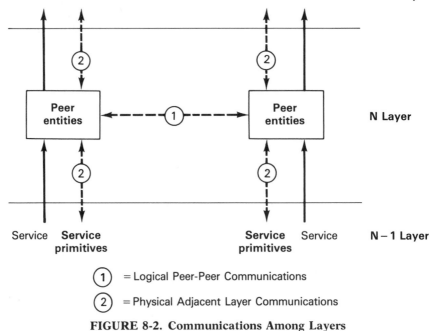

① = Logical Peer-Peer Communications

② = Physical Adjacent Layer Communications

FIGURE 8-2. Communications Among Layers

- An action is atomic if the process performing the action does not communicate with other processes while the action is being performed.
- An action is atomic if the process performing the action can detect no changes except those performed by itself and if it does not reveal its state changes until the action is complete.

To meet the principles of atomic actions, layered network protocols allow interaction between functionally paired layers in different locations without affecting other layers. This concept aids in distributing the functions to the layers. In the majority of layered protocols, the data unit passed from one layer to another is usually not altered, although the data unit contents may be examined and used to append additional data (trailers/headers) to the existing unit.

For example, layer N in Figure 8-2 might examine a field in a message that was inserted by layer N + 1. The field might contain a logical address of the recipient of the message. Layer N would translate this logical address to a node address. Then, perhaps layer N − 1 would interpret the node address into an actual physical communications line address. If the line became inoperable, layer N − 1 could make the necessary changes to a line address without affecting layers N or N + 1. This example illustrates one advantage of layered protocols: The layer can be changed without affecting those components that work with other layers.

Designations of the Layers

We need to clarify the rather cryptic notations N, N + 1, and N − 1. A layer in the OSI model is identified generally as an (N)-layer. The layer above it (if one exists) is designated as the (N + 1)-layer. The layer below the (N)-layer (if one exists) is designated as the (N − 1)-layer. These designations are relative. For example, in Figure 8–2, if we were referring to the transport layer, we refer to it as the (N)-layer. The layer above it, the session layer, is designated as the (N + 1)-layer. The layer below the transport layer is the network layer, and relative to the the transport layer, it is designated as the (N − 1)-layer. As another example, if the presentation layer is the layer of interest, it is designated as the (N)-layer and the layers above and below it are (N + 1) and (N − 1), respectively.

The advantage of using relative designators is that it allows the model to describe the interactions of the layers without regard to a specific layer. In other words, all layers communicate with a common set of conventions.

Using Facilities to Tailor Services

In many instances, a service provided by an (N)-layer can be tailored. A user can select certain desired services from a layer by passing identifiers to the layer known as *facilities*. Through the use of (N)-facilities, the specific attributes of a service can be selected. If an (N)-entity cannot support a service requested by an (N + 1) entity, it may call upon other (N)-entities to complete the service request.

Connection-End Points

The entities within a layer can be connected on as many-to-one, or a one-to many basis. That is to say, entities may service more than one entity or use the services of more than one entity. These services are provided at the (N)-service access point (SAP) and called an (N) *connection-end point*. In OSI, a connection is an association established by the (N)-layer between two or more (N + 1) entities, usually for data transfer.

The relationship of the layers is shown in Figure 8-2. Each layer contains entities that exchange data and provide functions (in a logical sense; see point 1) with peer entities at other sites in the network. Entities in adjacent layers interact through the common upper and lower boundaries (in a physical sense; see point 2) by passing parameters to define the interactions.

Typically, each layer at a transmitting station (except the lowest in most systems) adds "header" information to data. The headers are used to establish peer-to-peer sessions across nodes, and some layer implementations use headers to invoke functions and services at the N + 1 or N − 1 adjacent layers. The important point to understand is that at the receiving site, the layer entities use the headers created by the peer entity at the transmitting site to implement actions.

Now that we have described the principles, advantages, and goals in layered protocol design, let us examine the principles behind the layering concept as implemented in the OSI seven-layer model.

PRINCIPLES OF THE SEVEN-LAYER MODEL

The CCITT and ISO use several principles (P) to determine the number and nature of the layers [X.200]. These principles should be compared to the design principles explained in the previous section. The author has para-phrased the X.200 Blue Book explanations to clarify these points to the reader.

P1: For simplicity, keep the number of layers within a small limit.

P2: Create layer boundaries that minimize layer interactions and the description of services.

P3: Separate layers so that different functions are separated from each other. Also, layers that use different kinds of technology should be separated.

P4: Similarly, place similar functions in the same layer.

P5: Select layer boundaries that past experience shows have functioned successfully.

P6: As a complement to P4, localized functions should be established which allow a redesign with minimal effect to adjacent layers.

P7: Create boundaries that might permit the corresponding interface to be standardized.

P8: As a complement to P4, create a layer when the data must be handled differently.

P9: As a complement to P6, changes made in a layer should not affect other layers.

P10: Each layer has boundaries (interfaces) only to its upper and lower adjacent layers.

For the use of sublayers, similar principles apply and:

P11: As a complement to P3, P4, P6, P8, P9, and P10, create further subgrouping if necessary.

P12: Create sublayers to allow interface with adjacent layers.

P13: Sublayers may be bypassed if the services are not needed.

A close examination of these principles reveals they closely follow the design principles of structured techniques and atomic actions.

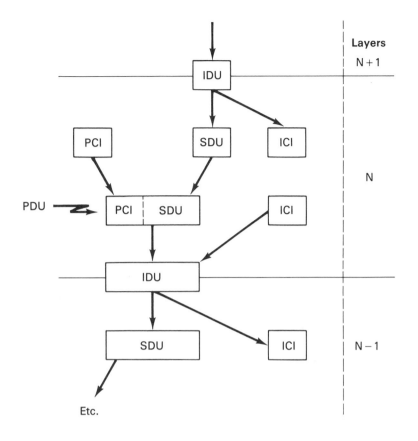

SDU	Service Data Unit
PCI	Protocol Control Information
PDU	Protocol Data Unit = PCI + SDU
IDU	Interface Data Unit = PDU + ICI
ICI	Interface Control Information

FIGURE 8-3. OSI Layer Components

Layer Primitives and Protocol Data Units (PDUs)

Networks are layered according to the structure in Figure 8-3. Each service provided by an (N)-layer can be tailored through the use of (N)-facilities. The cooperation between (N)-entities is controlled by (N)-protocols.

Please refer back to Figure 8-1. It shows the standard terminology for providing an interface with a layer or service provider. Four transactions, called primitives, are invoked to and from the layer through service access points (SAPs) (some sessions do not require all primitives):

• *Request*: Primitive by service user to invoke a function.

- *Indication*: Primitive by service provider to (a) invoke a function or (b) indicate a function has been invoked at a service access point (SAP).
- *Response*: Primitive by service user to complete a function previously invoked by an Indication at that SAP.
- *Confirm*: Primitive by service provider to complete a function previously invoked by a Request at that SAP.

A primitive is usually coded in software with a very specific format. For example, let us assume we wish to establish a "connection" to a network in order to access a computer in another city. Let us also assume the network communicates with us through primitives. We could request the connection with the following primitive:

N-CONNECT request (called address, calling address, quality of service parameters, user data).

This is a request primitive, or more precisely, a network layer (N) connect-request primitive. Notice the parameters associated with the connect request. The addresses are used to identify the called and calling parties. The quality of service (QOS) parameters inform the service provider about what type of services we wish to be invoked (expedited delivery, for example). It is possible that the primitive could contain many QOS parameters. The user data parameter contains the actual data to be sent to the called address.

The primitive is used by the layer to invoke the service entities and create any headers that will be used by the peer layer in the remote station. This point is quite important: *The primitives are used by adjacent layers in the local site to create the headers used by peer layers at the remote site.*

The Advantages of Abstract Primitives. One might question why the primitives are so abstract. Indeed, why are they not specific to a language, or at least to a convention, such as a subroutine call-by-value or a subroutine call-by-address? The abstract nature of the primitives makes good sense for the following reasons:

- They permit a common convention to be used between layers, without regard to specific vendor operating systems and specific languages.
- They give the vendor a choice as to how the primitives will be implemented on a specific machine. For example, the primitives are often implemented with a vendor's architecture-specific I/O calls.
- At the same time, if common languages and compilers are used among vendors, the standard primitives ease the task of layer transportability between different vendor machines.
- The use of standard primitives encourages the use of common for-

mats of the data units (packets, blocks, messages, frames, etc.). (The most common term today is protocol data units [PDUs]). This point is critical for achieving open systems interconnection (OSI), since common PDUs are quite important in achieving compatibility between different architectures. Returning to our simple example of a common language among all people: The imposition of a common tongue "encourages" the individual to think in that tongue and use a common syntax. Common protocol data units are to machines what common linguistics are to humans.

Components of Layered Communications

Five components are involved in the layers' communications process (see Figure 8-3). Their functions are:

- SDU (service data unit). Consists of user data and control information created at the upper layers which is transferred transparently by layer $N+1$ to layer N, and subsequently to $N-1$. The SDU identity is preserved from one end of an (N)-connection to the other.
- PCI (protocol control information). Information exchanged by peer (the same) entities at different sites on the network to instruct an entity to perform a service function (that is, headers and trailers).
- PDU (protocol data unit). The combination of the SDU and PCI.
- ICI (interface control information). A temporary parameter or parameters passed between N and $N-1$ to invoke service functions between the two layers. The primitive typically performs this function.
- IDU (interface data unit). The total unit of information transferred across the layer boundaries; it includes the PCI, SDU, and ICI. The IDU is transmitted across the service access point (SAP).

To assist the reader with these terms, consider the following:
- (N) to (N) remote entities use:
    PCI for control
    User data (SDU)
    PDU combines the PCI and SDU
- (N + 1) to (N) adjacent entities use:
    ICI for control
    User data (SDU)
    IDU combines the ICI and SDU

Elements of OSI Layers. The OSI model defines the elements of a layer's operation (see Box 8-1). The reader is strongly encouraged to study the contents of Box 8-1, because these elements are found (in one form or another) in several of the layers. The usefulness of several of the elements

BOX 8-1. Elements of Layers

- **Protocol identifier**: An identifier between communicating entities to select a protocol to be used in the logical connection.
- **Centralized/Decentralized multi-endpoint connection**: The ability to associate data from one to many and/or many to one connection-endpoint(s).
- **Multiplexing**: An (N)-layer function that uses one (N − 1) connection to support multiple (N)-connections.
- **Demultiplexing**: The reverse function of multiplexing.
- **Splitting**: An (N)-layer function that uses more than one (N − 1) connection to support multiple (N)-connections.
- **Recombining**: The reverse function of splitting.
- **Flow control**: A function to control the flow of data between adjacent layers or within a layer.
- **Segmenting**: An (N)-entity function that maps an (N)-service-data-unit into multiple (N)-protocol-data-units.
- **Reassembling**: The reverse function of segmenting.
- **Blocking**: An (N)-entity function that maps multiple (N)-service-data-units into one (N)-protocol-data-unit.
- **Deblocking**: The reverse function of blocking.
- **Concatenation**: An (N)-entity function that maps multiple (N)-protocol-data-units into one (N − 1) service-data-unit.
- **Separation**: The reverse function of concatenation.
- **Sequencing**: An (N)-layer function that preserves the order of data units submitted into it.
- **Acknowledgment**: An (N)-layer function that a receiving (N)-entity uses to acknowledge a protocol-data-unit from a sending (N)-entity.
- **Reset**: An (N)-layer function that returns correspondent (N)-entities to a state with possible loss or duplication of data.

may escape the reader. So, let us provide some additional discussion of those elements that may seem a bit abstract.
Notice the relationship between:

- Dealing with connections:
    multiplexing and demultiplexing
    splitting and recombining
- Dealing with data units (PDUs and SDUs):
    segmenting and reassembling
    blocking and deblocking
    concatenation and separation

As suggested in this list, these services deal with (a) the connections between entities (via a service access point [SAP]), and (b) the data units exchanged between entities. A layer may or may not furnish all these functions.

The OSI Model describes procedures for multiplexing more than one user session (connection) into one lower-level connection (see Figure 8-4(a)). This service can be useful (as an example) if an organization wishes to establish a connection to a network, and maintain the connection throughout an operating period. After the connection is established, multiple users can be multiplexed onto the ongoing network connection, and each user does not have to go through the delay and expense of obtaining a connection to the network. As shown in Figure 8-4(a), the OSI model also defines a complementary demultiplexing service at the receiving site.

In contrast to the multiplexing/demultiplexing services, a user may wish to establish multiple connections to a network (or some other layer). So, OSI defines the procedures for splitting a user connection into multiple lower connections (see Figure 8-4[b]). This service is useful when a user wishes to increase throughput and/or increase resiliency with multiple connections. If this service is invoked, the model defines procedures for recombining the lower-level connections into one connection at the receiving site.

Data units (such as packet frames) in different layers and vendor products are not always the same size. The Reference Model describes three methods for handling this problem. First, segmenting permits the mapping of a service data unit (SDU) into more than one protocol data unit (PDU) within the same layer. Figure 8-4(c) shows that the protocol control information (PCI) is appended to each protocol data unit. This PCI (header) is needed to preserve the identity of the unit, and to allow for reassembly at the receiving site.

Conversely, it may be desirable to block smaller service data units into one larger protocol data unit within the same layer (see Figure 8-4[d]). For example, some packet networks place smaller user packets into a larger packet for transmission through a network. The PCI must contain sufficient information to allow deblocking at the receiving site.

Lastly, the process of concatenation is similiar to blocking, except smaller protocol data units are placed into one larger service data unit. This function assumes the (N) PDUs are passed to a $(N-1)$ SDU. In other words, concatenation occurs between two layers, whereas blocking occurs within a layer. Concatenation/separation is often implemented with the connection multiplexing/demultiplexing procedures.

NETWORK LAYER ADDRESSING

The data communications industry uses the term "network address" to identify different things in the network. The OSI model (X.213) defines the network address in three contexts.

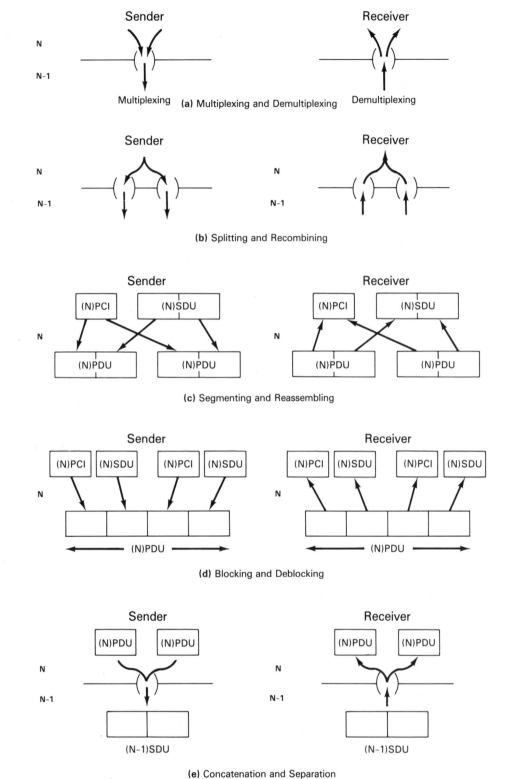

(a) Multiplexing and Demultiplexing

(b) Splitting and Recombining

(c) Segmenting and Reassembling

(d) Blocking and Deblocking

(e) Concatenation and Separation

NOTE: ( ) denotes a connection

FIGURE 8-4. OSI Management of Connections and Data Units

First, a network address identifies the interface to a public or private data network. The reader may recognize this address as the more common term DTE address. This definition of a network address does not pertain to an OSI service access point (SAP).

Second, a network address refers to the network service access point (NSAP). The N-CONNECT primitive uses the NSAP address in the called address, calling address, and responding address fields. As stated before, the SAP and primitives are conceptual and abstract. The OSI model does not specify a particular method of representing a SAP.

Third, a network address refers to field(s) within the network protocol control information (PCI). CCITT refers to this context as an address signal.

Since the primitives are used between adjacent layers for exchanging data and control, they are generally used to form the DTE addresses and/or the address in the PCI. Indeed, the DTE addresses and the address in the PCIs could be the same.

The NSAP address is an abstract concept used by OSI to identify the network service. The NSAP appears in the called address, calling address, and responding address parameters of N-CONNECT primitives. (It also appears in the source address and destination address of another primitive called N-UNITDATA, discussed in Chapter 14.)

A PRAGMATIC ILLUSTRATION

The OSI concept may be more easily understood by an examination of Figure 8-5. The abstract concepts of SDUs and PCIs are replaced with the words "user data" and "headers." As each unit traverses through the layers, it has a header added to it (encapsulation). This becomes the user data unit to the subsequent lower layers. Finally, the full protocol data unit (PDU) is transferred to the communications path. It arrives at the receiving site, coming up through the layers in the reverse order as it went through them from the sending site. The headers added at the peer layers at the transmitting site are used to invoke symmetrical and complementary functions at the receiving site. After the functions are performed, the protocol data unit is passed up to the next layer. The header that was added by the peer entity at the transmitting site is stripped off (decapsulated) by the peer entity at the receiving site. On close observation, it can be seen that the header is instrumental in invoking the functions across the network to the peer layer.

OVERVIEW OF THE SEVEN LAYERS OF OSI

This section provides a brief summary of the seven layers in the reference model. The following chapters explain each layer in more detail. Figure 8-6 illustrates the layers.

The lowest layer in the model is called the *physical layer*. The functions within this layer are responsible for activating, maintaining, and deacti-

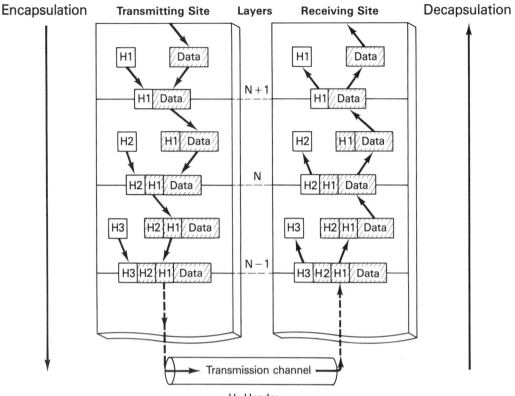

Encapsulation   **Transmitting Site**   **Layers**   **Receiving Site**   Decapsulation

H: Header

FIGURE 8-5. Communications Between Two Sites in a Network

vating a physical circuit between communicating devices. This layer includes specifications for physical signals (electrical, optical), cabling/wiring, and the characteristics of the connectors (plugs). Many standards are published for the physical layer. The most notable ones are EIA-232 and V.24.

The *data link layer* is responsible for the transfer of data over the channel. It provides for the synchronization of data to delimit the flow of bits from the physical layer. It also provides for the identity of the bits. It ensures that the data arrive safely at the receiving DTE. It provides for flow control to ensure that the DTE does not become overburdened with too much data at any one time. One of its most important functions is to provide for the detection of transmission errors and provide mechanisms to recover from lost, duplicated, or erroneous data.

The *network layer* specifies the interface of the user DTE into a network, as well as the interface of two DTEs with each other through a network. It also specifies network routing and the communications between networks (internetworking).

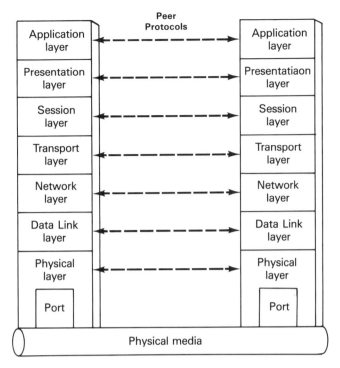

FIGURE 8-6. The OSI Layers

The *transport layer* provides the interface between the data communications network and the upper three layers (generally located at the user premises). This layer gives the user several options in obtaining certain levels of quality (and cost) from the network (i.e., the network layer). It is designed to keep the user isolated from some of the physical and functional aspects of the network. It also provides for end-to-end accountability.

The *session layer* serves as a user interface into the transport service layer. The layer provides for an organized means to exchange data between users. The users can select the type of synchronization and control needed from the layer.

The *presentation layer* provides for the syntax of data in the model; that is, the representation of data. It is not concerned with the meaning or semantics of the data. Its principal role, for example, is to accept data types (character, integer) from the application layer and then negotiate with its peer layer as to the syntax representation (such as ASCII). Thereafter, its functions are limited. The layer consists of many tables of syntax (teletype, ASCIII, Videotex, etc.).

The *application layer* is concerned with the support of an end-user application process. Unlike the presentation layer, this layer is concerned with the semantics of data. The layer contains service elements to support application processes such as job management, and financial data exchange. The layer also supports the virtual terminal and virtual file concept.

SUMMARY AND COMPARISON OF THE SERVICE DEFINITIONS BETWEEN LAYERS AND THE PROTOCOLS WITHIN THE LAYERS

Previous discussions in this chapter emphasized the importance of procedures to invoke services between the adjacent upper and lower layers (vertical communications). We learned that the services are requested, confirmed, etc. with primitives. We also learned that the primitives are used within the layer to create the header (PCI) for the protocol data unit (PDU). The PDUs and their PCIs are used by a remote peer layer to invoke specific operations (horizontal communications).

Figure 8-7 shows the most widely used service definitions. The majority of these protocols are published by the ISO, the CCITT, or the IEEE. In many instances, these different standards organizations' definitions are comparable. For example the ISO 8348 and CCITT X.213 documents are almost identical.

This figure also shows the principal protocols used within the layers. Please be aware that not all the protocols are shown. They are too numerous to show in one picture.

It should be noted that the IEEE service definition and the ISO 8802/X protocols are identical. Also, these protocols define both the service definitions and the operations within the layer.

CRITICISM OF THE OSI MODEL

This brief section describes some criticisms of the OSI model and includes some of the author's opinions on the subject.

The layers as presently specified by ISO and the CCITT require substantial computing resources to perform their functions, and it is fair to say they can be made more efficient. However, as more functions are provided to a user, more resources are required to provide the functions. Network services such as end-to-end reliability, fast response time, and high throughput do not happen with "vaporware." Software and hardware of sufficient power must be available to meet these requirements.

A close examination of the OSI architecture reveals (a) some duplications of functions and redundancy of primitives between and across several of the layers, and (b) considerable overhead in the headers and trailers used in several of the layers (especially the upper layers).

Regarding point (a), the redundant negotiation of services between and across layers is an area cited for improvement. However, it must be realized that a service performed at, say, layer 5 requires a request from an end-user residing above layer 7. How is this service to be requested and invoked if not by relaying the "parameters" to the responsible layer? It would appear the only other alternative is to pre-map the requests and services. They would then be invoked without the use of primitives. It is certainly an alternative and indeed it is used as an option in parts of the OSI model. It also degrades

IEEE Layer Protocol	CCITT Layer Protocol	ISO Layer Protocol	OSI Layer	ISO Service Definition	CCITT Service Definition	IEEE Service Definition
	X.400-X.430 MHS X.228 RTSE X.229 ROSE X.227 ACSE	9040 VT 8650 CCR 8571 FTAM 8649 CASE 8831 JTM	Application	8650	X.217	
	X.208 X.209 X.226	8824 8825 8823	Presentation	8822	X.216	
	X.225	8327	Session	8326	X.215	
	X.224	8073 8602	Transport	8072	X.214	
	Q.931 X.25 X.75 X.300–X.352	8208 8878 8473 8648	Network	8348	X.213	
802	LAPB I.440 / I.441 LAPD	7776 7809 3309 4335 8022	Data Link	8886, 8802/2	X.212	802.2
Many	Many	Many	Physical	8802/3, 8802/4, 880 2/5	X.211	802.3, 802.4, 802.5

FIGURE 8-7. The Most Prevalent Service Definition Protocols

Note: Entries do not represent all available standards, but a sample of the prevalent offerings.

287

the flexibility of requesting services dynamically. A practical approach is to pre-map the users' profiles as default options and use the parameters in the primitives only to override the defaults. Several of the OSI entities provide this flexibility.

Regarding point (b), the number of octets needed to construct PCI (protocol control information) in the layer headers could be reduced. The use of fields to indicate multiple functions with Boolean bit comparisons would reduce the number of overhead bits.

However, these schemes require more complex software and additional machine processing cycles to encode and decode the fields. The "slow-speed" channels that currently support networks can certainly benefit from a fewer number of overhead octets, but the increased channel throughput must be weighed against increased processing time.

Network managers face a dilemma. If OSI is altered and customized at this late date, it could lead to increased incompatibility. If it is not altered, it will continue to require substantial processing and transmission resources. The opponents to the changes to OSI state that the forthcoming faster processors and faster transmission systems will be capable of supporting a fully layered OSI network very effectively.

From the author's perspective, some of the OSI layers can be improved, but there is no such thing as a free lunch, and functionality requires resources. For example, after working with a variety of vendors' networks for several years, it is evident their richness of functions do not come without cost.

Frankly, many OSI applications will perform better if their programmers and designers are more skillful in how they implement the options available in many of the standards. Moreover, functions such as session control, segmentation, concatenation, end-to-end accountability, and resequencing cannot be implemented unless sufficient software and computing resources are available.

As a practical matter, many vendors and manufacturers simply choose to implement a specific part of the OSI layer or entity that they deem advantageous to their product.

U.S. GOVERNMENT OPEN SYSTEMS INTERCONNECTION PROFILE (GOSIP)

The U.S. Government Open Systems Interconnection Profile (GOSIP) is likely to play a major role in the future of the data communications industry. (One can only imagine the glee of the people who created this ironic acronym.) GOSIP is based on a series of workshops conducted at the National Bureau of Standards (NBS) and represents the final agreements on a set of OSI protocols for computer networking. Its importance lies in the fact that it is to be used by government agencies for product and services acquisition. To reinforce the importance of Part II of this book, GOSIP provides implementation specifications from standards issued by the ISO, CCITT, IEEE, ANSI, EIA, and others.

GOSIP Architecture

The U.S. government OSI architecture as seen through GOSIP is summarized in this section. Many of these specifications/recommendations are discussed in the following chapters. Our immediate purpose is to provide a framework for GOSIP in order to understand the implication of the U.S. government's efforts toward standardization.

To begin our examination of GOSIP, please examine Figure 8-8. A larger variety of network protocols exists at the lower levels. This implementation is necessary because different protocols are needed to handle different communications requirements, such as local and wide area networks. As OSI and GOSIP evolve, more protocols will be included in the upper levels. Presently, the major high-level protocols are X.400 and the FTAM recommendations. The following section is based on the GOSIP specification [GOSI87]. The specific references are provided in the chapters of this book that describe each specification. The reader is encouraged to contact the NBS for more detail on GOSIP.

GOSIP Layers

The physical layer is to be selected by the acquisition authority from the following protocols. In conjunction with the use of X.25, the choices are Interim MIL-STD-188-114 and EIA-232. In conjunction with the use of IEEE 802.2 Logical Link Control Type 1, the choices are IEEE 802.3 and IEEE 802.4.

The data link layer protocols are to be selected from the following specifications. High-Level Data Link Control (HDLC) and its "subset" LAPB will be used in conjunction with X.25. The Logical Link Control (LLC) IEEE 802.2 protocol is to be used in conjunction with IEEE 802.3 or IEEE 802.4.

The network layer can use the ISO connectionless internetwork protocol (IP). The IP must be implemented for the internetworking of concatenated networks and single networks as well. ISO 8348 and ISO 8473 are selected for connectionless networks. X.25 is selected for connection-oriented networks.

The transport layer must use the transport specifications from the ISO and CCITT, in accordance with the workshop agreements. Transport class 4 (TP4) is the preferred protocol class. Transport class 0 (TP0) is to be used in conjunction (and as appropriate) with CCITT X.400.

The upper three layers use both CCITT and ISO recommendations. The session layer uses ISO IS 8326 and IS 8327 or CCITT X.215 and X.225. The presentation layer uses ISO DIS 8822, DIS 8823, DIS 8824, and DIS 8825. The application layer uses FTAM and the X.400 Message Handling Systems set of protocols.

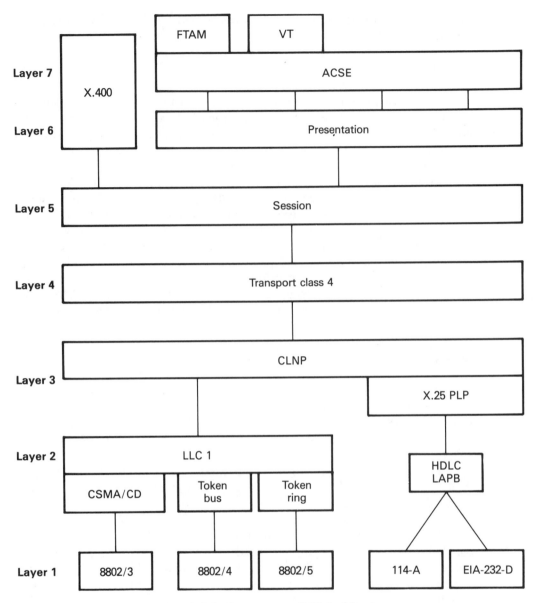

FIGURE 8-8. Government OSI Architecture

SYSTEMS NETWORK ARCHITECTURE

IBM introduced Systems Network Architecture (SNA) in September 1973 as its major commitment to communications systems and networks. By 1977, 350 SNA sites existed. At the end of 1978, the number had increased to 1250, and in 1978 over 4000 installations had SNA. Today, over 20,000 licensed

SNA sites are in operation. Even if the reader does not use SNA, it is a good idea to understand its basic features, since it is so pervasive in the industry.

SNA is a specification (of many, many documents) describing the architecture for a distributed data processing network. It defines the rules and protocols for the interaction of the components (computers, terminals, software) in the network.

SNA is organized around the concept of a domain (see Figure 8-9). A SNA domain is a Systems Services Control Point (SSCP) and all the resources controlled by it. These resources are physical units (PU), logical units (LU), data links, and devices. These features are described in the following paragraphs.

An IBM host node contains software identified as the virtual telecommunications access method (VTAM) and a subset called the System Services Control Point (SSCP). SSCP is the focal point in the network for managing the configuration, operation and sessions of components within the domain. Each SSCP in a network, which is performed by VTAM, has its own domain.

The communications controller node (COMC) is IBM's 3705, 3725, or 3745 front end with the Network Control Program (NCP). The reader can view the NCP as the operating system of the communications controller node. The cluster controller node (CLC) is a peripheral node (PN: like a terminal controller) that controls a variety of devices. IBM has developed several CLCs that perform special applications functions, such as banking and retail point-of-sale transactions. Finally, the terminal node (TN) is the farthest point out in SNA's distributed path, and describes pre-SNA devices such as Binary Synchronous Communications (BSC) 3270 devices.

SNA can best be introduced by a closer examination of the SSCP and two other fundamental parts of the architecture: physical units (PU) and logical units (LU). These three elements are called network addressable units (NAU), and they are the three essential components of SNA. In SNA, an NAU can be an originator or a receiver of traffic, and every NAU in the network is assigned a unique address. For example, an NAU is assigned to elements such as the host access method (VTAM), the front end network control program (NCP), cluster controllers, terminals, and applications. Communications lines are also assigned addresses, but they are not NAUs since they do not originate or receive traffic. An NAU is really a "logical port" into and out of the SNA network.

SSCP is the "heart and brains" of SNA. It is responsible for the SNA network. It resides in the host telecommunications access method (VTAM). Each part (domain) of a SNA network is assigned to a SSCP. To gain an appreciation of SSCP, consider its major functions:

- Establishing user sessions in the network
- Controlling resources in the domain
- Bringing up the network
- Bringing down the network

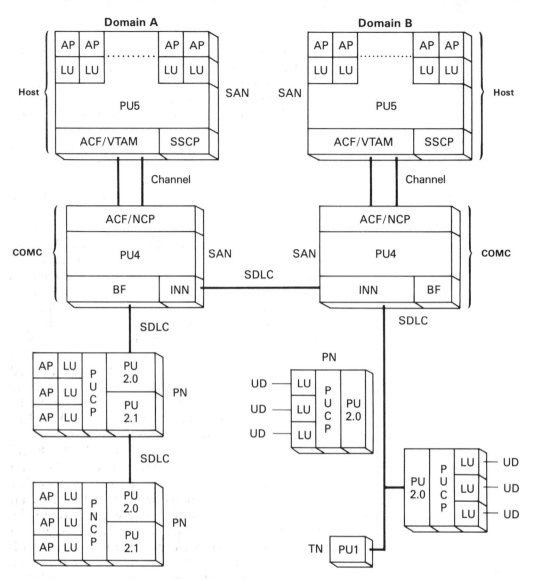

ACF/VTAM: Advanced Communication Function/Virtual Telecommunication Access Method
AP: Application Process (Program)
BF: Boundary Function
COMC: Communications Controller Node
INN: Intermediate Network Node
LU: Logical Unit
PN: Peripheral Node
PNCP: Peripheral Node Control Point
PU: Physical Unit
PUCP: Physical Unit Control Point
SAN: Subarea Node
SDLC: Synchronous Data Link Control
TN: Terminal Node
UD: User Device

FIGURE 8-9. An SNA Network

- Converting symbolic names to internal network addresses
- Scheduling error recovery
- Maintaining status of network
- Coordinating the interconnection of logical and physical units
- Coordinating the activities of the physical units (PUs) and logical units (LUs)
- Supporting devices directly attached to host node (channel-attached devices)

SSCP controls a SNA domain by sending commands to a PU, which then manages the resources attached directly to it. A PU is really a "partner" to SSCP and contains a subset of the SSCP capabilities. It performs functions such as recovery procedures, the activating of a data communications link and terminal control. The PU is responsible for management of each SNA node and provides the following functions: (a) controlling local stations; (b) activating and deactivating data links; (c) assisting in the recovery of failures; (d) providing control support for station operators; (e) generating diagnostic information; and (f) requesting downline loading of software into nodes.

SNA distinguishes between subarea nodes and peripheral nodes. A subarea node can route user data throughout the entire network. It uses the network address and a route number to determine a transmission line to the next node in the network. A subarea must contain either a host (Type 5 node) or a front-end with the network control program, NCP (Type 4 node). One or more nodes must contain an SSCP, or a subset of SSCP called a physical unit control point (PUCP).

A peripheral node (also called cluster controllers) is more locally oriented. It does not route between subarea nodes. The nodes are connected and controlled by synchronous data link control (SDLC). Messages are routed across the links to/from the nodes based on the address contained in the message. A peripheral node communicates only with the subarea node to which it is connected.

SNA Services and Layers

SNA networks use the layering concept. To add confusion to these matters, various IBM documents use different terms to describe the upper layers. Moreover, some of the layers' boundaries are ill-defined. Our convention in this book is to use the more recent terminology. Figure 8-10 illustrates the SNA layers, as well as comparing them to the OSI and DECnet layers (the DECnet layers are examined next).

SNA Function Management. This layer provides a very wide range of services. It corresponds to the OSI application and presentation services. The layer provides for common formats between end-users and device

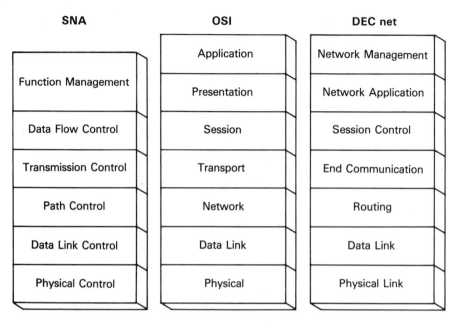

FIGURE 8-10. SNA, OSI, and DECnet Layers

control characters between dissimilar devices. The presentation services function provides compression and compaction facilities. It also provides for a common set of display screen formats between applications. (The application program need only transmit the name of the screen format.) This layer also performs sync-point processing and selected profiles for the user session. It is also responsible for providing network services.

Data Flow Control Layer. This layer is roughly analogous to the OSI session layer and supports full duplex dialogues between network addressable units It also supports sending a "chain" of data until it is complete. The chaining allows the layer to group unidirectional, related messages together and treat them as a whole. This is a useful feature when downline loading files or jobs to other sites in the network. The Data Flow Control Layer also provides for brackets. This permits grouping bidirectional, related messages that move between two logical units together. This keeps messages logically together that are related to one transaction.

Transmission Control Layer. This layer is similar to the OSI transport layer and maintains the status of an active session, provides for sequencing of the data messages, and paces the flow of data into and out of user sessions. It also routes data to appropriate points within a network unit. Transmission Control provides session window management by session-level pacing, which allows the LUs to control the number of messages processed. This prevents the overrun of LUs that have limited processing and buffering capabilities. Transmission Control also provides headers (request/response header, or RH) to the message for the chaining, bracket, and pacing functions. Encryption and decryption can also be obtained in this layer.

Path Control Layer. The Path Control Layer has two primary responsibilities: routing and flow control. Routing through the SNA nodes is accomplished by Path Control examining network names in the message and determining the appropriate link (or perhaps a group of links) in order for the message to move to its destination. The layer resolves addressing for both subareas and elements. Path Control also performs message segmenting, which is similar to the OSI segmenting functions discussed earlier. SNA allows different segment sizes for each link or group of links. In addition, Path Control also blocks messages together. This is a useful function for reducing channel input-output interrupts and operations. Path Control provides for various classes of service such as fast response, secure routes, or more reliable connections. Three transmission priorities (high, medium, and low) are provided.

Data Link Control and Physical Layers. These layers are equivalent to the two lower OSI layers. The data link layer is implemented with SDLC and the physical layer is available with RS-232-C, X.21, and other specifications.

DIGITAL NETWORK ARCHITECTURE
(DECnet or DNA)

DECnet is the major data communications network offering from the Digital Equipment Corporation. Developed as a distributed network, it supports a wide range of applications and programs. Digital has designed DECnet to achieve the following goals:

- Create a common user interface across varied applications and implementations.
- Provide resource-sharing capabilities to data, computers, and peripheral devices.
- Support distributed computation, allowing cooperating programs to execute in different computers in a network.
- Support a wide range of communication facilities such as Ethernet and X.25.
- Maintain a high level of availability, even in the event of node or link failure.

DECnet Layers

DECnet is designed around the concept of layered protocols (see Figure 8-10). It consists of eight layers.

Physical Layer. The lowest layer is called the Physical Link Layer. It is quite similar to the layers of other networks in that it encompasses specifications such as RS-232, X.21, and CCITT V.24/V.28.

Data Link Layer. The Data Link Layer is quite similar to the data link layer of other specifications. It controls the communications path between adjacent nodes. The data link layer ensures the error-free transmission of data across an otherwise error-laden link. Many of the data link layer functions are implemented through Ethernet and Digital Data Communication Message Protocol (DDCMP). Interestingly, DEC includes its X.25 module in the data link layer. We describe this seeming anomaly in Chapters 13 and 14.

Routing Layer. The Routing Layer (previously called the transport layer) provides the routing functions between nodes. It also is responsible for network congestion control and determining the lapsed time of a packet within the network.

End Communications Layer. The End Communication Layer (which was previously called the Network Services Layer) is similar to the Transport Layer of the ISO reference model. It is responsible for the end-to-end error control, segmentation, reassembly, and data flow control.

Session Control Layer. The Session Control Layer is responsible for logical communications between users. For example, it provides the mapping of node names to specific node addresses. It identifies end-users, and activates and deactivates sessions between users. It also validates sessions between users.

Network Application Layer. The Network Application Layer provides for higher-level functions such as remote file access, data transfer, and interactive terminal usage. The Network Application Layer contains functions similar to the application and presentation layers of the ISO reference model. This layer provides for the data access protocol (DAP) discussed later. It also provides the gateway access protocols to SNA and X.25, also discussed later.

Network Management Layer. The Network Management Layer is used principally for the controlling and monitoring of the network operations. For example, it permits downline loading of resources, testing links, setting and displaying the states of links and nodes.

User Layer.   Finally, the User Layer contains most of the user supplied routines. It also contains some DECnet systems such as the network control program, which is described later in this section. The User Layer has direct access to Network Management, Network Application, and Session Control Layers. The Network Management Layers have direct access to all the other layers.

DEFENSE DATA NETWORK (DDN)

In 1982 the Department of Defense (DOD) directed the establishment of the Defense Data Network (DDN), based on ARPANET technology. The ARPANET was designed under a 1969 Defense Advanced Research Projects Agency (DARPA) research and development program. It was designated as the ARPANET and was the pioneer of packet switching networks. Initially, ARPANET was designed as an experimental network to advance the embryonic computer resource sharing projects. It was also designed to provide communications between heterogeneous computers. As ARPANET evolved, it grew in functionality and complexity. In 1975, it was transferred to the Defense Communications Agency (DCA). Later in 1983, the DDN was established based on the ARPANET technology.

DDN is a packet switching network grouped into two major functional areas: (1) the backbone network which consists of the packet switches and the trunks between them and (2) the access network which consists of the user access lines connected to the backbone. Figure 8-11 illustrates the basic DDN layers and components. Hosts' systems can be connected to the packet switches using X.25 or the ARPANET 1822 interface specifications. The host trunks can operate at 9.6 to 56 Kbit/s. Each host system can be directly connected to one or more packet switches by one or more links. The host systems may also connect directly or through a host front-end processor.

The major layers and protocols of DDN are summarized in Box 8-2.

The DDN has been designed to provide survivability, security, and privacy. As a consequence, much of the equipment is configured with high-altitude electromagnetic pulse protection (HEMP) in the form of electromagnetic shielding, line isolation circuits, and surge suppressing components. Some of the nodes are configured with uninterrupted power supply (UPS). Several of the nodes are also configured with redundant equipment, to prevent a single failure from isolating a node.

DDN also is a dynamic routing network, and adjusts itself to any damage without disrupting service to the surviving subscribers. Distributed routing allows the nodes to automatically route the data around damaged, congested, or destroyed links and switches. DDN also provides extensive monitoring of the system and enables a graceful degradation in order to route around damaged or congested areas.

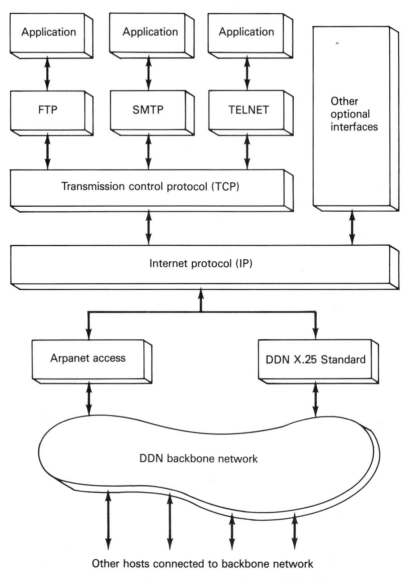

FIGURE 8-11. Defense Data Network (DDN)

DDN also provides secure traffic transmission, if needed, by using end-to-end encryption and other security measures. To provide this security, DDN is composed of two backbone networks. One segment is classified and the other is unclassified. The unclassified network uses encryption techniques based on the Bureau of Standards' Data Encryption Standard (DES). The classified network uses a higher-level, military-grade encryption service.

BOX 8-2. Layers and Protocols of DDN

- The DOD Standard Transmission Control Protocol/Internet Protocol (TCP/IP), which is used to permit the end-to-end flow control and accountability of data between two computer systems or between a computer system and a terminal access controller.
- The standard X.25 protocol and the ARPANET (1822) network access protocols
- The virtual terminal protocol TELNET is used to provide terminal access into the network using virtual terminal formats
- The file transfer protocol (FTP) which enables files to be transferred between computer systems
- The simple mail transfer protocol (SMTP) which provides the reliable transfer of electronic mail through the DDN

As depicted in Box 8-2, DDN users may use the DDN standard X.25 protocol (an adaptation of the CCITT specification) or the ARPANET (1822) interface protocol. Host computer systems must also use the TCP/IP protocol to communicate. Terminal users must use the TELNET to operate any DDN terminal on the network. The TELNET protocol permits terminals to communicate, not only with the host computers directly, but also indirectly with other host computers.

THE OSI DIRECTORY (X.500)

Directories have been in use in computer installations for over a decade. Some organizations have used them for simple operations such as storing source code for software programs. Others have built data directories to store the names and attributes of the organization's data elements. Some forward-thinking companies now use directories to show the relationships of data elements to data bases, files, and programs. The dictionary/directory is used to check all key automated systems for accuracy and duplication, and permits an organization to evaluate the impact of system changes to all the automated resources. The directory has become a vital component in an organization's management of its automated resources.

Typically, each organization and vendor has developed a unique and propietary approach to the design and implementaton of directories, which greatly complicates the management of resources that are stored in different machines and data bases. In the spirit of OSI, the purpose of the X.500 Directory is to provide a set of standards to govern the use of directories/dictionaries. This section provides an overview of the X.500 standards, and guides the reader to the specific, detailed references.

The X.500 standards were released as part of the CCITT 1988 Blue Book standards. They describe the operations of the *Directory*. It is designed to support and facilitate the communication of information between systems about *objects* such as data, applications, hardware, people, files, distribution lists, and practically anything else that the organization deems worthy of "tracking" for management purposes. X.500 is intended to allow the communication of this information between different systems.

X.500 actually encompasses eight standards, collectively known as X.500:

X.500: The Directory—Overview of Concepts, Models, and Services
X.501: The Directory Models
X.509: The Directory—Authentication Framework
X.511: The Directory—Abstract Service Definition
X.518: The Directory—Procedures of Distributed Operation
X.519: The Directory—Protocol Specifications
X.520: The Directory—Selected Attribute Types
X.521: The Directory—Selected Object Classes

Key Terms and Concepts

Referring to Figure 8-12, the information held in the Directory is known as the *Directory Information Base* (DIB). It is accessed by the Directory user through the *Directory User Agent* (DUA), which is considered to be an applications process. The DUA is so named because it acts as an agent to the end user vis-á-vis the DIB.

Figure 8-13 shows the entries in the DIB are arranged in a tree structure called the *Directory Information Tree* (DIT). The vertices in the tree represent the *entries* in the DIB. These entries make up a collection of information about one *object* (such as a person, a data element, a piece of hardware, a program and so on). The *alias* is also permitted; it points to an object entry.

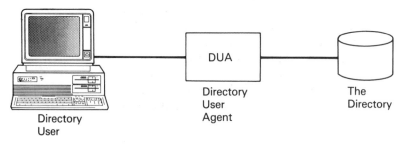

FIGURE 8-12. X.500 Directory Access

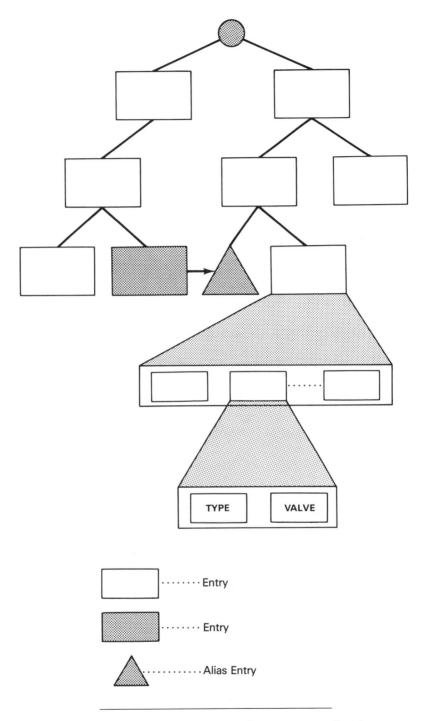

Entry

Entry

Alias Entry

FIGURE 8-13. The Directory Information Tree (DIT)

Each entry consists of *attributes*, and each attribute is made up of a *type* and one or more *values*. The attribute type also specifies the syntax and the data type of the value.

Each entry must have a *distinguished name*. This term means the name is unique and unambiguous in identifying the entry. The distinguished name is made up from the name of its superior entry (the entry above, in the tree), and some other meaningful identifier.

X.500 uses the term schema in a different context than other data base systems. A schema is a rule to ensure the DIB maintains its logical structure during modifications. It prevents inconsistencies in the DIB such as incorrect subordinate entries' class, attribute values, etc.

The DIB may return a request using more than one entry. To do so, X.500 uses a *filter*. It defines one or more conditions that must be satisfied by the entry if it is to be returned in the result to the user.

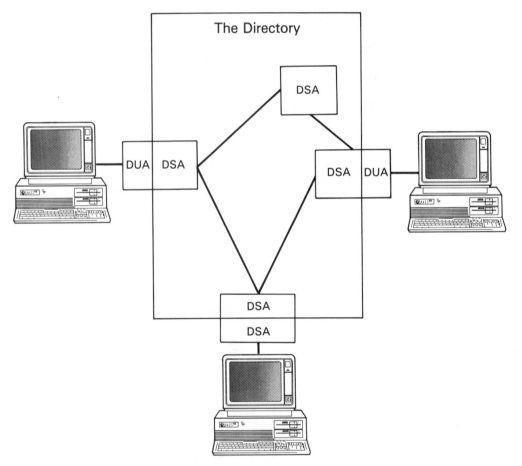

FIGURE 8-14. Directory System Agent (DSA)

X.500 assures the Directory can be distributed across a wide geographical area. To support this environment, the Directory System Agent (DSA) provides access to the DIB from the DUAs or other DSAs. Figure 8-14 shows the relationship of the distributed Directory. A DUA is permitted to interact with a single or multiple DSAs. In turn, the DSAs may internetwork with other DSAs to satisfy a request.

The DUAs and DSAs communications are governed by two protocols:

Directory Access Protocol (DAP): Specifies actions between DUA and DSA

Directory System Protocol (DSP): Specifies actions between DSAs

The Directory is administered by the *Directory Management Domain* (DMD), which consists of a set of one or more DSAs and zero or more DUAs. The DMD may be a country, a PTT, a network, or anything designated to manage the DIB.

Be aware that this is a very general overview of X.500 and the reader should obtain the X.500 document if more detailed information is needed.

SUGGESTED READINGS

We now have sufficient background information to examine each layer in more detail. For the reader who wishes additional information on OSI, [X.200] and [IS7498] should be studied. They contain the descriptions of the OSI reference model. [GOSI87] explains the GOSIP protocols. [DECN82] is a good overview of the DECnet architecture. [LINN87] is an excellent overview of SNA layers. [IEEE83] is a general survey of OSI and is highly recommended. [MART87] provides lucid descriptions of SNA.

QUESTIONS

TRUE/FALSE

1. The term network topology describes the conventions of how network components communicate with each other.
2. In the OSI model, sublayers may be bypassed if the services are not needed.
3. The network layer is responsible for actions within a network but is not responsible for internetworking actions.
4. GOSIP is a seven-layer model.
5. SNA describes its SSCP, LU, and PU as network addressable units.
6. Match the description to the appropriate term:

   Description

   a) Used on Ethernet systems

b) A typical SNA topology
c) A typical PBX configuration
d) Relatively immune to bottlenecks

Term

1. Hierarchical topology
2. Star topology
3. Mesh topology
4. Horizontal topology

7. Match the OSI component with the appropriate term:

Description

a) Preserved from an (N) connection to another (N) connection.
b) Unit of information transferred between the service access point (SAP) between an (N + 1) entity and an (N) entity. A combination of control and data.
c) Same as (b) except the term describes only control information.
d) Unit of information transferred between an (N) connection. A combination of control and data.
e) Same as (d) except the term describes only control information.

Terms

1. Interface data unit (IDU)
2. Interface control information (ICI)
3. Service data unit (SDU)
4. Protocol data unit (PDU)
5. Protocol Control Information (PCI)

8. Briefly describe the major performance goals of the network designer.
9. Explain the general concepts and goals of layered protocols.
10. Layered protocols are based on three principles of atomic actions. Describe these principles.
11. The figure on the facing page represents a structured, functional chart of program processes [BLAC87]. The boxes contain code that performs specific functions. The lines between the boxes show (a) the flow of control: the higher box in the hierarchy invokes the functions of a lower box and (b) the "coupling" of the functions: more lines indicate more functional relationships. Does this chart adhere to these OSI principles?
    a) Create layer boundaries that minimize layer interactions and the description of services.
    b) Localized functions should be established which allow a redesign with minimal effect to adjacent layers.
    c) Changes made in a layer should not affect other layers.
    d) Each layer has interfaces only to its upper and lower adjacent layers.
12. Referring to question 11, redraw the figure so that it represents a structure that supports the cited principles.

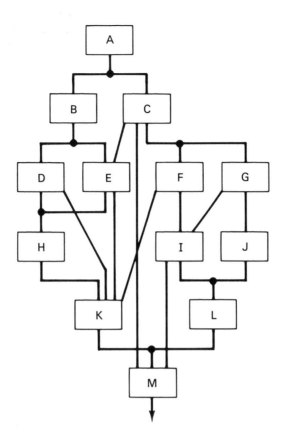

13. For reasons cited in this chapter, the OSI primitives are abstract. A specific system may use the primitives in the form of a program input/output statement, a function call, or a subroute call. Using the primitives described in this chapter, analyze the system you use and write a system-specific primitive for each of these OSI abstract primitives:
    a) CONNECT request (Addresses, QOS)
    b) DATA request (Data)
    c) DISCONNECT request (Addresses, QOS)

SELECTED ANSWERS

1. False. The correct term is protocol. Topology describes the shape of the network.
2. True. See OSI principle 13.
3. False. The network layer is responsible for subnetwork and internetwork actions.
4. True.
5. True.

6.
Description	Terms
a)	4
b)	1
c)	2
d)	3

7.
Component	Terms
a)	3
b)	1
c)	2
d)	4
e)	5

11. a) No. For example, function K has five different interface boundaries: D, H, E, F and M.

b) No. Several of the functions affect nonadjacent layers.

c) Unable to determine if this principle is met. Changes within a function (entity) may or may not affect others. If they do affect other layers/functions, they must adhere to the principles of atomic actions.

d) No. Functions E, D, K, C, F, G, I and M violate this principle.

12.

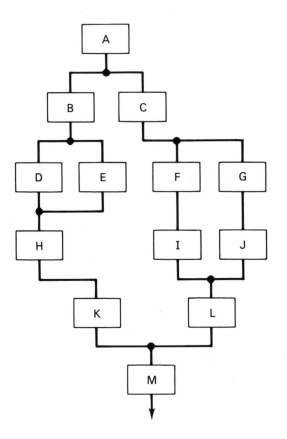

CHAPTER 9

The Physical Level

INTRODUCTION

The preceding chapters have described how signals are transmitted and received between computers, terminals, and other devices through the communications channel. We now focus our attention on the more commonly used conventions and recommended standards defining physical level interfaces. The reader is encouraged to review Chapter 3 since it introduces the physical level concepts of encoding, decoding, and modulation as well as several other terms that are used in this chapter.

The standards groups, the computer industry, and vendors have developed many specifications defining the interfaces of DCEs (such as modems and digital service units [DSUs]) with DTEs (such as terminals and computers). Their acceptance has made it possible to interface equipment from different vendors.

Our goal in this chapter is to gain an understanding of the concepts of physical level interfaces and to review the prevalent recommended standards and vendor products. The reader is encouraged to obtain the specific document if more detail is needed on an interface. These documents are cited at the end of the chapter.

Physical level protocols (or physical level interfaces) are so named because the DTE and DCE are physically connected with (a) wires and cables or (b) sky or ground wave signals through the atmosphere. Physical level interfaces perform several functions:

• Provide data transfer across the interface between the DTE and DCE
• Provide control signals between the devices

- Provide clocking signals to synchronize data flow and regulate the bit rate
- Provide for electrical ground
- Provide the mechanical connectors (such as pins, sockets, and plugs)

Most physical level protocols describe four attributes of the interface: electrical, functional, mechanical, and procedural. The electrical attributes describe the voltage (or current) levels, the timing of the electrical signals, and all other electrical characteristics (capacitance, signal rise time, etc.). The functional attributes describe the functions to be performed by the physical interface. Many physical level protocols classify these functions as control, timing, data, and ground. The mechanical attributes describe the dimensions of the connectors and the number of wires on the interface. Usually, the data, signalling, and control wires are enclosed in one cover. The procedural attributes describe what the connectors must do, and the sequence of events required to effect actual data transfer across the interface.

Where the Physical Level Resides

It is sometimes assumed that a physical level interface encompasses only the interchange circuit(s) between the DTE and the DCE. While this view is correct for some products and standards, the physical level also includes the signalling between the two DCEs (see Figure 9-1). The CCITT publishes the V Series physical level protocols to include (a) the DTE-to-DCE interface and

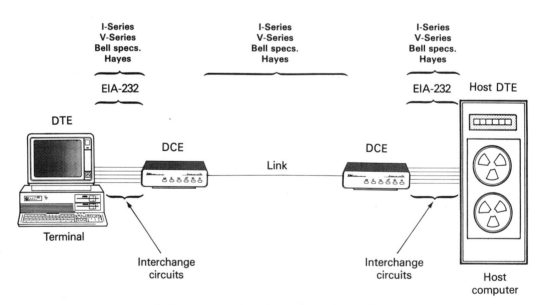

FIGURE 9-1. The Physical Level Interface

(b) the DCE-to-DCE interfaces. Other standards, such as EIA-232, encompass only the DTE-to-DCE side of the interface. Even though EIA-232 does not specify the DCE-to-DCE exchange, many vendors use the relevant portion of the CCITT V Series recommendations and/or the AT&T/Bell specifications to describe this part of the physical level interface. For example, this is a practice of the Hayes modem products. The I Series specifies a digital physical level interface.

Examples of DCEs

The DCE is typically a modem, multiplexer, or digital device (data service unit). We discussed the functions of these devices in previous chapters. A brief review is provided here as well as some examples of other DCEs. The digital DCE (I Series) is described in more detail in Chapter 19.

The modem is responsible for providing the translation and interface between the digital and analog worlds. The term modem is derived from (a) the process of accepting digital bits and changing them into a form suitable for analog transmission (modulation) and (2) receiving the signal at the other station and transforming it back to its original digital representation (demodulation). Modem is derived from the two words *mo*dulator and *dem*odulator. Modems are designed around the use of a carrier frequency. The carrier signal has the digital data stream superimposed on it at the transmitting end of the circuit. This carrier frequency has the characteristics of the sine wave discussed in Chapter 2.

The short-haul or limited-distance modem (LDM) is used for transmissions of a few feet to approximately 20 miles. The distance is highly variable and depends on the operating speed, type of transmission path, and configuration of the telephone company facilities. Typical LDMs use wire pairs or coaxial cables and some can operate at high data rates (19.2 Kbit/s to 1 Mbit/s). The use of a short-haul modem requires the removal of certain analog equipment on the telephone line. These machines are attractive due to their simplicity and low cost. Dedicated circuits are required.

Line drivers are dc machines and are often used to eliminate modems. Operating distances range from a few feet to several miles. The line driver is usually installed between two DTEs to replace the modems (on short distances). These machines are also attractive due to their very low price.

A null modem is actually an EIA-232 cable interface pinned to allow a direct connection between two devices when a modem is not required. Null modems provide no timing signals; consequently, they are used with asynchronous devices that derive their timing from start/stop bits.

A modem eliminator is used in situations where two synchronous devices (such as terminals, printers, plotters) are close together. The modem eliminator provides the interface and clocking for the devices.

Some people do not distinguish between a null modem and a modem eliminator. This writer uses the term null modem to describe an interface for asynchronous devices and the term modem eliminator as an interface for synchronous devices. The exact use of the terms is somewhat irrelevant as long as the conversing parties use the same term to describe the same device.

Acoustic couplers are yet another alternative for physical level signalling. These machines acoustically connect the terminal to the analog facilities. The telephone handset is placed into the coupler's transmit/receive device for connection. Portable terminals often contain acoustic couplers. The technique is very simple and very effective for low data rates (up to 1200 bit/s; usually no greater than 450 bit/s).

A Review of Clocking and Synchronization

Synchronization and clocking are important functions of the physical level. As discussed in Chapter 1, asynchronous and synchronous systems use different synchronization procedures. We learned that asynchronous transmission provides timing signals by the start-stop bits, and Chapter 3 introduced the idea of clocking for synchronous systems. We reiterate briefly these concepts and then delve into more detail.

Synchronous transmission provides timing signals by one of three techniques.

- Providing a separate clocking line
- Imbedding the clocking signal in the data stream with the data acting as a clock to a simple receiver circuit
- Imbedding the clocking signal in the data stream and using it to synchronize a receiver clock

A separate clocking line is a widely used technique for short distance connections. In addition to the data line, another line transmits an associated timing signal, which is used to "clock" the data into the receiver. The clocking line notifies the receiver when a bit is arriving.

However, the transmitting station does not always provide the clocking signal. Many configurations use the receiver to provide the clocking signal to the transmitting station. This signal from the receiver dictates the specific time for the transmitter to send data.

A separate clocking line is a common technique for synchronous interfaces between terminals/computers and their associated DCEs, such as modems and multiplexers. (As we shall see, the EIA-232 interface provides several options for synchronous transmission and clocking.) However, a separate clocking channel is not practical under certain conditions:

- Longer distances make a separate wire prohibitively expensive.
- Longer distances also increase the probability that the clocking line

will lose its synchronization with the data line, since each line has its own unique transmission characteristics.

- The telephone network does not provide clocking lines for a typical data subscriber since the lines are designed for voice.

The second approach is to embed the clocking signal in the data and have the receiver extract the clock from the received data stream. The receiver uses relatively simple circuitry for the clock extraction (a delay and rectifier circuit). In order to embed the clocking signal, the data bits are encoded at the transmitter to provide frequent transitions on the channel. Several encoding methods are employed; the more common schemes are explained in Chapter 3.

A digital phase locked loop (DPLL) is used to maintain bit synchronization with the third method. An oscillator is connected to the DPLL and operates at a rate considerably faster than the bit rate (16 or 32 clock periods per sample, for example). The fast sampling rate is used to detect the 1-to-0 or 0-to-1 transition as soon as possible. If the incoming bit stream and the local clock "drift" from each other, the frequent clock periods still provide a reasonably accurate indication of the line transition. Moreover, the DPLL readjusts if line transitions occur more or less often than the total clock periods/bit cell. The time periods between pulses are shortened or lengthened to keep the sampling close to the center of each bit cell. This technique allows the components in the data communications system to adjust to timing inaccuracies and remove timing jitter from the signals.

THE V SERIES RECOMMENDATIONS, ISO CONNECTORS, AND EIA-232

The majority of computer and terminal physical connections use the same type of physical interface. It is rather unusual when special connectors, circuits, clocking arrangements, encoding conventions, and electrical signals are required. Even if they are needed, it is often prohibitively expensive to implement them for a specific requirement. Consequently, it makes good sense to use a set of conventions for physical interfaces. By using the set, less variety will exist and different vendors' products are more likely to communicate with each other directly, without intervening converters.

The specifications for the operations of modems, digital service units, and other DCE type components with user devices (DTEs) are published by the CCITT, the Electronic Industries Association (EIA), the Institute of Electrical and Electronic Engineers (IEEE), and others. In addition, the International Standards Organization (ISO) publishes specifications on the mechanical connectors that connect DCEs with DTEs. In North America, the AT&T/Bell specifications have been accepted as de facto standards, and in the past few years, the Hayes modem specifications have taken a lion's share of the market with the PC-based modem product line.

The majority of data transmissions take place over the telephone line, or over lines that are engineered to the telephone line specifications. In recognition of this fact, the standards organizations have published many recommendations defining how these connections and communications are made. The CCITT V Series defines these connections. They are some of the most widely used physical level specifications in the world. It is quite likely that you have used these standards if you have a modem attached to your personal computer, and use it to access data bases and other computers.

Table 9-1 summarizes the most widely used V Series interfaces [BLAC86]. Many of the terms and concepts contained in the table have been explained previously. The remaining terms will be explained shortly. Also, a brief summary of Table 9-1 is provided for the reader in Box 9-1.

The ISO publishes many standards, some of which describe the mechanical connectors used by computers, terminals, modems, and other devices. Figure 9-2 shows the major ISO physical level connectors.

EIA-232-D is one of the most widely used physical interfaces in the world. It is sponsored by the Electronic Industries Association (EIA) and is most prevalent in North America. It specifies 25 interchange circuits for DTE/DCE use.

The circuits are actually 25 pin connections and sockets (see Figure 9-3). All the circuits are rarely used; most devices utilize eight or fewer pins. Later discussions in this chapter will examine EIA-232-D in more detail.

EIA-232-D and the ISO/CCITT Standards

Many people are perplexed by the many initials and acronyms in modem vendors' marketing material. Let us clear up these mysteries. They are really quite simple, once we understand the relationship of EIA-232-D and the ISO/CCITT standards.

The CCITT also publishes the V.24 specification, from which the ISO connector arrangements and EIA-232-D pin assignments are derived. The ISO establishes the specification for the mechanical dimensions of the pins and connector, and EIA-232-D uses the ISO 2110 connector. EIA-232-D also uses two of the V Series standards: V.24 and V.28.

At first glance, the EIA-232-D interface seems very confusing, but it simply uses the following CCITT/ISO recommendations:

Electrical: CCITT V.28
Functional: CCITT V.24
Mechanical: ISO 2110
Procedural: CCITT V.24

TABLE 9-1. CCITT V Series Interfaces [BLAC86]

Series Number	Line Speed	Channel Separation	Modulation Rate	Carrier Frequency	Use of V.2	FDX or HDX	Synchronous or Asynchronous	Modulation Technique	Bits Encoded
V.21	300	FD	300	1080 & 1750	Yes	FDX	Either	FS	1:1
V.22	1200	FD	600	1200 & 2400	Yes	FDX	Either	PS	2:1
V.22	600	FD	600	1200 & 2400	Yes	FDX	Either	PS	1:1
V.22 bis	2400	FD	600	1200 & 2400	ND	FDX	Either	QAM	4:1
V.22 bis	1200	FD	600	1200 & 2400	ND	FDX	Either	QAM	2:1
V.23	600	NA	600	1300 & 1700	ND	HDX	Either	FM	NA
V.23	1200	NA	1200	1300 & 2100	NkD	HDX	Either	FM	NA
V.26	2400	4-Wire	1200	1800	Yes	FDX	Synchronous	PS	2:1
V.26 bis	2400	NA	1200	1800	Yes	HDX	Synchronous	PS	2:1
V.26 bis	1200	NA	1200	1800	Yes	HDX	Synchronous	PS	1:1
V.26 ter	2400	EC	1200	1800	Yes	Either	Either	PS	2:1
V.26 ter	1200	EC	1200	1800	Yes	Either	Either	PS	1:1
V.27	4800	ND	1600	1800	Yes	Either	Synchronous	PS	3:1
V.27 bis	4800	4-Wire	1600	1800	Yes	Either	Synchronous	PS	3:1
V.27 bis	2400	4-Wire	1200	1800	Yes	Either	Synchronous	PS	2:1
V.27 ter	4800	None	1600	1800	Yes	HDX	Synchronous	PS	3:1
V.27 ter	2400	None	1200	1800	Yes	HDX	Synchronous	PS	2:1
V.29	9600	4-Wire	2400	1700	Yes	Either	Synchronous	QAM	4:1
V.29	7200	4-Wire	2400	1700	Yes	Either	Synchronous	PS	3:1
V.29	4800	4-Wire	2400	1700	Yes	Either	Synchronous	PS	2:1
V.32	9600	EC	2400	1800	Yes	FDX	Synchronous	QAM	4:1
V.32	9600	EC	2400	1800	Yes	FDX	Synchronous	TCM	5:1
V.32	4800	EC	2400	1800	Yes	FDX	Synchronous	QAM	2:1
V.35	48000	4-Wire	NA	100000	ND	FDX	Synchronous	AM-FM	NA

continued

TABLE 9-1 (continued). CCITT V Series Interfaces [BLAC86]

Series Number	Backward Channel	Switched Lines	Leased Lines	Use of V.25	Use of V.28	ISO Pine Connector	Equilization	Scrambler
V.21	ND	Yes	0	Yes	Yes	2110	ND	ND
V.22	ND	Yes	PP 2W	Yes	Yes	2110	Fixed	Yes
V.22	ND	Yes	PP 2W	Yes	Yes	2110	Fixed	Yes
V.22 bis	ND	Yes	PP 2W	Yes	Yes	2110	Either	Yes
V.22 bis	ND	Yes	PP 2W	Yes	Yes	2110	Either	Yes
V.23	Yes	Yes	0	ND	Yes	2110	ND	ND
V.26	Yes	No	PP MP 4W	ND	Yes	2110	ND	ND
V.26 bis	Yes	Yes	No	Yes	Yes	2110	Fixed	ND
V.26 bis	Yes	Yes	No	Yes	Yes	2110	Fixed	ND
V.26 ter	ND	Yes	PP 2W	Yes	Yes	2110	Either	Yes
V.26 ter	ND	Yes	PP 2W	Yes	Yes	2110	Either	Yes
V.27	Yes	No	Yes	ND	Yes	2110	Manual	Yes
V.27 bis	Yes	No	2W 4W	ND	Yes	2110	Adaptive	Yes
V.27 bis	Yes	No	2W 4W	ND	Yes	2110	Adaptive	Yes
V.27 ter	Yes	Yes	No	Yes	Yes	2110	Adaptive	Yes
V.27 ter	Yes	Yes	No	Yes	Yes	2110	Adaptive	Yes
V.29	ND	No	PP 4W	ND	Yes	2110	Adaptive	Yes
V.29	ND	No	PP 4W	ND	Yes	2110	Adaptive	Yes
V.29	ND	No	PP 4W	ND	Yes	2110	Adaptive	Yes
V.32	ND	Yes	PP 2W	Yes	Yes	2110	Adaptive	Yes
V.32	ND	Yes	PP 2W	Yes	Yes	2110	Adaptive	Yes
V.32	ND	Yes	PP 2W	Yes	Yes	2110	Adaptive	Yes
V.35	ND	No	Yes	ND	OS	ND	Adaptive	Yes

ND = Not Defined   NA = Not Applicable   OS = On Some Interchange Circuits

BOX 9-1. Explanation of Table 9-1 [BLAC86].

A V Series number may be entered into the table more than once. This means the recommended standard permits more than one option. The initials ND means not defined in the specification. The initials NA mean not applicable.

Entries	Explanation
Line Speed	Speed in bits per second (bit/s).
Channel Separation	If the recommended standard permits multiple channels, the method of deriving the channels is noted as: FD: Frequency Division 4-Wire: Each set of wires carries a channel EC: Echo Cancellation Note that the standard may also use a backward channel.
Modulation Rate	The rate of the signal change of the carrier on the channel; in baud.
Carrier Frequency	The frequency of the carrier or carriers used on the channel(s). The carrier(s)may be altered to yield different modulated frequencies. For example, the V.21 modem uses two mean frequencies of 1080 and 1750. Each carrier is then modulated with a frequency shift of $+100$ Hz for binary 1 and -100 Hz for binary 0.
Use of V.2	A CCITT specification, which establishes specified power ranges and levels.
FDX or HDX	FDX: Full Duplex, HDX: Half Duplex
Synchronous or Asynchronous	"Either" means the specification will work with one or the other.
Modulation Technique	The description of the modulation technique where: FS: Frequency Shift PS: Phase Shift QAM: Quadrature Amplitude Modulation AM: Amplitude Modulation TCM: Trellis Coded Modulation
Bits Encoded	Describes the number of bits encoded per signal change (baud). For example, 2:1 means two bits encoded per baud.
Backward Channel	Describes an alternate channel used for transmission in a reverse direction, at a lower rate, usually 75 baud. Its absence does not imply that the modem is only HDX, because a FDX modem may not use a backward channel.
Switched Lines	Describes the use of conventional dial-up circuits.
Leased Lines	0: Optional 2W: Two-wire PP: Point-to-point 4W: Four-wire MP: Multipoint
Use of V.25	A CCITT specification which describes the procedures for automatic dial-and-answer. May also offer features on call and answer beyond that of V.25.

Use of V.28	A CCITT specification which describes the electrical characteristics of unbalanced circuits.
ISO Pin Connector	Specifications from the International Standards Organization that describe the actual connector (dimensions, etc.) between the DTE and DCE.
Equalization	A technique to improve signal quality where: Fixed: Established when modem left the factory Adaptive: Changes and adjusts to received signal Either: Can be fixed or adaptive
Scrambler	A technique for altering the data stream to enhance the timing and synchronization between the two modems on the circuit.

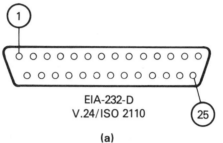

EIA-232-D
V.24/ISO 2110

(a)

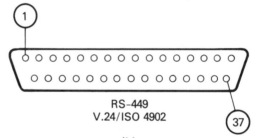

RS-449
V.24/ISO 4902

(b)

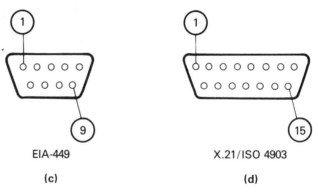

EIA-449

X.21/ISO 4903

(c)   **(d)**

FIGURE 9-2. ISO Connectors

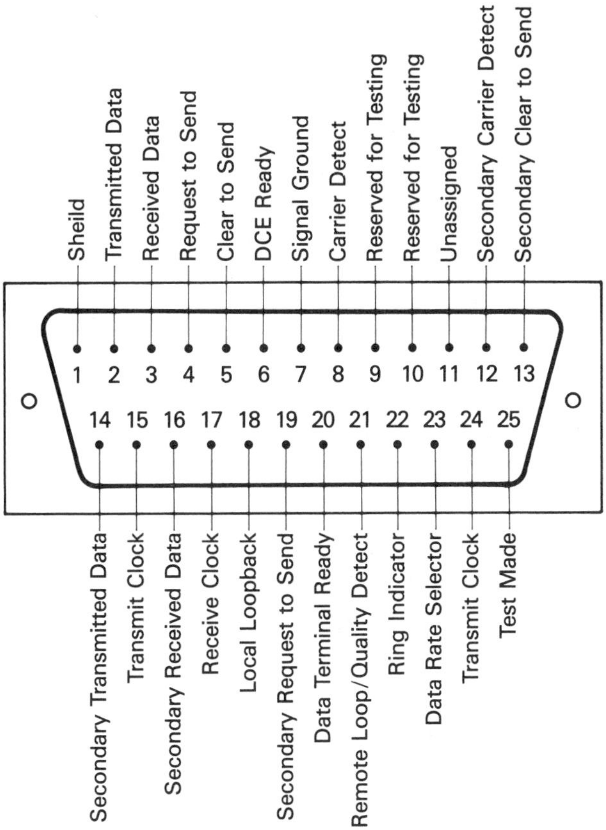

Pin	Circuit	Source	Description
1	AA	—	Shield
2	BA	DTE	Transmitted Data
3	BB	DCE	Received Data
4	CA	DTE	Request to Send
5	CB	DCE	Clear to Send
6	CC	DCE	DCE Ready
7	AB	—	Signal Ground
8	CF	DCE	Carrier Detect
9	—	—	Reserved for Data Set Testing
10	—	—	Reserved for Data Set Testing
11	—	—	Unassigned
12	SCF	DCE	Secondary Carrier Detect
13	SCB	DCE	Secondary Clear to Send
14	SBA	DTE	Secondary Transmitted Data
15	DB	DCE	Transmission Signal Element Timing
16	SBB	DCE	Secondary Received Data
17	D	DCE	Receiver Signal Element Timing
18	LL	—	Local Loopback
19	SCA	DTE	Secondary Request to Send
20	CD	DTE	Data Terminal Ready
21	RL/CG	DCE	Remote Loopback/Signal Quality Detector
22	CE	DTE	Ring Indicator
23	CH	DTE	Data Signal Rate Selector
23	CI	DCE	Data Signal Rate Selector
24	DA	DTE	Transmit Signal Element Timing
25	TM	—	Test Mode

FIGURE 9-3. EIA-232-D (DTE Connectors)

THE "FOUNDATION" V SERIES RECOMMENDATIONS

For purposes of compatibility and simplicity, most DCEs and DTEs use a set of "foundation" specifications and then add other V Series or Bell standards to achieve the actual data encoding and modulation. The major foundation V Series are summarized in Box 9-2.

As suggested in Box 9.2, V.24 defines the connecting circuits between the DTE and DCE. (Many systems also use V.24 for direct DTE-to-DTE or DCE-to-DCE interfaces.) The other V Series modems use V.24, as do standards such as EIA-232-D, although EIA-232-D uses different designations for the circuits. The V.24 100 series interchange circuits are listed in Table 9-2.

V.28 is applied to almost all interchange circuits operating below the limit of 20,000 bit/s. The recommendation provides specifications for other electrical interfaces as well. EIA-232-D uses this specification with some

---

BOX 9-2. Foundation V Series Recommendations

CCITT RECOMMENDATION

V.1	Brief description of terminology pertaining to signals, and binary symbols
V.2	Provides direction on permissible power levels to be used on equipment
V.5	Describes signalling rates (bit/s) over half duplex or duplex dial-up links
V.6	Describes signalling rates (bit/s) over dedicated links
V.10	Defines the electrical characteristics of an unbalanced interchange circuit
V.11	Defines the electrical characteristics of a balanced interchange circuit
V.24	Provides a list of definitions for the interchange circuits
V.25	Describes the conventions for automatic dial-and-answer interfaces. Uses four interchange circuits to transfer the dialed digit between DTE and DCE
V.25 bis	Describes the conventions for automatic dial-and-answer interfaces. Uses one interchange circuit to transfer the dialed digit between DTE and DCE
V.28	Defines the electrical characteristics for an unbalanced interchange circuit.

TABLE 9-2. V.24 Interchange Circuits

Interchange Circuit Number	Interchange Circuit Name
102	Signal ground or common return
102a	DTE common return
102b	DCE common return
102c	Common return
103	Transmitted data
104	Received data
105	Request to send
106	Ready for sending
107	Data set ready
108/1	Connect data set to line
108/2	Data terminal ready
109	Data channel received line signal detector
110	Data signal quality detector
111	Data signal rate selector (DTE)
112	Data signal rate selector (DCE)
113	Transmitter signal element timing (DTE)
114	Transmitter signal element timing (DCE)
115	Receiver signal element timing (DCE)
116	Select standby
117	Standby indicator
118	Transmitted backward channel data
119	Received backward channel data
120	Transmit backward channel line signal
121	Backward channel ready
122	Backward channel received line signal detector
123	Backward channel signal quality detector
124	Select frequency groups
125	Calling indicator
126	Select transmit frequency
127	Select receive frequency
128	Receiver signal element timing (DTE)
129	Request to receive
130	Transmit backward tone
131	Received character timing
132	Return to nondata mode
133	Ready for receiving
134	Received data present
136	New signal
140	Loopback/maintenance test
141	Local loopback
142	Test indicator
191	Transmitted voice answer
192	Received voice answer

minor variations. On a general level, the signals must conform to the characteristics described below.

For data interchange circuits, the signal is in the binary 1 condition when the voltage on the interchange circuit measured at the interchange point is more negative than minus 3 volts. The signal is in the binary 0 condition when the voltage is more positive than plus 3 volts.

For control and timing interchange circuits, the circuit is ON when the voltage on the interchange circuit is more positive than plus 3 volts, and shall be considered OFF when the voltage is more negative than minus 3 volts.

EIA-232-D

The Electronic Industries Association (EIA) sponsors the EIA-232-D standard. It is used extensively in North America, as well as other parts of the world and the reader should become familar with its characteristics. Table 9-3 describes the interchange circuits of EIA-232-D. These circuits are 25 pin connections and sockets (depicted in Figure 9-3). The terminal pins plug into the modem sockets. All the circuits are rarely used; many modems utilize only 4 to 12 pins.

The EIA-232-D circuits perform one of four functions:

- Data transfer across the interface
- Control of signals across interface
- Clocking signals to synchronize data flow and regulate the bit rate
- Electrical ground

The functional descriptions of the interchange circuits are summarized in Box 9-3. Each offering should be *examined carefully*, since many vendors do not use these circuits as specified by EIA-232-D.

EIA-232-D Operations

The actual operations of EIA-232-D are more involved than what might be inferred by reading Box 9-3. This section explains some of the more subtle operational features of the interface. You should find this information useful if you are installing a modem with your PC or workstation.

The transmit data interchange circuit (AA) does not operate unless the following interchange circuits are ON (but be aware that some vendors have modified their products not to use these circuits):

CA (Request to Send)
CB (Clear to Send)
CC (DCE Ready)
CD (DTE Ready)

TABLE 9-3. EIA-232-D Interchange Circuits

Interchange Circuit	CCITT Equivalent	Description	DATA			CONTROL		TIMING	
			End	From DCE	To DCE	From DCE	To DCE	From DCE	To DCE
AB	102	Signal ground/common return	X						
BA	103	Transmitted data			X				
BB	104	Received data		X					
CA	105	Request to send					X		
CB	106	Clear to send				X			
CC	107	DCE ready				X			
CD	108.2	DTE ready					X		
CE	125	Ring indicator				X			
CF	109	Received line signal detector				X			
CG	110	Signal quality detector				X			
CH	111	Data signal rate selector (DTE)					X		
I	112	Data signal rate selector (DCE)				X			
DA	113	Transmitter signal element timing (DTE)							X
DB	114	Transmitter signal element timing (DCE)						X	
DD	115	Receiver signal element timing (DCE)						X	
SBA	118	Secondary transmitted data			X				
SBB	119	Secondary received data		X					
SCA	120	Secondary request to send					X		
SCB	121	Secondary clear to send				X			
SCF	122	Secondary received line signal detector				X			
RL	140	Remote loopback					X		
LL	141	Local loopback					X		
TM	142	Test mode				X			

BOX 9-3. EIA-232-D Interchange Circuits

Circuit AB: Signal Ground or Common Return. This conductor establishes the common ground reference potential for all interchange.

Circuit BA: Transmitted Data. Signals are generated by the DTE and are transferred to the DCE.

Circuit BB: Received Data. Signals are generated by the receiving DCE to receiving DTE.

Circuit CA: Request to Send. Used to condition the local data communication equipment for data transmission and, on a half duplex channel, to control the direction of data transmission of the local data communication equipment.

Circuit CB: Clear to Send. Signals generated by the DCE to indicate whether or not the DCE is ready to transmit data.

Circuit CC: DCE Ready. Signals used to indicate the status of the local DCE.

Circuit CD: Data Terminal Ready. Controls connecting the DCE to the communications channel. The ON condition prepares the data communication equipment to be connected to the communications channel.

Circuit CE: Ring Indicator. Indicates that a ringing signal is being received on the communications channel.

Circuit CF: Received Line Signal Detector. The ON condition is presented when the DCE is receiving a signal which meets its suitability criteria. These criteria are established by the data communications equipment manufacturer.

Circuit CG: Signal Quality Detector. Indicates whether or not there is a high probability of an error in the received data. An ON condition is maintained whenever there is no reason to believe that an error has occurred.

Circuit CH: Data Signal Rate Selector (DTE Source). Selects between the two data signaling rates in the case of dual rate synchronous DCEs or the two ranges of data signalling rates in the case of dual range nonsynchronous DCEs.

Circuit CI: Data Signal Rate Selector (DCE Source). Selects between the two data signalling rates in the case of dual rate synchronous DCEs or the two ranges of data signalling rates in the case of dual range nonsynchronous DCEs.

Circuit DA: Transmitter Signal Element Timing (DTE Source). Provides the transmitting signal converter with signal element timing information.

Circuit DB: Transmitter Signal Element Timing (DCE Source). Provides the DTE with signal element timing information.

Circuit DD: Receiver Signal Element Timing (DCE Source). Provides the DTE with received signal element timing information.

Circuit SBA: Secondary Transmitted Data. Equivalent to Circuit BA (Transmitted Data) except that it is used to transmit data via the secondary (i.e., reverse or backward) channel.

Circuit SBB: Secondary Received Data. Equivalent to Circuit BB (Received Data) except that it is used to receive data on the secondary (i.e., reverse or backward) channel.

Circuit SCA: Secondary Request to Send. Equivalent to Circuit CA (Request to Send) except that it requests the establishment of the secondary channel instead of requesting the establishment of the primary data channel.

Circuit SCB: Secondary Clear to Send. Equivalent to Circuit CB (Clear to Send) except that it indicates the availability of the secondary channel instead of indicating the availability of the primary channel.

Circuit SCF: Secondary Received Line Signal Detector. Equivalent to Circuit CF (Received Line Signal Detector) except that it indicates the proper reception of the secondary channel line signal instead of indicating the proper reception of a primary channel received-line signal.

Circuit LL: Local Loopback. Controls LL test condition in local DCE. The ON condition causes the DCE to transmit to the receiving signal converter at the same DCE.

Circuit RL: Remote Loopback. Controls RL test condition in remote DCE. The ON condition causes the local DCE to signal the test condition to the remote DCE.

Circuit TM: Test Mode. Indicates whether the local DCE is in a test condition.

EIA-232-D requires the receive data interchange circuit (BB) be held in a marking condition at all times when the received line signal detector is in the OFF condition. Again, be aware that vendors vary in how this procedure is implemented.

The DCE ready interchange circuit (CC) is often misinterpreted. As suggested in Box 9-3, the circuit only indicates a status and not an end-to-end connection. It indicates:

Local DCE is connected to channel

Local DCE is not in test mode

Local DCE has completed any required timing functions

The data terminal ready interchange circuit (CD) is also used in automatic answering in conjunction with the ring indicator interchange circuit (CE) to "answer" a call.

Three other EIA-232-D interchange circuits are also frequently a source of confusion. These are the timing circuits.

DA - Transmitter signal element timing (DTE source)
DB - Transmitter signal element timing (DCE source)
DD - Receiver signal element timing (DCE source)

Several alternatives are available for the use of these circuits. Figure 9-4 depicts the scenarios.

In Figure 9-4 (a), the transmitting DTE A provides the timing to DCE A through interchange circuit DA (pin 24). At the receiving end, DCE B provides the timing to DTE A through interchange circuit DD (pin 17).

Figure 9-4 (b) shows a more common arrangement called external timing or an external clock. The transmitting DCE A furnishes the timing information to DTE A through interchange circuit DB (pin 15). The timing between DTE B and DCE B is the same as in Figure 9-4(a).

Figure 9-4 (c) depicts yet another timing scheme. The DCE furnishes the clock at both ends. It also uses one common clock within the DCE to provide the timing information to both the transmit data and receive data

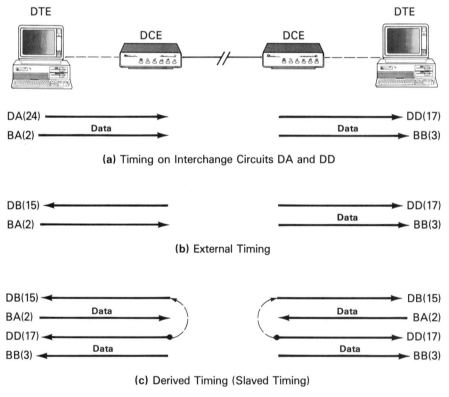

(a) Timing on Interchange Circuits DA and DD

(b) External Timing

(c) Derived Timing (Slaved Timing)

FIGURE 9-4. Timing Options on DTE/DCE Interface

circuits. In other words, the clock on one interchange circuit is "slaved" to the clock on the other circuit.

The EIA-232-D Unbalanced Interface

The EIA specification for the interchange circuits is shown in Figure 9-5. Please study the figure and note the relationship of circuits AB (Signal Ground) and the interchange circuit. The rules for the interchange circuit are summarized in Box 9-4.

The voltage levels of EIA-232-D are detected at the receiver by the relative voltage difference between the signal circuit and Signal Ground (circuit AB). This means voltage V_1 is measured relative to circuit AB. However, the transmitting and receiving stations usually have different logic ground due to different electrical characteristics of their components. As a consequence, a ground current can flow through the AB circuit. Obviously, the wire has electrical resistance, which produces a voltage drop. The voltage applied by the transmitter to the interchange circuit will appear differently to the receiver.

If the difference is small, this potential difference will not create any errors. However, a signal of $+5$ volts with a ground potential difference of $+3$ volts means the receiver would see $+2$ volts (an undefined, transition

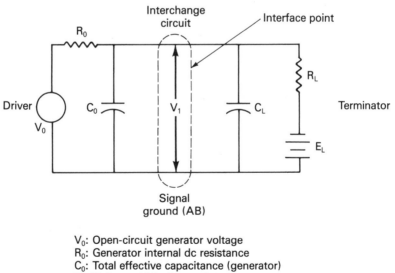

V_0: Open-circuit generator voltage
R_0: Generator internal dc resistance
C_0: Total effective capacitance (generator)
V_1: Voltage at interface point
C_L: Total effective capacitance (receiver)
R_L: Receiver load dc resistance
E_L: Open circuit receiver voltage

FIGURE 9-5. EIA-232-D Interchange Interface

- Interchange voltages are designated as (a) 1, marking or OFF, and (b) 0, spacing or ON.
- Interchange circuits are ON when voltage V_1 is more positive than $+3$ volts with respect to circuit AB and are OFF when V_1 is more negative than -3 volts a with respect to circuit AB.
- Load impedance is (R_2 and C_2) of receiver side of interchange circuit has a dc resistance of not less than 3000 ohms, measured with an applied voltage not greater than 25 volts and not more than 7000 ohms, measured with an applied voltage of 3-25 volts.
- Receiver side of interface circuit shall not exceed 2500 picofarads.
- The interchange circuit signals are in the marking condition when voltage (V_1) is more negative than -3 volts relative to signal ground (AB). For the spacing condition, the voltage (V_1) is more positive than $+3$ volts relative to AB.

region). A potential difference of -10 volts means the receiver mistakenly sees a 1 (mark) instead of the intended 0 (space).

The cable capacitance specification of EIA-232-D can also present a problem. The standard states that the circuit capacitance is to be less than 2500 picofarads. A cable length of 50 feet is the maximum permitted length because about 40-50 picofarads per foot is a common characteristic of a cable with multiple conductors. The end result of this problem could be that the transitions from marks (1s) to spaces (0s) might take a longer time than is permitted. This condition could result in a mark bit that is longer than a space bit (marking distortion) or a space bit that is longer than a mark bit (spacing distortion).

Comparisons of RS-232-C and EIA-232-D

In January 1987, RS-232-C was renamed EIA-232-D. The D version brings the specification in line with CCITT V.24, V.28, and ISO 2110. The revision also includes the addition of the local loopback, remote loopback, and test mode interchange circuits. Protective ground has been redefined and a shield has been added. Also, the term DCE is changed from data communications equipment (and data set) to data circuit-terminating equipment. The terms driver and termination are changed to generator and receiver respectively. Table 9-4 compares RS-232-C and EIA-232-D.

TABLE 9-4. Comparison of RS-232-C and EIA-232-D

| | RS-232-C | | | EIA-232-D | |
Pin	CCITT Number	EIA Name	Pin	CCITT Number	EIA Name
1	101	AA	1		
7	102	AB	7	102	AB
2	103	BA	2	103	BA
3	104	BB	3	104	BB
4	105	CA	4	105	CA
5	106	CB	5	106	CB
6	107	CC	6	107	CC
20	108.2	CD	20	108.2	CD
22	125	CE	22	125	CE
8	109	CF	8	109	CF
21	110	CG	21	140/110	RL/CG[1]
23	111/112	CH/CI	23	111/112	CH/CI[2]
24	113	DA	24	113	DA
15	114	DB	15	114	DB
17	115	DD	17	115	DD
14	118	SBA	14	118	SBA
16	119	SBB	16	119	SBB
19	120	SCA	19	120	SCA
13	121	SCB	13	121	SCB
12	122	SCF	12	122/112	SCF/CI[3]
			9	—	—
			10	—	—
			11	—	—
			18	141	LL
			25	142	TM

[1]CF no longer used

[2]See Pin 12

[3]If SCF not used then CI is on Pin 12

Examples of EIA-232-D Communications

Figures 9-6 and 9-7 are provided to illustrate the sequence of events at the EIA-232-D physical level interface for a full duplex synchronous operation (Figure 9-6) and a half duplex asynchronous operation (Figure 9-7). You are encouraged to study these figures carefully, because if you understand them, much of the "mystery" disappears about how physical level protocols actually operate.

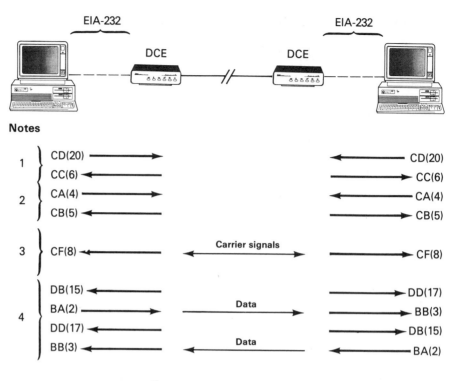

Notes

1: Initial Power Up

2: Initiate Controls for Transmission

3: Synchronize DCEs

4: FDX Operations

FIGURE 9-6. Full Duplex Operations Across DTE/DCE Interface

EIA RS-449 (RS-422-A and RS-423-A)

The EIA also sponsors RS-449. It was issued in 1975 to overcome some of the limitations of EIA-232. The EIA-232 standard has several electrical specifications that limit its effectiveness. For instance, EIA-232 is limited to a 20 Kbit/s and a few hundred feet spacing between the components. Actual distance depends on the size and quality of the circuits and is influenced by factors such as shielding and capacitance. EIA-232 also presents a noisy electrical signal which limits its data rate and distance. RS-449 provides 37 interchange circuits, and uses the ISO 4902 mechanical connector shown in Figure 9-2. In addition, the RS-449 specification establishes a bit rate up to 2 Mbit/s.

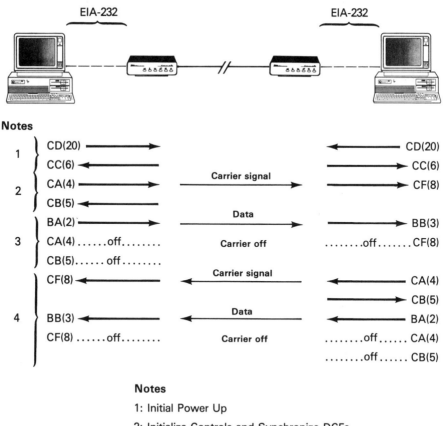

Notes

1: Initial Power Up

2: Initialize Controls and Synchronize DCEs

3: Send data, then turn off CA and CB

4: Repeat steps 1 & 2 in the other direction

FIGURE 9-7. Half Duplex Operations Across DTE/DCE Interface

RS-449 uses two companion specifications: RS-422-A and RS-423-A. The electrical interface RS-422-A is a balanced electrical interface (see Figure 9-8). RS-422-A is compatible with X.27. It is less noise sensitive and can transmit over a greater distance at a faster data rate than RS-423-A, which is a partially unbalanced electrical interface. The basic difference is that the balanced interface uses equipment that allows half the signal to be transmitted on each wire of the pair that is used. This approach is much less noise sensitive, because the receiver can invert the signals on each wire to cancel the noise. The unbalanced circuit provides for the transmission of the signal on one wire, with a common return for all wires, like EIA-232. Box 9-5 provides more information on this subject:

TABLE 9-5. Comparisons of EIA-232-D, V.35, EIA-449 Interfaces

EIA-232-D/CCITT V.24 25-Pin	CCITT V.35 37 or 15-Pin	EIA-449 37-Pin	EIA-232-D or EIA-449 9-Pin
1-Shield	1-Protective Ground	1-Shield 37-Send Common	1-Shield 9-Send Common
2-Transmitted Data	2-Transmitted Data	4-Send Data (A) 22-Send Data (B)	
3-Received Data	3-Received Data	6-Receive Data (A) 24-Receive Data (B)	
4-Request to Send	4-Request to Send	7-Request to Send (A) 25-Request to Send (B)	
5-Clear to Send	5-Ready for Sending	9-Clear to Send (A) 27-Clear to Send (B)	
6-DCE Ready	6-Data Set Ready	11-Data Mode (A) 29-Data Mode (B)	
7-Signal Ground		19-Signal Ground	5-Signal Ground (C)
8-Signal Detect	8-Receive Line Signal Detect	13-Receiver Ready(A) 31-Receiver Ready (B)	
9-Reserved for Testing		20-Receive Common	6-Receive Common
10-Reserved for Testing		10-Local Loop (A) 14-Remote Loop (A)	
11-Unassigned		3-SPARE 21-SPARE	
12-Sec. Carrier Detect		32-Select Standby	2-Sec. Receiver Ready
13-Sec. Clear to Send			8-Sec. Clear to Send
14-Sec. Transmitted Data			3-Sec. Send Data

TABLE 9-5. *(continued).* **Comparisons of EIA-232-D, V.35, EIA-449 Interfaces**

EIA-232-D/CCITT V.24 25-Pin	CCITT V.35 37 or 15-Pin	EIA-449 37-Pin	EIA-232-D or EIA-449 9-Pin
15-Transmit Clock (DCE Source)	15-TX Signal Element Timing	5-Send Timing (A) DCE Source, 23-Send Timing (B) DCE Source	
16-Sec. Received Data			4-Sec. Received Data
17-Receive Clock	17-RX Signal Element Timing	8-Receive Timing (A), 26-Receive Timing (B)	
18-Local Loopback		18-Test Mode (A), 28-Term in Service (A), 34-New Signal	
19-Sec. Request to Send			7-Sec. Request to Send
20-Data Terminal Ready		12-Terminal Ready (A), 30-Terminal Ready (B)	
21-Signal Quality Detector/Remote Loopback		33-Signal Quality (A)	
22-Ring Indicator		15-Incoming Call (A)	
23-Data Signal Rate Selector		2-Signalling Rate Indicator (A), 16-Signalling Rate Selector (A)	
24-Transmit Clock (DTE Source)		17-Terminal Timing (A), 35-Terminal Timing (B)	
25-Test Mode		36-Standby Indicator	

   The RS-422-A specification provides a balanced configuration with differential signalling over both wires. RS-423 uses a balanced differential receiver with a common return connected to signal ground only at the generator end. Both RS-422 and RS-423-A specify a balanced differential receiver even though they are different types of generators.

   EIA-232 employs a single-ended receiver with signal ground providing a common return. EIA-232 requires a very sharp rise time of the binary signal (less than 3% of the bit duration). As a consequence, considerable noise is created. RS-243 allows the rise time to be 30% slower and is not as noisy.

   To summarize the various recommended standards, some comparisons are provided in Table 9-5.

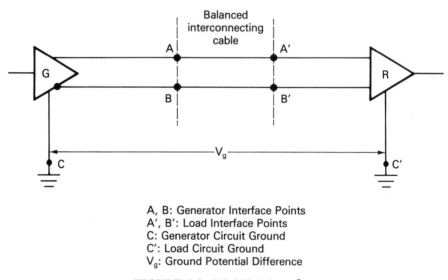

A, B: Generator Interface Points
A', B': Load Interface Points
C: Generator Circuit Ground
C': Load Circuit Ground
V_g: Ground Potential Difference

FIGURE 9-8. RS-422-A Interface

EIA-530, HIGH-SPEED 25-POSITION INTERFACE

EIA-530 is intended to replace EIA-232 for protocols that require higher data rates than 20,000 bit/s. It has been developed to serve as an interface to EIA-232-D and uses the EIA-232-D mechanical connector.

The standard can be used for data rates from 20 Kbit/s to 2 Mbit/s and is applicable to the following systems:

asynchronous or synchronous systems

switched, nonswitched, dedicated, leased, or private lines

two-wire or four-wire circuits

point-to-point or multipoint operations

EIA-366, DIAL AND ANSWER SYSTEMS

The EIA-366 specification defines the interface for an automatic call unit, a modem, and a DTE. The DTE and the ACU perform four major functions:

Ensure that the DCE is operable

Provide the telephone number (from the DTE)

Manage call abandonment

Monitor the call continuously to determine when to disconnect

Table 9-6 lists the EIA pins used for automatic dial and answer systems. A brief description of these pins follows.

The power indication (PWI) signal is used to determine if the automatic calling unit is powered up. The data line occupied circuit (DLO) is used to determine if the communications line is in use. These two circuits fulfill the function of ensuring the DCE is operable. The call request circuit (CRQ) must be activated to initiate control of the communications line: it "seizes" the line. In order to provide this service, the DTE checks the ACU to see if it has power on (PWI is ON) and if the line is free (DLO is OFF). If these conditions are met, DTE turns on CRQ to the automatic calling unit. A common scenario is the data terminal ready (DTR) signal is presented to the interface of the modem at this time. If this is the case, the communications line is in an off-hook condition (placed by the ACU). The telephone systems would then return a dial tone to the ACU.

Upon recognizing the dial tone, the ACU activates its present next digit circuit (PND) to the DTE. This informs the DTE the ACU is ready to accept the dialed numbers. In turn, the DTE presents the telephone numbers across four circuits labeled NB1, NB2, NB4, NB8. At the same time, the data lines are activated, a signal is provided on the digit present circuit (DPR). This is essentially a clocking signal. If the ACU accepts the telephone number, it so indicates by turning off the PND circuit.

TABLE 9-6. EIA-366-A Pins for Dial and Answer

Pin No.	Circuit	Direction	Description
1	FGD	Both	Frame ground
2	DPR	To ACU	Digit present
3	ACR	To Terminal	Abandon call & retry
4	CRQ	To ACU	Call request
5	PND	To Terminal	Present next digit
6	PWI	To Terminal	Power indication
7	SGD	Both	Signal ground
8			Unassigned
9			Unassigned
10			Unassigned
11			Unassigned
12			Unassigned
13	DSS	To Terminal	Data set status
14	NB1	To ACU	Digit lead
15	NB2	To ACU	Digit lead
16	NB4	To ACU	Digit lead
17	NB8	To ACU	Digit lead
18			Unassigned
19			Unassigned
20			Unassigned
21			Unassigned
22	DLO	To Terminal	Data line occupied
23			Unassigned
24			Unassigned
25			Unassigned

The PND circuit is turned on when the ACU has completed dialing the digit. This indicates that a new digit can be presented to the ACU. The process continues until the last number is dialed. Then the DTE places an end of number (EON) code on the digit lead. This informs the ACU that no more numbers are to be dialed and it can disconnect itself from the call set-up process.

To do this, the ACU turns a timer ON upon receiving the EON code. If the call is answered by the receiving DTE, a tone is sent back to the ACU and the timer is turned OFF. However, if the call is not answered, or if a problem occurs, the ACU will time-out and turn ON the abandoned call (ACR) circuit to the DTE. This informs the DTE that it is to disconnect itself from the line. The DTE performs this function by turning OFF the circuit CRQ.

If the call cannot be completed, a number of methods are used to clear the call set-up. One approach (CCITT V.25) sets an abandon call timer upon receiving the EON code. If the call is answered, the timer is stopped. If the call is not answered, or is answered by a person instead of a DTE, the timer stays ON. When it reaches a selected threshold, it turns on Abandon Call (ACR) which in turn drops the Call Request (CRQ) lead.

A considerable number of systems operate at the physical level with the CCITT X Series recommendations. These specifications are titled "Data Communications Network Interfaces." The X Series are found throughout the layers of the OSI Reference Model. This section explains the prevalent physical level recommendations.

X.24 Recommendations

X.24 is analogous to V.24 for the V Series in that it provides the descriptions of the interchange circuits used by the other X Series interfaces. Table 9-7 shows how the interchange circuits are used and designates them as data, control, or timing circuits.

The X.21 Recommendation

The X.21 recommendation is yet another interface standard that has received considerable attention in the industry. It is used in several European countries and Japan and has seen limited implementation in North America.

    The X.24 T and R circuits transmit and receive data across the interface. The data is either user or control signals. Unlike EIA-232-D and the V Series, X.21 uses the T and R circuits for user data and control. The C circuits provide an off/on signal to the network and the I circuit provides the off/on to the DTE. These two circuits serve to activate and deactivate the

TABLE 9-7. X.24 Interchange Circuits

Interchange Circuit Designation	Interchange Circuit Name	DATA From DCE	DATA To DCE	CONTROL From DCE	CONTROL To DCE	TIMING From DCE	TIMING To DCE
G	Signal ground or common return						
Ga	DTE common return				X		
Gb	DCE common return			X			
T	Transmit		X		X		
R	Receive	X		X			
C	Control				X		
I	Indication			X			
S	Signal element timing					X	
B	Byte timing					X	
F	Frame start identification					X	
X	DTE signal element timing						X

DCE-DTE interface session. The S and B circuits provide for signals to synchronize the signals between the DTE and DCE. The G circuit acts as a signal ground or a common return.

The X.21 bis Recommendation

X.21 bis is often used as the physical interface in an X.25 packet network. X.21 bis uses the V.24 circuits. It also has several options of how the ISO connectors and the other V and X interfaces are used. The electrical characteristics of the interchange circuits at both the DCE side and the DTE side of the interface may comply either with Recommendation V.28, using the 25-pin connector and ISO 2110, or with Recommendation X.26, using the 37-pin connector and ISO 4902. In North America, the V.28 convention is often used.

Other X Series Interfaces

Several X Series physical level interfaces are employed for the following functions:

X.20.	Interface between DTE and DCE for start/stop transmission services on public data networks.
X.20 bis.	Used on public data networks with data terminal equipment (DTE) which is designed for interfacing to asynchronous duplex V Series modems.
X.26.	Electrical characteristics for unbalanced double-current interchange circuits for general use with integrated circuit equipment. Functionally equivalent to V.10.
X.27.	Electrical characteristics for balanced double-current interchange circuits for general use with integrated circuit equipment. Functionally equivalent to V.11.

THE "BELL" MODEMS

Bell modems are widely used throughout North America and other parts of the world. The physical level interfaces in North America have been largely dictated by the "Bell System" specifications. The majority of vendors base their automatic dial-and-answer modems on the Bell 103/212A specifications, and the 103, 113, 201C, 208 A/B, 212A specifications are used by many manufacturers. A brief summary of these modems is provided below.

103/113 Series Modems

The 103 and 113 modems transmit and receive data at rates from 0 to 300 bit/s asynchronously utilizing FSK modulation. They operate full duplex on two-wire systems utilizing two distinct frequency bands: Transmit: Space 1070 Hz and Mark 1270 Hz; and Receive: Space 2025 Hz and Mark 2225 Hz.

The 103 can either originate or answer calls and can be used with a direct connection or by acoustic coupler. The 113 is a variant on the 103.

202 Series Modems

The 202 series modem operates at rates of 0 to 1800 bit/s on conditioned leased lines or 0 to 1200 bit/s on dial-up lines. It functions asynchronously utilizing FSK modulation. It is similar to CCITT V.23. The 202 modem operates half duplex on two-wire systems, or in a leased-line version on four-wire systems. When operating over a four-wire private line in point-to-point only configuration, modem control can be identical to 300 bit/s 103 operation. Both transmitters are strapped ON continuously and no line turn-arounds are involved.

201 Series Modems

The 201 modems operate at 2000 or 2400 bit/s. The 201A operates at 2000 bit/s and the 201B or 201C operates at 2400 bit/s. The 201 modem uses the CCITT V.26 PSK (four-level) modulation. Two bits (dibits) are used to encode four specific phase shifts. The 201 series operates half duplex on two-wire systems or full duplex on four-wire systems.

208 Series Modems

The 208 modems operate at 4800 bit/s. They use the CCITT V.27 modulation convention. The 208A is a private line modem; and the 208B is a dial-up modem. The modem uses PSK (eight-level) modulation. Three bits of information (tribits) are used to encode one of eight phase shifts. The 208 series of modems operates half duplex on two-wire systems or full duplex on four-wire systems. The 208A supports point-to-point or multipoint configurations. The training time is selectable at 50 or 150 milliseconds.

212A Series Modems

The 212A modem functions asynchronously with PSK modulation for 1200 bit/s mode of operation and FSK techniques for 0 to 300 bit/s mode of operation. The modem can also function as a synchronous device in the 1200 bit range. When the 212A functions in the 0 to 300 bit/s mode, it can communicate with the 103/113 series of modem. 212A operates full duplex on two-wire systems. For the 1200 bit/s option, the 212A modem uses the CCITT V.22 specification.

209A Series Modems

The 209A modem operates at 9800 bit/s, synchronously duplex over leased lines. It will accept serial data at 9600 bit/s or lower and perform the function of a multiplexer by splitting the bandwidth as:

One 7200 bit/s and one 2400 bit/s data stream
Two 4800 bit/s data streams
One 4800 bit/s and two 2400 bit/s data streams
Four 2400 bit/s data streams

V.29 Series Modems

This modem uses the CCITT V.29 specification summarized in Table 9-1.

THE HAYES MODEMS

The Hayes modems, developed by Hayes Microcomputer Products Inc., have become a de facto standard for low- and medium-speed autodialing modems. Hayes has several products available for full and half duplex com-

---

BOX 9-6.   The Hayes Modems

Smartmodem 300	Smartmodem 1200	Smartmodem 2400	Smartmodem 9600
300 bit/s (Bell 103)	1200 bit/s (Bell 212A and Bell 103 300 Bit/s)	300, 1200, 2400 bit/s	300, 1200, 2400, 4800
Frequency Shift Keying (PSK)	Phase Shift Keying (PSK)	300 bit/s: Bell 103	300 bit/s: Bell 103
1070-1270 Hz and 2025-2225 Hz	1200 and 2400 Hz	1200 bit/s: Bell 212A, CCITT V.22	1200 bit/s: Bell 212A, CCITT V.22
		2400 bit/s: CCITT V.22 bis	2400 bit/s: CCITT V.22 bis
			4800 bit/s: V.32 HDX
			9600 bit/s: V.32 FDX

---

munications, with a variety of options. Chapter 12 explains the Hayes modem in more detail and Box 9-6 summarizes the characteristics of the Hayes modems.

X.211 PHYSICAL SERVICE DEFINITIONS

The 1988 CCITT Blue Books have added the X.211 standard. It defines the services between the physical and data link layers of the OSI model. The X.211 standard specifies the use of six primitives to activate a physical connection (Phc), transfer data, and deactivate the connection.

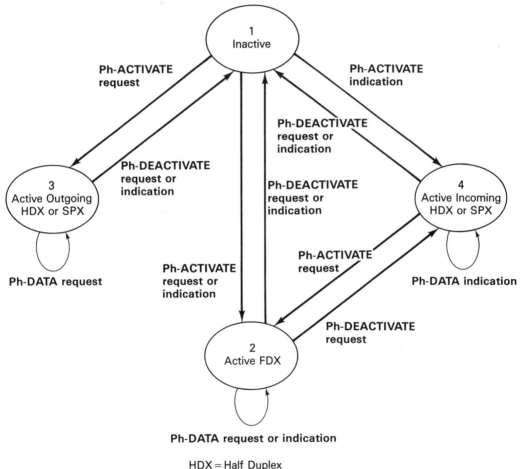

HDX = Half Duplex
SPX = Simplex
FDX = Full Duplex or Duplex

FIGURE 9-9. X.211 Composite State Diagram

Phase	Primitives
Phc Activation	Ph-ACTIVATE request
	Ph-ACTIVATE indication
Data Transfer	Ph-DATA request
	Ph-DATA indication
Phc Deactivation	Ph-DEACTIVATE request
	Ph-DEACTIVATE indication

The use of these primitives is governed by several state diagrams. Figure 9-9 depicts a composite state diagram for the X.211 Phc endpoints.

The publication of X.211 is one of the last pieces of the OSI service definitions. It is unclear at this time if it will really be used much, since most physical level products are in place and working without X.211. At this late date, a "retrofit" does not make much sense.

SUGGESTED READINGS

The EIA documents are referenced throughout this chapter. A general tutorial and basic reference guide on physical level interfaces is available from [BLAC86] and a more thorough and detailed explanation is found in [BLAC88]. The CCITT V Series modems are all covered in the CCITT Red Book Volume VIII, Fascicle VIII.1. [SHER85] provides several discussions and examples of EIA-232 and RS-449. [CAMP84] and [SEYE84] explain the practical uses of the RS-232-C interface. [ATT81] describes the "Bell System" DDS interface. [JURE81] provides a good tutorial on modems. One of the best books on physical level protocols is [MCNA82].

QUESTIONS ───────────────────────────────

TRUE/FALSE

1. EIA-232 describes the physical level interfaces between the DCEs.
2. EIA-232, while developed in North America, uses the CCITT/ISO specifications.
3. EIA-232 is an unbalanced interface.
4. It is possible for the DCE to provide the clocking signals at both transmit and receive for both EIA-232 and V.24.
5. One principal advantage of RS-422-A and RS-423-A over EIA-232 is that they are balanced interfaces.
6. Match the physical-level term to the appropriate description:

Description

    a) A 25-pin connector used on EIA-232.

    b) Compatible with X.27.

    c) Describes the functions of a family of interchange circuits.

    d) Associated with RS-232-C.

Term

    1. RS-442-A

    2. X.21 bis

    3. ISO 2110

    4. V.24

7. A physical-level protocol performs the following functions:

    a) control signalling   d) ground

    b) error checking   e) clock

    c) mechanical connectors   f) all of the above

8. From the standpoint of the interchange circuits, what is the principal difference between X.21 and EIA-232?

9. You are faced with the problem of connecting two DTEs. They are located in the same office, only a few feet apart. What are your options?

10. Describe the major attributes of EIA-232-D.

11. What are the differences between RS-232-C and EIA-232-D?

12. You personal computer is transmitting data to a printer. The printer output is garbled. What are some possible reasons for this problem?

SELECTED ANSWERS

1. False. EIA-232 only defines the interface between the DTE and the DCE.

2. True. CCITT V.28, CCITT V.24 and ISO 2110.

3. True.

4. True.

5. False. RS-423-A is an unbalanced interface at one end.

6.

Description	Term
a)	3
b)	1
c)	4
d)	2

7. All except (b) error check, which is usually performed at the link level.

CHAPTER 10

The Data Link Layer: Concepts and Functions

INTRODUCTION

The transfer of data across the communications link must flow in a controlled and orderly manner. Since communications links experience distortions (such as noise), a method must be provided to deal with the periodic errors that occur. The data communications system must provide each station on the link with the capability to send data to another station, and the sending station must be assured that the data arrive error-free at the receiving station. The sending and receiving stations must maintain complete accountability for all traffic. In the event the data are distorted, the receiver site must be able to direct the originator to resend the erroneous frame or correct the errors.

Data link controls (DLCs, also called line protocols) provide these services. They manage the flow of data across the communications path or link. Their functions are limited to the individual link. That is to say, link control is responsible only for the traffic between adjacent nodes/stations on a line. Once the data are transmitted to the adjacent node and an acknowledgment of the transmission is returned to the transmission site, the link control task is complete for that particular transmission.

DLCs typically consist of a combination of software and hardware. Several offerings are now available on a chip, and Chapter 12 describes several of the DLC chip sets.

The DLC provides the following functions:

- Synchronizing (logically, not physically) the sender and receiver through the use of flags/SYN characters.

- Controlling the flow of data to prevent the sender from sending too fast.
- Detecting and recovering from errors between two points on the link.
- Maintaining awareness of link conditions such as distinguishing between data and control and determining the identity of the communicating stations.

The data link layer rests above the physical layer in the OSI model. Generally, the data link protocol is medium independent, and relies on the physical layer to deal with the specific media (wire, radio, etc.) and the physical signals (electrical current, laser, infrared, etc.).

Hundreds of different link protocols are used by the data communications industry. The diversity of methods and offerings complicate the task of explaining them to the reader. Our approach will be to partition the descriptions into several chapters. This chapter provides a generic description with the use of two taxonomy trees (Figures 10-1 and 10-11) and also focuses on design and implementation considerations. Chapter 11 explains some of the most widely used link controls in the industry, with emphasis on several prevalent standards and vendor products. Subsequent chapters explain data link controls further with examples of their use in specific areas of data communications applications (satellites, local networks, personal computer systems, digital networks, etc.).

We begin our examination of data link controls with an explanation of their formats, which are broadly classified as asynchronous or synchronous. Figure 10-1 provides a simple taxonomy for our discussion.

ASYNCHRONOUS LINE PROTOCOLS

Asynchronous DLCs place timing bits around each character in the user data stream (see Figure 1-4 in Chapter 1 for a review). The start bit precedes the data and is used to notify the receiving site that data are on the path (start bit detection). The line is in an idle condition prior to the arrival of the start bit and remains in the idle state until a start bit is transmitted. The start signal initiates mechanisms in the receiving device for sampling, counting, and receiving the bits of the data stream. The data bits are represented as the mark signal (binary 1) and the space signal (binary 0).

The user data bits are placed in a temporary storage area, such as a register or buffer, and are later moved into the terminal or computer memory for further processing.

Stop bits, consisting of one or more mark signals, provide the mechanism to notify the receiver that all bits of the character have arrived. Following the stop bits, the signal returns to idle level, thus guaranteeing that the next character will begin with a 1 to 0 transition. Even if the character is all 0s, the stop bit returns the link to a high or idle level.

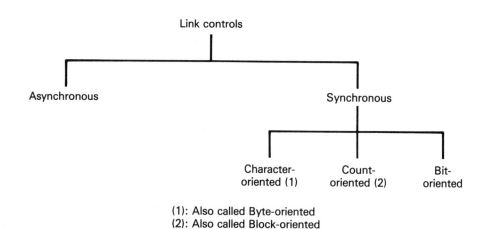

Link controls

Asynchronous   Synchronous

Character-   Count-   Bit-
oriented (1)   oriented (2)   oriented

(1): Also called Byte-oriented
(2): Also called Block-oriented

FIGURE 10-1. Formats of Data Link Protocols

This method is called asynchronous transmission due to the absence of continuous synchronization between the sender and receiver. The process allows a data character to be transmitted at any time without regard to any previous timing signal; the timing signal is a part of the data signal.

Asynchronous transmission is commonly found in machines or terminals such as teletypes or teleprinters and low-speed computer terminals. The vast majority of personal computers use asynchronous transmission. Its value lies in its simplicity.

SYNCHRONOUS LINE PROTOCOLS

Synchronous DLCs do not surround each character with start/stop bits, but place a preamble and postamble bit pattern around the user data. These bit patterns are usually called a SYN (synchronization) character, an EOT (end of transmission) character, or simply a flag. They are used to notify the receiver when user data are "arriving" and when the last user data have "arrived."

It should be emphasized that data communications systems require two types of synchronization.

- *At the physical level*: to keep the transmitter and receiver clocks synchronized.
- *At the link level*: to distinguish user data from flags and other control fields.

Character-Oriented Protocols

The character-oriented synchronous data link controls were developed in the 1960s and are still widely used today. The binary synchronous control (bisync) family are character-oriented systems. These protocols rely on a specific code set (ASCII, EBCDIC) to interpret the control fields; thus, they are code dependent. Box 10-1 summarizes the functions of the most common character-oriented control codes.

BOX 10-1. Typical Character-Oriented Control Codes

Character	Function
SYN	Synchronous idle (keeps channel active)
PAD	Frame pad (time fill between transmission)
DLE	Data link escape (used to achieve code transparency)
ENQ	Enquiry (used with polls/selects and bids)
SOH	Start of heading
STX	Start of text (puts line in text mode)
ITB	End of intermediate block
ETB	End of transmission block
ETX	End of text
EOT	End of transmission (puts line in control mode)
BCC	Block check count
ACK0	Acknowledges even-numbered blocks
ACK1	Acknowledges odd-numbered blocks
WACK	Wait before transmitting

If machines on a link use different codes (one with ASCII code and one with EBCDIC, for example) the user must deal with two variants of the link protocol, and some type of code conversion is required before the machines can communicate with each other. The problem is shown in Figure 10-2(a). Let us assume stations A and B use STX and ETX to represent start of (user) text and end of (user) text, respectively. It is evident that the two devices cannot communicate, since the ASCII and EBCDIC codes use different bit sequences. Consequently, code conversion must be performed by one of the machines.

It is also possible that a code recognized as control could be created by the user application process. For instance, assume in Figure 10-2(b) that a user program creates a bit sequence which is the same as the ETX (end of text) control code. The receiving station, upon encountering the ETX inside the user data, would erroneously assume the end of the transmission is signified by the user-generated ETX. The control would accept the ETX as a protocol control and attempt to perform an error check on an incomplete frame, which would result in an error.

Obviously, control codes must be excluded from the user text field. Character protocols address the problem with the DLE control code. This code is placed in front of the control codes such as STX, ETX, ETB, ITB, and SOH to identify these characters as valid line control characters (see Figure

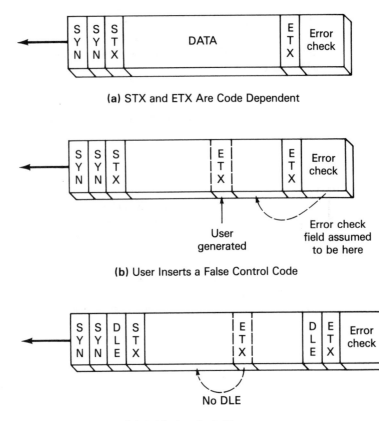

(a) STX and ETX Are Code Dependent

(b) User Inserts a False Control Code

(c) Achieving Code Transparency

FIGURE 10-2. Character-Oriented Protocols

10-2[c]). The simplest means to achieve code transparency is to use DLE.STX or DLE.SOH to signify the beginning of noncontrol data (user data) and DLE.ETX, DLE.ETB, or DLE.ITB to signify the end of user data.

The DLE is not placed in front of user-generated data. Consequently, if bit patterns resembling any of these control characters are created in the user text and encountered by the receiving station, the receiving station assumes they are valid user data, because the DLE does not precede the character in question.

The DLE presents a special problem if it is generated by the end-user application process, since it could be recognized as a control code. Character-oriented protocols handle this situation by inserting a DLE next to a data DLE character. The receiver discards the first DLE of two successive DLEs and accepts the second DLE as valid user data.

The character-oriented protocols have dominated the vendors synchronous line protocol products since the mid-1960s. While still widely used, they are being replaced by count and bit protocols.

Count-Oriented Protocols

In the 1970s, count-oriented protocols (also called block protocols) were developed to address the code dependency problem. These systems exhibit one principal advantage over character-oriented protocols in that they have a more effective means of handling user data transparency: they simply insert a count field at the transmitting station. This field specifies the length of the user data field. As a consequence, the receiver need not examine the user field contents, but need only count the incoming bytes as specified by the count field.

The count-oriented protocols are really a combination of character-oriented protocols and bit-oriented protocols. Figure 10-3 shows that certain control fields are code dependent and others are code transparent.

Count-oriented protocols may encounter problems when the signals are transmitted across a digital link. In Chapter 3, we learned that a digital system may delete a digital frame on a link to recover clocks and resynchronize. It may also insert timing/control data into the transmission. A count protocol loses its receive counter in such a situation, and the protocol must recover the lost data with retransmissions.

Bit-Oriented Protocols

Bit-oriented data link control protocols were developed in the 1970s and are now quite prevalent throughout the industry. They form the basis for most of the new link-level systems in use today.

Bit protocols do not rely on a specific code (ASCII/IA5 or EBCDIC) for line control. Individual bits within an octet are set to effect control functions. An 8-bit flag pattern of 01111110 is generated at the beginning and end of the frame to enable the receiver to identify the beginning and end of a transmission.

There will be occasions when a flaglike sequence, 01111110, is inserted into the user data stream by the application process. To prevent this occurrence, the transmitting site inserts a 0 bit after it encounters five continuous 1s anywhere between the opening and closing flag of the frame. This tech-

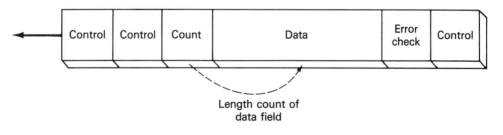

Length count of
data field

Note: Control codes are code dependent

FIGURE 10-3. Count-Oriented Protocols

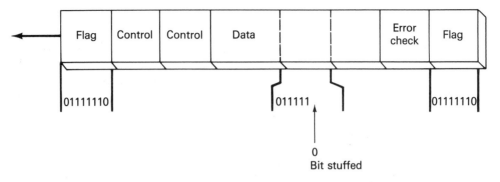

FIGURE 10-4. Bit-Oriented Protocols

nique is called bit stuffing and is similar in function to the DLE in character protocols and the count field in count protocols. As the frame is stuffed, it is transmitted across the link to the receiver. Figure 10-4 reviews the process.

The receiver continuously monitors the bit stream. After it receives a 0 bit with five continuous 1 bits following, the receiver inspects the next bit. If it is a 0 bit, it pulls this bit out; in other words, it "unstuffs" the bit. In this manner, the system achieves code and data transparency. The protocol is not concerned about any particular bit code inside the data stream. Its main concern is to keep the flags unique.

Bit-oriented protocols have virtually taken over the market for the newer products and offerings. Consequently, Chapter 11 discusses these systems in considerable detail.

Comparison of Synchronous Protocols

Box 10-2 provides a comparison of character-oriented, count-oriented and bit-oriented protocols. It is obvious that no clear distinction exists between all the attributes of the protocols. The count-oriented protocol is actually a hybrid of the other two protocols.

CONTROLLING TRAFFIC ON THE LINK

Asynchronous Systems

Traffic control on an asynchronous link may use the same techniques as a synchronous link. For example, some systems encapsulate an asynchronous data stream into the information field of a synchronous frame and transmit the frame with the synchronous protocol. These methods are examined shortly. For the present, we discuss two simple, yet widely used methods for controlling asynchronous traffic: (a) request to send/clear to send and (b) XON/XOFF.

BOX 10-2. Comparisons of Bit Protocols

Attribute	Character	Count	Bit
Start Framing	SYN SYN	SYN SYN	Flag
Stop Framing	Characters	Count field	Flag
Retransmissions	Stop-and-Wait	Go-Back-N or Selective Repeat	Go-Back-N or Selective Repeat
Window Size	1	Various (255)	Various (7-127)
Frame Formats	Several	Few	1
Line Mode	HDX	HDX or FDX	HDX or FDX
Text Transparency	DLE Code	Count Field	Bit Stuffing
Traffic Flow	TTD or WACK	Sliding Window	Sliding Window
Line Control	Full Character	Full Character and Bits	Bits

Request to send/clear (RTS/CTS) is considered a rather "low-level" approach to protocols and data communications. Nonetheless, it is widely used because of its relationship to and dependence upon the widely used physical interface, EIA-232.

The use of EIA-232 to effect communications between DTEs is most common in a local environment, because EIA-232 is inherently a short-distance interface, typically constraining the channel to no greater than a few hundred feet. Devices can control the communications between each other by raising and lowering the RTS/CTS signals on the circuits (pins 4 and 5, respectively). A common implementation of this technique is found in the attachment of a terminal to a simple multiplexer. The terminal requests use of the channel by raising its RTS circuit (pin 4). The multiplexer responds to the request by raising the CTS circuit (pin 5). The terminal then sends its data to the multiplexer through the transmit data circuit (pin 2).

Another widely used technique is XON/XOFF. XON is an ANSI/IA5 transmission character. The XON is usually implemented by DC1. The XOFF, also an ANSI/IA5, is represented by DC3. Peripheral devices such as printers, graphics terminals, or plotters can use the XON/XOFF approach to control incoming traffic.

The master station, typically a computer, sends data to the remote peripheral site, which prints or graphs the data onto an output media. Since the plotter or printer may be slow relative to the transmission speed of the channel and the transmission speed of the transmitting computer, its buffer may become full. Consequently, to prevent overflow, it transmits back to the computer an XOFF signal, which means stop transmitting or "transmit off."

The signals can be transmitted across an EIA connection, twisted-pair, or any type of media. As the buffers empty, the peripheral device transmits an XON to resume the data transfer.

Synchronous Systems

Regardless of the type of synchronous format used (character, count, or bit) the communications processes between stations are similar. This section provides a closer look at these processes by highlighting the following inter-related topics (these procedures are not used by all link protocols but are pervasive enough to warrant our attention):

> Flow control of traffic between the machines
> Sequencing and accounting of traffic
> Actions to be taken in the event of error detection

Figure 10-5 will get us started. This example illustrates several important points about data link (level 2) communications. It shows DTE A is to transmit data to DTE B. The transmission goes through an intermediate point, a computer located at C.

The most common approach is to pass the data, like a baton in a relay race, from site to site until it finally reaches its destination. One important aspect of the process is in event 2, where C sends an acknowledgment of the data received to A. This acknowledgment means station C has checked for possible errors occurring during the transmission of the frame, and as best it

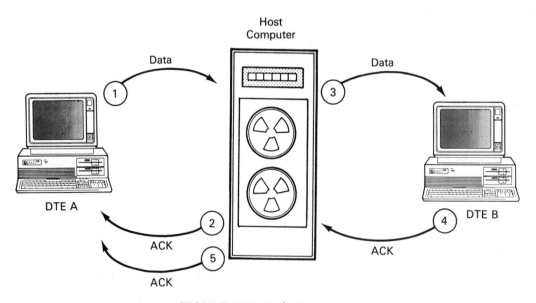

FIGURE 10-5. Link Operations

can determine, the data have been received without corruption. It so indicates by transmitting another frame on the return path indicating acceptance.

The data communications industry uses two terms to describe the event 2 response. The term ACK denotes a positive acknowledgment; the term NAK represents a negative acknowledgment. A NAK usually occurs because the signal is distorted due to faulty conditions on the channel (noise, etc.). The frame sent to A in event 2 will either be an ACK or a NAK. In the event of an error in the transmission, station A must receive a negative acknowledgment (NAK) so it can retransmit the data. It is also essential that the processes shown in events 1 and 2 are completed before event 3 occurs. If C immediately transmitted the data to B before performing the error check, B could possibly receive erroneous data.

If station A receives an ACK in event 2, it assumes the data have been received correctly at station B, and the communications system at site A can purge this data from its queue. (The application process often saves a copy on disk or tape for accounting, audit, or security reasons.)

Continuing the process in events 3 and 4, assume that an ACK is returned from B to C. The end-user at A may assume through event 2 that the data arrived at C. A false sense of security could result, because event 2 only indicates that the data arrived safely in C. If the data are lost between the C and B sites, the A user assumes no problem exists. This scenario provides no provision for an end-to-end acknowledgment. If an end-user wishes to have absolute assurance that the data arrived at the remote site, event 5 is required. Upon receiving event 4 at C, C sends another acceptance (ACK) to A.

The reader should be aware that the level 2 data link protocols do not provide end-to-end acknowledgment through multiple links. Some systems provide this service at level 3, the network layer. However, the OSI model intends end-to-end accountability to be provided by the transport layer (level 4).

Functions of Timers. Many link protocols use timers in conjunction with logic states to verify that an event occurs within a prescribed time. When a transmitting station sends a frame onto the channel, it starts a timer and enters a wait state. The value of the timer (usually called T1, no relation to a digital T1 carrier) is set to expire if the receiving station does not respond to the transmitted frame within the set period. Upon expiration of the timer, one to n retransmissions are attempted, each with the timer T1 reset, until a response is received or until the link protocol's maximum number of retries is met. In this case, recovery or problem resolution is attempted by the link level. If unsuccessful, recovery is performed by a higher-level protocol or by manual intervention and trouble-shooting efforts. (The retry parameter is usually designated as parameter N2.)

The T1 timer just described is designated as the acknowledgment timer. Its value depends on (a) round trip propagation delay of the signal (usually a small value, except for very long and very high-speed circuits); (b) the processing time at the receiver (including queuing time of the frame); (c) the transmission time of the acknowledging frame; and (d) possible queue and processing time at the transmitter when it receives the acknowledgment frame.

The receiving station may use a parameter (T2) in conjunction with T1. Its value is set to ensure that an acknowledgment frame is sent to the transmitting station before the T1 at the transmitter expires. This action precludes the transmitter from resending frames unnecessarily.

To illustrate the use of T1 and T2, the following algorithms [AT&T86A] describe a lower bound on T1 and an upper bound on T2 (T1 is started at the end of the transmission of a frame):

$$T1_T = \geq T2_R + PD + FPT_R + TT_{CUR} + TT_{ACK} + FPT_T$$
$$T2_R = \leq T1_T - PD - FPT_R - TT_{CUR} - TT_{ACK} - FPT_T$$

Where: T is the transmitter; R is the receiver; PD is the round-trip propagation delay; FPT is the frame processing time; TT_{ACK} is the admission time of the acknowledgment frame; TT_{CUR} is the time to complete the transmission of the ongoing frames that are already in the transmit queue and cannot be pushed down into the queue. (TT_{CUR} can also describe, if relevant to a particular protocol, the queue time at the receiver before the acknowledgment frame is "actioned" and T1 stopped.)

Figure 10-6 illustrates the use of the T1 timer and the T2 parameter. For the values shown in the figure, the T1 and T2 values are set properly:

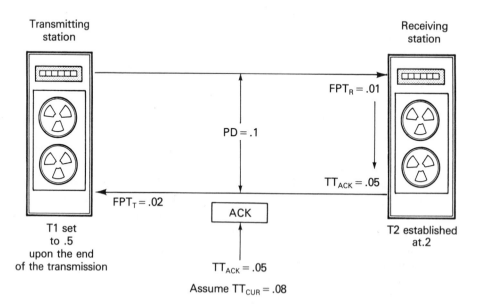

FIGURE 10-6. The T1 Timer and the T2 Parameter

$$\text{T1}_T \text{ or } .5 = \geq .2 + .1 + .01 + .08 + .05 + .02$$
$$.5 = \geq .46$$
$$\text{T2}_R \text{ or } .2 = \leq .5 - .1 - .01 - .08 - .05 - .02$$
$$.2 = \leq .24$$

The number of timers varies, depending upon the type of protocol and the designer's approach to link management. Some other commonly used timers are:

- *Poll timer (also called P bit timer)*: defines the time interval during which a polling station (i.e., a station requesting a frame from another station) shall expect to receive a response.
- *NAK timer (also called a reject or selective reject timer)*: defines the time interval during which a rejecting station shall expect a reply to its reject frame.
- *Link set-up timer*: defines the time interval during which a transmitting station shall expect a reply to its link set-up command frame.

The timing functions may be implemented by a number of individual timers and the protocol designer/implementer is responsible for determining how the timers are set and restarted.

Automatic Request for Repeat (ARQ)

When a station transmits a frame, it places a send sequence number in a control field. The receiving station uses this number to determine if it has received all other preceding frames (with lower numbers). It also uses the number to determine its response. For example, after it receives a frame with send sequence number = 3, it responds with an ACK with a receive sequence number = 4, which signifies it accepts all frames up to and including 3 and expects 4 to be the send sequence number of the next frame. The send sequence number is identified as N(S) and the receive sequence number is identified as N(R).

Half duplex (HDX) protocols need only use two numbers for sequencing, since they can have only one frame outstanding at a time. Most HDX protocols use the binary numbers 0 and 1 alternately. Full duplex (FDX) protocols typically use a greater range of sequence numbers because many frames may be outstanding at a time.

The term ARQ (automatic request for repeat) describes the process by which a receiving station requests a retransmission. As an example, the reception of a NAK with receive sequence number = 5 indicates that frame 5 is in error and must be retransmitted. The process is automatic, without human intervention (a somewhat antiquated term today). A stop-and-wait ARQ describes a similar half duplex protocol that waits for an ACK or NAK before sending another frame.

Inclusive Acknowledgment. One advantage of continuous ARQ is called inclusive acknowledgment. For example, a receiver might send an ACK of 5 and ACKs of 1, 2, 3, and 4 are not transmitted. The ACK of 5 means the station received and acknowledges everything up to and including 4; the next frame expected should have a 5 in its send sequence field. It is evident from this simple example that continuous ARQ protocols with inclusive acknowledgment can reduce considerably the overhead involved in the ACKs. In this example, one ACK acknowledges 4 frames considerably better than the stop-and-wait systems, in which an ACK is required for every transmission.

Piggybacking. The newer line protocols permit the inclusion of the N(S) and N(R) field in the same frame. This technique, called piggybacking, allows the protocol to "piggyback" an ACK (the N[R] value) onto an information frame (sequenced by the N[S] value). As an example, assume a station sends a frame with N(R) = 5 and N(S) = 1. The N(R) = 5 means all frames up to a number 4 are acknowledged and the N(S) = 1 means station B is sending a user information in this frame with a sequence of 1.

Flow Control with Sliding Windows. Continuous ARQ devices use the concept of transmit and receive *windows* to aid in link management operations. A window is established on each link to provide a reservation of resources at both stations. These resources may be the allocation of specific computer resources or the reservation of buffer space for the transmitting device. In most systems, the window provides both buffer space and sequencing rules. During the initiation of a link session (handshake) between the stations a window is established. For example, if stations A and B are to communicate with each other, station A reserves a receive window for B, and B reserves a receive window for A. The windowing concept is necessary to full duplex protocols because they entail a continuous flow of frames into the receiving site without the intermittent stop-and-wait acknowledgments. Consequently, the receiver must have a sufficient allocation of memory to handle the continuous incoming traffic. It can be seen that window size is a function of (a) buffer space and (b) the magnitude of the sequence numbers.

The windows at the transmitting and receiving site are controlled by state variables (which is another name for a counter). The transmitting site maintains a send state variable (V[S]). It is the sequence number of the next frame to be transmitted. The receiving site maintains a receive state variable (V[R]) which contains the number that is expected to be in the sequence number of the next frame. The V(S) is incremented with each frame transmitted and placed in the send sequence field (N[S]) in the frame.

Upon receiving the frame, the receiving site checks for a transmission error. It also compares the send sequence number N(S) with its V(R). If the frame is acceptable, it increments V(R) by one, places it into a receive sequence number field N(R) in an acknowledgment (ACK) frame and sends it to the original transmitting site to complete the accountability for the transmission.

If an error is detected or if the V(R) does not match the sending sequence number in the frame, a NAK (negative acknowledgment) with the receiving sequence number N(R) containing the value of V(R) is sent to the original transmitting site. This V(R) value informs the transmitting DTE of the next frame that it is expected to send. The transmitter must then reset its V(S) and retransmit the frame whose sequence matches the value of N(R).

A useful feature of the sliding window scheme is the ability of the receiving station to restrict the flow of data from the transmitting station by withholding the acknowledgment frames. This action prevents the transmitter from opening its windows and reusing its send sequence numbers values until the same send sequence numbers have been acknowledged. A station can be completely "throttled" if it receives no ACKs from the receiver.

Many data link controls use the numbers 0 through 7 for V(S), V(R), and the sequence numbers in the frame. Once the state variables are incremented through 7, the numbers are reused, beginning with 0. Because the numbers are reused, the stations must not be allowed to send a frame with a sequence number that has not yet been acknowledged. For example, the protocol must wait for frame number 6 to be acknowledged before it uses a V(S) of 6 again. The use of 0-7 permits seven frames to be outstanding before the window is "closed." Even though 0-7 gives eight sequence numbers, the V(R) contains the value of the next expected frame, which limits the actual outstanding frames to 7.

We just learned that many systems use sequence numbers and state variables to manage the traffic on a link. As a brief review, please refer to Box 10-3.

Other Considerations.   Three important goals of a line protocol are (a) to obtain high throughput, (b) to obtain fast response time, and (c) to minimize the logic required at the transmitting/receiving sites to account for traffic (such as ACKs and NAKs). The transmit window is an integral tool in meeting these goals. One of the primary functions of the window is to ensure that by the time all the permissible frames have been transmitted, at least one frame has been acknowledged. In this manner, the window is kept open and the line is continuously active. The timers discussed earlier are key to effective line utilization and window management.

One could argue that a very large window permits continuous transmissions regardless of the speed of the link and size of the frames, because the transmitter does not have to wait for acknowledgment from the receiver. While this is true, a larger window size also means that the transmitter must maintain a large queue to store those frames that have not been acknowledged by the receiver.

The concepts of continuous ARQ are relatively simple, yet it should be realized that with a large communications facility, the host computer or front-end processor is tasked with efficient transmission, data flow, and

Functions

    Flow Control of Frames (Windows)
    Detect Lost Frames
    Detect Out-of-Sequence Frames
    Detect Erroneous Frames

Uses

$N(S)$:	Sequence number of transmitted frame
$N(R)$:	Sequence number of the acknowledged frame(s). Acknowledges all frames up to $N(R) - 1$
$V(S)$:	Variable containing sequence number of next frame to be transmitted
$V(R)$:	Variable containing expected value of the sequence number $N(S)$ in the next transmitting frame.

response time between itself and all the secondary sites attached to it. The primary host must maintain a window for every station and manage the traffic to and from each station on an individual basis.

EXAMPLES OF CONTINUOUS ARQ PROTOCOL OPERATIONS

Figure 10-7 provides an example of operations on a data link, and will allow us to tie together some of the concepts in the previous discussions. Station A sends four frames in succession to station B. Station A increments the send state variable $V(S)$ with each transmission and places its value in the $N(S)$ field of each frame. Consequently, the four user data frames would have the $N(S)$ fields set as shown in the figure.

The illustration shows that station A's send state variable is incremented to the next frame to be transmitted and station B's receive state variable $V(R)$ is incremented upon receiving an error-free frame. Thus, the receive state variable should always equal the value of the next expected frame $N(S)$ field. Let us expand this idea further by moving to event 10 and seeing the effect of the receipt of the $N(R)$ field on station A.

In event 10, station A receives a frame from station B with $N(R) = 4$. Notice that station A's $V(S)$ of 4 equals the incoming $N(R) = 4$. Consequently, station A knows that all preceding traffic has been received without problems because its $V(S)$ equals the incoming $N(R)$ value. In other words, the

Event	Station A V(S)		Station B V(R)	
1	0		0	
2	0	N(S) = 0 →	0	
3	1		1	
4	1	N(S) = 1 →	1	
5	2		2	
6	2	N(S) = 2 →	2	
7	3		3	
8	3	N(S) = 3 →	3	
9	4		4	
10	4	← N(R) = 4	4	
11	4	N(S) = 4 →	4	
12	5		5	
13	5	← N(R) = 5, N(S) = 0	5	(Note 1)
14	5		5	
15	5	N(S) = 5 →	5	
16	6		6	
17	6	← N(R) = 6	6	
18	6	N(S) = 6 →	6	(Note 2)
19	7		6	
20	7	← NAK, N(R) = 6	6	
21	6		6	
22	6	N(S) = 6 →	6	
23	7		7	

Note 1: An example of piggybacking

Note 2: An error is detected

FIGURE 10-7. Sequencing the Frames on the Link

N(R) value is the value of the next expected frame, so it should equal the V(S), which is the value of the next frame to be transmitted.

The process is elegantly simple. Flow control and traffic accountability are maintained by the continuous checking, incrementing, and rechecking of the state variables and sequence numbers.

What happens in the event of an error? As we learned earlier, today's data link controls typically deal with transmission errors through ARQ (automatic request for repeat). User data is transmitted in frames with an error checking field created by the transmitting site and checked by the receiving site. This field allows the receiver to detect transmission errors and request the retransmission of erroneous frames. The transmitter automatically repeats these frames upon request from the data receiver.

In event 18, station A sends frame 6. However, station B detects an error in the frame. Due to the error, station B does not increment its receive state variable. Rather, it inserts the current value of this variable into the N(R) field and sends it back to station A with a NAK control code or a bit set to indicate a negative acknowledgment (event 20).

Station A then adjusts its state variables accordingly and retransmits the erroneous frame. In event 21, station A resets its send state variable to the received N(R) value of 6, and retransmits frame 6 in event 22. In event 23, the channel state variables and sequence numbers are once again synchronized, and the error has been resolved.

With this background information, we now examine several methods for dealing with errors.

EXAMPLES OF NEGATIVE ACKNOWLEDGMENTS AND RETRANSMISSIONS

To return to the scenario in Figure 10-7, event 20 can be implemented in a number of ways:

> Implicit reject
> Selective reject (SREJ)
> Reject (REJ) (or Go-Back-N)
> Selective reject/reject (SREJ/REJ)

Implicit reject uses the N(R) value to acknowledge all preceding frames and request the retransmission of the frame whose N(S) value equals the value in N(R). This technique works well enough on half duplex links but should not be used on full duplex systems. Since a full duplex protocol permits simultaneous two-way transmission, an N(R) value could be interpreted erroneously as either an ACK or a NAK. For example, if station A receives a frame with N(R) = 4 from station B and the station just sent a frame with N(S) = 4, station A does not know if B is NAKing or ACKing frame 4. On a half duplex, stop-and-wait link, the N(R) = 4 would clearly mean that frame 4 is expected next. Explicit NAKs are really preferable; they include selective reject, reject, and selective reject/reject.

Selective reject (SREJ) requires that only the erroneous transmission be retransmitted. Reject (REJ) requires that not only the erroneous transmission be repeated, but all succeeding frames be retransmitted (i.e., all frames "behind" the erroneous frame). Selective reject and reject are illustrated in Figure 10-8.

Both techniques have advantages and disadvantages. Selective reject provides better line utilization, since the erroneous frame is the only retransmission. However, as shown in Figure 10-8(b), site B must hold frames 3, 4, and 5 to await the retransmission of frame 2. Upon its arrival, frame 2 must be inserted into the proper sequence before the data is passed to the end-user application. The holding of frames can consume precious buffer space, especially if the user device has limited memory available and several active links.

Reject (also called Go-Back-N) is a simpler technique. Once an erroneous frame is detected, the receiving station discards all subsequent frames in the session until it receives the correct retransmission. Reject requires no frame queuing and frame resequencing at the receiver. However, its throughput is not as high as selective reject, since it requires the retransmission of frames that may not be in error. The reject ARQ approach is ineffective on systems with long round-trip delays and high data rates.

One principal disadvantage of selective reject is the requirement that only one selective reject frame can be outstanding at a time. For example, assume site A has transmitted frames 0,1,2,3,4, and 5, and site B responds with SREJ with N(R) = 2. This response frame acknowledges 0 and 1 and requests the retransmission of 2. However, let us suppose another SREJ frame were sent by site B before the first SREJ condition cleared. As the frame flow diagram in Figure 10-9 shows, multiple SREJs contradict the idea of the N(R) value acknowledging the preceding frames. In our example, site A does not know if the second SREJ of N(R) = 4 acknowledges preceding frames since it contradicts the previous SREJ of N(R) = 2. Again, the requirement for only one SREJ to be outstanding eliminates any ambiguity, but if the frame error rate is high and its occurrence exceeds the round-trip propagation delay between sites A and B, then the single SREJ convention can reduce the throughput on the channel. This problem stems from the fact that the channel may go idle while the stations wait for the first SREJ to clear. In our previous example, the SREJ N(R) = 4 could not be sent until site B had received its response to its first SREJ N(R) = 2. This effect is especially evident on circuits that experience long delays.

One relief to the SREJ dilemma is to use the SREJ N(R) = X to only refuse (NAK) the N(S) = X frame. That is, the SREJ has no acknowledgment functions. In our frame flow diagram, site A would assume that SREJ N(R)

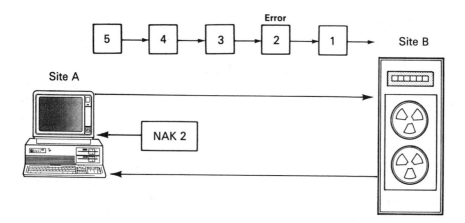

(a) Frames 1 Through 5 Transmitted with an Error in Frame 2

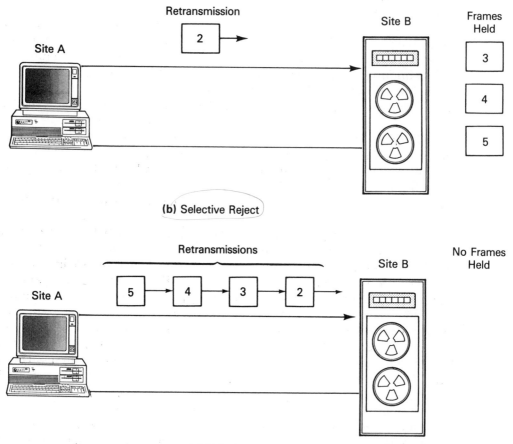

(b) Selective Reject

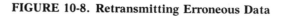

(c) Reject

FIGURE 10-8. Retransmitting Erroneous Data

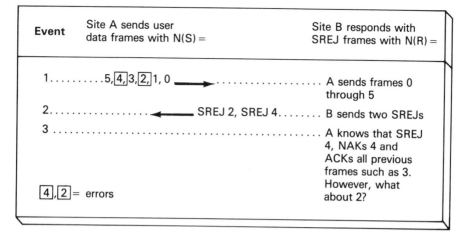

Event	Site A sends user data frames with N(S) =	Site B responds with SREJ frames with N(R) =
1.........5,4̲,3,2̲,1, 0 ⟶		A sends frames 0 through 5
2............... ⟵ SREJ 2, SREJ 4.......		B sends two SREJs
3		A knows that SREJ 4, NAKs 4 and ACKs all previous frames such as 3. However, what about 2?
4̲,2̲ = errors		

FIGURE 10-9. The Problem with Multiple Selective Rejects

= 2 and SREJ N(R) = 4 only NAK frames 2 and 4. Consequently, channel efficiency is not reduced significantly on (a) error-prone channels or (b) channels with long propagation delays.

However, if the SREJ has no positive acknowledgment as seen in our previous example, how is frame 3 acknowledged, if SREJ N(R) = 4 does not inclusively acknowledge preceding frames? The acknowledgment is through one of three alternatives. With the first, a subsequent REJ can be used to acknowledge previous frames. A second alternative can use a regular user data frame with the N(R) value acknowledging preceding frames.

The last approach, selective reject-reject (SREJ-REJ) has been proposed as an alternative to the other two techniques. SREJ-REJ performs like SREJ except that once an error is detected, it waits to verify the next frame as correct before sending the SREJ. If the receiver detects the loss of two contiguous data frames, it sends a REJ instead and discards all subsequently received frames until the lost frame is received correctly. Also, if another frame error is detected prior to recovery of the SREJ condition, the receiver saves (stores) all frames received after the first erroneous frame and discards frames received after the second erroneous frame until the first erroneous frame is recovered. Then, a REJ is issued to recover the second frame and the other subsequent discarded frames. SREJ-REJ is depicted in the frame flow diagram in Figure 10-10.

CATEGORIES OF DATA LINK CONTROLS

Even though link protocols vary widely in how they are implemented, the majority of systems can be described by one or a combination of the categories in Figure 10-11. A more complete description is available from other sources [BLAC87C] and Chapters 11, 19, 20, and 22 explain detailed aspects of link controls. This section is intended as a basic introduction to the sub-

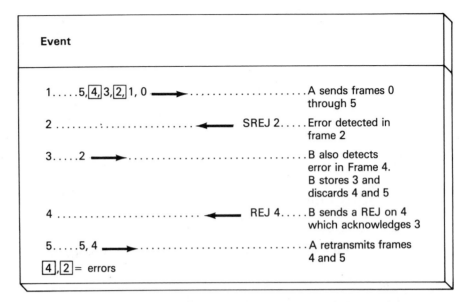

FIGURE 10-10. Using a Combination of Selective Reject and Reject

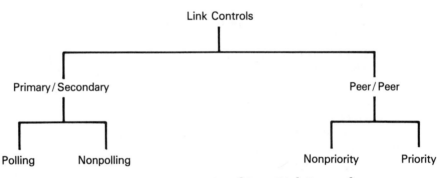

FIGURE 10-11. Categories of Data Link Protocols

ject. A more advanced reader may wish to skip to the next section, titled "Link Efficiency Considerations."

A widely used approach to managing the communications channel is through a primary/secondary (sometimes called master/slave) protocol. This technique designates one station as the primary site on the link. The primary station controls all the other stations and dictates when and if the devices can communicate.

The second major approach is a peer-to-peer protocol. This technique has no primary station and typically provides for equal status to all stations on the channel. However, stations may not have equal access to the link, since they can have pre-established priority over others. Nevertheless, the absence of a primary site usually provides for an equal opportunity to use network resources. Peer-to-peer systems are often found in local area networks (LANs) with ring, bus, and mesh topologies.

Primary/Secondary Protocols

Polling/Selection Systems. The most prevalent use of a primary/secondary system is polling/selection, usually shortened to polling. The configuration in Figure 10-12 shows a host computer at site A and a terminal

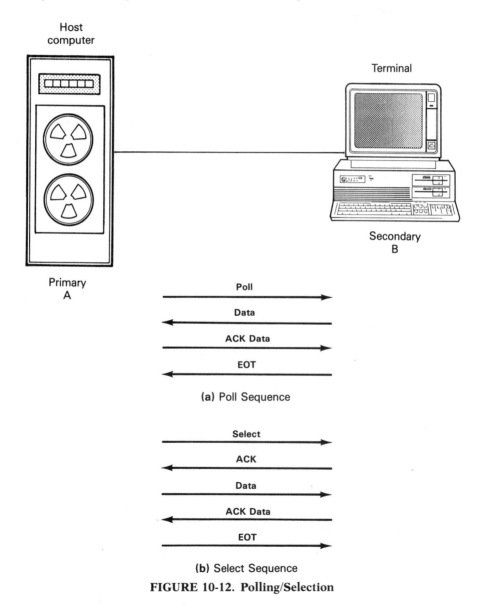

FIGURE 10-12. Polling/Selection

at site B. There could be many other configurations (for example, a multidrop line or a ring topology). Polling/selection works the same conceptually with computers linked to other computers; it is possible to have primary/secondary computers, as well as terminals.

Polling/selection systems revolve around two commands, poll and select. The purpose of the poll is to transmit data to the primary site. The purpose of the select is just the opposite: to transmit data from the primary site to the secondary site. Select commands are no longer needed on the newer protocols, because the master site reserves resources and buffers at the receiver during link establishment; thereafter, data is sent at the discretion of the master node.

A network often exists as an ordered form of a primary/secondary relationship. Poll and select are the principal commands needed to move data to any site on a channel or in the network. Let us examine how this is accomplished, referring to Figure 10-12 (a). First, a poll command is sent from the master site to secondary site 2. If data are to be transmitted, they are sent back to the polling site. The primary site checks for errors and sends an ACK if the data are acceptable or a NAK if they are incorrect. These two events (data and ACK/NAK) may occur many times until the secondary site has no more data to send. The secondary station must then send an indicator that it has completed its transmission, such as the end-of-transmission code (EOT), or a bit in a control field.

The select command is illustrated in Figure 10-12 (b). Select means the primary station has data for the secondary. The ACK to the select means the station is ready to receive data. The data are transmitted, checked for errors, and acknowledged. (As stated earlier, newer systems reserve resources at link establishment and assume the receiver can receive the data. Therefore, no selects are required with this approach.) The process can repeat itself. Eventually, an EOT control indicator is transmitted.

When a poll is issued to the secondary site, it could respond negatively if it has nothing to transmit. A system typically uses a NAK to indicate a negative response to a poll. In newer systems, the indication of a willingness to receive or transmit is called a receive ready (RR); unwillingness is called a receive not ready (RNR).

A disadvantage of a polling/selection system is the potential number of negative responses to polls, which can consume precious resources on the channel. This overhead is especially evident in systems without multiplexers or terminal cluster controllers that are used to manage local traffic.

Nonpolling Systems. Another approach to primary/secondary systems is the use of nonpolling protocols. One type that is widely used is time division multiple access (TDMA). This technique is a sophisticated form of time division multiplexing (TDM). Typically, a station is designated as a master station (often called the reference station [REF]). The responsibility of the reference station is to accept requests from the secondary stations, which are an indication that the secondary station wishes to use the channel. The requests are sent as part of the ongoing transmissions in a special control field. Periodically, the reference station transmits a control frame indicating which stations can use the channel during a given period. Upon receiving the permission frame, the secondary stations adjust their timing to transmit within the predesignated slot.

TDMA does not use a polling selection system. Nonetheless, it does fit into our classification of primary/secondary networks, because the TDMA reference station has the option of assigning or not assigning stations to a slot on the link.

Peer-to-Peer Protocols

The second major type of link control is the peer-to-peer system. Two examples are provided in this section: (a) nonpriority and (b) priority schemes.

Nonpriority Systems. The carrier sense (collision) protocol is an example of peer-to-peer nonpriority systems. Several implementations use this technique with the Ethernet specification and IEEE 802.3 standard. A carrier sense protocol considers all stations equal, so the stations contend for the use of the channel on an equal basis. (However, it is possible to introduce priority through different back-off times for different devices.) Before transmitting, the stations are required to monitor the channel to determine if the channel is occupied. If the channel is idle, any station with data to transmit can send its frame onto the channel. If the channel is occupied, the stations must defer to the passing signal.

Carrier sense networks are usually implemented on local area networks because the collision window lengthens with a longer channel. The long channel gives rise to more collisions and reduces throughput in the network.

In the event of a collision, wherein more than one station transmits at the same time, the stations detect the distorted signal. Each station is capable of transmitting and listening to the channel simultaneously. As the two signals collide, they create voltage irregularities on the channel which are sensed by the colliding stations. Both stations turn off the transmission, and after a randomized wait period attempt to seize the channel again. The randomized wait decreases the chances of the collision recurring, since it is unlikely that the competing stations will generate the same randomized wait time.

Priority Systems. Token passing is a widely used method for implementing both peer-to-peer nonpriority and priority systems. To illustrate the concepts, the priority systems are discussed here. The technique is found in many local area networks. Some token-passing systems are implemented with a horizontal bus topology; others are implemented with ring topology. The ring topology is covered in this section; later chapters discuss other topologies.

If the ring is idle (that is, no user data are occupying the ring), a "free" token is passed around the ring from node to node. The token is used to control the user of the ring by a free or busy indication. A busy token is an indication that a station has seized the ring and is transmitting data. The token is passed sequentially from node to node around the ring.

Each system attached to a token network has a priority assigned to it. Typically, eight priorities are assigned. The object of the token-passing priority scheme is to give each station an opportunity to reserve the ring for the next transmission around the ring. As the token and data circle the ring, each node examines the token, which contains a reservation field. If the individual node's priority is higher than the priority number in the reservation field, it raises the reservation field number to its level, thus reserving the token on the next round. If another node does not make the reservation field higher, then the station is allowed to use the token and channel on the next pass around the ring.

The station seizing the token is required to store the previous reservation value in a temporary storage area at its location. Upon releasing the token when it completes a complete loop around the ring, the station restores the network to its previous lowest priority request. In this manner, once the token is made free for the next round, the station with the highest reservation is allowed to seize the token. Token-passing priority systems are widely used in local area networks (LANs) and are explained in more detail in Chapter 20, which highlights the IEEE 802.5 token ring standard and the IBM token ring.

LINK EFFICIENCY CONSIDERATIONS

Window Sizes

Window size is important to link efficiency for the following reasons: A large window requires the receiver to reserve more storage for the incoming frames, yet it also provides a means to keep the channel active because the larger windows allow a greater range of sequence numbers to be used. More numbers simply reduce the possibility of a transmitting site having to close its transmit window, because it has used all its send sequence number values. In contrast, a small window size decreases the amount of storage required at the receiver for the incoming frames. Yet, it also increases the possibility of a closed transmit window.

Interestingly, a network that is busy or congested benefits from a small window size, because with the Go-Back-N (REJ) technique, lost frames and all succeeding frames are retransmitted. The best performance by a busy/congested network is obtained by using a small window for the following reason: The large window commits a large number of frames to be outstanding at any one time. Consequently, in the event of an error (with Go-Back-N [REJ]) the erroneous frame and all those that followed must be retransmitted. Obviously, a small window size prohibits the number of frames that can be outstanding at any one time, and limits the frames that might be retransmitted.

Some systems have only one frame on the link at a time. A high-speed, short-distance network, such as a local area network, is an example. When a station begins a transmission, the receivers detect it with very little delay. Therefore, local networks generally transmit only one frame on the link at a time. Satellite networks operate at the other extreme. Due to the long preparation delay, satellite channels must have multiple frames on the link at the same time; otherwise the link goes idle and its efficiency decreases.

Window sizes can be calculated in a number of ways. This discussion examines a relatively simple process entailing three interrelated factors:

T: transmission rate of channel (in bit/s)
D: round-trip delay of signal (in seconds)
L: length of user information frame (the I frame; in bits)

Round-trip delay includes not only the propagation delay on the circuit, but the delay encountered at the receiver with tasks such as error checking, sequencing, buffer management, frame construction, etc. Some tasks are performed very rapidly with hardware; others may take more time due to software execution, queue management, and contention for resources at the station. Designers use different factors to determine D; some are more significant than others; for example:

- Propagation delays of frame to receiver and acknowledgment from receiver. The effect of piggybacking (the ACK is returned in a data frame) plays a significant role in link efficiency and some designers do not factor in the acknowledgment time.
- Time to transmit a frame onto the link in both directions.
- Processing time at the receiver for the data frame and the transmitter for the acknowledgment frame. This factor may also be insignificant unless the stations are busy and queue the frames for a time.

The window size should allow for a sufficient number of outstanding frames (K) to keep the transmit window open. K is the smallest integer not less than r (window size) and is calculated as follows (more detailed equations are presented later):

$$r = \frac{T * D}{L}$$

A higher channel speed or a longer propagation delay requires a larger window. Conversely, a longer frame decreases the window size requirement. Here are some examples:

1. T = 4800; D = .7;   L = 1056; r = 3.1
2. T = 9600; D = .7;   L = 1056; r = 6.3
3. T = 9600; D = 1.1; L = 1056; r = 10

Example 1 shows a 4800 bit/s line using a typical frame of 1056 bits (128 bytes in a packet; 4 bytes in the control frame around the packet: 132 * 8 = 1056) with a round-trip delay of .7 second. The minimum window requirement is 4. Example 2 illustrates the use of a higher-speed line which necessitates a larger window size of 7. Example 3 shows the effect of a longer round-trip propagation delay (1.1 seconds). Notice the minimum window size is now 10. A round-trip delay of .5 to 1.0 second can occur on a satellite circuit, for example.

A more rigorous analysis is provided here for the reader who wishes more detail [FIPS80]. The minimum window size for a reject protocol is defined as:

$$M_I = 2 + \frac{S_I(T_{I-r} + T_{r-I} + T_{rproc} = T_{Iproc})}{I_I} + \frac{3\,I_rS_I}{2\,I_IS_r}$$

Where: I_I = local station's average I frame length, including flags, address field, control field, and frame check sequence (bits); I_r = remote station's average I frame length, including flags, address field, control field, and frame check sequence (bits); M_I = minimum modulus of sequence number necessary to support continuous I frame transmissions by the local station; S_I = local station's transmission speed (bit/s); S_r = remote station's transmission speed (bit/s); T_{Iproc} = time required by local station to process a received frame (seconds); T_{I-r} = propagation time from local to remote station (seconds); T_{rproc} = time required by remote station to process frame (seconds); T_{r-I} = propagation time from remote to local station (seconds).

As an example, assume two stations are operating at 2400 bit/s with I frames of 2400 bits in length. The channel experiences a delay of 50 ms. Each station processes a frame in 1 ms. A simple substitution and calculation yields an answer of 3.602 which is rounded to 4. Since a typical sequencing is modulo 8, the window is sufficient for continuous transmission.

For selective reject, the minimum window is:

$$M_I = 5A + 2 + \frac{S_I(A + 1)(T_{I-r} + T_{r-I} + T_{rproc} = T_{Iproc}}{I_I} + \frac{(A + 3)I_rS_I}{2I_IS_r} + \frac{ARS_I}{I_IS_r}$$

Where: A = number of transmissions required before I frame is successfully received; R = length of SREJ frame, including flags, address field, control field, and frame check sequence field.

As another example, assume the medium is a satellite channel which experiences a propagation delay of .25 second in each direction. In this situation, SREJ is used and one continuous transmission is to occur through at least one retransmission attempt. The SREJ formula reveals that $M_I = 11$.

Consequently, the window of seven is insufficient for continuous transmission and the sequence numbers and state variables must be increased.

Medium Length

Two parameters used in analyzing link performance are T, the transmission rate of the link and D, the propagation delay between the stations on the link (which is proportional to distance). The product of T and D (i.e., T * D) is an important factor in the analysis: efficiency is the same for a 10 Mbit/s, .6 mile link (1 Km) as it is for a 5 Mbit/s, 1.2 mile (2 Km) link!

Of equal importance is the concept of medium length, which is the length of the transmission channel described in bits. It describes the number of bits that can be on the link between two stations at any one specific time.

Before we examine the medium length formula, propagation velocity is described. The propagation delay D is partially dependent on the type of medium. Generally, the following equation is used to calculate propagation delay (PV) on a wire medium:

$$PV = 6.6 * 10^8 \text{ feet per second } (2 * 10^8 \text{ meters per second})$$

Estimating Link Efficiency

Referring to the earlier equation on window sizing, the length of the link (a) is proportional to r and is derived from the same formula of T * D / L. Also, a can be stated as follows because L/T is the time taken by the transmitter to place the frame on the link:

$$a = D / (L/T)$$

In other words, a = propagation time/transmission time.

The following method for determining link efficiency [STAL86] is based on the supposition that a is the single most important factor, and other factors, such as processing line and queue waiting, are relatively insignificant. In most cases, the supposition is correct.

$$u = 1 / (1 + 2d)$$

From this formula, we can easily determine the utilization efficiency of the link.

COMPARISON OF ARQ ERROR CONTROL SCHEMES

Conventional ARQ

Earlier discussions in this chapter explained the ARQ schemes. In this part of the book, the throughput performance of the following error control schemes are explored [LIN84].

Stop-and-Wait ARQ

Go-Back-N (reject) ARQ

Selective reject ARQ

Selective reject/reject ARQ

Hybrid ARQ

The equations defined herein use the following notations: λ = idle time between two successive transmissions; δ = data rate of transmitter; P_c = probability that a received n bit word contains no error; K/n = rate of the code word used (K information bits; n code word bits); T = average number of bits that must be transmitted for a code word to be received correctly; N = number of code words.

The throughput for Stop-and-Wait ARQ is calculated as:

$$TP_{sw} = P_c (K/n)/1 + \lambda\delta/n$$

The throughput for Go-Back-N is:

$$TP_{GBN} = P_c (K/n)/P_c + (1 - P_c) N$$

The throughput for selective reject is:

$$TP_{SR} = P_c (K/n)$$

Several observations can be made about these equations. The Stop-and-Wait ARQ is quite inefficient for systems with long propagation delays. The Go-Back-N ARQ is acceptable for short propagation delays and relatively low data rates. However, it is inefficient in the other situations, especially if the error rate is high. The selective reject works best because the throughput does not depend upon the round-trip propagation delay. Figure 10-13 compares Go-Back-N and selective reject [LIN84]. The comparison is made on a satellite channel at 1.544 Mbit/s data rate and a round-trip delay of 700 ms.

Since selective reject retains frames until the "earlier" frame is retransmitted, it may require considerable buffering capacity. Indeed, for a very large window, the buffering would be intolerable. It also requires more logic to reinsert the retransmitted frame into the proper place in a queue (that is, in front of its succeeding frame with greater N[S] values). Moreover, most systems utilize circuits with relatively low data rates and propagation delays. Consequently, the Go-Back-N (reject) method is more commonly used than is selective reject.

Modified ARQ

Other ARQ approaches yield even better results. Earlier in this chapter, the selective reject/reject technique was examined (see Figure 10-10). A varia-

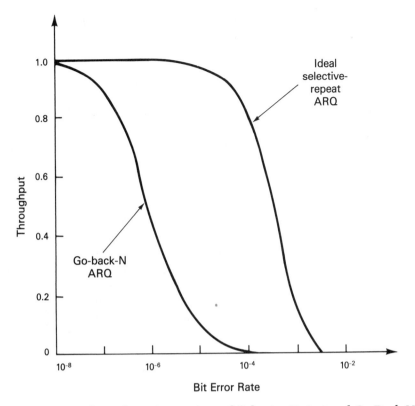

FIGURE 10-13. Throughout Comparison of Selective Reject and Go-Back-N
[LIN84]

tion on this theme (called by the same name) is shown in Figure 10-14. It
differs from the scenario in Figure 10-10 in that the retransmitted frame
must be retransmitted once again. But the principles are the same: (a) move
from selective reject to Go-Back-N reject and (b) upon executing event 4,

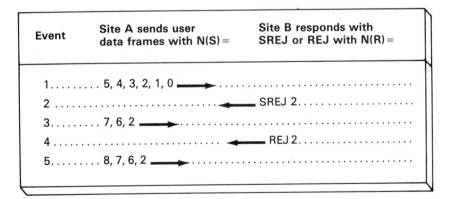

Event	Site A sends user data frames with N(S) =	Site B responds with SREJ or REJ with N(R) =
1	5, 4, 3, 2, 1, 0 ⟶	
2		⟵ SREJ 2
3	7, 6, 2 ⟶	
4		⟵ REJ 2
5	8, 7, 6, 2 ⟶	

FIGURE 10-14. Reject the Same Frame More Than Once

discard succeeding frames (to preserve buffer) until the erroneous frame is once again retransmitted (one hopes correctly, eventually).

The throughput for selective reject/reject is:

$$TP_{SR/R} = P_c \, (K/n) \, / \, 1 + (N - 1)(1 - P_c)^{V + 1}$$

Where: V = retransmission in the selective reject mode allowed before switching to Go-Back-N reject mode.

Figure 10-15 plots the throughput performance of selective reject/reject against selective reject and reject. As V increases, the throughput performance increases.

ERROR PROTECTION PERFORMANCE OF CRC

As a practical matter, it makes sense to question how far one should go to detect errors. That is, what is the incremental cost to obtain incremental gains in the error control? The cost must be evaluated in terms of a specific system. The incremental gains can be determined by examining several tables [FIPS80], dubbed by some people as the "Murphy's Law" tables. (Please note: all tables assume that the bits may take any random pattern.)

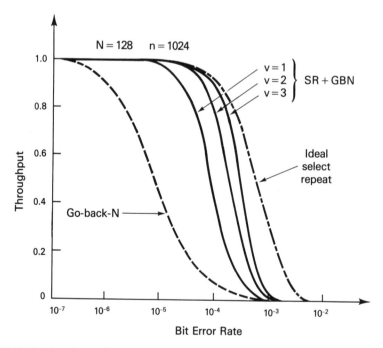

FIGURE 10-15. Throughout Comparison at Selective Reject, Go-Back-N and Others [LIN84]

Table 10-1 shows the probability of a pattern of errors that will not be detected by a 16-bit frame check sequence (FCS). For a typical frame of 1122 bits (128 octets * 8 bits of user data + 3 octets * 8 bits of packet header + 5 octets * 8 bits of internal network header + 4 octets * 8 bits of frame header and trailer = 1122 bits, rounded to 1000), the probabilities of an undetected error are approximately $5 * 10^{-10}$ for a link operating in a relatively poor 10^{-4} bit error rate.

Table 10-2 shows the maximum undetected bit error rate resulting from (a) a flag destruction and (b) the subsequent interpretation of the last 16 bits of the longer frame as a correct FCS. For our frame of 1122 bits, the maximum undetected bit error rate is approximately $1 * 10^{-11}$.

Table 10-3 depicts the maximum undetected bit error rate resulting from (a) data in a frame garbled into a flag pattern; which (b) divides the frame into two shorter frames; in which (c) the last 16 bits of either of the two frames pass the FCS check. The 1122 bit frame shows a $9 * 10^{-8}$ maximum undetected error rate.

Table 10-4 shows yet another possibility for an undetected error to occur. Two situations are covered in this table. First, a transmission error causes the receiver to leave a stuffed bit in a frame. For example, a bit stream of 111110 (where: 0 is a stuffed bit) is corrupted to 101110. Second, a group of bits is corrupted to resemble a stuffed bit, for example, a bit stream of 111101 is corrupted to 111110 (where: 0 appears to be a stuffed bit). In both cases, the last 16 bits are interpreted as a correct FCS pattern. The 1122 frame at a 10^{-4} bit error rate exhibits a $3 * 10^{-7}$ maximum undetected error rate.

Finally, Table 10-5 is an estimate of the overall undetected error rate expected on a link. Our example of the 1122 bit frame on the 10^{-4} link shows a very resilient $4 * 10^{-7}$ overall undetected error rate.

To place this data in perspective, it should be recognized that the chances of an undetected error certainly exist even though they do not occur frequently. As better systems are placed in operation using optical fibers and forward error correction (FEC), these systems will yield even better results.

TABLE 10-1. Undetected Bit Error Rate from Errors Within Frames

Bits in Frame	Bit Error Rate				
	10^{-3}	10^{-4}	10^{-5}	10^{-6}	10^{-7}
100	1×10^{-8}	1×10^{-9}	1×10^{-10}	1×10^{-11}	1×10^{-12}
300	9×10^{-8}	9×10^{-9}	9×10^{-10}	9×10^{-11}	9×10^{-12}
1000	7×10^{-9}	5×10^{-10}	4×10^{-11}	4×10^{-12}	4×10^{-13}
3000		2×10^{-11}	1×10^{-12}	1×10^{-13}	1×10^{-13}
10000		1×10^{-10}	2×10^{-11}	2×10^{-12}	2×10^{-13}
30000		$\sim 10^{-5}$	$\sim 10^{-6}$	$\sim 10^{-7}$	$\sim 10^{-8}$

TABLE 10-2. Undetected Error Rate from Scrambled Single Flag Between Frames

Bits in Frame	Bit Error Rate				
	10^{-3}	10^{-4}	10^{-5}	10^{-6}	10^{-7}
100	1×10^{-9}	1×10^{-10}	1×10^{-11}	1×10^{-12}	1×10^{-13}
300	4×10^{-10}	4×10^{-11}	4×10^{-12}	4×10^{-13}	4×10^{-14}
1000	1×10^{-10}	1×10^{-11}	1×10^{-12}	1×10^{-13}	1×10^{-14}
3000	4×10^{-11}	4×10^{-12}	4×10^{-13}	4×10^{-14}	4×10^{-15}
10000	1×10^{-11}	1×10^{-12}	1×10^{-13}	1×10^{-14}	1×10^{-15}
30000	4×10^{-12}	4×10^{-13}	4×10^{-14}	4×10^{-15}	4×10^{-16}

TABLE 10-3. Undetected Error Rate from Fictitious Flag

Bits in Frame	Bit Error Rate				
	10^{-3}	10^{-4}	10^{-5}	10^{-6}	10^{-7}
100	9×10^{-8}	9×10^{-9}	9×10^{-10}	9×10^{-11}	9×10^{-12}
300	3×10^{-7}	3×10^{-8}	3×10^{-9}	3×10^{-10}	3×10^{-11}
1000	9×10^{-7}	9×10^{-8}	9×10^{-9}	9×10^{-10}	9×10^{-11}
3000	3×10^{-6}	3×10^{-7}	3×10^{-8}	3×10^{-9}	3×10^{-10}
10000	9×10^{-6}	9×10^{-7}	9×10^{-8}	9×10^{-9}	9×10^{-10}
30000	3×10^{-5}	3×10^{-6}	3×10^{-7}	3×10^{-8}	3×10^{-9}

TABLE 10-4. Undetected Error Rate from Zero Bits Errors

Bits in Frame	Bit Error Rate				
	10^{-3}	10^{-4}	10^{-5}	10^{-6}	10^{-7}
100	2×10^{-7}	2×10^{-8}	2×10^{-9}	2×10^{-10}	2×10^{-11}
300	9×10^{-7}	9×10^{-8}	9×10^{-9}	9×10^{-10}	9×10^{-11}
1000	3×10^{-6}	3×10^{-7}	3×10^{-8}	3×10^{-9}	3×10^{-10}
3000	1×10^{-5}	1×10^{-6}	1×10^{-7}	1×10^{-8}	1×10^{-9}
10000	3×10^{-5}	3×10^{-6}	3×10^{-7}	3×10^{-8}	3×10^{-9}
30000	1×10^{-4}	1×10^{-5}	1×10^{-6}	1×10^{-7}	1×10^{-8}

SUGGESTED READINGS

[CONA80] provides a good introduction to character-oriented protocols. [BLAC82] is also a general review of the topic. [STAL86] is a very good description of how to determine link efficiency. [GREE86] describes techniques for link monitoring. Several equations in this chapter are from [LIN84], which contains an excellent survey of ARQ error-control schemes.

TABLE 10-5. Approximate Overall Undetected Bit Error Rate

Bits in Frame	Bit Error Rate				
	10^{-3}	10^{-4}	10^{-5}	10^{-6}	10^{-7}
100	3×10^{-7}	3×10^{-8}	3×10^{-9}	3×10^{-10}	3×10^{-11}
300	1×10^{-6}	1×10^{-7}	1×10^{-8}	1×10^{-9}	1×10^{-10}
1000	4×10^{-6}	4×10^{-7}	4×10^{-8}	4×10^{-9}	4×10^{-10}
3000		1×10^{-6}	1×10^{-7}	1×10^{-8}	1×10^{-9}
10000		4×10^{-6}	4×10^{-7}	4×10^{-8}	4×10^{-9}
30000		$\sim 10^{-5}$	$\sim 10^{-6}$	$\sim 10^{-7}$	$\sim 10^{-8}$

QUESTIONS

TRUE/FALSE

T 1. The principal function of wide-area data link controls is error detection.

F 2. Count-oriented protocols achieve code independence.

T 3. The DLE control code and the bit-stuffing technique are both used to prevent incorrect interpretation of the user data field.

F 4. A data link protocol provides error detection and end-to-end acknowledgment across multiple links.

F 5. Inclusive acknowledgment and piggybacking must be used together.

6. Match the description with the appropriate term:

Description

2 a) Uses a peer-to-peer nonpriority protocol.

4 b) Employs the concept of primary and secondary stations.

1 c) Employs the concept of primary and secondary stations without polling.

3 d) Uses a peer-to-peer priority protocol.

Term

1. Time division multiple access (TDMA)
2. Carrier sense/collision detect
3. Token passing
4. Polling/Selection

7. Match the description with the appropriate term (a term may be used more than once):

Description

4 a) Achieves code transparency with DLE.

5 b) May or may not be self-clocking.

2 c) Uses start/stop bits for synchronization.

d) Self-clocking systems
e) Achieves code transparency with flag.
f) Achieves code transparency with length indicator.

Term

1. Bit-oriented protocols
2. Asynchronous protocols
3. Count-oriented protocols
4. Character (Byte)-oriented protocols
5. Synchronous protocols

8. Describe the differences between asynchronous and synchronous data link controls.

9. A bit-oriented protocol transmitter examines the following bit stream within the user data field: 010011111101111101011. How would this data stream appear after it had been zero stuffed?

10. Briefly contrast the T1 timer and the T2 parameter.

11. Match the description with the appropriate term:

Description

a) The selective reject has no acknowledgment functions.
b) Retransmission technique for some half duplex links.
c) Erroneous frame retransmitted.
d) Erroneous frame and preceding frames retransmitted.

Term

1. Reject (Go-Back-N).
2. Selective reject.
3. Implicit reject.
4. Selective reject/reject.

SELECTED ANSWERS

1. True. However, some local area data link controls do not perform error detection.

2. False. Code independence is achieved in the user text field, but most systems use control characters that are code dependent.

3. True.

4. False. The data link control only provides error detection and acknowledgment across an individual link.

5. False. While most continuous ARQ protocols use both techniques, it is not a necessity.

6.

Description	Term
a)	2
b)	4
c)	1
d)	3

7.

Description	Term
a)	4
b)	5
c)	2
d)	2
e)	1
f)	3

CHAPTER 11

Data Link Control: Standards and Products

INTRODUCTION

In Chapter 10 we introduced data link protocols and examined two data link classification schemes, as well as several equations for calculating link efficiency. This chapter continues this discussion and also covers several prevalent data link standards and products.

BINARY SYNCHRONOUS CONTROL (BSC)

In the mid-1960s, IBM introduced the first general-purpose data link control to support multipoint or point-to-point configurations. This product, the binary synchronous control protocol (BSC), has found widespread use throughout the world. Indeed, it is one of the most widely used synchronous line protocols in existence. IBM's product families, designated as 3270 and 3780, were originally based on BSC. Practically every vendor has some version of BSC implemented in a product line, and the standards organizations publish specifications on the protocol. (Some people use the term bisync to describe the protocol.)

BSC is a half duplex protocol, in that transmissions are provided two ways, alternately. The protocol supports point-to-point and multipoint connections, as well as switched and nonswitched channels. BSC is a code-sensitive protocol, and every character transmitted across a channel must be decoded at the receiver to determine if it is a control character or a data character. Code-dependent protocols are also called byte or character protocols.

BSC Formats and Control Codes

The BSC frame formats and control codes are shown in Figure 11-1. The figure does not show all the possibilities for the format of a BSC frame, but is a sampling of some of the major implementations.

Since BSC is a character-oriented protocol, it is possible that a code recognized as BSC control could be created by the user application process. For instance, assume a user program creates a bit sequence which is the same as the ETX (end of text) control code. The receiving station, upon encountering the ETX inside the user data, would assume that the end of the transmission is signified by the user-generated ETX. BSC would then accept the ETX as a protocol control character and attempt to perform an error check on an incomplete BSC frame. An error would result.

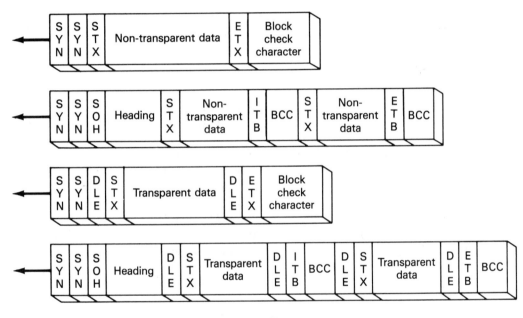

BSC Control Character:

Character	Function
SYN	Synchronous idle (keeps channel active)
DLE	Data link escape (used to achieve code transparency)
ENQ	Enquiry (used with polls/selects and bids)
SOH	Start of heading
STX	Start of text (puts line in text mode)
ITB	End of intermediate block
ETB	End of transmission block
ETX	End of text
EOT	End of transmission (puts line in control mode)
BCC	Block check count

FIGURE 11-1. BSC Formats and Control Codes

Control codes must be excluded from the text and header fields and BSC addresses the problem with the DLE control code. This code is placed in front of the control codes to identify these characters as valid line control characters. The DLE is not placed in front of user-generated data. Consequently, if bit patterns resembling any of these control characters are created in the user text and encountered by the receiving station, the receiving station assumes they are valid user data, because the DLE does not precede them. The DLE places the line into a transparent text mode, which allows the transmission of any bit pattern.

The DLE presents a special problem if it is generated by the end-user application process, since it could be recognized as a control code. BSC handles this situation by inserting a DLE next to a data DLE character. The receiver discards the first DLE of two successive DLEs and accepts the second DLE as valid user data.

The headers illustrated in Figure 11-1 are optional. If they are included, the SOH code is placed in front of the header.

Line Modes

The BSC channel or link operates in one of two modes. The *control mode* is used by a master station to control the operations on the link, such as the transmission of polling and selection frames. The *message* or *text mode* is used for the transmittal of an information block or blocks. Upon receiving an invitation to send data (a poll), the slave station transmits user data with either an STX or SOH in front of the data or heading. These control characters place the channel in the message or text mode. Thereafter, data is exchanged under the text mode until an EOT is received, which changes the mode back to control. During the time the channel is in text mode, it is dedicated to the exchange of data between two stations only. All other stations must remain passive.

The polls and selects are initiated by a frame with the contents: Address.ENQ (where address is the address of the station). The control (master) station is responsible for sending polls and selects.

BSC also provides for contention operation on a point-to-point circuit. In this situation, one of the stations can become the master by "bidding" to the other station. The station accepting the bid becomes the slave. A point-to-point line enters the contention mode following the transmission or reception of the EOT.

The ENQ code plays an important role in BSC control modes. To summarize its functions:

Poll: Control station sends with an address prefix.

Select: Control station sends with an address prefix.

Bid: Point-to-point stations send to contend for control station status.

BSC has a rather unusual way of indicating if its control frames are selects or polls. The lower-case code of a station address is used to indicate a select, and the upper-case code is used to indicate a poll.

Line Control

The transmitting station knows the exact order of frames it transmits, and it expects to receive ACKs to its transmissions. The receiving site transmits the ACKs with sequence numbers. Only two numbers are used, a 0 and a 1. This sequencing technique is sufficient, since the channel is inherently half duplex and only one frame can be outstanding at one time. An ACK0 indicates the correct receipt of even-numbered frames; and ACK1 indicates the receipt of odd-numbered frames.

In addition to the frame-format control codes in Figure 11-1, BSC uses several other line control codes:

ACK0   Positive acknowledgment to even-sequenced blocks of data or a response to a select or bid.

ACK1   Positive acknowledgment to odd-sequenced blocks or data.

WACK   (Wait before transmit—positive acknowledgment) Receiving station temporarily unable to continue to process or receive transmissions. Signifies a line reversal. Also used as a positive acknowledgment of a transmission. Station will continue to send WACK until it is ready to receive.

RVI   (Reverse interrupt) Indicates station has data to send at the earliest opportunity. This causes an interruption of the transmission process.

DISC   For switched lines, forces a disconnection.

TTD   (Temporary text delay) Indicates sending DTE cannot send data immediately, but wishes to maintain control of line (for example, its buffer is being filled or its card hopper is empty).

Box 11-1 provides several examples of BSC control traffic flow on the link.

OTHER "BSC-LIKE" SPECIFICATIONS

ISO 2110, ISO 1745, and ISO 2628

While BSC is probably the best-known character-oriented protocol, other similar products and standards are widely used. The ISO protocols are examples. ISO 2111, ISO 1745, and ISO 2628 are complementary protocols which define the following link activities [WATK81].

BOX 11-1. Examples of BSC Link Activity

Transmission: ENQ SYN SYN →
Meaning: A point-to-point station seeks a connection establishment and acquires control of the line. If both stations transmit this signal at the same time, a predesignated primary station is allowed to retry.

Transmission: ENQ Station Address SYN SYN EOT SYN SYN →
Meaning: With a multipoint link, the primary station uses this format to send a poll (station address is uppercase) or a select (station address is lowercase).

Transmission: ACK0 SYN SYN →
Meaning: Station is ready to receive traffic.

Transmission: ACK0/1 SYN SYN →
Meaning: Station ACKs transmission and/or is ready to receive traffic.

Transmission: NAK SYN SYN →
Meaning: Station NAKs transmission and/or is not ready to receive traffic.

Transmission: WACK SYN SYN →
Meaning: Station requests other station to try again since it is temporarily not ready. This format is also used to acknowledge previous traffic.

Transmission: RVI SYN SYN →
Meaning: ACKs previous traffic and requests other station to suspend transmissions since receiving station needs the link itself.

Transmission: ENQ STX SYN SYN →
Meaning: Sending station is experiencing a temporary delay but does not wish to relinquish the line. Also used when a polled station is not ready to transmit but wants the polling station to wait. This format this called a temporary text delay (TTD).

Transmission: EOT SYN SYN →
Meaning: This is a negative response to a poll and is also used when a sending station has completed its transmission.

ISO 2111 describes the transmission control characters to manage the data link. These codes are the same as BSC codes (STX, DLE, ETB, etc.), so they are not explained again here.

The ISO 1745 (1975) specification defines the actual link operations; that is to say, the functions of the control codes. ISO 1745 allows either asynchronous start/stop or synchronous transmission. Duplex or half duplex links are allowed. The link is actually managed by the "states" of the attached stations: master, slave, neutral.

ISO 2628 specifies the recovery, abort, and interrupt procedures to complement ISO 2111 and ISO 1745. The standard defines a number of timers.

These character-oriented protocols are being replaced by bit protocols for four reasons: (1) dual interpretations of codes; (2) the necessity to use the DLE to provide code transparency; (3) the flexibility and efficiency of bit protocols; and (4) the overhead in the character protocol. Consequently, the focus of the remainder of this chapter is on bit-oriented link protocols.

HIGH-LEVEL DATA LINK CONTROL (HDLC) AND ADVANCED DATA COMMUNICATION CONTROL PROCEDURES (ADCCP)

HDLC is a bit-oriented line protocol specification published by the International Standards Organization (ISO) as ISO 3309 and ISO 4335. It has achieved wide use throughout the world. The recommended standard provides for many functions and covers a wide range of applications. It is frequently used as a foundation for other protocols that use specific options in the HDLC repertoire. For this reason, HDLC is covered in considerable detail in this chapter. ADCCP is published as ANSI X3.66. With minor variations, it is identical to HDLC. To keep matters simple, we only examine HDLC since its use is more widespread.

This section addresses the main functions of HDLC. It also covers some of the more important "subsets," such as SDLC, LAP, LAPB, LAPD, and LLC. The reader is encouraged to check with specific vendors for their actual implementation of HDLC. Most vendors have a version of HDLC available, although the protocol is often renamed by the vendor or designated by different initials (except for the Honeywell Data Link Control).

HDLC Characteristics

HDLC provides for a number of options to satisfy a wide variety of user requirements. It supports both half duplex and full duplex transmission; point-to-point and multipoint configuration; and switched or nonswitched channels. An HDLC station is classified as one of three types:

- The *primary station* is in control of the data link. This station acts as a master and transmits command frames to the secondary stations on the channel. In turn, it receives response frames from those stations. If the link is multipoint, the primary station is responsible for maintaining a separate session with each station attached to the link.
- The *secondary station* acts as a slave to the primary station. It responds to the commands from the primary station in the form of

responses. It maintains only one session, that being with the primary station, and has no responsibility for control on the link. Secondary stations cannot communicate directly with each other; they must first transfer their frames to the primary station.

- The *combined station* transmits both commands and responses and receives both commands and responses from another combined station. It maintains a session with the other combined station.

HDLC provides three methods to configure the channel for primary, secondary, and combined station use:

- An *unbalanced* configuration provides for one primary station and one or more secondary stations to operate as point-to-point or multipoint, half duplex, full duplex, switched, or nonswitched. The configuration is called unbalanced because the primary station is responsible for controlling each secondary station and for establishing and maintaining the link.
- The *symmetrical* configuration is used very little today. The configuration provides for two independent, point-to-point, unbalanced station configurations. Each station has a primary and secondary status, and therefore each station is considered logically to be two stations: a primary and a secondary station. The primary station transmits commands to the secondary station at the other end of the channel and vice versa. Even though the stations have both primary and secondary capabilities, the actual commands and responses are multiplexed onto one physical channel.
- A *balanced* configuration consists of two combined stations connected point-to-point only, half duplex or full duplex, switched or nonswitched. The combined stations have equal status on the channel and may send unsolicited frames to each other. Each station has equal responsibility for link control. Typically, a station uses a command in order to solicit a response from the other station. The other station can send its own command as well.

The terms unbalanced and balanced have nothing to do with the electrical characteristics of the circuit. In fact, data link controls should not be aware of the physical circuit attributes. The two terms are used in a completely different context at the physical and link levels.

While the stations are transferring data, they communicate in one of the following three modes of operation:

- *Normal response mode* (NRM) requires the secondary station to receive explicit permission from the primary station before transmitting. After receiving permission, the secondary station initiates a response transmission which may contain data. The transmission may consist of one or more frames while the channel is being used by the secondary station. After the last frame transmission, the secondary station must again wait for explicit permission before it can transmit again.

- *Asynchronous response mode* (ARM) allows a secondary station to initiate transmission without receiving explicit permission from the primary station. The transmission may contain data frames, or control information reflecting status changes of the secondary station. ARM can decrease overhead because the secondary station does not need a poll sequence in order to send data. A secondary station operating in ARM can transmit only when it detects an idle channel state for a two-way alternate (half duplex) data flow, or at any time for a two-way simultaneous (duplex) data flow. The primary station maintains responsibility for tasks such as error recovery, link set-up, and link disconnections.
- *Asynchronous balanced mode* (ABM) uses combined stations. The combined station may initiate transmissions without receiving prior permission from the other combined station.

Normal response mode (NRM) is used frequently on multipoint lines. The primary station controls the link by issuing polls to the attached stations (usually terminals, personal computers, and cluster controllers). The asynchronous balanced mode (ABM) is a better choice on point-to-point links since it incurs no overhead and delay in polling. The asynchronous response mode (ARM) is used very little today.

The term asynchronous has nothing to do with the format of the data and the physical interface of the stations. It is used to indicate the stations need not receive a preliminary signal from another station before sending traffic. Referring to Figure 10-1 in Chapter 10, HDLC uses synchronous formats in its frames.

Frame Format

HDLC uses the term frame to indicate the independent entity of data (protocol data unit) transmitted across the link from one station to another. Figure 11-2 shows the frame format. The frame consists of four or five fields:

Flag fields (F)	8 bits
Address field (A)	8 or 16 bits
Control field (C)	8 or 16 bits
Information field (I)	variable length; not used in some frames
Frame check sequence field (FCS)	16 or 32 bits

All frames must start and end with the flag (F) sequence fields. The stations attached to the data link are required to continuously monitor the

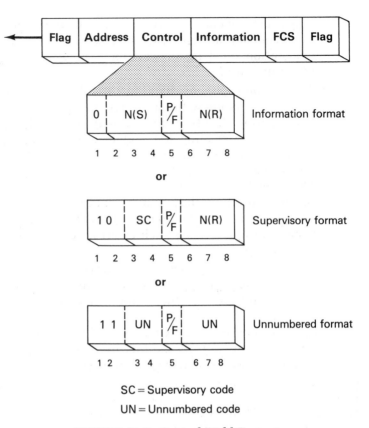

SC = Supervisory code
UN = Unnumbered code

FIGURE 11-2. Control Field Formats

link for the flag sequence. The flag sequence consists of 01111110. Flags are continuously transmitted on the link between frames to keep the link in an active condition.

Other bit sequences are also used. At least seven, but less than fifteen continuous 1s (abort signal) indicate a problem on the link. Fifteen or more 1s keep the channel in an idle condition. One use of the idle state is in support of a half duplex session. A station can detect the idle pattern and reverse the direction of the transmission.

Once the receiving station detects a nonflag sequence, it is aware that it has encountered the beginning of the frame, an abort condition, or an idle channel condition. Upon encountering the next flag sequence, the station recognizes it has found the full frame. In summary, the link recognizes the following bit sequences as:

01111110	=	Flags
At least 7, but less than 15 1s	=	Abort
15 or more 1s	=	Idle

The time between the actual transmission of the frames on the channel is called interframe time fill. This time fill is accomplished by transmitting continuous flags between the frames. The flags may be 8-bit multiples and they can combine the ending 0 of the preceding flag with the starting 0 of the next flag.

HDLC is a code-transparent protocol. It does not rely on a specific code (ASCII/IA5, EBCDIC, etc.) for the interpretation of line control. For example, bit position n within an octet has a specific meaning, regardless of the other bits in the octet. On occasion, a flaglike field, 01111110, may be inserted into the user data stream (I field) by the application process. More frequently, the bit patterns in the other fields appear flaglike. To prevent "phony" flags from being inserted into the frame, the transmitter inserts a 0 bit after it encounters five continuous 1s anywhere between the opening and closing flag of the frame. Consequently, 0 insertion applies to the address, control, information, and FCS fields. This technique is called bit stuffing. As the frame is stuffed, it is transmitted across the link to the receiver.

The procedure to recover the frame of the receiver is a bit more involved (no pun intended). The "framing" receiver logic can be summarized as follows: The receiver continuously monitors the bit stream. After it receives a 0 bit with five continuous, succeeding 1 bits, it inspects the next bit. If it is a 0 bit, it pulls this bit out; in other words, it unstuffs the bit. However, if the seventh bit is a 1, the receiver inspects the eighth bit. If it is a 0, it recognizes that a flag sequence of 01111110 has been received. If it is a 1, then it knows an abort or idle signal has been received and counts the number of succeeding 1 bits to take appropriate action.

In this manner, HDLC achieves code and data transparency. The protocol is not concerned about any particular bit code inside the data stream. Its main concern is to keep the flags unique.

Many systems use bit stuffing and the non-return-to-zero-inverted (NRZI) encoding technique to keep the receiver clock synchronized. With NRZI, binary 1s do not cause a line transition but binary 0s do cause a change. It might appear that a long sequence of 1s could present synchronization problems since the receiver clock would not receive the line transitions necessary for the clock adjustment. However, bit stuffing ensures that a 0 bit exists in the data stream at least every 5 bits. The receiver can use them for clock alignment.

The address (A) field identifies the primary or secondary station involved in the frame transmission or reception. A unique address is associated with each station. In an unbalanced configuration, the address field in both commands and responses contains the address of the secondary station. In balanced configurations, a command frame contains the destination station address and the response frame contains the sending station address.

The control (C) field contains the commands, responses, and sequence numbers used to maintain the data flow accountability of the link between the primary stations. The format and the contents of the control field vary, depending on the use of the HDLC frame.

The information (I) field contains the actual user data. The information field only resides in the frame under the information frame format. It is usually not found in the supervisory or unnumbered frame, although one option of HDLC allows the I field to be used with an unnumbered frame.

The frame check sequence (FCS) field is used to check for transmission errors between the two data link stations. The FCS field is created by a cyclic redundancy check described in Chapter 7 and summarized here. The transmitting station performs modulo 2 division (based on an established polynomial) on the A, C, and I fields plus leading 0s and appends the remainder as the FCS field. In turn, the receiving station performs a division with the same polynomial on the A, C, I, and FCS fields. If the remainder equals a predetermined value, the chances are quite good the transmission occurred without any errors. If the comparisons do not match, it indicates a probable transmission error, in which case the receiving station sends a negative acknowledgment, requiring a retransmission of the frame.

The Control Field

Let us return to a more detailed discussion of the control field (C) because it determines how HDLC controls the communications process (see Figure 11-2). The control field defines the function of the frame and therefore invokes the logic to control the movement of the traffic between the receiving and sending stations. The field can be in one of three formats, information transfer, supervisory, and unnumbered:

- The *information transfer format* frame is used to transmit end-user data between the two devices. The information frame may also acknowledge the receipt of data from a transmitting station. It also can perform certain other functions such as a poll command.
- The *supervisory format frame* performs control functions such as the acknowledgment of frames, the request for the retransmission of frames, and the request for the temporary suspension of the transmission frames. The actual use of the supervisory frame is dependent on the operational mode of the link (normal response mode, asynchronous balanced mode, asynchronous response mode).
- The *unnumbered format* is also used for control purposes. The frame is used to perform link initialization, link disconnection, and other link control functions. The frame uses five bit positions, which allows for up to 32 commands and 32 responses. The particular type of command and response depends on the HDLC class of procedure.

The actual format of the HDLC determines how the control field is coded and used. The simplest format is the information transfer format. The N(S) (send sequence) number indicates the sequence number associated with a transmitted frame. The N(R) (receive sequence) number indicates the sequence number that is expected at the receiving site.

Piggybacking, Flow Control, and Accounting for Traffic

HDLC maintains accountability of the traffic and controls the flow of frames by the state variables and sequence numbers discussed in Chapter 10. To briefly summarize: The traffic at both the transmitting and receiving sites is controlled by these state variables. The transmitting site maintains a send state variable (V[S]), which is the sequence number of the next frame to be transmitted. The receiving site maintains a receive state variable (V[R]), which contains the number that is expected to be in the sequence number of the next frame. The V(S) is incremented with each frame transmitted and placed in the send sequence field in the frame.

Upon receiving the frame, the receiving site checks the send sequence number with its V(R). If the CRC passes and if V(R) = N(S), it increments V(R) by one, places the value in the sequence number field in a frame and sends it to the original transmitting site to complete the accountability for the transmission.

If the V(R) does not match the sending sequence number in the frame (or the CRC does not pass), an error has occurred, and a reject or selective reject with a value in V(R) is sent to the original transmitting site. The V(R) value informs the transmitting DTE of the next frame that it is expected to send, i.e., the number of the frame to be retransmitted.

The Poll/Final Bit

The fifth bit position in the control field is called the P/F or poll/final bit. It is only recognized when set to 1 and is used by the primary and secondary stations to provide a dialogue with each other:

- The primary station uses the P bit = 1 to solicit a status response from a secondary station. The P bit signifies a poll.
- The secondary station responds to a P bit with data or a status frame, and with the F bit = 1. The F bit can also signify end of transmission from the secondary station under Normal Response Mode (NRM).

The P/F bit is called the P bit when used by the primary station and the F bit when used by the secondary station. Most versions of HDLC permit one P bit (awaiting an F bit response) to be outstanding at any time on the link. Consequently, a P set to 1 can be used as a checkpoint. That is, the P = 1 means, "Respond to me, because I want to know your status." Checkpoints are quite important in all forms of automation. It is the machine's technique for clearing up ambiguity and perhaps discarding copies of previously transmitted frames. Under some versions of HDLC, the device may not proceed further until the F bit frame is received, but other versions of HDLC (such as LAPB) do not require the F bit frame to interrupt the full duplex operations.

How does a station know if a received frame with the fifth bit = 1 is an F or P bit? After all, it is in the same bit position in all frames. HDLC provides an elegantly simple solution: The fifth bit is a P bit and the frame is a command if the address field contains the address of the receiving station; it is an F bit and the frame is a response if the address is that of the transmitting station.

This destination is quite important because a station may react quite differently to the two types of frames. For example, a command (address of receiver, P = 1) usually requires the station to send back specific types of frames.

A summary of the addressing rules follows:

- A station places its own address in the address field when it transmits a response.
- A station places the address of the receiving station in the address field when it transmits a command.

HDLC Commands and Responses

Table 11-1 shows the HDLC commands and responses. They are briefly summarized here.

The *Receive Ready* (RR) is used by the primary or secondary station to indicate that it is ready to receive an information frame and/or acknowledge previously received frames by using the N(R) field. The primary station may also use the Receive Ready command to poll a secondary station by setting the P bit to 1.

The *Receive Not Ready* (RNR) frame is used by the station to indicate a busy condition. This informs the transmitting station that the receiving station is unable to accept additional incoming data. The RNR frame may acknowledge previously transmitted frames by using the N(R) field. The busy condition can be cleared by sending the RR frame.

The *Selective Reject* (SREJ) is used by a station to request the retransmission of a single frame identified in the N(R) field. As with inclusive acknowledgment, all information frames numbered up to N(R) − 1 are acknowledged. Once the SREJ has been transmitted, subsequent frames are accepted and held for the retransmitted frame. The SREJ condition is cleared upon receipt of an I frame with a N(S) equal to V(R).

An SREJ frame must be transmitted for each erroneous frame; each frame is treated as a separate error. Only one SREJ frame can be outstanding at a time; since the N(R) field in the frame inclusively acknowledges all preceding frames, to send a second SREJ would contradict the first SREJ because all I frames with N(S) lower than N(R) of the second SREJ would be acknowledged.

The *Reject* (REJ) is used to request the retransmission of frames starting with the frame numbered in the N(R) field. Frames numbered N(R) − 1 are all acknowledged. The REJ frame can be used to implement the Go-Back-N technique.

TABLE 11-1. HDLC Control Field Format

Format	1	2	3	4	5	6	7	8	Commands	Responses
					CONTROL FIELD BIT Encoding						
Information	0	—	N(S)	—	=	—	N(R)	—	I	I
Supervisory	1	0	0	0	=	—	N(R)	—	RR	RR
	1	0	0	1	=	—	N(R)	—	REJ	REJ
	1	0	1	0	=	—	N(R)	—	RNR	RNR
	1	0	1	1	=	—	N(R)	—	SREJ	SREJ
Unnumbered	1	1	0	0	=	0	0	0	UI	UI
	1	1	0	0	=	0	0	1	SNRM	
	1	1	0	0	=	0	1	0	DISC	RD
	1	1	0	0	=	1	0	0	UP	
	1	1	0	0	=	1	1	0		UA
	1	1	0	1	=	0	0	0	NR0	NR0
	1	1	0	1	=	0	0	1	NR1	NR1
	1	1	0	1	=	0	1	0	NR2	NR2
	1	1	0	1	=	0	1	1	NR3	NR3
	1	1	1	0	=	0	0	0	SIM	RIM
	1	1	1	0	=	0	0	1		FRMR
	1	1	1	1	=	0	0	0	SARM	DM
	1	1	1	1	=	0	0	1	RSET	
	1	1	1	1	=	0	1	0	SARME	
	1	1	1	1	=	0	1	1	SNRME	
	1	1	1	1	=	1	0	0	SABM	
	1	1	1	1	=	1	0	1	XID	XID
	1	1	1	1	=	1	1	0	SABME	

LEGEND:

I	Information	NR0	Non-Reserved 0
RR	Receive Ready	NR1	Non-Reserved 1
REJ	Reject	NR2	Non-Reserved 2
RNR	Receive Not Ready	NR3	Non-Reserved 3
SREJ	Selective Reject	SIM	Set Initialization Mode
UI	Unnumbered Information	RIM	Request Initialization Mode
DISC	Disconnect	FRMR	Frame Reject
RD	Request Disconnect	SARM	Set Async Response Mode
UP	Unnumbered Poll	SARME	Set ARM Extended
RSET	Reset	SNRM	Set Normal Response Mode
XID	Exchange Identification	SNRME	Set NRM Extended
DM	Disconnect Mode	SABM	Set Async Balance Mode
=	The P/F Bit	SABME	Set ABM Extended

The *Unnumbered Information* (UI) format allows for transmission of user data in an unnumbered (i.e., unsequenced) frame. The UI frame is actually a form of connectionless-mode link protocol in that the absence of the

N(S) and N(R) fields precludes flow-controlling and acknowledging frames. The IEEE 802.2 logical link control (LLC) protocol uses this approach with its LLC Type 1 version of HDLC.

The *Request Initialization Mode* (RIM) format is a request from a secondary station for initialization to a primary station. Once the secondary station sends RIM it can monitor frames but can only respond to SIM, DISC, TEST, or XID.

The *Set Normal Response Mode* (SNRM) places the secondary station in the Normal Response Mode (NRM). The NRM precludes the secondary station from sending any unsolicited frames. This means the primary station controls all frame flow on the line.

The *Disconnect* (DISC) places the secondary station in the disconnected mode. This command is valuable for switched lines; the command provides a function similar to hanging up a telephone. UA is the expected response.

The *Disconnect Mode* (DM) is transmitted from a secondary station to indicate it is in the disconnect mode (not operational).

The *Test* (TEST) frame is used to solicit testing responses from the secondary station. HDLC does not stipulate how the TEST frames are to be used. An implementation can use the I field for diagnostic purposes, for example.

The *Set Asynchronous Response Mode* (SARM) allows a secondary station to transmit without a poll from the primary station. It places the secondary station in the information transfer state (IS) of ARM.

The *Set Asynchronous Balanced Mode* (SABM) sets mode to ABM, in which stations are peers with each other. No polls are required to transmit since each station is a combined station.

The *Set Normal Response Mode Extended* (SNRME) sets SNRM with two octets in the control field. This is used for extended sequencing and permits the N(S) and N(R) to be seven bits in length, thus increasing the window to a range of 1-127.

The *Set Asynchronous Balanced Mode Extended* (SABME) sets SAMB with two octets in the control field for extended sequencing.

The *Unnumbered Poll* (UP) polls a station without regard to sequencing or acknowledgment. Response is optional if poll bit is set to 0. Provides for one response opportunity.

The *Reset* (RESET) is used as follows: the transmitting station resets its N(S) and receiving station resets its N(R). The command is used for recovery. Previously unacknowledged frames remain unacknowledged.

HDLC Timers

The vendors vary in how they implement link level timers in a product. HDLC defines two timers, T1 and T2. Most implementations use T1 in some fashion. T2 is used, but not as frequently as T1. The timers are used in the following manner:

- T1: A primary station issues a P bit and checks whether a response is received to the P bit within a defined time. This function is controlled by the timer T1 and is called the "wait for F" time out.

- T2: A station in the ARM mode that issues I frames checks whether acknowledgments are received within a timer period. This function is controlled by timer T2 and is called "wait for N(R)" time out.

Since ARM is not used much today, timer T1 is typically invoked to handle the T2 functions.

To examine T1 further, refer to Figure 11-3. The state diagram for a primary station's time out functions is illustrated (with a normal response mode [NRM]). Box 11-2 explains the use of the timer for NRM [ECMA79].

BOX 11-2.   T1 Activity at Primary Station [ECMA79]

Action	*Reason*
Start T1 from 0	When a command is sent with P = 1
Restart T1 from 0	When a response is received with F = 1
Reset T1 to 0	When a response is received with F = 1
Retransmit command with P = 1	T1 expires

HDLC "SUBSETS"

Many other link protocols are derived from HDLC. While they are referred to as subsets, they sometimes include other capabilities not found in HDLC. The major subsets are summarized in this section. The overall HDLC schema is shown in Figure 11-4. Two options are provided for unbalanced links (Normal Response Mode [UN] and Asynchronous Response Mode [UA]) and one for balanced (Asynchronous Balanced Mode [BA]).

In order to classify a protocol conveniently, the terms UN, UA, and BA are used to denote which subset of HDLC is used. In addition, most subsets use the functional extensions. For example, a protocol classified as UN 3,7 uses the unbalanced normal response mode option and the selective reject and extended address functional extensions.

LAP—Link Access Procedure

LAP (Link Access Procedure) is an earlier subset of HDLC. LAP is based on the HDLC Set Asynchronous Response Mode (SARM) command on an

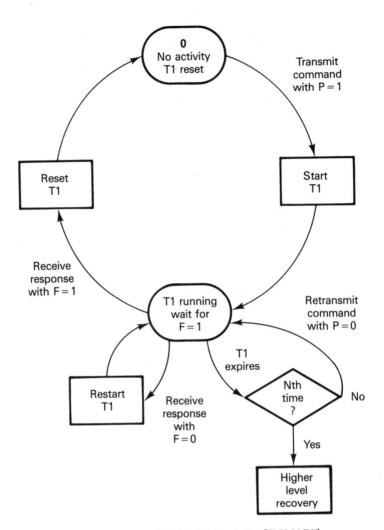

FIGURE 11-3. HDLC T1 Activity [ECMA79]

unbalanced configuration. It is classified UA 2,8 except it does not use the
DM response. LAP is still used to support some X.25 network links.

To establish a LAP data link, the sending end (primary function) transmits a SARM in the control field to the receiving end (secondary function).
Concurrent with the transmission of the SARM, the primary function will
start a no-response timer (T1). When the secondary function receives the
SARM correctly it transmits an acknowledgment response (UA: unnumbered acknowledgment). Receipt of the UA by the primary function confirms
the initiation of one direction of the link and resets the T1 timer. The receipt
of the SARM in a given direction will be interpreted by the secondary func-

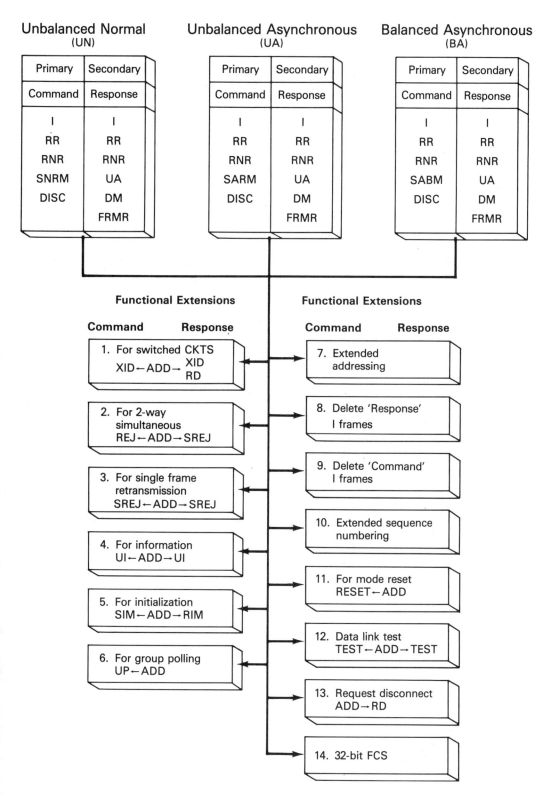

FIGURE 11-4. HDLC Schema/Set

tion as a request to initiate the other direction of transmission so the procedure may be repeated in the other direction, at the discretion of the secondary function.

LAPB—Link Access Procedure, Balanced

LAPB (Link Access Procedure, Balanced) is used by many private and public computer networks throughout the world. LAPB is classified as a BA 2,8 or BA 2,8,10 subset of HDLC. Option 2 provides for simultaneous rejection of frames in a two-way transmission mode.

Option 8 does not permit the transmitting of information in the response frames. This restriction presents no problem since in asynchronous balanced mode, the information can be transferred in command frames, and since both stations are combined stations, both can transmit commands. Moreover, with LAPB, the sending of a command frame with the P bit = 1 occurs when the station wants a "status" frame and not an information frame. Consequently, the responding station is not expected to return an I field.

LAPB is the link protocol layer for an X.25 network. It is used extensively worldwide and is found in many vendor's ports on a chip, with the X.25 network level software. Since the protocol is so pervasive, we examine it in more detail. This discussion is derived from [BLAC86A].

LAPB implements the HDLC protocol with the following refinements:

The LAPB link is set up by the user device (DTE) or the packet exchange (called data circuit-terminating equipment or DCE in the X.25 specification). The SABM/SABME commands set up the link. Either station may set up the link. A station indicates it is able to set up the link by transmitting continuous flags. Prior to link set-up, either station can send DISC to make certain all traffic and modes are cleared. If the link cannot be set up, DM must be returned.

X.25 requires the LAPB address field to designate the DTE as A and DCE as B (where A = 11000000 and B = 10000000).

LAPB has specific procedures for the use of the P/F bit. The station, upon receiving a SABM/SABME, DISC, Supervisory, or I frame with the P = 1, must set the F to 1 in the next response it transmits. The following conventions apply:

Frame Sent with P Bit Set to 1	Response Required with F Bit Set to 1
SABM/SABME,DISC	UA,DM
I (Information Transfer)	RR,REJ,RNR,FRMR
I (Disconnected Mode)	DM
Supervisory (RR,RNR,REJ)	RR,REJ,RNR,FRMR

BOX 11-3. LAPB Actions in the Information Transfer State

Frame Received or an Event Occurs	Frame Sent	Change State To:
I, P = 1	RR, F = 1	-
RR, P = 1	RR, F = 1	-
REJ, P = 1	RR, F = 1	-
RNR, P = 1	RR, F = 1	Remote Station Busy
RNR, P = 0	RR, F = 0	Remote Station Busy
SABM, P = 0 or 1	UA, F = P	-
DISC, P = 0 or 1	UA, F = P	Disconnected
RR, F = 1	SABM, P = 1	Link Set Up
REJ, F = 1	SABM, P = 1	Link Set Up
RNR, F = 1	SABM, P = 1	Link Set Up
RNR, F = 0	-	Remote Station Busy
UA, F = 0 or 1	SABM, P = 1	Link Set Up
DM, F = 1 or 0	SABM, P = 1	Link Set Up
FRMR, F = 1 or 0	SABM, P = 1	Link Set Up
Local Start	SABM, P = 1	Link Set Up
Local Stop	DISC, P = 1 or 0	Disconnect Request
Station Becomes Busy	RNR, F = P	Station Busy
T1 Expires	RR, P = 1	Waiting Acknowledgment
N2 Exceeded	SABM, P = 1	Link Set Up
Invalid N(S) Received	REJ, F = P	REJ Frame Sent
Invalid N(R) Received	FRMR, P = 1	Frame Reject
Unrecognized Frame Rec'd	FRMR, P = 1	Frame Reject

Like many communications protocols, LAPB is state-driven. While executing a specific state, it (a) accepts certain types of frames for action; (b) rejects other frames that are logically inconsistent with the state; and (c) ignores frames that have no bearing on the state and the activities on the link. An example of the actions pertaining to one state (the information transfer state) is shown in Box 11-3 [MOTO86].

LLC—Logical Link Control (IEEE 802.2)

LLC (Logical Link Control) is a standard sponsored by the IEEE 802 standards committee for local area networks (LANs). The standard permits the interfacing of a local area network to other local networks as well as to a wide area network. LLC uses a subclass of the HDLC superset. LLC is classified as BA-2,4.

LLC permits three types of implementations of HDLC: Type 1, using the UI frame (Unacknowledged Connectionless Service); Type 2, using the conventional I frame (Acknowledged Connection-oriented service); and Type 3, using AC frames (Acknowledged Connectionless Service).

		Commands	*Responses*
Type 1		UI	
		XID	XID
		TEST	TEST
Type 2	(I Format)	I	I
	(S Format)	RR	RR
		RNR	RNR
		REJ	REJ
	(U Format)	SABME	
		DISC	UA
			DM
			FRMR
Type 3		AC	AC

LLC is designed to interact with the IEEE local area networks. These networks are discussed in Chapter 20. Consequently, the details of LLC are deferred to that chapter.

LAPD—Link Access Procedure, D Channel

LAPD (Link Access Procedure, D Channel) is another subset of the HDLC structure, although it has extensions beyond HDLC. It is derived from LAPB. LAPD is used as a data link control for the integrated services digital network (ISDN).

ISDN provides LAPD to allow DTEs to communicate with each other across the ISDN D channel. It is specifically designed for the link across the ISDN user-network interface.

LAPD has a very similar frame format to HDLC and LAPB. Moreover, it provides for unnumbered, supervisory, and information transfer frames. LAPD also allows a Modulo 128 operation. The control octet to distinguish between the information format, supervisory format, or unnumbered format is identical to that of HDLC.

LAPD provides for two octets for the address field (see Figure 11-5). This is valuable for multiplexing multiple functions onto the D channel. Each ISDN basic access can support up to eight stations. The address field is used to identify the specific terminal and service access point (SAP). The address field contains the address field extension bits, a command/response indication bit, a service access point identifier (SAPI), and a terminal endpoint identifier (TEI). These entities are discussed in the following paragraphs.

The purpose of the address field extension is to provide more bits for an address. The presence of a 1 in the first bit of an address field octet signals that it is the final octet of the address field. Consequently, a two-octet

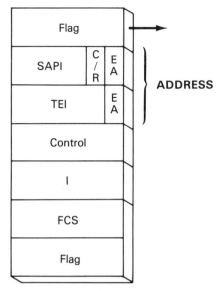

```
        8 7 6 5 4 3 2 1

                Flag

                    C  E
        SAPI        /  A
                    R        }  ADDRESS

        TEI            E
                       A

               Control

                  I

                 FCS

                Flag
```

FLAG = 01111110
  EA = Address Field Extension Bit
 C/R = Command/Response Bit
SAPI = Service Access Point Identifier ⎫ Data Link Connection
 TEI = Terminal Endpoint Identifier   ⎭ Identification (DLCI)
   I = Information Field
 FCS = Frame Check Sequence

FIGURE 11-5. The LAPD Frame

address would have a field address extension value of 0 in the first octet and a 1 in the second octet. The address field extension bit allows the use of both the SAPI in the first octet and the TEI in the second octet, if desired.

The command/response (C/R) field bit identifies the frame as either a command or a response. The user side sends commands with the C/R bit set to 0. It responds with the C/R bit set to 1. The network does the opposite—it sends commands with C/R set to 1 and responses with C/R set to 0.

The service access point identifier (SAPI) identifies the point where the data link layer services are provided to the layer above (that is, layer 3). (If the concept of the SAPI is vague, review Chapter 8.)

The terminal end-point identifier (TEI) identifies a specific connection within the SAP. It can identify either a single terminal (TE) or multiple terminals. The TEI is assigned by a separate assignment procedure. Collectively, the TEI and SAPI are called the data link connection identifier (DLCI), which identifies each data link connection on the D channel. As stated earlier, the control field identifies the type of frame as well as the sequence numbers used to maintain windows and acknowledgments between the sending and receiving devices.

Presently, the SAPI values and TEI values are allocated as follows:

SAPI Value	SAPI Related Entity
0	Call Control Procedures
16	Packet Procedures
32-47	Reserved for National Use
63	Management Procedures
Others	Reserved

TEI Value	TEI User Type
0-63	Non-Automatic Assignment
64-126	Automatic Assignment

Two commands and responses in LAPD do not exist in the HDLC schema. These are sequenced information 0 (SI0) and sequenced information 1 (SI1). The purpose of the SI0/SI1 commands is to transfer information using sequentially acknowledged frames. These frames contain information fields provided by layer 3. The information commands are verified by means of the end (SI) field. The P bit is set to 1 for all SI0/SI1 commands. The SI0 and SI1 responses are used during single frame operation to acknowledge the receipt of SI0 and SI1 command frames and to report the loss of frames or any synchronization problems. LAPD does not allow information fields to be placed in the SI0 and SI1 response frames. Obviously, information fields are in the SI0 and SI1 command frames.

LAPD differs from LAPB in a number of ways. The most fundamental difference is that LAPB is intended for point-to-point operating (user DTE-to-Packet Exchange [DCE]). LAPD is designed for multiple access on the link. The other major differences are summarized as follows:

LAPB and LAPD use different timers.

As explained earlier, the addressing structure differs.

LAPD implements the HDLC unnumbered information frame (UI).

LAPB uses only the sequenced information frames.

LAPD Primitives. LAPD uses a number of primitives for its communications with the network layer, the physical layer and a management entity which resides outside both layers. The primitives are summarized in Box 11-4.

SDLC—SYNCHRONOUS DATA LINK CONTROL: IBM'S LEVEL 2 PROTOCOL

SDLC (Synchronous Data Link Control) is IBM's widely used version of the HDLC superset. SDLC uses Unbalanced Normal Response Mode, which means the link is managed by one primary station. In addition, it uses sever-

BOX 11-4. LAPD Primitives

Primitive	Function
DL-ESTABLISH (level 2/3 boundary)	Issued on the establishment of frame operations
DL-RELEASE (level 2/3 boundary)	Issued on the termination of frame operations
DL-DATA (level 2/3 boundary)	Used to pass data between layers with acknowledgments
DL-UNIT-DATA (level 2/3 boundary)	Used to pass data with no acknowledgments
MDL-ASSIGN (level management/2 boundary)	Used to associate TEI value with a specified end point
MDL-REMOVE (level management/2 boundary)	Removes the MDL-ASSIGN
MDL-ERROR (level management/2 boundary)	Associated with an error that cannot be corrected by LAPD
MDL-UNIT-DATA (level management/2 boundary)	Used to pass data with no acknowledgments
PH-DATA (level 2/1 boundary)	Used to pass frames across layers
DH-ACTIVATE (level 2/1 boundary)	Used to set up physical link
PH-DEACTIVATE (level 2/1 boundary)	Used to deactivate physical link

al options of the superset. One of its classifications, for example, is UN-1,2,4,5,6,12, but it does use other subsets.

Loop Operations

The term superset becomes blurred when discussing SDLC, because it uses several commands that are not found in HDLC products or standards. These commands and responses provide the ability to establish a loop topology and perform loop or ring polling operations.

Figure 11-6 (a) illustrates a loop configuration. The primary station is connected only to the first and last stations on the loop. A station passes data around the loop to the next station. The primary station can send data to one or more secondary stations, but the secondary stations can send data only to the primary station.

Some IBM equipment uses the hub go-ahead configuration shown in Figure 11-6 (b). The secondary stations are daisy-chained through the inbound channel. The primary station communicates with the secondary stations through the outbound channel.

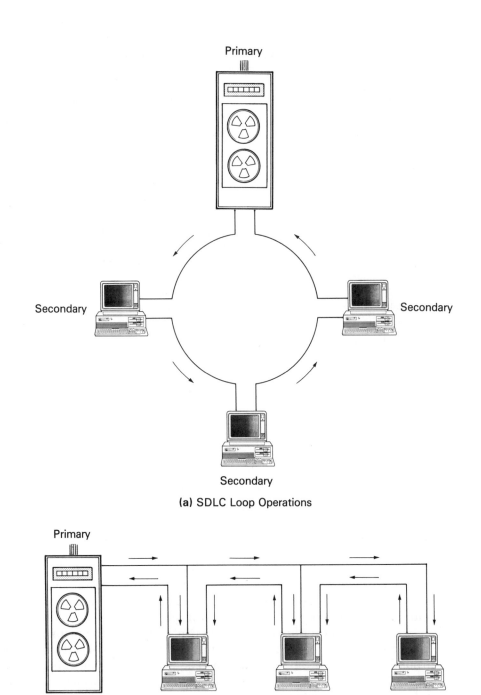

(a) SDLC Loop Operations

(b) Hub Go-Ahead Operations

FIGURE 11-6. SDLC Operations

SDLC uses the addressing rules of HDLC but adds some additional features to manage multipoint links: (a) individual address, (b) group addresses, and (c) broadcast addresses. The individual address is used in the same manner as in HDLC. The secondary station sends its own address; the primary station sends the address of the secondary station. The group address is used to send traffic to more than one station, i.e., a group of stations. If all stations are to receive the traffic, a broadcast address can be placed in the address field of the frame. All stations would then copy the broadcast frame.

SDLC Frames

SDLC uses the same frame format as HDLC (Figure 11-2). The information (I) field contains SDLC control data or the basic transmission unit (BTU) that is passed down from the path control layer.

SDLC allows an extension of the single byte address field. The address extension is implemented by setting the last bit of the address byte to 1. This setting indicates another address byte follows. The last address byte sets the last bit in its byte to 0.

EXAMPLES OF LINK OPERATIONS

Figures 11-7 through 11-10 are provided as examples of HDLC, LAPB, and SDLC link operations. Each figure is accompanied by a short explanation of the events taking place on the link. The reader should note that the figures are drawn with the frames occupying the link in nonvarying time slots. This is usually not the case, but this approach keeps the illustrations relatively simple and the illustrations are conceptually accurate. The figures depict the following link configurations:

Figure 11-7:   Link set up with SABM and half duplex operations
Figure 11-8:   A typical SDLC error recovery with a NRM link
Figure 11-9:   A LAPB error recovery with an ABM link
Figure 11-10: A SDLC multipoint operation

DDCMP—DIGITAL DATA COMMUNICATIONS
MESSAGE PROTOCOL: DEC'S LEVEL 2 PROTOCOL

The Digital Data Communications Message Protocol (DDCMP), developed by DEC in 1974, is an example of a character-count protocol. It does not have the problem of data/text transparency since it specifies the length of the user data field with the count field. The receiver need not examine the contents of the text but merely count the specified number of bytes in the field. It then knows the next field is the error-check (data checksum field).

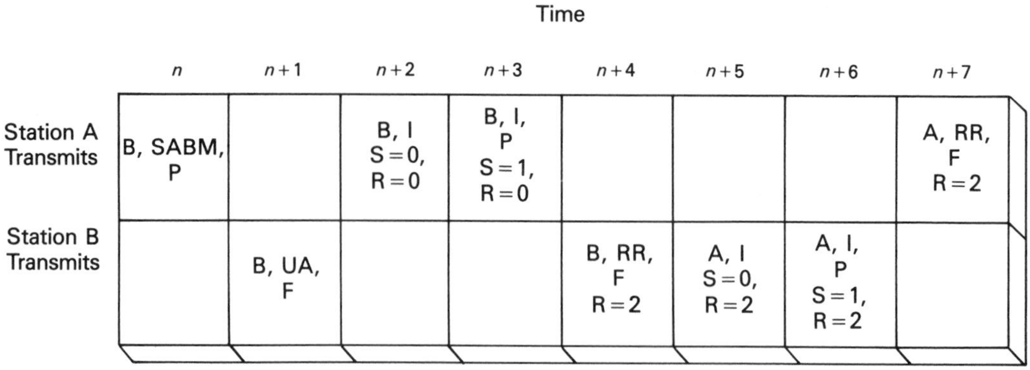

Time

	n	$n+1$	$n+2$	$n+3$	$n+4$	$n+5$	$n+6$	$n+7$
Station A Transmits	B, SABM, P		B, I S=0, R=0	B, I, P S=1, R=0				A, RR, F R=2
Station B Transmits		B, UA, F			B, RR, F R=2	A, I S=0, R=2	A, I, P S=1, R=2	

Legend (I means I field present):

n: Station A transmits *Set Asynchronous Balanced Mode* (SABM) command with P bit set.

$n+1$: Station B responds with an *Unnumbered Acknowledgment* (UA) response with F bit set.

$n+2, 3$: Station A sends information frames 0 and 1, sets P bit.

$n+4, 5, 6$: Station B acknowledges A's transmission by sending 2 in the receive sequence number field. Station B also transmits information frames 0 and 1, and sets P = 1.

$n+7$: Station B acknowledges A's frames of 1 and 2 with N(R) = 2 and responds to P = 1 with F = 1.

FIGURE 11-7. Asynchronous Balanced Mode with Half Duplex Data Flow (using P/F for checkpointing)

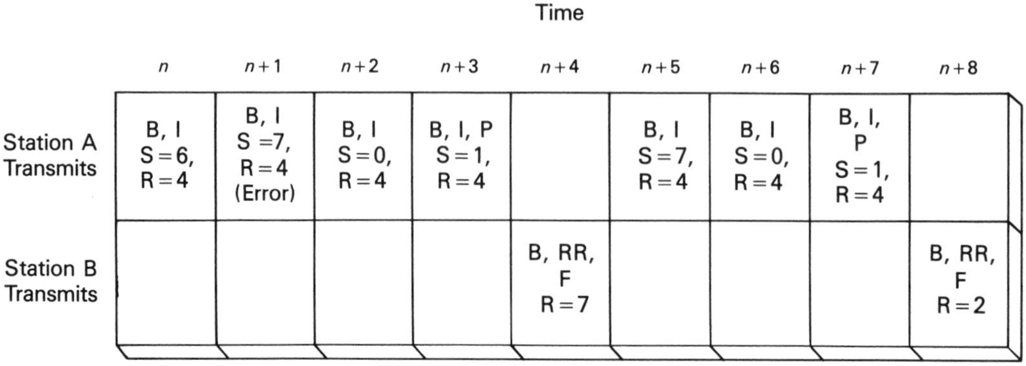

Time

	n	$n+1$	$n+2$	$n+3$	$n+4$	$n+5$	$n+6$	$n+7$	$n+8$
Station A Transmits	B, I S=6, R=4	B, I S=7, R=4 (Error)	B, I S=0, R=4	B, I, P S=1, R=4		B, I S=7, R=4	B, I S=0, R=4	B, I, P S=1, R=4	
Station B Transmits					B, RR, F R=7				B, RR, F R=2

Figure Illustrates an Ongoing Session

Legend (I means I field present):

$n, n+1, 2, 3$: Station A sends information frames 6, 7, 0, and 1

$n+4$: Station B returns a *Receive Ready* (RR) with a send sequence number of 7 and a final bit. This means station B is expecting to receive frame 7 again (and all frames transmitted after 7).

$n+5, 6, 7$: Station A retransmits frames 7, 0, and 1 and sets the P bit for a checkpoint.

$n+8$: Station B acknowledges frames 7, 0, and 1 with a *Receive Ready* (RR) and a receive sequence number of 2, and sets the F bit.

FIGURE 11-8. An SDLC Error-Recovery Operation

Time

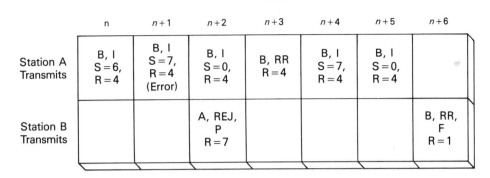

Figure Illustrates an Ongoing Session

Legend (I means I field present):

n, *n* + 1, 2: Station A sends information frames 6, 7, and 0. Station B detects an error in frame 7, and immediately sends a *Reject* frame with a receive sequence number of 7. Notice the use of the address field and P bit to depict a command frame.

n + 3, 4, 5: Station A returns an RR and retransmits the erroneous frames.

n + 6: Station B acknowledges the retransmission.

FIGURE 11-9. An LAPB Error-Recovery Operation

DDCMP Messages

DDCMP has a simpler message format convention than BSC. It has one message format and uses the class field in the frame to designate one of three message types:

SOH: Designates a data message.

ENQ: Identifies the message as a control message with the control field replacing the count field (more on the control field shortly).

DLE: Identifies the message as a maintenance message used for special purposes.

Data Message

The formats for the DDCMP data message are illustrated in Figure 11-11. (DEC uses the term message to describe its protocol data unit; we have been using the term frame.) The fields within the message provide the following functions:

- The SOH identifies the message as a data message.
- The count field gives the length of the data field from 1 to 16,383 bytes.

Figure Illustrates an Ongoing Session

	n	$n+1$	$n+2$	$n+3$	$n+4$	$n+5$	$n+6$	$n+7$
Station A Transmits	C, RR, P R=0	B, I, S=0, R=0	B, I, S=1, R=0		B, RR, P R=0		C, RR, P R=3	B, RR, P R=2
Station B Transmits						B, I S=0, R=2	B, I, F S=1, R=2	
Station C Transmits		C, I, S=0, R=0	C, I, S=1, R=0	C, I F S=2, R=0				

Legend (I means I field present):

n: Station A uses *Receive Ready* command to poll station C with poll bit set.

$n+1, 2$: Station A sends frames 0 and 1 to B, which station C responds to the previous poll and sends frames 0 and 1 to A on the other subchannel of the full-duplex circuit.

$n+3$: Station C sends information frame 2 and sets final bit.

$n+4$: Station A polls B for a checkpoint (confirmation).

$n+5$: Station B responds by acknowledging A's 0 and 1 frames with a receive sequence of 2. Station B also sends information frame 0.

$n+6$: Station A acknowledges C's frames 0, 1 and 2 with a *Receive Ready* (RR) and a receive sequence of 3. Station B sends frame 1, and sets F to 1 in response to the P bit in $n+4$.

$n+7$: Station A acknowledges B's frames 0 and 1 with a *Receive Ready* (RR) and a receive sequence of 2.

FIGURE 11-10. An SDLC Multipoint Operation

- The flags are called the sync flag and the select flag. The sync flag indicates the frame will be followed by SYN characters. The select flag is used on half duplex and multipoint lines to indicate the last data message in a transmission.
- The transmit (NUM) and receive (RESP) numbers are used to sequence the transmitted messages and acknowledge previously received messages.
- The address field identifies a specific station on a multipoint line. The field is not used on a point-to-point line.
- The BLKCHK1 field is used to perform a CRC-16 frame check sequence on the message header. A separate check is performed on the header to ensure that the count field is not damaged.

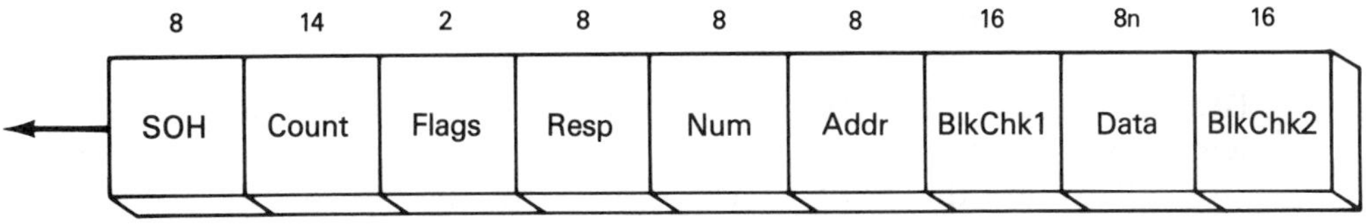

```
   8      14      2      8      8      8      16     8n     16
```

| SOH | Count | Flags | Resp | Num | Addr | BlkChk1 | Data | BlkChk2 |

SOH: Identifies a Data Message
Count: Length Indicator of Data Field
Flags: Special Uses (See Text)
Resp: Received Sequence Number
Num: Send Sequence Number
Addr: Link Station Address
BlkChk1: Header Error Check
Data: User Data
BlkChk2: Data Field Error Check

FIGURE 11-11. DDCMP Data Message Format

- The data field contains the user data and the BLKCHK2 is the CRC-16 frame check sequence on the data field.

Control Messages

DDCMP uses five control messages to manage the link activity. These messages perform the following tasks on the link:

- *Acknowledge message (ACK):* This message acknowledges the data messages that have passed the FCS check. The message is utilized when no data messages are forthcoming from the station. The message conveys the same information as the RESP field in the data message.

- *Negative acknowledged message (NAK):* This message is used to convey a negative acknowledgment (NAK) to the transmitting DDCMP module. A NAK TYPE is available to indicate the cause of the error. Like several other protocols discussed in this chapter, the NAK message also acknowledges previously transmitted messages.

- *Reply to message number (REP):* This message is used to request a status message from the other station. The message is sent under three conditions: (a) the transmitting station has sent a data message, or (b) it has not received an acknowledgment of the data message, or (c) the time allotted for an acknowledgment has expired.

- *Start message (STRT):* This message is used for initial contact, and establishment of the link and synchronization. The DDCMP station sends this message during the initial link set-up.

- *Start acknowledge message (STACK):* This message is sent in response to the start message. It informs the other DDCMP station that the transmitting node has completed its initialization. This message is quite similar to the HDLC/SDLC UA frame.

DDCMP Link Operations

DDCMP operates like HDLC in several respects. For example, it uses sliding windows, inclusive acknowledgments, and piggybacking. DEC has designed DDCMP around three functional components for link operations: (a) framing, (b) link management, and (c) message exchange. The framing component is similar to the functions of framing and other protocols discussed in this chapter. It locates the beginning and end of the message. It also locates certain bit, byte, or messages within the communications signal itself. DDCMP uses the conventional start/stop transmissions to synchronize individual bytes on asynchronous links. It uses the bisync type character SYN for synchronization on synchronous links. It also synchronizes messages by searching for one of the three starting bytes after achieving byte synchronization. These bytes are: SOH, ENQ, and DLE.

The link management module of DDCMP is responsible for the ongoing transmission and reception of messages between the stations on the link. It manages the conventional link management functions of data flow, window management, addressing, etc.

The last module of the DDCMP is the message exchange module. This module is used for sequencing operations and error checking. It is invoked after framing is accomplished.

DDCMP also allows window control in the sense that several data messages may be sent before requiring an acknowledgment of the first data message. As stated before, acknowledgment of the highest numbered message implies acknowledgment of all lower numbered messages.

MULTILINK PROCEDURES (MLP)

In recent years, many manufacturers have developed link-level protocols to manage more than one link. The advantages are obvious. First, additional throughput can be achieved, and second, a faulty link can be replaced easily by a predefined back-up link.

In 1984, LAPB was amended by the CCITT to include provisions for multilink procedures (MLP). The MLP protocol is quite similar to SNA's transmission groups.

Each single link channel behaves just as we have learned in this chapter and Chapter 10. Basically, MLP adds one additional component: a sequence number for all the multilinks. This sequence number is used to manage the windows and flow control across all the links that are identified to the multilink. The multilink sequence number ranges from 0-4095 in order to accommodate many links possibly operating at high data transfer rates. Figure 11-12 shows the relationships of the multilink and single link layers.

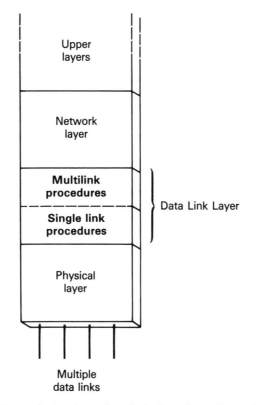

FIGURE 11-12. Relationship of Multilink and Single Link Procedures

The MLP specification is not very "user friendly" in that it is difficult to read. The following discussion is intended as a guide to the basic concepts of MLP. Readers who do not wish detailed information on this protocol can skip to the section entitled "Example of an MLP Operation."

The flow control, sequencing, and window management of MLP closely follow the concepts of individual single links. The main difference is MLP's management of the multiple physical links as if they were one logical link. MLP uses the following sequence numbers and state variables to accomplish multilink management:

MV(S)   Multilink send state variable
MN(S)   Multilink send sequence number
MV(T)   Multilink transmitted frame acknowledgment state variable
MV(R)   Multilink receive state variable
MW   Multilink window size
MX   Multilink receive window guard region
MV   Multilink system parameter

MV(S) identifies the sequence number of the next send sequence number (MN[S]) to be given to a SLP. It is incremented by 1 with each frame assignment.

MN(S) contains the value of the sequence number of the multilink frame. Note that it is not the same as the N(S) in the SLP control field. The two values perform independent functions. The N(S) sequences the frame on the single link and the MN(S), acting as a higher-level sequence number, sequences the frame traversing the multiple links. The MN(S) is used at the receiver to resequence incoming frames that may have arrived out of order across the multiple links (due to SLP retransmission) and to check for duplicate frames (due to the transmitting MLP placing a copy of the frame on more than one SLP to increase the probability of delivery).

MV(T) is maintained at the transmitting station. It identifies the oldest multilink frame that has not yet been acknowledged from the remote station. Due to the existence of more than one link at the interface, it is possible that multilink frames with sequence numbers higher than MV(T) may have been acknowledged.

MV(R) is maintained at the receiving station to identify the next expected in-sequence frame to be delivered to the next layer (usually, X.25, X.75 or a vendor's proprietary network layer). As previously stated, multilink frames with sequence numbers higher than MV(R) may have been received.

MW is the window of frames that the transmitting site can give to its SLPs and the receiving site can give to its next higher level. The MW window parameter is significant for both the transmit and receive sites. Its value is affected by factors such as propagation delay, frame lengths, the number of links, the SLP T1 timer and N2 retry parameter. The multilink MW is defined as:

Transmit MW = MV(T)→M(V)T + MV − 1 inclusive
Receive MW = MV(R)→M(V)R + MV − 1 inclusive

MLP permits any received multilink frame whose MN(S) is within the window to be released to the upper level. Of course, the MN(S) must also equal the multilink receive state variable MV(R).

The MX parameter identifies a range of multilink sequence numbers beginning at MV(R) + MW. The parameter permits the receiving station to accept multilink frames that are outside its receive window.

The MV is a parameter to denote the maximum number of sequentially numbered frames that the transmitting station can give to the SLPs beyond the value of MV(T) (the oldest multilink frame awaiting an acknowledgment). The value is established at both sites on the link and is the same value for a given direction of transmission. Its purpose is to prevent overrunning the receiver's window guard region. Therefore, it is not allowed to exceed maximum MN(S) value less the value of the window guard region: MV ≤ 4095 − MX.

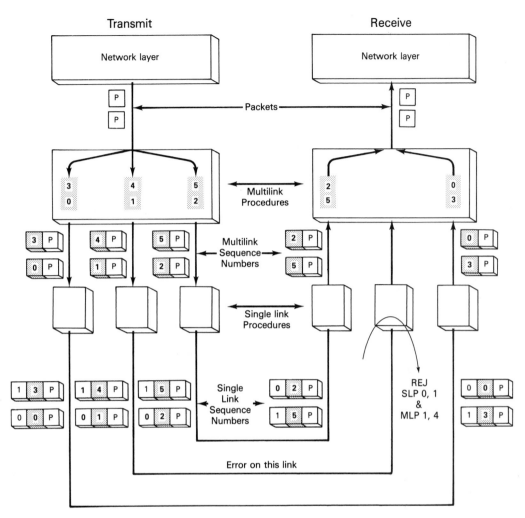

Note: Shaded Boxes Represent MLP Sequence Numbers

FIGURE 11-13. Multilink Operations

Example of an MLP Operation

These numbers and variables can be quite perplexing to the uninitiated. So, let us develop a practical example of MLP operations. Figure 11-13 shows two stations (computers, switches, front-ends, etc.) connected with three physical links. Each link is controlled by a single link protocol, such as LAPB. The receiving single link protocols only deliver the protocol data units (PDUs, or frames) to the MLP sublayers when the FCS error-check passes, and all edits on the control fields are satisfactory. Then, the MLP sublayer resequences the data before sending them to their next upper layer (usually, the network layer).

In Figure 11-13, we assume link 2 experiences some problems (such as noise) and the transmitting SLP retransmits its SLP frames 0 and 1, which are MLP frames 1 and 4. In the meantime, SLP frames 2 and 3 have been delivered to MLP. However, it may hold these data units until it receives a frame with an MLP sequence of 1. Upon receipt of this unit, it passes MLP 1, then 2, then 3 to its next layer. In this example, it resequences the traffic from the single links.

BOX 11-5.   Data Link Service Primitives

Connection-Oriented

DL-CONNECT.request (Called Address, Calling Address, Expedited Data Selection, Quality of Service Parameters)

DL-CONNECT.indication (Called Address, Calling Address, Expedited Data Selection, Quality of Service Parameters)

DL-CONNECT.response (Responding Address, Expedited Data Selection, Quality of Service Parameters)

DL-CONNECT.confirm (Responding Address, Expedited Data Selection, Quality of Service Parameters)

DL-DISCONNECT.request (Originator, Reason)
DL-DISCONNECT.indication (Originator, Reason)
DL-DATA.request (User-Data)
DL-DATA.indication (User-Data)
DL-EXPEDITED-DATA.request (User-Data)
DL-EXPEDITED-DATA.indication (User-Data)
DL-RESET.request (Originator, Reason)
DL-RESET.indication (Originator, Reason)
DL-RESET.response
DL-RESET.confirm
DL-ERROR-REPORT.indication (Reason)

Connectionless

DL-UNITDATA.request (Source Address, Destination Address, Quality of Services, User-Data)

DL-UNITDATA.indication (Source Address, Destination Address, Quality of Services, User-Data)

DATA LINK SERVICE DEFINITION
WITH ISO DIS 8886 OR CCITT X.212

To complete our discussion of data link controls, it should be noted that the ISO has published a data link service definition. It is DIS 8886. As we have learned, the services are defined by primitives and 8886 provides for both connection-oriented and connectionless services. These primitives are summarized in Box 11-5.

The CCITT added the link level service definition to its 1988 Blue Book Recommendations. It is similar to ISO 8886, but some of the parameters in the primitives are different. There are also several other relatively minor differences between the two standards. The reader can study Appendix I of the X.212 recommendation for a detailed description of the differences between ISO 8886 and X.212.

SUGGESTED READINGS

In the final analysis, the most informative reading about a data communications system is the actual source document. However, most data link level source specifications are not very "user friendly," in that they are written as specific references, with minimal tutorial prose. Nonetheless, the reader is directed initially to the source documents.

The HDLC specification is available in ISO 3309 and ISO 4335. Each vendor publishes its own version of the Bisync protocol. IBM's source documents are [IBM70] and [IBM81]. The LAPB specification is contained in CCITT X.25. LAPD is described in CCITT I.440 and I.441. [WATK81] provides an excellent description of the ANSI character-oriented protocols. [MART87] describes SDLC quite thoroughly.

QUESTIONS

TRUE/FALSE

1. Binary Synchronous Control (BSC) operates in either control mode or text mode.
2. A BSC select performs the sole function of placing the selected station into a slave mode.
3. HDLC is used as a foundation for LAPB and LAPD.
4. The HDLC balanced option is complemented by the physical level balanced interface.
5. Match the definition with the appropriate HDLC term:

   Definition

   a) Combined station can transmit without prior permission.
   b) Secondary station can transmit without prior permission.
   c) Secondary must receive permission to transmit.

Term

1. Normal response mode (NRM)
2. Asynchronous balanced mode (ABM)
3. Asynchronous response mode (ARM)

6. The BSC ENQ code performs the following functions:
   a) Polls
   b) Bids
   c) Selects
   d) All of the above
   e) None of the above

7. Describe the principal functions of the ISO 2628 no-response timer, receive timer, and no-activity timer.

8. HDLC allows the following station types:
   a) Secondary
   b) Combined
   c) Master
   d) Slave

9. Why would a HDLC link encounter problems if it were established as a multipoint balanced link?

10. Describe the main functions of the HDLC information format, supervisory format, and unnumbered format.

11. What is the function of the HDLC P/F (poll/final) bit?

12. Describe the rules for using the address field in a HDLC frame.

SELECTED ANSWERS

1. True.
2. False. It may also place other stations on a multipoint link into a passive state.
3. True.
4. False. It has no relationship.
5.

Definition	*Term*
a)	2
b)	3
c)	1

6. d)

10. The information format frame is used to transmit end-user data between two devices. It may also acknowledge the receipt of data from a transmitting station, and perform other functions such as polls. The supervisory format frame performs control functions such as acknowledgment, request for retransmission of frames and the request for the temporary suspension of the transmission frames. The unnumbered format is also used for control purposes. The frame is used to perform link initialization, link disconnection and other link control functions. The frame uses five bit positions, which allows for up to 32 commands and 32 responses.

CHAPTER 12

The Port

INTRODUCTION

A friendly word of caution is in order about this chapter. Due to the nature of the subject, the chapter focuses on "bit level" discussions. The reader who is not interested in this level of detail can skip this chapter and not suffer any ill effects.

The connection of the user device to the modem, multiplexer, or data service unit and the communications link is provided through a combination of hardware and firmware functions called the communications port. Other names are used to designate the port. Some commonly used terms are: communications adapter interface, serial port, serial board, board, UART (universal asynchronous receiver/transmitter), USART (universal synchronous/asynchronous receiver/transmitter).

A port is usually a microprocessor with its own separate clock, memory, registers, and a central processing unit (in other words, a full-fledged microcomputer). The intelligence of the port is highly variable, depending on the type of interface needed. A port represents only one communications interface to a link, so a computer may have many ports (see Figure 12-1).

The main purpose of the communications port is to physically connect the communications channel with the user device and provide the support functions of transferring data into and out of the device. In order to perform those services, the port supports many of the physical level functions described in Chapter 9. Moreover, many ports are also manufactured to include the data link layer functions explained in Chapters 10 and 11.

The first section of this chapter is a tutorial on communications input/output operations (I/O). The second section describes a simple physi-

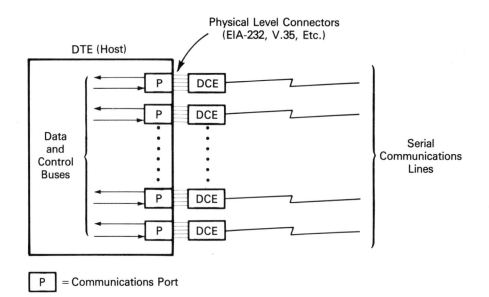

FIGURE 12-1. The Communications Ports on a DTE

cal level port chip. Two examples are provided: (a) an introductory illustration and (b) a more detailed illustration of the IBM Personal Computer port and its interface with the Hayes modem. The reader who wishes only an overview of the port can study example (a) and skip example (b). The reader who needs the details should study both examples. Example (b) should be of particular interest to the reader who uses a personal computer. After these examples, a data link/physical level chip is described that uses the LAPB protocol. Lastly, a simple example is provided of a BASIC program and its "communications" instructions.

POLLING AND INTERRUPTS

Input/Output (I/O) is controlled at the port through one of two techniques, polling or interrupts. With the polling technique, a software program in the machine periodically and continuously checks certain bits of the port registers to ascertain if the port should be serviced: i.e., does it have data to transmit or has it received data. The program periodically scans the status bits in the register to determine if it is to invoke an input or output function to the port.

The interrupt approach does not require software to continuously search the status of the port registers. Instead, the port is designed to send certain signals to the DTE I/O control program when a specific event occurs. The DTE's I/O control is executed only when it receives a signal from an interrupt line. While this would appear to have decided advantages over polling, it must be remembered that an interrupt can be received at any time during a machine's processing. As a consequence, the DTE operating system must be able to suspend the task on which it is operating and service the interrupt. We have more to say about these techniques as we proceed through this chapter.

The polling approach is implemented by setting a bit in one of the registers in the port (usually, the interrupt enable register bit). This action prevents the port from generating an interrupt to the system; therefore, the program repeatedly checks the status register to determine when traffic is to be emptied from the receive buffer.

To handle the interrupt method, a special program is executed, commonly known as an interrupt handler. When this approach is used, the computer operating system branches to the the interrupt handler when it receives an interrupt signal from the port. In most machines, the operating system provides addresses to areas in memory for the interrupt handler to examine and determine further actions.

Upon being activated, the interrupt handler knows nothing except that it is executing. Consequently, it must examine the status registers at the port to see what caused the interrupt. For example, the data-ready bit may have been turned on, which means data have been received at the register, and this information determines the actions of the interrupt handler. The data may be available in a memory buffer, but typically they are still in a receive register which the interrupt handler may access and then transfer to a memory location for assembly into a complete user message.

The interrupt may also indicate that data should be sent to the port because the transmit register is empty or soon to be empty.

THE PORT AT THE PHYSICAL LEVEL

Most communications ports in computers and terminals use an input/output (I/O) interface chip called the universal asynchronous receiver/transmitter (UART) or the universal synchronous/asynchronous receiver/transmitter (USART). This large-scale integrated (LSI) device performs the following functions:

- Accepts parallel data from the DTE and converts them to serial data for the communications link.
- Accepts serial data from the link and converts them to a parallel form for the DTE.
- Performs some limited problem detection (parity, no stop bit, character overrun).
- Provides for transmitter and receiver clocks.
- Detects a byte or block of data from the link or from the DTE.
- Selects number of stop bits for an asynchronous system.

- Selects number of bits per character.
- Selects odd or even parity.

The UART is usually packaged in a 40 pin DIP (dual in-line package) (see Figure 12-2 and Table 12-1), and the pins are inserted into a board which becomes part of the port logic. The device is used by both the DTE and DCE to control the communications process. The pins are set to a high or low state to provide the functional signals described in Table 12-1. The pins are also used with other components on the port. These components are discussed shortly.

A simple USART interface is shown in Figure 12-3. We will use this figure to examine how data are transferred through the port. Data are transferred across the physical level connector (pin 3 of EIA-232) from the modem and communications link to an eight-bit UART or USART receive buffer register. Upon the buffer being filled, the data are moved across a parallel bus to the DTE for further processing. (Some high-performance chips store a full block of data [for example, 128 bytes] before transferring it out of the communications interface.)

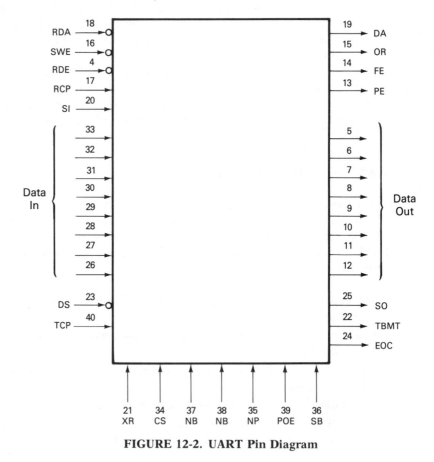

FIGURE 12-2. UART Pin Diagram

TABLE 12-1. UART Pin Functions

Pin Number	Name	Mnemonic	Functions
1	—	—	Power
2	—	—	Power
3	Ground	GND	Electrical ground
4	Received Data Enable	RDE	Gates the received data onto pins 5-12
5-12	Received Data	RD	Data out
13	Parity Error	PE	Parity error indicator
14	Framing Error	FE	No valid stop bit
15	Overrun	OR	Data overrun in the buffer
16	Status Word Enable	SWE	Places PE, OR, TBMT, FE, DA on output lines
17	Receiver Clock	RCP	Input line for an external clock
18	Reset Data Available	RDA	Resets DA
19	Received Data Available	DA	Data character has been received
20	Serial Input	SI	Incoming data
21	External Reset	XR	Resets UART chip
22	Transmit Buffer Empty	TBMT	Transmit register can be loaded with a character
23	Data Strobe	DS	Loads data into transmit register
24	End of Character	EOC	Goes low when last bit of character transmitted
25	Serial Output	SO	Outgoing data
26-33	Data Input	DB	Data in
34	Control Strobe	CS	Places certain information into holding register
35	No Parity	NP	No parity checks
36	Two Stop Bits	SB	Indicates number of stop bits
37, 38	Number of Bits	NB	Number of bits in character
39	Parity Select	POE	Indicates type of parity
40	Transmitter Clock	TCP	Input line for external clock

On the transmit side, data are transferred after the DTE has filled the transmit buffer register and sent a control signal to instruct the chip to send the data onto the link (usually on pin 2 of EIA-232).

The address selection logic allows the host to select the individual port and the registers at the port for either reading or writing. The interrupt control logic allows the host to service an interrupt request by the USART or UART chip.

The registers are set and/or examined by the host I/O program to manage the communications process. Each bit in the registers can be individually programmed to configure the communications process to suit the user's need.

The UART or USART logic is controlled by the DTE (host) with I/O programming. The chip and the DTE are interfaced to each other by the use of programmable registers, which we explain shortly.

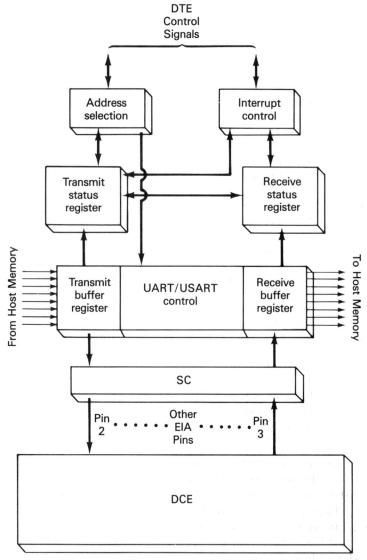

SC: Signal Converter

FIGURE 12-3. The Communications Port

An Example of the Port

A description of the commonly used bit positions in the registers should help the reader to understand how this communications interface works. The bit usages vary, depending on specific protocols such as asynchronous, synchronous, character-oriented, count-oriented, or bit-oriented systems.

This section provides an overview of a port and is derived from [MCNA82]. Be aware that while UARTs and USARTs are similar, most manufacturers have implemented additional features and registers and/or have adapted the UARTs/USARTs to their own microprocessors.

The reader is encouraged to compare the EIA-232 interchange circuits described in Chapter 9 to the bit functions in the registers. The signals on the EIA-232 pins are used with many of these bits.

In our general example, five registers are used by the UART/USART and the host I/O program. The contents and functions of the registers are explained in Tables 12-2 through 12-6. As these registers are examined, they should be compared with the EIA circuits in Figure 9-3 in Chapter 9.

Transmit status register	Table 12-2
Receive status register	Table 12-3
Transmit buffer register	Table 12-4
Receiver buffer register	Table 12-5
Parameter status register	Table 12-6

TABLE 12-2. Transmit Status Register

Bit Position	NAME	*Transmit Status Register Bit Functions* FUNCTION
0	BRK	Permits the sending of a special signal from the DTE, like a terminal's break signal
2	MAIN	Loops the transmitter's output to the receiver's input for diagnostic purposes
3	HDX	Used with interface to a half duplex DCE
4	SEND	Used to activate the transmitter logic; traffic is sent when this bit is set
5	DNA IE	Allows an interrupt if bit 15 is set
6	XMIT IE	Allows the UART (through bit 7) to generate an interrupt to the I/O program
7	XMIT RDY	Indicates that transmit logic is ready to accept another character
9	XMIT ACT	Signals to I/O program that request to send to DCE can be dropped
10-14	TIME	Indicates how the transmitter and receiver logic are to obtain their clocking (from modem, from DTE, etc.)
15	DNA	Indicates that data are not available for transmission. Generates an interrupt if bit 5 is set

The transmit status register is used to control the output side of the port. The computer's I/O program sets and reads the bits in the register to handle interrupts, transmit data, and communicate with the EIA-232 interchange circuits. As Table 12-2 shows, other bits are used to provide testing, to establish breaks, and to set the link to half duplex operations.

TABLE 12-3. Receive Status Register

Bit Position	NAME	Receive Status Register Bit Functions — FUNCTION
1	DTR	Indicates data terminal ready lead to DCE is on or off
2	REQ SND	I/O program sets this bit to put the request to send circuit to the DCE in an on or off state
4	SCH SYN	Used to instruct receiver logic to look for synchronization signals (SYN, Flags)
5	DS IE	Allows an interrupt to the I/O program, when bit 15 set. Program may first examine bits 13 and 12
6	RVCR IE	Allows the UART (through bit 7) to generate an interrupt signal to DTE
7	RVCR DONE	Signals that a received character is available for transfer to DTE memory
8	ST SY	Indication to discard remaining SYNC characters, once synchronization has been achieved
9	DS RDY	Indicates DCE is operational and has turned on its data set ready lead to DTE
11	RCVR ACT	Indicates the receive active bit is on
12	CAR DET	Indicates that carrier detect lead from DCE has changed state
13	CLR SND	Indicates clear to send lead is on from the DCE
14	RING	Indicates ringing signal is coming across the ring lead from the modem
15	DS INT	Set when bits 11 or 12 change state; causes an interrupt if bit 5 is set

TABLE 12-4. Transmit Buffer Register

Bit Position	NAME	Transmit Buffer Register Bit Functions — FUNCTION
0-7		Stores the character that is to be transmitted
8	SOM	Instructs interface to send flags, if data are not available for sending
9	EOM	Instructs interface to send out a flag after it finishes transmitting a character
10	XMIT ABRT	I/O program uses this bit to instruct transmitter to send abort signals

TABLE 12-5. Receiver Buffer Register

Bite Position	Name	Receiver Buffer Register Bit Functions FUNCTION
0-7	None	Stores received character
8	SOM	Indicates data in bits 0-7 represent the first character of a synchronous frame (SDLC, HDLC, etc.) bit-oriented protocol
9	EOM	Indicates flag has arrived in bits 0-7; prompts an examination of bit 12 to detect an error
10	RCV ABRT	Indicates a synchronous bit-oriented protocol is sending abort signals
12	PE or CRCE	Signals a parity error, if parity checking is used Signals a CRC error, if CRC used
13	FE	Framing error indication: in asynchronous transmission start and stop bit not detected accurately, not used with synchronous systems
14	OE	Overrun indication: previous data not moved to memory before current data arrived. This previous data character is last
15	ERR	Can be used by I/O program to test any combination of bits 12, 13, and 14

TABLE 12-6. Parameter Status Register

Bit Position	Name	Parameter Status Register Bit Functions FUNCTION
0-7	SYNC	Specifies the bit stream of the SYNC character
8	PS	Set to 1 to indicate even parity; 0 indicates odd parity
9	PE	Enables or disables parity
10-11	WRD	Indicates length of character (word)

The receive status register controls the input side of the port. It is also used to handle interrupts and to connect with the EIA-232 interface. It supports other activities as well. For example, it is used to alert the receiver logic to accommodate to SYN or flag signals. It is also used to indicate the receiving DCE is generating a ring sequence (on a dial-and-answer configuration).

The transmit and receive buffer registers store the data as it is received or transmitted through the port. Several of the bits in these registers are also used to control the ongoing input/output operations between the I/O program and the port.

Finally, the parameter status register contains the bit values of the SYNC character as well as the values to indicate the use (or non-use) of parity checking, and the length of the data character (5, 6, 7, or 8 bits per character).

The IBM Personal Computer (PC) Port and the Hayes Modem

Since the IBM PC is an asynchronous DTE, it uses a UART chip at its communications ports. A PC communicates with the Hayes modem (or a Hayes compatible device) via the PC bus, then through the PC UART, and then to the modem's microprocessor. The PC controls the transfer of information by reading and writing from/to the UART registers. Even though these registers reside at the port and are actually on the board of an in-board modem (our example), they are considered as part of the PC I/O address space.

The PC allows two I/O address spaces for two asynchronous devices. The devices are designated COM1 and COM2. The Hayes modem occupies one of these addresses. COM1 and COM2 are controlled by their respective registers and are accessed by hexadecimal addresses (3F8 - 3FF for COM1 and 2F8 - 2FF for COM2).

The IBM PC UART registers are illustrated in Figure 12-4. The interface utilizes the following registers (all registers are 8 bits):

> Line Control Register (LCR)
> Divisor Latch (DLL) - least significant byte
> Divisor Latch (DLM) - most significant byte
> Line Status Register (LSR)
> Modem Control Register (MCR)
> Modem Status Register (MSR)
> Receiver Buffer Register (RBR)
> Transmitter Holding Register (THR)
> Interrupt Enable Register (IER)
> Interrupt Identification Register (IIR)
> Modem Speed Register (MSR)

The line control register (LCR) indicates the character format. The LCR can be written or read. Bit positions 1 and 2 are designated as word length bits (WLS1, WLS0). They are used together to define the size of the ASCII characters. The permissible values are a word length of 5 bits, 6 bits, 7 bits, or 8 bits. The bits are turned on as:

> 00   5 bits
> 01   6 bits
> 10   7 bits
> 11   8 bits

Bit 2 of the LCR register designates the number of stop bits per character. The permissible values are 2, 1-1/2, or 1 stop bit for each character. Bit position 3 of the register enables or disables parity generation and checking. Bit position 4 can be used to designate even or odd parity. If this bit is used,

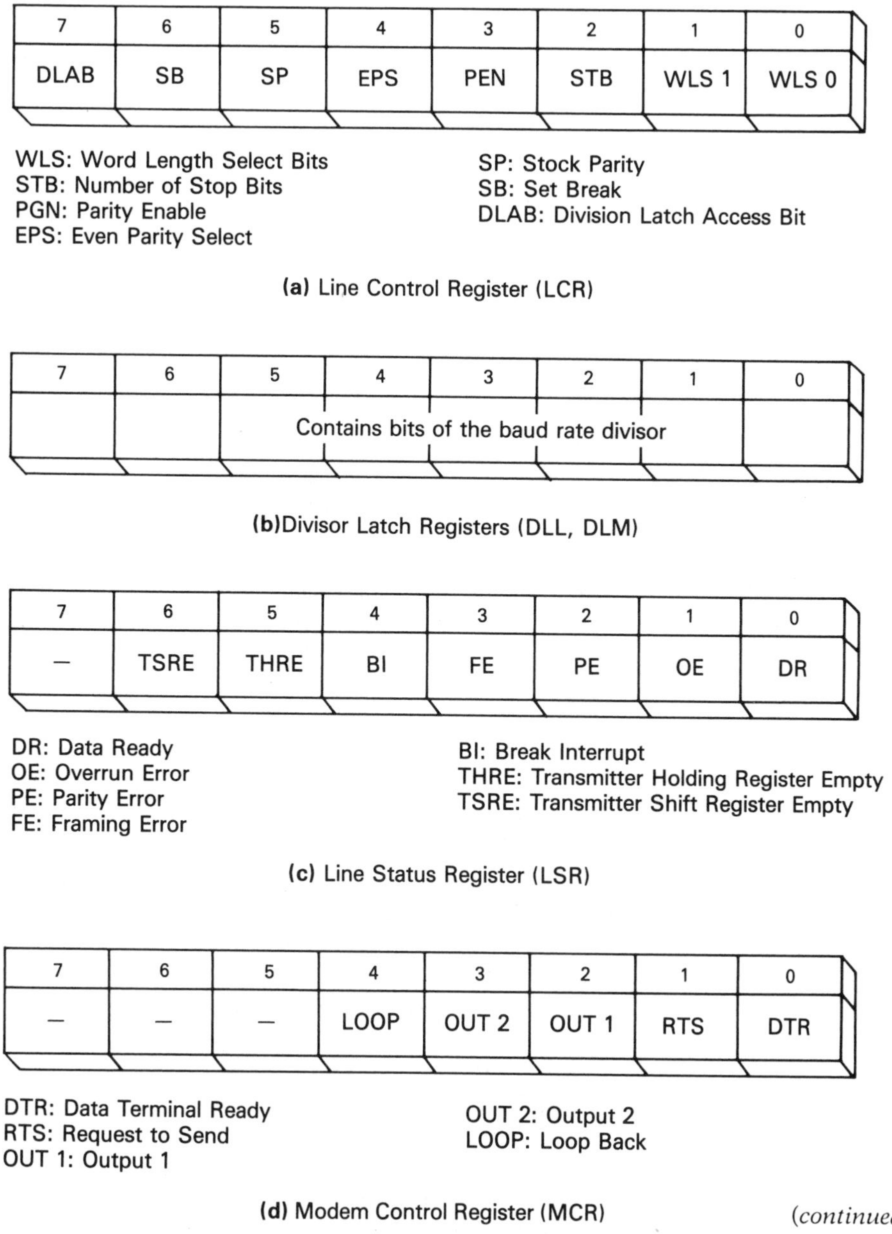

7	6	5	4	3	2	1	0
DLAB	SB	SP	EPS	PEN	STB	WLS 1	WLS 0

WLS: Word Length Select Bits
STB: Number of Stop Bits
PGN: Parity Enable
EPS: Even Parity Select

SP: Stock Parity
SB: Set Break
DLAB: Division Latch Access Bit

(a) Line Control Register (LCR)

7	6	5	4	3	2	1	0
			Contains bits of the baud rate divisor				

(b) Divisor Latch Registers (DLL, DLM)

7	6	5	4	3	2	1	0
—	TSRE	THRE	BI	FE	PE	OE	DR

DR: Data Ready
OE: Overrun Error
PE: Parity Error
FE: Framing Error

BI: Break Interrupt
THRE: Transmitter Holding Register Empty
TSRE: Transmitter Shift Register Empty

(c) Line Status Register (LSR)

7	6	5	4	3	2	1	0
—	—	—	LOOP	OUT 2	OUT 1	RTS	DTR

DTR: Data Terminal Ready
RTS: Request to Send
OUT 1: Output 1

OUT 2: Output 2
LOOP: Loop Back

(d) Modem Control Register (MCR)   (*continued*)

FIGURE 12-4. IBM PC UART Registers

7	6	5	4	3	2	1	0
RLSD	RI	DSR	CTS	DRLSD	TERI	DDSR	DCTS

DCTS: Delta Clear to Send
DDSR: Delta Data Set Ready
TERI: Trailing Edge Ring Indicator
DRLSD: Delta Received Line Signal Detect

CTS: Clear to Send
DSR: Data Set Ready
RI: Ring Indicator
RLSD: Received Line Signal Detect

(e) Modem Status Register (MSR)

7	6	5	4	3	2	1	0
		Receiving and sending characters					

(f) Receiver Buffer (RBR) and Transmitter Holding Registers (THR)

7	6	5	4	3	2	1	0
—	—	—	—	EDSSI	ELSI	ETBEI	ERBFI

ERBFI: Enable Received Data Available Interrupt
ETBEI: Enable Transmitter Holding Register Empty Interrupt
ELSI: Enable Receiver Line Status Interrupt
EDSSI: Enable Modem Status Interrupt

(g) Interrupt Enable Register (IER)

7	6	5	4	3	2	1	0
—	—	—	—	—	IID	IID	IP

IP: Interrupt Pending   IID: Interrupt ID

(h) Interrupt Identification Register (IIR)

FIGURE 12-4. *(continued).*

then bit position 3 must also be set to 1. Bit position 5 is used to determine if stick parity is to be set. Bit position 6 is designated the set break bit and it causes the modem to either transmit a continuous break signal or if turned to a 0, it stops the transmission of the break signal. The last bit of register LCR is the divisor latch access bit. This bit is turned to 1 to enable access to the divisor latches (discussed shortly) during a read/write operation. If it is set to a 0, it enables access to the receiver buffers, the transmitting holding registers, and the interrupt enable registers. Let us examine the divisor latch registers to determine the function of this bit.

The two divisor latch registers are designated as divisor latch DLL for the least significant byte and the divisor latch DLM for the most significant byte. Both registers can be read or written. The DLL contains the low-order bits of the baud divisor used to select the variable baud generator at the interface. The DLM contains the upper 8 bits of the baud divisor. These two bits are used in conjunction with each other to determine the baud of the interface.

It should be noted that the specifications use baud inappropriately here. The divisor latches deal with the bit rate. The particular method of implementation depends on the speed allowed at the basic modem and chip set level. In order to use either of these registers, bit position 7 of the line control register (LCR) must be set to 1. The two values of these registers are used together to compute a desired "baud."

The line status register (LSR) is used to provide status of error conditions and the data transfer. As Figure 12-4 illustrates, bits 0 through 5 can be used to produce an interrupt provided that the interrupt enable register is set to true (1). If the reader examines the line status register in Figure 12-4, it will be obvious that this UART interface is quite similar in this area to the generic UART port discussed earlier. Let us examine the functions of the bits of LSR.

Bit position 0 is the data ready (DR) bit position. When set to a 1, it indicates a character has been received and is being held in the receiver buffer register. The PC sets this to 0 when the data is read from the register. Bit position 1 is the overrun error position (OE). When set to 1, it indicates that the character in the receiver buffer register was not read before the next character was received. Of course, this means that the previous character was destroyed. This bit is reset to 1 whenever the line status register is read. Bit position 2 is the parity error bit (PE). A value of 1 indicates a parity problem. In other words, the character received does not match the parity specified by the line control register. Bit position 3, the framing error bit (FE), is set to a 1 to indicate that the received character lacks a valid stop bit. It is reset to 0 when the register is read.

Bit position 4 is the break interrupt bit (BI). When set to a 1, it indicates a break signal has been received. Bit position 5 is the transmitter holding register empty bit (THRE). It indicates the UART chip is ready to accept a new character for transmission. This bit position is reset to 0 when the transmitter holding register is loaded. (This register is described shortly.) Bit position 6 is the transmitter shift register empty (TSRE). A value of 1 indicates the last character in the transmitter shift register has been transmitted. This bit is set to 0 when data transfer occurs from the transmitter holding register to the transmitter shift register. We shall see shortly that the transmitter shift register is part of the UART parallel to serial converter. It is used in conjunction with the transmitter holding register to actually transfer a character. Bit position 7 is not used and is set to 0.

The modem control register (MCR) is also used for reading or writing. It manages the interface with the Hayes modem. Only the first five bits of this register are used. Some of the bits work with the physical level interface, which is described in Chapter 9. (The reader may wish to review Chapter 9 before examining this register.) Bit position 0 is the data terminal ready bit (DTR). It enables the DTR lead between the modem and the PC. It is used in conjunction with switches at the interface at the modem to indicate to the modem that the PC is ready to accept data. When the bit 0 is 1, it means the DTR lead is ON and the modem is enabled. If the DTR is set to 0, the modem can neither accept commands nor answer calls. Bit position 1 is the request to send bit (RTS). Request to send is not used by the Hayes modem. It is used by many other interfaces; however for this discussion it makes no difference whether the bit is 0 or 1. Bit 2 is called the output 1 bit (OUT 1). If set to a 1, this action resets the modem; it is equivalent to providing a power off to the modem. In order for this action to occur, the interface requires that the 1 be held for at least 50 ms. The Hayes modem command set can be used to set this bit. Bit position 3 is the output 2 bit (OUT 2). When set to 1, this enables the interrupt line drivers; that is, it allows the UART to interrupt the computer for certain functions. If the bit is set to a 0, it disables the interrupt line drivers. The last bit used in this register is called the loop bit. It is used when set to a 1 to activate loopback testing for diagnostic work with the UART. It is set to a 0 for normal operations. (Loopback testing is described in more detail in Chapter 7.)

The modem status register (MSR) should also be compared to the generic UART described earlier. Some of the bits are quite similar. The MSR is responsible for providing the status of control signals from the modem. Bits 0 and 1, the clear to send (CTS) and data set ready (DSR) bits are not used by the Hayes/PC interface. Bit position 2 is the trailing edge ring indicator bit (TERI). It indicates that an incoming call utilizing a ring indicator (bit 6) has been changed from 1 to 0. In other words, it indicates the modem has detected a ringing signal on the line if bit position 6 equals 1. Bit position 2 indicates there is no longer a ringing signal on the line. Bit position 3 is the delta received line signal detect (DRL). It indicates that the receive line signal detect has changed states. (Chapter 9 describes the function of the receive line signal detector, if the reader needs more information at this time.) Bits 4 and 5, the clear to send (CTS) and data set ready (DSR) bits, are not used by the Hayes modem/IBM PC interface.

The reader might wonder why bits 0, 1, 4, and 5 are not used since they can be viewed as an integral function of modem and DTE signalling. These bits are not needed because the port operates in full duplex; consequently, the clear to send and data set ready are unnecessary to perform control functions.

Bit position 6 is the ring indicator bit. As discussed earlier, when set to 1, it indicates that the modem has detected a ringing signal on the telephone link. Finally, bit position 7 is the receive line signal detector (RLSD). When set to a 1 it indicates that the modem has detected a carrier signal on the link. When set to a 0 it indicates there is no carrier signal on the link.

The receiver buffer register (RBR) has many similarities to our earlier general example. This register contains the character that was just received from the data communications link. The reader may wish to review bit 7 of the line control register (LCR) because this bit must be equal to 0 if the receiver buffer register can be accessed.

The transmitter holding register (THR) contains the next character to be transmitted onto the link. As discussed in the previous paragraph, bit position 7 of LCR must be equal to 0 in order for this register to be accessed.

The interrupt enable register (IER) is used to control the interrupts across the interface. Presently, the first four bits are used for this activity. Bit position 0 is the enable received data available interrupt (ERBFI). When set to a 1, the UART chip generates an interrupt whenever the data ready bit (DR) of the line status register is set to a 1. Bit position 1 is the enable transmitter holding register empty interrupt (ETBEI). When set to a 1, this bit causes the UART chip to generate an interrupt if bit position 5 (THRE) of line status register is set to a 1. Bit position 2 is the enable receiver line status interrupt bit (ELSI). When set to a 1, this causes the UART to generate an interrupt when the following occurs: a parity error, a framing error, a break interrupt, or an overrun error. Again, this is quite similar to our previous generic example. Finally, the last bit used on this register is the enable modem status interrupt (EDSSI). When set to 1, the UART generates an interrupt if bit position 7 of the modem status register (RLSD) is also set to 1.

The interrupt identification register (IIR) utilizes the low order three bits to assist in managing interrupts. Bit position 0, the interrupt pending bit, indicates that an interrupt condition has occurred. Bit positions 1 and 2 are used in conjunction with each other to indicate the priority of the interrupt condition. Their bit configurations provide the following information (priority of the interrupts is highest for 11 and worst for 00):

11 An interrupt source is (a) overrun error (OE), or (b) parity error (PE), or (c) framing error (FE), or (d) break interrupt (BI)

10 The interrupt source is the DR bit on the line status register

01 The interrupt source is the THRE bit on the line status register

00 The interrupt source is (a) ring indicator (RI) or (b) received line signal detect (RLSD) on the modem status register

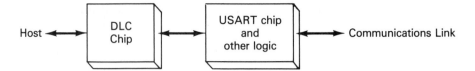

FIGURE 12-5. The Data Link and Physical Layers in the Communications Port

The last register is the modem speed register (MSR). This register is used by the Hayes modem; it is not on the UART register. Bit position 0 of this register is used to indicate the modem's speed of operation. It is comparable to pin 12 of EIA-232.

THE PORT AT THE DATA LINK CONTROL (DLC) LEVEL

It is common practice today to place the data link control layer on LSI chips. The chips are then connected into the physical level chips (USARTs, or programmable USART-oriented registers) and the physical and data link control logic become part of the communications port (see Figure 12-5). The port logic is controlled by the vendor's I/O programs and/or the network layer.

This section examines a communications interface port [MOTO86] that supports the data link layer and the LAPB protocol (explained in Chapter 11).

An efficient method for the host software (I/O program) and the DLC chip set to communicate is through shared memory. This permits a limited

Station Table

• Time out limits
• Retries limits
• Outstanding frames limits	Written by Host to Instruct DLC
• Remote address
• Local address
• Pointers to user data

• V(S) and V(R) contents
• LAPB mode description
• Pointers to user data	Written by DLC to Inform Host of Activity
• Received FRMR field
• Link status
• Frame reject description

FIGURE 12-6. Communications with Shared Memory

number of instructions to be used, and it also minimizes the number of registers required for the interface. The shared memory table (hereafter called the station table) is shown in Figure 12-6. The top part of the table is the host processor area; it is written by the host and read by the DLC logic. The bottom part is used by the DLC to inform the host of the state of the communications activity at the port. The contents of this table should be familiar to the reader who has read Chapters 10 and 11.

Two other tables are used by the host and the DLC chip (see Figure 12-7). The transmit frame table queues the data (I field) for DLC in buffers located throughout memory. The table contains transmit frame specification blocks which describe the location of the buffers. The pointers in the

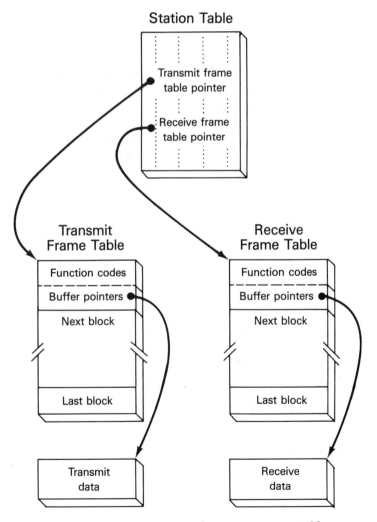

FIGURE 12-7. Transmit and Receive Frame Tables

station table point to the first specification block and the DLC logic uses the block to locate the data in memory.

To transmit a frame, DLC copies the remote address from the station table into a first-in, first-out (FIFO) queue. This table entry becomes the address field in the frame. DLC then constructs the control field and places it in FIFO. The I field is processed next; DLC uses a transmit buffer pointer register to access the data and place it into FIFO. The DLC uses a function code from the table to direct its operations. The cyclic redundancy check (CRC) processes the A, C, and I fields, then creates the FCS field, which is attached to complete the frame. The data is then presented to the physical level chip-set (through setting the bits in the status registers and sending the data to the transmit buffer register).

The DLC updates its V(S) upon each transmission and manages the use of the T1 timer. The process is repeated until the end of the chain is detected in the transmit frame table or until the transmit window is closed because acknowledgments have not been received.

The receive frame table is used by the receiving device host and DLC to manage the incoming traffic. It queues data in receive buffers for the DLC and points to the location of the data throughout memory. The DLC uses the pointers to store incoming I frames. It also uses the function codes in the receive frame table to direct its operations.

As data are passed from the communications link and the USART, the DLC compares the address field to the remote and local address registers in the station table. If the address is correct, the N(S) is compared with the DLC V(R). If the sequencing is correct, and the FCS check passes, the V(R) is incremented and the I field is passed to the receive memory buffer. When the end of the receive frame specification table is reached, the DLC sets bits in the station table to notify the host of the incoming data. The DLC chip performs other functions described in Chapter 11, such as sending back N(R)s to acknowledge traffic and issuing RR, RNR frames to control the flow of traffic.

WRITING A COMMUNICATIONS PROGRAM

If the reader has access to a personal computer and understands the rudiments of programming, it might prove interesting and enlightening to write a communications program. A detailed discussion on communications programming is beyond the scope of this book, but an examination of the communications I/O instructions of the BASIC language will provide a means to tie together the concepts discussed earlier in this chapter.

To begin the discussion, we examine the BASIC OPEN instruction. It operates like any other BASIC OPEN except it uses some different parameters:

OPEN "COM1: 2400,N,8,1" as 1 LEN = 128

Where: COM1 = the identifier of the port; 2400 = speed of bit transfer rate in bit/s; N = no parity checking; 8 = 8 bits per character; 1 = designation of one stop bit; as 1 = logical "file" identifier used with I/O statements; LEN = 128 specifies size of buffer in characters.

Several of the parameters need not be coded since BASIC defaults to predetermined values. To ensure their proper execution, it is recommended they be coded, since several versions of BASIC handle the parameters differently.

To program an IBM Personal Computer to use interrupt I/O, the bits in the Interrupt Enable Register (IER) must be set to enable interrupts. With these bits properly set, the computer typically branches to a software routine (which could be written by you or your personnel). The software examines other bits in the registers to determine the reason for the interrupt. For example, bit 1 of the line status register set to 1 would indicate that data has arrived and a program could then read the data from the receiver buffer register.

If a polling I/O convention is used, a software routine must set the interrupt enable bit to 0. Then the following actions must be programmed into the software:

- *Transmitting:* Continue sending as long as there are characters to send. Check various bits in the register to determine that the lines and modem are operational.
- *Receiving:* Continue testing to determine when a character is received. Program must also check to determine when all data has been received.

To perform actual I/O operations, the BASIC input and output instructions are used. For example, INPUT #1, AREA$ is an instruction to obtain input from file #1, which is moved into a buffer identified by AREA$.

To communicate with the registers at the port, the BASIC instruction INP is used for reading a register and OUT is used for writing a register.

Here are some examples of instructions that read and write the port registers:

MODSTST = INP(&H3FE)	Reads register 3FE (modem status register) into variable MODSTAT
OUT(&H3F8,DATA)	Sends the character stored in the variable data to the transmitter holding register (3F8)

With a little imagination, you can alter the registers stored in memory with BASIC statements to control the port and modem communications operations. However, be aware that many off-the-shelf programs are readily available for you to use. The coding of a full-function I/O program is time consuming and deceptively complex. So, you may wish to experiment with your own program, but load another program for your ongoing "production" runs.

SUGGESTED READINGS

Surprisingly, little literature exists on ports beyond the vendors' technical references. The Hayes Company [HAYE83] has an instructive manual on its interface with the IBM Personal Computer. [GOFT86] describes the port from the perspective of the UART chip and the BASIC language. Perhaps the best overall reference on the subject is [MCNA82].

QUESTIONS

TRUE/FALSE

1. A port's input/output operations are controlled by either polling or interrupt operations.
2. A programmer is not given access to the port control registers.
3. The IBM personal computer communications port is typically an asynchronous interface.
4. The port services only the physical level.
5. Shared memory is an efficient method of communications between host I/O software and the DLC chip set.
6. Describe the characteristics of I/O control with polling and interrupts. Explain the advantages and disadvantages of each.
7. Describe the main functions of a UART chip.
8. Examine Figure 12-6. The entries in shared memory reflect the data link control (DLC) level actions between a host machine and the DLC logic. From the knowledge gained in Chapters 10, 11, and 12 describe the functions of each entry.

SELECTED ANSWERS

1. True.
2. False. The registers are designed to be manipulated by program control.
3. True.
4. False. Some ports have integrated both the physical level and data link level functions.
5. True.

CHAPTER 13

The Network Layer

INTRODUCTION

This chapter examines the network layer and its principal functions: routing and switching. The layer is also responsible for overall management of the network and this important task is explained. As with other chapters in Part II, several major standards and vendor products are also discussed.

Three switching techniques are explained: (a) circuit switching; (b) message switching; and (c) packet switching. We concentrate on packet switching since it has become the prevalent approach for switched data networks and for control networks in telephone systems. The broadcast networks are examined in Chapter 19.

The reader should also remember that we are building design methodologies for networks, and the earlier chapters dealing with traffic engineering and queuing theory will be referenced in this chapter with the assumption that the reader has read the sections in Chapters 5 and 6 titled "Traffic Engineering" and "Multiplexer Capacity" respectively.

Before delving into the actual switching and routing technologies and examples, we will take a look at the OSI convention for defining network services.

DEFINING NETWORK SERVICES WITH X.213

The 1988 Blue Book X.213 recommendation is quite similar to the 1984 Red Book version. The principal difference is the addition of an appendix on network addresses. Appendix 13A in this chapter covers this topic.

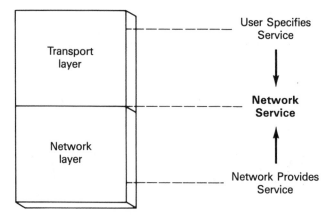

FIGURE 13-1. Network Service Provisions

The interconnection between the transport and network layers is of special significance to an end user because these layers represent the delineation between the network (lower three layers) and the user (upper four layers). The relationship of the layers is shown in Figure 13-1. In this section, we learn how the layers communicate. CCITT X.213 is used as the example for this subject. The ISO publishes a similar document designated DIS 8348.

The network layer is responsible for providing transparent transfer of data between the network service users. Ideally, the users do not know about the specific characteristics of the underlying services. For example, the network service users are unaware of the underlying subnetwork or subnetworks. Indeed, the subnetworks might be dissimilar (heterogeneous).

The network service is responsible for providing routing and relaying functions between the two users. The network service is not concerned with the format, syntax, semantics, or content of the data it transfers.

As with other layers, the network layer allows the network service user to request certain qualities of service (QOS). In addition, the network service provides addressing schemes that allow the network service users to refer to each other without ambiguity.

The network layer allows two network service users to exchange data with each other through one network connection or multiple network connections. The network service user may also be flow-controlled by the network service through the use of queues at the NSAPs (see Figure 13-2). This depends entirely on the type, quality, and speed of the underlying subnetworks. In some instances, the network service user may wish to transfer data with expedited protocol data units as well. The network services may also include (a) specific acknowledgments of data; (b) release of network connection (in which case the data may be destroyed); (c) resets; and (d) synchronization procedures. All these important concepts are explained in this chapter.

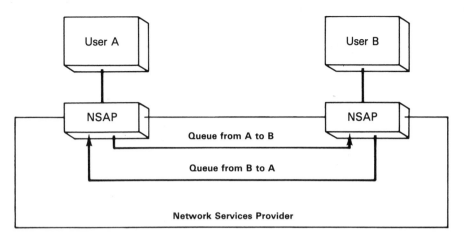

NSAP: Network Service Access Point

FIGURE 13-2. Network Connection Queue Model

Network Service Primitives and State Diagrams

From the discusions in previous chapters, the reader may now have an idea of how the network services are invoked. As with all OSI layers, they are invoked with primitives. Once again, we return to this subject, because it is fundamental to the concept of layered protocols. The primitives used by the network service are illustrated in Table 13-1. The parameters are also shown with the primitives. These primitives are used in various sequences to perform network establishment, network release, and of course, data transfer. The parameters required in the primitives are described next.

The addresses in the parameters are all NSAP addresses. (Again, refer to Figure 13-2.) These addresses are variable length, with a maximum length of 32 characters. The called address identifies the receiving NSAP. The calling address parameter identifies the requesting address of the NSAP. The responding address identifies the address of the NSAP to which the actual network connection has been established.

The receipt confirmation selection parameter stipulates if the network connection will use receipt confirmation. If this parameter is accepted by the local and remote network service users, then subsequent data primitives can request the confirmation of actual data through the use of the confirmation request parameter of the N-DATA request protocol data unit. The expedited data selection parameter stipulates the use of expedited data transfer during the actual network connection. Expedited data is used for higher priority traffic. The quality of service (QOS) parameters are invoked during session establishment. These parameters are explained later.

Figure 13-3 summarizes the network primitives and the various ways that they can be used. A brief description is provided here to explain each possibility.

TABLE 13-1. Network Service Primitives (X.213)

Primitive	Parameters
N-CONNECT	(Called Address, Calling Address, Receipt Confirmation Selection, Expedited Data Selection, Quality of Service Parameter Set, NS User-Data.)
N-CONNECT indication	(Called Address, Calling Address, Receipt Confirmation Selection, Expedited Data Selection, Quality of Service Parameter Set, NS User-Data.)
N-CONNECT response	(Responding Address, Receipt Confirmation Selection, Expedited Data Selection, Quality of Service Parameter Set, NS User-Data.)
N-CONNECT confirm	(Responding Address, Receipt Confirmation Selection, Expedited Data Selection, Quality of Service Parameter Set, NS User-Data.)
N-DATA request	(NS User-Data, Confirmation request.)
N-DATA indication	(NS User-Data, Confirmation request.)
N-DATA ACKNOWLEDGE request	—
N-DATA ACKNOWLEDGE indication	—
N-EXPEDITED-DATA request	(NS User-Data.)
N-EXPEDITED-DATA indication	(NS User-Data.)
N-RESET request	(Reason.)
N-RESET indication	(Originator, Reason.)
N-RESET response	—
N-RESET confirm	—
N-DISCONNECT request	(Reason, NS User-Data, Responding Address.)
N-DISCONNECT indication	(Originator, Reason, NS User-Data, Responding Address.)

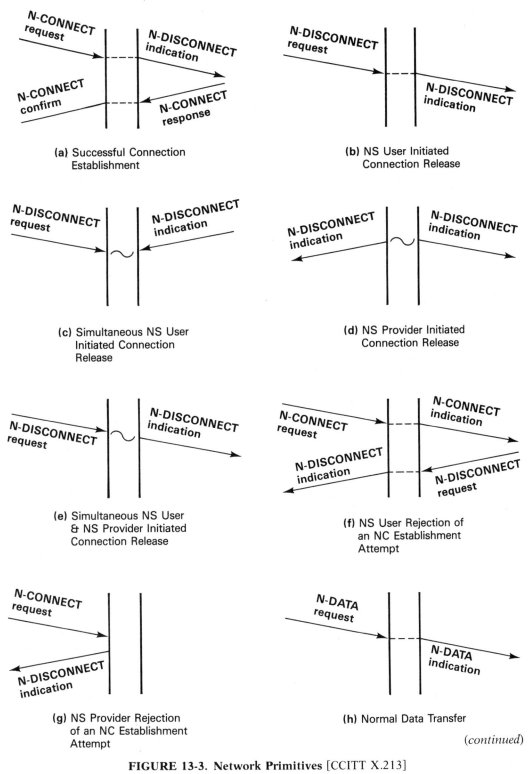

(a) Successful Connection
Establishment

(b) NS User Initiated
Connection Release

(c) Simultaneous NS User
Initiated Connection
Release

(d) NS Provider Initiated
Connection Release

(e) Simultaneous NS User
& NS Provider Initiated
Connection Release

(f) NS User Rejection of
an NC Establishment
Attempt

(g) NS Provider Rejection
of an NC Establishment
Attempt

(h) Normal Data Transfer

(continued)

FIGURE 13-3. Network Primitives [CCITT X.213]

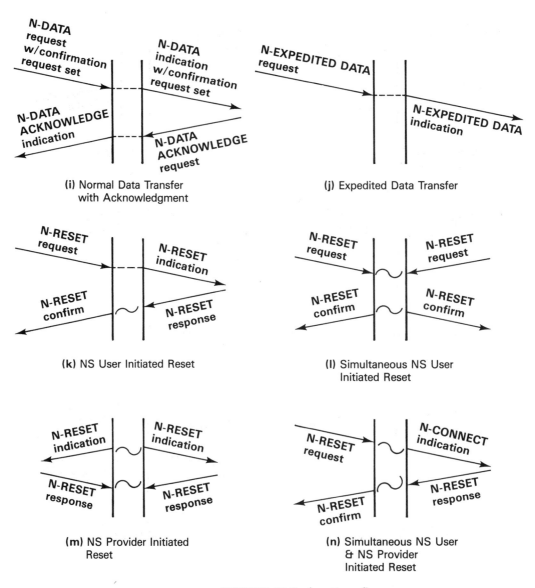

(i) Normal Data Transfer
with Acknowledgment

(j) Expedited Data Transfer

(k) NS User Initiated Reset

(l) Simultaneous NS User
Initiated Reset

(m) NS Provider Initiated
Reset

(n) Simultaneous NS User
& NS Provider
Initiated Reset

FIGURE 13-3. *(continued).*

It is recognized that these figures may seem somewhat abstract. However, later in this chapter we relate these primitives to actual protocols and data flows. With that in mind, let us examine the permissible primitive sequences.

Figure 13-3(a) depicts a typical successful connection procedure where the two end users provide the necessary primitives for the network connection establishment. Figure 13-3(b) depicts a typical connection release occurring at the initiation of the network service user.

It is possible for both network service users to initiate a connection release at approximately the same time. This situation is depicted in Figure 13-3(c). The figure shows that both users initiate the release simultaneously. Figure 13-3(d) illustrates the network provider initiating the release. The release is in the form of an N-DISCONNECT indication primitive to both users. Yet another possibility is shown in Figure 13-3(e), where the network provider and the network service user initiates the release at approximately the same time. Figure 13-3(f) shows an establishment attempt that is rejected by the end user. In contrast, Figure 13-3(g) shows the rejection coming from the network.

Figure 13-3(h) depicts a normal data transfer between the two users. In this situation, there is no acknowledgment of the traffic. Figure 13-3(i) shows the normal data transfer with acknowledgment back to the originator of the traffic, and Figure 13-3(j) shows an expedited data transfer mode.

As stated earlier, the network connection can be released. Figure 13-3(k) shows a reset occurring from the network service user. Figure 13-3 (l) shows the users both initiating a reset. Figure 13-3(m) shows the network issuing a reset. Figure 13-3(n) shows the release occurring simultaneously between the network service user and the network service provider.

The concepts illustrated in Figure 13-3 require considerable thought in their implementation. For example, the various possibilities of reset shown in Figures 13-3(k) through 13-3(n) require that the network provider and both end users are aware of the reset at the proper time and that all data units are recovered. These seemingly simple tasks offer many potential pitfalls to the unwary and considerable material in this chapter and Chapters 14 and 15 will provide the reader with more detailed information on the actions shown in Figure 13-3.

To complete this description of the network services, Figure 13-4 shows the state diagram for the various primitive sequences of a network connection.

Quality of Services (QOS) Parameters for Network Layer

The quality of service parameters for the transport layer are generally mapped directly to the complementary quality of services parameters for the network layer.

Several important aspects of the QOS parameters are depicted in Table 13-2. Most of the parameters deal with speed or reliability of the service. Table 13-2(a) shows the performance-oriented parameters and Table 13-2(b) shows the nonperformance-oriented parameters.

Functions of the QOS Parameters. The QOS parameters depicted in Table 13-2 perform the network services described in this section for the network connection between two end points. Once the connection is established, the network service users have the same knowledge of the QOS. This pertains to a connection through one network or multiple subnetworks.

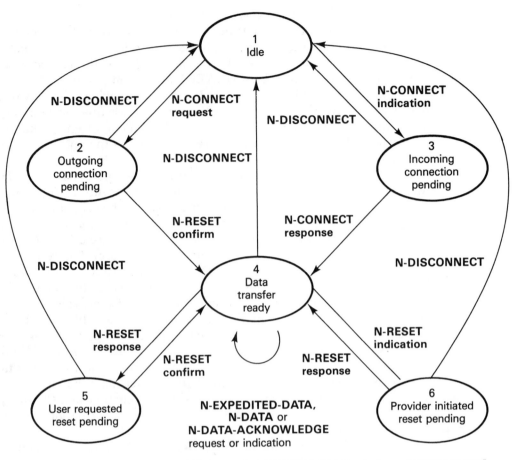

FIGURE 13-4. State Diagram for CCITT X.213 Procedures [CCITT X.213]

TABLE 13-2(a). QOS Performance Parameters

| *Phase of* | PERFORMANCE CRITERIA | |
Connection	*Speed*	*Accuracy/Reliability*
NC Establishment	NC Establishment Delay	NC Establishment Failure Probability (includes misconnection/refusal)
Data Transfer	Throughput Transit Delay	Residual Error Rate NC Resilience Transfer Failure Probability
NC Release	NC Release Delay	NC Release Failure Probability

TABLE 13-2(b). QOS Nonperformance Parameters

NC Protection
NC Priority
Maximum Acceptable Cost

The reader should examine these parameters carefully, because they are used by many networks today. They are also part of the ubiquitous X.25 protocol (discussed later).

NC Establishment Delay is the maximum acceptable delay between the issuance of the N-CONNECT request primitive and the associated N-CONNECT confirm primitive. This delay also includes the delay encountered at the remote user. Simply stated, it places a time limit on how long a user will wait to get a connection.

NC Establishment Failure Probability is the ratio of total connection failures to total connection attempts. The failure could occur for a number of reasons such as remote end refusal, expiration of an establishment delay timer, etc. It is a useful parameter for ascertaining the quality of the network service.

Throughput is measured for each direction of transfer through the network. Many private and public networks allow a user to "negotiate" throughput for each connection. Typically, the provision for a higher throughput rate will increase the cost to the user. Consequently, this QOS parameter allows a user to make cost/performance trade-offs for each network session.

Transit Delay is the time between the N-DATA request and its associated N-DATA indication. The time includes only successfully transferred NSDUs. Many public networks provide this feature as an option. It is becoming increasingly important as users become more conscious of network performance and response time.

Residual Error Rate is the total number of incorrect, lost or duplicate NSDUs to the total number of NSDUs transferred. It is defined as:

$$RER = [n(e) + n(l) + N(x)]/N$$

Where: RER = Residual error rate; $n(e)$ = incorrect NSDUs; $n(l)$ = lost NSDUs; $N(x)$ = duplicate NSDUs; N = total NSDUs transferred. This QOS parameter is useful when a user wishes to obtain a quantitative evaluation of the network service reliability. The reader may keep this formula in mind as the other layers are described; it is repeated in other specifications (to obtain consistency through the layers).

Transfer Failure Probability is the ratio of total transfer failures to total transfers. The ratio is calculated on an individual network connection. A failure is defined by an observed performance that is worse than the specified minimum level and is measured against three other QOS parameters: (a) Throughput; (b) Transit Delay, and (c) Residual Error Rate.

Network Connection Resilience is defined as the probability of (a) the network service provider invoking a disconnect and (b) the provider invoking a reset. Both actions come as a result of network actions and not a user request; see Figure 13-3. This parameter is quite important in evaluating the quality of a network. Several public networks publish their performance data relating to connection resilience.

Network Connection Release Delay is the maximum acceptable delay between a user disconnect request and a receipt of a disconnect indication (see Figure 13-3[g]); that is, when the user is able to initiate a new network connection request. This is an important consideration for users that need fast connections after "logging off" from a previous network session.

Network Connection Release Failure Probability is defined as the probability that the user is not able to initiate a new connection with a specified maximum release delay. It is the ratio of total network connection release failures to total release attempts.

Network Connection Protection is a qualitative QOS parameter to determine the extent to which the network service provider attempts to present unauthorized use of data This parameter, if used by a public network, is not often revealed to a user.

Network Connection Priority is defined as (a) the order in which the connections have their QOS degraded and (b) the order in which connections are broken. Typically, once a user obtains a network connection, it remains stable for the duration of the session.

Maximum Acceptable Cost, as its name implies, specifies the maximum acceptable cost to the user for a network connection. The costs are specified by the network in relative or absolute terms.

In summary, X.213 (and ISO 8348) serve as a model for defining network interfaces and network services. The X.213 and ISO 8348 primitives, QOS parameters, and queue concepts are used by a number of network vendors in their product lines.

We now examine the concepts of switching and routing and analyze several vendor products, as well as some recommended standards published by the CCITT and other groups.

CIRCUIT SWITCHING

Circuit switching provides a direct connection between two components. The direct connection of a circuit switch serves as an open "pipeline," permitting the two end users to utilize the facility as they see fit—within bandwidth and tariff limitations. Many telephone networks use circuit switching systems.

Circuit switching is arranged in one or a combination of three architectures: (a) concentration (more input lines than output lines), (b) expansion (more output lines than input lines), and (c) connection (an equal number of

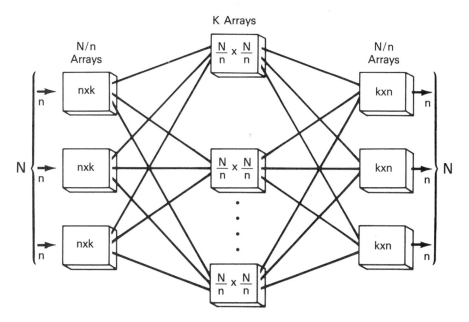

FIGURE 13-5. Circuit Switching (A basic set-up)

input and output lines). In its simplest form, a circuit switch is a N × M array of lines that connect to each other at crosspoints. In a large switching office, the N lines are input from the subscriber (terminals, computers, etc.), and the M lines are output to other switching offices.

Circuit switching is usually performed in more than one array or stage in order to reduce the number of crosspoints. If N lines are to be connected as in Figure 13-5, then N^2 crosspoints are required. Multistaging switches are economical for networks when $N \geqq 16^3$ [AMOS79]. Multistage networks are designed with fewer crosspoints, yielding a more economical arrangement.

A three-stage, multistage switch is shown in Figure 13-5. The input and output lines are divided into subgroups of N inputs and N outputs. The input first stage consists of n × k matrices. The k output is connected to one of the k center matrices. The third stage consists of k × n matrices connected from the center stage to the n outlets.

The center stage matrices are all N/n by N/n arrays that permit connections from any first stage to any third stage.

The total number of crosspoints for this three-stage switch is [BELL82]:

$$N_x = 2Nk + k(N/n)^2$$

Where: N_x = total number of crosspoints; N = number of input and output lines; n = size of each input/output group; k = number of center stage arrays.

Circuit switching only provides a path for the sessions between data communications components. Error checking, session establishment, frame flow control, frame formatting, selection of codes, and protocols are the responsibility of the users. Little or no care of the data traffic is provided in the circuit switching arrangement. Consequently, the telephone network is often used as the basic foundation for a data communications network, and additional facilities are added by the value-added carrier, network vendor, or user organization. Subsequent examples of other switching technologies (e.g., message and packet) often use circuit switching as the basic transmission media, and then provide additional functions and facilities such as store-and-forward services, protocol conversion, etc.

Dynamic Routing for Circuit-Switched Traffic

Many circuit switching systems are nondynamic; that is to say, the switching hierarchy cannot be changed to exploit traffic variations. In North America, AT&T and Northern Telecom have implemented dynamic routing methods. This new technology is not constrained by a fixed hierarchical structure, but allows a choice of path based on heavy overflow traffic from the fixed topology. Dynamic circuit-switched routing will replace much of the hierarchical network by 1990. Dynamic circuit-switching will result in fewer busy signals and faster connections to the end user.

Dynamic Nonhierarchical Routing (DNHR). AT&T's DNHR is based on differing time zone usages of the network (see Figure 13-6[a]). A day is divided into 10 time periods (load set periods), and a different preset routing sequence is set for each period. When a call is placed into the network, a preferred route is attempted. If the connection is unsuccessful, alternate routes will be attempted, depending on the time of day. A "crankback" signal is sent back to the originator in the event the call is unsuccessful.

DNHR is not real time, but a technique called the trunk status map (TSP) has been proposed for real time dynamic routing. TSP makes real time measurements of the trunks to determine the optimal route for the calls.

Dynamically Controlled Routing (DCR). Northern Telecom's DCR uses a centralized controller to manage the routing decisions of the exchanges (see Figure 13-6[b]). Every 10 seconds, the participating exchanges send status information to the network processor. This information is based primarily on exchange load and the availability of outgoing trunks.

DCR uses four exchange classifications within the network:

N: Stored program control, capable of dynamic routing. Used as a tandem for I/N exchanges.

I: Stored program control, capable of dynamic routing. Not used as a tandem.

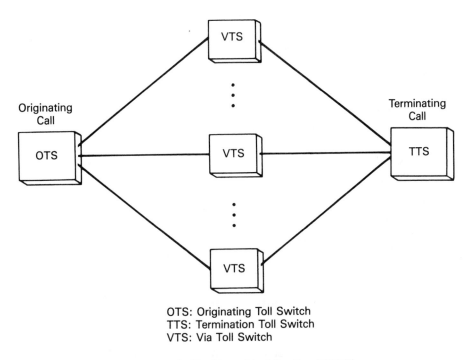

OTS: Originating Toll Switch
TTS: Termination Toll Switch
VTS: Via Toll Switch

(a) Dynamic Nonhierarchical Routing (DNHR)

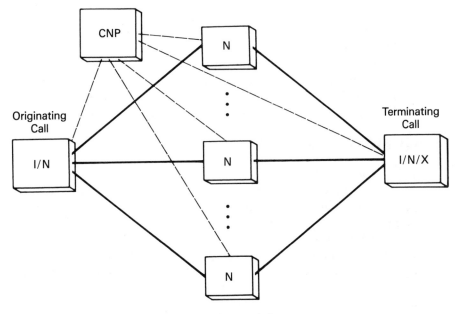

CNP: Control Network Processor

(b) Dynamically Controlled Routing (DCR)

FIGURE 13-6. Dynamic Routing for Circuit-Switched Traffic

X: Limited capability exchange. Used only as a destination exchange.

Z: All other exchanges.

A call set-up proceeds in a manner similar to DNHR. A primary route is attempted first, then the remaining tandem routes are chosen based on the status of the exchange and its outgoing trunk capacity.

Box 13-1 provides a comparison of DNHR and DCR. (Routing algorithms are discussed in more detail later in this chapter.) Both systems will most likely evolve to include other enhanced techniques ([HEGG85], [LIPP85], and [NARE82]).

The use of CCITT Signalling System No. 7 (SS7; see Chapter 5) provides a powerful tool for passing status information between these exchanges. Interestingly, DCR uses the X.25 protocol for the exchange of network processor information between the exchanges.

MESSAGE SWITCHING

In the 1960s and 1970s, the pervasive method for switching data communications traffic was message switching. The technology is still widely used in certain applications, such as electronic mail. (A message was defined as a complete unit of data, such as a bank transaction.) The switch is typically a specialized computer. It is responsible for accepting traffic from attached terminals and computers (through dial-up or leased lines). It examines the address in the header of the message and switches (routes) the traffic to the receiving station. Unlike circuit switching in telephone networks, message switching is a store-and-forward technology: the messages are stored temporarily on disk units at the switches.

Since the data are usually stored, the traffic is not considered to be interactive or real time. However, selected traffic can be sent through a message switch at very high speeds by establishing levels of priority for different types of traffic. High-priority traffic is queued for a shorter period than low-priority traffic. This approach can support interactive applications.

The disk queuing also provides a method to smooth traffic by queuing the lower-priority traffic during peak periods. The queuing also decreases the chances of blocking traffic due to network congestion. For example, the traffic can be stored temporarily and later routed to stations when they are available to accept it.

Message switching has served the industry well, but it suffers from three deficiencies. First, since it is inherently a master/slave structure, the entire network can be lost if the switch fails, because all traffic must go through the message switch. Consequently, many organizations install a duplicate (duplexed) switch, which assumes the role of the primary switch in the event of failure. The second major deficiency stems from the hub arrangement of a message switch. Since all traffic must go through one switch, the switch itself is a potential bottleneck. Degraded response time and decreased throughput can result from such an arrangement. Third, message switching does not utilize the communications lines as efficiently as other techniques discussed in the next section.

PACKET SWITCHING

Because of the problems with message switching, the industry began to move toward a different data communications switching structure in the 1970s: packet switching. Packet switching distributes the risk to more than one switch, reduces vulnerability to network failure, and provides better utilization of the lines than does message switching.

Packet switching is so named because user data (for example, messages) are divided into smaller pieces. These pieces, or packets, have protocol control information (headers) placed around them and are routed through the network as independent entities.

A packet switching network is illustrated in Figure 13-7. The topology is obviously different from message switching. First, more switches allow the network load to be distributed to multiple switching sites. Second, additional communications lines are attached to the switches. The arrangement provides the opportunity to perform alternate routing around failed or busy nodes and channels. As a consequence, a packet switching network exhibits high availability to end users.

Packet switching gained interest initially as a means to provide secure voice transmissions. The technology of packet voice transmission did not develop at that time. It was too complex and the switches were too slow to handle real time voice traffic. However, as we shall see later in the book (Chapter 19), packet voice is now a reality.

It was recognized that packet switching would work well with data communications traffic, because many devices, such as keyboard terminals,

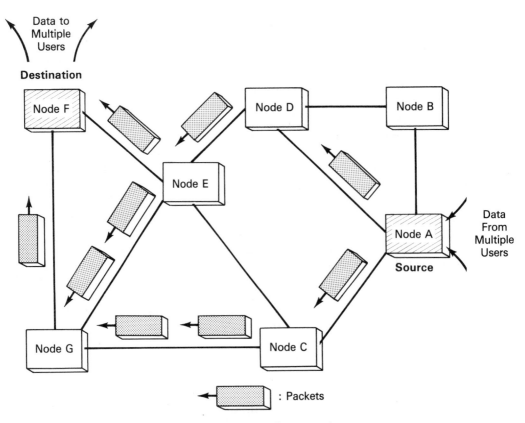

FIGURE 13-7. Packet Switching

transmit traffic in bursts. The data is sent on the channel, which is then idle while a terminal user inputs more data into the terminal or pauses to think about a problem. The idle channel time translates into wasted line capacity. One of the concepts of packet switching is to interleave multiple transmissions from several terminals onto one channel; in effect, packet switching achieves statistical time division multiplexing across a communications line. This approach provides better use of the expensive communications channel.

Packet switching goes one step further than simple multiplexing of the communications lines. Packet logic can also multiplex multiple user sessions onto a single communications port of the computer. Instead of dedicating a port to one user, the system interleaves the bursts of traffic from multiple users across one port. The user perceives a dedicated port is being used when actually the user terminal or program is sharing a port with other users.

Studies have revealed that communications traffic is often asymmetrical; that is, transmissions occur more in one direction between two devices than in the other. A good example of asymmetrical communications is in computer-to-terminal traffic: the terminal often transmits less data than it receives from the computer. Packet switching provides a facility to smooth the asymmetrical flow across the channel by interleaving multiple users onto the channel. For instance, in Figure 13-7, what might be a computer at B and a terminal at D from one user session could be reversed by having another user share the same line with the opposite structure: a terminal at B and a computer at D. Packet switching balances the traffic across many channels by switching traffic among the many users to decrease the asymmetrical aspect of the traffic flow.

Packet switching also provides an attractive feature for connecting the terminals and computers together for a session. In a circuit-switched telephone structure, connect time is often slow. A switched telephone call requires that a number be dialed and that all circuits be set up for the call to be routed to the destination. However, with a packet-switching system, dedicated leased lines are available for multiple users to transmit and receive their data traffic. The lines do not require any circuit set-ups, since they are permanently connected through the system. The technique can improve the slow connect time associated with multiple telephone circuit switches.

In summary, the major goals of packet switching are:

- Provide for statistical multiplexing capabilities of the channel and the port
- Smooth the asymmetrical traffic among multiple users
- Provide for fast response time to all users of the facility
- Provide for high availability of the network to all users
- Provide for distribution of risks and sharing of resources

When and When Not to Use Packet Switching

How does an organization know when to use or not to use packet switching systems? With the preceding discussion in mind, one way to address this question is to compare the following four alternatives for connecting DTEs:

Public telephone dial-up system
Private, nonswitched channels
Public packet networks
Private packet networks

Organizations with relatively low data-transfer rates benefit from using public dial-up lines. If sessions between DTEs are short and the connections between the DTEs are local, the dial-up approach makes good sense if the user does not mind the dial-up delay and an occasional busy signal. Since dial-up charges are based on time and distance, infrequent and short-distance transmission favor the use of the public telephone system.

Private leased lines are a viable option for organizations that experience heavy, constant traffic throughout a 24-hour period and/or cannot tolerate the delays of dial-up. The organization can use the permanently connected leased lines continuously. Moreover, companies that establish multidrop connections on their private channels usually benefit from using the leased channel option, because the multidrops permit a more effective sharing of the channel.

Public packet networks (several of which are discussed in this chapter) are sometimes called value-added carriers (VACs) because they provide value-added services to their customers. For example, VACs lease lines from the telephone carrier, add packet switches and protocol converters to the lines, and sell the service to any customer willing to pay the fees. Organizations with low to medium traffic volumes can usually benefit from subscribing to a public packet network. Also, for organizations that are spread out over a large geographical area, the public packet network may be better economically, since most of the public packet carriers charge primarily on volume of traffic, not on the distance between user stations.

Many organizations have established private packet networks or private circuit-switched systems. There are several reasons for private systems. For medium to high traffic volumes, private networks are more cost effective than dedicated private lines.

The reader should be aware that changing carrier offerings and tariffs require a careful analysis of the options vis-à-vis a company's needs. Moreover, the value-added aspects of packet networks could alter a user organization's decisions to favor a packet network alternative.

Choosing the Packet Route

In this section, we examine one of the principal functions of the network layer: routing of traffic. The literature on this subject is vast and several references are cited at the end of this chapter.

Packet switched networks are designed to route user traffic based on a variety of criteria, generally referred to as *least-cost routing*. The name does not mean that routing is based solely on obtaining the least-cost route in the literal sense. Other factors are often part of the routing algorithm:

- Capacity of the link
- Number of packets awaiting transmission onto the link
- Load leveling through the network
- Security requirements for the link
- Type of traffic vis-à-vis the type of link
- Number of intermediate links between the transmitting and receiving stations
- Ability to reach (connect to) intermediate nodes, and of course, the final receiving station

Whatever the least-cost criteria may be, the network designer's goal is to determine the least-cost, end-to-end path between any two communicating stations.

Even though networks vary in least-cost criteria, three constraints must be considered: (a) delay, (b) throughput, and (c) connectivity. If delay is excessive or if throughput is too little, the network does not meet the needs of the user community. The third constraint is quite obvious: the communications devices must be able to reach each other; otherwise, all other least-cost criteria are irrelevant.

The algorithms used to route the packets through the network vary. As we shall see in this chapter, some algorithms are set up at a central site or executed at each individual packet switch. They may provide a static, end-to-end path between the two users of the network, or they may route the traffic through different packet switches. We shall also see that they vary in how they adapt to changing network conditions. Some algorithms adapt only to failures, and some adapt as traffic conditions change.

The data communications industry has focused attention on two classes of packet routing algorithms. The first technique, called bifurcated routing, is designed to minimize the average network delay. The second technique, called shortest-path routing, provides a least-cost path between the communicating pair of users. Shortest-path routing is designed to minimize the delay to the users. Since bifurcated routing is not used much, we mention it in passing only. For further information, the reader can examine [SCHW77].

Routing Algorithms. The shortest-path algorithms are classified as follows [SCHW80]:

Algorithm A
Algorithm B
Algorithm B, Decentralized Version

Algorithm A is one of the most widely used routing techniques and is used as our model. It has also been used to establish optimum designs and network topologies. The concepts discussed here are from [DIJK59] and [AHO74].

Figure 13-8 shows an example of how algorithm A is applied, using node A as the source and node J as the destination (sink). (Please be aware that the topology represented in the figure was prepared for illustrative purposes, not for implementation.) Algorithm A is defined generally as one in which:

- Least-cost criteria weights are assigned to the paths in the network (Figure 13-8[a]).
- Each node is labeled (identified) with its least-cost criteria from the

source along a known path. Initially, no paths are known, so each node is labeled with infinity.

- Each node is examined in relation to all nodes adjacent to it. (The source node is the first node considered and becomes the working node) (see Figure 13-8[b]). This step is actually a one-time occurrence, wherein the source node is initialized with the costs of all its adjacent nodes.

- Least-cost criteria labels are assigned to each of the nodes adjacent to the working node. Labels change if a shorter path is found from this node to the source node.

- After the adjacent nodes are labeled (or relabeled), all other nodes in the network are examined. If one has a smaller value in its label, its label becomes permanent and it becomes the working node (see Figure 13-7[c]).

- If the sum of the node's label is less than the label on an adjacent node, the adjacent node's label is changed, because a shorter path has been found to the source node. In Figure 13-7(d), node E is relabeled because node D is a shorter route through node C.

- Another working node is selected and the process repeats itself until all possibilities have been searched. The final labels reveal the least-cost, end-to-end path between the source and the other nodes. These nodes are considered to be within a set N as it pertains to the source node.

The following general statements describe the preceding discussion [SCHW87]:

1. Let $D(v)$ = sum of link weights on a given path
2. Let $c(i,j)$ = the cost between node i and j
3. Set $n = \{1\}$
4. For each node (v) not in N, set $D(v) = C(1,v)$
5. For each step, find a node w not in N for which $D(w)$ is a minimum; add w to set N
6. Update $D(v)$ for all nodes still not in N by:
   $$D(v) \leftarrow \min [D(v), D(w) + c(w,v)]$$
7. Repeat steps (4) through (6) until all nodes are in set N.

The use of the algorithm is shown in Table 13-3. The steps are successively performed until all nodes are in N. The process is performed for each node, and a routing table created for the node's use. Each node's table is constructed in the manner just discussed.

The routing topology for node A is shown in Figure 13-9. The numbers in parentheses represent the order of selection as reflected in Table 13-3.

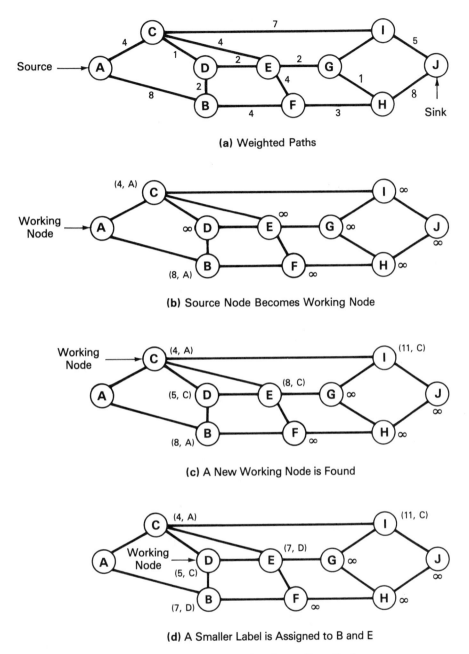

(a) Weighted Paths

(b) Source Node Becomes Working Node

(c) A New Working Node is Found

(d) A Smaller Label is Assigned to B and E

FIGURE 13-8. Determining Least-Cost Path

It should prove useful to pause momentarily and examine the weighted paths in Figure 13-9. One might question why certain paths are weighted with large or small numbers. As an explanation, consider that node A could have two communication links available for transmission. The link from A

TABLE 13-3. Choosing the Nodes

Step	N	A(B)	A(C)	A(D)	A(E)	A(F)	A(G)	A(H)	A(I)	A(J)
Initial	{A}	8	4	∞	∞	∞	∞	∞	∞	∞
1	{A,C}	8	(4)	5	7	∞	∞	∞	11	∞
2	{A,C,D}	8	4	(5)	7	∞	∞	∞	11	∞
3	{A,C,D,B}	7	4	5	(7)	11	∞	∞	11	∞
4	{A,C,D,B,E}	(7)	4	5	7	11	9	∞	11	∞
5	{A,C,D,B,E,F}	7	4	5	7	11	(9)	14	11	∞
6	{A,C,D,B,E,F,G}	7	4	5	7	11	9	(10)	10	∞
7	{A,C,D,B,E,F,G,H}	7	4	5	7	11	9	10	(10)	18
8	{A,C,D,B,E,F,G,H,I}	7	4	5	7	(11)	9	10	10	15
9	{A,C,D,B,E,F,G,H,I,J}	7	4	5	7	11	9	10	10	(15)

to C could be a microwave land link and the A to B link could be a satellite circuit. If an interactive user application were being routed through node A, the satellite link would be heavily weighted to discourage its use. As another example, the user data may need a secure link and the A to B line may not use encryption/decryption devices. It should also be recognized that networks may not route traffic based on factors such as security, or other quality of service parameters, but rely on performance criteria such as minimum delay.

The network capacity is like a chain, which is no stronger than its weakest link. A network has no more capacity than a specific combination of its lowest-capacity resources.

One might argue that packet switching provides the means to route traffic around nodes and links that are either saturated or of insufficient capacity to handle the load. Nonetheless, at some point the traffic will reach an "area" within the network that is a bottleneck. This bottleneck limits the throughput of the entire network.

To determine why this limit exists, assume the least-cost weights in Figure 13-8 represent the maximum link and node capacities for traffic flow in one direction. A set of nodes and links can be identified that act as the lowest common resource for network capacity.

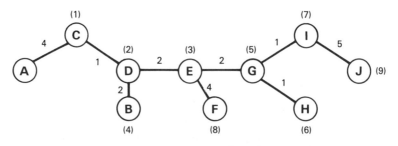

FIGURE 13-9. Routing Topology from Node A

One method to obtain this information is the *cut*. A cut is defined as the removal of connections (the paths) between two nodes such that the two nodes are disconnected. In other words, they cannot reach each other.

Network designers look for a minimum cut through a network. This term describes an area with the minimum capacity and thus the potential bottleneck. Each cut is given a capacity which is the sum of the weights of the links in the cut. The cut with the lowest sum is the minimum cut.

Figure 13-10 shows several possible cuts of our example. (Other cuts are possible, but are not shown in order to keep the figure simple.) It is obvious that cuts 1 and 3 are the potential bottleneck since their maximum capacity of 12 is less than that of the other cuts. Indeed, if the traffic from the source exceeds the minimum cut capacity, then the potential bottleneck becomes a real bottleneck. (However, in our example the source itself is a minimum cut, which is a simple method to manage congestion.)

Delay Analysis in Packet Networks

It is evident that packet networks rely on queues. Basic queuing theory is introduced in Chapters 5 and 6. We continue these discussions and expand them to examine several equations relating to delay analysis. It is assumed the reader has studied the queuing material in those chapters.

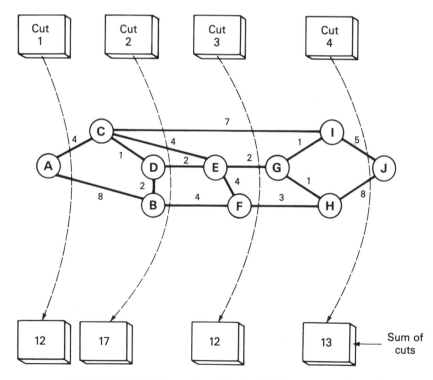

FIGURE 13-10. Some Possible Cuts (all cuts not shown)

First, recall that the probability of n users (i.e., packets) arriving at a switch during an interval of length t with a λ mean arrival rate, is defined by the Poisson process:

$$P_n(t) = \frac{(\lambda t)^n}{n!} \, e^{-\lambda t}$$

Where: $P_n(t)$ = probability of n customers arriving at an interval of length t; λ = mean arrival rate.

The delay analysis is also based on a model of a queue called the M/M/1 queue. The notation takes the form of A/B/C, where A = the arrival distribution; B = the service distribution, and C = the number of servers. The M/M/1 model has the attributes of: Poisson arrivals/general service distribution/a single server.

The M/M/1 queuing system possesses a remarkable quality: the probability of the remaining service time of an object (e.g., packet) in a queue is independent of how long the object has been in the queue. The system can be fully depicted by the objects in the systems, that is to say, (a) the mean arrival rate (λ) and (b) the mean service rate (μ).

It can be demonstrated that the M/M/1 queue model can be used to define several equations to determine the time delay through the packet switch queue. A simple formula (Little's formula) is used [LITT61]:

$$N = \lambda \, T$$

Where: N = average queue length; λ = average arrival rate; T = mean time delay in the system.

Using Little's formula and other equations in Chapters 5 and 6, the total waiting time (t) in a packet switch queue is [TANE81]:

$$T = \frac{N}{\lambda} - \frac{P/\lambda}{1-p} - \frac{1/\mu}{1-p} - \frac{1}{\mu-\lambda}$$

This equation can be rewritten to reflect the service time in bits per second:

$$T_i = 1/\mu C_i - \lambda_i$$

Where: T_i = queuing and transmission time; i = channel$_i$; C_i = capacity of channel i in bit/s.

We must recognize that the circuits in a packet network are not isolated from each other. For example, the queue outputs of several M/M/1 servers could be the input to another queue. Fortunately, analysis has shown:

- The output of several M/M/1 servers into another is also a Poisson process [BURK56].
- A network of M/M/1 queues can be analyzed as if the queues are isolated from each other, if the mean input rate is known [JACK57].

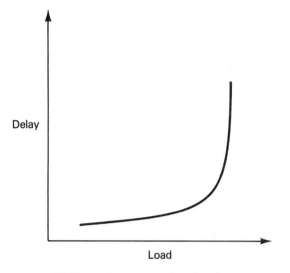

FIGURE 13-11. Load and Delay

The queuing and transmission time equations again demonstrate what we learned in earlier discussions on queuing (see Figure 13-11):

- As the load in a network increases, so does the throughput, to a certain point.
- The average number of packets in the queues leads to an increased time delay in the queues.
- It is quite difficult to achieve short delay and high throughput at the same time.

Let us return to the earlier discussion on minimum cuts. As traffic is increased in a network, the smallest cut is the first to saturate. To provide some relief to the bottleneck, it is possible to load split the traffic and route some of it around the smallest capacity link (node) in the cut to the other routes. While this would provide more capacity, the minimal cut is still the bottleneck to the network. Nevertheless, the use of packet routing can certainly overcome temporary congestion problems. With this thought in mind, let's move to the subject of packet routing.

Packet Routing Methods

Network routing entails the use of logic (software, hardware, or microcode) at the switches to move the data packets through the network to the end destination. Network routing is generally based on three primary goals:

1. Provide for the shortest possible delay and highest throughput
2. Route the packet through the network at the least cost

3. Provide each packet with the maximum possible security and reliability

Network routing can be categorized in a number of ways (see Figure 13-12). Two contrasting categories are centralized and distributed routing. The centralized routing network provides for a network control center (NCC) to determine the routing of the packets through the network. The packet switches are not as intelligent as the central site, which can translate into decreased costs at the switching nodes. Centralized control suffers from the possible vulnerability of one central site to possible failure. Consequently, NCCs are usually duplicated (duplexed) for back-up.

Distributed routing requires more intelligent nodes in the network. However, it provides more network resiliency, because each node makes its own routing decisions without regard to a centralized network control center. Distributed routing is also more complex, as we will see shortly.

Before discussing the actual routing schemes, it is necessary to define some terms.

- *Traffic multiplication effect* (TME): A given packet generates additional, identical packets
- *Node "route-around"*: Bypassing a failed or busy node or channel
- *Packet die-out (packet kill)*: Diminishing the effect of TME

Most packet networks perform routing by the use of a routing directory or table. The directory contains addresses that the switch uses to transmit a packet to one of several possible output channels at the switch. Packet network directories are organized around three approaches.

- *Fixed (or static) directory*: Changes at system generation time only. Remains static for every user session
- *Session-oriented or "Logon" directory*: Changes with each user session. Static for an individual session

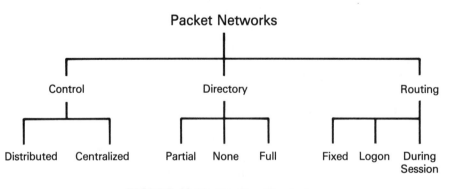

FIGURE 13-12. Routing Strategies

• *Adaptive or dynamic directory*: Changes within each user session

The directory systems are further classified as partial-path directory or full-path directory. A partial-path directory usually contains only the adjacent nodes to a particular switch, i.e., those nodes connected directly to the switch. A full-path directory contains the entire set of intermediate nodes for the packet to traverse to its final destination. Another alternative is the absence of a directory, in which case routing decisions are made by some other means.

The routing techniques described herein illustrate the wide diversity of methods used by network designers. Some of these techniques are widely used; others are not used much or are subjects of research projects.

"Directory-less" Routing. As the name implies, a directory-less network does not use a routing directory. One approach to "directory-less" network routing is packet flooding. Every possible path is used between a transmitting and receiving station; duplicate packets are sent on all output channels and routed through the network. An advantage to flooding is that, since every path through the network is used, the first copy of the packet to arrive at the end site will have gone through the shortest delay (which meets one of the major goals of network routing). However, the traffic multiplication effect (TME) is quite severe with packet flooding, and the load on the network is proportional to the connectivity of the network, i.e., more channels and alternate paths create more traffic. Notwithstanding, packet flooding provides for a highly resilient network since a packet copy will always get through to the end destination as long as one path exists between the sending and receiving stations. Some military networks use this technique because it is very robust.

The traffic multiplication effect (TME) can be diminished by adding some additional bookkeeping logic at each switch. For example, the design can be set up as follows: If each receiving node recognizes a duplicate packet, it discards the packet and does not send any additional copies of the packet. In other words, it forwards only one copy of the packet. This process is called die-out (or packet kill), and substantially reduces TME. Packet copies gradually disappear as the packets make their way toward the end destination.

Flooding is part of the United States Defense Communication Agency (DCA) Defense Switched Network (DSN) [HEGG85]. DSN uses the CCITT Signalling System No. 7 (SS7) from the originating exchange to send Search-Out messages to all possible routes to the final destination. The destination exchange returns a Search-Back message to the originator to identify the best route for the call.

Directory Routing. Most packet networks use some type of directory routing. The directory contains information used by the packet switch to choose the best path to the next node in the network. The directory may contain information about all nodes (a full directory), or may contain information only about the adjacent nodes (a partial directory).

Network routing is typically performed based on a number of criteria called least-cost routing. As we learned earlier, the name does not mean the routing decisions are made solely on the basis of cost factors. Other factors are usually part of the process, such as delay, etc.

The directories typically remain static and are changed if the network undergoes a topology change, or a link or node fails. Some networks use adaptive and dynamic methods to update the directories to reflect traffic conditions and the switches' queue lengths. With such a method, the packets may take different paths through the network and arrive out of order at the final destination. The network then resequences the packets before passing them to the end user.

The taxonomy depicted in Figure 13-12 is further examined in the next section.

EXAMPLES OF NETWORK LAYERS

This section describes the network layer protocols of three private and public network vendors. The following systems are chosen for review, because they are illustrative of the various approaches:

The SNA Path Control Layer
The DECnet Routing Layer
ARPANET

SNA ROUTING WITH THE PATH CONTROL LAYER

SNA uses a static and partial directory to manage the routing of the data between remotely connected LUs. Figure 13-13 depicts a typical SNA topology.

SNA is organized around the concept of domains and nodes. Nodes constitute domains. Two kinds of nodes exist. The subarea node consists of a mainframe computer and a front end. The subarea contains the programs that make routing decisions. Peripheral nodes contain cluster controllers and/or terminals and do not make routing decisions.

When a user wishes to use the SNA network, a class of service (COS) is defined for the user. The COS can be assigned each time the session is established or it can be predefined as part of the "logon mode" and remain the same for each session.

The user defines a preferential route and a preferential level of service (i.e., a class of service [COS]). For example, the preferential route could contain (a) a request for land lines instead of satellite links because of

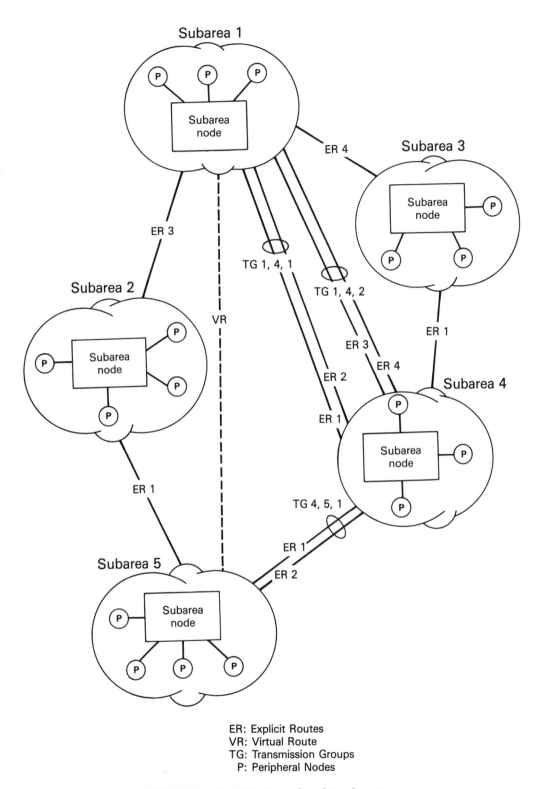

ER: Explicit Routes
VR: Virtual Route
TG: Transmission Groups
P: Peripheral Nodes

FIGURE 13-13. SNA Virtual and Explicit Routes

response time considerations, (b) explicit routing over certain links that are more secure than others, and/or (c) the bypassing of certain nodes, etc.

The class of service (COS) defines a list of preferential routes, called virtual routes (VR). A virtual route is a logical route between two end points. It is quite similar to the X.25 virtual circuit concept. The VR is the logical connection of all the tandem links and subarea nodes between the two users. Figure 13-13 shows a virtual route between subareas 1 and 5.

A user session is assigned to an operational VR in the class of service table. Each virtual route is then mapped into a table to create explicit routes (ERs). An explicit route is a portion of the path between the end-user subarea nodes.

Up to eight explicit routes can be defined between each pair of subarea nodes. To achieve flexibility and prevent bottlenecks, many SNA networks are configured with more than one explicit route between subareas. As shown in Figure 13-13, alternate explicit routes are available between subareas 1 and 4. When the explicit route is chosen, it usually remains the same for the duration of the session. However, a different route can be selected if problems occur during the session between the LUs.

Routing through SNA is session-oriented and with logon mode may be fixed at the time the user's profile is generated into the routing table. As with all packet-switching networks, alternate routing entries in the table are provided in the event of problems with nodes or channels.

SNA provides an additional feature called transmission groups (TGs). This term describes the grouping of parallel links between adjacent subarea nodes. The transmission groups consist of links using the same technology (for example, land lines or satellite links). The transmission group is identified by the two subarea nodes it connects and its own number. Figure 13-13 illustrates four explicit routes between subareas 1 and 4 which comprise two transmission groups.

As stated earlier, the SNA directory is partial—no single subarea has an understanding of the complete end-to-end path. As the table in Figure 13-14 shows, the subarea only knows the adjacent nodes to which it is to route traffic, because it routes traffic based on the next node entry in the table. The explicit routes are broken down into route segments. A change in network configuration and topology (for example, adding new nodes or removing nodes from the network), necessitates changing only the transaction routing tables of the adjacent nodes. Other nodes are not affected.

Each explicit route is defined in a transit routing table (see Figure 13-14). The routing table contains the destination of the subarea addresses as well as explicit route numbers.

The transit routing table consists of three fields: the destination subarea (DSA); explicit route numbers (ERNs); and the next node/transmission group (NN/TG) field. When an SNA message, called a path information unit (PIU), is processed by a subarea node, the node checks the PIU header for a DSA and an ER number. It finds the corresponding entries in the table and places the message in the appropriate outgoing queue. In Figure 13-14, the

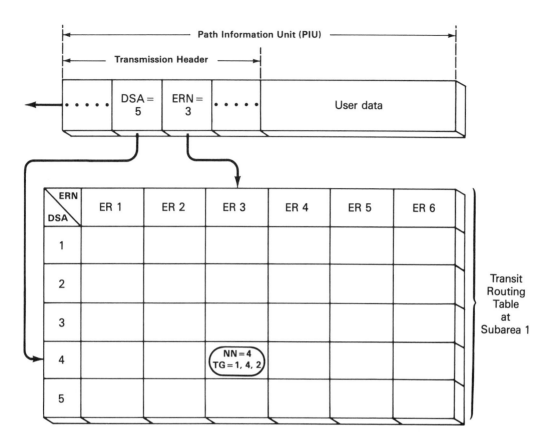

DSNA: Destination Subarea
ERN: Explicit Route Number
ER: Explicit Route
NN: Next Node
TG: Transmission Group

FIGURE 13-14. Routing from Subarea 1 to Subarea 5

transmission header contains DSA = 5 and ERN = 3. The table look-up yields NN = 4 and TG = 1,4,2. The process is repeated at subarea 4. A transit routing table is accessed to reveal the next node and transmission group. In this example, the next node is the final destination.

DECnet ROUTING WITH THE ROUTING LAYER

The DECnet Routing Layer uses a distributed routing strategy. It also uses a datagram service: the packets are delivered on a best-effort basis and the routing layer makes no guarantee against the packets being lost, duplicated, or delivered out of order. DECnet's next layer, the End Communication Layer, is responsible for these tasks.

DECnet selects routes based on network topology and operator-assisted costs. Although DECnet adapts to circuit or node failures, it does not adapt to changing traffic conditions. The Routing Layer does not examine the amount of traffic on the circuit as part of its routing algorithm. However, DECnet does determine the best path for a packet, if more than one path exists to the destination node. The major functions of DECnet routing are summarized in Box 13-2.

Before we examine DECnet routing in more detail, a few definitions are needed:

- The logical distance from one node to another node is a hop.
- The distance between the source to destination nodes is the path length and is measured in hops.
- The maximum number of hops permitted is called maximum visits.

The DECnet network manager assigns a cost to each circuit connected to a node. The cost factor is not specifically a cost, per se, but an integer number to determine the best path for the packet. It is identical to the concept of "least-cost path" discussed earlier. The routing layer routes packets to the circuit with the least-cost path length to the destination, even though it may not be the path with the fewest number of nodes. Figure 13-15 [DECN82A] illustrates the routing process.

BOX 13-2.   DECnet Routing Layer Functions

Service	Component
Packet Paths:	Determines path for packets, if more than one path exists.
Topology Changes:	Alternate paths are used if a node or circuit fails; routing modules are changed to reflect changes.
Packet Forwarding:	Forwards packet to End Communication Layer at destination node, or the next node if packet is not destined for the local node.
Node Visits:	Limits number of nodes that a packet can visit.
Buffer Management:	Manages buffers at nodes.
Packet Return:	Returns packets to End Communication Layer if packets are addressed to unreachable nodes (if requested by End Communication Layer).
Data Link Monitoring:	Monitors errors detected by the data link layer.
Statistics:	Gathers event data for Network Management Layer.
Node Verification:	If requested by the Network Management Layer, exchanges passwords with adjacent node.

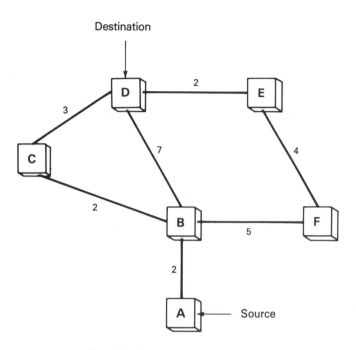

Possible Routes:

1. A→B→D=9 is Path Cost
2. A→B→C→D=7 is Path Cost
3. A→B→F→E→D=13 is Path Cost

Therefore, Route 2 is chosen.

FIGURE 13-15. DECnet Least-Cost Routing [DECN 82A]

It should be emphasized that DECnet does not provide:

* Adaption to changing traffic
* Distinction among different classes of traffic (high priority for example)
* Guaranteed delivery (performed at other layers)

Figure 13-16 shows the DECnet routing layer, sublayers and function components. The layer is organized as follows:

Control Sublayer

The routing function consists of four major processes: (a) decision, (b) update, (c) forwarding, and (d) receive. The function operates with the DECnet routing data base and the forwarding data base. A description of each process follows.

End Communication Layer

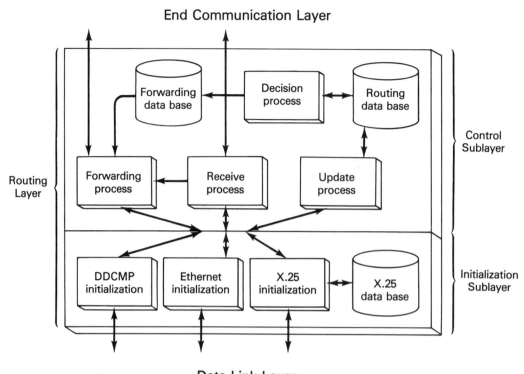

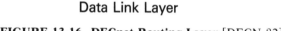

Data Link Layer

FIGURE 13-16. DECnet Routing Layer [DECN 82]

The decision process selects routes to each destination in the network. It uses a connectivity algorithm to maintain path lengths and a traffic assignment algorithm to maintain path costs. The decision process uses the routing data base and forwarding data base (discussed later) to determine the route. The decision process does not control all the parameters in these data bases. The network manager must set several parameters in the routing data base for the decision process to use.

The update process constructs and transmits routing messages, which contains path cost and path length for all destinations. The forwarding process manages the buffers in the DECnet nodes. It performs table-lookups to determine the route to the adjacent node. It returns (or discards) a packet if the destination is unreadable. It also performs several editing functions such as packet reformatting.

The receive process examines the packet header and sends the packet to the End Communications Layer or to a component within the Routing Layer.

The congestion control function limits the number of packets in a queue for each circuit. If a queue reaches a predetermined threshold, congestion control discards any additional packets. It prevents locally generated packets from congesting the network. It also checks the packet size of each packet to be transmitted.

The packet lifetime function contains three major processes. The loop detector counts the number of nodes a packet has visited and removes a packet when it exceeds a threshold. The node listener determines that a minimum level of activity has occurred between its node and an adjacent node. If the minimum activity violates a threshold, the adjacency between the nodes is considered down. The node talker provides the minimum level of activity for each adjacent node listener. It also tests the circuit. "Hello" messages are sent periodically in the absence of other traffic to check the link and ensure that a minimum level of activity occurs.

Initialization Sublayer

This sublayer is a start-up and monitor procedure for adjacent nodes. It adapts to the characteristics of the circuit and identifies the neighbor nodes. The actual operations are dependent upon the type of node and circuit (Ethernet, DDCMP, X.25).

ARPANET

ARPANET (implemented by the Department of Defense [DOD]) is an example of adaptive or dynamic directory routing. It also illustrates the concept of distributed packet systems. Each node maintains an awareness of the entire network topology and independently computes the optimum (least delay) path to each destination node and the final node.

Adpative networks function on the concept of node-adjacency knowledge; that is, a particular node is aware of the status of those nodes adjacent to it.

The ARPANET routing scheme has each node maintain two vectors (directories): (a) a delay vector (D_i) for the node (i), and (b) a successor node vector (S_{ij}) for the node $_i$. The vector D_i contains d_{ij}: the current estimate of the minimum delay from node $_i$ to node $_j$. The vector S_i contains the next node in the current minimum-delay route from i to j.

In ARPANET, delay is the performance criterion for the least-cost path (the older version used queue length). Each packet is time-stamped upon arrival at a node, and its departure time is recorded as well. If a positive acknowledgment is received from the neighbor node, the delay for the packet is received as:

$$D = DT - AT + TT + PD$$

Where: D = delay; DT = departure time; AT = arrival time; TT = transmission time; PD = propagation delay.

Every 10 seconds, a node computes the average delay on each link and uses flooding to notify all other nodes if any significant changes have occurred. When a node receives new information, it recomputes its vectors with a forward-search algorithm [STAL85].

X.25

In 1974, CCITT issued the first draft of X.25. It was revised in 1976, 1978, 1980, 1984, and again in 1988 with publication of the "Blue Book" recommendations. Since 1974, the standard has been expanded to include many options, services, and facilities. X.25 is now the predominant interface standard for wide area packet networks, and the data communications professional should have an understanding of its features. The standard is relatively stable and the 1988 Blue Book release is not much different from the 1984 Red Book version. These revisions are examined later in this section.

The placement of X.25 in packet networks is widely misunderstood. X.25 is *not* a packet switching specification. It is a packet *network interface* specification (see Figure 13-17). X.25 says nothing about the routing within the network. Hence, from the view of an X.25 user, the network is a "cloud." For example, the X.25 logic is not aware if the network uses adaptive or fixed directory routing. The reader may have heard of the term "network cloud." It is derived from these concepts.

X.25 defines the procedures for the exchange of data between a user device (DTE) and a network node (DCE). Its formal title is "Interface Between Data Terminal Equipment and Data Circuit Terminating Equipment for Terminals Operating in the Packet Node on Public Data Networks." In X.25, the DCE is actually a packet exchange or a network node. However, we will use the term DCE to stay consistent with X.25.

X.25 has achieved wide use for several reasons. First, the adoption of a common standard among vendors provides for an easier way to interface different vendor products. Second, the X.25 standard has gone through numerous revisions and is relatively mature. (X.25 is now revised every four years.) It has seen considerable use since 1980, and several systems were implemented as early as 1976. Consequently, the changes and adaptations made to the 1984 document reflect a substantial amount of experience relating to interfaces with packet networks. Third, a widely used standard such as X.25 can decrease network costs, since off-the-shelf software and hardware are readily available from many vendors. Fourth, it is much easier to write a request for proposal to a vendor stating the network must conform to X.25 than to write a lengthy specification document.

X.25 and the Physical Layer

The reader may wish to review Chapter 9 before reading this section. The X.25 packet-level recommendation is one of the recommended standards for

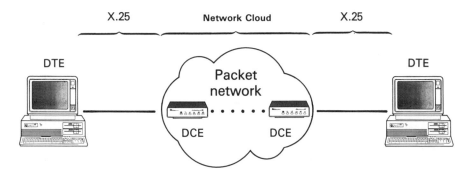

DTE: Data Terminal Equipment (User Equipment)
DCE: Data Circuit-Terminating Equipment (Network Node or Packet Exchange)

FIGURE 13-17. The X.25 Network Interface

the network (third) layer of ISO's model (see Figure 13-18). It actually encompasses the third layer as well as the lower two layers. The recommended physical layer (first layer) interface between the DTE and DCE is X.21.

Since few countries have implemented X.21, X.25 also provides a provision to use the EIA-232 or V.24/V.28 physical interface. In X.25, this physical level interface is called X.21 bis. In order to use X.21 bis, X.25 requires that the V.24 circuits 105, 106, 107, 108, and 109 be in the ON condition. Data is exchanged on circuits 103 and 104. If these circuits are off, X.25 assumes the physical level is in an inactive state and any upper levels (such as Data Link and Network) will not function. X.25 networks can operate with other physical layer standards (for example, RS449 and V.35).

The physical level plays a very small role in the control of an X.25 network. In essence, it is an electrical path through which the packets are transported.

The principal EIA-232 and V.24 circuits required for X.25 are as follows (reference, timing, signal grounds, etc. are not shown):

	EIA-232	*V.24*
Send Data	BA	103
Receive Data	BB	104
Request to Send	CA	105
Clear to Send	CB	106
Data Set Ready	CC	107
Data Terminal Ready	CD	108.2
Carrier Detect	CF	109

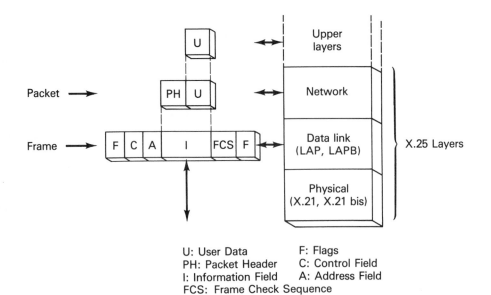

U: User Data   F: Flags
PH: Packet Header   C: Control Field
I: Information Field   A: Address Field
FCS: Frame Check Sequence

FIGURE 13-18. X.25 Layers and Protocol Data Units

X.25 and the Data Link Layer

X.25 assumes the data link layer (second level) to be LAPB (discussed in detail in Chapter 11). This line protocol is a subset of HDLC. Some vendors also use other data link controls, such as Bisync (Binary Synchronous Control), for the link layer.

The X.25 packet is carried within the LAPB frame as the I (information) field. LAPB ensures that the X.25 packets are transmitted across the link from/to the DTE/DCE, after which the frame fields are stripped and the packet presented to network layer. The principal function of the link level is to deliver the packet error-free despite the error-prone nature of the communications link. Once again, we delineate between a *packet* and a *frame*. A packet is created at the network level and inserted into a frame which is created at the data link level.

Logical Channels and Virtual Circuits

X.25 uses logical channel numbers (LCNs) to identify the DTE connections to the network. As many as 4095 logical channels (i.e., user sessions) can be assigned to a physical channel, although not all numbers are actually assigned at one time due to performance considerations. In essence, the LCN serves as an identifier for each user's packets that are transmitted through the physical circuit to and from the network cloud.

An aspect of X.25 that many people find confusing is its use of the terms logical channel and virtual circuit. Figure 13-19 illustrates the principal difference:

Logical Channel: Has local significance
Virtual Channel: Has end-to-end significance

X.25 explains quite specifically how logical channels are established but allows the network administration considerable leeway in how the virtual circuit is created. However, the network administration must "map" the two logical channel connections together through the network so they can communicate with each other. How this is done is left to the network administration, but it must be done if X.25 is to be used as specified.

X.25 Interface Options

We introduce X.25 in more detail by discussing the options for establishing sessions between DTEs and the packet network. The standard provides four mechanisms to establish and maintain communications (see Figure 13-20):

Permanent virtual circuit (PVC)
Virtual call (VC)
Fast select call
Fast select call with immediate clear

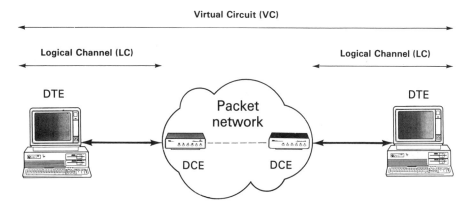

LC: Logical Channel = Local Significance
VC: Virtual Circuit = End-to-End Significance

FIGURE 13-19. X.25 Logical Channels and Virtual Circuits

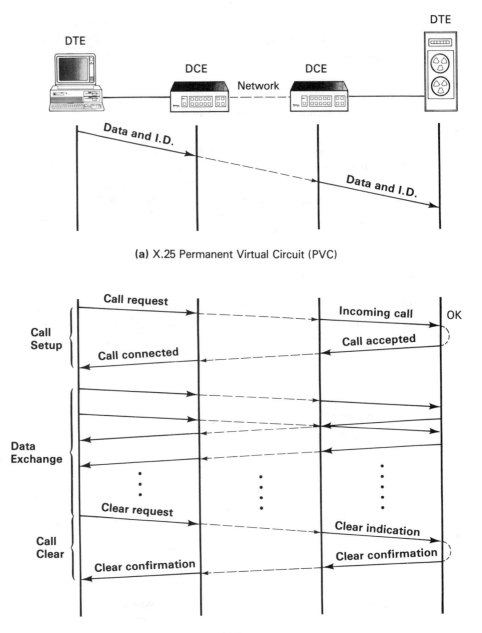

(a) X.25 Permanent Virtual Circuit (PVC)

(b) X.25 Virtual Call (VC)

FIGURE 13-20. X.25 Interface Options

Permanent Virtual Circuit (PVC). A permanent virtual circuit is somewhat analogous to a leased line in a telephone network: The transmitting DTE is assured of obtaining a connection to the receiving DTE

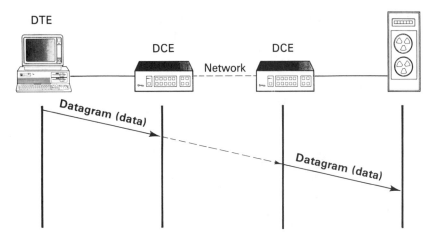

(c) Datagram (Not Supported in X.25)

(d) X.25 Fast Select Call

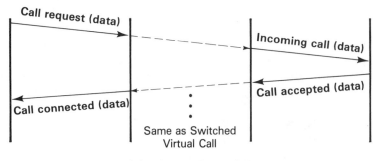

(e) X.25 Fast Select with Immediate Clear

FIGURE 13-20. X.25 Interface Options

through the packet network. X.25 requires that a permanent virtual circuit be established before the session begins. Consequently, an agreement must be reached by the two users and the network administration before a permanent virtual connection will be allocated. Among other things, this includes the reservation of an LCN for the PVC user.

Thereafter, when a transmitting DTE sends a packet into the packet network, the logical channel number in the packet indicates that the requesting DTE has a permanent virtual circuit connection to the receiving DTE. Consequently, a connection will be made by the network and the receiving DTE without further arbitration and session negotiation. PVC requires no call set-up or clearing procedures, and the logical channel is continually in a data transfer state.

Virtual Call (VC). A virtual call (also called a switched virtual call) resembles some of the procedures associated with telephone dial-up lines. The originating DTE issues a call request packet to the network with a logical channel number. The network routes the call request packet to the destination DTE. The destination DTE receives the call request packet as an incoming call packet from its network node with an LCN.

If the receiving DTE chooses to acknowledge and accept the call request, it transmits the network a call accepted packet. The network then transports this packet to the requesting DTE in the form of a call connected packet. The channel enters a data transfer state after the call establishment. To terminate the session, a clear request is sent by either DTE. It is received as a clear indication, and confirmed with the clear confirm packet.

Datagram Deleted. The datagram facility is a form of connectionless service discussed earlier. No call set-up and clear are required, nor is (network) error recovery stipulated. Datagram service was supported in an earlier release of the standard (1980). However, it received little support from the commercial industry because of its lack of end-to-end integrity and security. Consequently, the 1984 release of X.25 standard does not contain the datagram option.

Fast Select. The basic premise of the datagram (eliminating the overhead of the session establishment and disestablishment packets) makes good sense for certain applications, such as those with very few transactions or short sessions on the network. Consequently, the fast select facility was incorporated into the standard. The 1984 release of X.25 provides the fast select as an essential facility, which means that vendors or manufacturers implementing X.25 should implement fast select in order to be a certified X.25 network supplier. Most vendors have implemented fast select.

Fast select provides for two options. The first option is fast select call. A DTE can request this facility on a per-call basis to the network node (DCE) by means of an appropriate request in the header of a packet. The fast select facility allows the call request packet to contain user data of up to 128 bytes (octets). The called DTE is allowed to respond with a call accepted packet, which can also contain user data. The call request/incoming call packet indicates if the remote DTE is to respond with clear request or call accepted. If a call accepted is transmitted, the X.25 session continues with the normal data transferring and clearing procedures of a switched virtual call.

Fast Select with Immediate Clear. Fast select also provides for a fourth call connection feature of the X.25 interface, the fast select with immediate clear. As with the other fast select option, a call request contains user data. This packet is transmitted through the network to the receiving DTE, which upon acceptance transmits a clear request (which also contains user data). The clear request is received at the origination site as a clear indication packet. This site returned a clear confirmation. The clear confirmation packet cannot contain user data. Thus, the forward packet sets up the network connection and the reverse packet brings the connection down.

The idea of the fast selects (and the defunct datagram) is to provide support for user applications that have only one or two transactions such as inquiry/response applications (point of sale, credit checks, funds transfers). These applications cannot effectively use a switched virtual call because of the overhead and delay required in session establishment and disestablishment. Moreover, they cannot benefit from the use of a permanent virtual circuit because their occasional use would not warrant the permanent assignment of resources at the sites and the extra costs involved. Consequently, the fast selects have been incorporated into X.25 to meet the requirement for specialized uses of a network and to provide for more connection-oriented support than the datagram offered. Both DTEs must subscribe to fast select or the network will block the call within the DCE, sending back a clear indication packet to the DTE.

Other Packet Types

In addition to the packets described in the previous discussion, the X.25 recommendation uses several other packet types (see Figure 13-21). These packets are used for data transfer, diagnostics, and control functions such as resetting a session. A more complete description is available in [BLAC87C].

Packet Formats

The default user data field length in a data packet is 128 bytes (octets), but X.25 provides options for other lengths (see Figure 13-22). The following options are also available: 16, 32, 64, 256, 512, 1024, 2048, and 4096 octets. The latter two sizes were added in the 1984 revision. If the user data field in the packet exceeds the network permitted maximum field, the receiving DTE will reset the virtual call by issuing a reset packet. Each logical channel can have a different packet size.

Packet Type		Service	
From DCE to DTE	From DTE to DCE	VC	PVC
Call Set-up and Clearing			
Incoming call	Call request	X	
Call connected	Call accepted	X	
Clear indication	Clear request	X	
DCE clear confirmation	DTE clear confirmation	X	
Data and Interrupt			
DCE data	DTE data	X	X
DCE interrupt	DTE interrupt	X	X
DCE interrupt confirmation	DTE interrupt confirmation	X	X
Flow Control and Reset			
DCE RR	DTE RR	X	X
DCE RNR	DTE RNR	X	X
	DTE REJ	X	X
Reset indication	Reset request	X	X
DCE reset confirmation	DTE reset confirmation	X	X
Restart			
Restart indication	Restart request	X	X
DCE restart confirmation	DTE restart confirmation	X	X
Diagnostic			
Diagnostic		X	X
Registration			
Registration confirmation	Registration request	X	X

VC = Virtual Call   PVC = Permanent Virtual Circuit

FIGURE 13-21. X.25 Packets

Every packet transferred across the DTE/DCE interface to the network must contain at least three octets (bytes). The three octets comprise the packet header. Other octets may also be used to make up the header. The first four bits of the first octet of the header contain the logical channel group number (introduced earlier and discussed in more detail shortly). The last four bits of the first octet contain the general format identifier (GFI). Bits 5 and 6 of the general format identifier are used to indicate the sequencing for the packet sessions. Two sequencing options are allowed in X.25. The first option is Modulo 8 which permits sequence numbers 0 through 7. Modulo 128 is also available. This option permits sequence numbers ranging from 0 through 127. The seventh bit or Delivery-Option (D) bit of the general format identifier is used only with certain packets. (We discuss the D bit shortly.) The eighth bit is the Qualifier (Q) bit and is used only for special packets. The network does not "act upon" a packet with Q = 1, but passes it to the destination. (Q bit is discussed in relation to X.29 in Chapter 18.)

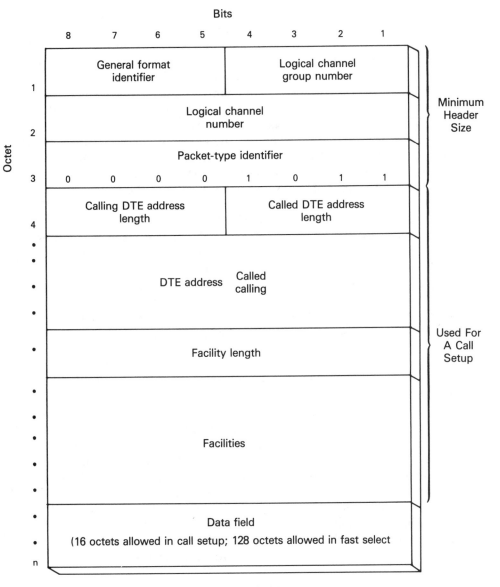

(a) Packet For a Call Request

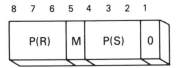

(b) Third Octet in a Data Packet

FIGURE 13-22. X.25 Packet Formats

The second octet of the packet header contains the logical channel number (LCN). This 8-bit field combined with the logical channel group number provides the complete logical channel identification of 12 bits which provide a total possibility of 4095 logical channels (256 × 16 less the 0 channel). The 0 LCN is reserved for control use (restart and diagnostic packets). Networks use the logical channel fields in various ways. Some networks use the two together; other networks treat them as separate fields.

The assignment of LCNs is only pertinent to the DTE and its packet exchange DCE. At the other end of the network, the very same packet may contain a different LCN. Of course, the network must remember that the two different LCNs are the identifiers for the DTE-to-DTE communications.

The third octet of the X.25 packet header is the packet type identifier octet for nondata packets and sequencing octet for data packets. This field identifies the specific nondata packet types.

Additional fields may exist inside the X.25 packet. For call establishment packets, the DTE addresses and address lengths are included. The address fields can be in the fourth through nineteenth octet (maximum length) of the call request packet. The address fields are needed during a call establishment in order for the network to know the calling and called DTEs. Once the call is established, the logical channel numbers are used to identify the DTE-to-DTE session. Some networks do not require the calling address field.

In addition, the facility fields may also be used in the event the DTEs wish to use the facility options contained in the X.25 standard. (These facilities are explained shortly.)

Finally, user call data may exist in the packet. The maximum limit in the call request packet for user data is 16 octets. This field is useful for entries such as passwords and accounting information for the receiving DTE. This field is also used by X.25 for additional protocol identification. For instance, a PAD uses this field to identify itself as a PAD when it is calling a host DTE. In this context, this field is not an ordinary user data field. For the option of a fast select, 128 octets of user data are allowed.

The packet header is modified to facilitate the movement of user data through the network. The third octet of the header, normally reserved for the packet type identifier, is broken into four separate fields for user data packets:

Bits	Description or Value
1	0
2-4	Packet send sequence: P(S)
5	More data bit (the M bit)
6-8	Packet receive sequence: P(R)

The functions of these fields are as follows: The first bit of 0 identifies the packet as a data packet. Three bits are assigned to a send sequence number P(S). One bit is assigned to a M bit function. (More about this later.) The three remaining bits are assigned to a receiving sequence number P(R). Note that sequence numbers exist at both this level (network) and the data link level (HDLC/LAPB).

The sending and receiving numbers are used to coordinate and acknowledge transmissions between the DTE and DCE. As the packet travels through the network from node to node, the sequence numbers may be altered as the packet traverses the network switching nodes. Nonetheless, the receiving DTE or DCE must know which packet receiving sequence number to send back to the transmitting device to properly acknowledge the specific packet. X.25 is similar to the features found in the second ISO level, data link control; the use of P(R) and P(S) at the network level requires the P(R) to be one greater than the P(S) in the data packet.

Remember that both HDLC/LAPB and X.25 provide for independent (R) and (S) sequencing. However, the difference between the link and network sequencing is significant. The link level sequence numbers are used to account for all users' traffic on the communications link, and to manage flow control on the link. The network level sequence numbers can be used to manage the traffic of each DTE (or anything that has a logical channel number).

Logical Channel Assignments

Logical channel numbers are used to identify the DTE to the packet node (DCE) and vice versa (see Figure 13-23). The numbers may be assigned to: (a) permanent virtual circuits; (b) one-way incoming calls; (c) two-way calls; and (d) one-way outgoing calls. The term "one way" refers to the direction in which the call establishment occurs.

It is possible that the DTE and DCE may use the same LCN when beginning a communication process. For example, DTE call request could use the same LCN as a DCE call connection. To minimize this possibility, the network (DCE) looks for a number starting at the low-order end and the DTE starts at the high-order end. If the outgoing call (call request) from a DTE may have the same LCN an incoming call (call connected) from the network DCE, X.25 stipulates that the incoming call be cleared and the call request processed.

The D, M, Q and L Bits

The D Bit. The D bit facility was added to the 1980 version of X.25. It is used to provide for one of two capabilities (see Figure 13-24). First, when the bit is set to 0, the P(R) value indicates that acknowledgment of receipt of the data packets is by the network. The second alternative is used when D is set to 1; the P(R) field is used to provide for an end-to-end acknowledgment of the packet, i.e., from one DTE to the other DTE.

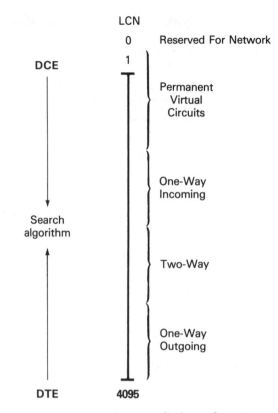

FIGURE 13-23. X.25 Logical Channel Assignments

The end-to-end acknowledgment confirms that the packets did indeed arrive at the remote DTE. However, the delay in obtaining end-to-end acknowledgment translates into a greater number of outstanding packets and the requirement for larger window sizes.

Be aware that some networks do not allow the user to specify end-to-end confirmation.

The M Bit. The M (more data) bit of the general format identifier identifies a related sequence of packets traversing through the network. This capability aids the network and DTEs in preserving the identification of blocks of data when the network divides these blocks into smaller packets (see Figure 13-25). For example, a block of data relating to a data base needs to be presented to the receiving DTE in the proper sequence. The capability is quite important when networks are internetworking each other, a topic discussed later.

The Q Bit. This bit is optional and may be used to distinguish between user data and control information. Since one of the PAD standards,

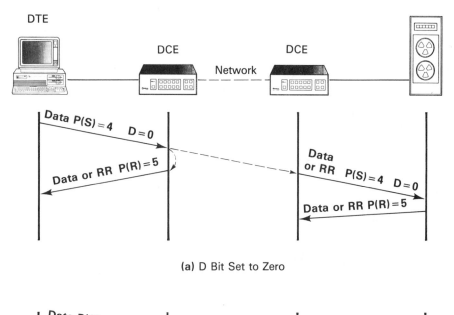

(a) D Bit Set to Zero

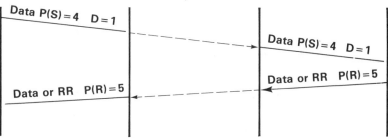

(b) D Bit Set to One

FIGURE 13-24. The D Bit

X.29, uses the Q bit, we will defer discussion of this bit until we discuss the PAD standards in Chapter 18.

   The L Bit.   The 1988 Blue Book release of X.25 allows the eighth bit of the first octet to be used during session establishment to stipulate that longer address fields will be used for the session. This addition is intended to accommodate the ISDN addresses described in CCITT E.164.

Flow Control and Windows

X.25 uses flow control techniques and window concepts that are quite similar to HDLC, LAPB, and SDLC which reside at the data link control or line

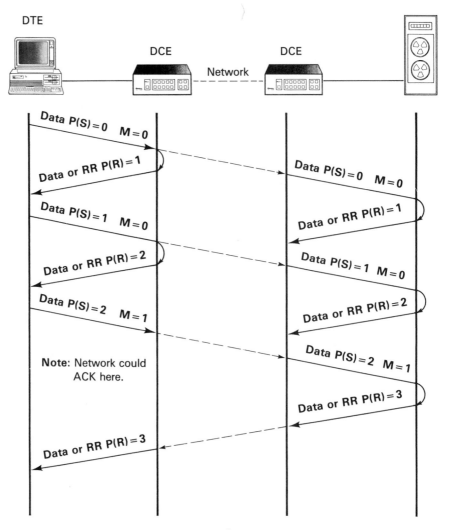

FIGURE 13-25. The M Bit Option

protocol level. A data packet combines two sequence numbers (send and receive) to coordinate flow of packets between the DTE and DCE. The extended numbering scheme allows for a sequence field to contain a maximum number of 127, using Modulo 128. At the DTE/DCE interface, the data packets are controlled separately for each direction, based on the authorizations coming from the user in the form of the receive sequence numbers and/or the receive ready (RR) and receive not ready (RNR) control packets.

With X.25, a standard window size of 2 is recommended for each direction of flow; although other window sizes can be made available by networks. The value of 2 limits the flow of packets that are outstanding at any one time. This limitation also necessitates faster acknowledgment of the packets from the receiving DCE.

X.25 Facilities (Quality of Service [QOS])

The 1984 release of X.25 contains a number of quality of service features called facilities. Some of these features are not required for a vendor to be "X.25 certified," yet they provide some very useful functions to end users and some are considered essential to a network. The facilities are requested by specific entries in the call request packet. However, most networks require the user to identify the requested facilities at subscription time. They are then invoked by coding values in the facilities field of a call request packet. Some facilities can be dynamically allocated.

The X.25 facilities include such features as reverse charging, call redirection, throughput negotiation, and variable packet sizes. Additional information on the X.25 facilities is available in [BLAC87C].

Building the Packet and Frame

The reader may wish to review Figure 13-18 which shows the relationships of the user data, the X.25 packet, and the LAPB frame. We now turn our attention to how the data, packet, and frame are transmitted from the X.25 user station to the packet exchange. Remember that X.25 uses the term DCE to describe the actual packet exchange. Unfortunately, the term DCE has more than one meaning. From the context of X.25, it refers to the packet exchange. But from the context of other interfaces, it refers to devices such as modems and multiplexers.

Figure 13-26 depicts the user equipment (such as an X.25 terminal) and the X.25 packet exchange. The user application passes the data to the user X.25 network layer (NL), which performs the X.25 functions previously described, such as establishing a call request, verifying user ID, selecting facilities, and selecting a logical channel number. This layer adds the X.25 packet header (PH) to the user data and passes the unit to the data link layer. Here, LAPB appends the error-check FCS field after it adds the appropriate link level address and controls fields. The X.25 packet is placed into the I field of the frame and transmitted out of the physical port, through the X.21 bis (or EIA-232/V.24 or X.21) interface to the modem. The modem modulates the data onto the channel, or a data service unit (DSU) sends the signals in digital form.

The data is received at the packet exchange, where it is checked for errors by LAPB at the data link layer. LAPB performs several other important functions such as link level flow control and link level sequencing. After its tasks are complete, the LAPB frame is then stripped away and the I field (the packet) is passed to the network layer of the packet exchange. This layer

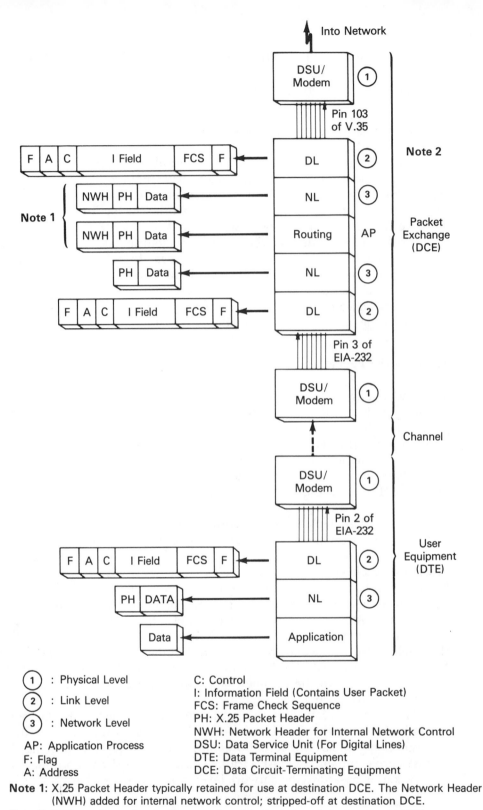

FIGURE 13-26. Operations at the X.25 Network Interface

Into Network

DSU/Modem ①

Pin 103 of V.35

Note 2

| F | A | C | I Field | FCS | F |

DL ②

| NWH | PH | Data |

NL ③

Note 1

| NWH | PH | Data |

Routing   AP

Packet Exchange (DCE)

| PH | Data |

NL ③

| F | A | C | I Field | FCS | F |

DL ②

Pin 3 of EIA-232

DSU/Modem ①

Channel

DSU/Modem ①

Pin 2 of EIA-232

User Equipment (DTE)

| F | A | C | I Field | FCS | F |

DL ②

| PH | DATA |

NL ③

| Data |

Application

① : Physical Level
② : Link Level
③ : Network Level

AP: Application Process
F: Flag
A: Address

C: Control
I: Information Field (Contains User Packet)
FCS: Frame Check Sequence
PH: X.25 Packet Header
NWH: Network Header for Internal Network Control
DSU: Data Service Unit (For Digital Lines)
DTE: Data Terminal Equipment
DCE: Data Circuit-Terminating Equipment

Note 1: X.25 Packet Header typically retained for use at destination DCE. The Network Header (NWH) added for internal network control; stripped-off at destination DCE.

Note 2: X.25 usually not invoked here, unless it is the last node to the remote DTE.

FIGURE 13-26. Operations at the X.25 Network Interface

maps the logical channel number, accepts the user data, performs other X.25 functions, and then passes the data unit out of the X.25 interface logic to a vendor-specific routing algorithm.

The vendor routing software selects the appropriate output link, and if X.25 is used inside the network, passes the data back to the network layer of X.25, which selects a logical channel number of the outbound packet. It usually uses the incoming packet header to construct an outgoing packet header for the packet.

The vendor may or may not use X.25 within the network. In the majority of networks, it is not used inside the network cloud. The reader should remember that X.25 does not define the internal workings of the packet network.

The packet is then passed to the outbound data link layer, where the frame is again reconstructed with the appropriate address, control, and FCS fields. LAPB may not be used inside the network, but substituted with another link protocol. The frame (with the packet in the I field) is sent to the next packet switch or a user device, by transmitting the packet out of the physical level, such as V.35.

Notice that the process is very structured and orderly. The data unit passes through each of the layers at the packet exchange as shown in Figure 13-26. At no time is a layer bypassed. The reader may wish to compare the events in Figure 13-26 with the concepts of encapsulation and decapsulation in Chapter 8.

SUGGESTED READINGS

An introductory, yet thorough description of the network layer is provided in [SCHW87]. [DECN82] provides an excellent description of DECnet's routing protocols. [TANE81] gives a lucid description of routing algorithms, as do [LITT61] and [SCHW80] and [STAL85]. [BLAC87C] provides a full chapter on X.25, and [BELL82] gives a full explanation of both circuit and packet switching. More specific and detailed references are available from [SCHW77], [SCHW80], [DIJK59], and [AHO74].

APPENDIX 13A
ADDRESSING PLANS

Network Layer Addressing

Recall from earlier discussions in this chapter that a network address can take one of three forms.

- An address is the end user interface to a network, referred to as a subnetwork address. An example is a user DTE address to an X.25 packet network.
- An address is the Network Service Access Point (NSAP). Examples are the called address, calling address, responding address parameters in the network level N-CONNECT primitive. Other examples are the source address and destination address in the connectionless-mode N-UNITDATA primitives.
- An address is the address code found in the network protocol control information (N-PCI). Typically, the NSAP address is mapped into the N-PCI address code in the protocol data unit. An example is an addressing convention, such as X.121 or E.164 (discussed in next section).

ISO 7498/PDAD 3 and the 1988 release of X.213 (Annex A) describe a hierarchical structure for the NSAP address. Figure 13A-1 shows the hierarchical concept of an inverted tree diagram. The term global network addressing domain refers to all NSAPs in the OSI environment. The domain can be divided further into subdomains, which are called network addressing domains.

These domains correspond to a specific type of network such as an ISDN, a telephone network, an X.25 public network, etc. They can also correspond to networks within a geographical region, or to a specific organization, such as the International Telecommunications Union (ITU).

ISO 8348/DAD 2 (Draft Addendum 2) specifies the structure for the NSAP address (see Figure 13A-2). It consists of four parts:

- *Initial Domain Part* (IDP): Contains the Authority Format Identifier (AFI) and the Initial Domain Identifier (IDI)
- *Authority Format Identifier* (AFI): Contains a two-digit value between 0 and 99. It is used to identify (a) the IDI format and (b) the syntax of the Domain Specific Part (DSP). Table 13A-1 contains the AFI and DSP values.
- *Initial Domain Identifier* (IDI): Specifies the addressing domain and the network addressing authority. Table 13A-2 contains a summary of the IDI formats and contents.
- *Domain Specific Part* (DSP): Contains the address determined by the network authority. It is an address below the second level of the addressing hierarchy. It can contain addresses of user end systems on an individual subnetwork.

The ISO 8348/DAD 2 and X.213 scheme are not perfect, and do not solve all addressing problems. However, they do provide a flexible and coherent framework for network addressing and will simplify future work in this important area.

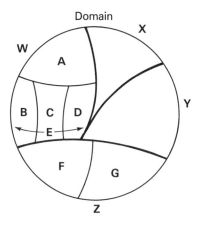

OR:

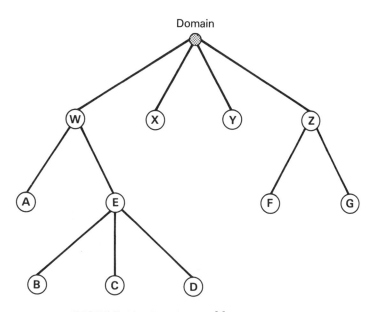

FIGURE 13A-1. NSAP Address Structure

X.121: International Numbering Plan
for Public Data Networks

This recommendation has received considerable attention throughout the world because its intent is to provide a universal data network addressing scheme, allowing users to communicate with each other through multiple networks. X.121 establishes a standard numbering scheme for all countries' networks and individual users within those networks.

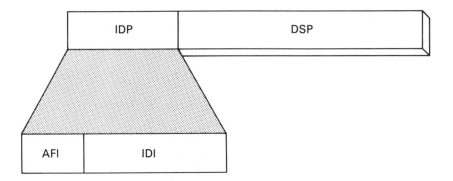

IDP: Initial Domain Part
DSP: Dominion Specific Part
AFI: Authority Format Identifier
IDI: Initial Domain Identifier

FIGURE 13A-2. NSAP Address Format

TABLE 13A-1: Allocated AFI Values

	DSP SYNTAX				
IDI Format	*Decimal*	*Binary*			
X.121	36	37			
ISO DCC	38	39			
F.69	40	41			
E.163	42	43			
E.164	44	45			*National*
				Character	*Character*
ISO 6523	46	47			
Local	48	49		50	51

A DTE within a public data network is addressed by an international data network address. The international data network address consists of a data network identification code (DNIC) plus a network terminal number (NTN). Another option is to provide the international data number as the data country code (DCC) plus a national number (NN).

The four codes consist of the following identifiers: the DNIC consists of four digits—the first three digits identify the country and can be regarded as a data country code (DCC). The fourth digit identifies a specific data network within a country. The network terminal number can consist of 10 digits or, if in place of the NTN, a national number (NN) is used; 11 digits are allowed. The scheme works as follows:

TABLE 13A-2: IDI Formats

IDI format	DSP syntax	Binary DSP encoding (octets)	Decimal DSP encoding (digits)
X.121	Decimal	20	40
	Binary	17	39
ISO DCC	Decimal	20	40
	Binary	17	40
F.69	Decimal	20	40
	Binary	17	40
E.163	Decimal	20	40
	Binary	17	39
E.164	Decimal	20	40
	Binary	18	40
ISO 6523-ICD	Decimal	20	40
	Binary	16	39
Local	Decimal	20	40
	Binary	16	40
	Character	20	40
	Nat'l Character	15	37

```
P + DNIC + NTN
P + DCC + NN
```

The P is a prefix indicator of one or more digits. It allows the selection of different formats and is not part of the number. It is not carried over a network boundary to another network. In addition, an escape code can be used for the same purpose, but it must be carried across the network boundaries. For example, an escape code of 0 is used to go from an X.121 numbering plan to the G.164 numbering plan.

E.164: International Numbering Plan for ISDN

The E.164 numbering plan is similar to X.121. It consists of the following structure:

```
CC + NDC + SN
```

where: CC = country code, NDC = national destination code, and SN = subscriber's number. The number is of variable length, and can be as long as 15 digits.

TRUE/FALSE

1. A network service is concerned with the semantics and content of the user data.
2. Circuit switching is a store-and-forward technology.
3. X.25 is a packet-switching protocol.
4. Packet switching exploits the "bursty" characteristics of many data communications devices.
5. Least-cost routing does not refer only to the cost of the route.
6. Match the term to the appropriate description (more than one term may apply to a description):

    Description

    a) Designed for data traffic.
    b) Designed for voice traffic.
    c) Uses statistical multiplexing.
    d) Accommodates applications that require fast response time.

    Term

    1. Circuit switching
    2. Packet switching
    3. Message switching

7. Match the term to the appropriate definition.

    Definition

    a) Directory remains the same for each session.
    b) Generation of duplicate packet copies.
    c) Directory changes with each session.
    d) Reducing duplicate copies.
    e) Directory changes during session.

    Term

    1. Traffic multiplication effect
    2. Logon directory
    3. Packet die-out
    4. Fixed routing directory
    5. Adaptive directory

8. Message switching is quite flexible but exhibits some deficiencies. Briefly describe them.
9. List viable criteria for a least-cost routing algorithm.
10. Define a network "cut." What is its purpose?

11. The mean arrival rate of packets into a packet switch is 1000 packets per second. The mean service rate is 1025 packets per second. What is the total waiting time, including service time?

12. What is the mean queuing time for the packets using the switch (in question 11)?

13. List the four major services of SNA's Path Control Layer.

14. DECnet uses several "control" messages in its Routing Layer. Briefly describe their functions.

15. The X.25 recommendation provides the following DTE/DCE interface options:
    a) Permanent virtual circuit (PVC)
    b) Fast select
    c) Datagram
    d) Switched virtual call (SVC)
    e) all of the above

16. Explain the difference between a logical channel and a virtual circuit.

17. Assume your application needs an end-to-end acknowledgment through an X.25 network. How can this service be obtained? What are the advantages and disadvantages of using this service?

18. Draw a state diagram based on the following description of the X.25 DTE/DCE interface.

    The interface is in the flow control ready state. Either the DTE or DCE can initiate reset operations out of the d1 state.

    The DTE experiences a transition from the d1 state to the DTE reset request state (d2) upon signalling a reset request packet. The DTE remains in the d2 state until the DCE sends a reset indication packet to the DTE. This action returns the DTE to the flow control ready state (d1).

    The DCE experiences a transition from the d1 state to the DCE reset indication state (d3) upon signalling a reset indication packet. The DCE remains in the d3 state until the DTE sends a reset confirmation packet to the DCE. This action returns the DTE to the flow control ready state (d1).

19. After reviewing the answer to question 18, add the following information to the state diagram:

    During the d2 state, the DTE may reissue a reset request packet and return back to the d2 state.

    During the d3 state, the DCE may reissue a reset indication packet and return to the d3 state.

SELECTED ANSWERS

1. False. These concerns are handled by upper layers.

2. False. Circuit switching is designed as a direct connect.

3. False. X.25 does not specify packet-switching techniques or algorithms. X.25 is an interface protocol between a packet network node (DCE) and user device (DTE).

4. True.

5. True.

6.

Description	Term
a)	2,3
b)	1
c)	2
d)	1,2

7.

Definition	Term
a)	4
b)	1
c)	2
d)	3
e)	5

10. A network cut is the removal of paths between two nodes such that they are disconnected from each other. Its purpose is to determine the capacity through the paths of a network and the potential bottlenecks.

11. The mean arrival rate is λ = 1000 packets per second. The mean service time is μ = 1025 packets per second. Since T = $1/(\mu - \lambda)$, T = $1/(1025 - 1000)$ = 0.04 second.

15. (a), (b), (d)

17. End-to-end acknowledgment can be accomplished by using the D bit option in the X.25 facility features. This allows the destination DTE to return a packet with a P(R) value to acknowledge the transmitting DTE's packets. Of course, the advantage of the use of D bit = 1 is that it does provide end-to-end accountability. This allows the two users to periodically checkpoint the traffic to see if it has arrived safely and in sequence. However, with some thought it can be seen that the D bit could have some disadvantages. For example, if the X.25 network requirement places a small window on the transmitting DTE (for example, two) the user DTE is at the "mercy" of the receiving remote DTE to provide rapid turnaround of the packet acknowledgments. Moreover, if the network cloud is slow, this could introduce additional delay. Another factor to be considered is that the remote device may have no data packet to send back to the submitting site. However, in order to keep the window open, non-data packets must be sent (for example, receive ready packets) with the P(R) value set for acknowledgment. If the network charges on a per volume basis, these non-data packets traversing the network are still considered as chargeable packets.

18. and 19.

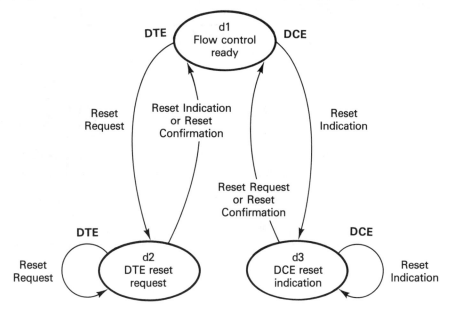

CHAPTER 14

The Network Layer, Internetworking

INTRODUCTION

Data communications networks were developed to allow users to share computer and information resources, as well as a common communications system. As organizations have brought the computer into almost every facet of business, it has become obvious that a single network, although very useful, is inadequate to meet the burgeoning information needs of businesses and individuals. For example, a user of one network often needs to access computers and data bases that "belong" to another network. It is prohibitively complex and expensive to merge all resources into one network (not to mention the political and organizational problems of merging the disparate organizations' vital information resources).

As shown in Figure 14-1, an alternative is interconnecting the networks to obtain the required resources. Hereafter, the network is also called a subnetwork. The subnetwork forms an autonomous whole. It consists of a relatively homogeneous collection of equipment, physical media, and software which is used to support the user community. Some examples of subnetworks are privately owned networks, public networks (TELENET, Tymnet, Datapac), and local area networks.

Problems with Internetworking

As illustrated in Figure 14-1, several difficult issues and problems arise in providing internetworking services:

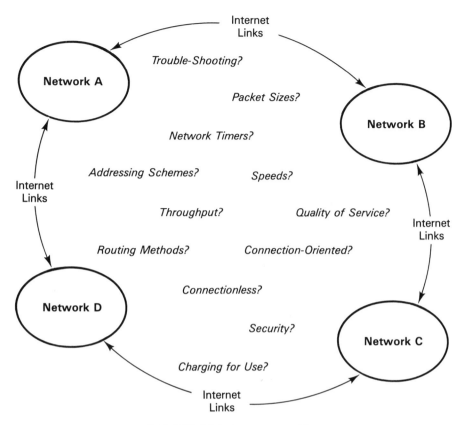

FIGURE 14-1. Internetworking

- The subnetworks may use different sizes and formats for protocol data units (PDUs). If different sizes are supported, the subnetworks must provide for the segmentation and reassembly of the data units. In so doing, the identity of the data units must not be lost. The varying sizes of the data units do not eliminate the requirement to maintain a sequence number relationship on an end-to-end basis.

- The timers, timeouts, and retry values often differ between subnetworks. For example, assume network A sets a wait-for-acknowledgment timer when a data unit is sent into the "cloud." The timer is used to ensure that an end-to-end acknowledgment occurs within a specified period. The data unit is passed to network B, but this network does not have an end-to-end timer. Thus, we have a dilemma. Should network A return the ACK upon passing the data unit to network B and assume the second network will indeed deliver the data unit? A false sense of security would result in network A's user, since the data unit may not arrive at the end destination.

- The subnetworks may provide different types, levels, and quality of service (QOS). For example, one network may support reverse charging and another may not allow the feature. Internetworking usually requires the QOS to be supported to the lowest common denominator—not a very attractive alternative for the user of the high-QOS network.

- The subnetworks may use different addressing conventions. For example, one may use logical names, and another may use physical node names. In such a case, address resolution and mapping would differ between the two subnetworks. Indeed, most networks use network-specific addresses. For example, an SNA address simply does not equate to a DECnet address.

- The subnetworks may exhibit different levels of performance. For example, one subnetwork may be slower and exhibit more delay and less throughput than another network.

- The subnetworks may employ different routing methods. For example, one may use a fixed routing directory and another may use an adaptive routing directory. In the former case, the network logic for resequencing is sparse. In the latter case, resequencing logic is extensive.

- The subnetworks may require different types of user interfaces. For example, a subnetwork may employ a connection-oriented, DTE-to-subnetwork interface and another may use a connectionless, datagram protocol. The interface type influences error recovery and flow control.

- The subnetworks may require different levels of security. For example, one network may require encryption and another may only support clear-text transmissions.

- Troubleshooting, diagnostics, and network maintenance (a) may differ between the subnetworks and (b) may not be used across more than one network. A problem created in one subnetwork may affect another subnetwork, yet the affected network may have no control in the error analysis and correction.

- The question of charging/billing is yet another problem. Which subnetwork(s) reap the revenue? How are costs allocated?

Clearly, the internetworking task is not simple, and it requires considerable analysis and forethought before it is implemented. Yet the problems are not insurmountable. As we shall see in this chapter, the vendors and standards organizations have developed and implemented many effective internetworking techniques. In this chapter, we examine several fundamental internetworking concepts/products from the standard groups and network vendors.

Dividing the Network Layer

In its DIS 8648 specification, ISO divides the network layer into three functional groups (see Figure 14-2). This division provides a convenient method to identify internetworking operations. Moreover, several vendors are now using this convention in their commercial offerings. At the top is the *subnetwork independence convergence protocol* (SNICP), which provides the relay and routing services for internetworking. This sublayer contains the internetwork protocols to effect data transfer between networks.

The middle group is the *subnetwork dependent convergence protocol* (SNDCP), which may be used to bring the interconnecting networks up to a level needed for the interconnection. The interconnecting networks (subnetworks) may not provide a needed service, so SNDCP provides a "mapping" of the required service, or it may operate an explicit protocol to provide the convergence. At its most basic level, SNICP serves as a network protocol converter. This sublevel is sometimes a source of confusion to some people, so let us examine a "real life" situation.

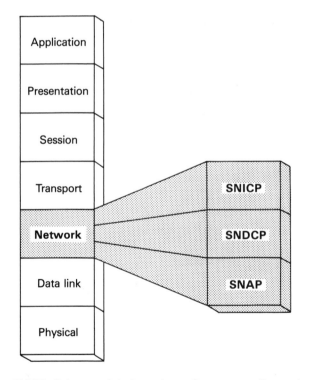

SNICP: Subnetwork Independence Convergence Protocol
SNDCP: Subnetwork Dependence Convergence Protocol
SNAP: Subnetwork Access Protocol

FIGURE 14-2. Sublayers of the Network Layer

The ISO publishes DIS 8878 as a SNPCP. It is used to support a 1980 X.25 network that does not have all the features of a 1984 X.25 network. It adds information to the 1980 packet in order to obtain the added services of the 1984 version.

The lowest sublayer is the *subnetwork access protocol* (SNAP), which contains the services relevant to each of the interconnecting networks. For example, SNA, the X.25 network interface, and CSMA/CD are SNAPS. The SNAP provides the data transfer between the DTE and the DCE. It also manages the connections and receives the quality of service requests from the end user.

Summary of Internetworking Specifications

Several internetworking specifications/standards are now being used. The standards that have received the most attention are briefly summarized here. Several are explained in more detail in this chapter.

- *ISO 8348:* describes a connection-oriented network service (CONS) with an X.25 packet layer protocol (PLP)
- *ISO 8881:* specifies the use of X.25 in a LAN station attached to a local area network or a packet switched data network
- *ISO 8473:* specifies a connectionless internetworking protocol either with connection-oriented or connectionless subnetworks
- *ISO 8208:* specifies the use of X.25 packet level procedures (PLP) for direct DTE-to-DTE communications
- *ISO 8880 part 2:* describes the provision and support of connection-mode network service
- *ISO 8880 part 3:* describes connectionless network service, in general
- *ISO 8878:* describes the convergences of protocols between sub-networks (using 1980 X.25)
- *ISO 8645:* describes the internal organization

Preview of Internetworking Protocols

The remainder of this chapter explains several of the prevalent internetworking standards used in the industry. It also describes several protocols available from IBM and DEC. The following standards/products are covered:

Connectionless-Mode Network Service (ISO 8473)
The Internet Protocol (IP)
X.75 Internetworking
Internetworking SNA and X.25
Internetworking DECnet and SNA

Internetworking DECnet and X.25

Internetworking X.25 and IEEE 802 LANs (ISO 8881, ISO 8208)

Internetworking ISDNs and X.25 (X.31)

X. 300 Internetworking Recommendations

X. 122 Internetworking Addressing Plan

CONNECTIONLESS-MODE NETWORK SERVICE (ISO 8473)

Introduction

The connectionless-mode network service attempts to manage user protocol data units (PDUs) as independent and separate entities. No relationship is maintained between successive data transfers and very few records are kept of the ongoing user-to-user communications process through the network(s). The term "datagram" network is also associated with a connectionless network. Figure 14-3 contrasts connectionless and connection-oriented networks.

By its very nature, connectionless service achieves (a) a high degree of user independence from specific protocols within a subnetwork; (b) considerable independence of the subnetworks from each other; and, (c) a high degree of independence of the subnetwork(s) from the user-specific protocols. However, as we shall see in this section, connectionless systems are not completely connectionless and they do consume more overhead (in relation to headers versus user data) than their connection-oriented counterparts.

Our discussion will focus on the ISO 8473, a specification that describes the architecture for connectionless-mode network service. It is also called the connectionless network protocol (CLNP).

ISO 8473 has been designed to operate within the DTEs attached to public and private networks. As will be seen, the protocol does not involve itself with the particular characteristics of the underlying subnetworks. The basic idea is to demand little in the way of services from the subnetworks except to transport the protocol data unit.

The protocol communicates by exchanging internetwork protocol data units (IPDUs) in a connectionless (datagram) fashion. Each IPDU is treated independently and does not depend on the state of the network for any particular establishment connection time (since no connection exists in a connectionless network). Generally, routing decisions are made independently by each forwarding internetworking node. It is also possible for the source user to determine the routing by placing the routing information in the IPDU source routing field.

The ISO 8473 connectionless-mode network service is provided by two primitives: N-UNITDATA Request and N-UNITDATA Indication (see Figure 14-4). These two primitives are quite similar to the primitives used by the IP

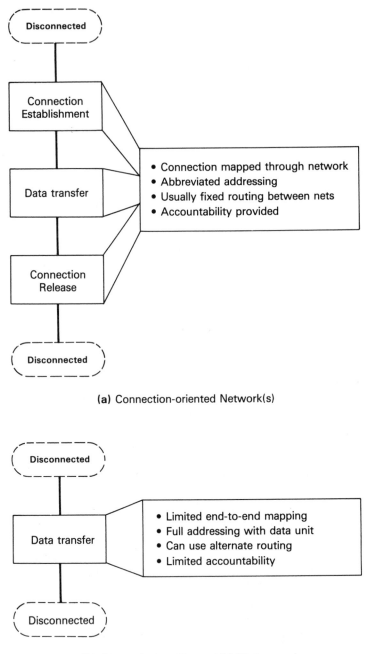

(a) Connection-oriented Network(s)

(b) Connectionless Network(s) (Datagrams)

FIGURE 14-3. Connecting into Networks

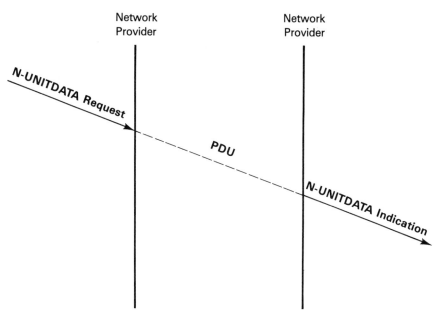

PDU: Protocol Data Unit

FIGURE 14-4. The Two Connectionless-Mode Primitives

(Internet Protocol), discussed next. The reader should note that the protocol uses no connection and clear primitives, which is a rather obvious indication of its connectionless attributes. Each of the two primitives contains four parameters: NS-Source-Address; NS-Destination-Address; NS-Quality-of-Service; and NS-Userdata. All parameters are explained shortly.

Layer Interaction

ISO 8473 is resplendent with acronyms and specialized terms. Consequently, let us use Figure 14-5 to illustrate the actual use of several of the terms. It will also provide the opportunity to see how the primitive parameters are placed into the fields of the protocol data units, which is one of the key concepts of the OSI model and layered protocols.

The connectionless network protocol (CLNP) receives the N-UNITDATA Request from the transport layer. The parameters with the request are used to construct a protocol data unit (PDU). The address parameters contain the source and destination NSAP address parameters.

The underlying service to support ISO 8473 is also defined by two primitives: SN-UNITDATA Request and SN-UNITDATA Indication. The primitives are used by the ISO 8473 machine to interface with an actual network (SNAP), an intervening layer (SNDCP), or an actual data link protocol.

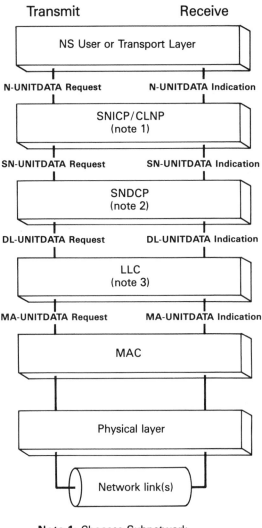

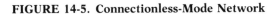

Note 1: Chooses Subnetwork
Note 2: May Not Be Used
Note 3: SNAP Could Be Evoked Here

FIGURE 14-5. Connectionless-Mode Network

When the appropriate subnetwork has been selected, the SN-UNITDATA Request is issued by the CLNP to the local SNDCP. It then maps the request parameters to a DL-UNITDATA.request, which is used by ISO 8802 (IEEE 802.2 Type 1; known as LLC or logical link control; discussed in Chapter 20). It must then invoke a procedure to create an HDLC/LLC unnumbered information (UI) frame. The SN-Userdata is placed into the I field (information) of the frame. The LLC frame is then given to the MAC sublayer with the MA-UNITDATA.request.

The receiving node reverses the process just described. Its LLC receives a MA-UNIT DATA.indication and passes the protocol data unit (frame) to the SNDCP. It decapsulates the UI frame and derives the addresses and user data. It then maps these addresses onto the SN-Destination-Address and SN-Source-Address parameters of the SN-UNITDATA indication primitives. It also maps the I field onto the SN-Userdata parameter of the SN-UNITDATA indication.

The destination SNDCP then receives the data unit, and notifies the receiving CLNP via a SN-UNITDATA indication. The NSAP address in the PDU is then checked to determine if it corresponds to any of the NSAP addresses serviced by the receiving CLNP. If so, the PDU is decomposed and an N-UNITDATA indication is passed to the NS user. If the protocol data unit has not yet reached its destination, routing and forwarding functions are executed for internetwork transfer. The data are transferred transparently between the subnetworks.

The ISO 8473 Protocol Data Unit

The fields of the protocol data unit (see Figure 14-6) provide the functions described in Box 14-1. The reader should review these functions since they are used to explain the internetworking session.

Quality of Service (QOS) Functions

An underlying subnetwork may provide several quality of service (QOS) functions. The services are negotiated when the primitives are exchanged between layers. Of course, the primitive parameters must be based on a priori knowledge of the availability of the services within the subnetwork. It does little good to ask for a quality of service features if it is known that the subnetwork does not provide it. Be aware that the values of QOS apply to both ends of the network connections (NCs), even though the NC may span several subnetworks that offer different services.

Use of ISO 8348. For Quality of Service choices, ISO 8473 uses the following QOS functions described in ISO 8348:

- *Transit delay:* Establishment of the elapsed time between a data request and the corresponding data indication. This QOS applies only to successful PDU transfers. The delay is specified by a desired value up to the maximum acceptable value. All values assume a PDU of 128 octets. User-initiated flow control is not measured in these values.

- *Residual error rate:* The ratio of total incorrect, lost, or duplicated PDUs to total PDUs transferred:

$$RER = \frac{N(e) + N(1) - N(x)}{N}$$

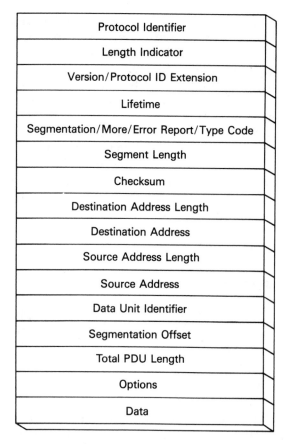

| Protocol Identifier |
| Length Indicator |
| Version/Protocol ID Extension |
| Lifetime |
| Segmentation/More/Error Report/Type Code |
| Segment Length |
| Checksum |
| Destination Address Length |
| Destination Address |
| Source Address Length |
| Source Address |
| Data Unit Identifier |
| Segmentation Offset |
| Total PDU Length |
| Options |
| Data |

FIGURE 14-6. The ISO 8473 Protocol Data Unit (PDU)

Where: RER = residual error rate; N(e) = PDUs in error; N(1) = lost PDUs; N(x) = duplicate PDUs; N = PDUs.

- *Cost determinants:* A parameter to define the maximum acceptable cost for a network connection. It may be stated in relative or absolute terms. Final actions on this parameter are left to the specific network provider.
- *Priority:* Used to determine preferential service in the subnetwork. Outgoing transmission queues and buffers are managed based on the priority values contained in the PDU header options field.
- *Protection against unauthorized access:* Used to direct the subnetwork to prevent unauthorized access to user data.

Protocol Functions

ISO 8473 includes several optional or required protocol functions. Each function provides a specialized service to the network user. In a sense, the

BOX 14-1. **Functions of Fields in 8473 Protocol Data Unit**

Network layer protocol identifier: This field identifies the protocol as ISO 8473. *Length indicator:* This field describes the length of the header. *Version/protocol identifier extension:* This identifies the version of ISO 8473.

Lifetime: This field represents the lifetime of the PDU. It is coded in units of 500 milliseconds. *Segmentation permitted:* This bit indicates if segmentation is permitted. The originator of the PDU determines this value and it cannot be changed by any other entity.

More segments: This bit indicates if more user data is forthcoming. It is used when segmentation takes place. When the bit equals 0, it indicates that the last octet of the data in this PDU is the last octet of the user data stream (the network data service unit [NSDU]).

Error report: This bit is set to 1 to indicate that an error report is to be generated back to the originator if a data PDU is discarded. *Type code:* These five bits describe the PDU as a data PDU or an error PDU.

PDU segment length: This field specifies the entire length of the PDU (header and data). If no segmentation occurs, the value of this field is identical to the value of the total length field.

Checksum: The checksum is calculated on the entire PDU header. A value of 0 in this field indicates that the header is to be ignored. A PDU is discarded if the checksum fails.

Address length and addresses: Since the source and destination addresses are variable in length, the length fields are used to describe their length. The actual addresses are Network Service Access Points (NSAPs). *Data unit identifier:* This field identifies an initial PDU in order to correctly reassemble a segmented data unit.

Segmentation offset: If the original PDU is segmented, this field specifies the relative position of this segment in relation to the initial PDU.

PDU total length: This field contains the entire length of the original PDU, which includes both the header and data. It is not changed for the lifetime of the PDU.

Option part: Optional parameters are placed in this part of the PDU. The source routing addresses are placed here as are the records of the path the PDU takes through the subnetworks to the destination. This field also can be coded to show quality of service parameters, priorities, buffer congestion indication, padding characters, and designation of security levels (specific security procedures are left to service implementation).

Data: This field contains the user data.

ISO 8473 protocol functions are similar to quality of service (QOS) features, except they are performed as an integral part of the protocol. The next section explains the use of the major functions, and the interested reader can refer to Appendix 14A for a more thorough description of each function.

Traffic Management Between Subnetworks

This section provides an illustration of how an 8473 connectionless-mode internetwork protocol transfers data between subnetworks. While different vendors use various techniques for the provision of connectionless service, many use the concepts described herein.

When the protocol receives the NS-Source-Address and NS-Destination-Address parameters in the N-UNITDATA Request primitive from an upper layer, it uses them to build a source address and destination address in the header of the PDU. The source address and NS-Quality-of-Service parameters are used to determine which optional functions are to be selected for the network user. At this time, a data unit identifier is assigned to uniquely identify this request from other requests. This identifier must remain unique for the lifetime of the initial PDU and any segmented PDUs in the network(s). Subsequent and/or derived PDUs are considered to correspond to the initial PDU if they have the same source address, destination address, and data unit identifier. At first glance, this rule may appear to be connection-oriented, but it applies only to PDUs created as a result of segmentation.

The protocol data unit is then forwarded through the subnetwork(s). Each hop examines the destination address to determine if the PDU has reached its destination. If the destination address equals an NSAP (network service access point) served by the network entity, it has reached its destination. Otherwise, it must be forwarded to the next node.

When the PDU reaches its destination, the receiver removes the PCI (protocol control information) from the PDU. It also uses the addresses in the header to generate the NS-Source-Address and NS-Destination-Address parameters of the UNITDATA indication primitive. It preserves the data field of the PDU until all segments (if any) have been received. The options part of the PDU header is used to invoke any quality of service parameters at the receiving end.

Unlike connection-oriented networks, an ISO 8473 connectionless-mode network has more flexibility in terminating service to a user. For example, if a new network connection request is received with a higher priority than an ongoing data transfer, the network may release the lower priority transfer. Moreover, users may also have priorities established for the data transfers. The network connections (NC) with a higher priority will have their requests serviced first and the remaining resources of the network are used to attempt to satisfy the lower priority network connections.

User data is given a specific "lifetime" in the network(s). This mechanism is useful for several reasons. First, it prevents lost or misdirected data from accumulating and consuming network resources. Second, it gives the transmitting entity some control over the disposition of aged data units. Third, it greatly simplifies congestion control, flow control and accountability logic in the network(s). (It should be emphasized that discarded data units can be recovered by the transport layer.)

The lifetime field in the PDU header is set by the originating network entity. The value also applies to any segmented PDUs and is copied into the header of these data units. The value contains, at any time, the remaining lifetime of the PDU. It is decremented by each network entity that processes it. The value is represented in units of 500 milliseconds and is decremented by one unit by each entity. In the event delays exceed 500 milliseconds, the value is decremented by more than one unit.

If the lifetime value reaches 0 before the PDU reaches its destination it is discarded. If the error report bit is on, an error report data unit is generated to inform the originator of the lost data. This feature may be considered by some to be a connection-oriented service. Whatever its name, it is obviously very useful if end-to-end accountability is needed.

In addition to discarding aged data units, the network may also discard data for other reasons:

- Checksum reveals an error (if checksum is used).
- A PDU that contains an unsupported function such as a QOS is received.
- Local congestion occurs at the receiver.
- Header cannot be interpreted accurately.
- A PDU cannot be segmented and it is too large for the underlying network to handle.
- The destination address is not reachable or a path route is not acceptable to the network serving the PDU.

The protocol data unit is transferred on a hop-to-hop (next node) basis. The selection of the next system in the route may be influenced by the quality of service parameters and other optional parameters. For example, the next hop might be chosen because it supports the QOS requests.

Internetwork Routing. The routing technique in ISO 8473 is called *source routing*. The route is determined by the originator of the PDU by placing a list of the intermediate routes in the options part of the PDU header. The route indicators are called titles. The relaying is accomplished by each network entity routing the PDU to the next title in the list. The indicator is updated by each relay point to identify the next stage of the route.

The protocol provides two types of routing: complete source routing and partial source routing. Complete source routing requires that the specified route be used in the exact order as in the route list. If this route cannot be taken, the PDU must be discarded with the option of returning an error report to the originator. Partial source routing allows a system to route to intermediate systems that are not specified in the list.

Another routing option, called the record route function, requires the intermediate systems to add their title to a record route list in the options field of the header. The list is built as the PDU is forwarded to its destination. This list can be used for troubleshooting internetwork or subnetwork problems. It can also be used as a tool for efficiency analysis, audit trails or simply as a "directory" for a returning PDU.

If this option is invoked, either complete route recording or partial route recording is used. With the former, all intermediate systems are recorded and PDU reassembly is performed only if all derived PDUs took the same route. Otherwise, the PDU is discarded. The partial route recording also requires the full list but does not require that the derived PDUs visit the same intermediate systems.

An Example of Internetwork Routing

Figure 14-7 provides an example of connectionless internetwork routing. Two scenarios are provided. In Figure 14-7(a) the source network A stipulates the record route function (any route) to network G for its 512 octet-size data units. No segmentation is allowed, and the source requests a QOS transit delay time. Furthermore, its lifetime field is set to 800 ms and the error report is to be generated in the event problems occur.

The gateway at network A must route the data to the intermediate network B because network C does not support a transit delay QOS function and network D does not support a 512 octet data unit. We assume the gateway in network B then chooses network E as the next and final hop before the destination network G.

In this example, the data unit experiences a transit delay of 300 ms in network B and 600 ms in network E. Since the data unit's lifetime is 800 ms, network E discards the data and generates an error report. Network E examines the record route list to determine the predecessor network. It sends the error report back to network B, which gives it back to the source, network A.

In an automatic-recovery network, the error report can evoke the generation of a primitive to a recovery routine: (a) a module complementary to the internetwork protocol; (b) a user program; or (c) a transport layer program. Typically, the data unit is retransmitted, but it might take a different route if network E is deemed to be an excessive bottleneck. However, the very fact that the data unit had a lifetime value may preclude its retransmission.

One possible alteration is illustrated in Figure 14-7 (b). Even though network C does not support the transit delay, QOS, it is the shortest overall hop-to-hop path to the final destination. It is conceivable that the upper layer protocol would "turn off" its transit delay QOS request to give network C the opportunity to provide the hop service. Network A could also use the complete source routing option to stipulate the exact order of the internetwork route.

It can be seen that connectionless networks as described by ISO 8473 present the user and network managers with many options, but at the cost of increased complexity. However, the complexity may be warranted by the additional functionality and flexibility that these systems offer.

THE INTERNET PROTOCOL (IP)

Introduction

The internet protocol (IP) is a networking protocol developed by the Department of Defense (see Figure 14-8). The system was implemented as part of the DARPA internetwork protocol project, and is widely used throughout the world. IP is an example of a connectionless service. It permits the exchange

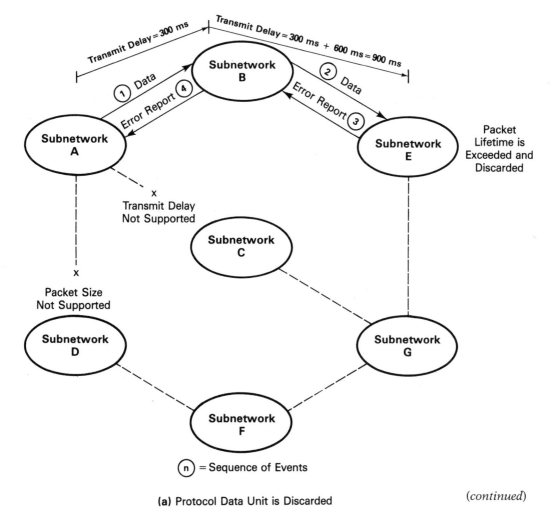

(a) Protocol Data Unit is Discarded

(continued)

FIGURE 14-7. Connectionless-Mode Service Features

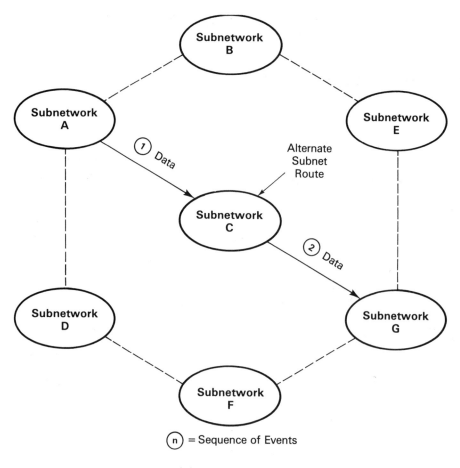

(n) = Sequence of Events

(b) Alternative Route

FIGURE 14-7. (*continued*)

of traffic between two stations without any prior call set-up. (However, these two stations do share a common connection-oriented transport protocol.)

IP is quite similar to the ISO 8473 specification explained in the previous part. Many of the ISO 8473 concepts were derived from IP. Before reading about IP, you should first read the material on ISO 8473.

The data sent by the station is encapsulated into an IP datagram. The IP header identifies the global station address of the receiving station. The IP datagram and header is further encapsulated into the specific protocol of the transit network. After the transit network has delivered the traffic to an IP gateway, its control information is stripped away. The gateway then uses the datagram header to determine where to route the traffic. It may then encapsulate the datagram header and user data into the headers and trailers of another network. Eventually, the datagram arrives at the final destination, where it is delivered to the receiving station.

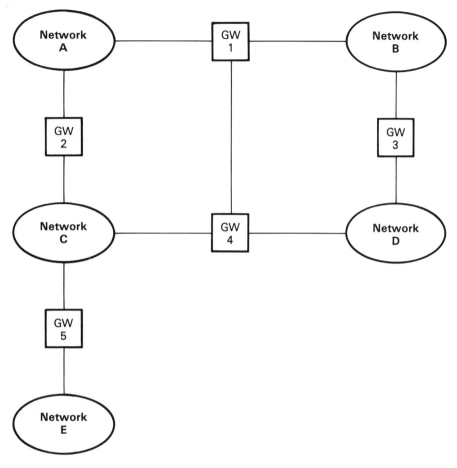

FIGURE 14-8. Internet Protocol and Gateways

IP Routing

In most instances, the IP gateway must make routing decisions. For example, if the destination station resides in another network, the IP gateway must decide how to route to the other network. Indeed, if multiple hops are involved in the communications process then each gateway must be traversed and the gateway must make decisions about routing the traffic.

Figure 14-8 shows network A may choose gateway 1 or gateway 2 to reach other networks. If the destination station is directly attached to the network serviced by the gateway, it is called directly connected. If the station is on an adjacent network to the gateway it is referred to as a neighbor gateway. If more than one gateway is required to reach the final destination, it is called a multiple hop session.

Each station and gateway maintains a routing table that contains the next gateway to the final destination network. These tables may be static or dynamic, although both approaches provide alternate routes in the event of problems at a gateway.

The IP uses the source routing, route recording, fragmentation and reassembly functions explained with ISO 8473. It also uses a datagram life-time feature as well as an error report in the event data units are discarded.

Since the IP is a connectionless protocol, it is possible that the datagrams could be lost between the two end users' stations. For example, the IP gateway generally enforces a maximum queue length size, and if this queue length is violated, the buffers will overflow. In this situation, the additional datagrams are discarded in the network. For this reason, the higher-level transport layer is essential.

Routing Tables. IP controls routing through the use of routing tables stored at each station and each gateway. The table enables a gateway to determine the next gateway to which a protocol data unit is to be sent. In the event a gateway fails, the neighbors of the gateway issue a time-out and send status reports to other gateways and stations. This status report identifies the problem IP gateway and allows gateways and stations to change their routing tables to reflect the change.

Since many networks may be involved in the communications between two user stations, it is likely that individual packet sizes will exist in the end-to-end process. To accommodate this requirement, IP permits datagrams to be fragmented through the system. Each of the fragmented data units is provided with an identifier to uniquely identify it with the other associated packets. In addition, a length indicator (LI) is placed in the protocol data unit to identify the relative position in the original datagram.

IP uses two primitives to communicate with the end user. The transmitting user utilizes the Send primitive to request the services of the network. In turn, IP uses the Deliver primitive to notify the destination user of the arrival of data. The interface of IP with the network layer is quite simple, because IP is designed to operate with several diverse kinds of networks. Because of this requirement, the IP network interface performs relatively few functions.

It should prove instructive to compare the IP protocol data unit (Figure 14-9) with the ISO 8473 protocol data unit (Figure 14-6). Again we see many similarities between the two protocols. A description of the IP data unit field is provided in Box 14-2.

Internet Control Message Protocol (ICMP)

IP contains a module called the internet control message protocol (ICMP) (see Figure 14-10). The responsibility of ICMP is to provide status messages and diagnostics to IP regarding certain activities in the network. The ICMP notifies the IP when datagrams cannot be delivered, when gateways direct traffic on shorter routes, or when the gateway might not have sufficient buffering capacity to forward protocol data units. The ICMP also notifies the

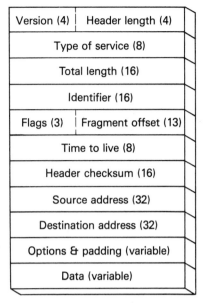

(n) = Number of bits

FIGURE 14-9. Internet Protocol Data Unit (IP Diagram)

IP if a destination is unreachable, is responsible for managing or creating a time-exceeded message in the event that the lifetime of the datagram expires, and performs certain editing functions in the event the protocol data unit header is in error.

In order to ascertain if two stations can communicate, ICMP also supports the echo and echo reply messages. An echo message recipient must return an echo reply message. The two protocol data units are used to determine if the two destinations can be reached from each other

ICMP also supports time stamp and time stamp reply messages. These data units provide a means for examining and calculating the delay characteristics of the network. The sender of the data unit can place a time stamp

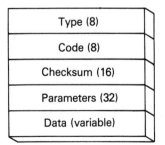

FIGURE 14-10. The Internet Control Message Protocol Data Unit

The *version field* identifies the version of IP. The *internet header length* specifies the length of the IP header. A header must be at least 20 octets in length. The *type of service* field stipulates functions similar to ISO 8473 such as transit delay, throughput, priority and reliability. The *total length field* specifies the total length of the IP datagram, including the header.

The *identifier* is used with the address fields to uniquely identify the data unit. It serves the same function as the ISO 8473 data unit identifier.

The *flags* are used to indicate that (a) more data is forthcoming for a fragmented data unit or (b) fragmentation is prohibited. The *fragmentation offset* describes where the datagram belongs within the original protocol data unit. It is measured in 64-bit units, so a datagram (except the last perhaps) must be at least 64 bits in length.

The *time to live* field is identical to the function of the ISO 8473 lifetime field, except it is measured in number of gateway hops and not in 500 ms increments.

The *protocol* field is used to identify a next-level protocol that is to receive the user data at the final destination. This field serves the same functions as the NSAPs in ISO 8473. The *header checksum* is used to perform an error check on the header.

The *source and destination address* fields identify the networks and the specific stations within the network. The address field lengths are 32 bits but can be used in combinations for variable addressing.

The *option* field is used to request additional services for the IP user. It is similar to the option part field of ISO 8473. The *padding* field is used to give the header a 32-bit alignment.

Finally, the *user data* field contains user data. The user data field and the header cannot exceed 65,535 octets.

---

in the message, or the receiver can append its time stamp and transmit this back to the originator of the traffic. ICMP also provides for source/squelch messages. This allows either a user station or a gateway to stop transmitting traffic or reduce the rate in which the traffic is transmitted. The source/squelch message contains the header of the datagram that created the problem.

The contents of the ICMP are shown in Figure 14-10. The type field specifies the type of ICMP message. The code field is used to identify parameters in the message. If this field is not long enough, the parameters field is also used. The information field provides additional information about the ICMP message. The checksum field performs an error check on the entire ICMP message.

In summary, ICMP uses these types of messages to perform the following functions:

Time exceeded on datagram lifetime

Parameter unintelligible

Destination unreachable (for a variety of reasons)

Source "squelch" for flow control

Echo and echo reply

Redirect for routing management

Time stamp and time stamp reply

X.75 INTERNETWORKING

Introduction

X.25 is designed for users to communicate with each other through one network. However, two users operating on two separate X.25 networks may need to establish communications to share resources and exchange data. X.75 is designed to meet this need. It is also used to connect packet exchanges within a network. The standard has been in development for almost ten years; it was published as a provisional recommendation in 1978, and amended in 1980, 1984, and 1988.

The objective of X.75 is to allow internetworking. It provides a gateway for a user to communicate through multiple networks with another user (see Figure 14-11). As mentioned before, it is also used to connect exchanges within a network. The standard works best when user stations, networks and packet exchanges use X.25 packets, because X.75 uses the X.25 packet headers that are created in the subnetworks.

X.75 is quite similar to X.25. It has many of its features, such as permanent virtual circuits, virtual call circuits, logical channel groups, logical channels and several of the control packets. The architecture is divided into physical, link and packet levels, with X.75 sitting above X.25 in the network layer.

X.75 defines the operation of international packet switched services. It describes how two terminals are connected logically by an international link while each terminal is operating within its own packet mode data network. X.75 uses a slightly different term for the network interface. In the description of X.25, we used the term data circuit-terminating equipment (DCE) to describe an X.25 packet exchange. The X.75 terminology defines this device as a signalling terminal (STE), even though it may be the same as the X.25 device.

Like X.25, the physical level can be implemented with appropriate V series recommendations (such as V.35). X.75 requires the signalling to be performed at 64 Kbit/s. (An optional rate is 48 Kbit/s.) Of course, many vendors use other link speeds (56 Kbit/s, 1.544 Mbit/s, etc.). The second level of X.75 uses the HDLC subset LAPB. X.75 does not support LAP.

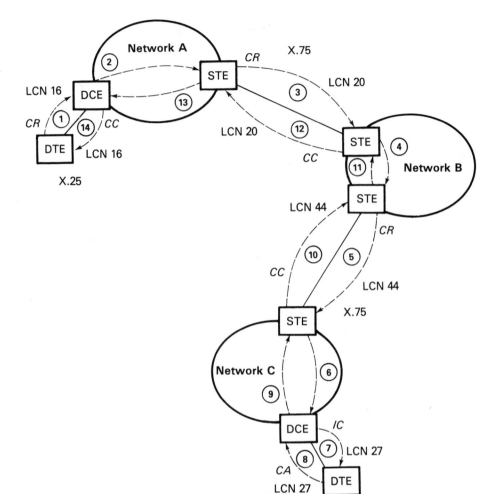

(n) = Sequence of Events

CR: Call Request
CC: Call Connected
IC: Incoming Call
CA: Call Accepted
LCN: Logical Channel Number

FIGURE 14-11. Internetworking X.25 Networks with X.75 (Connection Establishment)

X.75 and Multilink Procedures (MLP)

The X.75 link level frequently uses the multilink procedure (MLP). This procedure provides for the use of multiple links between STEs. MLP establishes the rules for frame transmission and frame resequencing for delivery to/from the multiple links. Multilink operations allow the use of parallel communications channels between STEs in such a manner that they appear as one channel with a greater capacity. The multilink operation provides for more reliability and throughput than can be achieved on a single channel.

Multilink procedures (MLP) exist at the upper part of the data link level. The X.25 network layer perceives it as connected to a single link and the LAPB single links operate as if they were connected directly to the network layer. MLP is responsible for flow control between layers 2 and 3, as well as resequencing the data units for delivery to the network layer. The network layer operates with a perceived higher capacity in the data link layer. MLP is described in more detail in Chapter 11.

X.75 Packet Types

X.75 does not use the variety of packet types that are found in X.25, primarily because the STE-to-STE communication has no relationship to the "other side of the cloud." In X.75, there is no other side, since the communication is only between two STEs and not two sets of DCEs/DTEs. The X.75 protocol uses the following packet types:

- Call Set-up and Clearing
    Call Request
    Call Connected
    Clear Request
    Clear Confirmation
- Data and Interrupt
    Data
    Interrupt
    Interrupt Confirmation
- Flow Control and Reset
    Receive Ready
    Receive Not Ready
    Reset Confirmation
- Restart
    Restart
    Restart Confirmation

The X.75 packet format is almost identical to the X.25 format. The address fields are specifically defined as international data numbers (X.121). The logical channels have significance only for the STE-to-STE interface.

The similarities and differences between X.25 and X.75 can be seen by an examination of Figure 14-11. The DTE in network A is initiating a call to a DTE in network C. The call set-up packet and logical channel relationships are depicted for each phase of the connection establishment.

The X.75 packet carries an additional field called network utilities. Its purpose is to provide for network administrative functions and signalling. In many situations, a request in the X.25 user packet facility field invokes the use of an X.75 network utility.

INTERNETWORKING SNA AND X.25

Introduction

X.25 networks are growing in use and the protocol is now used in many network and non-network interfaces. In recognition of this fact, IBM has developed several major products to internetwork SNA and X.25. These products fall into two categories: (1) the use of X.25 as the primary transit interface between SNA and X.25 devices (Figure 14-12[a]); and (2) the use of SNA as the primary transit network between SNA and X.25 devices (Figure 14-12[b]). This section discusses the use of X.25 as the transit network. The next section explains how SNA serves as the transit network to connect X.25 and SNA devices.

Using X.25 as the Transit Network

The IBM X.25 NCP packet switching interface (NPSI) provides an interface for SNA users through a packet switched data network. NPSI appears to SNA to be a series of switched or nonswitched SDLC links. When used as an interface to an X.25 network, NPSI provides communications between the following DTEs:

SNA host node to SNA peripheral node
SNA host node to SNA host node
SNA host node to non-SNA X.25 node
SNA host node to X.28 node
SNA host node to other non-SNA node

NPSI provides a key service called the virtual circuit manager (VCM). This manager supervises all virtual circuits at the NPSI packet switched interface. It is responsible for managing all connections using switched virtual circuits. It is also responsible for handling error recovery procedures on the virtual circuits. The virtual circuit manager functions are controlled by the systems services control point (SSCP) or by X.25 control packets from

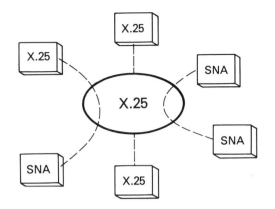

(a) Using X.25 as the Transit Network

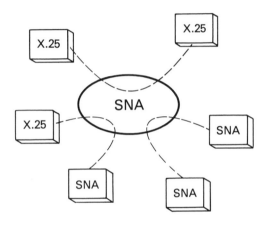

(b) Using SNA as the Transit Network

FIGURE 14-12. Internetworking SNA and X.25

the packet network. VCM allows the SNA user to communicate with either remote SNA nodes or remote non-SNA nodes.

The X.25 NPSI supports several types of X.25 virtual circuits. The various support functions are classified with respect to the type of DTE at the remote end of the connection. To give the reader an idea of the X.25/SNA interfaces, two systems are analyzed:

Type 0 virtual circuits: Connections to non-SNA DTEs

Type 3 virtual circuits: Connections to SNA subarea nodes

Type 0 Virtual Circuits. As shown in Figure 14-13, Type 0 virtual circuits are supported by the host communicating with NPSI over an SNA session between the SSCP located in the access method and the physical unit (PU) located in the front-end processor. In turn, a logical unit session is developed between the LU (and the application program) and the LU in NPSI. The Type 0 virtual circuit connection is supported by a section of code within NPSI called the protocol converter for non-SNA equipment (PCNE). This code converts outgoing SNA commands to X.25 packets and incoming X.25 packets to SNA commands.

PCNE is invoked for the virtual call set-up and clear. Once the virtual circuit is established, the LU-to-LU session is invoked to manage the data flow between the host application and the packet switching interface. The PCNE is involved in converting outgoing SNA protocol data units (PIUs) into data packets; it also converts the incoming X.25 data packets to SNA PIUs and sends them to the application program through the LU-to-LU session. The data packet actually contains the X.25 packet header and an SNA request response unit (RU).

Now that we have introduced an SNA/X.25 interface, it should prove useful to examine why IBM (and many other vendors) use this approach. The

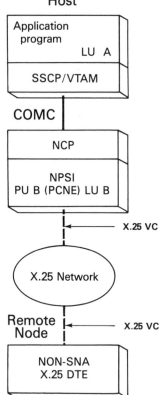

FIGURE 14-13. Type 0 Virtual Circuit

salient fact is that the remote device (a) is not an SNA device and (b) is an X.25 device. Consequently, IBM developed the PCNE module to perform the very complex task of translating between the SNA and X.25 protocols. PCNE must keep the X.25 protocol isolated from any of the SNA functions and vice versa. For example, an incoming X.25 call request packet must be translated ("mapped") to a comparable SNA command, if one exists. If it does not exist, it must create a command to keep SNA functioning properly and return an X.25 call connected packet to the X.25 module to keep it running. It takes little imagination to grasp how powerful a protocol converter like PCNE must be.

Does this configuration ensure that the application data is accepted at the remote device? The answer depends on which layers are involved. This approach provides for compatibility up to the network level. However, it does not provide assurance of upper layer compatibility. The reader should be aware that the upper levels must still resolve the fact that a non-SNA device is logically attached to an SNA host. Consequently, it will be necessary to create upper level activities to resolve problems such as incompatible codes, different cursor control commands, etc.

Type 3 Virtual Circuits A Type 3 virtual circuit is also an example of how SNA provides connections through an X.25 network to a SNA peripheral node (as in Type 2). However, this approach uses an additional feature called boundary network node qualified logical link control (BNN QLLC). This feature interprets and processes the SNA PIUs flowing between the host through the X.25 network and the peripheral nodes. BNN QLLC is responsible for placing the SNA PIUs destined for the peripheral node into the X.25 packet. For incoming packets, BNN QLLC removes the PIUs from the packets and sends them to the host.

Another possibility for the Type 3 virtual circuits is to communicate between two SNA subarea nodes, as shown in Figure 14-14. This requires two types of SNA sessions to be associated with this connection. The first one is a SSCP-SSCP session between the two hosts communicating together. The other session is an LU-LU session between the LU and one host or peripheral node and the LU in the other host or peripheral node. In contrast to remote peripheral node set-up, which uses the BNN QLLC, this implementation uses an NPSI module called the intermediate network node qualified logical link control (INN QLLC). This module is responsible for interpreting and processing the PIUs flowing between the SNA host and the adjacent SNA device assigned to the virtual circuit. The INN QLLC is responsible for placing PIUs into the X.25 packet for out-putting to the remote node. In turn, it removes PIUs from the incoming packets and sends them to the host. What is the rationale for this configuration? Simply put, IBM uses the concepts of encapsulation and decapsulation to achieve internetworking.

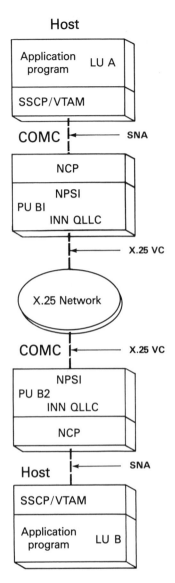

FIGURE 14-14. Type 3 Virtual Circuit

Using SNA as the Transit Network

IBM's X.25 SNA Interconnect (XI) gives a user the ability to use SNA as the transit network. In other words, it provides the "cloud" between X.25 and SNA devices. The XI network is made up of a set of communicating devices with the XI node residing in a front-end processor using the network control program (NCP) and NPSI. The X.25 packets or SNA protocol data units are routed between XIs using the conventional SNA network services. XI is not needed at SNA intermediate nodes; XI is only installed where the X.25 DTE interfaces connect to the 3725.

The Session Pipe. In providing X.25 service through SNA, a fundamental question had to be addressed. How are logical units (LUs) to be used, since the logical unit concept is integral to SNA? It might appear that a logical unit session could be related to each X.25 virtual call. However LU-to-LU sessions provide more functions for the user than does an X.25 logical channel connection. An SNA session entails considerable resources for set-up and management. A comparable X.25 VC does not require this type of resource. As a consequence, it is impractical to set up an LU for each virtual call, because the cost would simply be prohibitive.

The XI concept is based on a session as a "pipe." The X.25 logical channel networking procedures are performed completely within XI. All these logical channel communications occur through a single session between two XIs supporting the process. Consequently, the system services control point (SSCP) resources are not needed for each VC. The concept is illustrated in Figure 14-15(a). Each XI node exists within a 3725 and each XI node has an LU for each XI with which it is communicating. Multiple virtual calls are carried within one session of the XI. In other words, XI multiplexes the VCs across the XI-XI link.

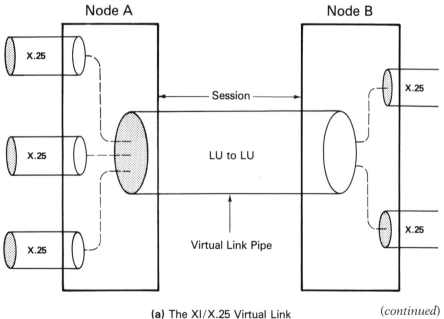

(a) The XI/X.25 Virtual Link   *(continued)*

FIGURE 14-15. The XI/X.25 Session Pipe

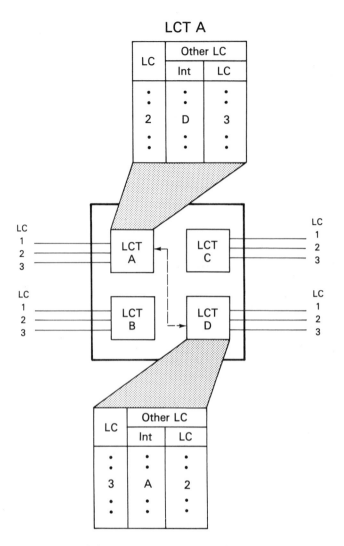

(b) Logical Channel Tables (LCT)

FIGURE 14-15. (*continued*)

The operation of XI is centered on the concept of logical channel switching as illustrated in Figure 14-15(b). Each XI module maintains a logical channel table, which has an entry for each logical channel defined to that node. In this figure, LC 2 in logical channel Table A is mapped with LC 3 in logical channel Table B. A logical channel table entry provides a pointer associating its logical channel to the other logical channel within the XI node. This pointer is established at call set-up time and is used to route the data packets through the XI's sessions with each other. There is no restriction in the pairing of the logical channels and the logical channels can be switched in any manner.

The interface in Figure 14-15(b) can represent one of these possible entities: (1) An LAPB physical link can be an interface (or both interfaces) if the communicating users are within the same node; and (2) the interface may be an "external interface" in that the packets can be treated as if they have arrived from another network.

As stated earlier, the LU is simply a pipeline for the virtual calls. Once these sessions are established between two logical channels, they can be switched only between each other. XI does not permit switching to another LC on another session during this process. Of course, this would be a very powerful capability, but it would be extraordinarily complex and costly.

INTERNETWORKING DECnet AND SNA

Introduction

Many internetworking products are offered by vendors to connect to an IBM product. DEC is no exception. It has several systems that provide the following SNA/DEC interconnections:

- Access from a DECnet host to an IBM host through an SNA network.
- Support of programs in the DECnet host that act as logical units to SNA.
- Support of the features offered by the SNA transmission Control and Data Flow Control layers.
- Ability to communicate with SNA by emulating an SNA Physical Unit Type 2 (PU2).
- Use of an emulated PU2 from another DECnet system to communicate with SNA resources.

DECnet/SNA Gateway

DECnet/SNA internetworking products provide two methods to connect to an IBM SNA network, the DECnet/SNA Gateway, and the VMS/SNA Software.

The DECnet gateway allows DECnet nodes in a DEC network to communicate with IBM systems in an SNA network. From the perspective of the SNA view, DEC's gateway is an SNA Type 2 Physical Unit (PU2). DEC provides two methods to implement the gateway. One approach is called the DX24 gateway. This approach allows the DECnet SNA gateway to be attached point-to-point to the DECnet host system. The second approach is called the DECSA gateway. This structure is established for direct connection of the DECnet host to an Ethernet local area network. The DX24 gateway and the DECSA gateway remain transparent to the DECnet users.

The two approaches are shown in Figure 14-16. The DX24 gateway in Figure 14-16(a) acts as the connector between the DECnet and the SNA. Typically, the DECnet gateway connects to the IBM communications controller such as a 3725. The DECSA gateway shown in Figure 14-16(b) also attaches to the IBM communications controller. In this figure the gateway acts as a node attachment to the Ethernet cable.

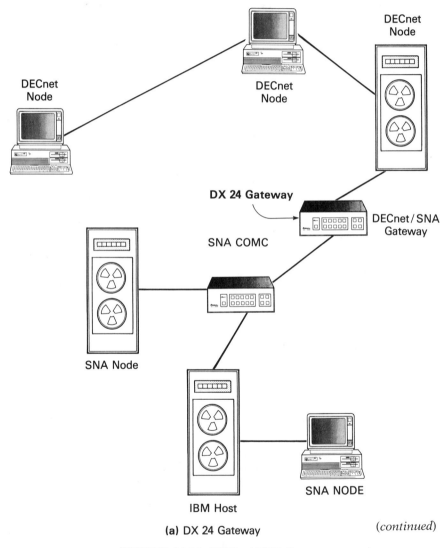

(a) DX 24 Gateway   (*continued*)

FIGURE 14-16. DECnet/SNA Gateway

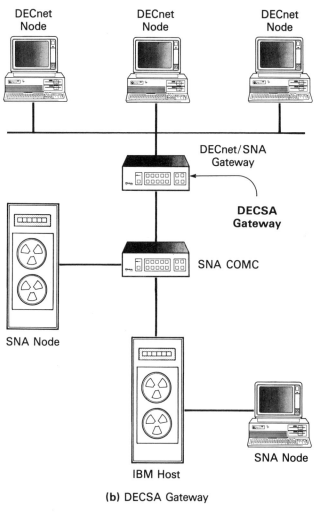

FIGURE 14-16. (*continued*)

VMS/SNA Software

In the past, DEC provided gateways to IBM and SNA through the means of a conventional DECnet gateway. Today it is possible to offer the gateway through DEC's MicroVAX. DEC VMS/SNA software provides the DEC-to-IBM connection without the intervening DEC network. (However, it should be emphasized that both options are available to a user.) To a SNA host, the attached MicroVAX simply appears to be a SNA node operating as a cluster controller or as a physical unit Type 2 (PU2).

The MicroVAX can also perform both communications and applications functions. This capability differs from the DECnet/SNA gateway, which is a dedicated communications processor. The reader is cautioned that the MicroVAX CPU connection may not support a large amount of traffic. Eventually, the more powerful DECnet/SNA gateway might have to be used. In this discussion, we assume either product is being used. The complementary software in the two techniques allows a user to run either package. For purposes of brevity, the systems are referred to as DECnet/SNA gateway.

Relationships Between DECnet and SNA Layers for Gateway Operations

The DECnet local node is a secondary logical unit (SLU) using SNA protocols such as RJE, 3270, etc. The data from this node is passed to DEC's Network Application Layer (the SNA Gateway Access Module).

This module accepts the SNA data and passes it to the DECnet layers. The data is passed to the gateway and received by DEC's Gateway Server Module, which is the PU-to-SNA. The Gateway Server Module acts as the go-between. It acts on requests of both the local node (SLU) and the IBM host node (PLU). It also uses the services of the SNA protocol emulator to gain access to the SNA network.

The SNA protocol emulator emulates the activities of SNA's Path Control and Data Link Control layers. SNA recognizes it as a PU2 node. The emulator also performs the necessary functions to communicate with SNA's SSCP (System Services Control Point.)

DX24

The DX24 gateway allows one or two communications links from the DECnet nodes. Several DCE types are available as well as various line speeds. For planning considerations, the user should be aware that various components can be used such as modems, modem eliminators, or direct coaxial connections. The connections require synchronous modems using EIA-232-D or an equivalent V.24/V.28 interface. Optionally, a modem eliminator is allowed, or a direct coaxial connection can be used. Generally, the lower speed CCITT V modems can be used as well as the Bell modems. The physical level interfaces generally do not present a serious problem as long as they are coordinated and planned before the installation.

The other major aspect for the installation at the DX24 gateway is loading the DEC software properly to the gateway node. This requires generating the software parameters in accordance with the DEC specifications (the appropriate DECnet/SNA gateway management guides).

INTERNETWORKING DECnet AND X.25

Introduction

DEC provides two major gateway products for connecting DEC equipment (which may or may not use DECnet) to an X.25 network. The two products are called VAX PSI and VAX PSI Access.

The VAX PSI system operates in one of two modes, native mode and multihost mode (see Figure 14-17). The native mode allows a direct access to

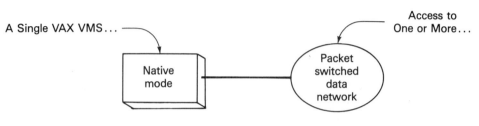

(a) Example of Native Mode

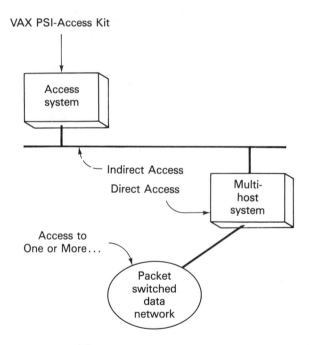

(b) Example of Multi-host Node

FIGURE 14-17. VAX PSI and PSI Access

one or more X.25 packet networks from a single VAX system. The multihost mode provides direct access into one or more X.25 public networks. It also provides indirect access for other systems. DEC requires that all systems must have the VAX PSI system installed and all systems must be running DECnet.

The VAX PSI Access software operates in one mode: access mode. The access mode provides system access to any X.25 packet data network to which multimode system is connected. DEC requires that both systems use DECnet. DEC also provides a combination system which permits the same VAX machine to run both VAX PSI and VAX PSI Access.

Another very useful feature for the DEC X.25 gateway is the ability to configure the VAX to operate as either a DTE or a DCE. Other vendors have this approach as well. It is very useful for communicating with another system that may not have X.25 DCE software.

A single VAX PSI provides considerable flexibility because it permits a VAX machine to connect to more than one packet network. Moreover, the gateway provides the ability to use multiple physical lines into one or more networks.

DECnet manages X.25 virtual circuits (switched and permanent) through the network management layer. The network management commands the routing layer to initialize X.25 circuits. This is performed by DECnet's routing initialization sublayer. The sublayer contains a data base which is maintained by network management. This data base maps the routing layer circuits to X.25 permanent and switched circuits. The data base contains information on X.25 calls such as addresses, the X.25 packet sizes, call attempts, etc. An outgoing call to an X.25 network is serviced by the routing initialization sublayer which provides the necessary parameters to the X.25 header. These parameters are used to communicate directly with the X.25 network mode.

In the case of the incoming X.25 call, routing initialization determines whether to accept the call or reject it. It performs this function principally by examining the DTE addresses in the X.25 incoming call packet. The routing initialization sublayer may also segment and combine DNA datagrams in the packets. The sublayer also appends an error check field to every packet to check for transmission errors at the other end of the link.

The routing initialization sublayer is also responsible for monitoring the X.25 connections. Some of the events monitored are X.25 clears, restarts, and resets. In the event any of these packets are transmitted to the routing initialization sublayer, it sets the circuit as inoperable, informs its routing control sublayer, and then attempts to reinitialize the X.25 circuit.

DECnet Layer Operation with X.25

While considerable X.25 gateway logic resides at the DECnet Network Application Layer, the routing layer also provides several services. The initialization sublayer (see Chapter 13 and the section on DECnet routing layer) contains a data base maintained by the network management layer. It is used to map between the routing layer circuits and X.25 permanent virtual circuits and switched virtual circuits. The data base contains parameters such as DTE addresses, maximum packet size, retries on failed calls, etc. The initialization sublayer also performs the following other functions:

- Segments or assembles DECnet datagrams into X.25 packets
- Appends checksum to each X.25 packet
- As with other circuits, monitors X.25 circuits for errors (X.25 resets, restarts, clears)

The network application layer uses several facilities to provide the X.25 gateway access service. Their relationships to the other DECnet layers are shown in Figure 14-18.

INTERNETWORKING AN X.25 STATION ON A LAN

Introduction

At first glance, it might appear that placing an X.25 station onto a local area network would be a relatively simple process. After all, if all components use standard primitives with the LAN and perform encapsulation and decapsulation functions, the process should be fairly straightforward. Unfortunately, the problem is more involved. Consider the following:

- Since X.25 is written from the network (DCE) perspective, a user must define some of the specific actions of the DTE.
- LAN stations generally communicate symmetrically (i.e., on a DTE-to-DTE basis). We have learned that X.25 is asymmetric: DTE-to-DCE on each side of the network cloud.
- X.25 is basically point-to-point with the DTE and DCE as the two points. Many LANs are broadcast systems, and the LAN DTEs connect logically through the broadcast medium.
- X.25 uses the very reliable, connection-oriented data link layer, LAPB. Most LANs use the logical link control, type 1 specification from the IEEE (IEEE LLC1, 802.2). LLC1 is connectionless, and allows the use of unnumbered information (UI) frames. Consequently, LLC1 differs significantly from LAPB.
- Many X.25 public packet network vendors administer the X.25 facilities. LAN stations often need to control some of the facilities directly. Moreover, some X.25 DCEs are very powerful, offering several thousand simultaneous virtual calls to the attached DTEs. Many LANs do not have this kind of capacity.

- With a connectionless link-level LAN (LLC1), the idea of an X.25 level 2 (LAPB) link connection does not exist. Reinitializing the link from the context of X.25 is simply not in the repertoire of LLC1's commands and responses.

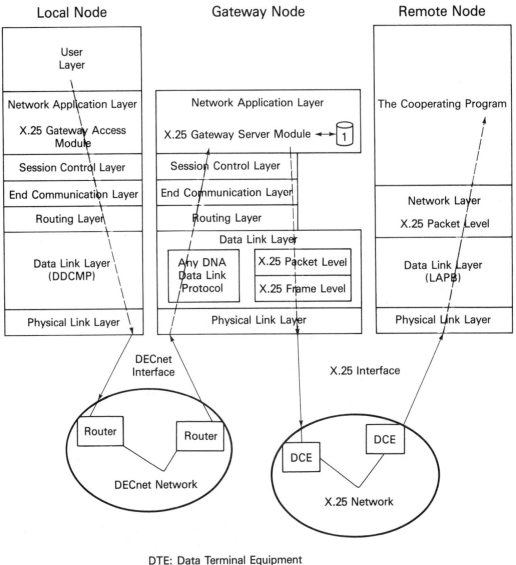

DTE: Data Terminal Equipment
DCE: Data Circuit Equipment
Router: A DNA Node Performing Switching
①: Incoming Call Mapping Database

FIGURE 14-18. DECnet Facilities and DECnet Layer Relationships [DECN82A]

Nonetheless, it is possible to internetwork X.25 with LANs. Fortunately, the ISO 8881 (annex A) provides several scenarios for the internetworking of X.25 LAN stations. Figure 14-19 depicts four possibilities:

1. One gateway between a LAN and an X.25 WAN
2. Two gateways between a LAN and an X.25 WAN
3. One gateway that connects two LANs
4. Two gateways that connect two LANs

A LAN station in Figure 14-19 is to communicate with another station which is not on its LAN. It must communicate with an internetworking unit (IWU) located on its LAN. The IWU provides the requisite gateway functions to support the internetworking. As discussed in the introductory section of this book and in Chapter 8, the protocols below X.25 PLP on the right and

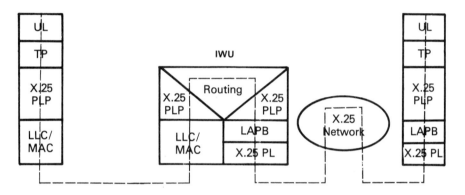

(a) Gateway Between LAN and WAN

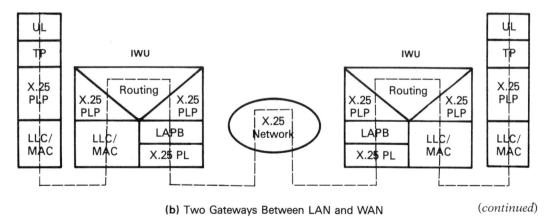

(b) Two Gateways Between LAN and WAN   (*continued*)

FIGURE 14-19. X.25 and LAN Gateways

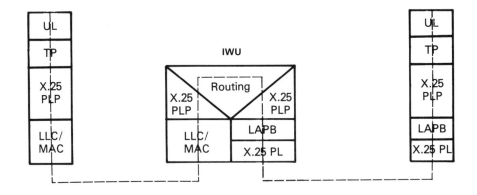

(c) Gateway Between Two LANS

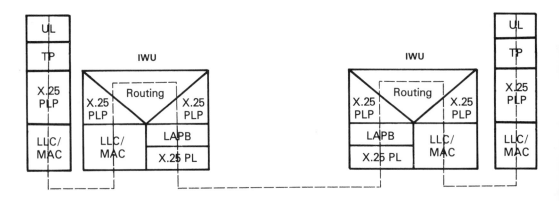

(d) Two Gateways Between Two LANS

FIGURE 14-19. (*continued*)

left sides of each other are independent of each other. ISO 8881 (Annex A) describes how the right and left sides of the X.25 PLP levels can be coupled. It does not address the lower levels.

The LAN station acts as an X.25 DTE and each station communicates in a point-to-point mode as stipulated by ISO 8208. The packet level (PL) entity of the DTE-to-DTE is identified by the media across control (MAC) address of the two LAN stations.

The IWU is responsible for mapping the logical channel numbers across the two sides of the PLP levels. This task is the same as any wide area X.25 network that must map the LANs across both sides of the network cloud. However, the IWU performs two different roles: It emulates a DCE on the terminal side and a DTE on the network side.

Call Set-up and Clearing

The IWU performs the functions of an X.25 network cloud. It receives call set-up and clear packets from both sides of the gateway, performs several editing functions and maps the packet types to other packet types.

During a call set-up, the IWU will receive an incoming call packet from either the LAN or an X.25 network. (These networks have already processed the request from a user, created the call request packet, and sent it to the X.25 PLP, where it is mapped to the incoming call packet.) The IWU checks the packet (including facilities requests). It matches the window sizes and packet sizes to relate the incoming call packet to those available on the other interface. If the IWU does not have segmentation and reassembly capabilities, it must ensure that the packet sizes on the two interfaces are equal or clear the call. If segmenting and reassembly are supported by the IWU, it dictates the sizes. It maps the MAC addresses at the LAN interface and the X.25 address at the packet interface (X.25 address fields and address extension fields).

The IWU determines the recipient of the packet and maps the address across both sides of the IWU. It must also select a free logical channel on the other side of the IWU and store the association of the two logical channels in order to transfer the ongoing data packets to the proper recipient during the data transfer state. It then transmits a call request to the outgoing side of the IWU. The receiving station maps this packet into an incoming call packet.

If the call request is successful, the IWU receives a call connected packet from the called station. It then transmits a call accepted packet to the calling interface, using the logical channel corresponding to the original incoming call packet. The IWU handles unsuccessful calls with clear request and clear indication packets.

From the preceding discussion, it can be concluded that the IWU acts as an intermediary between the two communicating stations. For example, it recreates the call request packet from the originating station in one direction and recreates the call accepted packet in the other direction.

ACCESSING X.25
NETWORKS THROUGH THE ISDN

The ISDN CCITT recommendation X.31 provides two scenarios for the interface of an X.25 packet mode terminal into an ISDN node: (1) the minimum integration scenario and (2) the maximum integration scenario. (The reader may wish to read the ISDN section in Chapter 19 before reading this material. It is included in this chapter because it is an internetworking protocol.)

Minimum Integration. Figure 14-20(a) illustrates the minimum integration scenario. It supports a very rudimentary and basic service. The

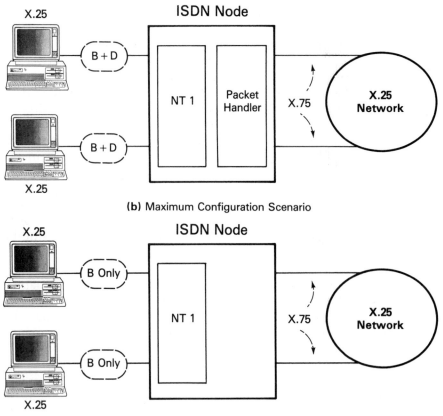

(b) Maximum Configuration Scenario

(a) Minimum Configuration Scenario

FIGURE 14-20. ISDN and X.25 Configurations

ISDN provides a transparent handling of the packet calls from the DTE to the X.25 network. The minimum integration scenario only supports B Channel access. Moreover, if two local DTEs wish to communicate with each other, their packets must be transmitted through the ISDN and through the X.25 network, before the packets can be relayed to the other DTE. The minimum integration scenario uses the B Channels for all call management. This is performed using ISDN signalling procedures prior to initiating the X.25 level 2 and level 3 procedures. In essence, the ISDN node passes the X.25 call transparently to the X.25 network.

Maximum Integration. The maximum integration scenario provides several additional functions, as depicted in Figure 14-20(b). The ISDN provides a packet handling (PH) function within the node. Actual implementations of the maximum integration scenario use two separate facilities for the interconnection. The ISDN switch is provided through a vendor's ISDN NT1 product and the packet handler function is provided by the vendor's packet switch itself.

The maximum integration scenario permits two options: (1) access via the B Channel, and (2) access via the D Channel. With the first option, more than one terminal can be supported at the customer site, and any one of the terminals is able to use the B Channel to establish calls. This scenario permits multiple terminal operations of packet devices using multiplexing techniques. The access through the D Channel is the implementation that is being used in more vendors' products today. All active logical channels are established through a D Channel connection and all X.25 packets, including connection set-ups, connection disconnects, and data packets must be transmitted on the D Channel on the LAPD link. In effect, the D Channel access provides the preferred method of out of channel (out of band) signalling characteristic.

THE X.300 INTERWORKING STANDARDS

The CCITT publishes a series of standards in the 1988 Blue Books pertaining to the internetworking of various types of networks. They encompass several documents numbered X.300 through X.370, generally called the X.300 Interworking Standards. You may have noticed that we have introduced a new word, *interworking*. The CCITT uses this word in place of internetworking.

Perhaps one of the most useful features of X.300 is its explanation of how the X-Series Recommendations fit into interworking. Figure 14-21 is a simplified view of the X.300/X-Series framework. The standards are divided into three categories:

Aspects of interworking pertinent to different cases
Aspects of interworking pertinent to each case
Aspects of internetwork signalling interfaces

This book examines the signalling interface standards in previous sections and chapters. Our task here is to examine the X.300 specifications.

Categories of Interworking

The X.300 transmission capability between two networks is divided into two categories:

- *Call Control Mapping*. Call control information used for switching in one subnetwork (including addressing) is mapped into call control information in the other subnetwork.
- *Port Access*. Call control information is used by one network to select the interworking point. Then, a convergence protocol is used at this network and the call control information is mapped into call control information in the other subnetwork.

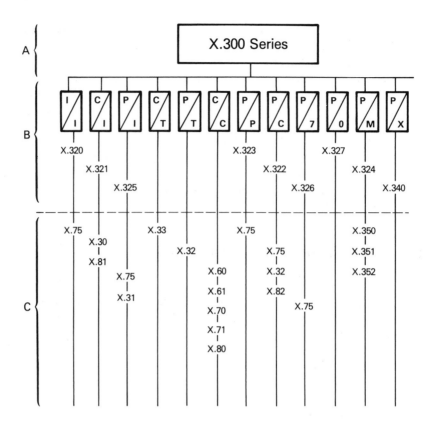

Legend:
A: Arrangements generic to different cases
B: Arrangements for each case
C: Interwork signalling interfaces

Abbreviations:
C: Circuit switched data network
I: ISDN
M: Mobile network
O: Privately owned network
P: Packet switched data network
T: Telephone network
X: Telex network
7: Signalling system No 7

FIGURE 14-21. The X-Series Framework

Transfer of Addressing Information

One of the more important parts of the X.300 recommendations is contained
in X.301: rules for the transfer of addressing information. X.301 defines how
X.121 and E.164 addresses are used between two networks. (See Chapter 13,
Appendix 13A, for X.121 and E.164 descriptions.)

Figure 14-22 shows the X.301 set-up for addressing when the interworking function (IWF) is interworking an X.121 address-based network and an E.164 address-based network. Table 14-1 depicts the permissible address forms for the call establishment phase. The prefixes P1 through P6 are not passed over the IWF, and their form and use is an internal network matter. The escape digits E1 and E2 indicate that the succeeding address is a different numbering plan. The prefixes may or may not precede the escape digit.

The CCITT Blue Books now contain X.122. It is a complementary standard to X.301. Among other functions, it describes the escape codes to be used between data networks, telephone networks, and ISDNs. The escape codes are used as follows:

- Escape code 0: Escape from X.121 to E.164 and request a digital interface at destination network.
- Escape code 9: Escape from X.121 to E.164/163 and request an analog interface at destination network.

It is also permissible to use another field to indicate the type of address present. This element in the protocol is called the *Number Plan Indicator/Type of Address* (NPI/TOA). The form of this field depends upon the specific network access protocol employed.

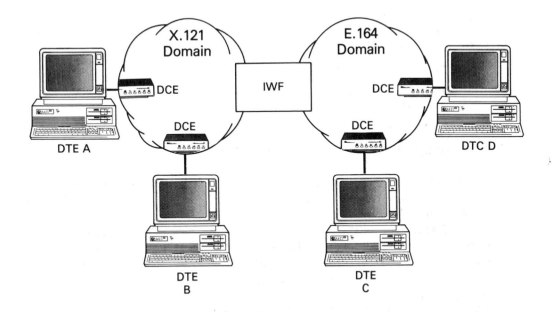

IWF: Interworking Function

FIGURE 14-22. Interworking Function (IWF) Between Two Addressing Domains

TABLE 14-1. Call Establishment Phase Address Forms

Direction (DTE to DTE)	Form of Address	Extent of Validity
A to B	NTN	Network
A to B	P1 + NTN	Network
A to B	DNIC + NTN	Internetwork
A to B	P2 + DNIC + NTN	Internetwork
A to B	NTN + [NPI/TOA]	Network
A to B	DNIC + NTN + [NPI/TOA]	Internetwork
C to D	SN	Network
C to D	P3 + SN	Network
C to D	CC + (NDC) + SN	Internetwork
C to D	P4 + CC + (NDC) + SN	Internetwork
C to D	SN + [NPI/TOA]	Network
C to D	CC + (NDC) + SN + [NPI/TOA]	Internetwork
A to C	E1 + CC + (NDC) + SN	Internetwork escape to E.164/E.163
A to C	P5 + E1 + CC + (NDC) + SN	Internetwork escape to E.164/E.163
A to C	CC + (NDC) + SN + [NPI/TOA]	Internetwork
C to A	E2 + DNIC + NTN	Internetwork escape to X.121
C to A	P6 + E2 + DNIC + NTN	Internetwork escape to X.121
C to A	DNIC + NTN + [NPI/TOA]	Internetwork

where: CC = country code   NPI = numbering plan indi-
                                                             cator
         NDC = national destination   TOA = type of address
               code
         NTN = network terminal   DNIC = data network identi-
               number   fication code

X.122 Numbering Plan for Internetworking

To provide specific guidance on using numbering plans between data networks, telephone networks, and ISDNs, X.122 was released by CCITT in 1988 as part of its Blue Books.

X.300 uses several of the X.122 conventions for escape codes (discussed in the previous section). In addition, X.122 establishes the protocol for the numbers. It does not stipulate the call set-ups between the networks.

Figure 14-23 provides an example of how the numbers are carried between two X.25 DTEs and packet and ISDN networks. The originating DTE enters the number of the called DTE with an escape code of 0 plus the E.164 address of DTE B. Its calling address uses X.121. The 0 + E.164 is used by the packet data network for routing to the correct network interface.

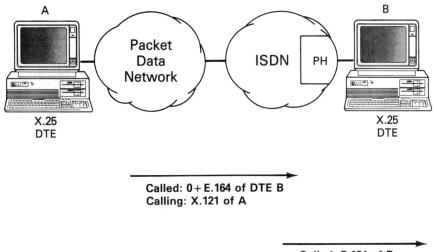

Called: 0+ E.164 of DTE B
Calling: X.121 of A

Called: E.164 of B
Calling: 0+X.121 of A

FIGURE 14-23. An X.122 Scenaro of Address Resolution

The ISDN receives the packet and places an escape code in front of the X.121 calling address. The packet is passed through the ISDN packet handler to the called DTE.

SUGGESTED READINGS

The reader is probably best served by reading the actual source documents on internetworking. Please refer to the list of this material in the section titled "Summary of Internetworking Specifications" in this chapter. In addition [NBS80] provides a discussion on IP and [CERF78] examines the issue of internetworking packet networks. [STAL85] has a very good chapter on internetworking. [STEW84] explains local area network bridges, and [CALL83] provides a comparison of IP and X.25.

APPENDIX 14A
THE ISO 8473 PROTOCOL FUNCTIONS

A connectionless protocol is sometimes viewed as having no support functions at all. However, as this material demonstrates, the 8473 network provides a wide variety of options for the user. The 8473 protocol can be analyzed by an examination of its major functions. Each is summarized in this Appendix.

The *PDU composition function* establishes the rules for construction of the protocol data unit. It establishes a procedure for creating the addresses and other data unit identifiers. The function provides the procedures for building the fields of the PDU.

The *PDU composition function* establishes the rules for interpreting the protocol control information (PCI) from the PDU and for mapping to the N-UNITDATA Indication (with the parameters for the primitive as well).

The *header format analysis function* determines if the full ISO 8473 protocol is to be employed or if the specific subset is to be used. It also provides the rules for the use of an inactive subset of the protocol.

The *PDU lifetime control function* is used to manage the lifetime of the PDU in the system. It determines whether a PDU shall be discarded because its lifetime has expired.

The *route PDU function* is used to determine the specific network entity that is to receive a protocol data unit if it is forwarded. It determines the underlying service that is to be used to reach the specific network entity. Furthermore, if segmentation is performed, this function determines where the segments will be sent (that is, to which underlying service).

The *forward PDU function* is responsible for issuing the SN-UNITDATA Request primitive to supply the subnetwork or the SNDCF with the addresses for routing. In other words, it identifies the next system that is to receive the PDU.

The *segmentation function* describes the procedures for segmenting a protocol data unit if it is larger than the maximum size supported by an underlying service. It also describes the use of the segmentation fields in the actual PDU.

The *reassembly function* provides complementary guidance on the rules for reassembling the segmented PDUs into the full PDU. It describes procedures for reassembly times and reassembly lifetimes in the system.

The *discard PDU function* is responsible for freeing resources which have been reserved when various situations have been encountered. For example, the protocol procedure has been violated; local congestion prevents delivery; a checksum is inconsistent; etc.

The *error reporting function* describes the procedures for creating the error report portion of the protocol data unit. This function is described in more detail shortly.

The *PDU header error detection function* is used to check the contents of the entire PDU header with a checksum. It can be used to verify the header at each point where the PDU header is processed. It protects against the corruption of the PDU header through the entire system.

The *padding function* simply provides space in the PDU header for the reservation of any other support function that may be invoked.

The *security function* is used to provide for certain protection services in the system. For example, data authentication and confidentiality of the data can be invoked. It is left up to the specific network provider to interpret how the security functions are actually used.

The *source routing function* can be invoked to allow the originator to specify the path for a specific protocol data unit. This function provides the rules for creating the addresses to designate the route of the PDU. These addresses are placed in the contents of the PDU itself. Examples in the main body of this chapter show the use of this function.

The *record route function* is used to record the paths that are actually taken by the PDU as it traverses through the subnetworks to the final destination. More detail is provided on this important function in the body of the chapter.

The *quality of service and maintenance function* is used to assist the subnetworks to make routing decisions where certain quality of service functions are to be invoked. It is used to attempt to provide a consistent level of service through the subnetworks (where possible). Obviously, if the subnetworks cannot provide the required quality of services, then the services cannot be met.

The *priority function* allows a PDU with a higher priority value to be treated preferentially over lower priority PDUs. The specific network entity is free to implement this function in the specific manner it chooses.

The *congestion notification function* is used to allow the network service users to take appropriate action when congestion is experienced. The congestion function provides a flag in the quality of service parameter in the PDU header. The flag can be set to 1 by any underlying system processing the PDU to indicate that it is actually experiencing congestion. How the congestion is handled is dependent upon the specific subnetworks and is considered a local matter.

QUESTIONS

TRUE/FALSE

1. From the perspective of internetworking, a subnetwork is also called a network.
2. The connectionless-mode network service manages packets as independent entities.
3. The use of all the ISO 8473 protocol functions is required for an internetworking transmission.
4. X.75 was designed to support connectionless networks.
5. The SNA NCP packet switching interface (NPSI) supports internetworking through either an SNA or X.25 interface.

6. Match the appropriate network protocol description to the appropriate terms. More than one description may fit the term:

   Description

   a.) Used in SNA/X.25 internetworking.
   b.) Often interconnects X.25 networks.
   c.) Used in DECnet/X.25 internetworking.
   d.) A connectionless-mode protocol.
   e.) Used in ISDN/X.25 interfaces.

   Term

   1. XI
   2. DX24
   3. ISO 8473
   4. X.31
   5. NPSI
   6. X.75
   7. DECSA
   8. IP

7. List several problems that are associated with internetworking.

8. What are the three sublayers of the network layer? What are their functions?

9. What are the major differences between connection-oriented and connectionless services?

10. The ISO 8473 connectionless-mode network service stipulates several quality of service options. Briefly describe these options.

11. Connectionless-mode networks may establish a "lifetime" for a packet in the network(s). Describe the rationale for this feature.

12. The Internet Control Message Protocol (ICMP) is a complementary protocol to IP. Describe the functions of ICMP.

13. Describe the SNA/X.25 internetworking technique called logical channel switching.

14. The internetworking unit (IWU) provides a critical function to the LAN/X.25 internetworking interface. Explain this function.

SELECTED ANSWERS

1. True.

2. True.

3. False. Some functions are optional.

4. False. X.75 was originally designed to support X.25 networks, which are connection-oriented.

5. True.

6.

Description	Term
a)	1, 5
b)	6
c)	2, 7
d)	3, 8
e)	4

8. The top sublayer is the subnetwork independence convergence protocol (SNICP). It provides the relay and routing services for internetworking. It contains the internetwork protocols to effect data transfer between networks. The middle sublayer is the subnetwork dependent convergence protocol (SNDCP). It is used to bring the interconnecting networks up to a level needed for the interconnection. The SNDCP may provide a mapping into the required service, or it may operate an explicit protocol to provide the convergence. The third sublayer is the subnetwork access protocol (SNAP). It contains the services relevant to each of the interconnecting networks.

11. The use of a lifetime option gives the connectionless-mode network service a means to control the amount of traffic that accumulates in the network(s). By deleting aged data units it prevents lost or misdirected packets from accumulating and consuming buffer and computing resources. It also allows the transmitting user to establish a lifetime to control the disposition of old data units. In certain applications, old data units become useless. Without question, the lifetime feature simplifies congestion control and flow control, since aged data units simply are discarded and/or accumulation of large queues can be managed by "throwing away" the packets.

13. Since the use of a logical unit session with each X.25 logical session is expensive, the SNA XI system uses an ongoing LU-to-LU session pipe. This session remains in existence for the duration of the internetworking connections. Each XI module maintains a logical channel table, which contains an entry for each logical channel that is defined to a particular node. Logical channel switching occurs when two end users are mapped to each other. Their respective logical channel tables are updated to reflect they are communicating through the associated logical channel tables. Inside the logical channel tables is an association of the logical channel numbers. These pointers are established at call set-up time and then used during the ongoing data session to route the data packets through the LU pipe.

CHAPTER 15

The Transport Layer

INTRODUCTION

Previous chapters emphasized that not all data link (level 2) protocols recover from corrupted data. Examples are some local area network protocols and HDLC's unnumbered information (UI) frame option. We also emphasized that various network layer (level 3) protocols do not recover from certain problems. Our examples in Chapter 13 with X.25 and the clear, restart, and reset packet types showed how data packets may be discarded. Moreover, some networks are inherently unreliable. For example, various types of connectionless networks, several types of mobile radio networks, and packet radio networks do not guarantee delivery of traffic. Certain user data require absolute assurance that all protocol data units have been delivered safely to the destination. Furthermore, the transmitting user may need to know the traffic has been delivered without problems.

The mechanisms to provide these important services reside at the transport layer. Perhaps the best approach is to think of the transport layer as a security blanket. It takes care of the user data, regardless of the goings-on in the underlying layers and networks.

As we shall see, the transport layer performs several functions other than end-to-end data integrity. One of its principal jobs is to shield the upper layers from the details of the lower layers' operations. Indeed, the user may be completely unaware of the physical network(s) that are supporting the user's activities, because the transport layer is providing the transparent interface between the user and the network(s).

It should also be noted that some applications do not need a transport layer (or for that matter, any of the upper layers). Some machines and applications do quite well with just the physical and data link layers.

SUPPORT FOR NETWORKS

The job of the transport layer may be quite complex. For example, in some systems, it must accommodate to a wide array of network characteristics. Some of the networks may be connection-oriented, and some may be connectionless; some may be reliable, and some may be unreliable. Some offer different quality of service (Q05) features. Consequently, these networks have different operating characteristics and experience different kinds of problems.

This section provides examples of how the transport layer deals with these major problems:

Establishing and terminating a network session
Detecting duplicate, lost, and mis-sequenced data
Controlling the flow of data

Establishing and Terminating a Network Session

In order to establish a virtual circuit through a network (or networks), a connection request protocol data unit is relayed to the remote user. Typically, this user returns a connection confirm unit to the requester, and the virtual circuit is now in operation and ready to transfer data. A number of problems can occur in this seemingly simple process. Figure 15-1 shows one example. We assume that the connection for this virtual circuit has been terminated previously. A late-arriving, duplicate connection request unit for this specific virtual circuit is accepted by the receiver as a valid and new connection request. (The duplicate connection request could be the result of the retransmission of connection request units.) The receiver returns a connection confirm in response to the defunct connection request. However, when a new and valid connection request is received, it is discarded, and the receiver either ignores the request or sends a disconnect signal back to the originator to terminate the session set-up procedure. In either case, the receiver is not aware of the erroneous connection request, and it may then discard subsequent data units.

Other connection management problems can be cited. For example, what happens if the connection confirm is lost, or arrives late at the requestor? What happens if the disconnect unit is late?

Clearly, measures must be taken to provide a reliable connection management procedure. The answer to the problem in our example is to use a sequence number and an identifier in the connection request and connection

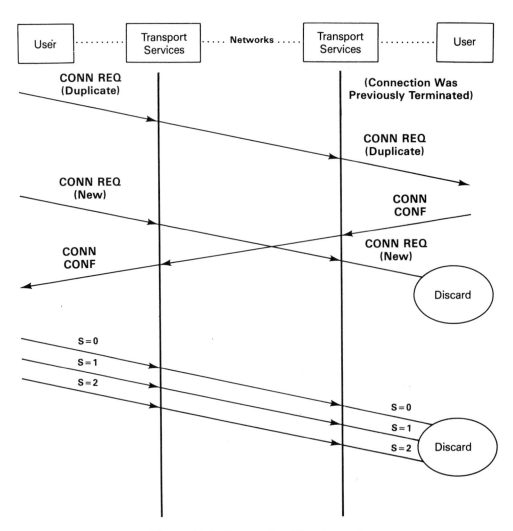

Figure 15-1. Connection Management

confirm units to explicitly acknowledge a request and a confirm. These identifiers must be unique and contain the same values across both directions of
the virtual circuit set-up. Furthermore, the identifiers and sequence numbers must not be reused within a time in which they could be misinterpreted
as belonging to a disconnected virtual circuit. In our example, the duplicate
connection request would have been detected and discarded by the receiver
checking the unique identifiers.

The use of explicit acknowledgments and sequence numbers for connection management is known as a *three-way handshake*, because signals are
exchanged between the two remote users three times. The use of identifiers

that cannot be reused and thus lose their unique identity is referred to as *frozen reference* numbers. Later discussions on the CCITT and ISO standards will show examples of these connection management procedures.

Detecting Duplicate, Lost, and Mis-sequenced Data

Many networks throw away packets that have exceeded the time-to-live value, and from the perspective of the network, the packets are lost and not recovered. Additionally, networks that use adaptive routing schemes may present the packets in a mis-sequenced order at the receiving end-user site. The transport layer is tasked with detecting and correcting these problems.

Figure 15-2 depicts an example of the problem. This example assumes a send window of 5 and a sequence number range of 0–6. The data unit with a send sequence number (S) = 1 is delayed in the network(s). (Referring to Figure 15-2, notice its delayed arrival.) Also, before the receiver has an

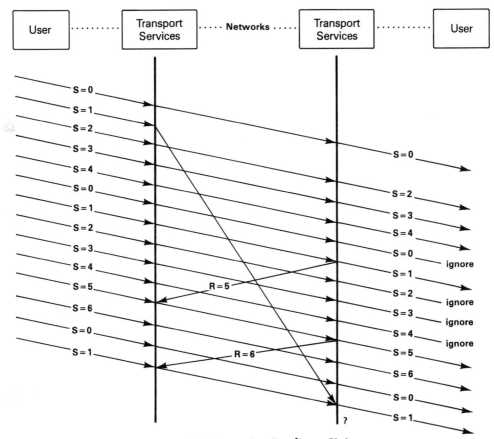

Figure 15-2. Detecting Duplicate Units

opportunity to acknowledge the data units with a receive sequence number (R), the transmitter exhausts its window of 5 (because data units 0–4 are still unacknowledged) and retransmits the data. These events could occur because the transmitter's wait-for-acknowledgment timer is set to a value that is too small, or the receiver is not responding fast enough, due to congestion or other reasons.

Whatever the reason for the timeout, data units 0, 2, 3, and 4 are detected as duplicates and ignored. The receiver accepts data unit 1, and sends back an acknowledgment of R = 5 to inclusively acknowledge units 0 through 4. The R = 5 also states it is next expecting data unit with S = 5.

As ill luck would have it, the late-arriving data unit with S = 1 finally arrives and is erroneously detected as valid. It is actually a duplicate that is not detected at the receiver. As Figure 15-2 illustrates, the sequence numbers have been reused and the cycling sequence is back to 1, or S = 1 appears to be correct.

What is the solution to the problem? Easily enough, it is to use a wide range of sequence numbers. If the value of S = 1 is not reused for an extended time, the arrival of the data unit will be detected as a duplicate. This approach is similar to the use of frozen references for identifying session names. In this situation we employ frozen sequence numbers.

While all these possibilities will improve matters, they require each machine to keep a considerable amount of history about past events. This approach costs money, and if a machine fails, the history is lost. Yet another solution is to establish a time-to-live value that ensures the delayed unit is discarded before it reaches the receiver. However, this action could create additional problems if the networks become congested and experience delay. As a consequence, the data units would be discarded, and they would have to be retransmitted, creating still more traffic. It is certainly possible that all this nonproductive activity could seriously degrade response time and throughput.

It should be evident that the transport layer designers must give careful consideration to windows, sequence numbers, timers, and time-to-live values.

Controlling the Flow of Data

Network congestion can be controlled with conventional schemes, such as withholding the issuance of the data units with the R value incremented. However, the R values are also used for acknowledgment. It is preferable to decouple flow control and acknowledgment, because the two functions provide different (if complementary) services.

Flow control is rather complex at the transport layer because: (a) multiple entities are involved (users, networks, gateways, etc.), and (b) the delay in all these entities introduces more queues and a wider range of delay times. Figure 15-3 illustrates some of the problems.

First, the user, transport and network queues are affected by any flow control mechanisms in place across the peer entities (peer entity control). For example, a user application will control the flow of records in a file transfer from a remote peer application. Second, the service provider (the N-1 layer) will control the flow of protocol data units from the service user (the N layer) at the local and remote sites (adjacent layer control). Third, the first two relationships affect each other. For example, if a user application stops the flow of data into it from the transport layer, it is possible that the transport layer will then flow control its adjacent network layer, which will in turn, flow control its remote network peer layer, and so forth.

To accommodate to this rather convoluted situation, the transport layer manages flow control with a concept called *credits* (C). The credit is a field carried in the transport protocol data unit (TPDU), separately from the S and R fields. Its value (C = n) informs the other transport entity it has the option of sending n TPDUs, without regard to any acknowledgment restrictions. This approach decouples flow control from acknowledgment. It allows the credit allocation to change at any time, at the discretion of either transport entity.

Figure 15-4 shows how credit allocation operates. The remote entity sends a TPDU with R = 2, and C = 3. This means: (a) it acknowledges units 0 through 1, (b) it is expecting 2 next, (c) it is giving the local transport entity the option of sending three more TPDUs.

The credit concept is an optimistic approach, because the entity that issues the credit is stating that it will be able to accommodate to whatever it sets as the C value. If it cannot, it must discard the excess data units. Therefore, the credits must be established with some forethought.

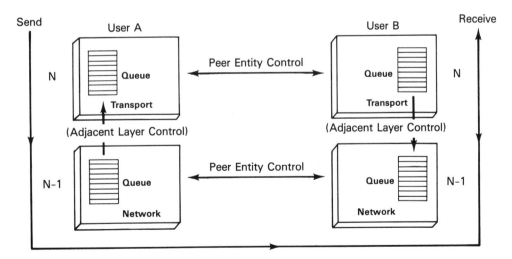

Figure 15-3. Flow Control and Queues

It should also be noted that it is possible for the credit TPDUs to be delayed and arrive out of order. For example, the first transmitted data unit could have C = 5, and its next unit could reduce the credit with C = 1. However, the C = 1 arrives first. When the delayed data unit with C = 5 arrives, it appears the credit has been increased, when in fact the exact opposite action was intended. The solution is to use sequence numbers on the credit TPDUs. In this manner, the receiving transport entity can make rational decisions about the credit values.

With this background information, we now examine the prevalent OSI transport layer standards and several conventions used by the vendors.

CCITT TRANSPORT LAYER

The CCITT approved the transport layer June 25, 1984, as part of its Red Books and it is now implemented in many vendor products. Other organiza-

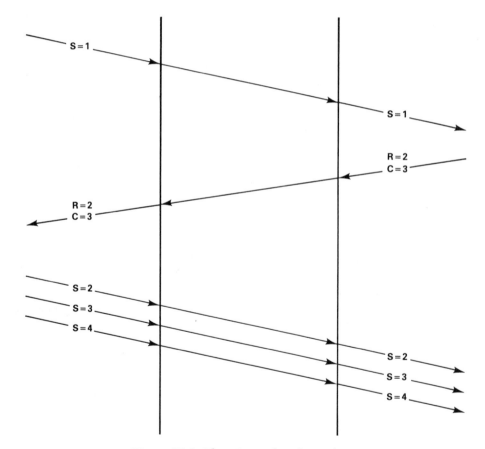

Figure 15-4. Flow Control with Credits

tions such as NBS and ANSI have made significant contributions to the specification.

The importance of this protocol lies in the fact that it is the end user's first opportunity to choose how an underlying network serves the user. Its primary purpose is to provide a reliable, end-to-end service for the user (and upper layers). As we learned in the introduction, it shields the user from the details of the lower levels and the types of networks used at these levels.

The CCITT transport layer functions are described in X.224. In addition, X.214 describes how to invoke the services of the transport level from the session level. For purposes of continuity and simplicity, our discussions incorporate these two recommendations. The ISO publishes similar specifications in ISO 8072 and ISO 8073. This discussion also includes the 1988 Blue Book changes.

Types of Networks

The transport layer requires the user to specify a quality of service (QOS) to be provided by the underlying network(s). Consequently, the transport layer must know the types of services offered by the network(s) below it. Upon receiving the user's request for a network connection and quality of service associated with the connection, the transport layer selects a class of protocol to match the user's quality of service parameters in relation to the supporting network(s). Even though a variety of networks exist (connection oriented, connectionless, etc.), the transport layer attempts to provide a consistent level of service to the end user. As we shall see, the QOS parameters are passed by the transport user to the transport layer, which uses them to pass parameters to the network layer to invoke the requested services.

The quality of network services rests on the types of networks available to the end user and the transport layer. Three types of networks are defined by CCITT and ISO recommendations.

- A Type A network provides acceptable error rates and acceptable rates of signalled failures (acceptable quality). Packets are assumed not to be lost. The transport layer need not provide recovery or resequencing services.
- A Type B network provides for acceptable error rates, but an unacceptable rate for signalled failures (unacceptable signalled errors). The transport layer must be able to recover from errors.
- A Type C network connection provides an error rate not acceptable to the user (unreliable). The transport layer must recover from failures and resequence packets. A Type C network could include some local area networks, mobile networks, and datagram networks.

The idea in defining network types is to recognize that different qualities of networks exist, yet the user is provided with a consistent level of service, regardless of network type. For example, a Type C network could be one in which the transmissions take place in a connectionless mode. On the other hand, a Type B network would likely be one using X.25 functions and capabilities. The layer also gives the user options to obtain network services at a minimum cost on a per-connection basis.

The existence of a Type A network means the transport layer has an easy job. However, most of the complexity of this layer stems from the fact that many networks exhibit the characteristics of Type B or Type C networks.

The transport layer service definition uses primitives to specify what services are to be provided through the network. The parameters associated with each primitive action provide the specific actions and events to be provided by the network. During the connection establishment phase, the characteristics of the connection are negotiated between the end users and the transport layer. The primitives and the parameters of the primitives are used to support the negotiation. It is possible that a connection will not be made if the network or an end user cannot provide the requested quality of service. Moreover, the requested services may be negotiated down to a lower level.

After the parameters are accepted between the two negotiating parties, data transfer is provided at the local site from the transport layer through the network layer, data link layer, physical layer, and finally, through the channel. At the remote site, the data passes up through the physical layer, data link layer, network layer, and the transport layer to the user or another upper layer.

Classes of Protocol

As stated earlier, the transport layer is responsible for selecting an appropriate protocol to support the quality of service (QOS) parameters established by the user. Since the transport layer knows the characteristics of a network (Types A, B, or C) the layer can choose five classes of protocol procedures to support the QOS request from the user. The procedures are:

Class 0: Simple class
Class 1: Basic error recovery class
Class 2: Multiplexing class
Class 3: Error recovery and multiplexing class
Class 4: Error detection and recovery class

The *class 0* protocol provides for a very simple transport connection establishment to support a Type A network. Class 0 provides for a connection-oriented support, both during the network connection and release phases. It does not provide for any support or user transfer data during connection establishment. This protocol is able to detect and signal protocol errors, but it does not recover from errors. If the network layer signals an error to the transport layer, the transport layer releases the connection to its network layer. In so doing, the end user is informed about the disconnection. The CCITT developed this class for its Teletex standard.

The *class 1* protocol is associated with networks such as an X.25 packet network. In contrast to class 0, the TPDUs are numbered. The class 1 protocol provides for segmenting of data if necessary, retention of all data, and acknowledgment. It allows resynchronization of the session in the event of an X.25 reset packet. The protocol is also required to support expedited data transfer. It responds to disconnect requests and to protocol errors. It is also responsible for resynchronization and performing reassignments in the event of a network failure (i.e., an X.25 restart packet).

It is possible to transmit user data in a class 1 connection request. Also, each data unit is sequenced to aid in ACKs/NAKs and error recovery. The ACKs release the copies of the data units at the transmitting sites. Class 1 also provides for either user acknowledgment or network receipt acknowledgment.

The *class 2* protocol is an enhancement to class 0 that allows the multiplexing of several transport connections into a single network session. It also provides for flow control to prevent congestion from occurring at the end DTE sites. Class 2 provides neither error detection nor recovery. If an X.25 reset or clear packet is detected, this protocol disconnects the session and the user is so informed. The class 2 protocol is designed to be used over very reliable Type A networks. The flow control provided in this protocol uses the concept of credit allocation (discussed shortly). User data can be transmitted in the connection request data unit.

The *class 3* protocol provides for the services included in the class 2 structure. It also provides recovery from a network failure, without requiring the notification of the user. The user data are retained until the receiving transport layer sends back a positive acknowledgment of the data. This class has a very useful mechanism to retransmit data. The packets in transit through a network are given a maximum "lifetime" through timers. All data requiring a response are timed. If the timer expires before an acknowledgment is received, retransmission or other recovery procedures can be invoked. The class 3 protocol assumes a Type B network service.

The class 4 protocol includes the flow control functions of classes 2 and 3. Like class 3, expedited data is allowed and the ACKs are sequenced. This protocol allows for "frozen" references (a reference is a connection identifier). Upon a connection release, the corresponding reference cannot be reused, since the network layer could still be processing late-arriving data associated with the references. The class 4 protocol is designed to work with Type C networks.

In summary, the protocol classes and the associated network types are:

Class	Network Type
0	A
1	B

2	A
3	B
4	C

Error Detection

One option in the transport layer is the use of a checksum for error-detection. The option is valuable if the link layer does not perform this function or if the link level does not signal its detection of an error. It is always used in a connection request protocol data unit and all other data units if the communicating parties so indicate. The checksum uses integer arithmetic and is not as effective in detecting errors as the cyclic redundancy check (CRC) explained in Chapter 7. However, it is more efficient and is designed to be executed in software. The CCITT checksum is summarized here. [FLET82] provides more detail on the arithmetic checksum, and X.224 also uses these algorithms for developing the checksum parameters.

$$\sum_{i=1}^{L} a_i = 0 \text{ (modulo 255)}$$

$$\sum_{i=1}^{L} i^a i = 0 \text{ (modulo 255)}$$

Where: i = position of an octet within the TPDU; a_i = value of octet in position i; L = length of TPDU in octets.

Connection Management and Data Transfer

The transport layer functions can be divided into two categories: connection management (establishment and release) and data transfer. The connection establishment is shown in Figure 15-5. The T-CONNECT request primitive is passed from the upper layer (the session layer, for example) to the transport layer. The primitive contains the parameters used to create a transport connection request (CR) protocol data unit (TPDU). Table 15-1 summarizes the primitives and parameters. As we shall see later, these parameters are mapped into certain fields of the TPDU for use at the destination transport entity.

The transport service provider receives the T-CONNECT request. During this phase, the parameters (for example, the quality of service [QOS] parameter) can be reduced by the transport provider (new parameters would appear in the T-CONNECT indication to the user) or by the transport user. Whatever the case, the proposed parameters are coded in the T-CONNECT response, placed in a connect confirm PDU, which is sent through the network and then mapped into the T-CONNECT confirm primitive.

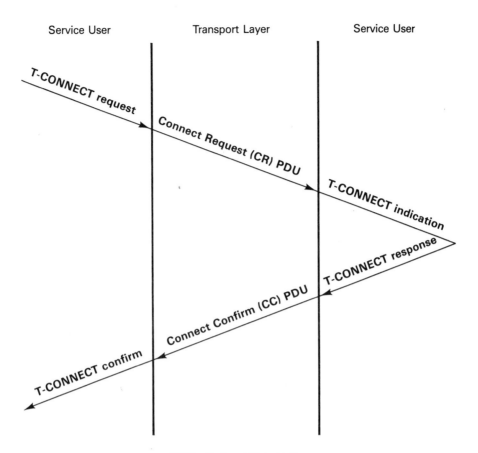

Service User   Transport Layer   Service User

T-CONNECT request

Connect Request (CR) PDU

T-CONNECT indication

T-CONNECT response

Connect Confirm (CC) PDU

T-CONNECT confirm

PDU = Protocol Data Unit

FIGURE 15-5. Connection Establishment

The transport connection release follows a similar pattern (see Figure 15-6), except additional disconnection scenarios are allowed. A typical disconnect occurs when one transport entity issues a T-DISCONNECT request. This is mapped to a T-DISCONNECT indication at the receiving transport entity (Figure 15-6[a]). Another possibility is the issuance of the T-DISCONNECT request at both ends of the transport connection (Figure 15-6[b]). This release is not coordinated and neither end knows the other end is issuing the disconnect. This absence of a time and dependency relationship is noted by the symbol ~. Another possibility is the release initiated by the transport services provider (Figure 15-6[c]). Finally, Figure 15-6(d) shows the release initiated simultaneously by the transport services user and the transport services provider.

These disconnections can occur for a variety of reasons. As examples: the data cannot be delivered; the user decides to terminate the communications dialogue; one of the entities has exhausted the required resources to

Table 15-1. Transport Layer Primitives and Parameters

Phase	*Primitive*	*Parameters*
TC establishment	T-CONNECT request	(Called address, calling address, expedited data option, quality of service, TS user-data)
	T-CONNECT indication	(Called address, calling address, expedited data option, quality of service, TS user-data)
	T-CONNECT response	(Responding address quality of service, expedited data option, TS user-data)
	T-CONNECT confirm	(Responding address quality of service, expedited data option, TS user-data)
Data transfer	T-DATA request	(TS user-data)
	T-DATA indication	(TS user-data)
	T-EXPEDITED DATA request	(TS user-data)
	T-EXPEDITED DATA indication	(TS user-data)
TC release	T-DISCONNECT request	(TS user-data)
	T-DISCONNECT indication	(Disconnect reason, TS user-data)

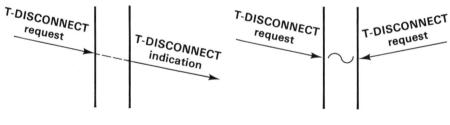

(a) Disconnect By One Entity

(b) Disconnect By Both Entities

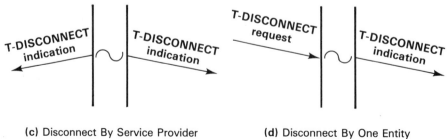

(c) Disconnect By Service Provider

(d) Disconnect By One Entity and Service Provider

FIGURE 15-6. Possible Transport Level Disconnects

support the process; the quality of service is at an unacceptable level; etc. Although no reason must be given for the disconnection, a "reason" parameter is available in the T-DISCONNECT indication primitive to convey the problem and reason for the disconnection. This information is mapped into the reason field of the disconnect request (DR) TPDU and transmitted to the receiving transport entity.

The data transfer takes place with the T-DATA request and T-DATA indication primitives. In addition, the transport layer can utilize expedited data transfer with the use of the T-EXPEDITED-DATA request and T-EXPEDITED-DATA indication primitives. The permissible transport layer primitive sequences are shown in Table 15-2 and the state diagram in Figure 15-7).

Certain options (protocol classes) in the transport layer permit the transport entities to acknowledge the successful receipt of TPDUs between each other. This capability is provided with the acknowledge (AK) TPDU. The AK TPDU can be implemented to provide an ACK with each unit of

TABLE 15-2. Transport Layer: Primitive Sequences

An initial primitive:

May be followed by:	T-CONNECT request	T-CONNECT confirm	T-CONNECT indication	T-CONNECT response	T-CONNECT request	T-CONNECT indication	T-EXPEDITED-DATA request	T-EXPEDITED-DATA indication	T-DISCONNECT request	T-DISCONNECT indication
T-CONNECT request	NP	NP	NP	NP	NP	NP	NP	NP	NP	NP
T-CONNECT confirm	+	NP	NP	NP	NP	NP	NP	NP	NP	NP
T-CONNECT indication	NP	NP	NP	NP	NP	NP	NP	NP	NP	NP
T-CONNECT response	NP	NP	+	NP	NP	NP	NP	NP	NP	NP
T-CONNECT request	NP	+	NP	+	+	+	+	+	NP	NP
T-CONNECT indication	NP	+	NP	+	+	+	+	+	NP	NP
T-EXPEDITED-DATA request	NP	+	NP	+	+	+	+	+	NP	NP
T-EXPEDITED-DATA indication	NP	+	NP	+	+	+	+	+	NP	NP
T-DISCONNECT request	+	+	+	+	+	+	+	+	NP	NP
T-DISCONNECT indication	+	+	+	+	+	+	+	+	NP	NP

+: Possible
NP: Not Possible

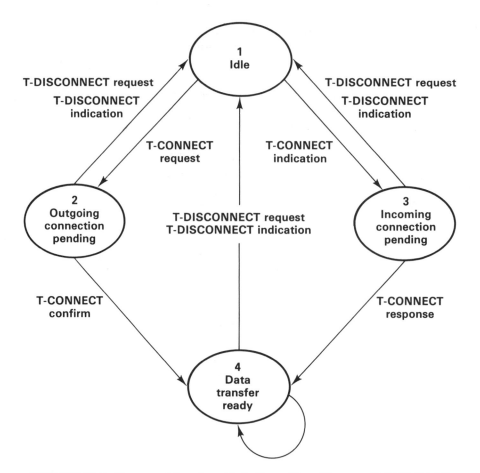

FIGURE 15-7. Transport Services State Transition Diagram [CCITT X.214]

data. Using this option, a data unit is given to the transport layer as a T-DATA request primitive. Another choice is for the transport user to present user data with one T-DATA request primitive and the remote transport layer to issue a T-DATA indication primitive after receiving a complete data unit. These two choices are diagrammed in Figure 15-8.

Transport Layer Protocol Data Units (TPDUs)

The transport layer protocol uses ten transport protocol data units to perform its functions. All TPDUs have a similar structure, which consists of four parts (see Figure 15-9a):

1. *Length Indicator (LI):* Length of header in octets
2. *Fixed Part of Header:* Control fields

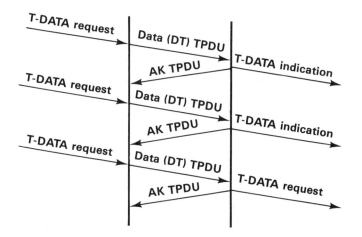

(a) Single TPDU Message

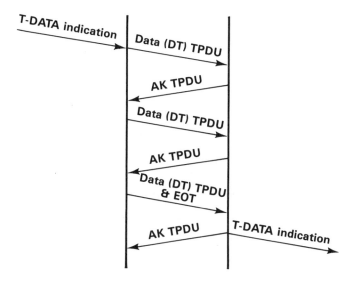

(b) Multi TPDU Message

FIGURE 15-8. Acknowledge Options with Class 4

3. *Variable Part of Header:* Control fields (if present)
4. *Data Field:* User data (if present)

The data fields in the TPDU contain all the headers (Protocol Control Information or PCIs) that have been added from higher layers and, of course, end-user data if appropriate. The transport level control fields are used to (a)

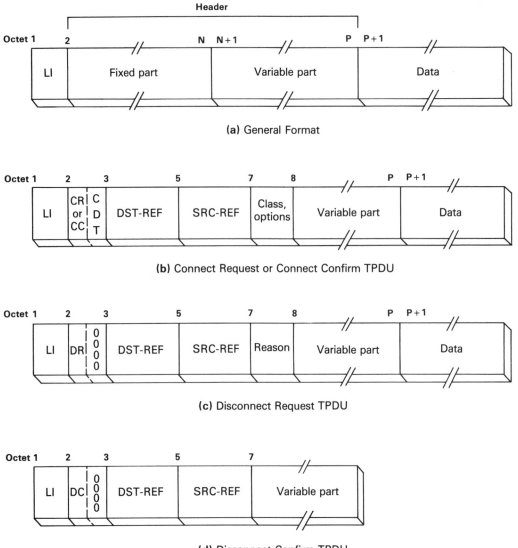

(a) General Format

(b) Connect Request or Connect Confirm TPDU

(c) Disconnect Request TPDU

(d) Disconnect Confirm TPDU

FIGURE 15-9. Formats for Transport Layer Protocol Data Units (TPDUs)

negotiate the level of service between the transmitter and receiver during a connection establishment, (b) manage the ongoing data transfer, and (c) provide the termination of the connection. The specific kind of TPDU is identified by the type code in the second octet of the header.

Connection Request (CR) and Connection Confirm (CC) TPDU. The connection request (CR) unit is illustrated in Figure 15-9(b). The length indication (LI) was explained earlier. The second octet contains the type code in bits 8–5 and the initial credit allocation code (CDT) in bits 4–1. (The CDT is explained later.) The destination-reference (DST-REF) octets are not used for a connection request and are set to all 0s; they are used with subsequent TPDUs.

The source-reference (SRC-REF) octets are used by the originator of the connection request to identify the originator. The DST-REF and SRC-REF are short IDs that identify the two communicating entities during data transfer (quite similar to the logical channel numbers in the X.25 packet header). For a connection set-up, the complete destination and source addresses are placed in the variable part of the CR header and the sending and receiving transport entities usually map these addresses to the DST-REF and SRC-REF addresses. Thereafter, the longer addresses are not needed. Both transport entities use the abbreviated addresses in the DST-REF and SRC-REF fields.

The class, options octet performs two functions: (a) it defines the preferred transport protocol class (0 through 4); and (b) it defines other options within the protocol class such as extended formats for the data units and the stipulation for flow control procedures between the transport entities.

The variable part of the header contains the less frequently used parameters. The length of the contents of this field is detected by the LI and fixed length part of the header. The parameters (depicted in Table 15-3) are coded with each parameter structured as follows:

Octet N + 1	=	Parameter code
Octet N + 2	=	Parameter length indication (m)
Octet N + 2 + M =		Parameter value

The quality of service (QOS) parameters in Table 15-3 are derived from the QOS parameters provided in the T-CONNECT request primitive explained in Figure 15-5. In turn, these parameters are used to create the N-CONNECT request primitive for the lower network layer. This concept is emphasized once again to ensure that the reader understands that a primitive is used to create the PCIs (headers) in the layer's protocol data unit (PDU).

Let us pause to examine the parameters in Table 15-3. They reveal much about the services of the transport layer. The transport service access points (TSAPs) contain the identifiers of the calling and called TSAPs. They are mapped into these fields during call establishment.

The TDPU size parameter is coded in powers of 2 to identify the size of the TPDU. The values range from 128 (0000 0111: 2^7) to 8192 (0000 1101: 2^{13}). X.224 places certain restrictions on sizes permitted within these ranges.

The security parameter is user defined. The checksum parameter was discussed earlier. The additional options parameter stipulates the use of network expedited data transfer, receipt confirmation, use of a checksum, and use of transport expedited data transfer. The alternative protocol

TABLE 15-3. Parameters for Variable Parts of the TPDU

Parameter Description	Parameter Length of Octets	Notes
Identifier of calling TSAP	Variable	1
Identification of called TSAP	Variable	1
TPDU size	1	2
Security	Variable	3
Checksum	Variable	4
Additional options	1	
Alternative protocol class(es)	Variable	5
Acknowledge time	2	4
Throughput	12 or 24	5
Residual error rate	3	5
Priority	2	5
Transit delay	8	5
Reassignment time	2	6

Notes:

1. If a TSAP ID is in a request, it may also be returned in the confirmation.
2. Default is 128 octets; sizes range from 128–8192 octets.
3. User defined.
4. Used only with class 4.
5. Not used for class 0.
6. Not used for classes 0, 2 or 4.

class(es) parameter permits the identification and negotiation of another protocol class.

The acknowledge time parameter is used to provide guidance to the receiving transport entity. It indicates a maximum time which can elapse from the time the transport entity receives the TPDU from the network layer to the time it transmits an acknowledgment. It conveys the maximum values for the acknowledgment timers, which are explained later.

The throughput parameter is coded in octets per second (usually passed down from a user-initiated primitive). It allows throughput to be negotiated as (a) maximum and/or (b) average. These values are negotiated and may be reduced by the called entity. They cannot be negotiated up.

The residual error rate parameter defines the loss of transport data units that are not reported. The three octet field is defined as follows: (a) target value, (b) minimum acceptable value, and (c) length of TPDU. Octets 1 and 2 are expressed in a power of 10, octet 3 is expressed in a power of 2.

The priority parameter is not defined concisely. It refers to the order in which the connections are to have their QOS degraded, if necessary, or the order in which communications will be broken, if necessary. The use of the parameters depends upon how a network administration chooses to apply it.

The transit delay parameter describes the negotiated delay between the two entities. Values are expressed in milliseconds and are based on a TSDU of 128 octets.

The reassignments time parameter is used in protocol classes 1 and 3 to commence recovery after the network layer has signalled a failure (i.e., a disconnect).

The CC TPDU uses the same format as the CR TPDU except the DST-REF field is filled in by the remote entity (see Figure 15-9).

Disconnect Request (DR) and Disconnect Confirm (DC) TPDU. The format for the DR TPDU is shown in Figure 15-9(c). The fields previously explained are not explained again. The reason for the disconnections are given in the reason field. Table 15-4 describes the coded values in the reason field.

The variable part of the DR TPDU consists of the parameter code 1110 0000, the parameter length, and the parameter value, which is user defined. The user data field cannot exceed 64 octets. It is used to hold TS-user data and their delivery is not guaranteed by the transport layer. Class 0 cannot carry the user data field. The checksum parameter can be carried in the variable part if the checksum is used.

The DC TPDU is shown in Figure 15-9(d). The variable part contains the checksum, if applicable.

Table 15-4. Reasons for Transport Disconnection

Reason	Notes
Normal disconnect initiated by session entity	1, 4
Remote congestion at transport entity during CC	1, 4
Failed connection negotiation	1, 3
Duplicated source reference for same NSAP pairs	1, 4
References are mismatched	1, 4
Protocol error	1, 4
Reference overflow	1, 4
Connection request refused	1, 4
Header or parameter length invalid	1, 4
No reason specified	2, 4
Congestion at TSAP	2, 4
TSAP and session entity not attached	2, 3
Unknown address	2, 3

Notes:

1. Used for classes 1 to 4.
2. Used for all classes.
3. Reported to TS-user as persistent.
4. Reported to TS-user as transient.

Data (DT) TPDU. Several data (DT) TPDUs are used in the transport layer. The format of the TPDU depends on the following factors:

> Normal format for classes 0 and 1
> Normal format for classes 2, 3 and 4
> Extended format for classes 2, 3 and 4
> Normal format for expedited TPDUs for classes 1, 2, 3, and 4
> Extended format for expedited TPDUs for classes 2, 3, and 4

Figure 15-10 illustrates the formats for the latter two TPDUs. As can be seen, all are variations on the same theme. We now discuss the fields in Figure 15-10 as they pertain to each format.

The EOT bit (bit 8 in octet 5) is set to 1 to indicate that the current DT TPDU is the last data unit of a sequence, i.e., the end of a complete TSDU.

The TPDU send sequence number (TPDU-NR) is used to sequence each data unit. It uses the following octets (less the EOT bit):

> Normal format: octet 5
> Extended format: octets 5–8

The TPDU-NR is used only for flow control in class 2 because the network layer performs resequencing. In class 4, it is also used to reorder DT TPDUs and to detect lost or duplicate TPDUs. The number is incremented by one with each transmission of a data unit. These services are explained shortly.

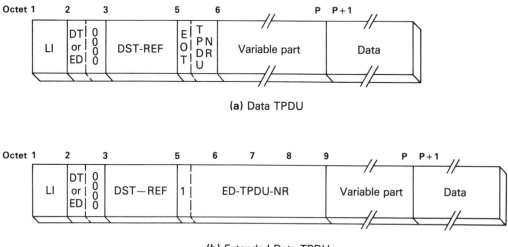

(a) Data TPDU

(b) Extended Data TPDU

FIGURE 15-10. Data Transport Layer Protocol Data Units (TPDUs)

The variable part of the DT TPDU contains the checksum parameter, if relevant. The user data field contains the user data and is restricted to the negotiated size. It is no greater than 16 octets for an expedited (ED) TPDU.

Elements of Procedure

Table 15-5 provides a list of the transport layer elements of procedure within each class. Notice that these elements of procedure are invoked based on the protocol class. Class 0 provides relatively few elements, but class 4 provides many because class 4 is used with unreliable and/or connectionless networks. For example, retransmissions, resequencing, and checksums are used with the class 4 protocol. The reader is cautioned that the elements within different classes may not be identical, and the CCITT or ISO documents should be read to understand the specific differences. Many of these procedures are self-explanatory but Appendix 15A provides a description of each element of procedure. The reader may wish to study this appendix if more detail is needed. These important parts of the CCITT transport layer remain largely the same in the 1988 Blue Book release.

Class 4 (TP4)—A Closer Look

TP4 (Transport protocol class 4) has received considerable attention and is now used in many systems. As noted earlier, it provides mechanisms for detecting and recovering from errors that might occur at the lower levels. It assumes that the underlying network may lose, duplicate, or mis-sequence data units. As with other protocols that are responsible for these kinds of functions, TP4 uses end-to-end acknowledgment in combination with several timers, retry parameters, and timer parameters. They are summarized in Table 15-6 and described in more detail in this section.

One of the primary tools used by TP4 is T1. It is quite similar to the link level T1 described in Chapter 10, but in this case, T1 encompasses all point-to-point delays and processing times through the end-to-end transport connection. It is used to determine the appropriate time for the transport entity to retransmit a protocol data unit. The value of T1 is bound on the time the transport entity will wait for an acknowledgment from the other transport entity. The T1 is defined as:

$$T1 = X + E_{LR} + A_R + E_{RL}$$

Where: X = the local time required to process the TPDU; E_{LR} = expected maximum transit delay from the local to remote entity; A_R = processing time required at the remote entity to acknowledge the TPDU; and E_{RL} = expected maximum transit delay from remote to local entity.

The values of E_{LR} and E_{RL} depend on the performance of the network or networks that support the transport connection. The speeds and delay of each component must be considered. For example, the propagation delay for

TABLE 15-5. Elements of Procedure

Protocol Function	Variant	0	1	2	3	4
Assignment to network connection		X	X	X	X	X
TPDU transfer		X	X	X	X	X
DT TPDU length and segmenting		X	X	X	X	X
Concatenation and separation			X	X	X	X
Connection establishment		X	X	X	X	X
Connection refusal		X	X	X	X	X
Normal release	Implicit	X				
	Explicit		X	X	X	X
Error release		X		X		
DT TPDU numbering	Normal		X	X	X	X
	Extended			O	O	O
Expedited data transfer	Normal		X	X	X	X
	Expedited		O			
Association of TPDUs with TC		X	X	X	X	X
Reassignment after failure			X		X	
Retention until acknowledgment of	Confirmation		O			
TPDUs	Receipt AK		X		X	X
Resynchronization			X		X	
Multiplexing and demultiplexing				X	X	X
Explicit flow control						
With				X	X	X
Without		X	X	O		
Checksum (use of)						X
(non-use of)		X	X	X	X	O
Frozen references			X		X	X
Retransmission on time out						X
Resequencing						X
Inactivity control						X
Treatment of protocol errors		X	X	X	X	X
Splitting and recombining						X

TPDU = Transport Protocol Data Unit

O = Optional

a wide area network is a much more significant factor than a local area network; and a session traversing several subnetworks requires a larger T1 value than a connection involving only one network.

Table 15-6. Class 4 Timer Parameters

Symbol	Use
A_L	Time lapse between receipt of TPDU by local entity and transmission of acknowledgment.
A_R	Time lapse between receipt of TPDU by remote entity and transmission of acknowledgment.
E_{LR}	Maximum expected delay of NDSUs from local to remote transport entity.
E_{RL}	Maximum expected delay of NDSUs from remote to local transport entity.
I	Time lapse between last received TPDU and the initiation of a release.
L	Time lapse between transmission of any TPDU and the receipt of any acknowledgment related to it.
M_{LR}	Maximum time between the local transmission of a NDSU and a receipt of any copy of it at the remote entity.
M_{RL}	Maximum time between the remote transmission of a NDSU and a receipt of any copy of it at the local entity.
N	Maximum number of retransmission attempts of a TPDU.
R	Maximum time a transport entity will attempt retransmission of a TPDU that requires acknowledgment.
T1	Maximum wait time a transport entity will attempt retransmission of a TPDU that requires acknowledgment.
W	Time lapse between successive window updates.
X	Time to process TPDU.

Retransmission Procedures. If T1 expires, the data unit is retransmitted and T1 is restarted. After the retry value of N is reached, the release procedure is executed and the transport service user is informed.

The T1 can be maintained per each TPDU or it can be associated with each transport connection. In the latter case, the transport entity starts T1 upon sending a TPDU requiring acknowledgment. It restarts T1 upon receiving an acknowledgment of any one of the TPDUs that are outstanding. It stops T1 upon receiving an ACK of the last outstanding data unit. The use of T1 must take into consideration the throughput implications. Obviously, an ACK of every data unit will affect throughput.

Retransmission can be accomplished by one of two methods: (a) only the first DT TPDU is retransmitted or (b) all TPDUs waiting for acknowledgment (to the upper window edge) are retransmitted.

Reference Time for the Data Unit. TP4 must have some means of calculating the maximum length of time a TPDU might be expected to remain in the network(s). As we learned earlier, the source and destination references must not be reused if a chance exists that the TPDU is still in the system. This situation can occur with datagram networks.

To handle this situation, TP4 implements a reference time L. It represents the bound for the maximum time between the transmission and/or retransmission of a TPDU and the receipt of any acknowledgment relating to it. It also represents the time during which a sequence number or reference number cannot be reused. The bound on references and sequence numbers (i.e., L) is:

$$L = R + M_{LR} + A_R + M_{RL}$$

Where: R = the time required to retransmit the maximum number of TPDUs (where $R = T1 * [N - 1]$) (the R value is known as persistence time or the give-up timer); M_{LR} = maximum time between transmission and receipt of NSDUs in the underlying network from the local remote entity; A_R = remote acknowledgment time; and M_{RL} = maximum time between transmission and receipt of NSDUs in the underlying network between the remote and the local entity.

Another timer used for flow control is the window timer (W). It is the bound for the maximum time the transport entity will wait before retransmitting a protocol data unit that updates the windows.

TP4 recommends that after N transmissions of a DT TPDU, the transport entity should wait a period of time before entering the release phase. This time lapse provides for the possibility of receiving an ACK before the release is made. The recommended wait is $T1 + W + M_{R2}$. For TPDUs other than DT TPDUs, the recommended wait period is $T1 + M_{RL}$.

TP4 also uses an inactivity timer (I) to protect against a break in a network connection. Its value is several times the window timer (W). It is reset any time a TPDU from the remote entity is received. The window timer (W) is similar to a receive ready (RR) at the lower levels in that it ensures some units (AK TPDUs) flow between the transport entities in the absence of data units. The use of the inactivity and window timers is defined as:

$$I = 2 * N * max(T1 \text{ or } W)$$

Flow Control. TP4 is unique among the protocols discussed in this book in its method of flow control. It uses the credit (CDT) field for the receiver to indicate to the transmitter how many data units it is willing to receive. This credit allocation scheme can be reduced or expanded as deemed necessary. The initial credit is provided by connection request and connection confirm PDU and carried in the CDT fields. (The reader may recall that other layers (data link and network) control flow with one or a combination of the following three methods: (a) pre-established agreements, (b) negotiated window sizes, and (c) receive ready (RR) and receive not ready (RNR) frames/packets.)

TP4 uses a sliding window concept similar to the data link and network layers (see Figure 15-11). The acknowledgment PDU contains the value of

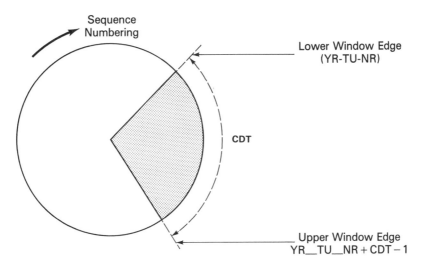

FIGURE 15-11. Credits and Windows

the next expected data unit (in the YR-TU-NR field) and the number of data units that can be sent (in the CDT field). The class 4 protocol also uses the YR-TU-NR to implicitly and inclusively acknowledge the correct receipt of all lower-numbered data TPDUs.

Connection Establishment. A TP4 connection establishment must follow the connection establishment and connection refusal elements of procedure as well as these additional procedures:

1. A successful connection requires a three-way handshake (see Figure 15-12). The sender of a CR TPDU must respond to the incoming CC TPDU by sending a ST, ED, DR, or AK protocol data unit. This rule is quite important for two reasons. First, if the sender of the CR goes down and does not transmit the AK, the entity that issues the CC might wait indefinitely for the next protocol data unit. However, with a three-way handshake, if the remote entity can time-out and retransmit the CC, eventually its N value can be exhausted and it will know the connection did not take effect. Second, it is possible in datagram network(s) that duplicate CR TPDUs could be entered into the network(s). The remote transport entity could possibly send a second CC TPDU when the associated connection had been released. However, through the use of frozen references and the third handshake, the local entity can be programmed to reply with a disconnect request (DR) TPDU.

2. The retransmission procedures (previously explained) must be used during connection establishment.

3. A CC TPDU using a frozen reference requires a response of DR TPDU.

4. If a duplicate CR TPDU is received, a CC TPDU is transmitted. If the three-way handshake has been completed, the CR TPDU is to be ignored.

TRANSMISSION CONTROL PROTOCOL (TCP)

Another widely used transport layer protocol is the transmission control protocol (TCP). It was developed for use in ARPANET but is used throughout the industry and is found in several commercial networks as well as networks in research centers and universities. It has many similarities to the CCITT transport protocol. A number of its features were incorporated into TP4.

The goals of TCP are quite similar to TP4. Its job is to deliver and receive data across network boundaries. It recovers from damaged, duplicated, or mis-sequenced data units. As depicted in Figure 15-13 the TCP fits into the transport layer and rests below the upper layers (designated as ULP) and above the internet protocol (IP) below. (The internet protocol is described in Chapter 14).

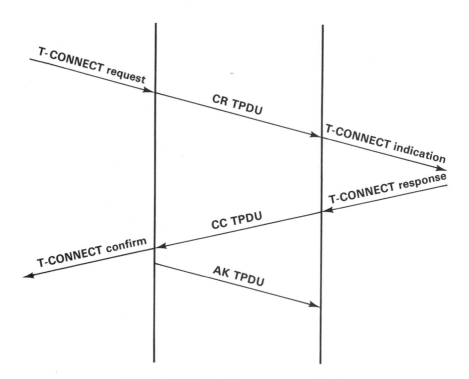

FIGURE 15-12. A Three-Way Handshake

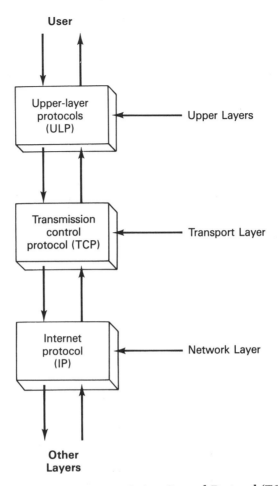

FIGURE 15-13. Transmission Control Protocol (TCP)

TCP works in a fashion quite similar to TP4 in that it requires a three-way handshake. One principal difference is the manner in which a connection is opened by the ULP. Two forms of connection establishment are permitted. The passive open mode allows the ULP to tell the TCP it is to wait for the arrival of connection requests from the remote system. This type of protocol could be used to accommodate data base accesses from remote users. The second form of connection establishment is the active mode. In this situation the ULP designates specifically another transport layer through which a connection is to be established.

Both TCP and TP4 provide for sequencing during the data transfer. As we learned earlier, TP4 sequences transport protocol data units. TCP uses a different scheme, providing sequence numbers of the data octets within a block of data. In this manner, each data octet is numbered sequentially.

Table 15-7. TCP Primitives

Service Request Primitives (ULP to TCP)

PRIMITIVE	PARAMETERS
UNSPECIFIED-PASSIVE-OPEN	Source port, ULP timeout (∗), timeout action (∗), precedence (∗), security (∗)
FULL-PASSIVE-OPEN	Source port, destination port, destination address, ULP timeout (∗), timeout action (∗), precedence(∗), security (∗)
ACTIVE-OPEN	Source and destination ports, destination address, ULP timeout (∗), ULP timeout-action (∗), precedence (∗), security (∗)
ACTIVE-OPEN-WITH DATA	Source and destination ports, destination address, ULP timeout (∗), ULP timeout-action (∗), precedence (∗), security (∗), data, data length, push flag, urgent flag (∗)
SEND	Local connecting name, data, data length, push flag, urgent flag, ULP timeout (∗), ULP timeout-action (∗)
ALLOCATE	Local connection name, data length
CLOSE	Local connection name
ABORT	Local connection name
STATUS	Local connection name

∗ Optional.

Service Response Primitives (TCP to ULP)

PRIMITIVE	PARAMETERS
OPEN-ID	Local connection name, source port, destination port, destination address
OPEN-FAILURE	Local connection name
OPEN-SUCCESS	Local connection name
DELIVER	Local connection name, data, data length, urgent flag
CLOSING	Local connection name
TERMINATE	Local connection name, description
STATUS RESPONSE	Local connection name, source port and address, destination port and address, connection state, receive and send window, amount-waiting-ack and -receipt, urgent mode, timeout, timeout-action
ERROR	Local connection name, error description

BOX 15-1. Principal Differences Between TP4 and TCP	
TP Class 4 (TP4)	*Transmission Control Protocol (TCP)*
Data placed in specific units and transmitted as discrete service data units (SDUs).	Data flow in an ongoing stream-oriented basis.
Expedited data dequeued and may arrive before data sent earlier (on same session).	Expedited data remain in queue.
Uses OSI Service Access Point (SAP) addressing concept.	Uses IP 32-bit address and a TCP port number.

TCP accepts data from the upper layer protocols in a stream-oriented fashion. There is no specific block structure such as the CCITT transport service data unit. The data is sent from the ULP and transmitted to the network level as appropriate, depending on the buffer management techniques at the TCP level. A push function is available to force the TCP to send data immediately. This function is used to ensure that traffic is delivered to avoid deadlock at the other end. TCP has a feature similar to the TP4 expedited data structure. Its term is the urgent data service. This service requires the receiving ULP to pay special attention to the traffic designated as urgent data.

TCP Primitives

TCP also works with the primitive concept. Some of the primitives are similar to TP4 as Table 15-7 illustrates. Two types of primitives are implemented with TCP. The service request primitives are used from ULP to the TCP and the service response primitives are used from the TCP to the ULP. Table 15-7 also lists the parameters associated with each primitive.

The principal differences between TP4 and TCP are summarized in Box 15-1.

SNA'S TRANSPORT LAYER—TRANSMISSION CONTROL

The SNA Transmission Control Layer is somewhat similar to the OSI transport layer model. Functions such as sequencing, segmentation and pacing are found in both specifications. The two layers also differ in many of their functions.

To begin our analysis of this layer, please examine Figure 15-14. Transmission Control constructs the request/response header (RH) based on the information it receives from the Data Flow Control Layer (request/response

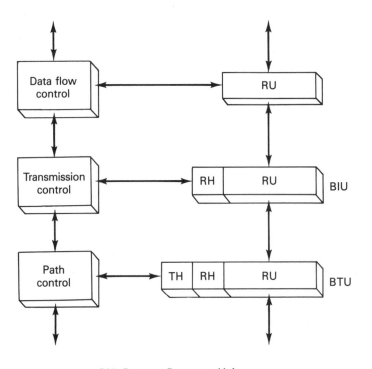

RU: Request Response Unit
RH: Request Response Header
TH: Transmission Header
BIU: Basic Information Unit
BTU: Basic Transmission Unit

FIGURE 15-14. BIU and BTU Construction

unit [RU]). The RH is appended to the RU to form the basic information unit (BIU). The BIU is passed to Path Control. A receiving Transmission Control Layer uses the RH to perform several functions. It then strips off the RH and passes the remaining RU to the data flow control layer. Again, this figure emphasizes that SNA uses the concepts of encapsulation and decapsulation.

Request/Response Header (RH)

The RH is three octets in length. Its format is shown in Figure 15-15 and Table 15-8. Perhaps the best way to understand SNA's Transmission Control Layer is to examine the RH; so let us begin with an analysis of the functions of the RH fields.

The request/response indicator bit identifies the RU as a request or a response and the next two bits designate the RU category. SNA provides four possible categories for an incoming or outgoing RU. Since RUs are not

Bit

Octet	7	6	5	4	3	2	1	0
0	End chain	Begin chain	Sense data	Format indicator	Not used	RU category		R-R indicator
1	Pacing	QR	Not used	Not used	ER	DR 2	Not used	DR 1
2	Not used	Padded data	Enciphered data	Code selection	Not used	Change direction	End bracket	Begin bracket

(a) SNA Request Header Format

Bit

Octet	7	6	5	4	3	2	1	0
0	Not used	Not used	Sense data	Format indicator	Not used	RU category		R-R indicator
1	Pacing	QR	Not used	Not used	ER	DR 2	Not used	DR 1
2	Not used	Not used	Not used	Not used	Not used	Not used	Not used	Not used

(b)   SNA Response Header Format

FIGURE 15-15. SNA Request/Response Header (RH)

used by logical units, these two bits are defined to indicate the destination as follows:

00: Function management
01: Network control
10: Data flow control
11: Session control

The next bit is designated as the format indicator bit. This bit is set to 1 when the RU is to be used for session control, network control, or data flow control. A value of 0 indicates that no network service header or character coding exists (this subject is discussed later). If the RU is destined for function management, as part of a LU-to-LU session, the bit indicates whether or not the FM header is to be used. If the function management services are part of a SSCP-to-SSCP session, or SSCP-to-PU session, or SSCP-to-LU ses-

Table 15-8. Contents of Request/Response Header (RH)

CONTENTS OF REQUEST HEADER

Contents	Octet 1
Request/Response Indicator	0
RU Category	1–2
Not Used	3
Format Indicator	4
Sense Data Included Indicator	5
Begin Chain Indicator	6
End Chain Indicator	7

	Octet 1
Definite Response 1 Indicator	0
Not Used	1
Definite Response 2 Indicator	2
Exception Response Indicator	3
Not Used	4–5
Queued Response Indicator	6
Pacing Indicator	7

	Octet 2
Begin Bracket Indicator	0
End Bracket Indicator	1
Change Direction Indicator	2
Not Used	3
Code Selection Indicator	4
Enciphered Data Indicator	5
Padded Data Indicator	6
Not Used	7

CONTENTS OF RESPONSE HEADER

Contents	Octet 0
Request/Response Indicator	1
RU Category	1–2
Not Used	3
Format Indicator	4
Sense Data Included Indicator	5
Not Used	6–7

	Octet 1
Definite Response 1 Indicator	0
Not Used	1
Definite Response 2 Indicator	2
Exception Response Indicator	3
Not Used	4–5
Queued Response Indicator	6
Pacing Indicator	7

	Octet 2
Not Used	0–7

sion, this value indicates the presence of a network service header and field formatting (again, this material is covered shortly).

The sense data indicator bit is used to indicate a problem during the session. This bit is turned on to indicate that there is information about the error and it is included in the request/response unit (RU).

Most data communications networks provide the ability to chain data units together. We learned that this important feature is provided in X.25 with the more data bit (the m bit). This can be done for a number of reasons. For example, it may be desirable to store related units in a buffer until they all have arrived. This permits the releasing of a full logical transaction to a data base update or CRT screen. SNA uses two bits, called chain control indicators, to indicate that request units are logically tied together. Transmission Control provides this information by coding the chain indicator bits as follows:

10: First RU in chain
00: Middle RU in chain
01: Last RU in chain
11: Only RU in chain

The bits in the first part of octet one in the RH are used to instruct the receiver that (a) no response is needed, (b) a response is needed if an error occurs, or (c) a response is always needed. These instructions are coded in the definite response 1 indicator, the definite response 2 indicator, and the exception response indicator.

The queued response indicator bits instruct the system as to whether this response can be queued or whether the response is to bypass queues. In the latter case the bit is set to 0, in the former case it is set to 1.

The pacing indicator bit is similar to the credit allocation function of the CCITT transport protocol class 4. With SNA, it is used to provide session level pacing. This function is implemented to ensure that a receiving node does not request more units than it can accommodate. It specifies a maximum number (N) of data units that can be transferred before a response is received. When the originating node transmits the unit with the pacing indicator set, it is asking for permission to send yet another group of end data units to the receiver. The receiving node will send back the response unit with the pacing indicator on if it is willing to accept another group of N requests.

The first bits of octet two are designated as the bracket control indicators. This allows data flow control to group a sequence of chains into a logical unit called the bracket. The two bits identified in octet two are used to signify the beginning and the ending of the bracket. Chapter 16 (on session control) describes the bracket control indicators in more detail.

The change direction indicator bit is only used during the half duplex communication function. It is set to 1 to instruct the receiving node that it is now able to transmit data units.

Box 15-2. DECnet NSP Messages

Data	Carries part of session control message
Data, Interrupt	Carries urgent data and optionally, data
Data, Request	Carries flow control and optionally, an acknowledgment
Data, Interrupt Request	Carries interrupt flow control and optionally, an acknowledgment
Acknowledgment	Carries ACK of Connect Confirm, and data
Other Acknowledgment	Carries ACK of Interrupt Request, Interrupt, Data, and Data Request
Acknowledgment, Connect	Carries ACK of Connect Initiate
Control (Connect Initiate and Retransmitted Connect Initiate)	Carries logical link connect request
Connect Confirm	Carries Connect Acceptance
Disconnect Initiate	Carries connect rejection or disconnect request
No resources	Carries NAK to a Connect Initiate
Disconnect Complete	Carries ACK of receipt of Disconnect Initiate logical link
No Link	Carries a NAK for data on nonexistent logical link
No operation	Nothing

The code selection indicator bit is used to indicate if certain codes are being used, for example, ASCII or EBCDIC.

The enciphered data indicator bit indicates if the data are encrypted. The value of 1 indicates the data in the associated RU are encrypted, and a 0 indicates they are not encrypted.

The padded data indicator bit is used to indicate if the request response unit has been padded to provide an even octet alignment before encryption. A value of 1 indicates that it has indeed been padded.

DECnet's END COMMUNICATION LAYER

DECnet's End Communication Layer resides immediately above the Routing Layer and below the Session Layer. The layer is responsible for two users exchanging data reliably and sequentially. It makes no difference where they are located in the network. The controlling mechanism for the End Communication Layer is the network services protocol (NSP). The NSP manages each communications process on a connection basis. The connection is called a logical link. Logical link supports a two-way simultaneous transfer of normal data flow and independent two-way simultaneous transmission of interrupt traffic.

The NSP messages are divided into three categories: data, acknowledgment, and control. A summary of their functions is provided in Box 15-2. These messages are used for transfer of data, establishment of sessions, disconnection of sessions, resolution of errors, interrupts, and other flow control activities.

Functions of NSP

The NSP consists of four major functions:

1. Creation, management, and destruction of logical links
2. Segmentation of data from the session control layer, reassembly of the data at the receiving end
3. Acknowledgment and error control at each end of the logical link
4. Flow control through the logical link

The creation, management, and destruction of logical links is managed by NSP. The logical link is a full duplex, virtual circuit between two users. It is quite similar to the X.25 virtual circuit concept. The logical links are set up across actual physical links by the NSP. NSP ensures the users that the data will be sent in the proper order at both ends of the logical link connection. The NSP provides flow control and checking for errors, all of which are transparent to the user. NSP permits several logical links to exist at any time. The concept of logical links is illustrated in Figure 15-16.

Figure 15-17 shows a typical NSP link connection, data flow, and link disconnection scenario. NSP receives data from the session control layer and segments the data (if necessary) into smaller units. NSP also numbers each segment and sends it and other control information and the data segment message to the recipient NSP. At the receiving end, the NSP uses these sequence numbers to reassemble the data segments to present to the session control layer. Like many other protocols of this type, only normal data can be segmented. Interrupt data units cannot be segmented due to their limitation of size.

NSP provides for acknowledgment of traffic at each end of the logical link. A NSP may also negatively acknowledge (NAK) if the data unit does not meet certain criteria; for example, if it cannot be decoded, or if it is out of sequence, or if it is too big. In the event a negative acknowledgment is received by the transmitting NSP, or in the event nothing is received within a certain timeout interval, the sending NSP must retransmit the data.

Finally, the NSP is also responsible for flow control across the logical link. It is responsible for making certain that no data are lost and that no lock-outs occur between the two users. DECnet flow controls both normal and interrupt data units. DECnet uses a concept similar to that used by SNA

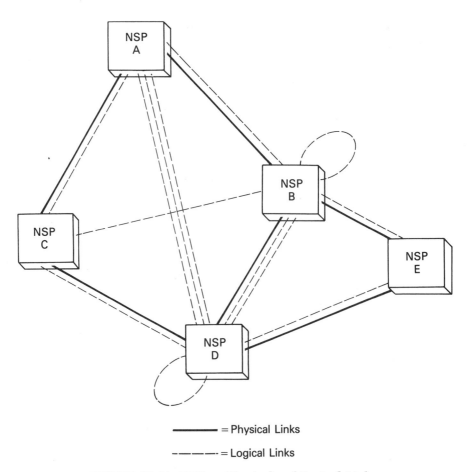

——— = Physical Links

————· = Logical Links

FIGURE 15-16. DECnet Physical and Logical Links

and the OSI transport layers in which the receiver sends a request count of the number of segments it will accept. In turn, the transmitter adheres to this value and does not exceed the flow window. NSP also allows the receiver to inform the transmitter to cease sending data units unconditionally or to resume the sending of the data units. Several of the control messages can contain acknowledgments for the data segments. In addition, the data acknowledgment message may also piggyback data units onto it. This approach reduces the number of overhead messages that must be transmitted between the two communicating NSPs.

CONNECTIONLESS TRANSPORT LAYER PROTOCOLS

This chapter has concentrated on systems that provide connection-oriented functions. Nonetheless, ISO has also issued standards on connectionless

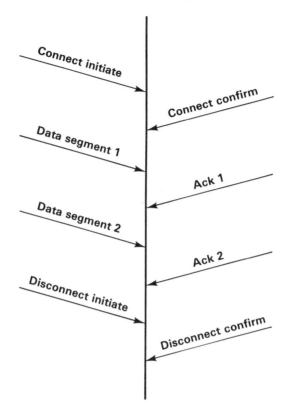

FIGURE 15-17. Message Exchange Between DECnet NSPs

transport services and protocols. These specifications are relatively new and have not found a wide following. The interested reader should obtain ISO 8072/DAD1 and DIS 8602 for more information.

SUGGESTED READINGS

For the reader who needs more detail on the CCITT transport layer X.200, X.214 and X.224 should be studied. The ISO 8072 and 8073 also contain similar information. [SCHW87] and [STAL85] provide a complete summary of the CCITT and NBS transport protocols. [MART87] and [CHAP87] describe the SNA transmission control layer. [FLET82] discusses several checksum algorithms.

APPENDIX 15A
CCITT TRANSPORT PROTOCOL ELEMENTS OF PROCEDURE

The transport layer uses many elements of procedure for its operations. Some of these procedures are required for the various protocol classes (0-4). The reader may wish to refer to Table 15-5 while studying the procedures.

Assignment to Network Connection. The procedure assigns transport connections to network connections. It also releases an assignment. It uses the N-CONNECT and N-DISCONNECT primitives. An originator may assign the transport connection to an existing or a new network connection. If it is an existing network connection, the assignment cannot override any classes or elements of procedure that currently exist. If classes 1 or 3 are used, an existing transport connection can be reassigned after a network connection failure.

TPDU Transfer. This procedure is simply a statement that a TPDU is to be conveyed in the data field of the network service primitives. While such a statement might appear obvious, a well-written specification does not allow the designer to assume a procedure is to be used; rather, it explicitly explains the procedure.

Segmenting and Reassembling. This procedure is used to map transport service data units (TSDUs) onto transport protocol data units (TPDUs). The procedure makes use of the DT TPDU and the end of TSDU parameter (explained later) to indicate if subsequent DT TPDUs exist in the sequence.

Concatenation and Separation. This procedure allows the transport entity to concatenate multiple TPDUs into one NSDU. The concatenated TPDUs may be from the same or different transport connections.

Connection Establishment. This procedure defines how a transport connection is established. (The procedure was described in general terms earlier in this chapter.) During the connection establishment, the transport entities choose a reference (a 16-bit field) to identify the specific transport connection. Also, the calling and called transport service access points (TSAPs) are exchanged, as are the following parameters (if relevant for the protocol class): initial credit, acknowledgment time, checksum parameter, and security parameter. During the connection establishment, the following services, procedures, and protocol classes can be negotiated:

- Protocols class (0–4)
- Transport protocol data unit (TPDU) size
- Normal or extended format
- Use of checksum
- These QOS parameters: throughput, transit delay, priority, residual error rate
- Non-use of explicit flow control (class 2)
- Network receipt confirmation
- Network expedited (for class 1)
- Expedited data transfer

Connection Refusal. This procedure is invoked when the transport entity refuses a connection request that was initiated with a CR TPDU. The refuser sends either a DR TPDU or an ER TPDU. These data units contain the reason (in the DR TPDU) or reject cause (in the ER TPDU). The source reference field (SRC-REF) is set to zero to indicate that the reference is unassigned.

Normal Release. This procedure describes the protocol for disconnecting the network sessions. The normal release procedure provides two variants for the release: the implicit variant and the explicit variant. Using the implicit variant (only for class 0), the transport entity can request the release by the network. The release occurs when either entity receives a N-DISCONNECT indication.

The explicit variant occurs using the DR and DC TPDUs. This procedure provides for the possibility that either transport entity may issue a disconnect request. As another possibility, one may have issued a disconnect and one may have issued a connect. The explicit variant provides for various scenarios to ensure that the two entities have terminated the session and both sides are aware that the connection has been released. It provides for more control across the two entities than is given with the implicit variant. Figure 15-2 was used earlier in the chapter to explain release scenarios.

Error Release. This procedure is used for classes 0 and 2 in the event the transport layer receives one of two primitives from the network layer: N-DISCONNECT indication or N-RESET indication. When the transport entity receives either of these primitives from the network layer, it considers the network connection released and must inform the upper levels, i.e., the transport service users. All other classes invoke error recovery procedures.

Association of TPDUs with Transport Connection. The purpose of this procedure is to associate a received NSDU as TPDU(s). The procedure uses the following network service primitives: N-DATA indication and N-EXPEDITED DATA indication. This detailed procedure stipulates how the received primitives are handled in the network layer. Generally, with ongoing data flow between the layers, the received TPDU is associated with the ongoing transport connection that is identified by the DST-REF parameter in the data unit.

However, if the DST-REF parameter identifies other connections, if the data unit is corrupted, or if the data unit cannot be interpreted, then the procedure defines the methods by which the disconnection is implemented or how to handle the unusual conditions. The protocol associated with this procedure varies depending on which class is being used for the connection.

Data TPDU Numbering. The numbering procedure states that (if used) the protocol data units will have sequence numbers associated with them. These sequences can be normal format sequence (2^7) or extended sequencing (2^{31}). These sequence numbers are used to maintain flow control sequencing between the two transport entities.

Expedited Data Transfer. The expedited data procedure is negotiated during connection establishment. Once established, this allows the user to create either a N-DATA primitive or a N-EXPEDITED DATA primitive. It defines how the receiver acknowledges the primitive with an expedited acknowledgment. This procedure restricts one expedited data unit at a time, i.e., only one of these units can be outstanding for each direction in each transport connection.

Reassignment After Failure. This procedure is used in protocol classes 1 and 3, and defines how recovery is made after receiving a disconnect indication primitive from the network layer. Generally, the transport connection is reassigned to another network connection and any lost TPDUs are retransmitted. The actual actions invoked are dependent on the transport connection waiting for reassignments or resynchronization, and is based on the current state of the following timers: TTR (time to try resynchronization/reassignment timer); and TWR (the time to wait for resynchronization/reassignment timer). Depending on the state of the timers, the transport entity will either release the connection and freeze the

Table 15A-1. TPDUs: Retention Until Acknowledgment

Retained TPDU	Retained TPDU Until Acknowledged By
CR	CC, DR, ER
DR	DC, DR
CC[1]	N-DATA ACKNOWLEDGE indication, RJ, DT, ED, EA
CC[2]	RJ, DT, AK, ED, EA
DT[1]	N-DATA ACKNOWLEDGE indication, from a N-DATA request
DT[2]	AK or RJ: if YR-TU-NR > TPDU-NR in DT
ED	EA: YR-EDTU-NR = ED-TPDU-NR in ED TPDU

[1]Confirmation of Receipt.

[2]AK.

reference or take some remedial actions. The reader should review the resynchronization procedure in relation to this procedure. Also, you might wish to review the timer procedure as well. These procedures are covered shortly.

Two timers are used in the reassignment after failure procedure: the TTR and the TWR. The TTR timer is used by the initiator of action. This procedure stipulates that its value will not exceed two minutes, less the total maximum disconnect propagation delay and the maximum transit delay of the network connections. The value of this timer can be negotiated during connection establishment. The TWR timer is managed by the receiver. Its parameter can also be negotiated in the connection request. The TWR value shall be greater than the TTR timer plus the maximum disconnection propagation delay plus the maximum transit delay through the network(s).

Retention Until Acknowledgment of TPDUs. This procedure describes the methods to retain data units (in classes 2, 3, and 4) to enable the recovery of TPDUs that may be lost. The procedure defines which types of protocol data units are to be retained and when they may be released. The following TPDUs must be retained for possible retransmission: CR, CC, DR, DT, ED. Table 15A-1 summarizes the rules for this procedure.

Resynchronization. This procedure is used in classes 1 and 3 to recover from a reset or a reassignment after failure. The class 4 protocol uses a different technique for its recovery. The procedure defines three methods for resynchronization: active resynchronization, passive resynchronization, and data resynchronization. The rules for invoking one of these procedures depend on whether (a) the transport entity is the responder or (b) the

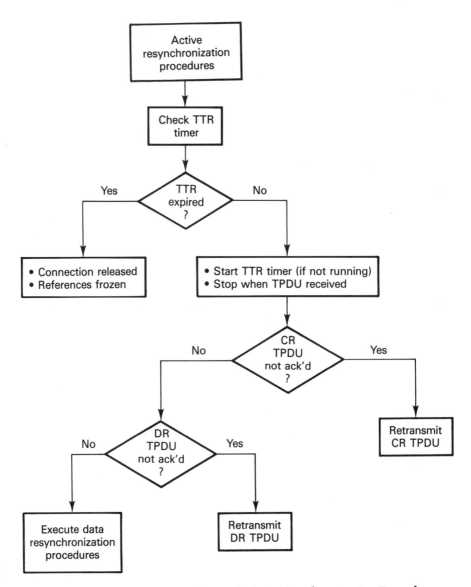

FIGURE 15A-1. Transport Layer Active Resynchronization Procedures

transport entity elects to reassign after failure. If the entity is a responder, passive synchronization occurs. If it has elected not to reassign, no synchronization occurs. Otherwise active synchronization occurs.

To give the reader an appreciation of the details of the transport layer, Figures 15A-1, 15A-2, and 15A-3 show the logic of the three synchronization procedures. Similar logic charts can be created for the other procedures.

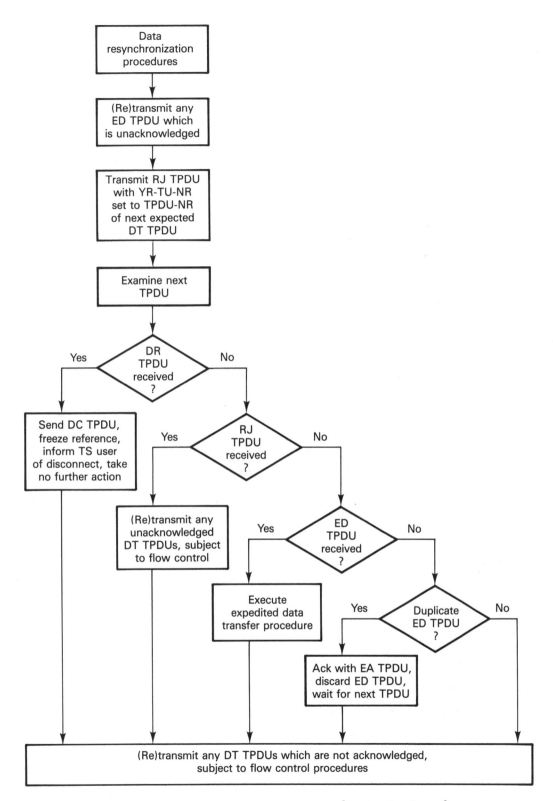

FIGURE 15A-2. Transport Layer Data Resynchronization Procedures.

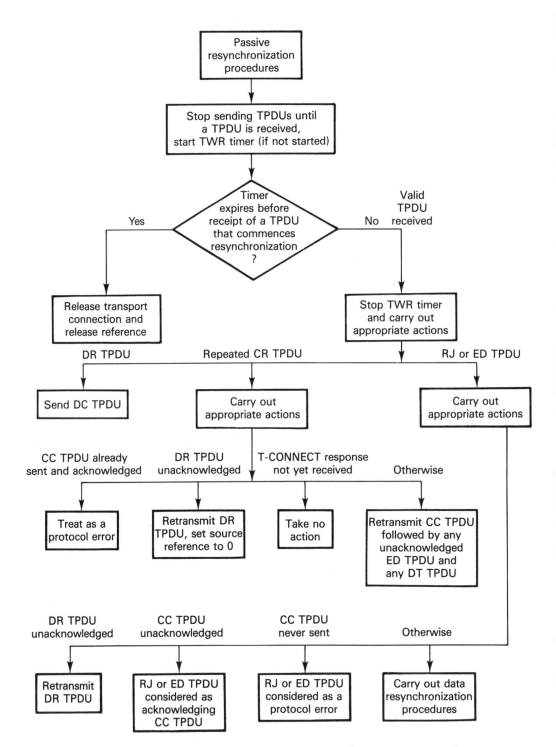

FIGURE 15A-3. Transport Layer Passive Resynchronization Procedures

This level of detail is quite helpful to designers because it decreases ambiguity and chances for misunderstanding the specification. If the reader needs this level of detail for other procedures, the CCITT transport layer document should be obtained and studied. Be aware logic charts are not in the document. The author drew these charts based on the CCITT specification.

Multiplexing and Demultiplexing. This procedure allows several transport connections to simultaneously share one network connection. The TPDUs belonging to different transport connections can be transferred in the same N-DATA primitive. The multiplexing operation uses the concatenation procedure and the demultiplexing operation uses the association of TPDUs with transport connections procedure.

Explicit Flow Control. This procedure is invoked to regulate the flow of the DT TPDUs between transport entities. This flow control acts independently from the flow control of the other layers. For example, the receive ready (RR)/receive not ready (RNR) flow control at the network layer (e.g., X.25) and data link layer (e.g., HDLC/SDLC) are fully independent flow control procedures. The flow control procedures vary with each protocol class. In a section of this chapter, this procedure is highlighted with a discussion of the class 4 protocol.

Checksum. This procedure was explained earlier. It is used only in the class 4 protocol if the users so agree during the connection establishment. It is always used with the CR TPDU.

Frozen References. In earlier discussions, the use of DST-REF (destination reference) and SRC-DEF (source reference) was explained. To briefly reiterate, these fields in the TPDU identify the two communicating transport entities. This procedure prevents a reference identifier from being reused. It is needed because a retransmission or out-of-sequence TPDU may arrive at the receiving entity after a connection release. The actions of this procedure depend upon the specific protocol class. For class 4, the reference must remain frozen for a time greater than L (maximum time between a TPDU transmission and its expected acknowledgment).

Retransmission Upon Timeout. This procedure is used only with protocol class 4 and is used to deal with lost TPDUs.

Resequencing. This procedure is used only with protocol class 4 and is used to resequence misordered TPDUs.

Inactivity Control. This procedure is used only with protocol class 4 and is used to handle an unsignalled termination of a network connection.

Treatment of Protocol Errors. Upon receiving an erroneous TPDU, a transport entity takes one of the following actions (which one is taken depends on the protocol classes used):

Transmit an ER TPDU
Reset network connection
Close network connection
Invoke protocol class-specific release procedures
Ignore the TPDU used on protocol class

Splitting and Recombining. This procedure is used only in class 4. It is invoked to increase throughput or provide more resilience to network failure. It makes use of multiple network connections and utilizes the assignment to network connections and resequencing procedures. We examine this procedure in the main part of this chapter and in chapter 8.

QUESTIONS

TRUE/FALSE

1. Transport-level protocols can recover from lost or erroneous protocol data units emanating from the applications level.
2. The CCITT transport-level elements of procedure vary in usage, depending on a protocol class.
3. The CCITT transport-level protocols allow the use of a checksum for error detection.
4. Frozen references are used only with TP4.
5. The CCITT TP4 and the transmission control protocol (TCP) have similar functions.
6. Examine Figure 15-15. To test your understanding of the SNA Request Response header, match the field in the header to its appropriate functions.

Function

a) Provides flow control
b) Indicates a problem has occurred
c) Controls a half-duplex session
d) Logically relates data units together
e) Controls acknowledgment options

Field

1. Chain indicators
2. Pacing indicator
3. Change direction indicator
4. Sense indicator
5. Response indicator

7. Your project leader is selecting the communications modules to operate a point-to-point link. The data link control (DLC) protocol recommendation is LAPB. The network level logic will not be used. The project leader recommends transport protocol, class 4 for the transport layer. What is your evaluation of this recommendation?

8. To continue the scenario in question 7: After further discussions, the idea of using a connectionless link level protocol is brought to your attention. The recommendation for the network and transport levels remain the same. What is your response?

9. The department managers in your organization wish to maintain control of their data and information systems. In this regard, one issue is their stipulation that end-to-end integrity reside in each application. Since each manager has a programming staff, it is planned that each department will write the necessary code to achieve end-to-end integrity. What are the advantages and disadvantages to this approach?

10. Briefly describe the differences between the TCP passive mode and active mode.

11. List the major differences between TP4 and TCP.

12. The abstract nature of the transport layer primitives permit considerable flexibility in their implementation. What method does DEC use for the OSI transport layer primitives?

13. Your application program at site A creates transactions for sending through the lower six layers to a complementary application at remote site B. The applications maintain copies of the transactions and periodically perform checks to account for all traffic between the applications. If a transport protocol is used at the transport layer, which class should it be, 0, 1, 2, 3 or 4? Why?

14. The following is an excerpt from the CCITT recommendation X.224: 6.14.4.1 Active resynchronization procedures:
The transport entity shall carry out one of the following actions:

a) if the TTR timer has been previously started and has run out (i.e., no valid TPDU has been received), the transport connection is considered as released and the reference is frozen;

b) otherwise, the TTR timer shall be started (unless it is already running) and the first applicable one of the following actions shall be taken:

    1. if a CR TPDU is unacknowledged, then the transport entity shall retransmit it;

    2. if a DR TPDU is unacknowledged, then the transport entity shall retransmit it;

    3. otherwise, the transport entity shall carry out the data resynchronization procedures.

To determine your ability to develop a program from CCITT specifications, write and draw a flow chart that describes the logic of the X.224 specification. Check your answer with Figure 15A-1.

15. The following is an excerpt from the CCITT recommendation X.224: 6.14.4.2 Passive resynchronization procedures:

The transport entity shall not send any TPDUs until a TPDU has been received. The transport entity shall start its TWR timer if it was not already started. If the timer runs out prior to the receipt of a valid TPDU which commences resynchronization, the transport connection is considered as released and the reference is released.

When a valid TPDU is received, the transport entity shall stop its TWR timer and carry out the appropriate one of the following actions, depending on the TPDU:

    a) if it is a DR TPDU, then the transport entity shall send a DC TPDU;

    b) if it is a repeated CR TPDU, then the transport entity shall carry out the action which is appropriate from the following:

    1. if a CC TPDU has already been sent and acknowledged: treat as a protocol error;

    2. if a DR TPDU is unacknowledged (whether or not a CC TPDU is unacknowledged): retransmit the DR TPDU, but set the source reference to zero;

    3. if the T-CONNECT response has not yet been received from the user: take no action;

    4. otherwise: retransmit the CC TPDU followed by any unacknowledged ED TPDU and any DT TPDU.

    c) if it is an RJ or ED TPDU, then one of the following actions shall be taken:

    1. if a DR TPDU is unacknowledged, then the transport entity shall retransmit it;

    2. otherwise, the transport entity shall carry out the data resynchronization procedures;

    3. if a CC TPDU was unacknowledged, the RJ or ED TPDU should then be considered as acknowledging the CC TPDU. If a CC TPDU was never sent, the RJ or ED TPDU should then be considered as a protocol error.

To determine your ability to develop a program from CCITT specifications, write and draw a flow chart that describes the logic of this X.224 specification. Check your answer with Figure 15A-2.

16. The following is an excerpt from the CCITT recommendation X.224:
4.4.3 Data resynchronization procedures:
The transport entity shall carry out the following actions in the following order:

   a) (re)transmit any ED TPDU which is unacknowledged;
   b) transmit an RJ TPDU with YR-TU-NR field set to the TPDU-NR of the next expected DT TPDU;
   c) wait for the next TPDU from the other transport entity, unless it has already been received. If a DR TPDU is received, the transport entity shall send a DC TPDU, freeze the reference, inform the TS-user of the disconnection and take no further action. If an RJ TPDU is received, (re)transmit any unacknowledged DT TPDUs, subject to flow control. It it is an ED TPDU, execute the expedited data transfer procedure. If it is a duplicated ED TPDU, the transport entity shall acknowledge it with an EA TPDU, discard the duplicated ED TPDU, and wait again for the next TPDU;
   d) (re)transmit any DT TPDUs which are unacknowledged, subject to any applicable flow control procedures (see Note).

To determine your ability to develop a program from CCITT specifications, write and draw a flow chart that describes the logic of the X.224 specification. Check your answer with Figure 15A-3.

SELECTED ANSWERS

1. False. The transport level protocols have no understanding of the actions and quality of service features of the upper levels. They are meant to recover from problems at the lower levels.

2. True.

3. True. See Table 15-5.

4. False. See Table 15-5.

5. True.

6.
Function	Field
a)	2
b)	4
c)	3
d)	1
e)	5

7. I would agree with the project leader's recommendation on the use of LAPB. LAPB functions quite well on point-to-point links. It is efficient and is available from a number of vendors of off-the-shelf products. The recommendation for using a null network level sounds reasonable, based on the information. The network level is generally most useful when there are network connections which must be made. A direct point-to-point link does not need the functionality associated with network level interfaces. The selection of the transport protocol class 4 presents potential problems. It is probably "overkill" for a point-to-point circuit. Many of the functions of

TP4 address the use of unreliable network clouds and unreliable links. LAPB provides a very reliable protocol at the link level, and there are no multiple links involved in a point-to-point link. That is, the end-to-end accountability normally associated with TP4 can be obtained through the use of LAPB.

14. See Figure 15A-1.
15. See Figure 15A-2.
16. See Figure 15A-3.

CHAPTER 16

The Session Layer

INTRODUCTION

To gain an insight into the functions of this important layer, let us assume you must design a system that manages the interactions between applications programs. For example, an application at a host computer must communicate with applications in other computers.

What would you consider to be the design issues? How would you coordinate the activities of each user application with the host application? Would you allow each application to send a file at any time? Should you provide periodic checkpoints to allow the applications to "back up" and recover from processing problems? Do you permit the applications to issue "reads" and "writes" at any time (full duplex), or must they restrict their input/output executions to an alternate two-way process (half duplex)? How do you pass control to the applications? Is it even necessary?

We could go on with these questions, but the point should be clear that designing a system to control the sessions between applications is a challenging task. Fortunately, several procedures have stood the test of time and are now available in vendors' products or in the standards organizations' specifications.

The session layer provides the aforementioned functions for the end user. It is so named because it manages the user application-to-application sessions. Most session layer systems provide the following services:

- Coordinating the exchange of data between applications by logically connecting and releasing sessions (also called dialogues).
- Providing synchronization points to structure the exchange of data.

- Imposing rules on the user application interactions.
- Providing a convention to take turns in exchanging data.

This chapter introduces session layer protocols with the CCITT and ISO recommendations. Then, the SNA and DECnet session layers are explained.

SESSION SERVICES FOR APPLICATIONS (X.215 AND X.225)

CCITT X.215 and X.225 define the protocols for the exchange of data between session service (SS) layer users. The principal parts of X.215 describe how the users establish a session through the session layer, exchange and account for data through synchronization points, use tokens to negotiate several types of dialogues, and release the session. X.225 describes the function and protocol data units of the session layer. For purposes of continuity, X.215 and X.225 are described together in this section. The ISO publishes comparable standards as ISO DIS 8326 and ISO DIS 8327.

The lower levels of a network generally assume they must execute rather elaborate mechanisms to provide a reliable service to the upper layers. In contrast, the session layer assumes it is receiving reliable data units from the network, so it uses few error control procedures. Moreover, when a lower level releases a session, any outstanding data units are discarded. The session layer will not release a session until all session service data units (SSDUs) have been delivered.

A key aspect to session level activities is the *token*. A token gives a user the exclusive right to use a service. It is dynamically assigned to one user at a time to permit the use of certain services. For example, a user can issue the Please token to another user to request the transfer of one or more tokens (that is to say, a use of a service or services). The relinquishing user could respond by passing back a Give token. If tokens are not available when the session is established between the session users, they remain unavailable for the session.

Tokens are not used for all the session service functions but are invoked for four specific functions:

Data exchange procedures

Releasing certain user dialogues

Supporting synchronization functions

Supporting an activity across more than one synchronization function

Synchronization (sync) points are another important part of the session layer. They are used to coordinate the exchange of data between session service users. Synchronization services are like checkpoint/restarts in a file transfer or transaction transfer operation. They allow the users to (a) define and isolate points in an ongoing data exchange and (b) if necessary, back up to a point for recovery purposes. Be aware that the session services do not actually save the session service data units (SSDUs) and do not perform the recovery operations. This activity is the responsibility of the application layer. The session layer merely decrements a number back to the sync point and the user must apply it to determine where to begin recovery procedures.

We now examine synchronization points in more detail. After defining some key terms, we will show a "real-life" example of how sync points can be used.

Two types of synchronization points are available: (a) minor synchronization points and (b) major synchronization points. As Figure 16-1 illustrates, the sync points are used in conjunction with the following dialogue units and activities:

- *Major sync point*: Structures the exchange of data into a series of dialogue units. Each major sync point must be confirmed and the user is limited to specific services until a confirmation is received. The sending user can send no more data until the receiving user acknowledges a major synchronization point.

- *Dialogue unit*: An atomic action in which all communication within it is separated from any previous or succeeding communications. A major sync point delineates the beginning and ending of a dialogue unit.

- *Minor sync point*: Structures exchange of data within a dialogue unit. This is more flexible than a major sync point. For example, each sync point may or may not be confirmed, and it is possible to resynchronize to any minor sync point within the dialogue unit. A confirmation confirms all previous minor sync points.

- *Activity*: Consists of one or more dialogue units. An activity is a logical set of related tasks, for example, the transferral of a file with

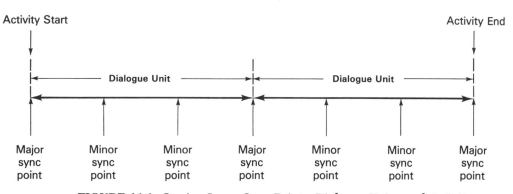

FIGURE 16-1. Session Layer Sync Points, Dialogue Units, and Activity

related records. A dialogue unit can be interrupted and later resumed.

Resynchronization.   A resynchronization allows a user to reestablish communications. It purges any undelivered data and sets a synchronization point number to a new value. It can be initiated by either user to provide one of three options: (a) the *set* option is invoked by the user to set the synchronization point serial number to any value the user chooses; (b) the *abandon* option sets the number to an unused value; (c) the *restart* option sets the synchronization point serial number to a used value. The value must be greater than a number which identifies the last major synchronization point.

Activity Rules.   The session layer restricts a session connection to one activity at a time, but several consecutive activities can be invoked during the session connection. An activity can perform resynchronization because it can span more than one session connection. It can be interrupted and reinvoked during another session connection.

An Example of Session Services

Let us assume an organization in Washington, D.C., must receive data each day from its 12 "districts" located throughout the country. (This is a common situation in both government and private enterprise, and our example is an actual operation.) The nature of the data is such that a district must successfully complete its transfer before another district can begin its transmission.

The central computing facility and the districts use session layer services to structure the file transfers as follows: The central site considers the 12 file transfers as one session level activity. Due to the nature of the activity service, the central site can interrupt the file transfer service (to perform maintenance in the evening, service higher priority jobs, etc.) and later resume the service without any loss of synchronization.

Within the activity are 12 dialogue units that begin and end with major synchronization points. The central site establishes and coordinates the sync point numbers to segregate the files from each district into a dialogue unit. This approach assures the districts and the central site that a file has been received and accepted from each district before another file is transmitted.

Within each dialogue, the specific district and central site use minor synchronization points to obtain flexible backup and recovery options. Since each file transfer is quite time consuming, it makes sense to use the minor sync points during the transfer to prevent the retransmission of large amounts of data.

We see that this operation uses many of the features of the session layer. It should also be obvious to the reader that the session layer services

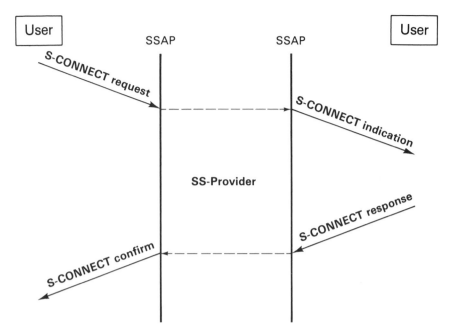

FIGURE 16-2. Session Connection Primitives

can be quite valuable to the end user. With this thought in mind, we now begin our more detailed analysis of the session layer protocols.

Session Service Phases

The session service layer is divided into three phases:

Session connection establishment phase
Data transfer phase
Session connection release phase.

Session Connection Establishment Phase. This phase establishes a connection between two session service (SS) users. During the phase, the tokens and parameters to be used are negotiated between the SS-users.

Figure 16-2 depicts the sequence of primitive exchanges to effect the session establishment. The primitives carry the negotiable parameters needed to support the connection. Presently, nine parameters are used, although not all of them are required in each primitive:

Session connection identifier
Calling SSAP address
Called SSAP address

Result
Quality of service
Session requirements
Initial synchronization point serial number
Initial assignment of token
SS-user data

A brief description of these primitive parameters follows. Boxes 16-1 and 16-2, and Table 16-1 are provided to assist the reader in understanding the session layer operations. It is recommended you study their contents as you read this section.

The session connection identifier, calling SSAP address, and called SSAP address identify the SS-users and the SSAPs. It consists of the calling and called references, a common reference, and additional reference information, if necessary.

The result parameter provides information about the acceptance or rejection of the connection establishment request. The reasons for the rejection may also be provided (such as SS-provider busy, called SS-user is unavailable, unknown SSAP, etc.).

The quality of service (QOS) parameters describe the services the SS-provider is to provide to the SS-users. Once the connection is negotiated and accepted, the communicating SS-users know the characteristics of their session with each other. The QOS parameters are either negotiated during the connection establishment or set up on an ongoing basis. Several of the QOS parameters are used in other layers and others are unique to the session layer. These parameters are summarized in Box 16-1.

The session requirements parameter may contain several entries pertaining to the use of *functional units*. The functional unit concept is a key aspect of the session layer. It is used to define and group related services offered by the layer. Presently, X.215 provides 12 functional unit services. Box 16-2 describes these units and Table 16-1 lists the actual services associated with each unit. We will examine these services shortly.

The initial synchronization point number is the proposed initial sync value (0–999999). This value is used for the major sync, minor sync, and resync functional units. The initial assignment of tokens contains the SS-user sides to which the tokens are initially assigned. The SS-user data are parameters containing user data. They range from 1 to 512 octets.

Data Transfer Phase. The data transfer phase is used to transfer data between two SS-users. The operations in this phase can be conveniently categorized by five major services. In this section, we examine each of them.

Data transfer
Token service

BOX 16-1. Quality of Service Parameters for Session Services Layer

---

Connection establishment delay:	Maximum acceptable delay between the connect request and connect confirm primitives.
Connection establishment failure probability:	Ratio of total connection failures to connection attempts.
Throughput:	Number of data octets transmitted between SS-users within a specified time.
Transit delay:	Delay between completion of request primitive and corresponding indication primitive.
Residual error rate:	Ratio of total incorrect, lost, or duplicate data units to total units transmitted.
Transfer failure probability:	Ratio of transfer failures to total transfers during a specific period.
Session connection release delay:	Maximum acceptable delay between abort request and its corresponding release.
Session connection release failure probability:	Ratio of total abort requests resulting in session failure to total abort requests.
Session connection protection:	Extent of effort to prevent unauthorized monitoring or manipulation of data.
Session connection priority:	Extent of importance of session.
Session connection resilience:	Probability of a non-orderly release of a session connection.
Extended control:	Options to use resyncs, aborts, interrupts, discards due to problems.[1]
Optimized dialogue transfer:	Option of concatenating certain service requests (SSDUs) and sending as one unit.[1]

[1]These parameters are not passed to the transport layer. All others are.

Synchronization and Resynchronization management
Error reporting
Activity service

For the *data transfer service*, session data units (see Figure 16-3) can be transferred in one of four ways. The first two are the normal or expedited rate. The latter option is free from any token control and flow control restrictions.

BOX 16-2. Session Services Functional Units

Kernal:	Provides five non-negotiable services.
Half duplex:	Alternate two-way transmission of data between SS-users. Data sent by owner of data token.
Duplex:	Simultaneous two-way transmission of data between SS-users.
Typed data:	Transfer of data with no token restrictions.
Exceptions:	Reporting of exceptional situations by either SS-user or SS-provider.
Negotiated release:	Releasing a session through orderly (normal) measures or by passing tokens.
Minor synchronize:	Invoking a minor sync point.
Major synchronize:	Invoking a major sync point.
Resynchronize:	Reestablish communications and reset connection.
Expedited data:	Transferring data that are free from token and flow control restarts.
Activity management:	Providing many functions (see write-up) within an activity.
Capability data exchange:	Exchanging a limited amount of data while not operating within an activity.

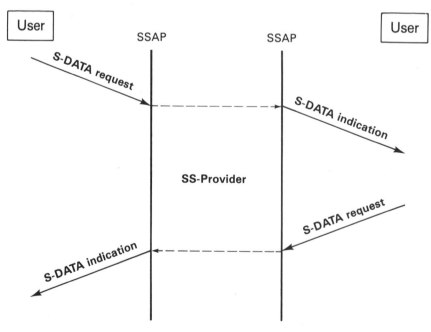

FIGURE 16-3. Session Layer Data Transfer

TABLE 16-1. Session Layer Functional Units and Associated Services

Functional Unit	Associated Services
Kernal:	Session connection, Normal data transfer, Orderly release, U-abort, P-abort
Half duplex:	Give tokens, Please tokens
Duplex:	No additional service
Typed data:	Typed data transfer
Exceptions:	Provider exception reporting, user exception reporting
Negotiated release:	Orderly release, Give tokens, Please tokens
Minor synchronize:	Minor sync point, Give tokens, Please tokens
Major synchronize:	Major sync point, Give tokens, Please tokens
Resynchronize:	Resynchronize
Expedited data:	Expedited data transfer
Activity management:	Activity start, Activity resume, Activity interrupt, Activity discard, Activity end, Give tokens, Please tokens, Give control
Capability data exchange:	Capability data exchange

Third, data units can also be transferred as typed data transfers. This option is subject to the same flow control restrictions as the normal rate but is not subject to token restrictions.

The fourth data transfer option is the capability data exchange service. It allows SS-users to exchange data outside an established activity (no activity is in progress). In the file transfer example, this service might be invoked between the districts and the central site in order to exchange control information.

With the *token service*, a user has the exclusive right to use certain services of the SS-provider. Four tokens are used to invoke these services:

- *Data Token*: Manages a half duplex connection in which the users take turns passing the token to each other to send data.
- *Release Token*: Releases a connection.
- *Sync-Minor Token*: Manages the setting of minor synchronization points.
- *Sync-Major Token*: Manages the setting of major synchronization points.

The use of tokens must be negotiated during the connection establishment phase. Interestingly, X.215 stipulates that a token is always in one of the following states:

- *Available*: Assigned to a user who then has exclusive rights to a service
- *Not available*: Neither user has a right to the service, but the token services are defined as:
  - *Inherently available*: Used for data transfer and release tokens.
  - *Not available*: Used for synchronization and activities.

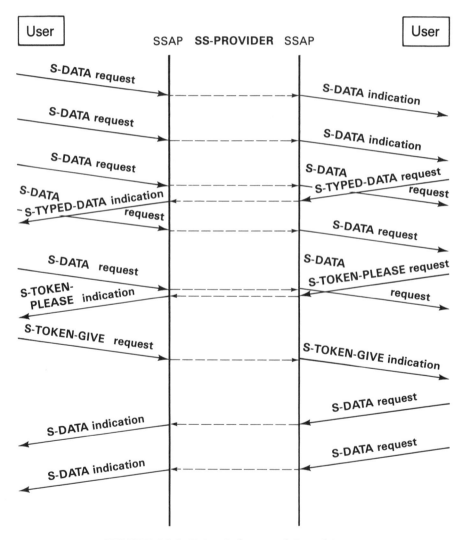

FIGURE 16-4. Using Tokens and Typed Data

Figure 16-4 provides an example of a typical connection between two users. Notice the use of the typed data exchange and the use of tokens to govern the half duplex dialogue. The figures shows how the Please token service is used to request the transfer of one or more tokens. The Give token surrenders the token(s). A third option is called the Give Control service. It allows a SS-user to surrender all available tokens to the other SS-user (not shown in Figure 16-4).

The *synchronization* and *resynchronization* services are used for managing the ongoing activities and for error recovery (see Figure 16-5). As we learned earlier, the major synchronization point service can be used to separate completely the data flow before and after a major synchronization point. After the SS-user issues the S-SYNC-MAJOR request, it may not initiate any other normal activities until the S-SYNC-MAJOR confirm is received. The SS-user may issue other "special" requests such as giving tokens, aborts, activity interrupts, etc. Likewise, the SS-user receiving the S-

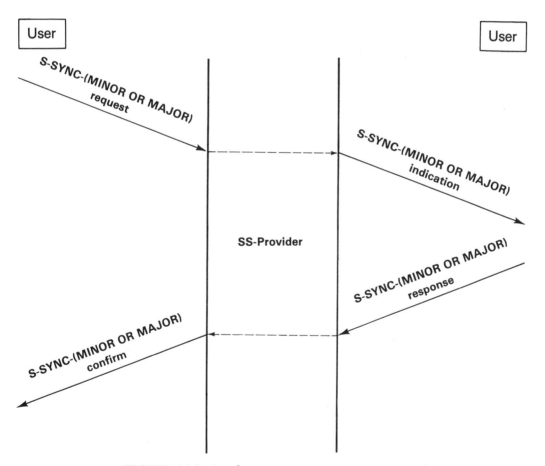

FIGURE 16-5. Synchronization Primitives (Minor and Major)

SYNC-MAJOR indication is restricted from initiating any syncs, activity interrupts, ends, or releases until it issues a S-SYNC-MAJOR response. This convention allows the SS-users to have a period (of no data flow) to determine if the communications flow is correct and continuous.

In addition to the major and minor synchronization point services, the resynchronize service is available to the SS-users. It is typically invoked following an error or disagreement between the SS-users. Its use sets the sync point number to an agreed value, and the session to an agreed state. This service purges all undelivered data.

The process for resynchronization allows for three options (See Figure 16-6):

- *Abandon*: Resynchronize the session connection to a new sync point number greater than or equal to the next sync point number. Do not recover; abort the current dialogue, but do not abort the connection.
- *Restart*: Return to an agreed sync point, as long as it is greater than the last confirmed major sync point.
- *Set*: Set sync point number to any value. Do not recover; abort the current dialogue but do not abort the connection.

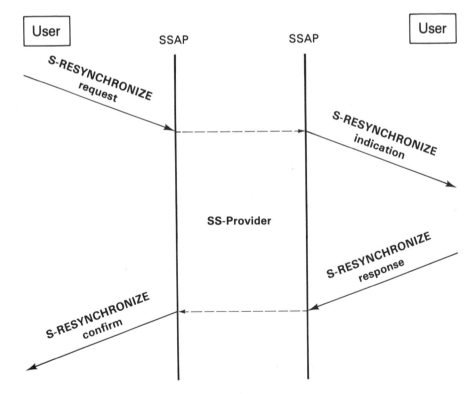

FIGURE 16-6. Resynchronization Primitives

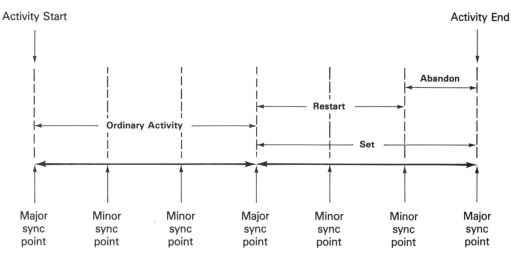

FIGURE 16-7. Resynchronization Options

Figure 16-7 depicts some options for the use of abandon, restart, and set for the resync procedure.

The procedures for synchronization are rather complex and detailed. The reader who wishes more information on the subject may refer to Appendix 16A.

The session services layer provides two *error reporting services*: (a) P-exception and (b) U-exception. The SS-provider uses the P-exception reporting service to notify the SS-users of any situations not covered by the other services. The P-exception forbids the users to initiate any other service until the error is cleared. They may do so by taking one of four actions: (a) resynchronization, (b) an abort, (c) an activity interrupt or discard, and (d) giving the data token. With the P-exception services, the SS-provider discards all outstanding data units.

The U-exception service is invoked by the SS-user to report an error condition. This service uses similar procedures as its SS-provider counterpart, the P-exception service.

The *activity service* is used to manage activities. The overall service is comprised of five major functions, which are summarized in Box 16-3.

The interrupt and discard activity services recommend that the SS-user that initiates the request provide a reason for the invocation of the service. A reason parameter is associated with the request primitive. Its value may be set to indicate: (a) SS-user may not be handling data properly, (b) local SS-user error, (c) sequence error, (d) demand data token, (e) unrecoverable procedure error, and (f) a non-specific error.

Session Connection Release Phase. The session connection release phase is achieved in one of three ways: (a) orderly release, (b) U-abort, and (c) P-abort (see Figure 16-8). The orderly release service allows the session

---

BOX 16-3. Session Layer Activity Services

Activity Start Service:	Starts a new activity. Sync point value is set to 1. Only used when no activity is in progress.
Activity Interrupt Service:	Terminates the current activity. Work is not lost and may be resumed later.
Activity Resume Service:	Resumes a previously interrupted activity.
Activity Discard Service:	Terminates the current activity. Previous work is cancelled.
Activity End Service:	Ends an activity and sets a major synchronization point.

---

connection to be released cooperatively between the two SS-users with complete accounting of all data. The S-RELEASE response and S-RELEASE confirm primitives must contain a result parameter indicating whether the release is accepted.

The U-abort and P-abort services are used by the SS-users and SS-provider respectively. Both services permit the session connection to be released immediately with the loss of all undelivered data. The S-P-ABORT indication primitive must contain a reason primitive to indicate the reason for the abort.

Summary of Session Layer Primitives

As you may now realize, all the layer services (in Table 16-1) are provided by the use of primitives passed from the presentation and application layers. We have just described the most commonly used primitives. All the primitives for the session layer are listed in Table 16-2. You will notice a one-to-one relationship between the primitives in Table 16-2 and the associated services in Table 16-1.

The reader may wonder why the data exchange primitives provide no confirmation services. First, the session layer uses the transport layer, which can be structured to provide for the guarantee and confirmation of delivery. Second, the use of token rights for sending data keeps both users informed about the passing of data.

It is important to note that, with two exceptions, the quality of service (QOS) parameters are passed directly to the transport layer. The reader should compare the session layer QOS parameters in Box 16-1 with the transport layer QOS parameters described in Chapter 15.

Most of the parameters have been explained in previous discussions. Those that have not been covered are:

Requirements: The functional units to be requested (see Table 16-1).

Serial number: The proposed initial synchronization number.

Token: The initial side for the assignment of tokens.

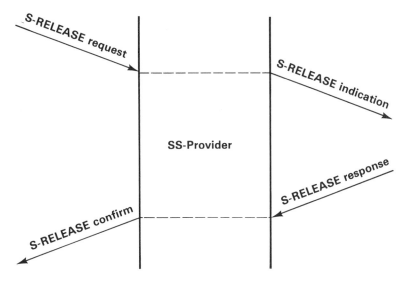

(a) Session Connection Release

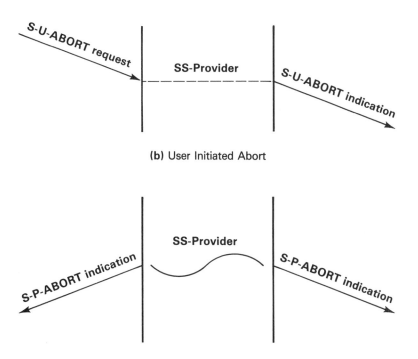

(b) User Initiated Abort

(c) Service-Provider Initiated Abort

FIGURE 16-8. Terminating a Session

TABLE 16-2. Session Layer Primitives

Primitive	Parameters
S-CONNECT.request	identifier, calling SSAP, called SSAP, quality of service, requirements, serial number, token, data
S-CONNECT.indication	identifier, calling SSAP, called SSAP, quality of service, requirements, serial number, token, data
S-CONNECT.response	identifier, called SSAP, result, quality of service, requirements, serial number, token, data
S-CONNECT.confirm	identifier, called SSAP, result, quality of service, requirements, serial number, token, data
S-DATA.request	data
S-DATA.indication	data
S-EXPEDITED-DATA.request	data
S-EXPEDITED-DATA.indication	data
S-TYPED-DATA.request	data
S-TYPED-DATA.indication	data
S-CAPABILITY-DATA.request	data
S-CAPABILITY-DATA.indication	data
S-TOKEN-GIVE.request	tokens
S-TOKEN-GIVE.indication	tokens
S-TOKEN-PLEASE.request	token, data
S-TOKEN-PLEASE.indication	token, data
S-CONTROL-GIVE.request	
S-CONTROL-GIVE.indication	
S-SYNC-MINOR.request	type, serial number, data
S-SYNC-MINOR.indication	type, serial number, data
S-SYNC-MINOR.response	serial number, data
S-SYNC-MINOR.confirm	serial number, data
S-SYNC-MAJOR.request	serial number, data
S-SYNC-MAJOR.indication	serial number, data
S-SYNC-MAJOR.response	data
S-SYNC-MAJOR.confirm	data
S-RESYNCHRONIZE-MINOR.request	type, serial number, tokens, data
S-RESYNCHRONIZE-MINOR.indication	type, serial number, tokens, data
S-RESYNCHRONIZE-MINOR.response	serial number, tokens, data
S-RESYNCHRONIZE-MINOR.confirm	serial number, tokens, data
S-P-EXCEPTION-REPORT.reason	indication
S-U-EXCEPTION-REPORT.request	reason, data

S-U-EXCEPTION-REPORT.indication	reason, data
S-ACTIVITY-START.request	activity, ID, data
S-ACTIVITY-START.indication	activity, ID, data
S-ACTIVITY-RESUME.request	activity ID, old activity ID, serial number, old SC ID, data
S-ACTIVITY-RESUME.indication	activity ID, old activity ID, serial number, old SC ID, data
S-ACTIVITY-INTERRUPT.request	reason
S-ACTIVITY-INTERRUPT.indication	reason
S-ACTIVITY-INTERRUPT.response	
S-ACTIVITY-INTERRUPT.confirm	
S-ACTIVITY-DISCARD.request	reason
S-ACTIVITY-DISCARD.indication	reason
S-ACTIVITY-DISCARD.response	
S-ACTIVITY-DISCARD.confirm	
S-ACTIVITY-END.request	serial number, data
S-ACTIVITY-END.indication	serial number, data
S-ACTIVITY-END.response	data
S-ACTIVITY-END.confirm	data
S-RELEASE.request	data
S-RELEASE.indication	data
S-RELEASE.response	result, data
S-RELEASE.confirm	result, data
S-U-ABORT.request	data
S-U-ABORT.indication	data
S-P-ABORT.indication	reason

Result: The indication of success or failure of a connect attempt.

Reason: The reason for use of several of the primitives.

Session Layer Protocol Data Units (SPDUs)

The session layer uses several protocol data units (PDUs) (see Figure 16-9). Three categories of PDUs exist and are summarized in Table 16-3.

Category 0:	Mapped one-to-one onto a TSDU or concentrated with one or more Category 2 SPDUs
Category 1:	Always mapped one-to-one onto a TSDU
Category 2:	Never mapped one-to-one onto a TSDU

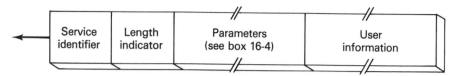

FIGURE 16-9. Session Protocol Data Unit (SPDU)

The structure of the SPDU is shown in Figure 16-9. Be aware that a different SPDU structure is used for each of the SPDUs, but all are variations of the structure in Figure 16-9.

The SI (service identifier) field identifies the type of SPDU (connect, data, token, etc.). The LI (length indicator) field represents the length of the parameter field. The parameter field contains the values used between the

TABLE 16-3. Session Layer Protocol Data Units (SPDUs)

Category 0	Category 1	Category 2
GIVE TOKENS SPDU	CONNECT SPDU	DATA TRANSFER SPDU
PLEASE TOKENS SPDU	ACCEPT SPDU	
		MINOR SYNC POINT SPDU
	REFUSE SPDU	MINOR SYNC ACK SPDU
	FINISH SPDU	
	DISCONNECT SPDU	MAJOR SYNC POINT SPDU
	NOT FINISHED SPDU	MAJOR SYNC ACK SPDU
	ABORT SPDU	
	ABORT ACCEPT SPDU	RESYNCHRONIZE SPDU
		RESYNCHRONIZE ACK SPDU
	GIVE TOKENS CONFIRM SPDU	
	GIVE TOKENS ACK SPDU	ACTIVITY START SPDU
		ACTIVITY RESUME SPDU
	EXPEDITED SPDU	ACTIVITY DISCARD SPDU
	PREPARE SPDU	ACTIVITY DISCARD ACK SPDU
	TYPED DATA SPDU	ACTIVITY INTERRUPT SPDU
		ACTIVITY INTERRUPT ACK SPDU
		ACTIVITY END SPDU
		ACTIVITY END ACK SPDU
		CAPABILITY DATA SPDU
		CAPABILITY DATA ACK SPDU
		EXCEPTION REPORT SPDU
		EXCEPTION DATA SPDU

SS-provider to support the session layer service. Many parameters are used, some of which are explained in Box 16-4. The data (if present) are placed in the user information field.

BOX 16-4.   Major Parameters of the SPDU

References and SSAPs:	Identifies SS-users and SSAPs
Protocol Options:	Indicates if concatenated SPDUs are to be used
TSDU Maximum Size:	Used to negotiate the maximum TSDU size
Initial Serial Number:	Value of serial number for use in sync point processing
Token Setting:	Indicates initial position of tokens (release, activity, sync minor, etc.)
Session User Requirements:	Identifies the functional units to be used with session
Reason Code:	Identifies reason for a disconnect, abort, etc.
Transport Disconnect:	Indicates if transport connection is to be kept
Enclosure Item:	Identifies if data unit is the beginning, middle, or end of a segmented SSDU
Token Item:	Indicates which tokens are being given by the sending-SS-user
Sync Type:	Indicates if confirmation is required for a sync point SPDU
Prepare Type:	Used to alert recipients to prepare for a sync or a resync

---

It may have occurred to the reader that the invocation of all the session layer services would likely be unnecessary for all applications. For example, our file transfers between Washington, D.C., and the districts certainly did not need all these services. In recognition of this fact, both the CCITT and the ISO divide the services described in Box 16-2 and Table 16-1 into subsets. The subsets are:

- *Kernal.* A minimum implementation of services, which must be provided. It does not invoke many of the session layer functions.
- *Basic Combined Subset (BCS).* Adds half duplex and duplex functional units.
- *Basic Synchronized Subset (BSS).* Adds the functional units needed for synchronization activities. This subset will likely be used in any applications.
- *Basic Activity Subset (BAS).* Uses most of the functional units.

To summarize the CCITT and ISO session layer protocols, Tables 16-4 and 16-5 show the relationships of the functional units and services to the four subsets.

TABLE 16-4.   Session Layer Subsets and Functional Units

Functional Unit	Basic Combined Subset (BCS)	Basic Synchronized Subset (BSS)	Basic Activity Subset (BAS)
Kernal	X	X	X
Half Duplex	X	X	X
Duplex	X	X	
Typed Data		X	X
Exceptions			X
Negotiated Release		X	
Minor Synchronize		X	X
Major Synchronize		X	
Resynchronize		X	
Expedited Data			
Activity Management			X
Capability Data Exchange			X

TABLE 16-5.   Session Layer Subsets and Services

Service	Kernal	Basic Combined Subset (BCS)	Basic Synchronized Subset (BSS)	Basic Activity Subset (BAS)
Session Connection	X	X	X	X
Normal Data Transfer	X	X	X	X[1]
Orderly Release	X	X	X	X
U-Abort	X	X	X	X
P-Abort	X	X	X	X
Give Tokens		X	X	X
Please Tokens		X	X	X
Expedited Data Transfer				
Typed Data Transfer			X	X
Capability Data Exchange				X
Minor Synchronization Point			X	X
Major Synchronization Point			X	
Resynchronize			X	
Provider Exception Reporting				X
User Exception Reporting				X
Activity Start				X
Activity Resume				X
Activity Interrupt				X
Activity Discard				X
Activity End				X
Give Control				X

[1]Half duplex

SNA'S SESSION LAYER—DATA FLOW CONTROL

IBM correlates its SNA Data Flow Control layer to the OSI session layer. As we shall see, the layers do indeed perform some functions that are similar to each other, but they also differ in many ways.

The Data Flow Control layer coordinates the activities between the Function Management and Transmission Control layer. It passes back-and-forth request/response units (RUs) in order to support the following functions:

Sequencing the RUs

Processing brackets

Processing chains

Controlling send/receive mode

Processing error recovery

Interrupting data flows

As a general practice, Data Flow Control does not create the RU. However, on specific occasions it will create an RU to pass to Transmission Control for certain control functions.

SNA Chaining

Data Flow Control is responsible for the management of chains. A chain is comprised of a series of request units used for synchronization and error recovery. If any unit in the chain cannot be processed, the complete chain is discarded (quite similar to the M bit in the X.25 protocol). Data Flow Control passes chains to Transmission Control and indicates the position of the RU in the chain. Transmission Control uses this information to set the values in the request header (begin chain indicator and end chain indicator, see Figure 16-10). The chain indicators identify a unit as the first, middle, or last (or only) RU in the chain. (Only normal flow request units can be chained.) Other units, such as expedited flow request and responses are sent as one unit.

Data Flow Control manages three types of chains based on the type of response expected to the RUs in the chain.

No-response chains

Exception-response chains

Definite-response chains

The no-response option means the recipient does not send a response to any RU in the chain. Exception-response chains require a response be sent only if an error is detected in any unit within the chain. The definite-response option requires a response be returned after the last RU in the

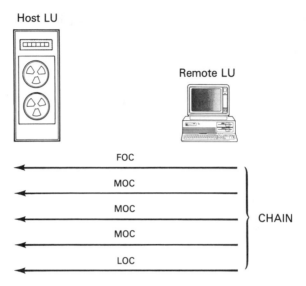

FOC: First on Chain
MOC: Middle on Chain
LOC: Last on Chain

FIGURE 16-10. SNA Chains

chain is processed. This procedure is accomplished by setting the response indicator (Figure 16-11) for the last RU in the chain to a definite response indication.

SNA Brackets

A group of chains can be grouped into brackets. (The chains must be normal flow chains.) A bracket is often used to group logically related request units together. For example, a data base update transaction, a CRT screen, a logical record from a file might require the use of multiple request units and chains.

Data Flow identifies brackets to Transmission Control by passing parameters to it. Transmission Control then sets the appropriate values in the begin bracket indicator and the end bracket indicator (bits 0 and 2 in the third octet of the request header format).

Request/Response Modes

Data Flow Control also manages the four SNA request/response modes. The modes are used to determine if only one RU or more than one RU can be sent before receiving a corresponding RU. The modes can differ in the two directions of the dialogue. The four modes are:

Immediate-request mode
Delayed-request mode

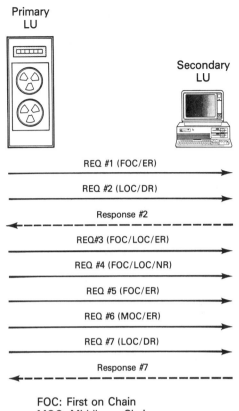

Primary
LU

Secondary
LU

REQ #1 (FOC/ER)

REQ #2 (LOC/DR)

Response #2

REQ#3 (FOC/LOC/ER)

REQ #4 (FOC/LOC/NR)

REQ #5 (FOC/ER)

REQ #6 (MOC/ER)

REQ #7 (LOC/DR)

Response #7

FOC: First on Chain
MOC: Middle on Chain
LOC: Last on Chain
DR: Definite Response Specified
ER: Exception Response Specified
NR: No Response Specified

FIGURE 16-11. SNA Chains and Response Options

Immediate-response mode
Delayed-response mode

The immediate-request mode allows a logical unit (LU) to send only one request chain at a time. A response must be received before another request can be issued. The originator is allowed to send successive chains if only the last chain stipulates a definite response. The delayed-request mode allows multiple request chains to be sent before receiving a response. The request can stipulate any form of response. The immediate-response mode specifies that responses are to be returned in the same order that the logical unit received the requests. The delayed-response mode allows the responses to be returned in any order.

Matching Requests and Responses

Data Flow Control is responsible for matching each response with the request(s) that is (are) related to it. It uses two tables and sequence numbers in the transmission header to accomplish the task. The two tables correlate normal data flow units and expedited data flow units. Each entry in the table relates to a chain, if chaining is used. Each table consists of two sets: one for outgoing responses and the other for the incoming responses. A sequence number is assigned by Data Flow Control when it receives a request unit. It passes the number (as a parameter) to Path Control which places it in the transmission header. At the receiver, an associated response is sent that contains the same sequence number as the request to which it is responding.

Figure 16-12 illustrates the use of the tables. When a request unit for a chain is sent, its sequence number is added to the receive responses table. For example, in Figure 16-12(a), sequence number 66 is added to the table. Also, when the first request unit of a chain is received, its sequence number is added to the send responses table. In Figure 16-12(a), the incoming sequence number of 92 is added to the table.

These entries to the tables are deleted only after the full chain has been sent or received. In Figure 16-12(b), the incoming response to a request 66 causes the entry to be deleted from the receive responses table and the sending of a response related to the request unit of 92 causes this number to be deleted from the send responses table.

It is possible that the entries in the tables could be quite limited. For example, a definite response chain with immediate mode requires that the response be received before another request is sent. If all traffic were of this type and mode, the tables would contain one entry. Obviously, the size of the tables depends upon the nature of the RUs being exchanged in the system.

Send/Receive Modes

Data Flow Control also establishes how the logical units exchange data with each other through a concept called the send/receive mode. These modes may be invoked for normal transmission and are completely independent of the modes of the same name that are used at the data link level with SDLC.

Half-duplex flip-flop
Half-duplex contention
Full duplex

Half-duplex flip-flop mode allows the logical unit half-sessions to alternate in the sending and receiving of data (a half-session is a set of sessions provided within a logical unit for LU-to-LU communications). The alternating process is controlled by the sending half-session inserting a flag in the charge direction indicator, in the request header of the last request unit.

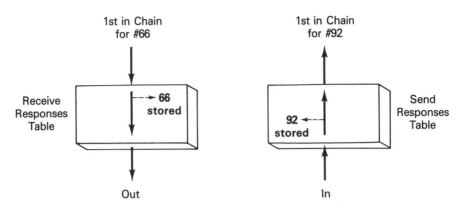

(a) Adding

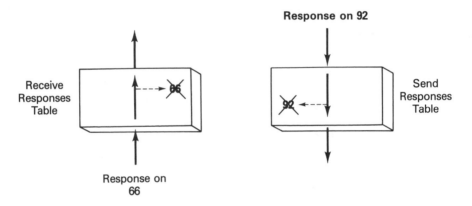

(b) Deleting

FIGURE 16-12. SNA Send Responses and Receive Responses Tables

This action indicates to the receiving half-session that it may begin transmission of its data units. The reader may recognize this function in the CCITT/ISO protocols with the use of the Give token.

If the half-duplex contention mode is used, either half-session can send request units. In the event of contention, the predesignated contention winner sends a negative response to the predesignated contention loser, which must then wait until the end of the request chain before attempting to retransmit its chain.

If the full-duplex mode is used, the half-sessions can send and receive requests at the same time. The overlapping two directions of data flow take place independently and Data Flow Control does not match the two directions.

DECnet SESSION CONTROL LAYER

DECnet's Session Control layer provides process-to-process communications functions that bridge the End Communication layer to the processes running in an operating system. The Session Control protocol provides four major functions:

- *Name and address mapping*: DECnet maintains a mapping table that defines the correspondence between a node name and a node address. An outgoing data unit is analyzed by Session Control and a destination node address or channel number is selected. The incoming data units are checked to determine the originating node.
- *User identification*: Incoming data units are checked to ensure the end-user process corresponds to the remote end-user process identified in the incoming data unit. It also passes the data unit to the proper user process.
- *Activating user process*: Session Control may also activate a user process (or create a new process) to accommodate an incoming connect request.
- *Validation and editing*: Session Control also performs various validation and editing functions for DECnet.

Connect Data Message Format

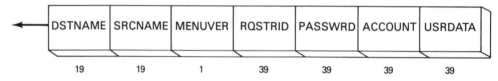

Reject/Disconnect Data Message Format

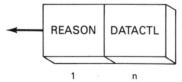

DSTNAME: The destination end user name
SRCNAME: The source end user name
MENUVER: The field format and version format
RQSTRID: The source user identification for access verification
PASSWRD: The access verification password
ACCOUNT: The link or service account data
USRDATA: The end user process connect data
REASON: A reason code
DATACTL: User data (length of field determined by the total length of reject or disconnect data received from the End Communication layer)

FIGURE 16-13. DECnet Session Control Layer Messages [DECN82]

Session Control is dependent upon the specific operations in the DEC workstation or computer. It isolates the levels from these operating systems. The protocol uses the protocol data units shown in Figure 16-13 to execute the session layer operations.

DECnet Session Layer Operations

When an end-user process requests a connection, the operating system passes the request to Session Control and maps the user name to a destination node address or channel number. It formats the data unit and sends a connection request to the End Connection layer. It may also start an outgoing connection timer to ensure the connection is acted upon within a specific time. Upon receiving an acceptance from the End Connection layer, it then passes data back and forth between the user process and the End Connection layer. Its operations on data are minimal.

The Session Control layer performs several functions when it receives an incoming connect request from the End Connection layer. It examines the incoming data unit to determine source and destination end user. It also validates some of the control information in the request. It then maps the source node's address to a node or channel name and identifies, creates, or activates the end-user process. It delivers the connect request to the end user. It may also start a timer to ensure the user process acts upon the requests within a specific time.

Session Control does not manage disconnect or abort requests. It passes these requests directly from/to the end-user process and to/from the End Communication layer.

The function code parameters can be used to invoke X.25 or non-X.25 functions. For example, the X.25 Q-bit, M-bit, and D-bit functions can be specified here.

SUGGESTED READINGS

The literature on the session layer is rather sparse, since in the past, each vendor has developed proprietary session level protocols. The ISO and CCITT specifications cited in this chapter are good references to introduce the reader to the subject: CCITT's X.215 and X.225 and ISO's 8326 and 8327.

APPENDIX 16A
AN EXAMINATION OF THE SYNCHRONIZATION PROCEDURES

Certain primitives contain the sync point serial number discussed in the main body of Chapter 16. It is used to identify a synchronization point. The numbers are assigned by the SS-provider and range from 0–999998.

The services are provided by the SS-provider through the use of four sync variables: V(M), V(A), V(R), and Vsc. V(M) is the value of the next sync point serial number to be used. V(A) is the value of the lowest serial number to which a sync point confirm is expected. If V(A) = V(M), no confirmation is expected. V(R) is the value of the serial number to which the resync and restart is permitted. The Vsc variable determines if the SS-user has the right to issue minor sync point responses.

If Vsc = true, the SS-provider can issue minor sync point response and V(A) = V(M). If Vsc = false, the SS-user cannot issue sync point responses.

Now, lucky reader, it is time to read another OSI specification. We have stressed the importance of learning how to comprehend the standards organizations' documents, so our next task will give you an opportunity to test your progress.

The following paragraphs are excerpted from CCITT X.215. They describe the rules for a minor synchronization point. These rules are drawn as a flow chart in Figure 16A-1. Please study them and compare them to the figure. Figure 16A-2 is also provided to show the rules for major synchronization points. After studying the text and graphics for the minor sync points, it is suggested that you examine Figure 16A-2 to test your understanding of major sync points.

When an S-SYNC-MINOR request is issued, the associated synchronization point serial number, which is indicated to the SS-user, is equal to V(M). V(R) remains unchanged. V(A) is set to V(M) if Vsc is true, otherwise V(A) remains unchanged. V(M) is then incremented by one and Vsc is set to false.

When an S-SYNC-MINOR indication is received, the associated synchronization point serial number, which is indicated to the SS-user, is equal to V(M). V(R) remains unchanged. V(A) is set to V(M) if Vsc is false, otherwise it remains unchanged. V(M) is then incremented by one and Vsc is set to true.

When an S-SYNC-MINOR response is issued, Vsc is true and the associated synchronization point serial number, which is supplied by the SS-user, must be less than V(M) and equal to or greater than V(A). V(A) is set to the serial number plus one. V(M), V(R), and Vsc remain unchanged.

When an S-SYNC-MINOR confirm is received, Vsc is false and the associated synchronization point serial number, which is indicated to the SS-user, is less than V(M) and equal to or greater than V(A). V(A) is set to the serial number plus one. V(M), V(R), and Vsc remain unchanged.

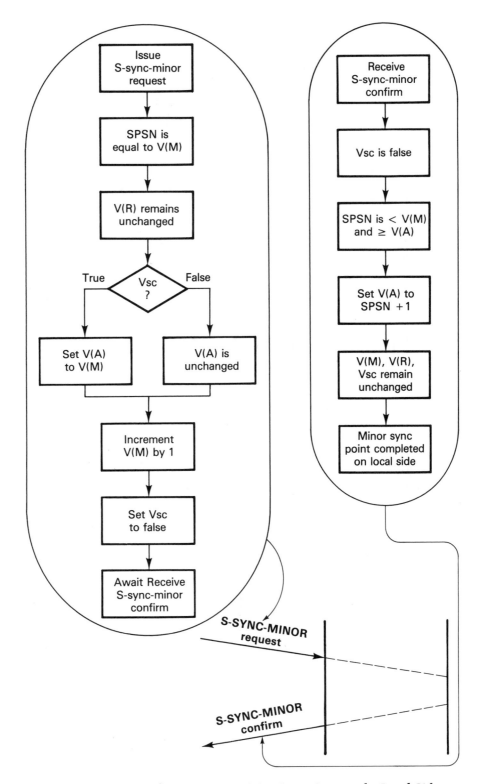

FIGURE 16A-1a. The Minor Sync Point Operations on the Local Side

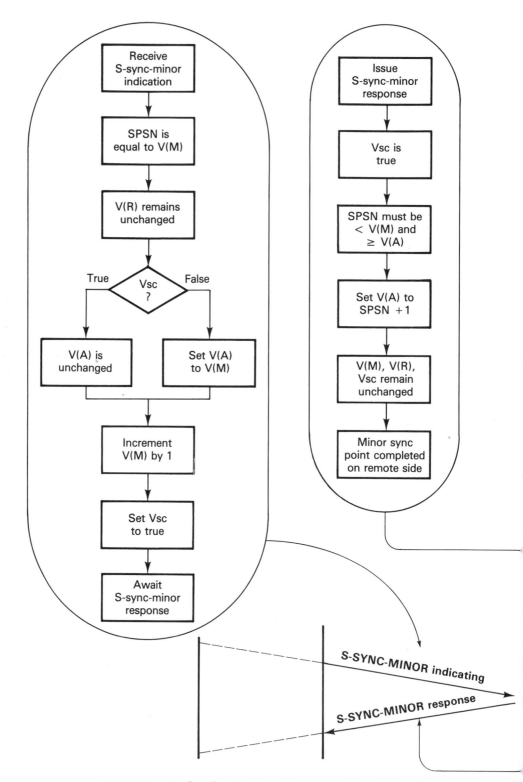

FIGURE 16A-1b. The Minor Sync Point Operations on the Remote Side

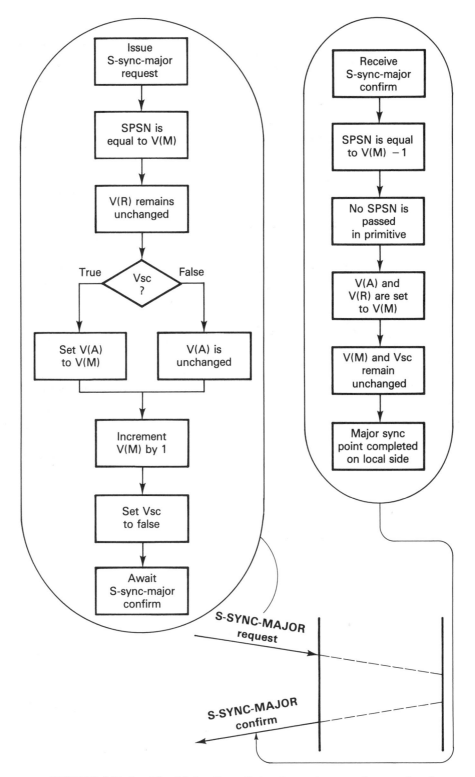

FIGURE 16A-2a. The Major Sync Point Operations on the Local Side

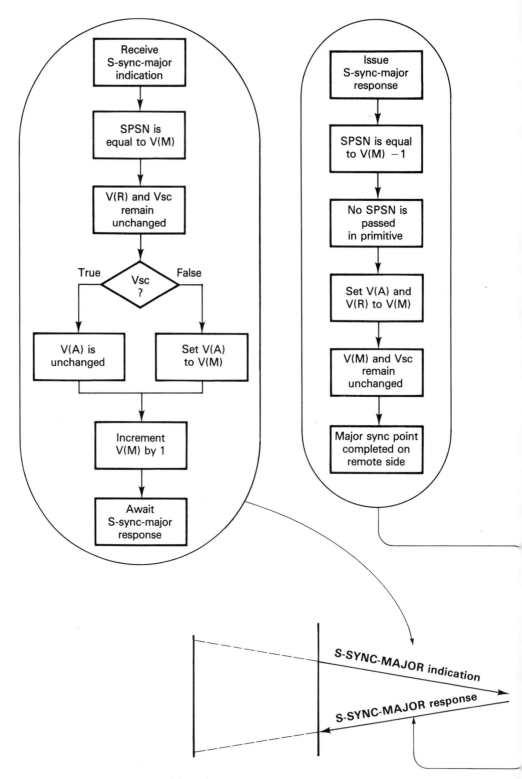

FIGURE 16A-2b. The Major Sync Point Operations on the Remote Side

TRUE/FALSE

1. Sync points are used to coordinate the exchange of data between session-service users.

2. A resynchronization does not purge undelivered data.

3. Synchronization and resynchronization services rely on sync variables for sync-point management.

4. SNA chains and brackets perform the same functions.

5. The DECnet session layer operates on the user data.

6. Match the session layer function to the appropriate term (use Figure 16-1):

    Function

    a) Structures exchange of data within a dialogue unit.
    b) Delineated by a major sync point.
    c) Structures data exchanges into dialogue units.
    d) Consists of dialogue units.

    Term

    1. Dialogue unit
    2. Major sync points
    3. Activity
    4. Minor sync point

7. Match the SNA Request/Response mode with the appropriate function:

    Function

    a) Responses sent in same order as the associated requests.
    b) Only one data unit can be outstanding at a time.
    c) Responses returned in any order.
    d) Multiple request chains maybe sent before receiving a response.

    Mode

    1. Immediate-request mode
    2. Immediate-response mode
    3. Delayed-request mode
    4. Delayed-response mode

8. Briefly describe the four major functions of DECnet's Session Control layer.

9. The following paragraphs are extracted from CCITT X.215:

    When an S-SYNC-MAJOR request is issued, the associated synchronization point serial number, which is indicated to the SS-user, is equal to $V(M)$. $V(R)$ remains unchanged. $V(A)$ is set to $V(M)$ if Vsc is true, otherwise it remains unchanged. $V(M)$ is then incremented by one and Vsc is set to false.

When an S-SYNC-MAJOR indication is received, the associated synchronization point serial number, which is indicated to the SS-user, is equal to $V(M)$. $V(R)$ and Vsc remain unchanged. $V(A)$ is set to $V(M)$ if Vsc is false, otherwise it remains unchanged. $V(M)$ is then incremented by one.

When an S-SYNC-MAJOR response is issued, the associated synchronization point serial number is equal to $V(M)$ minus one. No synchronization point serial number is passed with this primitive. $V(A)$ and $V(R)$ are set to $V(M)$. $V(M)$ and Vsc remain unchanged.

When an S-SYNC-MAJOR confirm is received, the associated synchronization point serial number is equal to $V(M)$ minus one. No synchronization point serial number is passed with this primitive. $V(A)$ and $V(R)$ are set to $V(M)$. $V(M)$ and Vsc remain unchanged.

To test your ability to comprehend a specification, draw a logic flow chart based on these X.215 sync point requirements. Check your response with Figure 16A-2 in Appendix 16A.

SELECTED ANSWERS

1. True.
2. False.
3. True.
4. False. Chains can be grouped into brackets.
5. False.
6.

Function	Term
a	4
b	1
c	2
d	3

9. See Figure 16A-2 for the answer.

CHAPTER 17

The Presentation Layer

INTRODUCTION

After using all the elaborate efforts and protocols provided by the lower levels, users may still be unable to communicate. Several reasons can be cited for this problem, and one is due to the different codes, syntax, and formats that exist in the end-user applications. To gain an appreciation of the problem, consider the following communications process between two end users.

User A transmits a protocol data unit (PDU) to user B using ASCII/IA5 code for alphabetic symbols and double precision floating point notation for the numeric symbols. We assume user B expects EBCDIC code for the alphabetic symbols and single precision floating point for the numeric symbols. Obviously, the process must use conversion routines to translate between the different symbol representations.

The conversion process is simplified considerably if both users agree to a common convention for both applications, for example all ASCII and all double precision. However, this agreement does not assure that the same protocol data units (PDU) can be used by both users, because they may be coded in different formats. For example, the PDU from user A could have field x placed before field y. If user B expects field y to precede field x, the wrong fields will be used by the user applications in their computations. This situation has happened so many times in the industry, that it is incalculable. In some instances, the result has had fantastic consequences, such as errors in million-dollar transactions.

In addition, the computer and communications vendors have implemented different methods for the placement of bits within a character (byte/octet). Some systems are coded with the low-order bit on the right side within the character code. Others place the low order bit on the left side.

One may think that the solution to the low-order/high-order problem is rather straightforward: just change the positions with a conversion program. It is not so simple. For example, the conversion of binary fields must be done differently than Boolean fields, which must be done differently than scientific notation fields. Moreover, the conversion program must know which type of field it is processing to perform the conversion correctly.

Therefore, describing the order of the data fields, the bits within the data fields, as well as the structure and syntax of the protocol data units is quite important. In software terms, the users adapt the same "data description" notations to represent the structure of the data.

In some computer systems, hundreds of different data structures are used daily. For example, a commercial bank needs different data structures to support check processing, loan payments, debit card transactions, etc., and each of these applications typically needs scores of different data structures. Indeed, one of the most important jobs of the data administrator in an organization is the management of the company's data structures, and the job may require several full-time positions.

Presentation Layer Functions

The presentation layer performs the services of data structure description and representation. It is not concerned with the meaning or semantics of the data. Rather, it accepts various data types and negotiates/converts the representation. It is concerned with (a) the syntax of the data of the sending application, (b) the syntax of the data of the receiving application, and (c) the data syntax used between the presentation entities that support the sending and receiving applications.

The latter service is called a *transfer syntax*. It is negotiated between the presentation entities. Each entity chooses a syntax that is best for it to use between it and the user's syntax, and then attempts to negotiate the use of this syntax with the other presentation layer entity.

We are really not discussing anything revolutionary about these services. Many organizations have been using common transfer syntax and formatting conventions for years. However, each organization has had its own unique method to describe syntax and offer translations between different types of structures.

These data structures are usually created and stored in a corporate "Data Dictionary" and used as if they were a community-wide resource. Indeed they are, because their creation is quite time consuming and programmers often forget where the numerous data structures are located or even if they exist. Usually the important job of creating data structures and acting as their "custodian" has been given to the organization's data administration entity (until recently, surely one of the most thankless tasks that ever befell a computer professional).

The OSI approach is to develop a standardized and limited set of syntax conventions to ease the task of describing data structures and data transfer operations between different machines and used applications. In this chapter, the prevalent ISO and CCITT presentation level protocols are examined. We also review graphics and videotex presentation protocols.

ASN.1 (ABSTRACT SYNTAX NOTATION ONE)

The ISO and CCITT have developed a presentation and transfer syntax to be used by application layer protocols. One widely used specification is ISO 8824. It is titled Abstract Syntax Notation One (ASN.1). In addition, ISO 8825 (the Basic Encoding Rules [BER]) provides a set of rules to develop an unambiguous bit-level description of data. That is to say, it specifies the representation of the data. In summary, ASN.1 describes an abstract syntax for data types and values and BER describes the actual representation of the data. ASN.1 and BER are collectively called ASN.1 by some people.

The CCITT specifies X.208 and X.209 for the presentation level. X.208 specifies the ASN.1 rules and X.209 specifies the basic encoding rules for ASN.1. In the 1988 Blue Books, the X.208 specification is aligned with ISO 8824, plus ISO 8824, Addendum 1 (except 8824 does not define some conventions on describing encrypted structures). X.209 is aligned with ISO 8825 plus ISO 8825, Addendum 1. This chapter uses X.208 and X.209 to describe the ISO presentation layer.

If the reader chooses to study this chapter, it is essential that the coding examples be studied carefully. They are actual illustrations of the use of abstract syntax notation. Once you have analyzed a couple of the examples (assuming you understand them), the subject matter becomes fairly simple.

PRESENTATION TRANSFER SYNTAX AND NOTATION

OSI Description Conventions

Each piece of information exchanged between users has a *type* and a *value*. The type is a class of information, such as numeric, Boolean, alphabetic, etc. (The term *datatype* is a synonym for type.) The value is an instance of the type, such as a number or a piece of alphabetic text. For example, if we describe "P of type integer" and "P: = 9," it means this instance of P has a value of 9. In an X.25 packet header example, the fields can be defined as of the integer or bit string type. In order for machines to know how to interpret data, they must first know the type of data (values) to be processed. Therefore, the concept of type is very important to the presentation layer services.

Another important feature of these standards is the use of *tags*. To distinguish the different types, a structure of values (for example, a data base record) or a simple element (for example, a field within the data base record) can have a tag attached that identifies the class. For example, a tag for a funds transfer record could be PRIVATE 22. This is used to identify the record, and inform the receiver about the nature of its contents. Tags could even identify libraries of job control language (JCL) to be used to invoke the execution of a predefined sequence of application programs. As we shall see, tags can be put to very clever uses.

X.208 uses Backus-Naur Form (BNF) to define the notation for a type of information. BNR is similar to the data definition statements found in languages such as Pascal, Ada, and C. The user applications use BNR to describe the syntax of the data. From the context of OSI, it is used to describe the syntax of one or more protocol data units (PDUs).

The best way to explain these ideas is through an example. We will first explain some basic conventions and then show how an X.25 Call Request packet header can be described with these standards. Two conventions must be explained immediately to get us started: (1) the pair of angle brackets ‹ › is a notation as a placeholder for an actual item; (2) the :: = means "defined as."

The following notation describes the rules for representing a *module* (which is one of several ASN.1 forms we will examine in this chapter).

‹ module name › DEFINITIONS :: = BEGIN
    ‹ module body ›
END

The module name identifies the module. The "DEFINITIONS" indicate the module is defined as the ASN.1 definitions that are placed between the "BEGIN" and "END." In other words, a module contains other ASN.1 definitions.

Within the modules are definitions of types. They have the following form:

‹ type name › :: = ‹ type definition ›

This notation is an example of a *simple type*. It is so named because it directly specifies the set of its values. The type name is the identifier of the type. The type definition describes the class and several other attributes, explained shortly.

The next example shows how four type definitions are coded within a module:

‹ module name › DEFINITIONS :: = BEGIN
    ‹ type name › :: = ‹ type definition ›
    ‹ type name › :: = ‹ type definition ›
    ‹ type name › :: = ‹ type definition ›
    ‹ type name › :: = ‹ type definition ›
END

This example is called a *structured type*. It contains a reference to one or more other types. The types within the structured type are called *component types*.

To complete the initial example, the placeholders are replaced with names and actual type definitions to describe the entries of an X.25 Call Request packet header (see Figure 13-22 in Chapter 13):

```
X25header DEFINITIONS ::= BEGIN
     Channelgroup ::= INTEGER
     Gfi ::= BIT STRING
     Channelnumber ::= INTEGER
     Packettype ::= INTEGER
END
```

As you can see, the fields in the header are named and typed as integer or bit string. This definition is quite straightforward, but it needs some more refinement. As indicated in Figure 13-22, the general format identifier (GFI) field consists of "subfields." Bits 5 and 6 are used to indicate modulo 8 or 128 numbering; bit 7 is used for the D (delivery confirmation) bit operation; and bit 8 is the L (extended length of the address) bit.

For most applications, it is necessary to further define the GFI field. ASN.1 provides several methods for this description. One option entails changing the module definition as follows:

```
X25header DEFINITIONS ::= BEGIN
     Channelgroup ::= INTEGER
     Gfi ::= SEQUENCE{
          Modulo ::= BIT STRING {first (0), last(1)}
          Dbit ::= INTEGER
          LBIT ::= INTEGER}
     Channelnumber ::= INTEGER
     Packettype ::= INTEGER
END
```

The GFI field is now defined as an ordered sequence of a series of the same or different data types. The sequence is bounded by the symbols { and }. The notation for the "modulo" explains that the bit string is of fixed length, consisting of two bits: the first bit is position 0 and the second bit is in position 1.

Several other options are available to decrease the amount of coding in our example. However, the example has been kept as simple as possible in order to give the reader the courage to read further, and learn about some of the more detailed and complex aspects of the presentation layer protocols.

BNR Rules and Conventions

BNR describes information with a series of replacement rules called *productions*. A production is a notation in which allowed sequences are associated with a name. The replacement rules allow any instance of information to be represented. Three classes of symbols appear in a production:

- *Terminal*: A symbol that actually appears in the information.
- *Non-terminal*: A symbol that can represent a series of symbols or several series of symbols.
- *Operator*: A symbol to assign a value to a non-terminal or to distinguish between alternative symbols' values for a non-terminal.

Presently, two operators are used in productions. The equivalence operator was introduced in the previous section. It is coded as ":: =". It assigns a value to a non-terminal. The alternative operator is "|". It distinguishes between several alternative symbols. For example, the BNF coding of Boolean symbols is:

Boolean Type :: = BOOLEAN
Boolean Value :: = TRUE|FALSE

The other conventions used are described in Box 17-1, and should be studied before proceeding further.

BOX 17-1. X.208 Conventions

String: A sequence of zero or more characters.

Identifier: A sequence of one or more characters, capital letters, small letters, decimal digits, and hyphens.

Number: A non-negative integer expressed as a decimal value or a hexadecimal value. In the latter case, the number is followed by an H. (For clarification, binary values may be subscripted with $_2$ and hex numbers with $_{16}$.) Both notations are used in this chapter.

Empty: A null or empty string of symbols.

Reserved words: Not used by user; noted with upper case letters.

Comments are embedded in notation, preceded and terminated by two hyphens.

Transfer Syntax for the Data Element

X.209 describes the actual encoding rules for the values of types, in contrast to X.208, which is concerned with the abstract structure of the information.

The transfer syntax convention is very useful in describing the structure of the data that is transferred between applications and machines.

Up to this point in the discussion, we have been examining the abstract syntax only. Hereafter, our examples will show both the abstract and transfer syntax.

Each transfer type is described by a standard representation. This representation is called a data element (or just element). It consists of three components, which appear in the following order:

Identifier Length Contents

The identifier distinguishes one type from another and specifies how the contents are interpreted. The length specifies the length of the contents. The contents (also called value) contains the actual information of the element. The element is also identified by the term TLV (Type-length-value). These components are explained shortly.

The transfer data element is illustrated in Figure 17-1. It can consist of a single TLV or a series of data elements, described as multiple TLVs. The

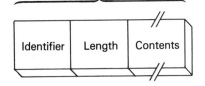

Data Element

| Identifier | Length | Contents |

(a) Single Element

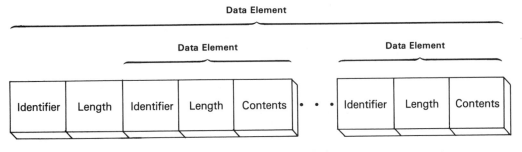

Data Element

Data Element

Data Element

| Identifier | Length | Identifier | Length | Contents | • • • | Identifier | Length | Contents |

(b) Multiple Elements

Note (1) The Identifier field is also called the type.
Note (2) The Contents field is also called the value.

FIGURE 17-1. X.209 Data Elements

element consists of an integral number n of octets, written with the most significant bit (MSB) (8) on the left and the least significant bit (LSB) (1) on the right:

XXXXXXXX
8 7 6 5 4 3 2 1

The identifier distinguishes four classes of type (information): universal, application-wide, context-specific, and private-use. We have more to say about these type classes later, but for now they are defined as:

- *Universal*: Application-independent types.
- *Application-wide*: Types that are specific to an application.
- *Context-specific*: Types that are specific to an application but are limited to a set within an application.
- *Private-use*: Reserved for private use, and not defined in X.209.

The identifier is coded as depicted in Figure 17-2(a). Bits 8–7 identify the four type classes by the following bit assignments:

Universal: 00
Application-wide: 01
Context-specific: 10
Private-use: 11

Bit 6 identifies the forms of the data element. Two forms are possible. A primitive element (bit 6 = 0) has no further internal structure of data elements. A constructor element (bit 6 = 1) is recursively defined in that it contains a series of data elements. The remaining five bits (5–1) distinguish one data type from another of the same class. For example, the field may distinguish Boolean from integer. If the system requires more than five bits, bits 5–1 of the first octet are coded as 11111_2 and bit 8 of the subsequent octets are coded with a 1 to indicate more octets follow and a 0 to indicate the last octet. Figure 17-2 (b) illustrates the use of single- and multi-octet identifiers.

The length (L) specifies the length of the contents. It may take one of three forms: short, long, and indefinite. The short form is one octet long and is used when L is less than 128. Bit 8 is always 0 and bits 7–1 indicate the length of the contents. For example, a contents field of 38 octets is described by the L field as: 00100110_2.

The long form is used for a longer contents field: greater than or equal to 128 and less than 2^{1008} octets. The indefinite form can be used when the element is a constructor. It has the value of 1000000_2 or 80_{16}. For the indefinite form, a special end-of-contents (EOC) element terminates the contents. The representation of EOC is 00000000_{16}.

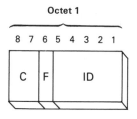

Octet 1

8 7 6 5 4 3 2 1

C | F | ID

(a) Single-octet identifier

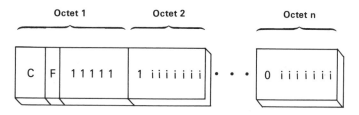

Octet 1   **Octet 2**   **Octet n**

C | F | 1 1 1 1 1 | 1 i i i i i i i • • • 0 i i i i i i i

(b) Multi-octet identifier

C: Class of the data type
F: Form of the element

FIGURE 17-2. X.209 Identifier

The contents (value) is the substance of the element, i.e., the actual information. It is described in multiples of eight bits and is variable length. The contents is interpreted based on the coding of the identifier (type) field. Therefore, the contents is interpreted as bit strings, octet strings, etc.

More About Classes

The 1988 Blue Book release of X.208 specifies several tags for the universal assignment. Remember, the tag is used to identify a class. The tag has two parts, a class identifier and a number. Table 17-1 depicts the universal class tag assignments as stipulated by X.208.

Built-in Types

X.208 defines several *built-in* types and two of these types (integer and bit string) were used in our initial example. A built-in type is one in which standard notation is provided for commonly used types. These built-in types are summarized in Box 17-2 and several are described in this section. The reader should obtain X.208 for more detail on each built-in type.

TABLE 17-1. X.208 Universal Class Tag Assignments

UNIVERSAL 1	Boolean type
UNIVERSAL 2	Integer type
UNIVERSAL 3	Bit string type
UNIVERSAL 4	Octet string type
UNIVERSAL 5	Null type
UNIVERSAL 6	Object Identifier type
UNIVERSAL 7	Object descriptor type
UNIVERSAL 8	External type
UNIVERSAL 9	Real type
UNIVERSAL 10	Enumerated type
UNIVERSAL 11	Encrypted type
UNIVERSAL 12–15	Reserved for future use
UNIVERSAL 16	Sequence and sequence-of-types
UNIVERSAL 17	Set and set-of-types
UNIVERSAL 18–22, 25–27	Character string types
UNIVERSAL 23–24	Time types
UNIVERSAL 28-...	Reserved for future use

The *Boolean built-in type* represents a logical quality of either true (1) or false (0). The notations are:

BooleanType :: = BOOLEAN
BooleanValue :: = TRUE/FALSE

The identifier is coded as a 1 to note a Boolean type. *False* is coded as all 0s. *True* is coded with any bit combination. An example of the Boolean built-in type to describe a false condition for "employed" is:

Identifier	*Length*	*Contents*
00000001_2	00000001_2	00000000_2

The *Integer type* represents an integer value (positive, zero, or negative), which can be followed by values and reference names assigned to them. The reference names begin with small letters. The contents is the value of the integer coded as a 2s complement binary number. The notations are:

IntegerType   :: = INTEGER|INTEGER{NamedNumberList}
IntegerValue   :: = number|-number|identifier
NamedNumberList :: = NamedNumber|Named NumberList,
                              NamedNumber
NamedNumber   :: = identifier (number)

BOX 17-2. Built-in Types

Type	Function
Boolean	Identifies logical data (true or false)
Integer	Identifies signed whole numbers
Bit String	Identifies binary data (ordered sequence 1s and 0s)
Octet String	Identifies text or data that can be described as a sequence of octets
Null	A simple type consisting of a single value. Could be a valueless place holder in which there are several alternatives but none of them apply.
Sequence	A structured type, defined by referencing an ordered list of various types.
Sequence of	A structured type, defined by referencing a single type. Each value in the type is an ordered list (if a list exists). Stated another way, a method of building arrays.
Set	A structured type; similar to Sequence type except Set is defined by referencing an ordered list of types. Allows data to be sent in any order.
Set of	A structured type; similar to Sequence of type except Set of is defined by referencing a single type. Each value in the type is an unordered list (if a list exists).
Choice	Models a data type chosen from a collection of alternative types. Allows a data structure to hold more than one type.
Selection	Models a variable whose type is that of some alternatives of a previously defined Choice
Tagged	Models a new type from an existing type but with a different identifier
Any	Models data whose type is unrestricted
Object Identifier	A distinguishable value associated with an object or a group of objects, like a library of rules, syntax, etc.
Character String	Models strings of characters for some defined character set
Enumerated	A simple type; its values are given distinct identifiers as part of the type notation
Real	Models real values (for example: $m \times B^e$, M = the mantissa, B = the base, and ^{e} = the exponent)
Encrypted	A type whose value is a result of encrypting another type

The identifier is coded as a 2 to note an Integer type. An example of the Integer built-in type to describe a value of 1 is:

Identifier	Length	Contents
00000010_2	00000001_2	00000001_2

An example of a list coded with the INTEGER{red(0), green(1), yellow(2)} to designate yellow is:

Identifier	Length	Contents
00000010_2	00000001_2	00000010_2

The *Bit String* type represents an ordered set of zero or more bits. The identifier code is 3 to denote integer. The notation for the bit string is a series of binary or hexadecimal digits enclosed in apostrophes and followed by a "B" for binary and an "H" for hexadecimal. The notations are:

Bit StringType	:: =	BIT STRINGIBIT STRING{NamedNumberList}
Bit StringValue	:: =	'string' BI'string' HI{identifierList}
NamedNumberList	:: =	NamedNumberINamedNumber-List,NamedNumber
NamedNumber	:: =	identifier(number)
IdentifierList	:: =	identifierIIdentifierList, identifier

If the binary form is primitive, the code is preceded by a binary number in the first two octets that encodes the number of unused bits in the contents.

As an illustration of a bit string, the value 'OC634521B' H is designated as:

Identifier	Length	Contents
00000011_2	000001102_2	$040C634521B0_{16}$

The value of 04 in the left-most part of the contents field stipulates that four bits of the field are not used. The 0 in the right-most position represents the binary string of 0000_2 which are coded to give a full octet alignment of six full octets. Notice the value '0C634521B' is only five and one-half octets in length.

The *Octet String* type represents a set of zero or more octets. The identifier is 4 to denote octet. The notation can take the form of binary (B) or hexadecimal (H). If any bits are unspecified in the last octet, they are assumed to be 0. The notations are:

Octet String Type :: = OCTET STRING
Octet String Value :: = 'string' BI'string' HI"string"

Let us use the Octet String type to examine both a primitive and a constructor (with the indefinite form). For example, an Octet String of '63E14C7832' H is coded as a primitive and constructor. Notice that the subscript of $_{16}$ is omitted from the contents field. This is the normal practice.

PRIMITIVE:

Identifier	Length	Contents
04_{16}	05_{16}	63E14C7832

CONSTRUCTOR:

Identifier	Length	Contents
24_{16}	80_{16}	63E14C7832

Octet String	Length	Contents
04_{16}	03_{16}	63E14C

Octet String	Length	Contents
04_{16}	02_{16}	7832

Identifier	Length
00_{16}	00_{16}

We now examine the constructor coding further. First, the identifier for a constructor is a 1 in bit position 6. Thus, the coding for the identifier is 00101000_2 or 24_{16}. Second, the length field for a constructor of indefinite form is 10000000_2 or 80_{16}. Last, the EOC (end of contents) element terminates the contents.

The *Null* represents a valueless place holder. The ID value is 5. The notations are:

```
NullType   :: = NULL
NullValue  :: = NULL
```

The *Sequence* represents an ordered set of zero or more values. Its identifier value is 16. These values are called the elements of the Sequence. The notation for the Sequence has three forms, each with different rules (constraints):

- Elements are variable in number, but of one type
- Elements are fixed in number and possibly of several types
- Elements are of multiple types and are optional

The notations are:

```
SequenceType     :: = SEQUENCE | SEQUENCE OF Type | SE-
                      QUENCE
                         {ElementTypes}
SequenceValue    :: = {ElementValues}
ElementTypes     :: = OptionalTypeList | empty
OptionalTypeList :: = OptionalType | OptionalTypeList,
                         OptionalType
```

OptionalType   :: = NamedType | NamedType **OPTIONAL** |
                             NamedType **DEFAULT** Value | Components
                             OF

NamedType   :: = identifier Type | Type

ElementValues   :: = NamedValueList | empty
NamedValueList :: = NamedValue | NamedValueList, Named
                             Value

NamedValue   :: = identifier Value | Value

The construct COMPONENTS OF can be used to form inclusive equivalencies between elements. For those readers who write software, it is quite similar to a FORTRAN EQUIVALENCE. For example, the sequence of:

I :: = SEQUENCE {A, B, C, D}
J :: = SEQUENCE {E, F, G, COMPONENTS OF I}

is the same as:

J :: = SEQUENCE {E, F, G, A, B, C, D}

An example of the sequence is illustrated with the IA5 string of "TOO STRUCTURED":

Sequence	Length	Contents
30_{16}	11_{16}	

	IA5 String	Length	Contents
	16_{16}	03_{16}	$544F4F_{16}$

	IA5 String	Length	Contents
	16_{16}	$0A_{16}$	$53545255435455524544_{16}$

Again, let us examine this notation more closely. The sequence code is 30_{16} or 00110000_2. This code translates to bit 6 = 1 to identify a constructor and bits 5 through 1 = 10000_2 to identify a 16 for the sequence identifier. The contents field are simply the hex equivalents of the ASCII/IA5 code. The length field of 11_{16} explains the length is 17 octets, which includes 13 octets for the IA5 string and 4 octets for the two sets of identifier and length fields.

The *Set* represents an ordered set of zero or more values. The values of the Set are called its members. The members of a Set may be variable in number but of one type, or a Set may have members that are fixed in number and of distinct types.

The notations for a Set are:

```
SetType          :: = SET|SET OF Type|SET MemberTypes
SetValue         :: = |MemberValues|
MemberTypes      :: = OptionalTypeList | empty
OptionalTypeList :: = OptionalType | OptionalTypeList,
                          OptionalType
OptionalType     :: = NamedType | NamedType OPTIONAL |
                          NamedType DEFAULT Value | ComponentsOF
NamedType        :: = identifier Type | Type
MemberValues     :: = NamedValueList | empty
NamedValueList   :: = NamedValue | NamedValueList, NamedValue
NamedValue       :: = identifier Value | Value
```

The *Tagged* represents a value that already exists and has already been tagged for identification. The type of value being tagged can be either explicit or implicit representation. The notations are as follows:

```
TaggedType  :: = TAG IMPLICIT Type| Tag Type
TaggedValue :: = Value
Tag         :: = [Class number]
Class       :: = UNIVERSAL | APPLICATION | PRIVATE | empty
```

Finally, the *Choice* represents a value whose type is selected (chosen) from a set of alternatives. The notations for Choice are:

```
ChoiceType          :: = CHOICE {AlternativeTypeList}
ChoiceValue         :: = identifierValue | Value
AlternativeTypeList :: = NamedType | AlternativeTypeList,
                             NamedType
NamedType           :: = identifier Type | Type
```

The X.208 Defined Types

X.208 also describes several defined types. A defined type is one specified with the standard notation.

1. The IA5 String type is formally defined as shown below. The characters allowed and their graphical depictions and 7-bit numeric codes are those specified for the International Reference Version of IA5 by Recommendation T.50. Each octet contains a single code. Bit 8 of each octet is 0, and bits 7–1 correspond to b_7–b_1 of the code (using the T.50 bit numbering convention).

2. A Numeric String represents an ordered set of zero or more charac-

ters that collectively encode numeric information in textual form. It models data entered from such devices as telephone handsets.

3. A Printable String represents an ordered set of zero or more characters chosen from a subset of the printable characters. It models data entered from devices with a limited character repertoire (for example, TELEX terminals).

4. A T.61 String represents an ordered set of zero or more characters and repesentation commands chosen from the set defined by Recommendation T.61. It models textual data suitable for processing by Teletex terminals.

5. A Videotex String represents an ordered set of zero or more alphabetic characters, pictorial characters, pictorial drawing commands, display attribute commands, etc., chosen from the set defined by the Data Syntaxes of Recommendation T.101 or the options from Recommendation T.100. It models textual and graphical data suitable for processing by Videotex terminals.

6. A Generalized Time represents a calendar date and time of day to various precisions, as provided for by ISO 2014, ISO 4031. The time of day can be specified as local time only, UTC time only (see Recommendation B.11), or as both local and UTC time.

7. The UTC Time type is a particular form of Generalized Time which is defined for use in international applications where the local time only is not adequate, and where the flexibility to use all of the possible forms of ISO 3307 and ISO 2014 is not required. The UTC Time type permits the time of day to be specified to a precision of one minute or one second. The notations for the X.409 defined types are shown in Box 17-3.

8. A graphic string represents an ordered set of graphic symbols.

9. A general string represent all graphic and character sets.

BOX 17-3.   X.409 Defined Types

(1) IA5String	:: = [UNIVERSAL 22] IMPLICIT OCTET STRING
(2) NumericString	:: = [UNIVERSAL 18] IMPLICIT IA5STRING
(3) PrintableString	:: = [UNIVERSAL 19] IMPLICIT IA5STRING
(4) T.61String	:: = [UNIVERSAL 20] IMPLICIT OCTET STRING
(5) VideotexString	:: = [UNIVERSAL 21] IMPLICIT OCTET STRING
(6) GeneralizedTime	:: = [UNIVERSAL 24] IMPLICIT IA5STRING
(7) UTCTime	:: = [UNIVERSAL 23] IMPLICIT GeneralizedTime
(8) GraphicString	:: = [UNIVERSAL 25] IMPLICIT GRAPHIC STRING
(9) GeneralString	:: = [UNIVERSAL 27] IMPLICIT GENERAL STRING

PRESENTATION PROTOCOLS FOR FACSIMILE TRANSMISSIONS

The use of standardized syntax for any type of communications is important. One of the most rapidly growing segments of the data communications industry is facsimile transmission. Most of these devices use presentation layer protocols in accordance with the CCITT recommendations. Specifically, the CCITT T-Series recommendations define the protocols and coding structure for various kinds of facsimile devices. Since Chapter 6 defines the most important facsimile coding structures in detail, we will not repeat the material here. The reader should read the CCITT T-Series if more detail is needed. T.0 through T.30 documents are relevant to presentation layer facsimile transmission.

INTERNATIONAL ALPHABET #5

The International Alphabet #5 (or ASCII code), is the most commonly used coding structure for data communications systems. It also plays a critical role in presentation layer protocols. This specification and coding structure, as well as IBM's EBCDIC code, is described in detail in Chapter 1. The reader may wish to refer to the Chapter 1 part titled "Codes" for more material on these control characters.

TELETEX GRAPHICS SET

The Teletex graphics set has been proposed as replacement for the TELEX International Alphabet #2 and the TWX 50 or 95 character set. Teletex research began in the mid-1970s when the West German government set up a commission to explore the possibilities of implementing a text communications service with improved capabilities over TELEX. The goal was to establish a terminal that offered text generation with communications capabilities and the full character-set repertoire of a typewriter. Also in the mid-1970s, the Swedish PTT Televerket began work on a system to support office equipment with word processing, communications, and document filing and retrieval capabilities. Studies such as these paved the way toward Teletex. Shortly thereafter, CCITT became involved in projects to improve TELEX and developed a series of detailed documents outlining recommended standards for Teletex systems. In 1980, the CCITT adopted the following recommended standards:

F.200 Teletex service
S.60 terminal equipment for use in the TELEX service
S.61 character repertoire and coded character sets for Teletex

S.62 control procedures for the Teletex service

S.170 network independent basic support service for Teletex

The Deutsche Bundepost of Germany introduced its Teletex system in 1980. Since that time, several countries have implemented Teletex services,

b8	0	0	0	0	0	0	0	0	1	1	1	1	1	1	1	1
b7	0	0	0	0	1	1	1	1	0	0	0	0	1	1	1	1
b6	0	0	1	1	0	0	1	1	0	0	1	1	0	0	1	1
b5	0	1	0	1	0	1	0	1	0	1	0	1	0	1	0	1
b4 b3 b2 b1	0	1	2	3	4	5	6	7	8	9	10	11	12	13	14	15
0 0 0 0 — 0			SP	0	@	P		p				°			Ω	K
0 0 0 1 — 1			!	1	A	Q	a	q			i	±	`		Æ	æ
0 0 1 0 — 2			"	2	B	R	b	r			¢	2	'		Đ	đ
0 0 1 1 — 3			⊚	3	C	S	c	s			£	3	v		ª	∂
0 1 0 0 — 4			⊚	4	D	T	d	t			$	x	~		H	ħ
0 1 0 1 — 5			%	5	E	U	e	u			¥	µ	–			ı
0 1 1 0 — 6			&	6	F	V	f	v			#	¶	˘		IJ	ij
0 1 1 1 — 7			'	7	G	W	g	w			§	·	•		Ŀ	l·
1 0 0 0 — 8			(	8	H	X	h	x			¤	÷	¨		Ł	ł
1 0 0 1 — 9			)	9	I	Y	i	y				⑦			Ø	ø
1 0 1 0 — 10			*	:	J	Z	j	z				°			CE	ce
1 0 1 1 — 11			+	;	K	[	k				≪	≫	‚		º	β
1 1 0 0 — 12			,	<	L		l	ı				¼	ⓞ		Þ	þ
1 1 0 1 — 13			–	=	M	]	m					½	"		Ŧ	ŧ
1 1 1 0 — 14			.	>	N		n					¾	˛		Ŋ	ŋ
1 1 1 1 — 15			/	?	O	®	o					¿	˙		'n	

Note 1: When interworking with Videotex, this code shall have the meaning *delimiter.*

Note 2: In the 1980 version of this Recommendation code 12/9 was allocated to represent the umlaut mark. The use of this facility is discouraged. Its removal is foreseen in the future.

Note 3: Non spacing underline is not a diacritical mark and may be combined with any graphic character of the Teletex repertoire.

Note 4: Teletex terminals should send only the codes 10/6 and 10/8 for graphic characters ♯ and ♮ respectively. When receiving codes 2/3 and 2/4 terminals should interpret them as ♯ and ♮.

FIGURE 17-3. Teletex Graphics Set [CCITT 84]

and Telecom Canada and Western Union (U.S.) have both announced Teletex systems.

The CCITT Teletex recommendations are meant to ensure compatibility among different manufacturers and vendors. In so doing, all Teletex terminals must use a standard graphic set. The Teletex graphic set is depicted in Figure 17-3. A receiving Teletex terminal must be capable of storing and responding to the entire Teletex graphic character set. This requirement was implemented to ensure that documents sent between countries can be received in all the different languages. As noted in Figure 17-3, the graphic set provides for symbols to handle some 35 different languages.

VIDEOTEX AND TELETEXT PRESENTATION STANDARDS

Of great importance for data communications is the use of standard presentation level syntax for video screens. Two standards are now evolving in the industry to define the screen representation for videotex and teletext devices.

The North American presentation level syntax (NAPLPS) is based on an AT&T presentation level protocol. The NAPLPS standard uses a technique called alphageometric coding. An alphageometric coding system displays characters with 2 x 3 picture elements. Each geometric element is coded with a mathematical description and hardware within the screen set produces a figure. The technique employs very high-quality graphics but requires complex coding/decoding units.

The alphamosaic coding scheme divides the CRT screen into 24 lines with 40 spaces on each line. In contrast to alphageometric coding, this approach uses one space for one character. A character is coded in a 7-bit code and displayed with an 8 x 10 dot pattern. The character may also be designated as a pictorial element. In this case, the character code is translated by a 2 x 3 pattern of squares.

Unfortunately, the two different approaches are incompatible. Consequently, efforts are under way to build a consensus and/or establish a specification that could encompass both approaches. The CCITT recommended standard T.101 has made inroads in this area by identifying three data syntaxes:

Data Syntax I
Data Syntax II
Data Syntax III

These syntaxes correlate to the current efforts under way in Japan, Europe, and North America respectively. At the present time, several studies are under way to provide more detailed coding of the syntax, protocol, and service elements for internetworking between videotex systems.

SUGGESTED READINGS

The CCITT specifications referenced in this chapter are recommended for the reader who is knowledgeable of presentation level syntax. [TYPE82] is a good overview of teletext and videotext graphics. [NEWM84] provides an excellent description of videotext syntaxes. The relevant ISO documents for the presentation layer are:

ISO DIS 8822	Service Definition
ISO DIS 8823	Protocol Specification
ISO DIS 8824	ASN.1 Notation
ISO DIS 8825	ASN.1 Encoding Rules

QUESTIONS

TRUE/FALSE

1. Under the convention of X.208, each piece of information has a type and a value.
2. An X.209 data element consists of an identifier, a length indicator and a contents description.
3. The presentation layer is concerned with the syntax and the values of the user data.
4. Match the X.208 built-in type function to the appropriate description:

    Function

    a) Models a valueless place holder.
    b) Models binary data.
    c) Models logical data.
    d) Models ordered collection of data called elements.
    e) Models signed whole numbers.
    f) Models a new type from an existing type.

    Term

    1. Integer
    2. Boolean
    3. Null
    4. Sequence
    5. Tagged
    6. Bit string

5. Code a Boolean type. The contents field (with a length of one) is true.
6. Code an Integer type of a contents field (with a length of one) with these possible values: {excellent (4), good (3), fair (2), poor (1)}. The contents field is: good. In this exercise, use hexadecimal notation.

7. Given a sequence of:
   TABLE A ::= SEQUENCE {I, J, K}
   TABLE B ::= SEQUENCE {L, M, N, Components of Table A}
   Code an equivalent definition of Table B.

8. Assume the type SEQUENCE {name IA5String, employed BOOLEAN} code the value {name "JONES", employed True}. Use Figure 1-5 in Chapter 1 to code "Jones".

SELECTED ANSWERS

1. True.

2. True.

3. False. The value of the user data is determined by the end-user application.

6.
Identifier	Length	Contents
02_{16}	01_{16}	03_{16}

7. TABLE B ::= {L, M, N, I, J, K}

CHAPTER 18

The Application Layer

INTRODUCTION

It is quite possible to devote an entire book to the application level. Its functions are broad and encompass protocols for office document systems, electronic mail, file transfer, and terminal control. Our objectives for this chapter are to examine the following major application layer protocol standards and vendor products:

Message Handling Systems (X.400–X.430)
SNA's Application Layer
DECnet's Application Layer
The Virtual Terminal (VT)
File Transfer, Access, and Management (FTAM)
Commitment, Concurrency, and Recovery (CCR)
Job Transfer and Manipulation (JTM)

Before we begin our examination of these subjects, it is necessary to define some terms and explain several key aspects of the upper layers of OSI.

The boundaries between the application, presentation, and session layers are different from those in the lower layers. The layers are not completely independent from each other, and in certain cases they perform complementary actions. The other difference pertains to the presentation layer. In several instances it is a "pass-through" layer between the application and session layers.

Some of the pass-through dialogue between the application and session layers do not use any services of the presentation layer. Hence, these services are directly mapped between the application and session layers. For example, the P-TOKEN-PLEASE and S-TOKEN-PLEASE are not used by the presentation layer and it is not affected by the passing of these primitives through its entities.

This concept is shown in Figure 18-1. An applications service request is passed to the application layer through an application primitive. Several of the parameters in this primitive are used at the application layer and several others are passsed directly to the presentation layer primitive. This process is also repeated at the next layer boundary with the session primitive. We examine these relationships in more detail later in this chapter.

Before further explanation of the upper layers, a few definitions are needed. These definitions are explained in more detail later in relation to the layers. Please refer to Figure 18-2 for a visual depiction of these terms.

- *Application Process* (AP): An end-user program, which is outside the scope of OSI.
- *Application Entity* (AE): Represents the AP within OSI.
- *User Element* (UE): Part of an Application Entity. It is specific to the application, and it represents the AP to the AE. It is concerned with the actual OSI services.
- *Application Service Element* (ASE): Part of an Application Entity that provides a defined OSI capability.
- *Common Application Service Element* (CASE): An ASE that provides services generally useful to a wide variety of applications.
- *Specific Application Service Element* (SASE): An ASE that provides services to a limited number of applications (perhaps only one).

An application entity (AE) operates through a single PSAP address with the presentation layer. However, it is quite possible that an end-user application process (AP) could use more than one application level protocol in a single session. As a consequence, the supporting application entity to the application process can contain (a) the single user element (UE); (b) a CASE kernal; *and* (c) multiple SASEs.

These brief definitions are explained further in this chapter. As we shall see, several of our subjects (VT, FTAM, JTM) are actually SASEs.

ELECTRONIC MAIL

Electronic mail is considered an application layer service. It is used extensively throughout the data communications industry. The technology offers

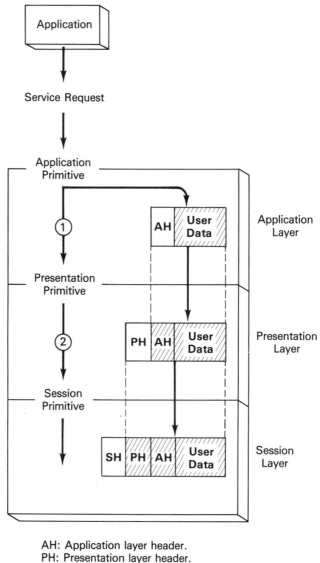

AH: Application layer header.
PH: Presentation layer header.
SH: Session layer header.

① : Parameters for presentation and session layers.

② : Parameters for session layer.

FIGURE 18-1. Relationships of Upper Three Layers

faster delivery than conventional mail-courier service and, as several studies indicate, costs are now beginning to favor electronic document deliveries over the postal service. Figure 18-3 depicts the major features of an OSI electronic mail system, referred to as a message handling system (MHS).

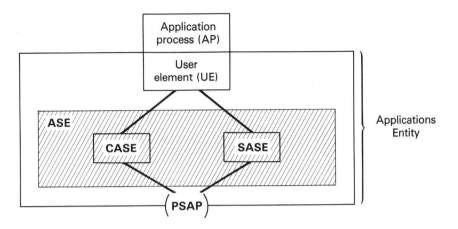

ASE: Applications Service Element.
CASE: Common Applications Service Elements.
SASE: Specific Applications Service Elements.

FIGURE 18-2. Application Layer Architecture

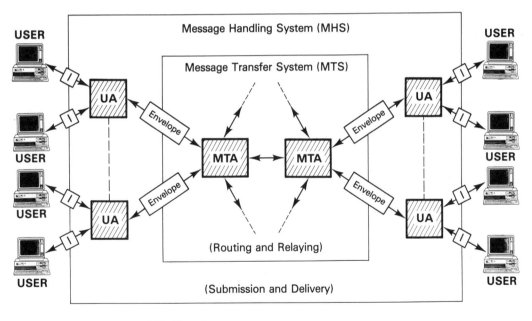

UA: User Agent.
MTA: Message Transfer Agent.
I: User Information (Contents Within Envelope).

FIGURE 18-3. MHS Model: Functional View

The *user agent* (UA) is responsible for directly interfacing with the end user. It prepares, submits, and receives messages for the user. It also provides text editing and presentation services for the end user. It provides for other activities, such as "user-friendly" interaction (for example, selective viewing), security, priority provision, delivery notification, and distribution of subsets of documents.

The *message-transfer agent* (MTA) provides the routing and relaying of electronic mail. This function is responsible primarily for the store-and-forward path, channel security, and the actual mail routing through the communications media. A collection of MTAs is called the Message Transfer System (MTS). These functions are usually specialized to a particular vendor's product, but recent efforts have pointed the way to more standardized systems.

X.400 MESSAGE HANDLING SYSTEMS (MHS)

The CCITT publishes a series of standards, entitled Message Handling Systems (MHS), in the X.400 documents. The term X.400 is used in this chapter as a general descriptor of recommendations X.400–X.430, unless otherwise noted. During our analysis of the X.400 specifications, it will be helpful to try to relate the MHS services to the mail services currently available in your office (manual and automated).

The vast majority of MHS systems in existence are based on the CCITT 1984 Red Books. Consequently, this discussion also uses these standards. The 1988 Blue Books release contains substantial editorial changes, but the overall MHS architecture remains the same. The most significant changes pertain to the addition of other functions and service elements. A detailed description of the difference between the 1984 and 1988 MHS recommendations can be found in Annex C of the 1988 X.400 document and Annex C of the 1988 X.419 document.

The MHS recommendations provide "mail" services with two principal features for end users: (a) the message transfer (MT) supports application-independent systems, which is responsible for the "envelope" of the letter, and (b) the interpersonal messaging service (IPM) which supports communications with existing CCITT, TELEX, and telematic services, and defines specific user interfaces with MHS. It is responsible for the contents of the letter within the envelope.

The MHS services are covered by the X.400 recommendations. Since X.400 is an involved and detailed specification, our analysis makes reference to each of the recommendations in order to guide the reader through the material.

X.400	System Model Service Elements
X.401	Basic Service Elements and Optional Facilities
X.408	Encoded Information Type Conversion Rules

X.409	Presentation Layer Transfer Syntax and Notation
X.410	Remote Operations and Reliable Transfer Server
X.411	Message Transfer Layer
X.420	Interpersonal Messaging User Agent Layer
X.430	Access Protocol for Teletex Terminals

Message handling systems (MHS) are considered to be an application of a specific application service element (SASE). As discussed earlier, SASE operates as part of the applications service elements (ASE) to support specific applications.

Layers and Protocols of MHS

MHS uses the principles of the OSI Reference Model. The entities and protocols reside in the application layer of the model. The MHS application is divided into two sublayers (see Figure 18-4):

- *User agent layer (UAL):* Contains the functions to manage message contents.
- *Message transfer layer (MTL):* Contains the functions to manage the message envelope and provide the transfer service. It is unaware of the contents of the message (similar to the postal service).

MHS distinguishes between the following terms (these terms are used throughout this section, so the reader should remember the location of this list for later reference):

- *UA (User agent):* Describes the general functions in the model
- *UAE (User agent entity):* Describes the specific protocol in the function
- *MTA (Message transfer agent):* Describes the general functions in the model

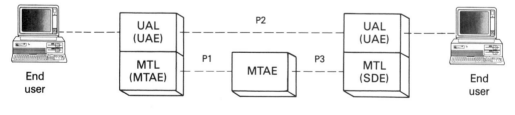

UAL: User Agent Layer.   MTAE: Message Transfer Agent Entity.
UAE: User Agent Entity.   SDE: Submission and Delivery Entity.
MTL: Message Transfer Layer.

FIGURE 18-4. Relationships of Interpersonal Message System Layers

- *MTAE (Message transfer agent entity):* Describes the specific protocol to support the MTL function
- *SDE (Submission and delivery entity):* Provides MTL services to the UAE. It interacts with a peer MTAE.

MHS Messages

The structure of the MHS messages consists of (a) an envelope which carries the information needed to transfer the message, and (b) the contents, which is the information the originating user agent (UA) wishes delivered to one or more UAs (see Figure 18-5). The contents consist of a heading and a body, which are collectively called the Interpersonal Message (IP). The UAs and MTAs use three types of envelopes for (a) submission, (b) relaying, and (c) delivery.

The submission envelope is provided by the originating UA to an MTA (see Figure 18-3). It contains the content of the message and the control information required for the MTS to perform its service. The delivery envelope is given to a receiving UA. It contains the message and control information related to the delivery of the message. The relaying envelope is used to

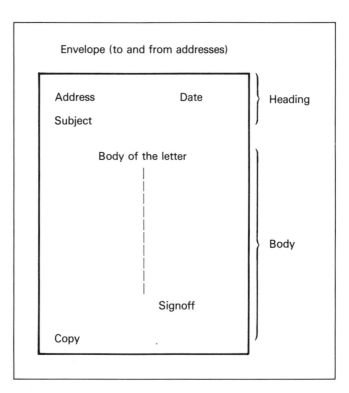

FIGURE 18-5. An Interpersonal (IP) Message

relay the message through other MTAs to the recipient UA. It should be emphasized that MHS relaying envelopes are intended for use between MTAs.

This upper-level routing is not part of the network-level packet routing, although the address created in the message could be used by a network to map to a network node or an X.25 interface address.

A specific class of UAs and MTAs make up the Interpersonal Messaging System (IPMS). The user agent provides the IPM service by acquiring *service elements* from the MTS.

Service elements are a key feature of MHS. They encompass the functions of a secretary, a word processor, and the office mail room. At a minimum, the IPM user agent should perform the following support/service functions:

- Preparation of messages
- Submission and delivery interaction with the message transfer system
- Message delivery to users
- Communication with other UAs to manage the messages

Naming and Addressing in MHS

MHS uses two kinds of names. A primitive name identifies a unique and specific entity such as an employee number or a social security number. A descriptive name denotes one user of the MHS, such as a job title. A descriptive name could identify different entities (in this example, people) as they move through a job. On the other hand, the primitive name is specific to the entity (a person). It may have global uniqueness (unique social security number in the United States) or it may not have global uniqueness (employee number). A name is permitted to have attributes, which further identify an end user (entity) with more detailed parameters.

The MHS address specifies the locations of the entities. The address specifies where the entity is located, rather than what entity is at the location.

The names in MHS are comprised of information that is related to the message originator/recipient (O/R). It may consist of four attributes: personal, geographical, organizational, and architectural (see Box 18-1). The management domain (MD) is responsible for ensuring that each UA has at least one name, and it must allow users to construct any attributes that are needed by other MDs.

MTL Services

As shown in Figure 18-4, the message transfer layer (MTL) provides user agent entities (UAEs) the means to transmit and receive messages. The service is invoked by a number of primitives that flow between the UAE and the MTAE, depicted in Figure 18-6. These primitives are used to support the service elements (described later).

For the reader who wishes more detail, each primitive and its function is described in Appendix 18A. On a more general level, these primitives are used to establish the following standard interfaces and procedures between the user agent and the message transfer agent:

1. Establishment and release of connection between the UAE and the MTL
2. Modification of parameters at the MTL by the UAE
3. Control by the UAE of the message types and lengths

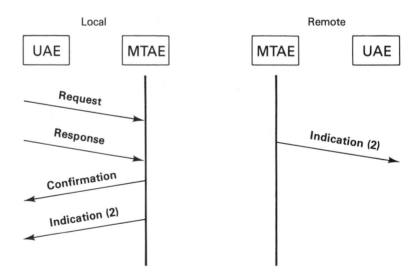

Note (1): See text for permissible combinations.
Note (2): Only a deliver indication primitive is permitted on the "remote" side.

FIGURE 18-6. Possible Scenarios for the MTAE and UAE Primitives (from the "local" perspective)

4. Submission of a message by UAE and the assignment of a unique number and time to each message
5. Determination if message can be delivered
6. Delivery by MTL of a message to a UAE
7. Non-delivery notification by MTL to UAE
8. Delivery notification by MTL to UAE
9. Cancellation by UAE of a submitted message

To summarize the MTL layer primitives, Figure 18-7 shows a session establishment between a UAE and its MTAE, the exchange of user messages/control messages, and the release with the LOGOFF primitives.

Interpersonal Messaging (IPM) User Agent Layer

The IPM (at the UA) uses the Interpersonal Messaging Protocol (P2) for UAEs to cooperate with others in exchanging messages. As depicted in Figure 18-4, this message exchange is performed by the UAEs (a) using P2 to construct the message and (b) using the primitives (Figure 18-7) to communicate with the servicing MTL.

The IPM user agent entities communicate with the end user to accept the user's message or send a message to the user. However, MHS does *not* define how the end user and the UAE communicate. It is considered a local matter. Consequently, a variety of user messaging systems could be serviced by a UA. The UA is responsible for changing the user message to a standard MHS format and transferring it to a peer UAE through the MTL services.

The IPM uses two types of protocol data units which become the contents within the MHS envelope: IP-message UAPDUs (IM-UAPDUs) and IPM-Status-report UAPDUs (SR-UAPDUs). The former contains the message of the user. It contains both the heading and the body. The latter is a control message used between the IPM UAEs. This idea is shown in Figure 18-8.

The heading of the IM-UAPDU is shown in Table 18-1. A number of service elements are invoked by the heading components. These service elements are described in detail in the next section of this chapter, so their functions are not iterated here. The body part contains the user message. Each part also carries an indication of encoded information type (IA5, videotex, etc.).

Sending and Receiving IP-messages. When the IPM user agent receives a message from the end user, it builds an IM-UAPDU and sends a SUBMIT.Request primitive to the message transfer layer (MTL). The message is transferred through the MHS to the destination. The recipient MTL sends a DELIVER.Indication primitive and the contents to the receiving UAE. The originating UAE must notify the end user if the submission failed and the reason for the failure. Appendix 18A provides more information on this procedure if the reader wishes more detail.

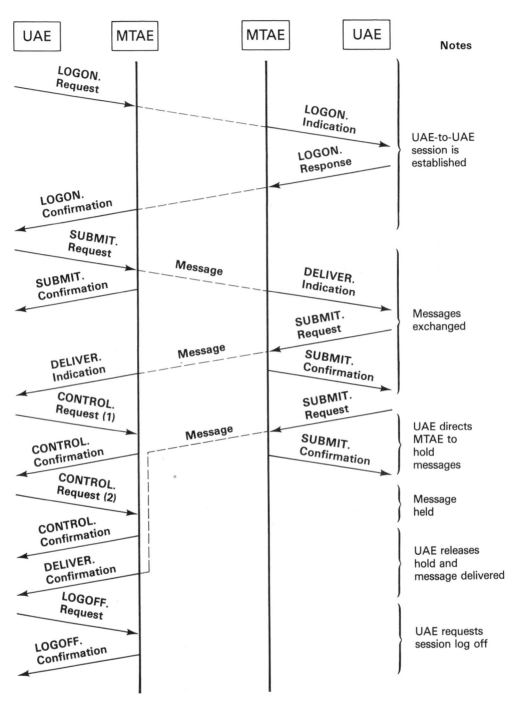

Note (1): Hold Messages
Note (2): Deliver Messages

FIGURE 18-7. Message Transfer Layer Services

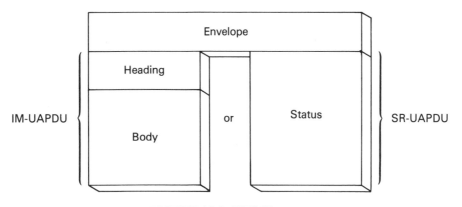

FIGURE 18-8. IPM Messages

MT and IPM: Service Elements

Several references have been made to the importance of the MHS *service elements*. We now examine them. A list of the MT and IPM service elements is provided in Tables 18-2(a) and 18-2(b) respectively. Since the service elements are the foundation of MHS, it is appropriate to analyze them in some detail. A short paragraph describing each service element follows.

MT Service Elements

The *access management* service element provides the support for the UA and MTA to communicate with each other through the identification and validation of names and addresses. This service element allows the UA to use its O/R name for access security. The MTS passwords used for this service element are different from any of those used by the UA itself to authenticate the end user.

    The *content type indication* service element supports an originating UA's indication of the content type (FAX, teletex, etc.) for each message. The recipient UA may have one or more content types delivered to it. The content type identification specifies the particular type.

    The *converted indication* service element is used by the MTS to inform a recipient UA that the MTS performed code conversion on a delivered message. The service element allows the recipient UA to be informed of the resulting code types.

    The *delivery time stamp indication* service element is used by the MTS to inform the recipient UA of the time and date the MTS delivered the message.

    The *message identification* service element is used by the MTS to give the UA the unique identification for each message sent to or from the MTS. The UAs and MTs use these values also to identify previously submitted

TABLE 18-1. Heading of the Interpersonal Message Protocol Data Unit (IM-UAPDU)

Heading Components	Service Element(s)
IP MessageId	IP message identification
originator	Originator indication
authorizingUsers	Authorizing users indication
primaryRecipients	Primary and copy recipients indication
copyRecipients	Reply request indication
	Receipt notification
	Non-receipt notification
blindCopyRecipients	Blind copy recipient indication
	Reply request indication
	Receipt notification
	Non-receipt notification
inReplyTo	Replying IP-message indication
obsoletes	Obsoleting indication
crossReferences	Cross referencing indication
subject	Subject indication
expiryDate	Expiry date indication
replyBy	Reply request indication
replyToUsers	
importance	Importance indication
sensitivity	Sensitivity indication
autoForwarded	Auto forwarded indication

TABLE 18-2(a). MT Service Elements

Service Group	Service Elements
Basic	Access management, Content type indication, Converted indication, Delivery time stamp indication, Message identification, Non-delivery notification, Original encoded information types indication, Registered encoded information types, Submission time stamp indication
Submission and delivery	Alternate recipient allowed, Deferred delivery, Deferred delivery cancellation, Delivery notification, Disclosure of other recipients, Grade of delivery selection, Multi-destination delivery, Prevention of non-delivery notification, Return of contents
Conversion	Conversion prohibition, Explicit conversion, Implicit conversion
Query	Probe
Status and Inform	Alternate recipient assignment, Hold for delivery

TABLE 18-2(b). IPM Service Elements

Service Group	Service Elements
Basic	Basic MT service elements, IP-message identification, Typed body
Submission and Delivery and Conversion	See Table 18-2(a)
Cooperating IPM UA Action	Blind copy recipient indication, Non-receipt notification, Receipt notification, Auto-forwarded indication
Cooperating IPM UA Information Conveying	Originator indication, Authorizing users indication, Primary and copy recipients indication, Expiry date indication, Cross-referencing indication, Importance indication, Obsoleting indication, Sensitivity indication, Subject indication, Replying IP-message indication, Reply request indication, Forwarded IP-message indication, Body part encryption indication, Multi-part body
Query	See Table 18-2(a)
Status and Inform	See Table 18-2(a)

traffic of other service elements such as confirmation and non-delivery notification.

The *non-delivery notification* service element is used by the MTS to inform an originating O/A if a message was not delivered to the receiving UA. The reason for the non-delivery is indicated as part of the service element.

The *original encoded information types indication* service element is used by the sending UA to identify the code type of the message submitted to the MTS. When the message is delivered to the recipient UA, it gives this UA the information about the information code.

In conjunction with the previous service element, the *registered encoding information type* service element is used by the sending UA to notify the MTS of the code types that can be delivered to the UA.

The *submission time stamp indication* service element is used by the MTS to inform the sending UA and the receiving UA of the date and time the message was submitted to the MTS.

The *deferred delivery* service element is used by the originating UA to inform the MTS that the message is to be delivered within a specified date and time. The MTS attempts to deliver the traffic as close to this period as possible. It does not deliver the traffic before the deferred delivery time and date stamp. The originator's management domain (MD) may place a limit on the parameters in the service element.

The *deferred delivery cancellation* service element is used by the originating UA to inform the MTS that it is to cancel a message which was previously submitted. The cancellation may or may not take effect. For example, if the message has already been forwarded within the MTS, it will not be cancelled.

The *delivery notification* service element is used for an end-to-end acknowledgment. This allows the originating UA to request that it be informed when the message has been successfully delivered to the recipient UA. This service element also stipulates the time and date of the actual delivery. The service element does not mean that the recipient UA has acted on the message or has even examined it. It only states that the delivery did occur. It is similar in concept to receiving a receipt of a delivery of a letter through the postal service. It merely means that the recipient has signed for the letter; it does not mean the recipient read the letter.

The *disclosure of other recipients* service element allows the originating UA to require the MTS to disclose the O/R names of all the other recipients after they have received the message. These names are originally supplied by the originating UA, and the MTS then informs the UA when each recipient receives the message.

The *grade of delivery selection* service element allows the sending UA to request the MTS to transfer the message on an urgent or non-urgent basis, rather than a normal basis. The service element does not stipulate the specific times for the grade of delivery selection.

The *multi-destination delivery* service element is used by the originating UA to stipulate that a message is to be submitted to more than one receiving UA. The specification does not place a limit on the number of UAs that can receive the message.

The *prevention of non-delivery notification* service element is used by the sending UA to inform the MTS not to return a non-delivery notification, if the message is not delivered. This situation is not unusual in electronic mail when non-priority bulletins are sent to various recipients.

The *return of contents* service element is used by the sending UA to request the content of its message be returned in any event of non-delivery. The return will not occur if the system has encoded the message into a different code.

The *conversion prohibition* service element is used by the originating UA to instruct the MTS that the message is not to have any code conversion performed on it. Two other service elements in this category provide complementary services.

The *implicit conversion* service element instructs the MTS to perform conversion for a period of time. It is so named because the UAs are not required to explicitly request the service. In contrast, the *explicit conversion* service element is used by the originating UA to instruct the MTS to perform conversion services. When using this service element, the sending UA is informed of the original code types as well as the newly encoded types of the message.

The *probe* service element is used by the sending UA to determine if a message can be delivered before it is actually sent. The MTS is responsible for providing the submission information by generating either non-delivery or delivery notifications. The useful aspect of the probe service element relates to the possibility that different codes, different message sizes, or even different content types might not be deliverable. In such a case, the UA might alter some of its size, content types, and codes as a result of the probe.

The *alternate recipient allowed* service element indicates that a "probe" may test the possibility of delivery to an alternate recipient.

The *alternate recipient assignment* service element gives the UA the capability to have certain messages delivered to it even when there is not an exact match in the attributes or descriptive names of the UA. In this situation, the UA is specified in specific attributes and also in other attributes for which any value would be acceptable. This is useful when a message is sent which contains the proper domain name and perhaps company name, but the person's name in the message does not match. This means the UA would still have the message delivered to it. The message will not be rejected, but manual procedures could be implemented to handle the notification to the person or to locate the individual.

The *hold for delivery* service element is quite similar to the postal department's holding mail for individuals. This allows the UA to require the MTS to hold its traffic for delivery as well as the notification. The UA can use this service element to inform the MTS when it is unavailable and when it is again ready to accept traffic. The hold for delivery service element is a temporary storage facility only. Unlike other forms of MHS, this is not used for permanent storage.

IPM Service Elements

The interpersonal messaging service (IPM) is used by the cooperating user agents (IPM UAs) to send end-user messages. The IPM service is reliant on the message transfer (MT) service.

A class of cooperating UAs manages the user's IP-messages. We have learned that the IPM UA is the user's direct bridge into the MHS. For example, IPM UA could edit the users input, provide filing support, allow the user to query for incoming messages, and provide store-and-forward of the messages to other end users. X.400 specifies a variety of IPM service elements. They are described here. It will be evident that many of these services are the tasks performed by secretaries and other office personnel.

The originating user requests his/her IPM UA to send a message to the recipient UA. The user specifies the O/R name of the recipient that is to receive the message. In turn, the IPM UA submits the traffic to the MTS for delivery to the end user.

The *basic message transfer identification* service element is used by the IPM UA to identify each IP message sent or received. The MHS does not specify the particular method by which this identifier is generated. However, it does suggest that the O/R name be included with the identifier to prevent any ambiguity in the addressing.

The *typed body* service element defines the attributes of the body of the IP message. For example, it may describe the type code (IA5), and whether it is a facsimile or a teletext document.

The *blind copy recipient indication* service element allows the originator of the message to provide the names of additional recipients of the traffic. These names are not disclosed to any of the other recipients.

The *non-receipt notification* service element is used by the originator to request that it be notified if an IP message was not delivered. This can be requested on an end-recipient basis. The receiving IPM UA must return a non-receipt if the message was forwarded to another recipient, if the recipient did not subscribe to the service, or if the message was discarded before the reception actually occurred. The non-receipt notification must contain the identification of the IP message involved in the non-delivery, as well as reasons for the non-delivery.

The *explicit conversion* service element allows the IPM UAs to exchange a unique identifier for each IP message.

The *receipt notification* service element is used by the originator to request that it be notified of the receipt of the IP message. The receipt notification must include the identifier of the message to which the notification is applicable, the time of destination receipt, the O/R name of the recipient, and an indication if any code conversion was performed.

The *auto-forwarded indication* service element is used to determine that an incoming IP message has been auto-forwarded. The auto-forwarded IP message may be accompanied by the information that was intended with its original delivery such as code conversion indications and time stamps.

The *originator indication* service element is used to identify the originator of the traffic. The MTS requires the transmitting UA to provide the proper O/R name to the receiver.

The *authorizing user indication* service element allows the originator to identify the names of one or more recipients of the traffic. The actual purpose of this service element is to give the receivers the identification of the people who are authorized to send the traffic (for example, a secretary or manager in an organization).

The *primary and copy recipients indication* service element is used by the originator to provide the names of the users who are the primary recipients of the IP message as well as the identification of the individuals who are copy recipients only. This is the familiar "to" and "cc" identifiers on a typical letter.

The *expiry date indication* service element is used by the originator to indicate the date and time when the IP message will no longer be valid. However, MHS does not specify what happens in the event the expiration time or date is exceeded.

The *cross-referencing indication* service element is used to identify associated IP messages. This is useful to allow the IPM UA to retrieve copies of the referenced messages.

The *importance indication* service element is used to establish a priority for the IP message. MHS defines three levels of priority: low, normal, and high. While this service element is used to indicate how important the traffic is, it is not related to the delivery selection service provided by the MTS itself. Moreover, MHS does not specify how to handle this service element.

The *obsoleting indication* service element is used by the originator to indicate that one (or more) IP messages previously sent is (are) no longer valid. The IP message identifying this situation supersedes the previous IP messages.

The *sensitivity indication* service element is used by the originator to provide guidelines for the security of the IP message. This service element indicates whether the recipient should have to identify itself before it receives the traffic; whether the IP message can be printed on a shared device; and whether the IP message can be auto-forwarded. The service specifies three levels of sensitivity: (a) *personal,* meaning the IP message is sent to an individual recipient; (b) *private,* meaning the IP message contains information that is to be used only by the recipient and no one else; and (c) *company confidential,* meaning the IP message contains information that should be used only according to company procedures.

The *subject indication* service element is used for the originator to indicate to the receiver the subject matter of the message.

The *replying IP message indication* service element is used to indicate that this IP message is sent in reply to another IP message. The reply may be sent only to the originator or to other users who received copies of the message.

The *reply request indication* service element is used by the originator to request that the receiver send an IP message and reply to the original message. This service element also allows the originator to specify the date on which to send the reply and the O/R names of those who should receive the reply. The recipient is responsible for deciding whether or not to reply to the traffic.

The *forwarded IP message indication* service element is used to forward the IP message as the body of the IP message. In a multipart body, the forwarded parts can be included along with the message body parts of other types of traffic.

The *body part encryption indication* service element is used by the originator to inform the receiver that the body part of the IP message has been encrypted.

The *multipart body* service element is used by the originator to send to the recipient an IP message that is in several parts. Each part can contain the nature, attributes, and type of the message.

Remote Operations and Reliable Transfer Service (RTS)

It is useful to remember that the MHS service elements are provided by the Interpersonal Message (IPM) and Message Transfer (MT) services. However, if the reader examines Figure 18-4, it should be evident that other MHS protocols are needed to transfer the messages between the MT services. Until now, we have been concerned with (a) the end-user interaction with the UA; (b) the UA interactions with the MT; and (c) the logical interactions between the cooperating UAs (with IPM).

It is now appropriate to examine the interactions between the MTAEs, and SDEs. In other words, what happens after the message leaves the local interfaces? What are the required interactions among these remote entities? The remainder of the material on X.400 discusses these areas.

Remote Operations. The specifications of remote interactive protocols are defined by the Reliable Transfer Service (RTS). Using this service, the protocol data units (PDUs) are transferred by the RTS as a service to an application entity (AE). RTS supports the MTAE by managing transfers between the MTAEs. The concept is really quite simple. As shown in Figure 18-9, a requestor AE sends an operation protocol data unit (OPDU) to a remote AE. In this data unit is a parameter that describes a requested operation. The remote AE (the server AE) performs the operation and then may or may not inform the requestor AE of the outcome.

An AE begins operations by transferring operation protocol data units (OPDUs). MHS defines four types of OPDUs:

Invoke OPDU

ReturnResult OPDU

ReturnError OPDU

Reject OPDU

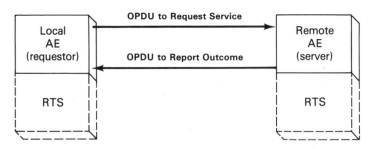

FIGURE 18-9. Logical Relationship of Local and Remote Application Entities (AEs)

The notation is:

OPDU   ::=   choice {[1] invoke, [2] Return Result, [3] Return Error, [4] reject}

The Invoke OPDU is used when an AE wishes to communicate with another AE. The OPDU contains an identifier which is used to ensure atomic actions of the OPDUs. The protocol data unit also specifies the operation to be performed. However, since the operation is application-specific, MHS does not define this aspect of the AE-AE process.

The notation for the Invoke OPDU is:

Invoke   ::=   SEQUENCE {invokeID INTEGER,OPERATION, argument ANY}

The ReturnResult OPDU reports the result of the AE-AE operation. It is sent if the result is successful. The ReturnError OPDU is sent if the operation is unsuccessful. The Reject OPDU is returned if the OPDU is rejected due to a content or formatting error. These OPDUs are coded as:

Return Result   ::=   SEQUENCE {invokeID INTEGER, result ANY}
Return Error   ::=   SEQUENCE {invokeID INTEGER, ERROR, parameter ANY}

Final Thoughts on the X.400 Recommendations

We have only touched the surface of the MHS X.400 functions. The final drafts of the 1988 recommendations number more pages than this book you are reading! The reader who wishes to learn more about MHS should study the 1988 X.400 document and X.400 Annex C.

SNA'S APPLICATION LAYER: APPLICATION AND FUNCTION MANAGEMENT LAYERS

Introduction

As we learned earlier in this book, the layers of SNA do not fit concisely into the ISO layers. Notwithstanding, several of IBM's upper layer systems are properly classified as application layer protocols. IBM's principal application layer protocols are explained here. Since many use the logical unit type 6.2 (LU 6.2), we begin with an explanation of this upper layer protocol.

LU 6.2

LU 6.2 is an advanced capability of SNA. It permits applications programs to communicate with each other. In previous SNA products, the user devices were assumed to be "dumb" terminals, which were connected to host-resident applications programs. SNA was designed to service this environment and to optimize the performance for the "dumb" device/host applications sessions. However, the advent and rapid proliferation of smart terminals, powerful personal computers, file transfer devices, and stand-alone networks created problems for SNA. It often resulted in poor performance to the end user.

One of IBM's answers to this problem is LU 6.2 APPC (advanced program-to-program communications). APPC supports applications-to-applications communications with an application program interface (API) (in SNA parlance, an application is an application transaction program [ATP]). Figure 18-10 illustrates the relationship.

LU 6.2 provides a method of achieving near-transparency between user programs. For example, one application might use a different syntax or programming language than another application. LU 6.2 requires these programs to translate their specific requests to LU 6.2 with protocol boundary verbs. Both applications must communicate with each other through LU 6.2 and a common set of these verbs. In other words, they must accept the LU 6.2 interface. In a sense, "protocol conversion" is moved to the application. This approach allows different programs that are in different systems to use LU 6.2 to interface with each other. The concept is aligned with the idea of OSI primitives discussed throughout Part II of this book.

LU 6.2 also enhances the applications' communications by requiring a base set of mandatory capabilities. All systems that use APPC must include these features. Additional LU 6.2 facilities are available and if a higher-level option is implemented, all lower-level facilities must also be supported. In

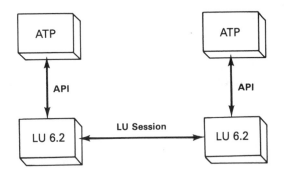

ATP: Application Transaction Program.
LU: Logical Unit.
API: Applications Program Interface.

FIGURE 18-10. SNA's ATP and LU 6.2

this manner, two products will be able to communicate at the highest level of their mutual subset of facilities.

An apt analogy is human communication wherein two language students speak to each other through their "nonnatural" language. One person has learned the past tense of the language's verb status and the other person has not yet learned this language subset. Consequently, the individuals communicate only in the present tense.

API acts as a protocol boundary between APPC and the ATPs. Its principal job is to support interapplications communications in a transparent manner. That is, the applications are unaware of the lower-level functions in APPC and Path Control.

LU 6.2 supports a conversation between two programs. The programs can communicate for a long time or a short period—perhaps the exchange of only one transaction. The key concept of an LU 6.2 conversation is that a series of conversations can use the same session. IBM also uses this idea in some of its internetworking protocols (see Chapter 14 on XI).

As mentioned earlier, LU 6.2 supports a macro language (a set of verbs) that resembles the instructions of a high-level programming language. The Function Management layer is responsible for interpreting the verbs.

LU 6.2 provides four categories of verbs:

Basic Conversation Verbs

Mapped Conversation Verbs

Type-independent Conversation Verbs

Control Operator Verbs

The Basic Conversation Verbs provide the fundamental parameters for the program-to-program communication. They correspond to basic LU 6.2 services and are used by the LU Service Transaction Programs (STPs). They are part of any LU 6.2 product implementation. The STPs (discussed later) include several of IBM's major products such as Document Interchange Architecture (DIA), SNA Distribution Services (SNADS), and the Change Number of Sessions Model (CNOS).

The Mapped Conversation Verbs are used with end-user high-level languages. They are easier to use because they perform formatting services that the Basic Conversations do not provide. They are designed for programs written in higher languages like COBOL or C. The mapped conversations are converted into a standard format called a generalized data stream. At the receiving end, they are converted back to the original form.

In a sense, these verbs are super macro instructions. They keep the applications programmer isolated from certain options and details. A brief description of the basic verbs is provided in Box 18-2 and should help the reader to understand how LU 6.2 operates. The Basic and Mapped Verbs are essentially the same, except the Mapped Verbs begin with a prefix MC-.

BOX 18-2.   LU 6.2 Verbs

- ALLOCATE (LU__name, ATP, Mode__name, Sync__level): Creates a new activity at a LU by building a conversation with a named partner program (ATP). The program is placed in execution and given addressability to the conversation that started it. Mode__name indicates the type of service (e.g., batch, interactive, etc.). Sync__level specifies none or confirm.

- SEND_DATA: Moves data to an output buffer and returns control to the program. Causes data to be sent to the partner program. The format for this data is defined under a LU 6.2 data stream called General Data Stream (GDS). The GDS record contains a length field (of the data) and the data themselves, which can range from 0 to 32,765 bytes.

- RECEIVE_AND_WAIT: Returns data from the conversation or control information to the program. If nothing has been received, the program waits. Causes data to be received by the partner program.

- DEALLOCATE: Ends a conversation. It deallocates a conversation from the transaction program.

- SEND_ERROR: Reports an error (called a detected-error notification) in the data being received. It terminates the incoming message, purges it, notifies the sender, and obtains the right to send. The other program is placed in a receive state.

- CONFIRM: Ends a message and asks the application partner for assurance that no errors have been detected in it. The verb is also used to synchronize the execution of the two transaction programs.

- CONFIRMED: Responds to the Confirm verb.

- SYNCPT and BACKOUT: Makes accumulated changes permanent. If changes are not to be made permanent, a rollback (removal of changes) is allowed.

- PREPARE_TO_RECEIVE: Marks the end of the current message being sent and gives up the right to send. The program changes from the send state to the receive state. The lower level LU session (layer 5) supports conversations with the half-duplex flip-flop protocol.

- FLUSH: Causes information in the buffer to be sent.

- REQUEST_TO_SEND: Asks application partner for the right to send. It notifies the remote program that it is requesting to enter a conversation send state.

- GET_ATTRIBUTES: Issuer of this verb receives conversation specific information such as local and remote LU names, synchronization levels, and mode name.

- POST_ON_RECEIPT: Requests the conversation when all information is available for the transaction program to receive.

- RECEIVE_IMMEDIATE: Does not wait for information to arrive. Receives any available information for a specified conversation.
- TEST: Used to check if a conversation has been posted. It is also used to ascertain if a REQUEST_TO_SEND notification has been received by the local LU.

Type-independent verbs are used for control functions such as sync points (periodic checks on status of the communications process) and back-outs (reversing the effects of previous communications transactions).

Since applications that process transactions may be located in different parts of a network, some means must be available for them to synchronize and coordinate their activities. LU 6.2 provides for three levels of synchronization. The first has no synchronization. The other two are:

- *Confirm synchronization:* This second option requires a definite response after each program has completed the processing of a transaction. It is an end-to-end acknowledgment. This level of synchronization provides nothing other than the confirm; it does not provide any method of error recovery in the event a problem occurs.
- *Sync point synchronization:* This LU 6.2 feature is the third and highest level of synchronization processing. The LU establishes certain resources as protected, and manages them accordingly. It then assumes responsibility for making the changes and committing the changes to protection. If an error occurs during the processing of a transaction, the LU is responsible to back out any changes that were made that might be unrecoverable. This feature requires the two LUs to exchange status information at the time of the failure and then perform the necessary actions to restore the resources to the state prior to the problem. The sync point synchronization feature uses the ideas of atomic action, commitment control, backout, and resynchronization that are discussed in sections of Chapters 8, 16, and 18.

Figure 18-11 provides an example of a LU 6.2 communications process.

LU 6.2 Support for IBM Products

IBM uses APPC LU 6.2 as the foundation for several higher-level protocols, distributed processing products, and office automation architectures. Like several specifications of the OSI, some of IBM's products span several layers (LU 6.2 for example). For ease of reference and because of their nature, they are discussed in this chapter.

This section examines the following major IBM products, which are also known as Transaction Services Architectures.

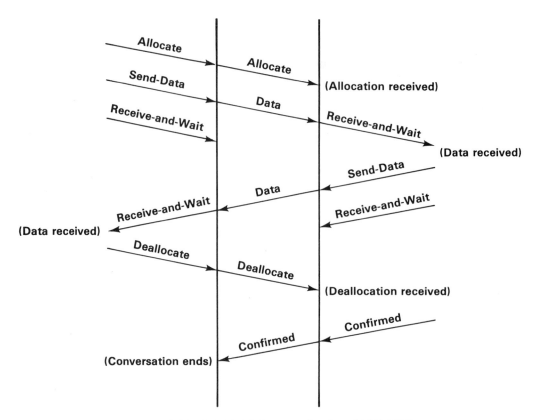

FIGURE 18-11. LU 6.2 Communications [MART87]

SNADS   SNA Distribution Services
DIA   Document Interchange Architecture
DCA   Document Content Architecture
DDM   Distributed Data Management
LEN   Low Entry Networking

SNADS (SNA Distribution Services). Most of the features of SNA are synchronous in that communicating users must be in a concurrently active session with each other. Higher-level protocols, especially in office systems, need to communicate in an asynchronous fashion wherein the traffic can be sent, queried, and perhaps delivered at a later time. SNADS fulfills this requirement.

SNADS is basically a store-and-forward service. It allows information to be stored until the path to the receiver and/or the resources at the receiver are available. The value of any store-and-forward service is that users do not have to be available to each other at the same time in order to communicate. The data are queued until the user requests the data.

SNADS is found in many electronic mail and document distribution systems. However, as a store/delivery service, it can deliver any type of data and need not be restricted to documents only.

SNADS also performs routing functions. Based on a user identification, it looks up a destination address in a routing table. It selects the most appropriate route by checking a control field that contains a priority, the required queuing capacity of the intermediate DSUs, and a security indicator.

SNADS provides the delivery mechanism for distribution between separate DSUs. Document delivery within the same machine does not need SNADS but relies on another system called DIA.

Document Interchange Architecture (DIA). The DIA provides document exchange between office system nodes (OSN) and source/recipient nodes (SRN). Figure 18-12 illustrates the relationship between OSNs, SRNs, and SNADS. Note that DIA is "locally oriented" and uses SNADS for "remote" distribution. DIA provides the following services for the user at the SRN:

- *Application Processing Services* (APS): Supports document processing, user program interfaces, and transformation of formats.

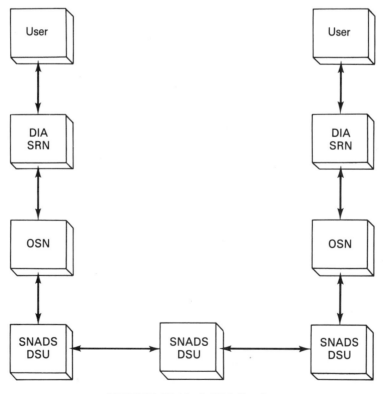

FIGURE 18-12. A DIA Session

- *Document Distribution Services* (DDS): Distributes copies of documents to recipients with option for priorities, distribution lists, and confirmations.
- *Document Library Services* (DLS): Supports the storing, retrieval, searching, and deletion of documents in the DIA library.
- *File Transfer Services* (FTS): Supports DLS in the file transfer operations.

The Office System Node (OSN) performs several functions which depend on whether the OSN is an originating or a destination node. An originating OSN assigns a unique name to each document request, stores requests, routes documents to their OSNs and provides status information to the DIA SRN. The destination OSN queues the distribution documents and delivers them to the recipient at a designated time. It also sends confirmations of delivery to the originating OSN.

Document Content Architecture (DCA). The DCA is somewhat similar in concept to CCITT X.208. It standardizes the representation of a document and the structure for formatting and interpreting the control information. The control information defines the actual format of the information on a page, such as page break, page width, etc. DCA allows a document to be represented in one of three forms:

- *Revisable Form Text* (RFT): Contains the document and the control information to allow a user to view this control and readily modify the text structure.
- *Final-form Text* (FFT): Contains the document in its final format as it would appear on an output device.
- *Mixed-form Text* (MFFT): A final-formed text that contains mixed information types, such as text and graphics.

Distributed Data Management (DDM). DDM supports the management of distributed data files: It uses a command language to (a) create a file: (b) remove a file; (c) delete a file; (d) load and unload a file; and (e) lock and unlock interconnected files.

DDM provides these functions for four record-oriented file systems: (a) direct; (b) sequential; (c) key; and (d) alternate index. In addition, it supports the following access methods for a file (if appropriate):

relative by record number
random by record number
combined relative and random by record number
relative by key

random by key

combined relative and random by key

combined relative and random by record number and key

Low Entry Networking (LEN). LEN gives SNA peripheral node (PN) the capability to operate as a network node. As such, it uses the PU Type 2.1 node capabilities and enhances them with LU 6.2.

The PU 2.1 is enhanced to allow a processor to operate autonomously under a peripheral node control point (PNCP). Moreover, the LEN network node is enhanced to support PU Type 4 intermediate network node functions.

COMPARISON OF SNA'S UPPER LAYERS AND PROTOCOL DATA UNITS

Figure 18-13 shows the SNA layers and SNA protocol data units [ROUT87A]. As with most layered protocols, SNA uses the concepts of encapsulation and decapsulation. The end-user document is encapsulated within the RFT DCA Data Stream and the process continues through the various SNA layers. At the data link layer, all information is encapsulated into the SDLC information (I) field.

DEC'S APPLICATION LAYER: THE NETWORK APPLICATION LAYER

DEC identifies a number of independent modules in a layer that are similar to the OSI application layer. DEC calls this layer the Network Application Layer. Many of these functions bear little resemblance to the pure OSI model, but several closely follow the OSI layered concept for the application level functions. DEC identifies five major modules for its network application layer. Their purpose is to provide data access, terminal access, as well as communications services to the users. They are summarized briefly in the following list and discussed in more detail in this part. This discussion is derived from [DECN82].

- The *network virtual terminal protocol* supports terminals connected to a host DECnet system to a remote host DECnet system.
- The *data access protocol (DAP)* supports remote file access and transfer across nodes independent of the specific I/O structure of the files.
- The *loopback mirror protocol* supports the transmission and reception of one message between the network management modules access routines.

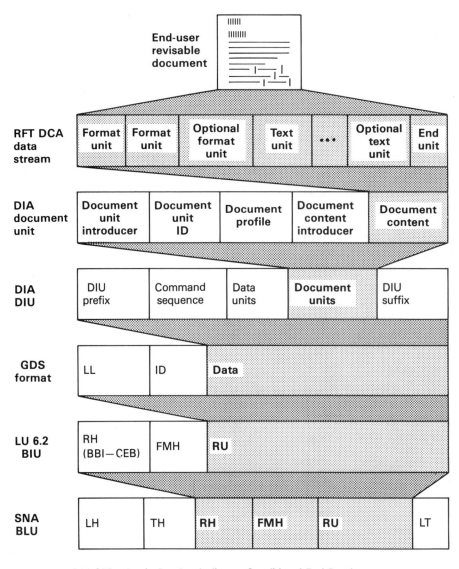

RFT DCA data stream

| Format unit | Format unit | Optional format unit | Text unit | ••• | Optional text unit | End unit |

DIA document unit

| Document unit introducer | Document unit ID | Document profile | Document content introducer | Document content |

DIA DIU

| DIU prefix | Command sequence | Data units | Document units | DIU suffix |

GDS format

| LL | ID | Data |

LU 6.2 BIU

| RH (BBI–CEB) | FMH | RU |

SNA BLU

| LH | TH | RH | FMH | RU | LT |

BBI-CEB = Begin Bracket Indicator-Conditional End Bracket
BIU = Basic Information Unit
BLU = Basic Link Unit
DIA = Document Interchange Unit
DIU = Distribution Interchange Unit
FMH = Function Management Header
GDS = General Data Stream
ID = Identifier
LH = Link Header
LL = Logical Link
LT = Link Trailer
RFT DCA = Revisable Form Text-Document Content Architecture
RH = Request/Response Header
RU = Request/Response Unit
TH = Transmission Header

FIGURE 18-13. SNA Layers and Protocol Data Units [ROUT87A]

- The *X.25 gateway access protocol* supports user written modules in a host DECnet system to communicate with other peer modules in a non-DEC system across an X.25 network.

- The *SNA gateway access protocol* supports user written modules in a host DECnet system to communicate with IBM host application programs within the SNA network.

The latter two DEC models are actually gateway functions, although they are written from the perspective of supporting the end-user application. Therefore, these modules are discussed in more detail in the Internetworking chapter.

Network Virtual Terminal (NVT)

DEC'S NVT is used to provide transparency between a terminal's applications. In effect, it is used to support different host systems, by allowing the different operating systems to communicate via common upper-level protocols (see Figure 18-14). The NVT offers several standard terminal services, and also provides a method to tailor the terminal's behavior in more detail. NVT is organized into two sublayers within the network application layer: the terminal communication protocol sublayer and the command terminal sublayer.

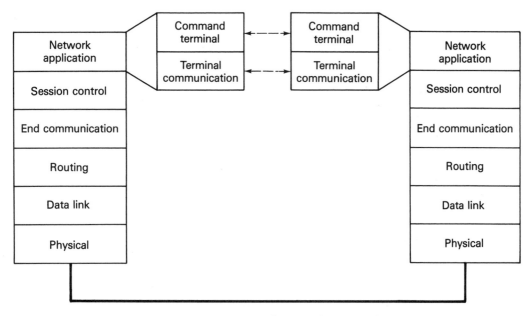

FIGURE 18-14. DEC Network Virtual Terminal Service.

The Terminal Communication Sublayer. This layer is responsible for managing the sessions between applications programs and the terminals. DEC has designed this sublayer to extend the DNA session layer module. It establishes DEC logical links between end points that are specific to the terminal services. DEC calls the end point in the host system a portal; the other end in the service system is called a logical terminal.

The Command Terminal Sublayer. This sublayer offers functions to support the input and output of hard copy, CRT, and video transmissions. It performs such tasks as reading lines of input (with echoing, if necessary), specifying line terminators, and enabling and disabling certain physical control features on the device. It provides some message handling functions described earlier in this chapter, such as accepting input even if a program has not issued a read. This means that it will save until the program issues a read request. DEC calls this its "type-ahead" function. This sublayer also takes action in response to certain characters struck from the terminal immediately as they are depressed instead of waiting for a buffer output. It provides for many other features such as the recognition of certain specific ASCII characters, determining and setting the terminal device characteristics, and managing the type-ahead input and output buffers.

Data Access Protocol (DAP)

DAP is an upper-layer protocol used to manage remote file access and file transfer. As stated earlier, it is designed to be independent of the input/output structure of the actual operating system. DAP consists of a set of messages that governs the exchange of files between two users. It is a functionally rich protocol that provides the following features:

- Supports heterogeneous files.
- Retrieves a file from an input device.
- Stores a file on an output device
- Transfers files between nodes.
- Supports deletion and renaming of remote files.
- Lists directories of remote files.
- Recovers from transient errors and reports fatal errors to the user.
- Allows multiple data streams to be sent over a logical link.
- Submits and executes remote files.
- Permits sequential, random, and indexed (ISAM) access of records.
- Supports sequential, relative, and indexed file organizations.

- Supports wild-card file specification for sequential file retrieval, file deletion, file renaming, and command file execution.
- Permits an optional file checksum to ensure file integrity.

DAP is executed with two users exchanging DAP messages. The users are (a) the user process and (b) a server process that acts on behalf of the remote user node. Several user I/O commands, which are used to access a remote file, are mapped into equivalent DAP messages and transmitted via a DEC logical link to a server of the remote node. In turn, the server interprets the DAP commands, and maps in to perform the actual file I/O. Next the server returns the status and, one hopes, the data to the user. DAP requires that the first message exchange in this process is a description of the operation system, the file systems, the buffer sized, the record sized, etc. This allows the software to adjust to varying calls about varying files and data bases.

DEC has implemented the following DAP-oriented remote file access facilities:

- *File Access Listener* (FAL). FAL receives user I/O requests at the remote node and acts on the user's behalf. This is the remote DAP-speaking server process.
- *Network File Transfer* (NFT). Operates at the user level, and interfaces to a DAP-speaking accessing process to provide DAP functions. NFT provides network-wide file transfer and manipulation services.
- *Record Management Services* (RMS). RMS is the standard file system for many of DEC's operating systems. RMS transmits and receives DAP messages over logical links. If an RMS file access request includes a node name in the file specification, RMS maps the access request into equivalent DAP messages. These DAP messages are sent to a remote FAL to complete the request. To the user, remote file access is handled identically to local file access, except that a remote node name and possibly access control information is necessary for remote file access.
- *Network File Access Routines* (NFARs). NFARs are a set of FORTRAN-callable subroutines. NFARs become a part of the user process; they cooperate with FAL, using DAP, to access remote files for user applications.
- *VAX/VMS Command Language Interpreter.* VMS commands pertaining to file access and manipulation interface with RMS to provide network-wide file access; hence, no separate NFT utility is required in VAX/VMS.
- *Network Management Modules.* Network Management modules use DAP services to obtain remote files for down-line loading other remote nodes and to transfer up-line dumps for storage.

THOUGHTS ON SNA, DECnet, AND OSI

It is evident that IBM and DEC have taken quite different approaches to the design of the application layer. It is also evident that SNA and DECnet are quite different from most of the entities in the OSI model.

Perhaps one of the most significant trends in the computer/communications industry today is the movement of vendors (such as IBM and DEC) to the OSI standards—all seven layers. Without question, this trend is good news for the end user.

In addition to the X.400 MHS recommendations, most vendors are developing (or planning to develop) products based on the standards discussed in the remaining part of this chapter. So, without further fanfare, let us take a look at them. (Be mindful that our examination is an overview of these standards.)

THE VIRTUAL TERMINAL (VT)

Even though you may not realize it, you probably use at least a rudimentary form of the virtual terminal (VT) concept in your home or office. The idea is to define the "behavior" of the terminal from the standpoint of its operating characteristics and network sessions. Ideally, the definition procedure is flexible enough to allow the terminal user to (a) readily change the behavior of the terminal and (b) to provide a means for a terminal to access a variety of computers and other terminals. The latter feature is especially difficult to provide, because most vendors' terminals use different upper-level protocols.

In this section, we examine two approaches for obtaining VT services:

- *Parameter model*: Use of codes and parameters to describe the terminal.
- *Object model*: Use of abstract objects to model the terminal characteristics and functions.

The parameter model is explained with the CCITT X.3, X.28, and X.29 protocols. The object model is explained with ISO 9040, ISO 9041, and the TELNET protocol from the U.S. Department of Defense (DOD).

The Parameter Model

As X.25 networks came into existence in the 1970s, it was recognized that the majority of terminals in operation were (and are) asynchronous devices. Obviously, an interface was needed to connect these terminals into packet networks. Consequently, standards were developed to provide protocol conversion and packet assembly-disassembly (PAD) functions for the asynchronous terminal. After the initial 1976 draft of the X.25 standard, the standards committees followed up in 1977 with recommendations for three specifications to support X.25 with asynchronous terminal interfaces: X.3, X.28, and X.29 (see Figure 18-15).

The PAD is actually a parameter-driven virtual terminal (VT). It provides protocol conversion for a user device (DTE) to a public or private network, and a complementary protocol conversion at the receiving end of the network. In so doing, it allows different types of terminals to communicate with each other. The goal is to provide a transparent service to user terminals through the network. While X.3 and its companion standards X.28

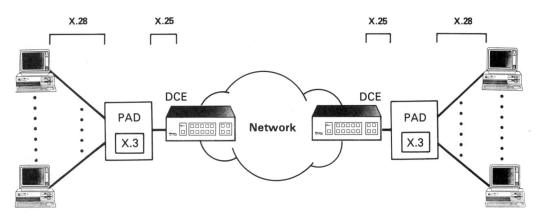

(a) Terminal-to-Terminal Communications

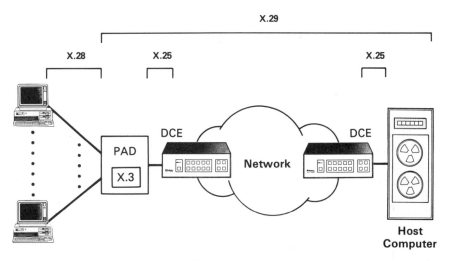

(b) Terminal-to-Host Communications

Note: DCE (Data Circuit-Terminating Equipment) is a Packet Exchange in X.25.

FIGURE 18-15. Use of X.3, X.28, and X.29 for Virtual Terminal Support

and X.29 address only asynchronous devices (which constitute many of the devices in operation today), many vendors offer other PAD services to support link-level protocols such as BSC and SDLC, and higher-layer functions as well.

X.3. The X.3 standard stipulates a set of 22 parameters the PAD uses to identify and control each terminal communicating with it. When a connection to a PAD from the DTE is established, the PAD parameters are used to determine how the PAD communicates with the user DTE. The parameters define certain attributes of the user terminal as well as several services that are provided by the PAD. The user also has options of altering the parameters after the logon is complete to the PAD device. Each of the 22 parameters consists of a reference number and parameter values. These parameters and references are explained in general terms in Table 18-3.

X.28. This recommendation defines the procedures to control the data flow between the user terminal and the PAD. Upon receipt of an initial transmission from the user DTE, the PAD establishes a connection and provides services according to the parameters in the X.3 table and the X.28 commands. The user terminal evokes X.28 commands to the PAD, which then requests an X.25 virtual call to a remote DTE. The PAD is responsible for transmitting the appropriate X.25 call request packet. Messages sent from the terminal to the PAD are called Command Signals and messages sent from the PAD to the terminal are called Service Signals. X.28 supports the procedures for:

> The establishment of the path
> The initialization of service
> The exchange of data
> The exchange of control information

X.28 specifies two profiles that can be defined for providing service to the user DTE. The transparent profile means that the servicing PAD is transparent to both DTEs: the DTEs perceive that they have a direct virtual connection to each other. In this situation, the remote DTE is responsible for some PAD functions such as error checking. The simple profile makes use of the fully defined X.3 standard and the parameter functions to satisfy the user DTE requests. The 1988 version of X.3 provides a user with the flexibility to tailor additional characteristics for a particular terminal.

X.29. This recommendation provides for the PAD and a remote DTE or PAD to exchange control information on an X.25 call. X.29 is quite useful in allowing the host computer (DTE) to change the PAD parameters of terminals connected to it. X.29 allows the exchange of information to occur at any time, either at a data transfer phase or any other phase of the virtual call.

TABLE 18-3. X.3 Pad Parameters

X.3 Parameter Reference Number	Description
1 Pad recall	Escape from data transfer mode to command mode in order to send PAD commands.
2 Echo	Controls the echo of characters sent by the terminal.
3 Data forwarding	Defines the characters to be interpreted by the PAD as a signal to forward data. Indication to complete assembly and forward a complete package.
4 Idle timer delay	Selects a time interval between successive characters of terminal activity as a signal to forward data.
5 Ancillary device control	Allows the PAD to control the flow of terminal data using XON/OFF characters.
6 Control of PAD service signals	Allows the terminal to receive PAD messages.
7 Operation of the PAD on receipt of breaking signal from DTE	Defines PAD action when a break signal is received from the terminal.
8 Discard output	Controls the discarding of data pending output to a terminal.
9 Padding after carriage	Controls PAD insertion of padding characters after a carriage return is sent to the terminal.
10 Line folding	Specifies whether the PAD should fold the output line to the terminal. Predetermined number of characters per line.
11 Binary speed of DTE	Indicates the speed of the terminal. Cannot be changed by DTE.
12 Flow control of the PAD	Allows the terminal to flow control data being transmitted by the PAD.
13 Linefeed insertion	Controls PAD insertion of linefeed after a carriage return is sent to the terminal.
14 Linefeed padding	Controls PAD insertion of padding characters after a linefeed is sent to the terminal.
15 Editing	Controls whether editing by PAD is available during data transfer mode (parameters 16, 17, and 18).
16 Character delete	Selects character used to signal character delete.
17 Line delete	Selects character used to signal line delete.
18 Line display	Selects character used to signal line display.
19 Editing PAD service signals	Controls the format of the editing PAD service signals.
20 Echo mask	Selects the characters which are not echoed to the terminal when echo (Parameter 2) is enabled.
21 Parity treatment	Controls the checking and generation of parity on characters from/to the terminal.
22 Page wait	Specifies the number of lines to be displayed at one time.

As introduced in Chapter 13, the X.25 Q bit controls certain functions of X.29. An X.25 packet contains user data fields and may also contain the Q bit. The Q bit (or data qualified bit) is contained in the header of the data packet. It is used by the remote DTE to distinguish between a packet containing user information (Q=0), or one containing PAD information (Q=1).

The X.29 protocol can be used to change a terminal's profile. In many instances, the terminal user (an accountant, a programmer, etc.) has no idea about the network and its many PAD parameters. The X.29 feature gives a host computer the capability to reconfigure certain characteristics of the devices that communicate with it through a PAD. Of course, how the PAD facilities are used is largely up to the creativity and imagination of the network managers and designers.

Figure 18-15 shows possible configurations for the use of a PAD in a network. Box 18-3 provides the reader with an example of how the X.3, X.28, and X.29 specifications could be used to provide a virtual terminal service.

The Object Model

The basic idea of an object model virtual terminal is as follows. Each terminal is described by (a) a data structure (or object) and (b) a profile. A profile may be part of the data structure. A profile is a set of parameters which define the characteristics of the terminal. The data structure not only describes the terminal's profile, but defines the specific terminal operation. The object model differs from the parameter model in that the object model terminal is considered to be much more intelligent, perhaps able to assume different profiles.

Figure 18-16 illustrates the use of the VT protocol and the data structures.

We assume in Figure 18-16 that an application program sends data to the terminal. The applications process provides a set of abstract instructions that are mapped by the VT protocol to device-specific commands.

The data structure copy of the application process is updated and a message is sent to the terminal. Its copy of the data structure is updated in the same manner and the terminal display is modified. Then, the terminal's data structure is updated to reflect the display change, and a message is sent back to the host, where the data structure is updated. The VT protocol ensures that the data structures are consistent after every change. In this manner, both devices are aware of the current state of the display. Figure 18-17 depicts a possible data structure for a VT protocol [TANE81].

The data structure in Figure 18-17 contains the following entries: The text contains the information displayed. The variables' xposition and yposition define the horizontal and vertical positions on the display. The size field entry describes how many positions are in the text field.

The rendition attribute models the actual characteristics of the display, such as screen color, the light intensity, etc. Each field in the text could be coded with different renditions.

BOX 18-3. Operations of the PAD

	ACTIONS OF	
Terminal	*PAD*	*Host*
Dial and answer: terminal/modem connect to PAD Port		
	PAD receives carrier, synchronizes port and returns carrier	
Terminal operator keys in predefined characters (e.g., carriage return [cr])		
	PAD analyzes characters to determine terminal's line speed, character set, and parity characteristics	
	PAD sends prompt to terminal	
Terminal operator keys in identification		
	Identification used to load X.3 table or:	
	Identification forwarded to host	
		Identification used to determine appropriate application to execute the proper X.3 profile
		X.29 control placed into X.25 packet and forwarded to PAD
	X.29 used to configure PAD to the specific terminal session (X.3 changed)	
	Service signals sent to terminal	
Command signals sent to PAD (control and data)	Creates packet for network use	Sends/Receives packets to/from network

The adjustment parameter defines the positioning of the text within the field. The next line of parameters describes the type of information accepted by the terminal.

The next line defines whether the field cannot be filled in (protected), part of the field must be filled in (Entry Required), or all the field must be filled in (Must Fill).

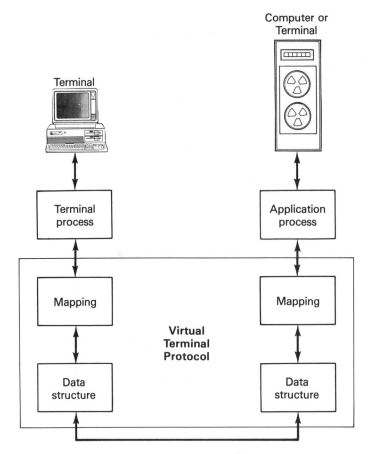

FIGURE 18-16. Virtual Terminal (VT) Concept

```
type field = record
        text: array [0 .. MaxText] of char;        {contents of the field}
        xposition: 0 .. MaxX;                       {horizontal position on screen}
        yposition: 0 .. MaxY;                       {vertical position on screen}
        size: 0 .. MaxSize;                         {size of the field}
        rendition: 0 .. MaxRendition;               {color, intensity, etc.}
        adjustment: (left, right);                  {positioning of text within field}
        lcletters, ucletters, numbers, space, special: boolean:    {allowed input}
        protected, EntryRequired, MustFill: boolean
end;
var datastruct: record
        display: array [0 .. MaxField] of field;    {collection of fields}
        cursor: record x: 0 .. MaxText; y: 0 .. MaxField end; {cursor position}
        TerminalType: (scroll, page, form);
        FlowMode: (alternating, FreeRunning);       {half or full duplex}
        turn: (mine, his);                          {who goes next (if half duplex)}
        state: (uninitialized, normal, interrupted)
end;
```

FIGURE 18-17. A Possible Data Structure [TANE81]

The data structure part represents the current contents of the display, the types of terminal (scroll, page, form), the type of communication (half or full duplex), and the state of the conversation.

ISO 9040 and ISO 9041. These two specifications describe a basic class virtual terminal service and protocol respectively. They are written for simple interactive applications alternating access (synchronous mode [S-mode]) or simultaneous access (asynchronous mode [A-Mode]). The ISO VT is considered to be a SASE (specific applications service element), which was introduced at the beginning of this chapter.

Virtual terminal users communicate with each other through a conceptual communication area (CCA) [FOLT87]. The CCA is shared by the VT users and information is exchanged by either VT user updating its contents and through the service provider, and making it available to the other VT user. This concept is quite similar to the data structure illustrated in Figure 18-16.

The ISO VT concept expands the ideas in Figure 18-16 with control objects and device objects (see Figure 18-18). The control object is used to manage the VT functions. The device object allows a user to specify certain physical device characteristics. The control and device objects collectively comprise the profile of a virtual terminal environment (VTE). The third object-type is called a display object, which describes the actual VT display images.

The display object is a one-, two-, or three-dimensional array of elements. The dimensions are called X, Y, and Z, and each is capable of handling one "character-box" graphic element. This element (a) is empty: nothing is assigned to it; (b) contains a primary attribute: a value that selects a specific graphic element; or (c) contains a secondary attribute: a value which selects attributes for the display object, such as color, intensity, blinking, font, etc.

Each array element is addressed by a display pointer and each element is completely independent of other elements.

Figure 18-18 depicts an ISO VT A-node operation. Input and output display objects are modeled independently of each other and are called conceptual data store (CDS). However, multiple device objects can exist for each display object and multiple control objects may exist for each device object. The control objects are called control, signalling, and status store (CSS).

The data structure definition (DSD) describes the virtual terminal objects. It stores the ongoing VT parameters for the VT session for all the objects. Finally, the access control store (ACS) contains the ongoing assignment of the VT's access rights. An access right is the ability to perform an operation (for example, a write operation).

As suggested in Figure 18-18, the display objects and control objects are mapped through the device objects to the actual VT device session.

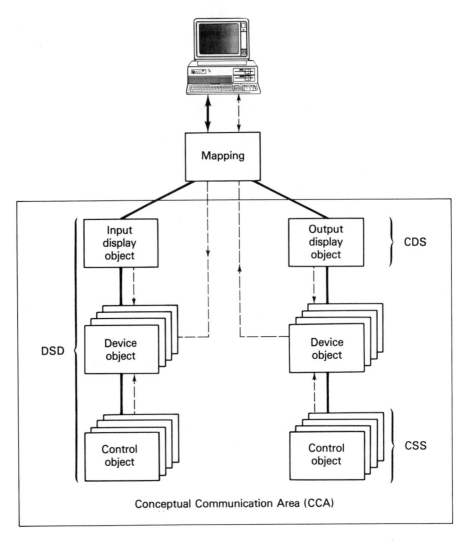

Note: Dashed Lines Show Mapping Relationships and Solid Lines Show Logical Relationships.

FIGURE 18-18. Virtual Terminal, A Mode

The VT users' session is governed by the VTE, which is controlled by the VT profiles. These profiles can be negotiated and changed, or a default profile may be used to describe the VTE. The actual virtual terminal communications process is managed through a number of VT facilities. They are summarized in Box 18-4. Most of these facilities functions can be understood by reviewing the material in Box 18-4, but a few explanatory notes are in order regarding the negotiation and access rights management facilities.

The negotiation facility permits two types of negotiation. The first type is called switch profile negotiation. It allows only one interaction of the

Name of Facility	Function of Facility
Establishment	Establishes a VT session, a VTE, and an association with an application entity (AE)
Termination	Terminates a VT association as (a) orderly and non-destructive; and (b) immediate and potentially destructive
Negotiation	Allows the selection, modification, and changing of a VTE
Data Transfer	Transfers updates to a display or control object
Delivery Control	Allows user to manage the updates (acknowledgment, synchronization)
Access Right Management	Allows VT users to control access rights

negotiation. The second type is multiple interaction negotiation, which allows a series of iterations in negotiating the VTE. Three categories of VTE negotiation are available:

- *VT-A (Kernal Subset)*: VT Basic Class services with initial profile only
- *VT-B (Switch Profile Negotiation Subset)*: VT-A plus switch profile negotiation
- *VT-B (Full Negotiation Subset)*: VT-B plus multiple interaction negotiation

As discussed earlier, an access right is the permission to perform some kind of operation. The VT Basic Class uses one access right called the WAVAR (Write Access Variable). It is reassigned between the users during the session. The access rights may also be established by a pair of access rights that are not reassigned during the session. The WACI (Write Access Connection Initiation) is always owned by the initiating VT user and the WACA (Write Access Connection Acceptor) is always owned by the user that receives the request for a VT association. S-mode uses WAVAR and A-mode uses WACI and WACA.

TELNET

TELNET was developed as part of ARPANET for use with asynchronous scroll-mode terminals. The TELNET protocol is two-way alternate (half duplex) with the use of ASCII/IA5 control characters.

A TELNET communications process may entail a negotiated option phase, provided by the following commands:

WILL X

- Users offer to begin performing option X.
- Do X or DONT X returned as positive or negative acknowledgments respectively.

DO X

- Also used to request other user to begin performing option X.
- WILL X and WONT X returned as positive or negative acknowledgments respectively.

TELNET has several predefined options which are called registered options. Each option is identified with a code. These options are similar to the functions of the X.3 PAD parameters (Table 18-3). They are summarized in Table 18-4.

TELEMATICS (TELETEXT AND VIDEOTEX)

The number of terminal- and personal-computer-based services has been increasing dramatically throughout the world. These services have a number of names attached to them: Teletext, Videotex, Teletex, public data banks, and information services.

The term telematics is used to describe two broad ranges of terminal-based service, Teletext and Videotex. Videotex describes the provision for two-way information services between a user's device and an information source. The term Teletext describes one-way transmission services. The Teletext technology uses a conventional TV broadcasting system to allow the one-way cycling of data into the user terminal. Typically, a page remains on the screen until a replacement page is automatically cycled or is requested by the user. In contrast, Videotex is a data communications system—a terminal keyboard is used to interact with a remotely located data base. Conventional components, such as modems and telephone networks, are used to provide the full two-way capability.

Telematics technology is fairly widespread throughout the industrialized world. The United States has been slower to embrace telematics due to the lack of a national organization such as a PTT to foster the use of the technology.

The basic idea of Videotex/Teletext is to provide a system with widespread dissemination capabilities for both graphic and text information. The information is disseminated by electronic means for display on low-cost terminals. The recipient of the information has selective control of the display by using easily understood procedures.

TABLE 18-4. TELNET Registered Options

Number	Function
0	Binary transmission
1	Echo
2	Reconnection
3	Suppress go ahead
4	Approximate message size
5	Status
6	Timing mark
7	Remote-controlled transmission and echoing
8	Output line width
9	Output page size
10	Output carriage-return disposition
11	Output horizontal tabstops
12	Output horizontal tab disposition
13	Output formfeed disposition
14	Output vertical tab stops
15	Output vertical tab disposition
16	Output line feed disposition
17	Extended ASCII
255	Extended options list

Telematics provides services which many of us may take for granted today. For example, the Teletext and Videotex uses involve these major applications:

News, weather, and sports

Shopping by terminal (teleshopping)

Advertising through Teletext broadcasts

Banking transactions through the use of a telephone or terminal

Electronic newspapers available in some cable TV areas

Financial information, such as stock market reports

Games and entertainment

Program captioning

Personal computer support

Electronic directories, such as shopping lists or mailing lists

Electronic mail

Telemetry

FILE TRANSFER, ACCESS, AND MANAGEMENT (FTAM)

Perhaps one of the greatest challenges to a communications or data processing organization is file management (usually called data management or data administration). While this fascinating subject is beyond the scope of this book, the transfer of files between two applications and/or data systems is certainly a communications process. Consequently, this section of the book examines the subject from the standpoint of file transfer, with emphasis on the ISO FTAM specifications. The subject is vast and complex, and references to more thorough studies are provided at the end of this chapter.

The FTAM Documents

The ISO FTAM specification is divided into four parts:

8571/1 Introduction to the FTAM concepts; discusses file transfer problems.
8571/2 Explains the terms, concepts, and vocabulary used in FTAM (file name, contents, access codes).
8571/3 Describes interface required between the two entities that participate in the file transfer process.
8571/4 Defines the specific rules for the activities in part 3.

The Virtual Filestore Concept

Although data usage often varies among different applications, a common model for all data files and data bases can provide a common foundation for file transfer, access, and management among diverse applications. This model is called the *virtual filestore*. Virtual filestore contains the file's characteristics, structure, and attributes. Its objective is to reduce the amount of detail needed to communicate with a file located in a remote part of the network.

The basic idea of virtual filestore is to provide a mapping of file definitions to/from actual files, which are called real filestores (see Figure 18-19). The filestore definitions form a schema (or set) of the file; subset descriptions of files form subschemas (or subsets). The concepts of schemas and subschemas are very well known and understood in the data base management industry. (The terms "sets" and "subsets" are used with virtual filestore.) The set provides a map of the data, shows the names of the attributes, and establishes relationships of data elements. It provides the overall view of the data base. It says nothing about the physical structure of the file or the physical access method. The subset is the specific user view of the data base, that is, the user subset of the set.

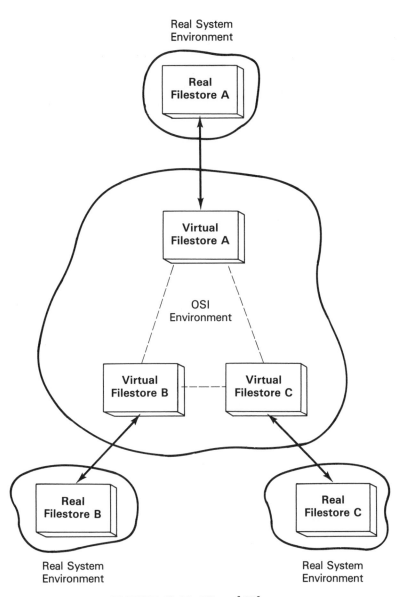

FIGURE 18-19. Virtual Filestore

Typically, organizations have hundreds of subsets and individual users often have multiple subsets to satisfy different kinds of retrieval and update requirements. This presents a challenging problem for the data base and network designers: They must provide for a physical design that satisfies all user "views" at all nodes in the network. The emerging ISO standards provide methods to join different subsets between systems at the presentation layer and additional procedures to manage file service dialogue at the session layer.

File Access Data Units (FADUs)

In virtual filestore, the conventional notion of a "data record" is called a data unit (DU). The DUs are related to each other through a hierarchical structure called file access data units (FADU). Operations on a file are performed in an FADU (see Figure 18-20). The DU is considered to be the smallest amount that can be transferred.

FTAM is also organized around the concept of the attribute, which describes the properties of a file. Presently, four groups of attributes are defined:

Kernel group:	Properties common to all files.
Storage group:	Properties of files that are stored.
Security group:	Properties for access control.
Private group:	Properties beyond FTAM scope.

The kernel group consists of the file name, a description of the file structure (sequential, hierarchical), access restrictions (deletion, reads, etc.),

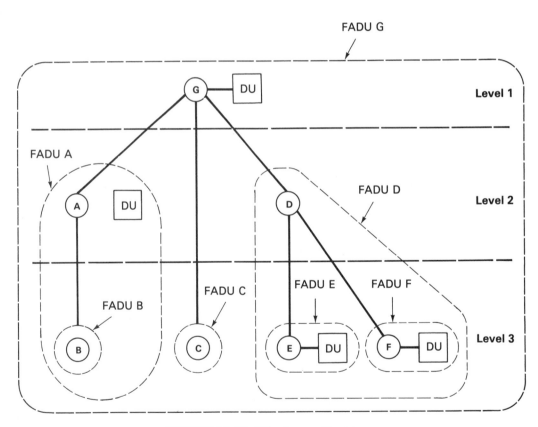

FIGURE 18-20. File Access Structure

location of the file user, and the identification of the application entities involved in the FTAM communications process.

The storage group describes several properties of a file. The properties are either (a) information about the ongoing characteristics of the file, or (b) information about the latest operations on the file. The following properties are included in the storage group:

- Date and time of last: (a) read; (b) change; (c) attribute change.
- Identification of: (a) creator; (b) last reader; (c) last modifier; (d) last attribute modifier.
- File size and availability.
- Identification of party to be charged for file storage and file access activities.
- Description of any locks on the file.
- Identification of initiating FTAM user.

The security group includes attributes on access permission criteria, encryption procedures, and legal qualifications (trademarks, copyrights, etc.).

The private group is not defined by the FTAM standard. It is used for files beyond the virtual filestore attributes.

FTAM Regimes

FTAM is organized around the concepts of regimes. The file service regimes define how FTAM primitives are used for the file activity. Regimes provide the protocol for file selection, file opens/closes, data transfer, and recovery operations. Figure 18-21 shows the relationships of the regimes and primitives. (The primitives are explained shortly.) Four types of file service regimes are defined:

- *Application association regime:* exists during the lifetime of application association of two file service users
- *File selection regime:* exists during the time in which a particular file is associated with the application association
- *File open regime:* exists during a particular set of presentation contexts, concurrency controls, and commitment controls in operation for data transfer (these concepts are explained shortly)
- *Data transfer regime:* exists when a particular access context and direction of transfer are in force

Virtual Filestore Actions. Virtual filestore defines two types of "actions" on files. The first encompasses actions to the contents of a file such as locating and reaching a file. This type also describes the protocol for (a)

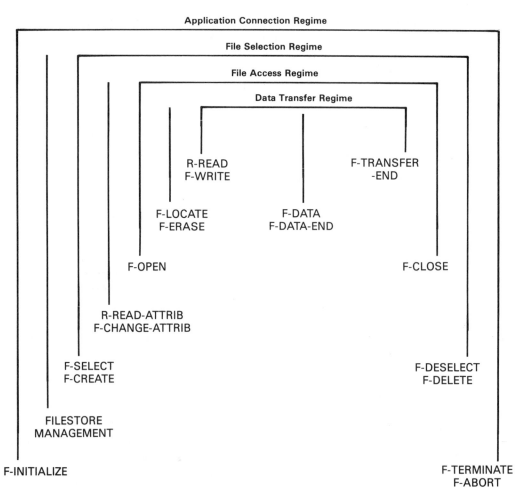

FIGURE 18-21. FTAM Regime [ISO8571]

inserting, (b) replacing, (c) extending, and (d) erasing a FADU within virtual filestores.

The second type defines actions on a complete file. For example, procedures describe the creation of a file, as well as its deletion. In addition, the read, open, close, and select attributes of the file are also defined within this action type.

File Service Primitives. FTAM services are managed with primitives. The ISO 8571 FTAM primitives invoke specific file services. These primitives and their associated parameters are summarized in Table 18-5. The functions of the parameters are described in more detail.in Appendix 18B.

TABLE 18-5. File Service Primitives

Primitive	Parameters
F-INITIALIZE	Diagnostic, Called address, Calling address, Responding address, Service type, Service class, Functional units, Attribute groups, Rollback availability, Communications QOS, Presentation context, Identity of initiator, Current account, Filestore password, Checkpoint window
F-TERMINATE	Charging
F-U-ABORT	Diagnostic
F-P-ABORT	Diagnostic
F-SELECT	Diagnostic, Filename, Attributes, Access control, Access passwords, Concur, Current access structure type, Current account
F-DESELECT	Diagnostic, Charging
F-CREATE	Diagnostic, Filename, Attributes, Access control, Access passwords, Concurrency control, Commitment control, Override, Current account, Delete password, Charging
F-READ-ATTRIB	Diagnostic, Attribute names, Attributes
F-CHANGE-ATTRIB	Diagnostic, Attributes
F-OPEN	Diagnostic, Processing mode, Presentation context name, Concurrency control, Commitment control, Activity identifier, Recovery mode
F-CLOSE	Diagnostic, Commitment control
F-BEGIN-GROUP	Threshold
F-END-GROUP	—
F-RECOVER	Diagnostic, Activity identifier, Bulk transfer number, Access control, Access passwords, Recovery point
F-LOCATE	Diagnostic, FADU identity, Concurrency control
F-ERASE	Diagnostic, FADU identity, Concurrency control

COMMITMENT, CONCURRENCY, AND RECOVERY (CCR)

The CCR specifications describe the actions for managing data base activity across multiple sites (data transfer, access, and update). Such a system must provide for consistent states for all data operating in virtual filestore. A consistent state means that all data bases are accurate and correct, and any replicated copies contain the same values in the data fields.

CCR assumes an upper-level protocol is available to assume the role of a master site (superior) to the other sites (subordinates). It further assumes that, even though the systems may be distributed, a "centralized" superior is controlling the data base activity.

An example of the complexities and problems of file transfer, access, and update is provided in Figure 18-22. Users A and B simultaneously access

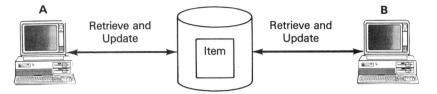

FIGURE 18-22. File Access Programs

and update an item in the data base. In the absence of control mechanisms, the data base reflects only the one update; the other update is lost. This happens when both users retrieve the data item, change it (add or subtract from the value), and write their revised value back into the data base.

Lockouts and the Deadly Embrace. The most common solution to this problem is preventing sites A and B from simultaneous executions on the same data. Through the use of lockouts, for example, site B would not be allowed to execute until site A had completed its transaction.

Lockouts work reasonably well with a centralized data base. However, in a distributed environment, the sites may possibly lock each other out and prevent either transaction from completing its task. Mutual lockout, often called deadly embrace, is shown in Figure 18-23. Users A and B wish to update base items Y and Z, respectively; consequently, user A locks data Y from user B and user B locks data Z from user A. To complete their transactions, both users need data from the other locked data bases. Hence, neither can execute further and the two sites are locked in a deadly embrace. Clearly, the deadly embrace is an unacceptable situation and the system must be able to detect, analyze, and resolve the problem. We address this problem shortly.

Failure and Recovery. The efforts to achieve resiliency in a distributed system are quite different than in a conventional centralized environment. The centralized approach assumes the availability of much information about a problem or failure. The operating system can suspend the execution of the problem program and store and query registers and control blocks, during which the problem component does not change.

In a distributed system, the time delay in gathering data for analysis may be significant; in some cases, the data may be outdated upon receipt by the component tasked with the analysis and resolution. The problem may not be suspended as in a centralized system, since some distributed systems have horizontal topologies and autonomous or near-autonomous components.

Let us assume an update was executed successfully at site A, but site B experienced problems due to a hardware or software failure. The update must be reversed in the site A copy. All items must be restored, transactions eventually reapplied, backup tapes made, and log files restored to the

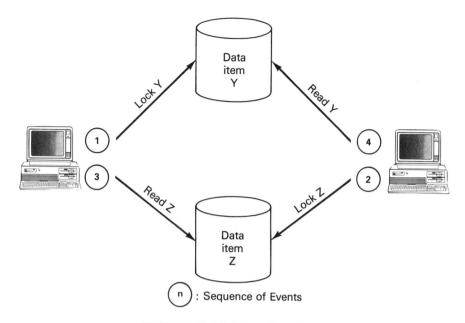

FIGURE 18-23. Mutual Lockout

preupdate image. In the meantime, other transactions must be examined to determine if they were dependent on the suspended transaction. Of course, one has the option of maintaining the site A update, continuing subsequent updates, and bringing the site B data up to date at a later time. Nonetheless, the affected nodes cannot independently make these decisions; all must be aware of each other if the data bases are to be properly synchronized.

A key question must be answered: Does the organization need timely data at the expense of consistency? Stated another way, must all copies be concurrent with each other? Practically speaking, certain classes of data (such as historical data) may be allowed to exhibit weak consistency: data are not kept concurrent. On the other hand, some classes of data (real-time data, for example) may need strong consistency. The designers must examine the user requirements very carefully. The benefits of strong consistency must be weighed against the increased costs of additional complexity.

The Two-Phase Commitment

The simple lockouts just described can be enhanced considerably by a two-phase commitment. We describe the idea with an example from [BERN81], and then examine the ISO Commitment, Concurrency, and Recovery (CCR) protocol.

    System Architecture. The network data base system is organized around the transaction manager or module (TM) and the data manager or module (DM). Each site has a computer running the TM and DM software (see Figure 18-24). The TM supervises transactions and all network action to satisfy the user's transaction request. The DM manages the data bases and the DBMS. The architecture functions through four operations at the transaction–TM interface:

1. *BEGIN:* TM sets up workspace for the user transaction (T). It provides temporary buffers for data moving into and out of the data bases.
2. *READ(X):* TM looks for a copy of data X in T's workspace. It returns it to T. If the data are not in the workspace, it issues a dm-read(x) command to one of the network DMs, which accesses the data and returns them to T's workspace.
3. *WRITE(X):* TM looks for a copy of X in T's workspace. If found, it updates the "old" copy with the current value of X. If the data are not in the work space, a copy of the current value is placed into it.

   Notice that no changes have yet been made to the data bases. That is, no dm-write(x) commands have been issued by the TM to the DMs. The system uses a two-phase commit procedure to assure (a) restart/recovery integrity, (b) adherence to atomic commitment, and (c) resiliency across nodes.

   • Restart/recovery: The DBMS can restart a transaction at any time before a dm-write(x) is executed.

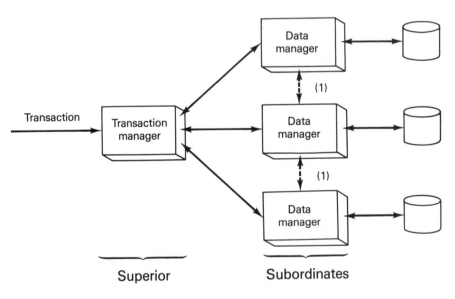

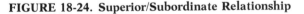

Superior   Subordinates

(1) Dialogues for Recovery from Transaction Manager Failure.

FIGURE 18-24. Superior/Subordinate Relationship

- Atomic commitment: Two-phase commit keeps all nodes' data base actions related to one transaction isolated from each other.
- Resiliency: Failure of a component during a Write does not lock up or bring down other components in the network.

4. *END:* For the first phase of the two-phase commit, TM issues a preWrite(x) to each DM in the network. The DM copies X from T's workspace onto some form of secure storage. At this point, the DM must have isolated the affected data and be committed to the action and a rollback, if necessary. After all DMs have executed the preWrite, the second phase of the commit begins by the TM issuing a dm-write(x) to the DMs. The DM then updates the data base from T's secure storage, and informs the TM of the success of the operation.

The prewrite commands specify all DMs that are involved in the two-phase commitment. Consequently, if a TM fails during the second phase, the DMs time-out, and check with other DMs to determine if a dm-write(x) had been received. If so, all other DMs use it as if it were issued by the TM. In the event of a DBMS failure during the Write, secure storage is used to recover data. If a DM operation fails, the TM so informs the DMs, which initiate a rollback and recovery.

The Commitment, Concurrency, and Recovery (CCR) specifications (ISO 8649, ISO 8650) operate in a manner similar to the previous example. CCR also uses a two-phase commitment operation:

Phase 1:   Superior informs subordinate of actions and subordinate agrees to perform the actions or it refuses.
Phase 2:   Superior orders the commitment or releases the resources to their beginning state.

CCR uses several primitives to invoke, process, and terminate an atomic action. These primitives are explained in Box 18-5. Please note the use of the presentation layer primitives. A normal sequence of the primitives is shown in Figure 18-25. In contrast, Figure 18-26 illustrates a situation in which the subordinate refuses to undertake the atomic action.

JOB TRANSFER AND MANIPULATION (JTM)

In a typical data processing environment, users and programmers submit "jobs" to the computer. These jobs are tasks for the computer to perform such as data retrieval, file updates, etc. In the past, most jobs were submitted by coding punched cards with job control language (JCL). Today, many jobs are submitted through a terminal by the execution of JCL statements previously stored on disk. The statements (generally called a catalogued procedure) are used to invoke the desired tasks. (A few years ago, a cartoon in a trade journal showed a JCL book stored in the mystery section of a library. Those readers who have coded JCL will appreciate this tidbit.)

BOX 18-5. CCR Primitives

Primitive Name	Function
C-BEGIN	Issued by initiator to begin atomic action. Not confirmed, but maps into a P-SYNC-MAJOR primitive.
C-READY	Responder issues when ready to commit to the action, *and* to roll back, if necessary. Maps to a P-TYPED-DATA. Confirm not required.
C-COMMIT	Issued by initiator to order the commitment. Maps to a P-SYNC-MAJOR. Confirm required.
C-PREPARE	Issued by initiator (optional) and issued by superior to determine if subordinate is prepared to commit. Maps to P-TYPED-DATA. Confirm not required.
C-REFUSE	Issued by responder up to a C-READY. It is a refusal to commit and maps to a P-RESYNCHRONIZE (ABANDON). Confirm not required.
C-ROLLBACK	Issued by initiator to revert back and restore the initial state before the commit. Maps to P-RESYNCHRONIZE (ABANDON). Confirm required.
C-RESTART	Issued by either initiator or responder to initiate recovery procedures. Maps to P-RESYNCHRONIZE (RESTART). Confirm required.

JCL directs the actions of the computer by identifying the programs and data files that are to participate in the "job." The JCL also directs the disposition of the programs, files, and job output, such as reports and listings.

The purpose of Job Transfer and Manipulation (ISO 8831) is to allow jobs submitted on any open system to run on any other open systems. It must be emphasized that the JTM does not address the standardization of job control languages. Indeed, it requires the user to specify the system where work is to be done. Furthermore, the user must know about the JCL, facilities, and functions where the work is to be done. So, the idea of JTM is (a) to specify the jobs to be executed on a system; (b) to control the movement of job-related data between systems; and (c) to monitor and manage the progress of the activity. Since JTM has not been adapted to a significant extent, we mention it only to provide continuity to this chapter.

The JTM layer architecture is depicted in Figure 18-27. Service primitives are used to invoke JTM procedures between the end users and the presentation layer. JTM uses the presentation services, the CASE kernal and the Commitment, Concurrency, and Recovery (CCR) protocol.

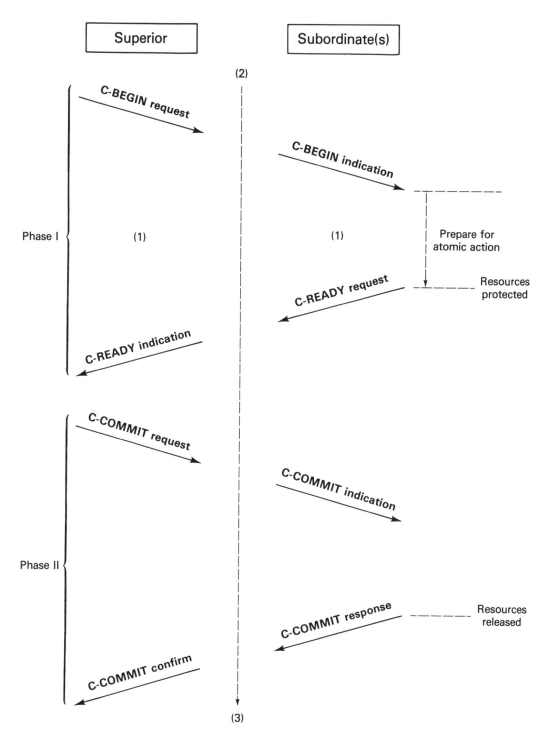

Note (1): Other Exchanges May be Made for Further Coordination.
Notes (2)-(3): Superior Responsible for Restart or Rollback.

FIGURE 18-25. Normal Commitment Procedure

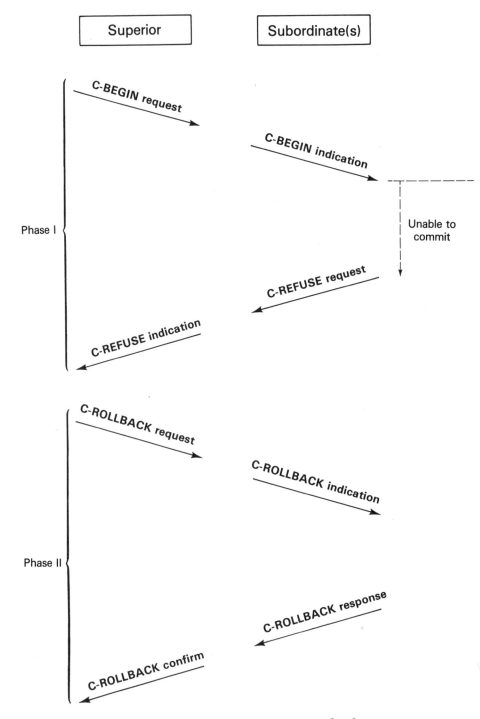

FIGURE 18-26. Atomic Action Refusal

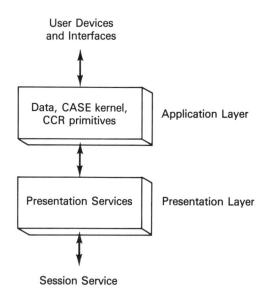

FIGURE 18-27. Job Transfer and Manipulation (JTM) Architecture

SUGGESTED READINGS

Since many application-level protocols are based on the CCITT and ISO standards, the reader should obtain these specifications for detailed information. The ISO documents pertaining to this subject are:

8571/3   Information Processing Systems—Open Systems Interconnection—File Transfer, Access, and Management. Part 3: File Service Definition.

8571/4   Information Processing Systems—Open Systems Interconnection—File Transfer, Access, and Management. Part 4: File Protocol Specification.

7498   Information Processing Systems—Open Systems Interconnection—Basic Reference Model.

8831   Information Processing Systems—Open Systems Interconnection—Job Transfer and Manipulation Concepts and Services.

8832   Information Processing System—Open Systems Interconnection—Specification of the Basic Class Protocol for Job Transfer and Manipulation.

8509   Information Processing Systems—Open Systems Interconnection—Service Conventions.

8822   Information Processing Systems—Open Systems Interconnection—The Presentation Service Definition.

8824   Information Processing Systems—Open Systems Interconnection—Abstract Syntax Notation One (ASN.1).

8825   Information Processing Systems—Open Systems Interconnection—Basic Encoding Rules for Abstract Syntax Notation One (ASN.1).

8326   Information Processing Systems—Open Systems Interconnection—The Basic Connection-Oriented Session Service Definition.

8649/3   Information Processing Systems—Open Systems Interconnection—Definition of Common Application Service Elements. Part 3: Commitment, Concurrency, and Recovery.

8650/3   Information Processing Systems—Open Systems Interconnection—Specification of Protocols for Common Application Service Elements. Part 3: Commitment, Concurrency, and Recovery.

APPENDIX 18A
THE MHS PRIMITIVES

The reader should analyze the MTL primitives (see Table 18A-1), understanding that their purpose is to establish a standard protocol for interactions between the user agent (UA) and the message transfer agent (MTA), regardless of the specific vendor architecture. Of course, we emphasize once again that this is the principal idea of the OSI model.

To initiate a session with a MTAE, a UAE issues a LOGON.Request primitive. This primitive contains the name of the O/R user that wishes access to the MTAE. It also contains a password for the UAE. The MTAE returns the LOGON.Confirmation primitive. It indicates if the logon request was successful. If successful, it also indicates the number of messages awaiting the UAE (if any) and their priorities. If the logon request fails, this primitive provides the reason for the rejection.

The MTL can also initiate a session (usually as a result of receiving messages from a remote UAE) by transferring a LOGON.Indication primitive to the local UAE. The primitive contains three parameters: (a) the name of the MTAE sending the primitive; (b) the number of messages awaiting delivery to the UAE; and (c) the password of the MTAE. The receiving UAE responds with the LOGON.Response primitive. It indicates if the logon is successful, and if not, the reason for its rejection (busy, faulty password, etc.).

The LOGOFF primitives are used to terminate a session between the UAE and the MTAE. The UAE issues the LOGOFF.Request and the MTAE returns the LOGOFF.Confirmation. They have no parameters associated with them.

The REGISTER.Request primitive is used by the UAE to change the values of its parameters that are maintained by the MTAE. The five parameters for this primitive convey the following information: (a) the types of messages the UAE can accept; (b) the length of the longest message the UAE

TABLE 18A-1. X.411 Message Transfer Layer Primitives

Issued by UAE	Issued by MTAE
LOGON.Request	LOGON.Configuration
LOGON.Response	LOGON.Indication
LOGOFF.Request	LOGOFF.Confirmation
REGISTER.Request	REGISTER.Confirmation
CONTROL.Request	CONTROL.Confirmation
CONTROL.Response	CONTROL.Indication
SUBMIT.Request*	SUBMIT.Confirmation
PROBE.Request*	PROBE.Confirmation
	DELIVER.Indication
	NOTIFY.Indication
CANCEL.Request	CANCEL.Confirmation
CHANGE-PASSWORD-Request	CHANGE-PASSWORD.Confirmation
	CHANGE-PASSWORD.Indication

* Also activates Message Dispatcher of Message Transfer Protocol.

can accept; (c) the default values for the parameters that can be established by the CONTROL.Request primitive; (d) the address of the UAE if it is needed; and (e) the O/R name of the UAE if it is needed. The MTAE returns the REGISTER.Confirmation primitive to indicate the success or failure of the REGISTER.Request.

The CONTROL.Request primitive is used by the UAE to change the restrictions currently in force with the MTL (what messages the MTL can send to the UAE). It only affects messages that are subject to the register parameters. This primitive is also used to direct the MTAE to hold messages for delivery. The CONTROL.Request primitive contains five parameters that perform the following functions: (a) the encoded information types (i.e., ASCII/IA5 code, TELEX code, etc.) that can be sent by the MTAE to the UAE; (b) the length of the longest message the UAE will accept; (c) the priority of the least urgent message the UAE will accept; (d) an indication if the UAE will accept messages; and (e) an indication if the UAE will accept notifications. The MTAE returns the CONTROL.Confirmation primitive to indicate if the CONTROL.Request was accepted or rejected. It also indicates if messages and notifications are waiting as a result of the CONTROL.Request.

The CONTROL.Indication is used by the MTAE to identify what messages it will accept from the UAE. It contains four parameters that perform the following functions: (a) the length of the longest message that the MTAE will accept; (b) the priority of the least urgent message that the MTAE will accept; (c) indication if the MTAE will accept a probe from the UAE (discussed later); (d) indication if the MTAE will accept messages from the UAE. The UAE, in turn, sends back the CONTROL.Response primitive. It has only one parameter to indicate if it is holding messages or probes due to the CONTROL.Indication primitive.

MHS uses three primitives to actually transfer messages between the UAEs and the MTAEs:

SUBMIT.Request

SUBMIT.Confirmation

DELIVER.Indication

The SUBMIT.Request is used by the UAE to send a message to the MTAE. The MTAE returns a SUBMIT.Confirmation primitive and forwards the message into the system. At the recipient node, the MTAE delivers the message to its UAE with the DELIVER.Indication. Several of the parameters of the SUBMIT.Request and DELIVER.Indication primitives are similar (see Table 18A-2). These parameters are listed side by side to give you an idea of which of the parameters are finally mapped to the remote user agent entity, but be aware some convey different information to the remote UAE.

The reader should study the entries and footnotes in Table 18A-2 to gain an understanding of the data and actual control signals passed between the UA and MT.

The SUBMIT.Confirmation primitive contains five parameters that perform the following functions: (a) an indication of the success of the SUBMIT.Request; (b) the time the MTAE accepted the request; (c) an identifier of the SUBMIT.Request; (d) the reason for the rejection (if it occurred); and (e) an identifier for the message contents that was generated by the UAE (UA-content-id).

The PROBE.Request primitive is used by the UAE to inquire if a SUBMIT.Request primitive (with the same parameters) would be a successful delivery. The primitive contains nine parameters that convey the following information: (a) recipient; (b) originator O/R names; (c) the content type; (d) the encoded information type(s) of the possible message to be transmitted; (e) indication of a conversion prohibition; (f) alternate recipient is allowed; (g) estimated length of probed message; (h) the UA-content-id; and (i) explicit-conversion. The MTAE sends back a PROBE.Confirmation primitive to inform the UAE of the success or failure of its probe.

It can be seen that the PROBE primitives do not convey the data but their estimated length (and other identifiers). This concept aids in decreasing the unsuccessful submission of the messages, which of course, is a wasteful exercise.

The NOTIFY.Indication primitive is used to inform the UAE whether or not a message was delivered. The primitive contains eleven parameters that convey the following information: (a) indication of delivery or non-delivery; (b) identification of the primitive that evoked this primitive; (c) identification of the original recipients related to the notification; (d) reason for non-delivery (if delivery was not performed); (e) time of delivery; (f) type of converted information type(s) (if conversion occurred); (g) O/R name of original recipient; (h) possible additional information; (i) the content of the returned message (if it was returned); (j) identification of UAE (private or owned by administration); and (k) the UA-content-id.

TABLE 18A-2. MHS Message Transfer Primitives and Parameters

SUBMIT.Request Primitive Parameters	DELIVER.Indication Primitive Parameters	Notes
Originator-O/R-Name	Originator-O/R-Name	
Recipient-O/R-Name	This-recipient-O/R-Name	
	Other-recipient-O/R-Names	
Content	Content	1
Content-type	Content-type	
Encoded-information-types	Original-encoded-information-types	2
	Converted-encoded-information-types	
Deferred-delivery-time	Delivery time	3
NDN-suppress		4
Priority	Priority	
Conversion-prohibited	Conversion-prohibited	5
Explicit-conversion		
Delivery-notice		6
Disclose-recipients		
Alternate-recipient-allowed	Intended-recipient-O/R-name	7
Content-return		8
UA-content-id		
	Submission-time	9
	Delivered-event-id	10

NOTES:

1. End-user information.
2. The type(s) of information sent and, if converted, the original encoded information type(s).
3. Earliest date/time permitted for delivery and the date/time delivered at receipt.
4. Suppress non-delivery notification.
5. Indicates a conversion to another type code is to be prohibited.
6. Requests notification of message delivery.
7. Submitter allows an alternate recipient, and receiver is notified of intended recipient.
8. Return message contents if it is not delivered.
9. Time the message was submitted for delivery.
10. The DELIVER.Indication event identifier.

The CANCEL.Request primitive is used by the UAE to request a delivery to be cancelled to a recipient UAE. The UAE is notified by the MTAE of the cancellation attempt with the CANCEL.Confirmation primitive, which indicates the success or failure of the request.

Finally, the three CHANGE-PASSWORD primitives are used to change a UAE's logon password or to indicate if the request was not successful. The primitives contain: (a) the current value; (b) the new value; and (c) an indication if it was changed successfully.

APPENDIX 18B
THE FTAM PRIMITIVE PARAMETERS AND FUNCTIONAL UNITS

This appendix provides a more detailed look at the FTAM primitive parameters and functional units. Each parameter is explained in a short paragraph. Be aware that the FTAM protocol has many other rules and conventions You may find it helpful to refer to Table 18-5 as you review this appendix.

Diagnostic: This parameter contains many codes to indicate the success or failure of an operation and the reason for the success or failure.

Calling and called address: These addresses identify the associations involved in the file transfer activity. The addresses identify the associated filestores.

Responding address: This address is used to reestablish the filestore association after a failure. It may or may not be the same as the called address.

Service type: This parameter allows the user to stipulate if error recovery procedures are to be provided transparently to the user or if the user is to directly control the error recovery procedures.

Service class: This parameter defines one of three file service classes: (a) file transfer; (b) file access; and (c) file management. The FTAM service classes are categorized based on the functional units. The functional units describe the specific services offered. For example, services are defined for filestore associations, file opens/closes, write and reading files, checkpointing, and several other tasks associated with file management (see the next parameter).

Functional units: As just mentioned, functional units describe the specific services of FTAM. The FTAM functional units are listed in Box 18B-1.

Attribute groups: This parameter negotiates optional file attribute groups for the association. Presently, two attribute groups are defined: (a) storage and (b) security.

BOX 18B-1.   FTAM Functional Units

Application Associations	File Selection/Description
File Open/Close	Read/Write Bulk Data
End/Cancel Data Transfer	Locate File Access Data Unit
Erase File Access Data Unit	File Creation/Deletion
Read/Change Attributes	Begin/End Grouping
Regime Recovery	Checkpointing
Restart Data Transfer	

Rollback availability: This parameter is used to indicate if the Commitment, Concurrency, and Recovery (CCR) mechanisms are to be used during this file transfer association.

Communications QOS: FTAM provides various quality of service features (QOS). This parameter is used to identify them.

Presentation context name: This parameter allows the initiator of the filestore action to indicate presentation context names requested by the initiator.

Identity of initiator: This parameter identifies the calling user.

Current account: The account that is charged for this association is identified in this parameter.

Filestore password: This parameter identifies and authenticates the initiator to the responder.

Checkpoint window: This parameter indicates the number of checkpoints which may remain unacknowledged. The range is 1 to 16.

File name: This is the name of the required file (in the request and indication primitives) and the file actually selected (in the response and confirm primitives).

Access control: This parameter describes the specific type of access on which the file is being selected. The bases for the access control are: read, insert as child or sister, replace, erase, create, change attribute, read attribute, delete file, and determine whether the action is required.

Access password: This parameter pertains to the actions associated with the access control parameter.

Concurrency control: This parameter allows the file users to define file selection relations to other activity on the same file. It is used in conjunction with the access control parameter.

Commitment control: The file service users pass commitment control information with this parameter. Its value is defined in the CCR part of this chapter.

Current account: This identifies the account to which the costs are charged. It relates to the regime which is being established for the activity.

Override: This parameter allows the user to select a file, if it already exists, or to delete a file and create a new one.

Delete password: Delete permission can be established with this parameter. It can be used, even though it was not requested when the file selection regime was established.

Processing mode: This parameter is used to indicate the types of primitives that are to be used as a result of access control and link data transfer requests.

Activity identifier: This parameter defines a unique identifier for the file activity that is to be performed within the open regime.

Recovery mode: This parameter identifies the error recovery facilities that are to be used for recovery. For example, the parameter could specify none, any active checkpoint, etc.

Threshold: This parameter specifies the number of primitives to be analyzed without errors within a group before any group can succeed.

Recovery point: This parameter identifies a checkpoint at which recovery is to take place. It can also specify that recovery is to begin at the start or end of the file.

FADU identity: This parameter provides the identity of the FADU with which the data transfer is associated.

QUESTIONS

TRUE/FALSE

1. The application layer provides no end-to-end acknowledgment services.
2. A MHS message consists of (a) an envelope and (b) the content.
3. A presentation layer protocol is used by the application level MHS.
4. IBM LU 6.2 is the cornerstone for SNA's "application" layer.
5. DEC's Network Virtual Terminal service is actually a two-layer protocol.
6. Match the term with the appropriate definition:

   Definition

   a) An application service element that provides general service to a wide variety of applications.
   b) An application service element that provides service to a limited number of applications.
   c) Part of an Application Entity (AE).
   d) Outside the scope of OSI.
   e) Represents the Application Process (AP) within OSI.

   Term

   1. Application Process (AP)
   2. Application Entity (AE)
   3. Common Application Service Element (CASE)
   4. User Element (UE)
   5. Specific Application Service Element (SASE)

7. Match the MHS System to its appropriate function(s).

   Function(s)

   a) Performs only MTA functions.
   b) Performs both MTA and UA functions.
   c) Performs only UA functions.

   System

   1. S2
   2. S1
   3. S3

8. MHS includes the protocols to define the actions between the UAL and MTL layers: P1, P2, and P3. Describe the interface defined protocol by each.

9. LU 6.2 uses a set of "verbs" to communicate with an application. Describe the purpose of these verbs.

10. Compare the LU 6.2 confirm synchronization and sync point synchronization services.

11. The Document Interchange Architecture (DIA) provides several services for an application process. Briefly describe these services.

12. Contrast DECnet's Terminal Communication Sublayer and Command Terminal Sublayer.

13. The CCITT X.3, X.28 and X.29 recommendations are examples of a parameter drivers virtual terminal (VT). Describe the functions of each protocol.

14. The ISO virtual terminal (VT) protocols (ISO 9040 and 9041) use three types of "objects" for terminal control and communications. Explain the functions of these "objects."

15. The File Transfer, Access and Management (FTAM) recommendations define four groups of attributes: kernel, storage, security, and private. Compare and contrast these groups.

16. Data base management often uses the ideas contained in the ISO Commitment, Concurrency and Recovery (CCR) specifications. CCR is based on a two-phase commitment operation. What does this operation accomplish?

SELECTED ANSWERS

1. False. Indeed, many applications-level protocols require end-to-end accountability.

2. True.

3. True. MHS uses the X.209 notation conventions.

4. True. Many of the SNA higher level protocols make use of LU 6.2.

5. True. It consists of the Command Terminal and Terminal Connection sublayers.

6.

Definition	Term
a)	3
b)	5
c)	4
d)	1
e)	2

7.

Definition	System
a)	1
b)	3
c)	2

11. DIA performs the following services: The Application Processing Services (APS) supports document processing and transformation of formats for documents. The Document Distribution Services (DDS) distributes copies of documents to recipients. The Document Library Services (DLS) supports the storing, retrieval, searching

and deletion of documents in the DIA library and the File Transfer Services (FTS), which supports DLS in the file transfer operations.

15. The kernel group consists of the file name, a description of the file structure, access rules, location of the file user and the identification of the application entities involved in the FTAM communications process.

    The storage group describes properties of a file: (a) information about the ongoing characteristics of the file, or (b) information about the latest operations on the file.

    The security group includes attributes on access permission criteria, encryption procedures and legal qualification (trademarks, copyrights, etc.).

    The private group is not defined by the FTAM standard. It is used for files beyond the virtual filestore attributes.

16. At the broadest level, the two-phase commitment provides atomic actions in the affected data elements. It is best explained by defining the two phases:

    Phase 1: Superior informs subordinate of actions and subordinate agrees to perform the actions or it refuses. If agreement is reached, subordinate commits resources for actions.

    Phase 2: Superior orders the commitment or releases the resources to their beginning state.

    The CCR primitives are used to manage the two-phase commitment. The primitives are passed back and forth between the superior and subordinates to ensure an action takes place correctly or is completely "backed out" of the system, and the affected objects restored to their states before the process began.

CHAPTER 19

Digital Networks

INTRODUCTION

We have been laying the foundations for this chapter in several other sections of this book. The subject is so diverse, it is not possible to restrict it to one chapter in a data communications text. For continuity, the reader may wish to review the following material in previous chapters before reading this chapter (titles are subject headings within the chapters):

Chapter 1: Synchronizing Data Communications Components
Chapter 2: Analog and Digital Signals
Chapter 3: Analog-to-Digital Conversion
            Digital-to-Digital Conversion
Chapter 5: Common Channel Interoffice Signalling (CCIS)
            Signalling System No. 7 (SS7)
Chapter 6: Time Division Multiplexing
            Statistical Multiplexing
Chapter 7: Link Access Procedure, D Channel (LAPD)

CHANNEL SERVICE UNITS (CSU) AND DATA SERVICE UNITS (DSU)

As depicted in Figure 19-1, digital transmission of data between computers and terminals occurs through devices known generally as customer premises equipment (CPE). Prior to deregulation, the CPEs were in the telephone

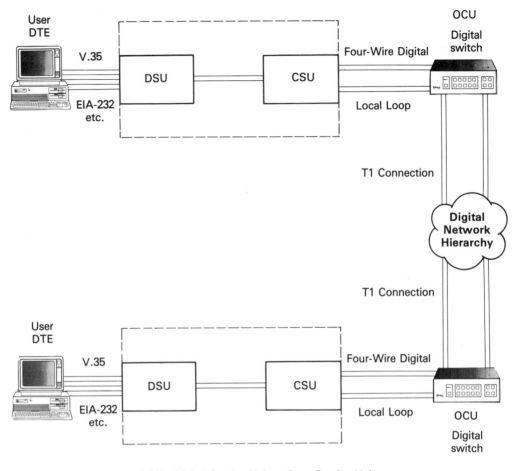

DSU = Digital Service Unit or Data Service Unit
CSU = Channel Service Unit
OCU = Office Channel Unit

FIGURE 19-1. Digital Circuit Structure

company's domain. As a result of Federal Communications Commission (FCC) rulings, neither AT&T nor the Bell Operating Companies (BOC) are permitted to install equipment a customer can provide. This equipment includes the digital CPEs.

In the 1970s and early 1980s, a user device was provided an interface into a digital channel with a Western Electric 500A, a combined channel service unit (CSU) and data service unit (DSU), or a combination of the two (CSU/DSU). The DSU converts the DTE signals into bipolar digital signals. The DSU also performs clocking and signal regeneration on the channel. The

CSU performs functions such as line conditioning (equalization), which keeps the signal's performance consistent across the channel bandwidth; signal reshaping, which reconstitutes the binary pulse stream; and loop-back testing, which entails the transmission of test signals between the CSU and the network carrier's office channel unit (OCU). As later discussions reveal, the CSU assumes other major responsibilities with the newer digital systems using the extended super frame (ESF).

THE T1 SYSTEM

The T1 System has become one of the most widely used high-capacity systems for transmission of voice and data. Originally conceived as a voice transmission technology in the early 1960s, it has evolved into a cost-effective and highly flexible means of transmitting both voice and data.

T1 is based on time division multiplexing 24 users onto one physical circuit. It usually employs a DSU/CSU. to accomplish the analog-to-digital conversion, and the multiplexing. At the inception of T1, it was known that solid copper cable was capable of providing frequencies above 100 KHz. Consequently, the earlier frequency division multiplexed (FDM) telephone system multiplexed 24 users onto one copper wire. Each user was assigned a different 4-KHz frequency band. The composite 24-voice channels totaled 96 KHz, which was within the capacity of twisted pair wires.

With the advent of analog-to-digital conversion and the cost-effective implementation of PCM techniques, AT&T and the Bell system began to implement digital voice systems in the early 1960s. These systems were designated as the T1 carrier and were initially constructed to connect telephone central offices together.

The T1 system is designed around a 1,544,000 bit/s rate, which in the 1960s, was about the highest rate that could be supported across twisted pair for a distance of approximately one mile. Interestingly, the distance of one mile (actually about 6000 feet) represented the spacing between manholes in large cities. They were so spaced to permit maintenance work such as splicing cables and the placing of amplifiers. This physical layout provided a convenient means to replace the analog amplifiers with digital regenerators.

The term T1 actually was devised by the telephone company to describe a specific type of equipment. Today, it is used to describe a general carrier system, a data rate, and various framing conventions.

As the T1 channel banks (T1 designation for multiplexers) increased in reliability and dropped in cost, the telephone companies recognized that customers with high-capacity requirements could be serviced with only two twisted pair cables instead of multiple lines. This approach resulted in "pulling" fewer physical wires to a high-volume user. It was also an important consideration in geographical areas where the local subscriber loops between the customer site and the T1 office were a long distance.

The T1 analog/digital conversion, while originally conceived to be used between central offices, has long since found its way in the cabinet that you see in your business neighborhood. These cabinets often contain the T1 channel bank.

Table 19-1 depicts the T1-based system that has evolved since 1962. The T carriers are also described by a digital signal designation (DS). The initial T1 central office systems used the D1 channel bank (a multiplexing terminal) and also a 7-bit sampling rate. In 1969, the new toll office channel bank was released. It uses an 8-bit sample, which allows 255 values per sample. This scheme established the familiar 64 Kbit/s voice-digitization rate (VDR) scheme. This change also made the D1 channel banks obsolete.

The earlier systems (D1 and D2) transmitted the digitized voice images in a somewhat pseudo-random manner. The newer D3 and D4 channel banks assign each user to a specific slot in a specific frame. For example, user 1 is always assigned the first slot in all the frames in the multiplexed transmission. Consequently, the D1 and D2 channel banks are basically incompatible with the D3 and D4 channel banks.

As Table 19-1 indicates, the initial T1 concept has been enhanced. AT&T has continued to increase the data rate and the time division multiplexing techniques. Today, many of the T1 systems have moved from copper and microwave to optical fiber-based systems.

Figure 19-2 illustrates the T1-based hierarchy. The D channel banks are used to support the DS rates. The multiplexing hierarchy in Figure 19-2 shows the DS designations on the left side of the page, the multiplexing arrangements in the middle, and the designation of the actual digital facili-

TABLE 19-1. AT&T Digital Facilities

System Name	Medium	Voice Grade Channels	Bit Rate (Mbit/s)	Repeater Spacing (miles)
T1	wire cable	24	1.544	1
T1C	wire cable	48	3.152	1
T2	wire cable	96	6.312	1–25
T4M	coaxial	4032	274.176	1.1
FT3	optic fiber	672	44.736	4
FT3C	optic fiber	1344	90.524	4
FT-4E-144	optic fiber	2016	140.0	8–12
FT-4E-432	optic fiber	6048	432.0	8–12

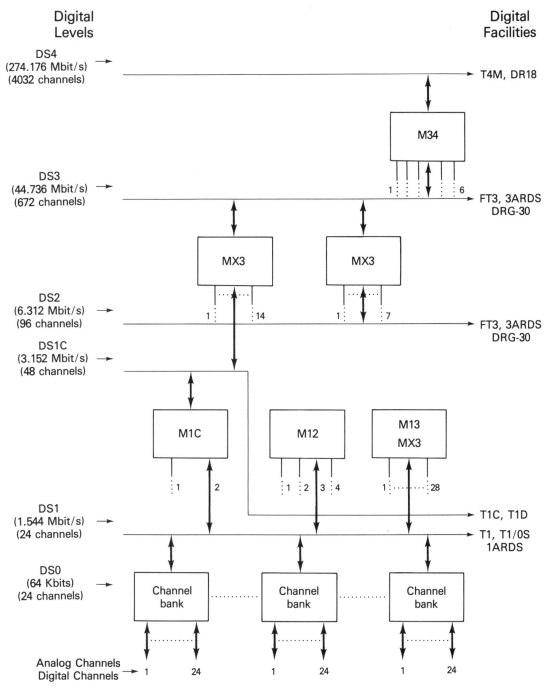

FIGURE 19-2. The T1 Hierarchy

ties on the right side of the page. (The optical fiber systems are not fully integrated into this picture.)

The majority of T1 offerings today digitize the voice signal through pulse code modulation (PCM), or adaptive differential pulse code modulation (ADPCM). Whatever the encoding technique, once the analog images are translated to digital bit streams, many T1 systems then time division multiplex voice and data together in 24 or 44 user slots within each frame.

We just learned that carriers transmit 24 voice or data channels together with time division multiplexed (TDM) frames. The T1 carrier system provides the multiplexing by sampling the 24 channels at a combined rate of 192,000 times per second (8000 times per second per channel $\times$ 24 channels = 192,000). Figure 19-3 shows how the 24 channels are multiplexed into a frame. The frame contains one sample from each channel, plus an additional bit for frame synchronization. Thus, the complete frame is 193 bits (8 bits per channel $\times$ 24 channels + 1 sync bit = 193 bits). Since a frame represents only one of the required 8000 samples per second, a T1 system operates at 1,544,000 to accommodate all 8000 frames (193 bits per frame $\times$ 8000 frames = 1,544,000). Each sample in the frame has a TDM slot of 5.2 microseconds($1/192,000 = 0.0000052$). In addition, each of the 24 channels requires a 64 Kbit/s rate: 8000 samples per second $\times$ 8 bits per sample = 64,000. As we learned in Chapter 3, newer systems use a reduced sampling rate or adaptive, companding schemes to reduce the bit transfer rate to 32, 24, or 16 Kbit/s.

T1 Frame Formats

The basic T1 frame consists of 24 eight-bit slots and a framing bit. The details of these slots and the framing are described in this section, with an emphasis on the following concepts:

Alternate Mark Inversion (AMI)
1s density requirements
Bit robbing
Binary 8 zero substitution (B8ZS)
The framing bit

Alternate Mark Inversion. The alternate mark inversion (AMI) concept is shown in Figure 19-4 (a). The reader may recognize this code as bipolar coding (described in Chapter 3). The T1 system requires that a 1 pulse must be sent as an opposite polarity from the preceding 1 pulse, regardless of the number of 0s in between the two 1s. The name "alternate mark inversion" is derived from the use of alternating polarities to represent binary 1s (marks).

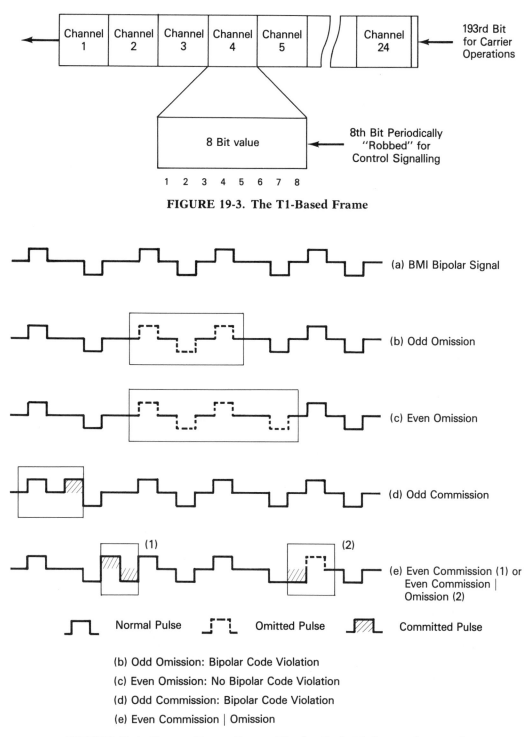

FIGURE 19-3. The T1-Based Frame

(a) BMI Bipolar Signal

(b) Odd Omission

(c) Even Omission

(d) Odd Commission

(1)   (2)   (e) Even Commission (1) or Even Commission | Omission (2)

Normal Pulse   Omitted Pulse   Committed Pulse

(b) Odd Omission: Bipolar Code Violation

(c) Even Omission: No Bipolar Code Violation

(d) Odd Commission: Bipolar Code Violation

(e) Even Commission | Omission

FIGURE 19-4. Format Errors Due to Bipolar Code Violations [VERI86]

The T1 System   **727**

This bipolar code performs well because it has no direct current (dc) component and therefore can be coupled with transformers. The scheme also makes efficient use of bandwidth.

1s Density Requirements. T1 provides no separate clocking signal. The timing or clocking information is embedded in the data stream. At the receiving end, the clock is recovered from the data stream by the detection of 1 pulses. Obviously, if the T1 data stream has insufficient 1 pulses embedded, the receiver can no longer produce reliable timing output.

To overcome this problem, a certain number of 1s must be present to ensure proper timing. This concept is called 1s density. The T1 facilities require that no more than 15 contiguous 0s shall be present in the frame. An additional requirement is that there must be at least three 1s in every 24 bits. Moreover, T1 requires a ratio of no less than 12.5% of 1s versus 0s, even though the 15-consecutive-0 rule is met. As we learned in Chapters 3 and 7, each pulse helps keep the clock aligned to a mid-bit sampling to eliminate or reduce systematic and waiting-time jitter. This convention is adequate to keep the receiver and the repeaters synchronized.

Due to noise, mechanical failures, etc., the bits may become distorted, which can cause a "violation" of the AMI rule. Bipolar violations or excessive errors are known as format errors because the errors are not in conformance with the required T1 format.

A bit distortion may not cause a format error. As Figures 19-4(b) through 19-4(e) show, the nature of the error determines if the bipolar violation is detected [VERI86]. The bipolar signal is altered with errors of omission (pulses are deleted) or errors of commission (pulses are added). The following possibilities exist:

Odd omission:	Creates a violation
Even omission:	Does not create a violation
Odd commission:	Creates a violation
Even commission:	Does not create a violation, or creates two violations

It is evident that, at best, only 50% of the errors can be detected. Unfortunately, the percentage is even worse if the signal passes through certain equipment before reaching the receiver. To illustrate, a T1 multiplexer may multiplex together two signals, both of which contain a code violation. In effect, the two errors "mask" each other when the multiplexer logic combines the signals into a single multiplexed stream.

The signal can be tested, but the transmission line must be taken out of service. Moreover, the majority of errors are transient in nature and the testing routines often do not find any problem.

The errored bits cause problems in voice transmission, especially if the frame's control bits are corrupted. For data transmissions, the corruption is even more serious. Clearly, the problem begs for a solution, and later discussions in this chapter examine several enhancements to address this problem.

Bit Robbing. The earlier T1 channel banks use the 8th bit in every slot for control signalling. Examples of control signalling are off-hook, on-hook, ringing, busy signals, battery reversal, etc. When the 256-step quantizers were initially conceived, it was thought the 8th bit would be used to represent all possible 256-step values ($2^8 = 256$). However, during the development of the D channel bank, the designers recognized that every 8th bit was not needed for signalling and chose to minimize the number of bits used. Consequently, the D2 channel banks (and later channel banks) use the 8th bit of every 6th and 12th frame to provide signalling information. The least significant bit in these frames is overwritten with a signalling bit. This concept is called *bit robbing*, and the respective 6th and 12th robbed frame bits are called the A and B bits.

The A and B bits are used in conjunction with each other. For example, an on-hook condition is indicated if the A and B bits equal 1 in both directions. When a caller goes off-hook, the A/B bits are then set to 0. Generally, the called end of the link responds by sending the 0s in both directions for a brief period of time. The scenarios are numerous, but this brief summary gives the reader an idea of the use of the A and B bits.

For the transmission of data, the 8th bit is unreliable. Consequently, most vendors have chosen to ignore this bit for data signalling. The majority of T1 and related systems use a 56 Kbit/s transmission rate instead of the 64 Kbit/s rate actually available.

This 8th bit is often a source of confusion, because it is also used to transmit status information. The office channel unit (OCU) inserts a 1 into bit position 8 when the customer is sending data. When the customer's device is idle, the OCU places a 0 in bit position 8 and 1s into bit positions 2–7. This technique provides the assurance that the signal has no more than seven consecutive 1s. Consequently, this convention effectively uses 8 Kbit/s of the transmission [LEE86].

B7ZS and B8ZS. To establish 1s density in the T1 signal, a technique called B7 zero code suppression is used [RUFF87]. As we have learned, a 1 is substituted in a T1 frame to prevent an occurrence of more than 15 consecutive 0s. It is possible that this substitution can occur with any bit in the frame. A voice channel can tolerate the loss of the 8th bit to signalling and can even tolerate the loss of the 7th bit to B7 substitution. However, a data channel cannot operate with this arrangement.

Practically speaking, it is not necessary to rob bits in a data channel since there is no telephone signal. However, it is quite possible to have all 0s in a data channel. Therefore, the data could be corrupted by the B7 zero code suppression technique. The insertion does not affect the voice channel but it certainly affects a data channel. To prevent this problem, a data channel generally only uses 7 bits and any 1 substitutions can be placed into the 8th bit. This prevents the B7 zero code suppression from corrupting the data channel. The reader may recognize this technique as an inband signalling technique or a non-clear channel. Clearly, this approach is undesirable and is being phased out with newer systems.

It is possible to enhance the older systems by changing the coding technique of the bipolar stream. The binary 8 zero substitution (B8ZS) has been applied to some of the older systems to address the all-0s word problem.

The rules for B8ZS are stated below and illustrated in Figure 19-5:

- If a pulse preceding the all-0s word is positive ($+$) the inserted code is: 000 $+$ $-$ 0 $-$ $+$.

- If a pulse preceding the all-0s word is negative ($-$) the inserted code is: 000 $-$ $+$ 0 $+$ $-$.

If a system is using the B8ZS convention, the DS1 terminating device must be capable of monitoring the incoming signals, and upon detecting the B8ZS (bipolar violations in the 4th and 7th bit position), replace it with eight 0s.

The Framing Bit—193rd Bit of the Frame. To decode the incoming data stream, a receiver must be able to associate each sample with the proper channel. At a minimum, the beginning and ending of the frame must be recognized. The function of the framing bit is to provide this delineation. This bit is located in the 193rd bit of each frame. It is not part of the user's information, but added by the system for framing. The use of this bit varies significantly depending on the type of T1 and the age of the technology.

The original D1 channel bank used the 193rd bit each time to locate the beginning of the frame. Since the 1960s, the succeeding frame format of D1, D2, D3, D4, and the extended super frame (ESF) format have been used to improve the T1 systems, all using the 193rd bit.

The D1 approach used alternating 1s and 0s in the 193rd position of the frame. It was fast and inexpensive, but the D1 banks were very susceptible to frame loss in the presence of 1,000 Hz test tones. These tones created a perfect alternating 1 and 0 pattern in every 193 bits. This problem is called false framing and can cause the receiver to "lock up" on the wrong frame or not lock up on any frame. (Carriers have since migrated to a 1004 Hz test tone.)

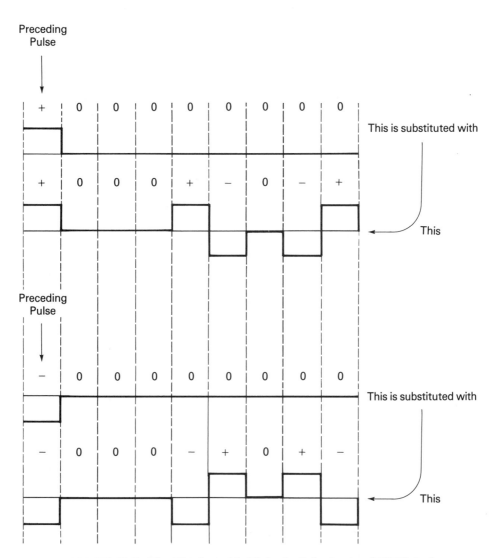

FIGURE 19-5. The Bipolar with Eight 0s Substitution (B8ZS) Code

The D2 channel banks had to deal with both the false frame problem and the A/B bit sequence. Consequently, D2 systems adapted a different sequence for the 193rd bit. Even though this technique was introduced with earlier D2 banks, today it is called the D4 frame format.

The D4 frame format is illustrated in Figure 19-6. The terminal framing (F_T) bits are used to align the receiving channel bank onto the proper sequence of the 24 channels. The channel bank searches for the F_T pattern to synchronize the incoming frames to the channel bank.

Value of 193rd Bit

Frame Number	F_T	F_S} $\longrightarrow$ SF	SF	ESF
1	1		1	DL
2		0	0	CRC
3	0		0	DL
4		0	0	F = 0
5	1		1	DL
6		1	1	CRC
7	0		0	DL
8		1	1	F = 0
9	1		1	DL
10		1	1	CRC
11	0		0	DL
12		0	0	F = 1
13				DL
14				CRC
15				DL
16				F = 0
17	Repeat Every 12 Frames	Repeat Every 12 Frames	Repeat Every 12 Frames	DL
18				CRC
19				DL
20				F = 1
21				DL
22				CRC
23				DL
24				F = 1

F_T: Terminal Framing Bit
F_S: Multiframe Alignment Bit (Signal Framing Bit)
SF: Superframe
ESF: Extended Superframe
DL: Data Link Bit
CRC: Cyclic Redundancy Check Bit
F: F_T and F_S Functions

FIGURE 19-6. D4 and Extended Super Frame Formats (193rd Bit)

The signal framing bits or multiframe alignment bits (F_S) indicate which frames are used for signalling bits (the robbed bits). They are also used to synchronize the timing between the channel bank multiplexer and the carrier's central office equipment.

The F_T and F_S framing bits are consolidated into the entire framing pattern that is used with a D4 channel bank. This composite framing convention, now known as the super frame (SF) format, is the D4 framing convention. This framing bit sequence repeats every 12 frames and constitutes the "super frame." To find the 193rd bit, the receiving channel bank looks for a repeating bit pattern of 100011011100.

Extended Super Frame (ESF).

Introduced by AT&T to address several problems, the ESF provides additional signalling capabilities, more diagnostics, and even error detection. The ESF format is also shown in Figure 19-6.

The 193rd bit is now used for (a) frame synchronization; (b) a data link control channel; and (c) a cyclic redundancy check (CRC).

The frame synchronization bits (F) occupy positions 4, 8, 12, 16, 20, and 24. They perform the combined functions of F_T and F_S and are coded as 001011. These 6 bits use 25% of the total numbered bits in the 193rd position of an 8000-frames-per-second-system. Consequently, the F-bit channel operates at 2 Kbit/s ($8000 * .25 = 2000$).

The data link control (DLC) bits are used to derive a time division multiplexed (TDM) channel of 4 Kbit/s. This channel is quite useful for control and diagnostic activity without disrupting the user subchannels. The DLC subchannel uses positions 1, 3, 5, 7, 9, 11, 13, 15, 17, 19, 21, 23 for a total of 12 bits, or 50% of the total number of the 193rd bit positions of the channel. Thus, it operates at a rate of 4 Kbit/s ($8000 * .5 = 4000$).

The data link subchannel typically uses a data link protocol such as HDLC, LAPB, etc., and the AT&T ESF system uses a simplified LAPB. The information (I field) is based on the Telemetry Asynchronous Block Serial protocol (TABS) from AT&T.

The CRC capability is a significant enhancement to the T1 system. It occupies positions 2, 6, 10, 14, 18, and 22 and operates at 2 Kbit/s.

CRC reduces the magnitude of the false frame problem. In the event of a framing problem, the CRC indicates an error and the channel bank is alerted to seek for a correct framing pattern. CRC is also used to evaluate the performance of the system. Since it detects logic errors instead of format errors, the line can be monitored for quality and performance.

An ESF Channel Service Unit (CSU) continuously monitors the data link for messages containing its address. It can be programmed to react to a variety of situations and messages, such as line failures, timer problems, and testing operations.

Increasing T1 Capacity

With the implementation of the 32 Kbit/s adaptive differential pulse code modulation (ADPCM), the T1 capacity of 24 channels to 44 channels can be increased on a single 1.544 Mbit/s (DS1) facility. In the United States, this capability is known as the M44 multiplexing interface specification [AT&T86]. It is in conformance with the ANSI T1Y1 requirements, and supports either a 12-frame super frame or the 24-frame extended super frame (ESF). It also supports the B8ZS code.

The 44 channels are "compressed" into the 193-bit T1 frame. The 32 Kbit/s channels are categorized as one of two types. The first is a voice band channel associated with the A and B signalling information. The allowed type is a 32 Kbit/s channel with no supervisory signalling. The scheme also allows the use of conventional 64 Kbit/s channels. The 64 Kbit/s channels may also be associated with or without supervisory signalling.

The 44 channels are compressed into the T1 frame as depicted in Figure 19-3. The links operate at 1.544 Mbit/s, but the multiplexed link is formatted as shown in Figure 19-7. The channels are grouped into 4-bit nibbles. Groups of 12 nibbles are grouped together to form a bundle.

The delta channel in each bundle contains the supervisory signalling bits and status information about the circuits in the bundle. The M44 delta channel also contains bundle framing, CRC-6 bits, and data link channel bits, which are used independently of the D4 or ESF DS1 framing carried in

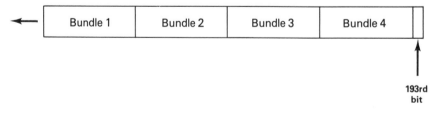

△ channel: Used for Control Signalling

FIGURE 19-7. 44-Channel DS1 Facility Format

the 193rd bit of the DS1 frame. These control bits restrict the system to 44 user channels.

T1 Networks

Figure 19-8(a) shows a typical T1 system. The pulse amplitude signals are created at each analog voice port, and then interleaved to a single analog PAM bus. Digital encoding is performed by all signals by one coder-decoder (codec). A central control circuit provides the synchronization. Conversely, at the receiving end the bit streams are interleaved onto a bus, the channel bank codec converts these to PAM signals, after which the ports receive their own pulses by waiting on a specific clocked period. The PAM signal is then converted to an analog waveform through the techniques described in Chap-

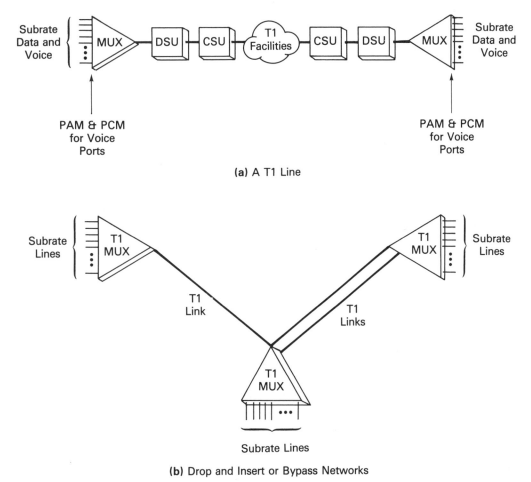

(a) A T1 Line

(b) Drop and Insert or Bypass Networks

FIGURE 19-8. T1 Networks

ter 3. The more recent channel banks do not use one codec. These systems digitize the channels at each port. This technique is known as the "codec on the card."

After the signals are digitized, they are multiplexed onto a digital bus. This is a significantly improved technique because data signals can be sent through the channel bank through data ports and do not have to pass through an analog stage. The digitized voice ports are found in many systems today, such as T1 multiplexers and PBXs. As previously discussed, the T1 can also be configured to support data.

Figure 19-8(b) shows how some T1 systems are evolving. The arrangement shown is called drop and insert, because the T1 multiplexers are configured to "insert" the data from subrate data lines onto T1 lines. Other configurations are possible. For example, the multiplexer may offer bypass capabilities wherein the data streams pass through the intermediate multiplexers to terminate at the destination node.

DIGITAL SWITCHING

Increasingly, digital-switching technology is being used to perform the routing and switching functions of digital voice and data traffic. From previous discussions in this chapter, we have learned that a PCM sampling speed is 8000 samples per second. A digital switch must be able to provide 8000 slots for each connection. Therefore, for n sessions, the switch must be switching at a speed of n $\times$ 8000. A very small system is capable of switching more than 2 million bits per second, which supports over 30 PCM channels.

Chapter 13 contains information on several switching techniques (circuit, message, and packet switching). Many concepts found in these switches are used in digital switching. Our focus in this chapter is on the form of digital switching called time division switching.

Time Division Switching

Time division switching transfers slots of data or voice between input and output lines. As indicated in Figure 19-9, the method actually employs time and space division switching. Channel 6 on link 1 is switched to channel 12 on link n; channel 1 on link n is transferred to channel 6 on link 1. Typically, this operation is exactly reversed for the voice transmission in the opposite direction.

Those readers familiar with programming computers should feel quite at ease with these concepts because time division switching basically entails writing and reading slots of voice/data into and out of memory. The time slots are interchanged and multiplexed into a single frame. The term *time slot interchange* (TSI) is derived from the process.

The TSI can be a nonblocking switch in that there are the same number of input slots available as there are output slots. A channel can be switched

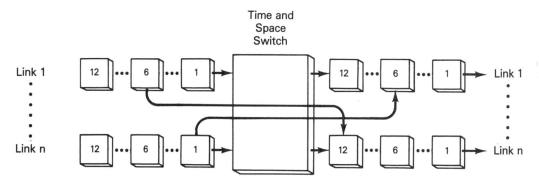

FIGURE 19-9. Time and Space Division Switching

from time position X in an input frame to time position Y in an output frame. With more complex systems, TSIs are connected together to form a digital switch called the time multiplexed switch (TMS). A TMS is essentially a n-by-n switch (n = number of connections). However, the TMS provides for another dimension: time. Unlike other switching systems and many PBXs, which leave the path open for the duration of a call, a TMS is changed for each of the n time slots in the digital frames coming from the time division multiplexer (such as a channel bank).

Because of the full duplex nature of the process, TSI requires a read and write for each channel slot that is supported through the switch. Thus, the maximum number of channels that can be supported by the TDM switch is [BELL82]:

$$C = 125 \div 2t_c$$

Where: C = maximum channels supported; 125 = slot time of an 8000 Hz noise sample (in microseconds); t_c = memory cycle time of processor (in microseconds).

Many systems in operation today maintain a one-to-one relationship between the output channels and the input channels. However, voice transmissions experience about 50% of the connect time with silence. Consequently, newer systems use dynamic slot arrangements, based on traffic demand and the allocation of the "silent" slots to other channels (for example, data transmissions).

INTEGRATED VOICE/DATA PACKET NETWORKS

At first glance it might appear that the integration of voice and data is a simple matter. After all, once the analog signals have been converted to digital images, all transmissions can be treated as data. However, if we examine the transmission requirements of voice and data, we find that they are quite different (see Box 19-1).

BOX 19-1. Characteristics of Packet Voice and Packet Data	
Voice	*Data*
High tolerance for errors	Low tolerance for errors
Network delay must be constant for all packets	Network delay can vary between packets
Some packets can be lost or discarded	Packets can rarely be lost or discarded
Queue length must be short to reduce delay, but allow occasional overflow	Queue length must be longer to prevent packet loss due to overflow

Voice transmissions exhibit a high tolerance for errors. If an occasional packet is distorted, the fidelity of the voice reproduction is not severely affected. In contrast, data packets have a low tolerance for errors. One corrupted bit is likely to change the meaning of the data.

Another difference between voice and data transmissions is in the matter of network delay. For the packetized voice to be translated back to an analog signal in a real-time mode, the network delay must be constant and generally must be low: less than 200 milliseconds. For data packets, the network delay can vary considerably. Indeed, the data packets can be transmitted asynchronously through the network.

Voice packets can afford (on occasion) to be lost or discarded. In the event of excessive delays in the network, overflowing buffers may cause the packets to be lost. Again, the loss does not severely affect voice fidelity if the lost packets are less than 1% of the total packets transmitted. As discussed before, data packets can ill afford to be lost or discarded.

Finally, voice transmissions require a short queue length at the network nodes in order to reduce delay (to reduce queuing) time. The short voice packet queue lengths can experience overflow occasionally, with resulting packet loss. However, data packets require longer queue lengths in order to prevent packet loss in overflow conditions.

Notwithstanding these problems, the integration of voice and data is an idea whose time has come. As we shall see in this section, the concept of packet switching plays a key role in integrated voice/data packet networks. Two concepts that have gained wide attention are *fast packet switching* (FPS) and *hybrid switching*.

Fast Packet Switching (FPS)

Fast packet switching (FPS) employs many of the conventional packet switching conventions, and also uses very-high-speed switches and high-capacity trunks [GREE87]. The technique relies on a session-oriented protocol that uses the same physical path through the network for the duration of the connection.

The network route is determined at the source node by the node accessing a network topology data base. The data base contains information on the current load on the switches and trunks in the network. Periodically, the data base is updated at each node to reflect the capacities and delays within the network.

When a call is requested at the source node, it uses the data base to choose a good route to the destination and builds a control packet that contains the identification of all successive nodes to the final destination point. It then sends this "exploratory" packet to the end user. The destination user returns a confirmation packet through the same route as the exploratory packet. Therefore, each packet associated with the call is routed through the same path as identified by the header in each packet. Each end uses the same physical path through the network.

When a route for a call is first calculated, the source node also calculates and stores several backup routes. In the event the connection request is not successful, the source selects the next best route and reinitiates the call. During a session, a failure of a node or link will cause the source node to choose a backup path. The destination node also follows suit and uses the same physical path.

Fast packet switching is an attractive combination of adaptive and non-adaptive packet switching. It chooses a path before a session begins (adaptive) and keeps the same path during the session (non-adaptive). The ongoing updates to the topology data base increase the speed of the call set-up since the route is predetermined. Moreover, since each node stores the topology data base, it is not necessary to route the call set-up request to a control center.

The FPS network must ensure that the voice packets experience as little delay as possible. The buffering of the voice bits at the source node is limited to about 30 ms and various groups and vendors place an upper bound of one-way delay of 80 to 160 ms [CCITT G.114]. Some researchers claim to have achieved a switching node delay of less than 10 ms, and a network transit delay of less than 55 ms [MIER86B].

One approach to managing delay is through the use of a total delay (T) parameter that is periodically adjusted [GREE87]. The source node initializes a packet lifetime field in the packet header to 0, and each node increments the field by its own delay value (see Figure 19-10). Since each node has a knowledge of the network topology, a reasonably accurate time can be calculated of a probable one-way delay. This one-way delay factor (C) is added to a variable amount of delay (V) and the accumulated delay (L) in order to equal T ($T = L + C + V$). On occasion, when $L + C + V$ exceed T, the packet is discarded because it has lost its value.

T is recalculated to keep the end-to-end delay low as well as to keep discarded packets below 1% of the total packets transmitted. V can be changed to keep the delay constant. If T exceeds a maximum threshold (for example 160 ms), voice calls will be blocked. Moreover, if network congestion occurs, some schemes "dynamically trim" the 32 Kbit/s adaptive differential pulse code modulation signal (ADPCM) to a reduced rate of 24 or 16 Kbit/s [MIER86B].

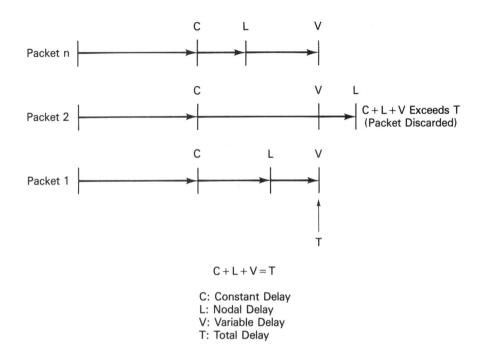

$$C + L + V = T$$

C: Constant Delay
L: Nodal Delay
V: Variable Delay
T: Total Delay

FIGURE 19-10. Fast Packet Switching (Delay Requirements)

Data packets are handled differently in FPS. Since they cannot be discarded, link-to-link or end-to-end protocols are invoked for retransmission of lost or corrupted data and for flow control. End-to-end flow control can be implemented with the credit allocation scheme described in Chapter 15 (Transport Protocol, Class 4). The data packets in FPS are assigned lower priority than voice packets.

Hybrid Switching

Hybrid switching uses a combination of circuit switching for voice connections and packet switching for data connections. The actual integration of the two technologies can be achieved in a number of ways. Generally, the integration is accomplished in the switch.

Hybrid switching uses the conventional concepts of time division multiplexing and framing (quite similar to the concepts discussed in the T1 section of this chapter). The bit stream on each trunk arrives in slots and the hybrid switch assigns these slots to different connections. The system is designed for each frame to be the standard T1 carrier length of 125 ms.

Figure 19-11 depicts a hybrid switch data unit. A frame consists of N slots (for example, in the T1 carrier, the frame is 24 slots). A specific number of these slots (N) are reserved for data packets. These slots cannot be used for voice transmissions. If multiple frames were examined, it could be seen that

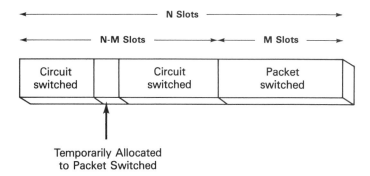

FIGURE 19-11. Hybrid Switching (Changing Slot Usage)

one data packet could be spread out over several contiguous and successive frames.

In hybrid switching, as in fast packet switching, the circuit switched connections have priority over the remaining slots in the frame (N-M). However, the packet traffic is allowed to use the N-M area of the frame, if the circuit switched traffic leaves any of these areas unused. As Figure 19-11 depicts, this provides for temporary additional packet capacity for the data.

The voice packets in a hybrid system are managed through an additional feature called digital speech interpolation (DSI). During the intervals in which two individuals do not speak, with periods of silence, the time intervals are filled with other transmissions. If circuit capacity is available and not needed for the DSI, the packet traffic will be allowed to "grab" some of the additional capacity. The attractive feature of DSI is that it is often possible to concentrate as many as twice the number of incoming circuits to the outgoing circuits, since more than half of a typical voice conversation is silence.

The call setup for hybrid switching is the same as the call set-up structure for fast packet switching. The data packet handling procedures for hybrid switching is also the same as that in FPS.

THE INTEGRATED SERVICES DIGITAL NETWORK (ISDN)

The communications facilities to support user applications are numerous and diverse. Figure 19-12 illustrates a typical user installation. The communications systems are supported by analog dial-up telephone lines (the POTS: plain old telephone service). These dial-up lines may support voice and/or data, which require different types of interfaces. In addition, many companies have dedicated leased lines, either analog or digital, or perhaps a combination of both. Added to these systems are the older TELEX services. Many organizations also have a facsimile service provided. To make matters

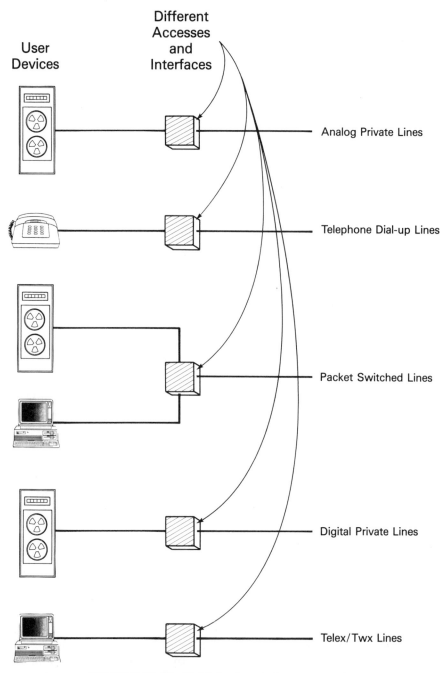

FIGURE 19-12. Multiple Access Arrangements

more complex, many organizations subscribe to public packet network carrier services or may have their own private packet network. Finally, some organizations have installed their own private circuit switched systems.

This melange of systems creates many types of access problems. Different access protocols are used for the voice and data carriers. In many instances, different physical connectors are used for the devices, and different protocols are required. Moreover, different types of lines are needed to support these services.

Presently, over 600 million telephone users can make a voice call practically anywhere in the world. Digital technology is extending this almost ubiquitous service to other forms of information. Ultimately, the integrated services digital network (ISDN) will provide this service for voice, data, text, graphics, music, and video.

In essence, ISDN is digital connectivity for the end user. As we just learned, virtually every subscriber local loop is analog. This is acceptable for voice communications. However, it is far too slow and unreliable for data communications. Data transmission now accounts for more than 10% of total network traffic and its use is growing in North America at a rate of 30% a year. ISDN is intended to extend digital technology over the subscriber loop to the end-user terminal by using common telephone wiring and a standard interface plug. Ideally, the numerous diverse interfaces shown in Figure 19-12 will be reduced (or eliminated) with a limited set of common conventions.

ISDN is centered on three main areas: (1) the standardization of services offered to subscribers in order to foster international compatibility; (2) the standardization of user-to-network interfaces in order to foster independent terminal equipment and network equipment development; and (3) the standardization of network capabilities in order to foster user-to-network and network-to-network communications.

Before we begin an analysis of ISDN, two terms must be defined:

- Functional groupings are a set of capabilities needed in an ISDN user-access interface. Specific functions within a functional grouping may be performed by multiple pieces of equipment and software.
- Reference points are the points dividing the functional groupings. Usually, a reference point corresponds to a physical interface between pieces of equipment.

The ISDN Terminal

To begin the analysis of ISDN, consider the end-user ISDN terminal in Figure 19-13. This device (called a DTE in this book) is identified by the ISDN term TE1 (terminal equipment, Type 1). The TE1 connects to the ISDN through a twisted pair 4-wire digital link. This link uses time division multiplexing (TDM) to provide three channels, designated as the B, B, and D channels (or 2B + D). The B channels operate at a speed of 64 Kbit/s; the D channel operates at 16 Kbit/s. The 2B + D is designated as the basic rate interface. ISDN also allows up to eight TE1s to share one 2B + D channel.

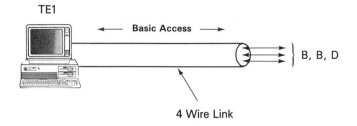

TE1: Terminal Equipment Type 1

FIGURE 19-13. An ISDN Terminal and Basic Access Interface (2B + D)

Figure 19-14 illustrates other ISDN options. In this scenario, the user DTE is a TE2 device, which is equipment currently in use in such as IBM 3270 terminals, TELEX devices, etc. The TE2 connects to the terminal adapter (TA), which allows non-ISDN terminals to operate over ISDN lines. The user side of the TA typically uses a conventional physical level interface such as EIA-232, or the V-series specification discussed in Chapter 9. It is packaged like an external modem or as a board that plugs into an expansion slot on the TE2 devices. The EIA or V-series interface is called the R interface in ISDN terminology.

Basic Access and Primary Access

The TA and TE2 devices are connected through the basic access to either an ISDN NT1 or NT2 device. (NT is network termination.) Figure 19-15 shows several of the options. The NT1 is a customer premise device which connects the 4-wire subscriber wiring to the conventional 2-wire local loop. ISDN allows up to eight terminal devices to be addressed by NT1.

The NT1 is responsible for the physical layer functions (of OSI), such as signalling synchronization and timing. It provides a user with a standardized interface.

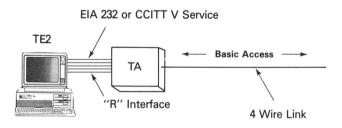

TA: Terminal Adapter
TE2: Terminal Equipment Type 2

FIGURE 19-14. ISDN Terminal Adapter and the R Interface

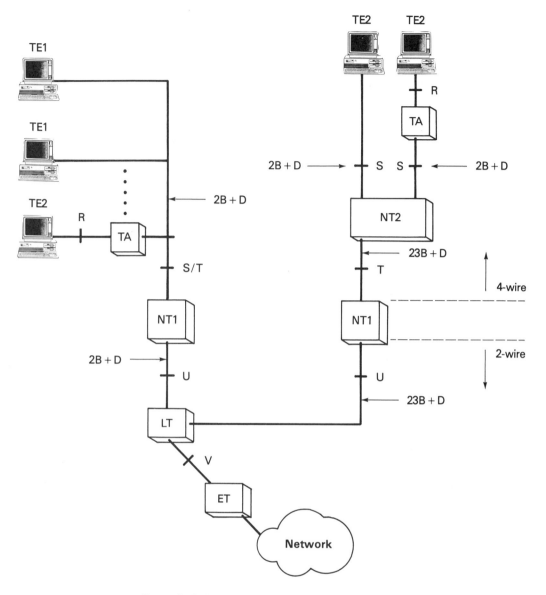

Note: S, T, U, R, V are the ISDN Reference Points.

FIGURE 19-15. An ISDN Configuration

The NT2 is a more intelligent piece of customer premises equipment. It is typically found in a digital PBX, and contains the layer 2 and 3 protocol functions. The NT2 device is capable of performing concentration services. It multiplexes 23 B + D channels onto the line at a combined rate of 1.544 Mbit/s. This function is called the ISDN primary rate access.

The NT1 and NT2 devices may be combined into a single device called NT12. This device handles the physical, data link, and network layer functions.

In summary, the TE equipment is responsible for user communications and the NT equipment is responsible for network communications.

ISDN Reference Points and Interfaces

Figure 19-15 also shows other ISDN components. The reference points are logical interfaces between the functional groupings. The S reference point is the 2B + D interface into the NT1 or NT2 device. The T interface is the reference point on the customer side of the NT1 device. It is the ISDN "plug in the wall." It is the same as the S interface on the basic rate access lines. The U interface is the reference point for the 2-wire side of the NT1 equipment. It separates a NT1 from the line termination (LT) equipment. The V reference point separates the line termination (LT) from the exchange termination (ET) equipment [FALE87].

The S and T reference points support 4-wire twisted pairs for a length of up to 3300 feet (1000 meters) or a point-to-point link of 500 feet (150 meters) on the multipoint configuration. The 2-wire U reference point is operated at full duplex with channel splitting accomplished with echo cancellation.

ISDN Channels

The most common ISDN interface supports a bit rate of 144 Kbit/s. The rate includes two 64 Kbit/s B channels, and one 16 Kbit/s D channel. In addition to these channels, ISDN provides for framing control and other overhead bits, which totals to a 192 Kbit/s bit rate. The 144 Kbit/s interfaces operate synchronously in the full duplex mode over the same physical connector. The 144 Kbit/s signal provides time division multiplexed provisions for the two 64 Kbit/s channels and one 16 Kbit/s channel. The standard allows the B channels to be further multiplexed in the subchannels. For example, 8, 16, or 32 Kbit/s subchannels can be derived from the B channels. The two B channels can be combined or broken down as the user desires.

The B channels are intended to carry user information streams. They provide for several different kinds of applications support. For example, channel B can provide for voice at 64 Kbit/s; data transmission for packet-switch utilities at bit rates less than or equal to 64 Kbit/s; and broadband voice at 64 Kbit/s or less.

The D channel is intended to carry control and signalling information, although in certain cases, ISDN allows for the D channel to support user data transmission as well. However, be aware that the B channel does not carry signalling information. ISDN describes signalling information as s-type, packet data as p-type, and telemetry as t-type. The D channel may carry all these types of information through statistical multiplexing.

The ISDN includes other kinds of channels (the E channel and H channels). These are intended for channels at faster speeds and are derived from multiple B channels. The E channel is a 64 Kbit/s channel used to carry signalling information for circuit switching. The H channels are categorized as:

HO: 384 Kbit/s
H11:   1536 Kbit/s
H12:   1920 Kbit/s

ISDN Local Loops

The ISDN uses the local loops currently in existence. Replacing the many millions of miles of unshielded copper wires comprising the local loop would entail astronomical costs. The voice signal is carried on the local loop over a frequency range from approximately 50 Hz to 4 KHz. The ISDN basic rate access operates at much higher frequencies, in the range of about 200 KHz.

In Chapters 2, 3, and 7, we learned that signal loss increases with higher frequencies. The high-frequency signal loss is quite significant for loops of medium to long distances. For example, a test by the Nynex regional telephone company revealed the following performances, on local loops using 26-gauge wire:

3700 feet: loss of 15 dB (decibels)
9000 feet: loss of 30 dB
18,000 feet: loss of 40 to 50 dB

Since the majority of local loops are longer than 9000 feet, it is obvious that the high-frequency ISDN signals present problems. Moreover, the Nynex test demonstrated that noise and crosstalk create significant distortion of ISDN frequencies.

The T1D1.3 working group has established a specification for local long basic access signalling that will ameliorate the problem. It is called 2 binary 1 quatenary (2B1Q). With 2B1Q, each signal change represents two binary bits. Consequently, a signalling rate of 80 KHz provides a D-bit transfer rate of 160 Kbit/s. The lower frequencies provide better performance over the loops.

ISDN Layers

The ISDN approach is to provide an end user with full support through the seven layers of the OSI model. In so doing, ISDN is divided into two kinds of services—the *bearer services*, responsible for providing support for the lower three levels of the seven-layer standard; and *teleservices* (for example, telephone, Teletex, Videotex message handling) responsible for providing support through all seven layers of the model and generally making use of the underlying lower-level capabilities of bearer services. The services are referred to as low-layer and high-layer functions, respectively. The ISDN functions are allocated according to the layering principles of the OSI and CCITT standards. The functions are depicted in Figure 19-16. Various entities of the layers are used to provide a full end-to-end capability. These layered capabilities may be supplied by PTTs, telephone companies, or other suppliers.

The Basic Rate Frames

The formats for the frames exchanged between the TE and the NT (reference points S and T) are shown in Figure 19-17. The formats vary in each direction of transfer, but are identical for point-to-point or multipoint configurations. The frames are 48 bits in length and are transmitted by the TE and NT every 250 ms. The first bit of the frame transmitted to the NT is delayed by

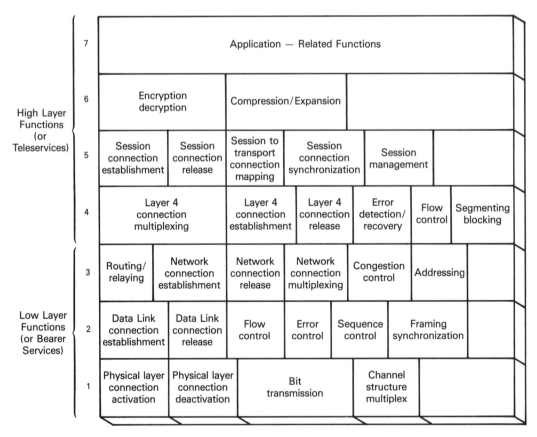

FIGURE 19-16. ISDN Layers

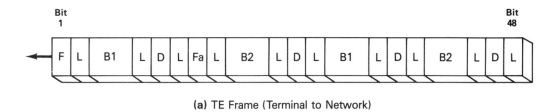

(a) TE Frame (Terminal to Network)

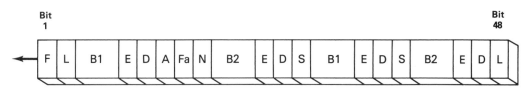

(b) NT Frame (Network to Terminal)

F: Framing Bit
L: DC Balancing Bit
B1: B1 Channel Bits
B2: B2 Channel Bits
D: D Channel Bits
Fa: Auxiliary Training Bit
E: Echo Bits

FIGURE 19-17. Basic Rate Frame Format

two bit periods with respect to the first bit of the frame received from the NT.

The 250 ms frame provides 4000 frames a second (1 second ÷ .000250 = 4000) and a transfer rate of 192 Kbit/s (4000 × 48 = 192,000). However, 12 bits in each frame is overhead, so the user data transfer rate is 144 Kbit/s (4000 × [48 − 12] = 144,000).

The first two bits of the frame are the framing bit (F) and the DC balancing bit (L). These bits are used for frame synchronization. In addition, the L bit is used in the NT frame to electrically balance the frame and in the TE frame to electrically balance each B-channel octet and each D-channel bit. The auxiliary framing bit (F_a) and the N bit are also used in the frame alignment procedures. Bit A is used for TE activation and deactivation.

The Primary Rate Frames

The ISDN specification defines two formats for the primary rate frame. Figure 19-18(a) shows the format for the 1.544 Mbit/s frame used in North America and Japan. Figure 19-18(b) shows the 2.048 Mbit/s frame used in Europe.

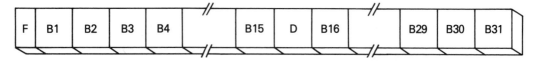

F = 001001 for multiframes of 24 frames long with the F value in every 4th frame.

(a) 1.544 Mbit/s Frame Format

F = 0011011 in positions 2 to 8 in channel time slot 0 of every other frame.

(b) 2.048 Mbit/s Frame Format

FIGURE 19-18. Primary Rate Frame Formats

LAPD

The ISDN provides a data link protocol to allow devices to communicate with each other across the D channel. This protocol is LAPD, a subset of HDLC and LAPB. (Chapter 11 provides a detailed discussion of HDLC and LAPB.) LAPD operates at the data link layer of the OSI architecture. The protocol is independent of transmission bit rate and requires a full-duplex bit transparent channel. Figure 19-19 depicts the LAPD frame format.

LAPD has a frame format similar to that of HDLC. Moreover, like HDLC, it provides for unnumbered, supervisory, and information transfer frames. Table 19-2 shows the LAPD commands and responses as well as a Modulo 128 operation. The control octet to distinguish between the information format, supervisory format, or unnumbered format is identical to that of HDLC. The LAPD unacknowledged information frames (UI) provide no flow control, windowing, or error recovery, but do give faster data transfer.

LAPD provides for two octets for the address field. This is necessary for multiplexing multiple sessions onto the D channel. The address field contains the address field extension bits, a command/response indication bit, a service access point identifier (SAPI), and a terminal end point identifier (TEI). The SAPI and TEI fields are known collectively as the data link control identifier (DLCI). These entities are discussed in the following paragraphs.

The purpose of the address field extension is to provide more bits for an address. The presence of a 1 in the first bit of an address field octet signals that it is the final octet of the address field. Consequently, a two-octet address would have a field address extension value of 0 in the first octet and

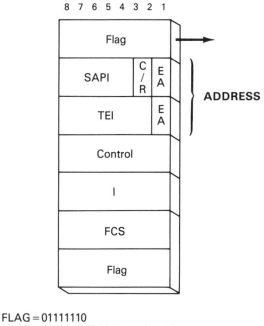

```
      8 7 6 5 4 3 2 1
```

Flag		

	C/R	EA
SAPI		

} **ADDRESS**

TEI	EA

Control

I

FCS

Flag

FLAG = 01111110
  EA = Address Field Extension Bit
 C/R = Command/Response Bit
SAPI = Service Access Point Identifier ⎫ Data Link Connection
 TEI = Terminal Endpoint Identifier ⎬ Identification (DLCI)
   I = Information Field
FCS = Frame Check Sequence

FIGURE 19-19. LAPD Frame Format

a 1 in the second octet. The address field extension bit allows the use of both the SAPI in the first octet and the TEI in the second octet, if desired.

The command/response (C/R) field bit identifies the frame as either a command or a response. The user side sends commands with the C/R bit set to 0. It commands with the C/R set to 1 and response with C/R set to 0. The network side uses the opposite values for commands and responses.

The service access point identifier (SAPI) identifies the entity where the data link layer services are provided to the layer above (that is, layer 3). (If the concept of the SAPI is vague, review Chapter 8.) At the present time, these SAPIs are defined in the ISDN:

SAPI Value	Frame Carries
0	Signalling Information
16	Data
63	Management Information

The Terminal End Point Identifier (TEI) identifies either a single terminal (TE) or multiple terminals. The TEI is assigned automatically by a separate assignment procedure. A TEI value of all 1s identifies a broadcast connection.

Table 19-2 shows two commands and responses which do not exist in the HDLC superset. These are sequenced information 0 (SI0) and sequenced information 1 (SI1). The purpose of the SI0/SI1 commands is to transfer information fields provided by layer 3. The information commands are verified by the means of the end (SI) field. The P bit is set to 1 for all SI0/SI1 commands. The SI0 and SI1 responses are used during single frame operation to acknowledge the receipt of SI1 and SI0 command frames and to report the loss of frames or any synchronization problems. LAPD does not allow information fields to be placed in the SI0 and SI1 response frames. Obviously, information fields are in SI0 and SI1 command frames.

Contending for Use of D Channel. In Figure 19-15, the user devices (TE1) are multidropped onto one circuit. With this configuration, it is possible that the terminals transmit at approximately the same time, which results in collisions. ISDN provides several features to determine if other devices are using the link at the same time. (Please refer to Figure 19-17 during this discussion.)

When the NT receives a D bit from the TE, it echoes back the bit in the next E bit position. The TE expects the next E bit to be the same as its last transmitted D bit. Under normal conditions, the TE continues to detect its own D bits in the E bits.

A terminal cannot transmit into the D channel until after it has detected a specific number of 1s (no signal) corresponding to a pre-established priority. If the number is reached, the TE can then send its D channel data.

If the TE detects a bit in the echo channel (E channel) that is different from its D bits, it must stop transmitting immediately. This indicates that another terminal has begun transmitting at the same time.

This simple technique ensures that only one terminal can transmit its D message at one time. After the successful transmission of the D message, the terminal has its priority reduced by requiring it to detect more continuous 1s before transmitting. A terminal is not allowed to raise its priority back to its previous value until all other devices on the multidrop line have had an opportunity to send a D message.

A telephone connection on the line has a higher priority and precedence over all user services. Signalling information is a higher priority than non-signalling information. Presently, the TE must detect 10 E bits of 1 before sending non-signalling information, but only 8 E bits before sending signalling information.

TABLE 19-2. LAPD Commands and Responses

Format	Commands	Responses	Control Field							
			8	7	6	5	4	3	2	1
Information Transfer	I (information)		— N(R) —			P	— N(S) —			0
Supervisory	RR (receive ready)	RR (receive ready)	— N(R) —			P/F	0	0	0	1
	RNR (receive not ready)	RNR (receive not ready)	— N(R) —			P/F	0	1	0	1
	REJ (reject)	REJ (reject)	— N(R) —			P/F	1	0	0	1
Unnumbered	SABM (set asynchronous balanced mode)		0	0	1	P	1	1	1	1
		DM (disconnect mode)	0	0	0	F	1	1	1	1
	SI0 (sequenced information 0)	SI0 (sequenced information 0)	0	1	1	P/F	0	1	1	1
	SI1 (sequenced information 1)	SI1 (sequenced information 1)	1	1	1	P/F	0	1	1	1
	UI (unnumbered information)		0	0	0	P	0	0	1	1
	DISC (disconnect)		0	1	0	P	0	0	1	1
		UA (unnumbered acknowledge)	0	1	1	F	0	0	1	1
		FRMR (frame reject)	1	0	0	F	0	1	1	1

ISDN Layer 3

The ISDN layer 3 specification (CCITT recommendations I.450 and I.451) encompasses circuit switch connections, packet switch connections, and user-to-user connections. I.450 and I.451 specify the procedures to establish, manage, and clear a network connection at the ISDN user-network interface (see Figure 19-20).

Circuit switched calls using layer 3 have some resemblance to the X.21 state diagrams discussed in Chapter 9. Table 19-3 is provided to give the reader a better understanding of the ISDN session procedures, as well as information transfer and disestablishment procedures for circuit-mode connections. The more widely used messages are summarized below. (Be aware that some carriers have not implemented all of the messages.)

The SETUP message is sent by the user or the network to indicate a call establishment. The message contains several parameters to define the circuit connection, and it must contain these three parameters:

- *Protocol discriminator*: Distinguishes between user-network call control messages and others, such as other layer 3 protocols (X.25, for example).
- *Call reference*: Identifies the ISDN call at the local user-network interface. It does not have end-to-end significance.
- *Message type*: Identifies the message function; that is to say, the types shown in Table 19-3.

As options, other parameters include the specific ISDN channel identification, originating and destination address, an address for a redirected call, the designation for a transit network, etc.

The SETUP ACKnowledge message is sent by the user or the network to indicate the call establishment has been initiated. The parameters for the SETUP ACK message are similar to those of the SETUP message.

The CALL PROCeeding is sent by the network or the user to indicate

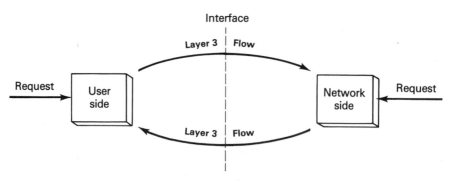

FIGURE 19-20. ISDN Interface

TABLE 19-3. ISDN Layer 3 Messages

Call Establishment Messages	Call Disestablishment Messages
ALERTing	DETach
CALL PROCeeding	DETach ACKnowledge
CONNect	DISConnect
CONNect ACKnowledge	RELease
SETUP	RELease COMplete
SETUP ACKnowledge	

Call Information Phase Messages	Miscellaneous Messages
RESume	CANCel
RESume ACKnowledge	CANCel ACKnowledge
RESume REJect	CANCel REJect
SUSPend	CONgestion CONtrol
SUSPend ACKnowledge	FACility
SUSPend REJect	FACility ACKnowledge
USER INFOrmation	FACility REJect
	INFOrmation
	REGister
	REGister ACKnowledge
	REGister REJect
	STATUS

the call is being processed. The message also indicates the network has all the information it needs to process the call.

The CONNect and the CONNect ACKnowledge messages are exchanged between the network and the network user to indicate the call is accepted between either the network or the user. These messages contain parameters to identify the session and the facilities and services associated with the connection.

To clear a call, the user or the network can send a RELease or DISConnect message. Typically, the RELease COMplete is returned, but the network may maintain the call reference for later use, in which case, the network sends a DETach message to the user.

A call may be temporarily suspended. The SUSPend message is used to create this action. The network can respond to this message with either a SUSPend ACKnowledge or a SUSPend REJect.

During an ongoing ISDN connection, the user or network may issue CONgestion CONtrol messages to flow-control USER INFOrmation messages. The message simply indicates if the receiver is ready or not ready to accept messages.

The USER INFOrmation message is sent by the user or the network to transmit information to a (another) user.

If a call is suspended, the RESume message is sent by the user to request the resumption of the call. This message can invoke a RESume ACKnowledge or a RESume REJect.

The STATUS message is sent by the user or the network to report on the conditions of the call.

The ISDN supports numerous facilities (see Table 19-4). They are managed with the following messages.

REGister REGister ACKnowledge and REGister REJect:	Initiates the registration of a facility (as well as confirmation or rejection)
FACility FACility ACKnowledge and FACility REJect	Initiates access to a network facility (as well as confirmation or rejection)
CANcel CANcel ACKnowledge and CANcel REJect:	Indicates a request to discontinue a facility (as well as confirmation or rejection)

Most of these facilities are self-explanatory; others are explained in the X.25 part of Chapter 13. It is evident that the connections of ISDN and X.25 have been given much thought by the standards groups.

TABLE 19-4. ISDN Layer 3 Facilities

Delivery of origin address barred
Connected address required
Supply charging information after end of call
Reverse charging requested
Connect outgoing calls when free
Reverse charging acceptance (allowed)
Call redirection/diversion notification
Call completion after busy request
Call completion after busy indication
Origination address required on outgoing calls
Origination address desired on incoming calls
Destination address required on incoming calls
Connect incoming calls when free (waiting allowed)
X.25 extended packet sequence numbering (modulo 128)
X.25 flow control parameter negotiation allowed
X.25 throughput class negotiation allowed
X.25 packet retransmission (allowed)
X.25 fast select (outgoing) (allowed)
X.25 fast select acceptance allowed
X.25 multilink procedure
X.25 local charging prevention
X.25 extended frame sequence numbering

Network Layer Message Format. The ISDN network layer protocol uses messages to communicate. The format for these messages is shown in Figure 19-21. The message consists of the following fields (these fields were explained with the SETUP message):

Protocol discriminator (required)

Call reference (required)

Message type (required)

Mandatory information elements (as required)

Additional information elements (when required)

Example of an ISDN Call. Figure 19-22 illustrates a typical procedure for a simple circuit switched call. Note the use of the ISDN messages that are listed in Table 19-3.

ISDN Progress

The countries in Europe have completed their initial ISDN trials, and several trials are either planned or are under way in North America. Each of the seven Bell regional companies is involved in ISDN prototypes, and vendors, such as AT&T and Northern Telecom, are very active in developing and implementing the pieces to ISDN. This writer believes ISDN will prove itself

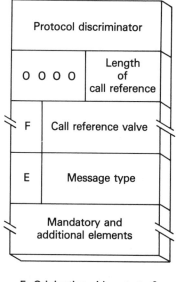

F: Origination side sets to 0
   Destination side sets to 1
E: Set to 0 (Extension Bit)

FIGURE 19-21. ISDN Message Format

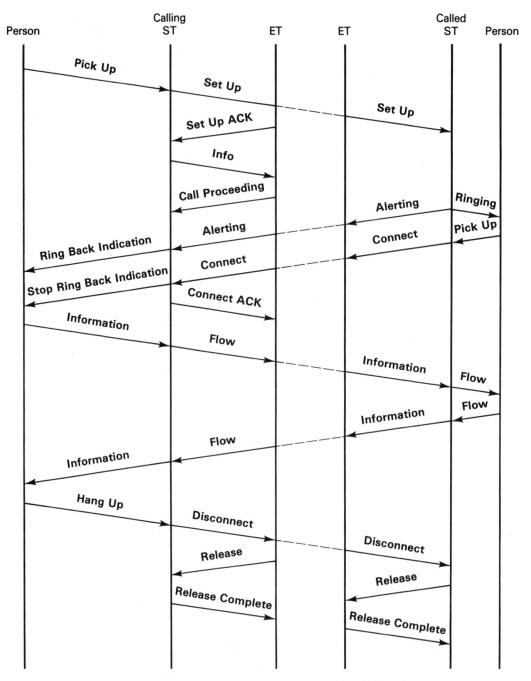

FIGURE 19-22. ISDN Circuit Switched Call [I451]

as a cost-effective and efficient technology. The telephone companies will benefit from ISDN within their own internal operations, regardless of what happens to the end-user interface. It is an idea whose time is overdue.

SUGGESTED READINGS

The literature on digital systems is almost overwhelming. Each week, a new book appears, and the trade journals contain many articles on digital systems, the T1 carriers, and ISDN. The reader will be well served by reading the following literature.

As in some other chapters [BELL82] is highly recommended. [RUFF87] is a good tutorial on T1 and ESF. [MIER85] provides a good discourse on T1 and its history.

[FLAN86] is an excellent, non-engineering textbook on T1. It is highly recommended to the reader. Verilink Corporation publishes a short, concise, and lucid description on ESF [VERI86].

Of course, there is no substitute for the original sources. The CCITT and AT&T documents on digital systems should be considered a primary source for the reader:

CCITT	I.110 - I.464	(ISDN)
AT&T	PUB 41459	(ISDN)
AT&T	PUB 54070	(T1.5, M44)
Bellcore	TA-TSY 000393	(ISDN)
Bellcore	TA-TSY 000397	(ISDN)
Bellcore	TA-TSY 000367	(ISDN)
Bellcore	TA-TSY 000419	(ISDN)
Bellcore	TA-TSY 000398	(ISDN)

QUESTIONS

TRUE/FALSE

1. T1 uses 24 or 32 time division multiplexed channels.
2. T1 is used exclusively on twisted pair or coaxial cable.
3. The newer T1 systems use a 32 Kbit/s transfer rate instead of the original 64 Kbit/s rate. The ANSI T1Y1 specification uses this scheme to double T1 capacity to 48 channels.
4. ISDN is intended to support any type of user application.
5. The ISDN D channel uses a collision-free protocol.
6. Match the following T1 function to the appropriate term:

   Function

   a) No more than 15 contiguous zeros are allowed.
   b) One pulse must be the opposite polarity of the preceding one pulse.
   c) Uses 8th bit for control.
   d) Supports multiframe alignment.

Term

1. Framing bit
2. 1s density
3. Bit robbing
4. Alternate mark inversion (AMI)

7. Match the ISDN function to the appropriate term:

Function

a) Current equipment
b) Performs physical layer functions
c) A protocol convertor
d) Performs higher level functions
e) An ISDN user terminal

Term

1. NT1
2. TE1
3. TA
4. TE2
5. NT2

8. The T1 framing bit with the extended super frame (ESF) format provides several powerful features. Describe these features with specific comments on the F_T, F_S, DLC, and CRC bits.

9. The extended super frame uses a data link control (DLC) channel. It operates at 4 Kbit/s. Refer to Figure 19-6 and explain how this data rate is derived from the T1 data rate.

10. What is the difference between an ISDN functional grouping and a reference point?

11. The following list describes the characters for voice and data systems. Check the appropriate entry for each characteristic.

Characteristics	*Voice*	*Data*
a) Transmission can be discarded.		
b) Queue length must be long.		
c) Low error rate required.		
d) Delay can vary.		

12. Compare the ISDN basic and primary rates.

13. What is the purpose of the LAPD address field? Why does it differ from LAPB's address field?

14. T1 and other similar digital systems stipulate a "1s density" for the transmitted signals. What is the reason for the 1s density requirement? What are its rules?

15. You are the person in charge of the communications operations in your company. Your board of directors has directed you to move to an all-digital technology and at the same time has reduced your budget. What is your response to these directives?

1. False. T1 is designed to carry 24 TDM channels.
2. False. T1 is used on other media, such as satellite channels.
3. False. Only 44 user channels are available. The other channels are used for control signals.
4. True. Its goal is to provide transparency to a user application.
5. True. It is implemented with the D and E bits in the basic rate frame.

6.

Function	Term
a)	2
b)	4
c)	3
d)	1

11.

Characteristic	Voice	Data
a)	X	
b)		X
c)		X
d)		X

15. These directives place a manager in a dilemma. It is accepted that future digital systems will be relatively less expensive than their analog counterpart. However, the initial transition will require the acquisition of new equipment and new software. It requires retraining many of the telephone analog-oriented personnel. In this case, there is no such thing as a free lunch. In order to save money in the future, your choice may have to be to spend money now. There really is no choice in the matter. What you should do as manager of this operation is to emphasize to the board of directors that they must forego some short-term gains in order to obtain long-term benefits. As we all know, this has been a problem that many boards of directors have ignored in the past decade. Therefore, your response to this proposal would be to do a cost-benefit study, noting that the up-front cost will yield results in later years.

CHAPTER 20

Local Area Networks

INTRODUCTION

The local area network (LAN) industry has grown at a dramatic rate during the past several years. It is estimated that in the U.S. alone, over 100 LAN vendors exist in the industry. In addition to the LAN vendors, other companies sell individual network components. Several hundred vendors are in the business of providing local area networks or the individual LAN components for the networks.

Due to the diversity of the LAN industry, it is impossible to cover all systems, standards, and products in one chapter. Chapter 22 examines the personal computer–based LANs and Chapter 23 discusses PBX-based LANs with emphasis on AT&T's ISN. This chapter provides a tutorial on LANs and then examines the IEEE LAN standards, the IBM token ring LAN and the Fiber Distributed Data Interface (FDDI) from ANSI.

Why LANs?

The driving force for the use of LANs is to increase employee productivity and efficiency and to share expensive hardware, like printers and disk units. Productivity can be increased and expenses can be decreased by giving employees easy, fast, and shared access to computers, terminals, and other workstations in the office. Moreover, with the distribution of computing resources (personal computers), it has become necessary to provide a means to connect these devices with the host computer. LANs are designed to provide these services.

Definitions of local networks are plentiful. While one definition has not gained prominence, most definitions include the following:

- The connections between the user devices are usually within a few hundred meters, to several thousand meters.
- The LAN transmits data (and often voice and video) between user stations and computers.
- The LAN transmission capacity is usually greater than that of a wide area network. Typical bit rates range from 1 Mbit/s to 20 Mbits/s.
- The LAN channel is typically owned by the organization using the facility. The telephone company usually is not involved in channel ownership or management. However, telephone companies are moving into this arena with their own offerings.
- The error rate on a LAN is considerably better than that on a wide area network-oriented telephone channel.

LAN COMPONENTS

A LAN contains four major components that transport data between end users: (1) channel; (2) the physical interface; (3) protocol; (4) user station (see Figure 20-1).

1. LAN channels (media) consist of coaxial TV cable, coaxial baseband twisted pair cable, or optical fiber. Coaxial cable TV (CATV) is used on many networks because it has a large transmission capacity, a good signal-to-noise ratio, low signal radiation, and low error rates ($1:10^7$ to 10^{11}). Twisted pair cable and microwave are also found in many LANs. Baseband coaxial is another widely used transmission

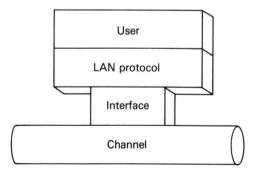

FIGURE 20-1. LAN Components

path, giving high capacity as well as low error rates and low noise distortion.

Thus far, optical fiber paths have seen limited application, but their positive attributes assure their increased use. The immediate use of lightwave transmission on local networks is for point-to-point, high speed connections of up to 10 miles (16 Km). A transfer rate of over 100 Mbit/s can be achieved on this type of path.

Infrared schemes using line of sight transmission are also used on the LAN channel. Several vendors offer infrared equipment for local loop replacement. Up to 100 Kbit/s over one mile (1.6 Km) distances are possible with infrared schemes.

2. The interface between the path and the user station can take several forms. It may be a single cable television (CATV) tap, infrared diodes, microwave antennas, or laser-emitting semiconductors for optical fibers. Some LANs provide regenerative repeaters at the interface; others use the interface as a buffer for data flow.

3. The protocol control logic component controls the LAN and provides for the end user's access onto the network. The LAN protocols employ methods and techniques discussed later in this chapter.

4. The last major component is the user workstation. It can be anything from a word processor to a mainframe computer. Several LAN vendors provide support for other vendors' products, and several layers of the ISO model are also supported by some LANs.

BROADBAND AND BASEBAND LANs

LANs are available as either broadband or baseband systems. A broadband network is characterized by the use of analog technology. It uses a high frequency modem (greater than 4 KHz) to introduce carrier signals onto the transmission channel. The carrier signals are then modified (modulated) by a user's digital signal. Because of the analog nature of the network, broadband systems are often frequency division multiplexed (FDM) to provide multiple channels (e.g., data, video, audio) on one path. (FDM is not mandatory, and a LAN with a single analog channel is called single channel broadband.) Broadband systems are so named because the analog carrier signals operate in the high frequency radio range (typically, in the 5 to 400 MHz range). They operate with widely used CATV 75-ohm coaxial cable.

The broadband LAN is unidirectional, that is, the signal travels in one direction. It is not economically feasible to construct amplifiers that operate in both directions, so the broadband LAN uses two separate channels to provide an inbound and outbound channel. Two configurations can be used to obtain the inbound and outbound channels: *dual cable* and *split channel*.

A dual cable configuration uses two separate cables, one for the inbound channel and one for the outbound channel. A headend connects the two cables and the connected station uses the same frequency to send and receive.

The split channel configuration uses two different frequencies for the inbound and outbound transmissions on one cable. The headend is responsible for converting the inbound frequencies to the outbound frequencies. It can be either an analog device (changes and amplifies signals) or a digital device (regenerates the digital signals).

Split channel configurations use various schemes to divide the frequency spectrum. Three common approaches are subsplit, midsplit, and highsplit multiplexing [STAL87]:

Direction	Subsplit	Midsplit	Highsplit
inbound	5 – 30 MHz	5 – 116 MHz	5 – 174 MHz
outbound	54 – 400 MHz	168 – 400 MHz	232 – 400 MHz

A split system is some 15 percent less expensive than a dual cable system [HOPK79], and it is convenient if only one cable is installed in a building. However, the dual cable system has over twice the capacity (bandwidth) of the split system, and it does not need a headend frequency translator.

The baseband network uses digital technology. A line driver introduces voltage shifts onto the channel to represent binary 1s and 0s. The channel then acts as a transport mechanism for the digital voltage pulses.

Baseband networks do not use analog carriers or FDM techniques. However, multiple access to the medium can be provided by a time division multiplexer (TDM) or by other protocols.

Baseband systems are bidirectional and use one cable. The technology is limited in distance (0.6 mile/1 Km is typical), because the digital pulse attenuates severely over longer distances.

Baseband LANs can use either coaxial cable or twisted pair. The coaxial scheme usually is implemented with 50 ohm cable (in contrast to broadband CATV 75 ohm cable) because it works well on multipoint lines and under conditions where low-frequency noise is present.

Baseband coaxial systems are configured with the following constraints (example is the Ethernet specification):

• Cable length of 500 m
• Stations attached with distances in between in multiples of 2.5 m
• A maximum of 100 taps per cable
• Cable length can be extended by replacing the terminators with digital repeaters.

Twisted pair baseband systems are attractive because they are simple to install, and are relatively inexpensive. But they do not have the capacity of coaxial systems. An unshielded twisted pair configuration often permits the use of existing wire inside a building (for example, telephone wiring). Shielded twisted pair, while more expensive, provides considerably more capacity and supports more drops on the channel.

Invariably, the question is asked, "Should I use baseband or broadband?" The answer is: it depends on the organization's needs and budget. In some cases, combinations of the two technologies may be the best approach. Like all automation and communications decisions, it comes down to an evaluation of the requirements versus the cost to meet the requirements. The summary in Box 20-1 provides the reader with the trade-offs of broadband and baseband systems.

BOX 20-1. Comparison of Broadband and Baseband LANs

	Broadband	*Baseband*
Advantages	Distance	Cost
	Capacity	Simplicity
	Multimedia (voice, TV)	
	Flexible configuration	
Disadvantages	RF modem costs	Capacity
	Propagation delay	One channel
	(Split channel or	One media
	dual capability)	Distance
	Complexity	

COMMON LAN PROTOCOLS

Local area networks operate using a variety of protocols. This section provides an overview of the more widely used techniques:

Carrier Sense Collision Detection
Token Ring
Token Bus
Carrier Sense Collision-Free
Register Insertion
Time Division Multiplexing
Polling/Selection

Carrier Sense Collision Detection

Carrier sense collision detection is widely used in local networks. Several vendors use this technique with Ethernet and the IEEE 802.3 specification (discussed later). A carrier sense LAN considers all stations as peers; the stations contend for the use of the channel on an equal basis. Before transmitting, the stations are required to monitor the channel to determine if the channel is active (that is, if another station is sending data on the channel). If the channel is idle, any station with data to transmit can send its traffic onto the channel. If the channel is occupied, the stations must defer to the station using the channel.

Figure 20-2 depicts a carrier sense collision detection LAN. Stations A, B, C, and D are attached to a channel (such as coaxial cable) by bus interface units (BIU). We assume stations A and B wish to transmit. However, station D is currently using the channel, so the BIUs at stations A and B "listen" and defer to the signal from station D. Upon the line going idle, A and B attempt to acquire the channel.

Since station A's transmission requires time to propagate to other stations, they may be unaware that a signal is on the channel. In this situation, station A could transmit its traffic even though another station has supposedly seized the channel. This problem is called the collision window. The collision window is a factor of the propagation delay of the signal and the distance between the two competing stations. (It is discussed later in this chapter.)

Carrier sense networks are usually implemented on short distance LANs because the collision window lengthens with a longer channel. The long channel provides opportunity for more collisions and can reduce throughput in the network. Generally, a long propagation delay (a long delay before each station knows the other is transmitting) coupled with

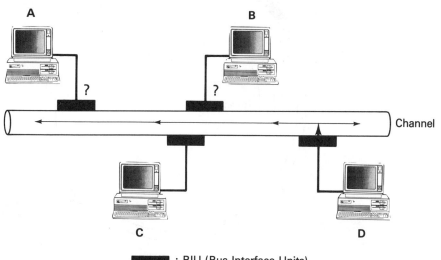

FIGURE 20-2. Carrier Sense Collision Detection Networks

short frames and high data transfer rates give rise to a greater incidence of collisions. Longer frames can mitigate the effect of long delay, but they reduce the opportunity for competing stations to acquire the channel.

Each station is capable of transmitting and listening to the channel simultaneously. As the two signals collide, they create voltage irregularities on the channel, which are sensed by the colliding stations. The stations must turn off their transmission, and through a randomized wait period, attempt to seize the channel again. The randomized wait decreases the chances of the collision recurring since it is unlikely that the competing stations will generate the same randomized wait time.

Carrier sense systems are explained in more detail with the IEEE 802.3 specification.

Token Ring

The token ring topology is illustrated in Figure 20-3. The stations are connected to a concentric ring through a ring interface unit (RIU). Each RIU is responsible for monitoring the data passing through it, as well as regenerating the signal and passing it to the next station. If the address in the header of the transmission indicates the data is destined for a station, the interface unit copies the data and passes the information to the user device.

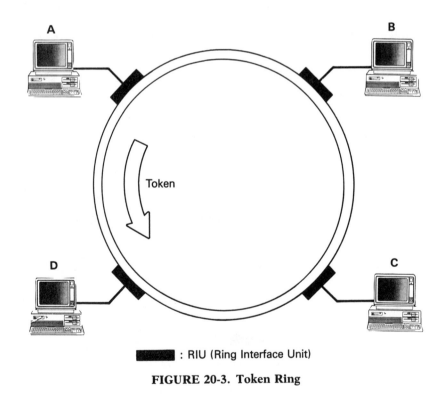

■■■■ : RIU (Ring Interface Unit)

FIGURE 20-3. Token Ring

If the ring is idle (that is, no user data is occupying the ring), a "free" token is passed around the ring from node to node. This token indicates the ring is available and any station with data to transmit can use the token to transmit traffic. The control of the ring is passed sequentially from node to node around the ring.

During the period when the station has the token, it controls the ring. Upon acquiring the token (i.e., marking the token busy), the transmitting station inserts data behind the token and passes the data through the ring. As each RIU monitors the data, it regenerates the transmission, checks the address in the header of the data, and passes the data to the next station. Upon the data arriving at the transmitting station, this station makes the token free and passes it to the next station on the ring. This requirement prevents one station from monopolizing the ring. If the token passes around the ring without being used, the station can once again use the token and transmit data.

Some systems remove the token from the ring, place the data on the channel and then insert the token behind the data. Other user frames can be placed behind the first data element to allow a "piggybacking" effect on the LAN with multiple user frames circling the ring. The approach requires that the token be placed behind the last data transmission. Piggybacking is useful for large-circumference rings that experience a long delay in the transmission around the ring, but the short propagation delay on a LAN is not worth the added complexity of a multiple token LAN.

Many token ring networks use priority schemes. The object of the priority is to give each station an opportunity to reserve the use of the ring for the next transmission around the ring. As the token and data circle the ring, each node examines the token, which contains a reservation field. If a node's priority is higher than the priority number in the reservation field, it raises the reservation field number to its level, thus reserving the token on the next round. If another node does not make the reservation field higher, the station is allowed to use the token and channel on the next pass around the ring.

The station with the token is required to store the previous reservation value in a temporary storage area. Upon releasing the token, the station restores the network to its previous lowest priority request. In this manner, once the token is made free for the next round, the station with the highest reservation is allowed to seize the token.

This overview is sufficient for the present time. Token passing priority systems are explained in more detail in the sections on the IEEE 802.5 specification, the IBM token ring, and the FDDI network.

Token Bus

Token bus LANs use a bus topology, yet provide access to the channel as if it were a ring. The protocol eliminates the collisions found in the carrier sense collision detection systems but allows the use of a bus-type channel. The token bus requires no physical ordering of the stations on the channel. The stations can be logically configured to pass the token in any order.

The protocol uses a control frame called an access token or access right. This token gives a station the exclusive use of the bus. The token-holding station uses the bus for a period of time to send and/or receive data. It then passes the token to a designated station called the successor station. In the bus topology, all stations listen and receive the access token, but the only station allowed to use the channel is the successor station. All other stations must await their turn to receive the token. The stations receive the token through a cyclic sequence, which forms a logical ring on the physical bus.

The token bus is explained in more detail in the section on the IEEE 802.4 specification.

Carrier Sense Collision-Free Systems

Carrier sense collision-free LANs are similar to carrier sense collision detection networks. The major difference is the use of timer or arbiter to prevent collisions from occurring. This device determines when a station can transmit without experiencing collisions. The timing is determined at each station; no master station exists to supervise the use of the channel.

Each station has a predetermined timing threshold. When the timing threshold expires, the LAN port uses a timing parameter to determine when to transmit. The timing can be established on a priority basis for the highest priority station to have its timer expire first. If this station does not transmit, the channel remains idle. When the next highest priority station senses the idle channel, it acquires the channel.

If the higher priority stations do not transmit, they create an idle condition on the channel, which allows the lower priority stations to use the channel. In conventional time division LANs, the idle time means wasted transmission opportunities. However, the collision-free LAN uses the arbiter to allow the next highest priority station on the link to use the otherwise idle time if it has data to transmit.

Register Insertion

A number of ring-based LANs use the register insertion technique to control traffic. Any station can transmit whenever an idle state exists on the link. If a frame is received on the input port while the station is transmitting on the output port, the frame is held in a register and transmitted behind the station's frame. This approach permits the "piggybacking" of multiple frames on the ring.

Time Division Multiplexing (TDM)

Time division multiplexing (TDM) is one of the simplest LAN protocols. Under a TDM system, each station is given a slot of time on the channel. The slots are divided equally or unequally among the stations and each user has the full use of the channel during the slot period. If a station has nothing to transmit, the channel remains idle during the station's slot period.

Polling/Selection

This type of protocol is widely used on long-haul networks (see Chapters 10 and 11). Some vendors have also implemented it in local networks.

Polling/selection systems revolve around two types of command frames: the poll and the select. The purpose of the poll command is to transmit data to the primary or master station. The purpose of the select command is just the opposite: to transmit data from the primary station to the secondary or slave station. Select commands are no longer needed on the newer protocols, because the master site reserves resources and buffers at the receiver during link establishment, thereby sending data at the discretion of the master node.

THE IEEE 802 RECOMMENDATIONS

The Institute of Electrical and Electronics Engineers (IEEE) publishes several widely accepted LAN recommended standards. These standards are very important because they encourage the use of common approaches for LAN protocols and interfaces. As a consequence, chip manufacturers are more willing to spend money to develop relatively inexpensive hardware to sell to (they hope) a large market. The IEEE LAN committees are organized as follows:

IEEE 802.1	High-Level Interface (and MAC Bridges)
IEEE 802.2	Logical Link Control (LLC)
IEEE 802.3	Carrier Sense Multiple Access/ Collision Detect (CSMA/CD)
IEEE 802.4	Token Bus
IEEE 802.5	Token Ring
IEEE 802.6	Metropolitan Area Networks
IEEE 802.7	Broadband Technical Advisory Group
IEEE 802.8	Fiber Optic Technical Advisory Group
IEEE 802.9	Integrated Data and Voice Networks

The IEEE standards are gaining wide acceptance. The European Computer Manufacturers Association (ECMA) voted to accept the 802.5 Token Ring as its standard. The NBS, the ISO, and ANSI have accepted these standards, and as we shall see, vendors and user groups are also using them.

It was apparent to the 802 committee that multiple systems were needed to satisfy different user requirements. Thus, the committee adopted the CSMA/CD, Token Bus, and Token Ring with the following media:

- *CSMA/CD*   Baseband (10 Mbit/s)
              (Broadband (10 Mbit/s)
              Twisted Pair (1 Mbit/s)

- *Token Bus* Broadband Coax (1, 5, 10 Mbit/s)
              Carrierband (1, 5, 10 Mbit/s)

- *Token Ring* Shielded Twisted Pair (1, 4 Mbit/s)

In 1987, the IEEE made revisions to the 802 specifications. Several changes were made to bring them into conformance with the OSI model. This chapter reflects these changes.

Relationship of the 802 Standards to the ISO/CCITT Model

Chapter 8 introduced the concept of layered protocols and the levels of the ISO network model (Open Systems Interconnection, or OSI). The IEEE efforts have emphasized the need to keep the OSI and 802 specifications as compatible as possible. The 802 committees split the data link layer into two sublayers: medium access control (MAC) and logical link control (LLC). As illustrated in Figure 20-4, MAC encompasses 802.3, 802.4, and 802.5. The LLC includes 802.2. This sublayer was implemented to make the LLC sublayer independent of a specific LAN access method. The LLC sublayer is also used to provide an interface into or out of the specific MAC protocol.

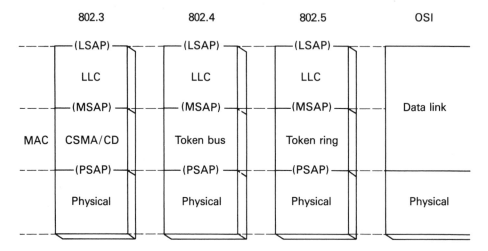

LLC: Logical Link Control
MAC: Medium Access Control
LSAP: LLC Service Access Point
MSAP: MAC Service Access Point
PSAP: Physical Access Point

FIGURE 20-4. IEEE 802 and OSI Reference Model Comparison

The MAC/LLC split provides several attractive features. First, it controls access to the shared channel among the autonomous user devices. Second, it provides for a decentralized (peer-to-peer) scheme that reduces the LAN's susceptibility to errors. Third, it provides a more compatible interface with wide area networks, since LLC is a subset of the HDLC superset. Fourth, LLC is independent of a specific access method; MAC is protocol-specific. This approach gives an 802 network a flexible interface with workstations and other networks.

Connection Options with LLC Types 1, 2, and 3

At the onset of the IEEE 802 work, it was recognized that a connection-oriented system would limit the scope and power of a local area network. Consequently, two connectionless models are now specified: acknowledged and unacknowledged.

Let us consider the reason for this approach. First, many local applications do not need the data integrity provided by a connection-oriented network. For examples: (a) Sensor equipment can afford to lose occasional data since the sensor readings typically occur quite frequently, and the data loss does not adversely affect the information content. As an illustration, the forest service in Canada uses a "connectionless" system to collect data on lightning strikes. Since several thousand strikes can occur in a very short time span, the loss of a few observations does not bias the data. (b) Inquiry-response systems, such as point-of-sale transactions, usually perform acknowledgment at the application level. These systems do not need connection-oriented services at the lower levels. (c) Packetized voice can tolerate some packet loss without affecting the quality of the voice reproduction.

Second, high-speed application processes cannot tolerate the overhead in establishing and disestablishing the connections. The problem is particularly severe in the local area network, with its high-speed channels and low error rates. Many LAN applications require fast set-ups with each other. Others require very fast communications between the DTEs.

An acknowledged connectionless service is useful for a number of reasons [FIEL86]. Consider the operations of a LAN in a commercial bank. As we learned in Chapters 10 and 11, a data link protocol usually maintains state tables, sequence numbers, and windows for each station on the link. It would be impractical to provide this service for every station on the bank's local network. Yet workstations like the bank's automated teller machines (ATMs) must be polled for their transactions. The host computer must also be assured that all transactions are sent and received without errors. The data are too important to use a protocol that does not provide acknowledgments. Additionally, the bank's alarm system needs some type of acknowledgment to assure that the computer receives notice of security breaches in the bank. It is too time-consuming to establish a "connection" before sending the alarm data.

DSAP: Destination Service Access Point Address.
SSAP: Source Service Access Point Address.

FIGURE 20-5. LLC Protocol Data Unit

Classes of Service. The 802 LAN standards include four types of service for LLC users:

Type 1   Unacknowledged connectionless service
Type 2   Connection-mode service
Type 3   Acknowledged connectionless service
Type 4   All of the above services

All 802 networks must provide unacknowledged connectionless service (Type 1). Optionally, connection-oriented service can be provided (Type 2). Type 1 networks provide no ACKs, flow control, or error recovery. Type 2 networks provide connection management, ACKs, flow control, and error recovery. Type 3 networks provide no connection set-up and disconnect, but they do provide for immediate acknowledgment of data units. Most Type 1 networks use a higher-level protocol (i.e., transport layer) to provide connection management functions.

Logical Link Control (LLC)—IEEE 802.2

As we have learned, LLC is the top sublayer of the 802 data link layer. It is common to all MAC modules in 802. It is independent of the MAC access methodology and medium.

The LLC protocol data unit is shown in Figure 20-5. The LLC unit contains a destination service access point address (DSAP), source service access point address (SSAP), control field, and information field. The standard also provides for the address field to identify a specific ring (on a token ring) and a specific node on the ring. The control field is quite similar to the HDLC control field explained in Chapter 11.

The HDLC-type commands and responses, established in the control field, depend on whether the LAN is Type 1, 2, or 3. The instruction sets allowed are shown in Table 20-1 (notice the UI frame for connectionless service and SABME for connection-oriented service). Since this material is covered in considerable detail in Chapter 11, we need not repeat the explanation here.

TABLE 20-1. LLC Commands and Responses

	Commands	Responses
Type 1	UI	
	XID	XID
	TEST	TEST
Type 2 (I Format)	I	I
(S Format)	RR	RR
	RNR	RNR
	REJ	REJ
(U Format)	SABME	UA
		FRMR
	DISC	DM
Type 3	AC0	AC0
	AC1	AC1

802 Layer Interactions Through Primitives

The 802 LANs use primitives to specify services. The primitives are defined for both the LLC and MAC sublayers. On a general level, four generic primitives are defined:

Request:	Passed from user to invoke a service.
Indication:	Passed from the service layer to user to indicate an event which is significant to the user.
Response:	Passed by user to acknowledge some procedure invoked by an indication primitive to the user.
Confirm:	Passed from the service layer to user to convey the results of previous service request(s).

The primitives are used in a variety of ways. Figure 20-6 illustrates the general time sequence diagrams for the LLC primitives. The examples in Figure 20-6 depict both the connection-oriented and connectionless service. The reader should note that the model provides for both locally confirmed service (Figure 20-6[b]), and provider-confirmed service (Figure 20-6[c]). In neither case does 802 imply that the data unit is received safely by the remote user. It only states that the data unit is delivered for the user to retrieve.

Table 20-2 lists each of the 802 primitives used with LLC and the following material describes them in more detail. The MAC primitives are also examined shortly.

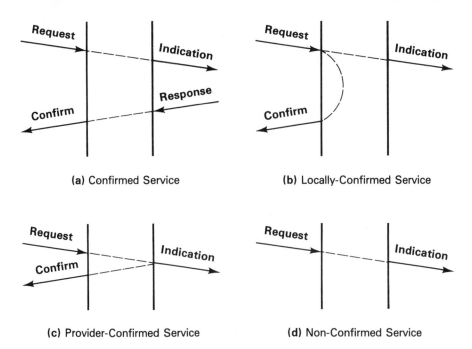

(a) Confirmed Service   **(b)** Locally-Confirmed Service

(c) Provider-Confirmed Service   **(d)** Non-Confirmed Service

FIGURE 20-6. Options for Data Transfer

TABLE 20-2. LAN Primitives

LLC PRIMITIVES

Connectionless Data Transfer
  DL-UNITDATA.request
  DL-UNITDATA.indication

Connection-Oriented Services
  DL-CONNECT.request
  DL-CONNECT.indication
  DL-CONNECT.response
  DL-CONNECT.confirm
  DL-DATA.request
  DL-DATA.indication
  DL-CONNECTION-FLOWCON-
  TROL.request
  DL-CONNECTION-FLOWCON-
  TROL.indication
  DL-RESET.request
  DL-RESET.indication
  DL-RESET.response
  DL-RESET.confirm
  DL-DISCONNECT.request
  DL-DISCONNECT.indication

MAC PRIMITIVES
  MA-UNITDATA.request
  MA-UNITDATA.indication
  MA-UNITDATA-STATUS.indication

Connectionless Unacknowledged Data Transfer. Two primitives are used for connectionless data transfer:

DL-UNITDATA.request (source-address, destination-address, data, priority)

DL-UNITDATA.indication (source-address, destination-address, data, priority)

The request primitive is passed from the network layer to LLC to request that a link service data unit (LSDU) be sent to a remote link service access point . The address parameters are equivalent to a combination of the LLC SAP and MAC addresses. The priority field is passed to MAC and implemented (except for 802.3, which has no priority mechanism). The indication primitive is passed from LLC to the network layer to indicate the arrival of a link service data unit from a remote entity. This relationship is depicted in Figure 20-6(d).

Setting Up a Connection. Four primitives are used to establish a connection-oriented session (Figure 20-6[a]):

- DL-CONNECT.request (source-address, destination-address, priority)
- DL-CONNECT.indication (source-address, destination-address, priority)
- DL-CONNECT.response (source-address, destination-address, priority)
- DL-CONNECT.confirm (source-address, destination-address, priority)

Once these primitives have been exchanged, it is the responsibility of the LLC entities to manage the flow control of the data units.

Connection-Oriented Data Transfer. Two primitives are used for connection-oriented data transfer.

- DL-DATA.request (source-address, destination-address, data)
- DL-DATA.indication (source-address, destination-address, data)

Interestingly, no confirmation primitives are returned to the sender. Generally, the MAC sublayer will deliver the frame data error-free and the LLC ensures that they are sent in the proper order. In the event of a problem, the protocol can issue disconnects or resets (discussed shortly).

Flow Control Procedures. The network layer can control the amount of data it receives from LLC and, likewise, LLC can flow-control the network layer. Two primitives are used for flow control:

- DL-CONNECTION-FLOWCONTROL.request (source-address, destination-address, amount)
- DL-CONNECTION-FLOWCONTROL.indication (source-address, destination-address, amount)

The amount parameter specifies the amount of data the affected entity is allowed to pass. It can be set with each issuance of the request or indication primitive. If set to zero, data transfer is stopped.

Resetting an LLC Connection. Four primitives are used to reset a connection:

- DL-RESET.request (source-address, destination-address)
- DL-RESET.indication (source-address, destination-address, reason)
- DL-RESET.response (source-address, destination-address)
- DL-RESET.confirm (source-address, destination-address)

A reset causes all unacknowledged data units to be discarded. LLC does not recover the lost data units, so a higher-level protocol must assume this responsibility.

Disconnecting a Session. Two primitives are used to disconnect the network/LLC session:

- DL-DISCONNECT.request (source-address, destination-address)
- DL-DISCONNECT.indication (source-address, destination-address, reason)

The reason parameter in the indication primitive states the reason for the disconnection. The disconnect can be initiated by either the LLC user or the LLC service provider. This action terminates the logical connection, and any outstanding data units are discarded.

Acknowledged Connectionless Data Transfer. The acknowledged connectionless service was added with the 1987 revision to the IEEE 802 standards. It consists of two services:

- DL-DATA-ACK An acknowleded delivery service with no prior connection establishment
- DL-REPLY A poll and response service with no prior connection establishment

The DL-DATA-ACK service allows an LLC user to request an immediate acknowledgment to a transmission. A service-class parameter in the primitive stipulates if the MAC sublayer is to participate in the acknowledgment (802.4 supports this feature). A status parameter is used by the remote peer LLC entity to indicate if the protocol data unit was/was not received successfully. The scenario in Figure 20-6(b) is used for this service.

The DL-REPLY service is quite useful when a user wishes to solicit data from another user. The LLC entity can hold a data unit and pass it to any user that polls for the data (Figure 20-6[c]), or a user can poll the remote user directly for the data (Figure 20-6[a]). As examples, the DL-DATA-ACK service would be useful for an electronic mailbox facility; the DL-REPLY service could be used to poll sensor devices on a factory floor.

LLC/MAC Primitives

The LLC and MAC sublayers use only three primitives to communicate with each other. The primitives operate as depicted in Figure 20-6[d].

- MA-UNITDATA.request (source-address, destination address, data, priority, service-class)
- MA-UNITDATA.indication (destination-address, source address, data, reception-status, priority, service-class)
- MA-UNITDATA-STATUS.indication (destination-address, source address, transmission status, provided-priority, provided-service-class)

The address parameters specify the MAC addresses. The reception-status parameter indicates the success of the transfer. An error would be reported to LLC, which might take remedial action. The transmission status parameter is also passed to LLC. Its value depends on a vendor's implementation.

Perhaps the most attractive feature of the LLC/MAC arrangement is that the MA-UNITDATA.request primitive is used to send any type of LLC data unit to any type of MAC network. In other words, the interface is portable across MAC protocols.

CSMA/CD and IEEE 802.3

The best-known scheme for controlling a local area network on a bus structure is carrier sense multiple access with collision detection (CSMA/CD). It is based on several concepts of the ALOHA protocol (Chapter 21). The most widely used implementation of CSMA/CD is found in the Ethernet specification. Xerox Corporation was instrumental in providing the research for CSMA/CD and in developing the first baseband commercial products [METC76]. The broadband network was developed by MITRE

[HOPK79],[HOPK80]. In 1980, Xerox, the Intel Corporation, and Digital Equipment Corporation jointly published a specification for an Ethernet local network. This specification was later introduced to the IEEE 802 committees and, with several modifications, has found its way into the IEEE 802.3 standard. (Be aware that the Ethernet and 802.3 interfaces differ in some signalling and formatting conventions.)

CSMA/CD Ethernet is organized around the concept of layered protocols (see Figure 20-7). The user layer is serviced by the two CSMA/CD layers, the data link layer and the physical layer. Each of the bottom two layers consists of two separate entities. The data link layer provides the actual logic to control the CSMA/CD network. It is medium independent; consequently, the network may be broadband or baseband. The 802 standard includes both broadband and baseband options.

The MAC sublayer consists of the following sublayers:

Transmit Data Encapsulation

• Accepts data from LLC.
• Calculates the CRC value and places it in the FCS field.

Transmit Media Access Management

• Presents a serial bit stream to the physical layer.
• Defers transmission when a medium is busy.
• Halts transmission when a collision is detected.
• Reschedules a retransmission after a collision.
• Inserts the PAD field for frames with a LLC length less than a minimum value.
• Enforces a collision by sending a jam message.

Receive Data Decapsulation

• Performs a CRC check.
• Recognizes and accepts any frame whose DA field is an address of a station.
• Presents data to LLC.

Receive Media Access Management

• Receives a serial bit stream from the physical layer.
• Discards frames that are less than the minimum length.

The physical layer is medium dependent. It is responsible for such services as introducing the electrical signals onto the channel, providing the

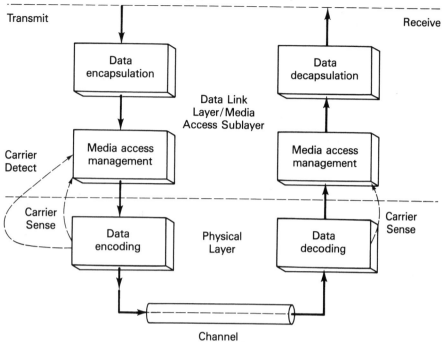

Note: The original Ethernet Channel Access sublayer is described as part of the Data Encoding and Data Decoding entities.

FIGURE 20-7. CSMA/CD Layers

timing on the channel, and data encoding and decoding. Like the data link layer, the physical layer is composed of two major entities: the data encoding/decoding entity and the transmit/receive channel access (although the IEEE 802.3 standard combines these entities in its documents). The major functions of these entities are:

Data Encoding/Decoding

- Provides the signals to synchronize the stations on the channel (this sync signal is called the preamble).
- Encodes the binary data stream to a self-clocking code at the transmitting site, and decodes the Manchester code back to binary code at the receiver.

Channel Access

- Introduces the physical signal onto the channel on the transmit side and receives the signal on the receive side of the interface.

- Senses a carrier on the channel on both the transmit and the receive side (which indicates the channel is occupied).
- Detects a collision on the channel on the transmit side (indicating two signals have interfered with each other).

In a CSMA/CD network, each station has both a transmit and receive side to provide the incoming/outgoing flow of data. The transmit side is invoked when a user wishes to transmit data to another DTE on the network; conversely, the receive side is invoked when data is transmitted to the stations on the network.

The CSMA/CD Frame. An MAC level CSMA/CD frame is shown in Figure 20-8. The preamble is transmitted first to achieve medium stabilization and synchronization. The start frame delimiter follows the preamble and indicates the start of the frame. The address fields contain the addresses of the source and destination. The destination address can identify an individual station on the network or a group of stations. The length field indicates the length of the LLC data field. If the data field is less than a maximum length, the PAD field is added to make up the difference. The FCS

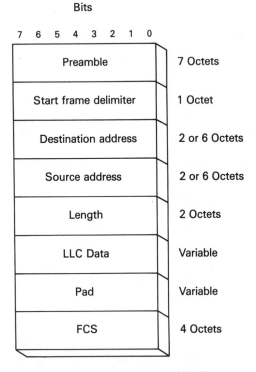

FIGURE 20-8. MAC CSMA/CD Frame

field contains the value of the CRC. The CRC is calculated on all fields except the preamble, SFD, and FCS. It is defined by the following polynominal:

$$G(x) = X^{32} + x^{26} + x^{23} + x^{22} + x^{16} + x^{12} + x^{11} + x^{10} + x^8 + x^7 + x^5 + x^4 + x^2 + x + 1$$

Token Ring—IEEE 802.5

The token ring technique has been used for several years. The IEEE 802.5 standard is now implemented in a number of vendors' products. IBM uses a variation of 802.5 in its token ring network.

The IEEE 802.5 protocol uses the single token scheme discussed previously. The IEEE 802.5 standard provides for three possible formats for the token ring. These formats are depicted in Figure 20-9. The token format (Figure 20-9[a]) consists of three bytes, the starting delimiter, the access control, and the ending delimiter. The purpose of the two delimiters is to indicate the beginning and ending of the transmission. The access control contains eight bits. Three bits are used for a priority indicator, three bits are used for a reservation indicator, and one bit is the token bit. When the token bit is set to 0, it indicates that the transmission is a token. When it is set to 1, it indicates that a data unit is being transmitted. The last bit in the access control byte is the monitor bit. This provides for a designated station to monitor the ring for error control and back-up purposes. Figure 20-9(b) shows an abort token consisting only of the starting and ending delimiter. This transmission can be sent at any time to abort a previous transmission.

The information-transfer format is illustrated in Figure 20-9(c). In addition to the starting delimiter, access control, and ending delimiter, the standard provides for additional fields. The frame control field defines the type of frame (MAC or LLC data unit) and can be used to establish priorities between two LLC peer entities. The address fields identify the sending and receiving stations. The information field contains user data. The FCS field is used for error checking and the frame status field is used to indicate that the receiving station recognized its address and copied the data in the information field.

The token ring provides for priority access to the ring through the following parameters and logic values. These are stored, updated, and checked at the ring interface units. It is suggested that the reader review these items before reading the following material.

RRR	Reservation bits allow high priority stations to request the use of the next token.
PPP	Priority bits indicate the priority of the token, and indicate which stations are allowed to use the ring.
Rr	Storage register for the reservation value.
Pr	Storage register for the priority value.
Sr	Stack register to store old values of Pr.

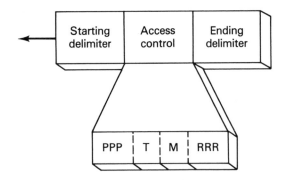

PPP: Priority Bits
T: Token Bit (0: Token, 1: Data)
M: Monitor Bit
RRR: Reservation Bits

(a) Token

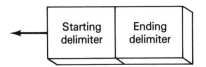

(b) Abort Token

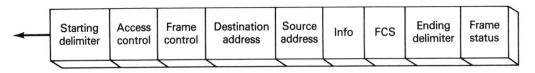

(c) Token and Data

FIGURE 20-9. IEEE 802.5 Ring Formats

Sx   Stack register to store new values of token that was transmitted.

Pm   Priority level of a frame queued and ready for transmission.

The priority bits (PPP) and the reservation bits (RRR) reside in the token. They give access to the highest priority frame ready for transmission on the ring. These values are also stored in registers Pr and Rr. The current ring service priority is indicated by the priority bits (PPP) in the token circulating around the ring.

The priority mechanism operates to provide equal access to the ring for all stations within a specific level. The same station that raised the service priority level of the ring (the stacking station) returns the ring to the original service priority. This guarantees that lower priority stations will have an opportunity to use the ring in the event the higher priority stations are idle. The Sx and Sr stacks are used to perform this function.

When a station has a frame to transmit, it requests a priority token by changing the reservation bits (RRR) as the station receives and transmits the token. If the priority level (Pm) of the frame that is ready for transmission is greater than the RRR bits, the station increases the value of RRR to the value of Pm. If the value of RRR is equal to or greater than Pm, the reservation bits (RRR) are transmitted unchanged.

After a station has claimed the token, the station transmits frames until it has completed transmission or until the transmission of another frame could not be completed before a timer expires. The station then generates a new token for transmission on the ring.

If the station does not have additional frames to transmit or if the station does not have a reservation request (contained in register Rr) which is greater than the present ring service priority (contained in register Pr), the token is transmitted with its priority at the present ring service priority and the reservation bits (RRR) at the greater of Rr or Pm. No further action is taken in this particular scenario.

On the other hand, if the station has a frame ready for transmission or a reservation request (Rr), either of which is greater than the present ring service priority, the token is generated with its priority at the greater of Pm or Rr and its reservation bits (RRR) as 0. Since the station has raised the service priority level of the ring, the station becomes a stacking station and must store the value of the old ring service priority as Sr and the new ring service priority as Sx. These values are used later to lower the service priority of the ring when there are no frames ready to transmit on the ring whose priority is equal to or greater than the stacked Sx.

The stacking station claims every token that it receives that has a priority (PPP) equal to its highest stacked transmitted priority (Sx). The RRR bits of the token are examined in order to raise, maintain, or lower the service priority of the ring. The new token is transmitted with its PPP equal to the value of the reservation (RRR) but no lower than the value of the highest stacked received priority (Sr). Remember (Sr) was the original ring priority service level. This approach assures that the highest priority gets access to the ring.

If the value of the new ring service priority (PPP equal to Rr) is greater than Sr, the RRR bits are transmitted as 0, the old ring service priority contained in Sx is replaced with a new value Sx equal to Rr, and the station continues its role as a stacking station.

However, if the Rr value is equal to or less than the value of the highest stacked received priority (Sr), the new token is transmitted at a priority value of the Sr, both Sx and Sr are removed from the stack, and if no other values of Sx and Sr are stacked, the station discontinues its role as a stacking station. This technique allows the lower priority stations to use the ring once the high priority stations have completed their transmissions.

LLC

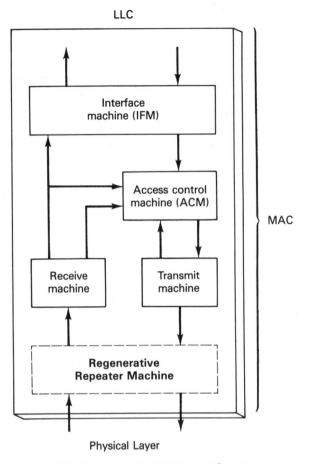

FIGURE 20-10. IEEE 802.4 Token Bus

Token Bus—IEEE 802.4

The token bus approach recommended by the IEEE 802.4 committee is illustrated in Figure 20-10. This MAC sublayer consists of four major functions: the interface machine (IFM); the access control machine (ACM); the receive machine (RxM); and the transmit machine (TxM).

The ACM is the heart of the token bus system. It determines when to place a frame on the bus and cooperates with the other stations' ACM to control access to the shared bus. It is also responsible for initialization and maintenance of the logical ring, including error detection and fault recovery. It also controls the admission of new stations.

The LLC frames are passed to the ACM by the interface machine (IFM). This component buffers the LLC sublayer requests. The IFM maps "quality of service" parameters from the LLC view to the MAC view and performs address checking on received LLC frames.

The TxM and RxM components have limited functions. The responsibility of the TxM is to transmit the frame to the physical layer. It accepts a frame from the ACM and builds a MAC protocol data unit (PDU) by prefacing the frame with the preamble and starting delimiter (SD). It also appends the FCS and the ending delimiter (ED). The RxM accepts data from the physical layer and identifies a full frame by detecting the SD and ED. It also checks the FCS field to validate an error-free transmission. If a received frame is an LLC type, it is passed from the RxM component to the IFM. The IFM indicates its arrival and then delivers it to the LLC sublayer. Once in the LLC sublayer, it goes through the necessary functions to service the end-user application, or another layer provided by ISO or HILI (IEEE 802.1).

The format of an 802.4 frame is identical to the token ring 802.5 frame, except that it has no access control (AC) field. Obviously, the AC is not needed, since this protocol does not use priority (PPP) and reservation (RRR) indicators.

Token Bus Operations. A token determines the right of access to the bus. The station with the token has control over the network. The IEEE 802.4 determines the logical ring of the physical bus by the numeric value of the addresses. A MAC or LLC data unit provides the facility for the lowest address to hand the token to the highest address. Then, the token is passed from a predecessor station to its successor station.

The token (right to transmit) is passed from station to station in descending numerical order of station address. When a station hears a token frame addressed to itself, it may transmit data frames. When a station has completed transmitting data frames, it passes the token to the next station in the logical ring. When a station has the token, it may temporarily delegate its right to transmit to another station by sending a request-with-response data frame.

After each station has completed transmitting any data frames it may have, the station passes the token to its successor by sending a token control frame.

After sending the token frame, the station listens for evidence that its successor has heard the token frame and is active. If the sender hears a valid frame following the token, it assumes that its successor has the token and is transmitting. If the token sender does not hear a valid frame following its token pass, it attempts to access the station of the network and may implement measures to pass around the problem station by establishing a new successor. For more serious faults, attempts are made to re-establish the ring.

Stations are added to an 802.4 bus by an approach called response windows:

- While holding the token, a node issues a solicit-successor frame. The address in the frame is between it and the next successor station.

- The token holder waits one window time (slot time, equal to twice the end-to-end propagation delay).
- If no response occurs, the token is transferred to the successor node.
- If a response occurs, a requesting node sends a set-successor frame and token holder changes its successor node address. The requester receives the token, sets its addresses, and proceeds.
- If multiple responses occur, another protocol is invoked to resolve the contention.

A node can drop out of the transmission sequence. Upon receiving a token, it sends a set-successor frame to the predecessor, with orders to give the token hereafter to its successor.

Options exist in the 802.4 standard to include class of service, which would make the system priority-oriented. The class of service option permits stations access to the bus based on one of four types of data to transmit:

Synchronous	Class 6
Asynchronous Urgent	Class 4
Asynchronous Normal	Class 2
Asynchronous Time-Available	Class 0

A token-holding station is allowed to maintain bus control based on priority timers. The timers give more time to the higher classes of traffic.

MAP AND TOP

Manufacturing Automation Protocol (MAP)

The Manufacturing Automation Protocol (MAP) was established by General Motors Corporation in 1962 and later transferred to the Society of Manufacturing Engineers. The intent of the specification is to provide for a common standard to achieve compatibility among communications devices that operate in manufacturing environments; for example, automobile assembly plants, petroleum manufacturing processes, and other factory floor devices.

In environments such as an automobile assembly plant, many vendors' products are connected together to provide the communications services to the workstations on the floor. The MAP specification was designed to provide for a common reference for the different vendors' products so that they can interface together without extensive protocol conversion facilities. By the end of the 1970s, GM found itself with over 20,000 programmable controllers, 2,000 robots, and 40,000 intelligent devices in its manufacturing operations. Approximately 15% of these devices could communicate outside their proprietary environment [THAC88]. Like many organizations, GM was spending an enormous amount of money on communications protocol converters.

General Motors developed the MAP specification in accordance with the Open Systems Interconnection (OSI) model. The MAP protocols correspond to the following OSI layers:

Layer 7   ISO CASE Kernel, Four ASEs: FTAM, Directory Service, Network Management, MMS
Layer 6   ISO 8822, 8823, 8824, 8825
Layer 5   ISO 8326, 8327, 8326/DAD2,8327/DAD2
Layer 4   ISO 8072 and 8073 Class 4
Layer 3   ISO Connectionless Internet 8473 and others
Layer 2   IEEE 802.2, various types and classes
Layer 1   IEEE 802.4 Broadband (10 MBit/s) and Carrierband (5MBit/s)

The majority of these layers have been discussed previously in this book. However, it should be noted that the MAP network utilizes connectionless services in the lower layers. Obviously, at the physical layer the idea of connectionless is irrelevant. However, at layers 2 and 3 the IEEE 802.2 Type 1 service uses the HDLC-type unnumbered information frame which precludes any type of connection-oriented acknowledgment. At layer 3, the Internet Protocol provides for only connectionless protocols. Consequently, the transport class 4 service is used at layer 4 to provide for the accountability of traffic.

Technical and Office Products System (TOP)

The Technical and Office Products system (TOP) was developed by Boeing Computer Services.and is now under SME. It is designed as a complementary local network to General Motors' MAP, and Boeing intends TOP to be compatible with MAP.

However, even though the two systems are very similar, some differences exist at certain levels. The common protocols for the TOP specifications are as follows:

Layer 7   ISO File Transfer, Access, and Management (FTAM) [ISO 8571/1-4]
Layer 5   ISO Session [ISO 8327]
Layer 4   ISO Transport [ISO 8073]
Layer 3   ISO Connectionless Internet [ISO 8473]
Layer 2   IEEE 802.2 Logical Link Control (LLC) [ISO 8802/2]
Layer 1   IEEE 802.3 CSMA/CD [ISO 8802/3]

The areas in which TOP and MAP differ are:

Layer 7   Manufacturing Messaging Format Standard (MMFS) are not required by TOP

Layer 7	Common Application Service Elements (CASE) are not defined for TOP
Layer 7	Network management and directory services are not defined for TOP
Layer 1	CSMA/CD Media Access Control (MAC) is defined for TOP, but not for MAP

THE IBM TOKEN RING

IBM announced its local area network token ring in the spring of 1986. Due to IBM's position in the industry, the announcement has received considerable attention. The following section provides an overview of the IBM token ring topology and protocol.

The token ring uses a combination of star and ring topology (see Figure 20-11). The physical ring provides for IEEE 802.5 unidirectional point-to-point transmission of signals to/from up to 250 workstations attached to one ring. The rings can be connected through several bridges which can also radiate through a building or office complex. IBM's principal reasons for developing this topology were (a) the ease in adding stations and links and (b) the simplification of troubleshooting problems on the links.

Each station attached to the ring is provided with a ring interface adaptor. This adaptor supports the line protocol and physical interface functions associated with any network. For example, the adaptor recognizes frames, buffers frames, generates and recognizes tokens, provides error detection, performs address decoding, and also provides for link error detection [STRO86].

The IBM topology permits several rings to be attached through the bridges. The bridges are then connected by a backbone ring. The bridge will provide a cross ring network function by copying frames that are forwarded from one ring to another ring. The bridge also provides for speed translations if rings are operating at different data rates by buffering the data. Moreover, each ring retains its own capacity and will continue operating in the event another ring on the bridge fails. Thus, the IBM token ring approach provides resiliency to station and link failure.

In addition to the bridge, a gateway is available to connect to wide area networks or other local area networks. The gateway performs speed conversions, address translations, and protocol conversions between the networks.

The fiber links are used to support point-to-point connections only. IBM has not chosen to provide multipoint or switching optic technology. The IBM optic transmitter utilizes light emitting diodes (LEDs). At the present time, laser transmitters are too expensive for the LANs and have not been specified by IBM.

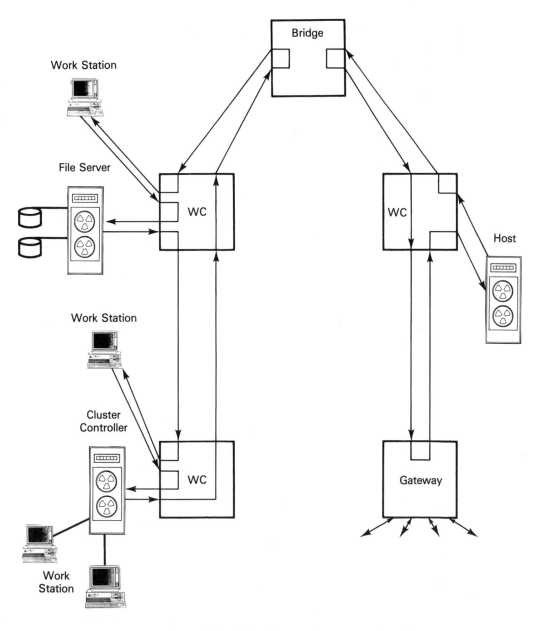

Work Station

File Server

Work Station

Cluster
Controller

Work
Station

Bridge

WC

WC

Host

WC

Gateway

WC: Wiring Concentrator

FIGURE 20-11. IBM Token Ring

Frame/Token Format

The IBM token ring frame format is quite similar to the IEEE 802.5 specification discussed earlier in this chapter (see Figure 20-9). The IBM token ring frame is depicted in Figure 20-12, which shows the following fields:

Physical Header

Starting delimiter
Starting physical control field
Destination address
Source address

Data

Data link control
Information (I)

Physical Trailer

Frame check sequence (FCS)
Ending delimiter
Ending physical control field

As with the IEEE 802.5 protocol, a node with data to transmit seizes a token and changes the token status field to identify the unit as an information frame. The frame is sent onto the ring. After the token makes one revolution of the ring, the originating station removes (absorbs) the frame from the ring and issues another token. It is not allowed to reuse the token, which allows other stations an opportunity to use the ring. Thus the IBM token ring protocol is deterministic. It gives uniform access to the ring.

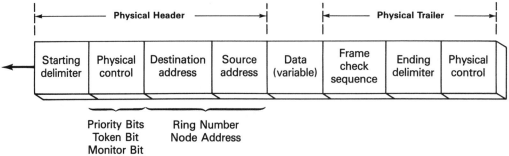

FIGURE 20-12. IBM Token Ring Format

Interfaces with LLC/MAC and SNA

IBM has replaced synchronous data link control (SDLC) at the link level. In place of SDLC for the token ring network, IBM uses the IEEE 802.2 standard, Logical Link Control (LLC) and Media Access Control (MAC). This change was necessary because SDLC uses the HDLC subset Normal Response Mode (NRM). With this technique, no peer-to-peer communications are provided on the channel. Rather, a primary station is responsible for maintaining traffic control with other stations. However with LLC, the Asynchronous Balanced Mode (ABM) is established, which allows peer-to-peer communications between any stations on the local channel. This means a station can send traffic at any time, independently of any commands coming from any other station. Of course, the "any time" transmission is subject to the MAC sublayer. For example, LLC may send a frame at any time to MAC via the DL-CONNECT.request primitive, but MAC must hold the data until it seizes a token. Therefore, LLC permits logical peer-to-peer interactions at the LLC level, subject to the constraints of the lower levels of MAC and the physical level.

The IBM token ring can also be integrated into IBM System Network Architecture (SNA). To accomplish this, SNA utilizes physical unit (PU) 2.1 for the token ring as well as its program-to-program communications protocol (APPC). The combination of these resources allows a direct connection of any two SNA nodes through the token ring network. Since SNA and the token ring use layered protocols, the SNA data unit is simply encapsulated into the I field of the token ring frame and transmitted transparently by MAC to the receiving station.

Source Routing

Previous discussions in this chapter have explained how the IEEE 802.5 protocol manages the transmission of traffic around a token ring. The IBM token ring closely adheres to the 802.5 convention. However, since IBM permits a multiple token ring network, one might ask how data are transmitted and received between rings. The answer is, by means of a concept IBM calls source routing. Source routing permits the internetworking of multiple rings and the transmission of data between these rings. In effect, it permits the networking of rings.

The routing logic for source routing is done by the insertion of routing information in the data before they are transmitted between the rings and bridges. This relieves the bridges and intermediate nodes of having to store and update complex routing tables, which in turn gives the bridges more latitude to perform other necessary functions, such as network management.

Source routing is performed in the IBM token ring below logical link control (LLC) 802.2. Consequently, the logic for inter-ring routing is a function resting between media access control (MAC) and the physical level.

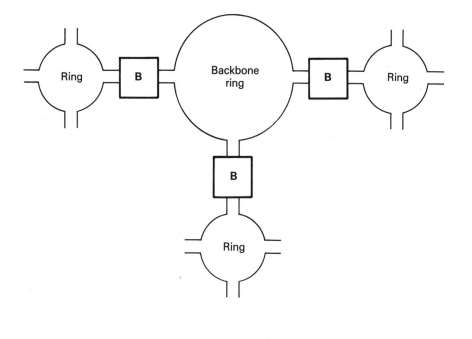

: Bridges

FIGURE 20-13. Internetworking Rings

Figure 20-13 illustrates the route of source routing. It shows a possible configuration on multiple rings that are connected to each other through bridges. The bridges, in turn, are connected through backbone systems, which can be media such as broadband frequency division multiplexed cable.

The transmitting station has four options in developing routing directions in the frames it transmits [BEDE86]:

- *Ring segment broadcast*. These frames are transmitted only within the ring and are not relayed by any of the interconnecting bridges.

- *Limited broadcast*. Frames are transmitted only once onto each ring in the network.

- *General broadcast*. These frames can be transmitted so that multiple copies may flow over the network. They must appear on each ring segment at least once. However, the list of bridges can be expanded such that multiple copies can be created. This concept is quite similar to packet flooding found in some packet switched networks.

- *Point-to-point routing.* This frame type can be transmitted such that frames travel specifically from one station to another over a designated route. There is no broadcast aspect to point-to-point routing. Only certain ring and bridge segments are involved.

Several advantages accrue to IBM's token ring source routing, the principal one being that the bridges do not have to be highly intelligent since routing information is contained in the frame that the bridge relays. The broadcast aspect of source routing also means that if a path fails, the multiple copies going on another path will reach the destination. Moreover, source routing allows flexible reconfiguration of the network. For example, if a station is relocated to another ring, a transmitting station can find the relocated device by using a general broadcast query through the network. The results of the query can be used to update the source node's routing table.

Multiple Ring Flow Control with Dynamic Windows

A link control protocol is used to accomplish several goals, three of which are: (a) high throughput, (b) fast response time, and (c) minimizing the logic required at the transmitting/receiving sites to account for traffic (such as ACKs and NAKs). The transmit window is an integral tool in meeting these goals. One of the primary functions of the window is to ensure that at least one frame has been acknowledged by the time all the permissible frames have been transmitted. In this manner, the window is kept open and the LAN station is continuously active.

One could argue that a very large window permits continuous transmissions regardless of the speed of the link and size of the frames, because the transmitter does not have to wait for acknowledgments from the receiver. While this is true, a larger window size also means that the transmitter must maintain a large queue to store those frames that have not been acknowledged by the receiver.

Interestingly, a network that is busy or congested benefits from a small window size, because the Go-Back-N (REJ) technique requires lost frames and all succeeding frames to be retransmitted. The best performance by a busy/congested network is obtained by using a small window for the following reason: the large window commits a large number of frames to be outstanding at any one time. Consequently in the event of an error (with Go-Back-N [REJ]), the erroneous frame and all those that follow must be retransmitted. Obviously, a small window size prohibits the number of frames that can be outstanding at any one time, and limits the number of retransmissions. From previous discussions, we learned that bridges serve the important function of relaying frames and providing the interconnection of multiple token rings in the network. As a consequence, considerable traffic passes through the bridges. Congestion can and sometimes does occur at the bridges. Congestion can cause errors because the bridge can become saturated and fail to deliver frames that have arrived at that bridge.

The idea of cross-network flow control is based on the concept of dynamic window management. With dynamic windowing, LLC must recognize when excess traffic accumulates in the network. It recognizes both congested and noncongested traffic conditions. Dynamic window management only involves the transmitting station. Consequently, unlike conventional subsets of HDLC, the receiver is not involved in helping the transmitter to manage the window. Moreover, the window management is not controlled by the bridge or the media access sublayer (MAC).

In order to manage traffic across the bridges and through the multiple token ring network, LLC detects when traffic is becoming heavy. This automatic congestion detection will then change the size of the transmit window dynamically. For example, as traffic conditions become heavier (or congested), LLC will decrease the size of the transmit window. The effect of this decision means that fewer frames will be outstanding at any one time and the amount of traffic passing through the bridges will be decreased. For example, if an error occurs or frames are noted out of sequence, only a limited number of frames have to be transmitted. Conversely, when traffic conditions are light and the network is noncongested, the window is expanded to permit a large number of frames to be transmitted and outstanding at any one time.

A transmit window is changed if a lost frame is confirmed at the transmitter. When the transmitter detects that the N(R) of the received frame is out of sequence with its expected transmit state variable (or it receives a reject frame), it reduces its window to one. As a consequence, it can send only one frame at a time. It must receive the acknowledgment before it sends another frame. In effect, LLC becomes a stop-and-wait protocol for a brief period. However, each successful transmission (wherein the transmitter receives back the N[R] number correctly), causes the transmitter to increase its window by one. Each increase eventually brings the window size back up to the original maximum value, which continues to be in effect until problems occur or a lost frame is detected.

Dynamic windows perform better than the fixed window algorithms. Figure 20-14 shows that throughput is increased substantially with dynamic windows [BUX86].

ANSI FIBER DISTRIBUTED DATA INTERFACE (FDDI)

ANSI (the American National Standards Institute) has developed a specification for an optical fiber local area network. It is called FDDI (Fiber Distributed Data Interface) and was written by ANSI Committee X3T9.5.

The use of optical fibers in local area networks can provide useful functions, and several reasons exist for placing DTEs on optical channels. First, computers operate at very high speeds. When computers are linked together,

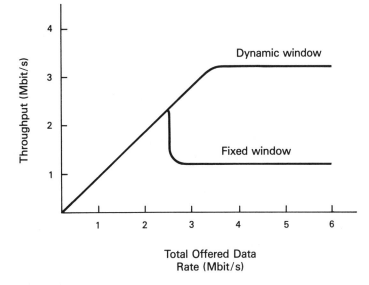

FIGURE 20-14. Dynamic versus Fixed Windows [BUX86]

the slow path between them can be a bottleneck. Consequently, the high-speed optical fiber can be a complementary path to the high-speed computer. Second, the improving technology of disk units will provide read/write speeds approaching 40 to 50 Mbit/s. This extraordinary capability can be hampered by the slow channel between the disk unit and the computer, and optical fibers can relieve this bottleneck. Third, digitized voice and video transmissions require a greater bandwidth than the typical telephone channel provides, especially if the conversations are in an interactive, real-time mode. Optical fibers provide the bandwidth capability to accommodate real-time voice transmissions.

The specifications for the FDDI are as follows: The optical fiber channel operates at 100 Mbit/s with a 1300 nm signal. Up to 1000 nodes can be placed on one optical fiber ring. The nodes can be spaced as far as 1.2 miles (2 km) apart, and the ring circumference can be up to 120 miles (200 Km). These limits minimize latency, that is, the time it takes the data (or signal) to travel around the ring.

FDDI also specifies a topology in which two independent, counterrotating optical fiber rings can be used (see Figure 20-15). The figure shows that the components (DTEs, such as terminals, computers, workstations, or graphics stations) are tied together through a wiring concentrator. The concentrator acts as a reconfiguration and concentration point for all optical wiring and data traffic. The inner channel connects only certain devices. These devices, which have inner and outer rings attached to them, are classified as A devices. The B devices are connected by only one ring. The attractive aspect of this specification is that it allows a user facility to designate those critical stations which need additional back-up. The other, less impor-

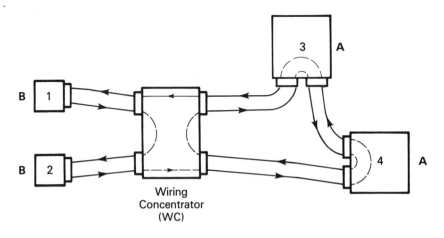

Class: **A** Inner and Outer Rings
Class: **B** Only Outer Rings
WC: Hub to Connect Stations } Reconfiguration and Backup: <u>Mixed Media</u>

FIGURE 20-15. Fiber Distributed Data Interface (FDDI)

tant DTEs, such as isolated workstations or low-priority terminals, can then be hooked up as class B stations, at a lesser cost.

The wiring concentrator allows a facility to connect stations and provide for reconfiguration. It also serves to isolate troubleshooting through the concentration point. FDDI does not specifically require that all the channels be optical fibers. The wiring concentrator could provide an interface in which a user installs optical fibers in one portion of the LAN and uses coaxial cable or twisted pair wiring in another portion of the network.

The connectors into the terminals and wiring concentrator are diodes which drive the fiber at a rate of over 100 MHz. Several years ago, these devices cost well over a hundred dollars. Light emitting diodes now can do the same task for under ten dollars each. FDDI stipulates a standard optical lightwave of 1300 nanometers, with multimode fiber.

In a building or plant, severed channels are not uncommon. Figure 20-16 depicts a possible reconfiguration in the event of a lost channel or channels. In the figure, the channel between devices 3 and 4 is lost. FDDI provides a reconfiguration by changing the loops through devices 3 and 4. As can be seen from the figure, the network remains intact. All devices have access to the net through the reconfiguration of the inner and outer loops from the wiring concentrator to devices 3 and 4.

If a station malfunctions and goes down, FDDI also stipulates that the node can be bypassed. In essence, a "mirror" directs the lightwaves through an alternative path. In Figure 20-16, if device 4 were to malfunction and become inoperable, the signals could be diverted away from the device by using the same channels and the mirrors.

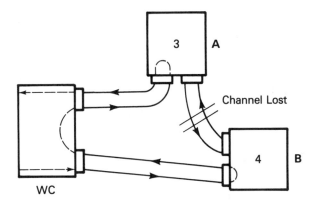

FIGURE 20-16. Channel Reconfiguration on FDDI

FDDI Token Protocol

FDDI permits multiple users to occupy the ring at one time. Figure 20-17 shows the multiple user operation. The token is passed to station B (Figure 20-17[a]), which captures the token and transmits its frame onto the ring (Figure 20-17[b]). It transmits a new token behind the frame. The frame circulates around the ring and is copied by the stations that are identified in the address field. If another station (say D) wishes to use the ring, it captures the token, and places its data behind station B's frame (Figure 20-17[c]). It then transmits a new token behind its frame. The frame is absorbed by the originating station as it circulates back around the ring (Figure 20-17[d]). The station examines the source address to determine if it should absorb the frame.

The 4B/5B Code

FDDI stipulates a unique approach to timing and clocking on the network. The reader may recall from previous discussions (Chapters 3 and 19) that the best code to be used in a network is one which provides frequent signal state changes. The changes provide the receiver with the ability to continue to adjust onto the incoming signal, thereby assuring that the transmitting device and the receiving device are synchronized with each other. The Manchester code used in the IEEE 802.3 standard is only 50 percent efficient, because every bit requires a two state transition on the line (i.e., two baud). Using Manchester code, a 100-megabit transmission rate requires 200 MHz rate. In other words, Manchester code requires twice the baud for its transmission rate.

ANSI, recognizing that the 200 MHz rate would create more expense in manufacturing the interfaces and clocking devices, devised a code called

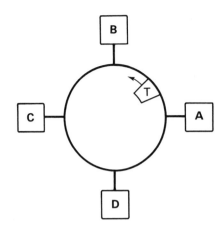

(a) Token Passed to Station **B**

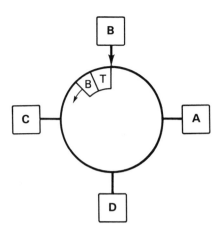

(b) Station **B** Transmits a Frame

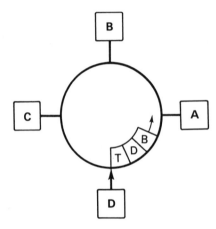

(c) Station **D** Transmits a Frame

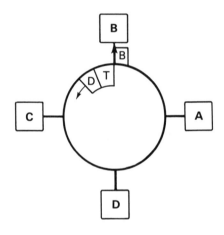

(d) Station **B** Absorbs (Removes) its Frame

T: Token

FIGURE 20-17. The FDDI Token Protocol

4B/5B, in which a 4-bit code is used to create a 5-bit code. For every 4 bits transmitted from a DTE, FDDI creates 5 bits. Consequently, the 100 Mbit/s rate on FDDI requires only 125 MHz of band.

The 4B/5B is transmitted onto the fiber with differential signalling techniques:

Binary 1:   Reverse of previous bit
Binary 0:   Same as previous bit

FDDI detects the absence or presence of light pulses, based on previous pulses. This technique is more reliable than comparing the signals to an absolute threshold.

Furthermore, since a binary 1 is always sent with a light pulse that is the opposite (present or absent) from the previous pulse, each 4B/5B code guarantees at least two signal transmissions and no more than three binary 0s in a row will occur. The 4B/5B differential signalling code provides a good clocking signal. The quality of the signal is further enhanced to reduce timing jitter (see Chapters 3 and 7) by the use of phase-locked loops and elastic buffers at each repeater.

LAN PERFORMANCE

Numerous studies have been performed to determine LAN performance with different topologies, protocols, and work loads. [STAL84] provides a good general description; [STUC83] describes the performance of the IEEE LANs; and [METC76] analyses CSMA/CD. This discussion is derived from these sources.

Consider the token ring and token bus. They can be analyzed together if the logical ordering is the same as the physical ordering. We assume a maximum propagation delay a; a network with N active stations; and each station ready to send traffic. Throughput is defined as:

$$S = T_1/(T_1 + T_2)$$

Where: S = throughput; T_1 = average time to transmit a packet; T_2 = average time to pass a token.

Consider CSMA/CD. The time on the channel is the maximum slot time from the start of transmission to detect a collision. Let us assume a station transmits with probability P. The CSMA/CD experiences: (a) a period of time (slots) with no user signals (collisions or no data) (this is called a contention interval), and (b) data transmission for 1/2a slots.

To determine the contention interval (average length):

$$A = (1 - 1/N)^{n-1}$$

If we assume the rules of CSMA/CD usage, throughput can be calculated as:

$$S = 1/[1 + 2a (1 - A)/A]$$

Figure 20-18 plots CSMA/CD and token throughput as a function of active workstations N. Interestingly, token passing performance improves with the increase in N because less time is spent in token passing [STAL85]. Conversely, throughput drops with CSMA/CD because of the increase in collisions.

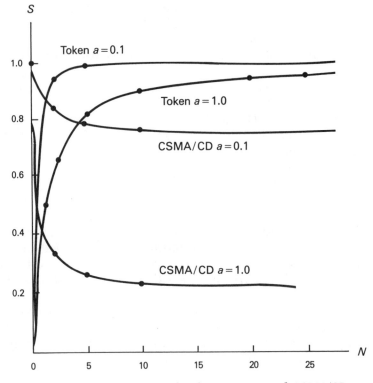

FIGURE 20-18. Comparison of Token Passing and CSMA/CD Throughput [STAL85]

To conclude this brief analysis, [STAL83] compares the IEEE 802 protocols: CSMA/CD, token bus and token ring. Figure 20-19 (a) and (b) depict the performance with one active station and 100 stations active out of a total of 100 attached to the network respectively. The actual data rate is the capacity of the network; the data rate is the actual rate of user data transmission. Several conclusions are noteworthy:

- All protocols perform well under light to medium loads.
- Token bus is less efficient under light loads because token passing delay is greater on the bus than on the ring.
- CSMA/CD is less efficient for heavy loads because of the increased collisions.
- Token ring is most efficient under varying work loads.

To refine this definition, [STAL84] normalizes time where packet transmission equals 1 and propagation time equals a. Then, throughput is a function of:

$$S = 1/(1 + a/N) \quad \text{for } a < 1$$
$$S = 1/[a (1 + 1/N)] \quad \text{for } a > 1$$

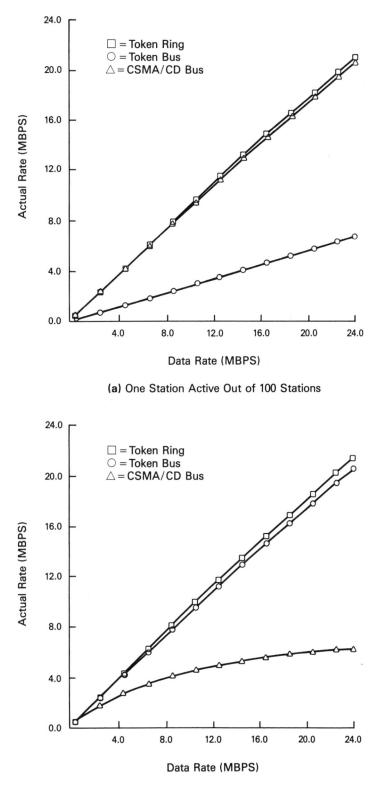

(a) One Station Active Out of 100 Stations

(b) 100 Stations Active Out of 100 Stations

FIGURE 20-19. Comparison of CSMA/CD, Token Bus, and Token Ring

SUGGESTED READINGS

Those readers wishing a general overview of local area networks should read [DERF83]. A text by [STAL84] provides a good tutorial as well as more detailed material. [STUL83], [STAL84], and [METC76] provide lucid descriptions of LAN performance. *Data Communications* magazine provides several excellent articles on the IBM token ring (see the February 1986 and March 1986 issues). Those readers wishing to know the details of IEEE LANs should review the following specifications (published also as ANSI and ISO Standards:

- *Logical Link Control:* ANSI/IEEE Std. 802.2 - 1987, ISO/DIS8802/2
- *Carrier Sense Multiple Access with Collision Detection:* ANSI/IEEE Std. 802.3 - 1987, ISO/DIS8802/3
- *Token-Passing Bus Access Method:* ANSI/IEEE Std. 802.4 - 1987, ISO/DIS8802/4
- *Token Ring Access Method:* ANSI/IEEE Std. 802.5 - 1987, ISO/DIS8802/5

The FDDI specification is published as X3.139 - 1987.

QUESTIONS

TRUE/FALSE

1. A local area network (LAN) can use either softwire or hardwire media, with either baseband or broadband schemes.
2. The IEEE protocols permit the bypassing of logical link control (LLC).
3. MAP and TOP use the same physical layer protocols.
4. A multi-network IBM token ring network is also a star network.
5. Dynamic windows provide better total throughput than fixed windows as the load increases on a network.
6. Match the LAN protocol description with the appropriate IEEE 802 protocol:

   Description

   a) Carrier sense, collision detection
   b) Top sublayer of data link control
   c) Uses a token ring
   d) Uses a token bus
   e) Bottom sublayer of data link control

Term

1. MAC
2. 802.3
3. LLC
4. 802.4
5. 802.5

7. While no one agrees on the exact definition of a local area network (LAN), several characteristics are unique to a LAN. What are these characteristics?

8. The decision to install a broadband or baseband LAN rests on several technical considerations. What are these considerations?

9. Draw the primitive flow in a time-sequence diagram to depict a connectionless exchange of data across a LAN.

10. Draw the primitive flow in a time-sequence diagram to depict a local node providing confirmation of a data unit.

11. Draw the same flow as in Question 10 except the confirmation is initiated from the remote side of the LAN.

12. What is the purpose of the jam signal on a Ethernet network?

13. The concept of source routing is being used in numerous wide area and local networks. Describe how IBM uses source routing on the IBM token ring network.

SELECTED ANSWERS

1. True. All options are available, but softwire media is not used much. Most LANs use twisted pair or coaxial cable.

2. False. The LLC provides the user interface to the MAC sublayer.

3. False. TOP uses IEEE 802.3 and MAP uses IEEE 802.4.

4. True.

5. True.

6.
Description	Term
a)	2
b)	3
c)	5
d)	4
e)	1

13. A user node maintains the routing addresses of those stations that the node accesses frequently. The routing information includes a list of the bridges that will relay the frame. It is used by the bridges to decide how to relay the traffic to the token rings. If a transmitting station wishes to reach a new station, it can send out a query through its local ring to determine if the station is on the ring. If it is not on the local ring, then a general query is

sent through the entire network. The response from this query contains the needed routing information which the transmitting station uses and inserts into the frame. This information is used by the intermediate bridges to determine how to route the traffic through the network.

CHAPTER 21

Satellite, Radio, and Television Systems

INTRODUCTION

In this chapter, we expand the discussions in Chapter 4, "Communications Media," and provide more detail on satellite, radio, and television systems. Nonetheless, this chapter is meant as an overview of these subjects. For more complete discussions, please refer to the bibliography at the end of the chapter.

Radio Waves

The radio wave and transmitting antenna are designed around the following operations (see Figure 21-1).

> Ground or surface wave
> Space wave
> Sky wave
> Satellite-based wave
> Scatter wave

The surface or ground wave is characterized by its propagation along the lower edge of the earth's surface. In effect, it follows the curvature of the earth. This signal is used generally in the low frequency bands (30 KHz–300 KHz). It is also used for broadcasting in the medium frequency band (300 KHz–3 MHz).

The long wavelengths of ground waves are relatively immune to terrestrial topography. For example, a 30-KHz signal has a wavelength of 6.2

miles (10,000 meters). Buildings or mountains do not affect the signal very much. However, a higher frequency signal will experience distortion and break-up from trees, mountains, and large buildings.

The space wave travels in a straight line between the transmitting and receiving antennas. It is considered to be a line-of-sight transmission (a direct wave). In addition, it has a component which travels by reflecting from the earth. This type of signal is used principally in TV broadcasting operation in the VHF/UHF/SHF bands.

The sky wave is transmitted upward into the ionosphere. Based on the ionospheric conditions, the signal or a portion of it is returned to earth and received at the ground station. This type of transmission is commonly used for high frequency radio communications devices (3 MHz–30 MHz). It has seen rather extensive use in radio broadcasting and long-distance telephone operations.

The satellite wave method uses a radio frequency transmitted to a satellite station which is amplified and then transmitted back down to earth at a different frequency. This technique is discussed in more detail later in this chapter.

The fifth method is called scatter propagation and is used on long-distance high frequency links. It also provides multi-channel telephone links. It is so named because the signal travels downward in a scatter approach toward the receiver.

COMMUNICATIONS PROTOCOLS FOR SATELLITES

Chapter 4 introduces satellite communications and describes the characteristics as a transmission medium. In this section, we examine satellite communications protocols and satellite-based applications.

Frequency Division Multiple Access (FDMA)

Communications between a satellite and the earth stations can be maintained with a number of techniques. One approach, frequency division multiple access (FDMA), is used on many systems. The entire channel spectrum is divided into subchannels, and users are assigned the various subchannels to transmit any traffic they wish within their prescribed spectrum space.

FDMA operates with either a single channel per carrier (SCPC) or a multiple channel per carrier (MCPC). SCPC is implemented with analog (FM) and digital (CVSD or PCM/PSK) modulation techniques, and is found in systems with only a few channels. MCPC uses similar modulation techniques and is used in larger systems [HEYD87].

Frequency division multiplexing has some significant drawbacks. First, some of the available bandwidth has to be utilized as a guardband to pre-

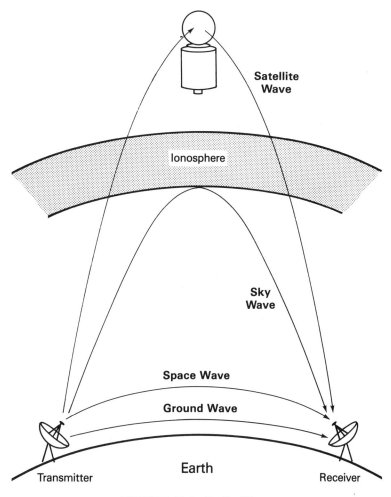

FIGURE 21-1. Radio Waves

vent adjacent channels from interfering with each other. Second, if the users are not all transmitting regularly, then much of the subchannel bandwidth is wasted because of the idle channel conditions. Third, multiple signals passing through the satellite simultaneously can create intermodulation distortion. Fourth, delay is encountered when frequency assignments are changed. An FDMA network is not very flexible in this regard. A new node requires rather extensive frequency clearance coordination.

Another approach is the use of time division multiplexing (TDM) in which the time spectrum is divided and users share time slots on the communications channel. The major shortcoming of time division multiplexing is similar to that of FDM. Since the capacity of the channel is preallocated to each potential user, the channel is wasted if the user is not transmitting regularly. We address these problems shortly when we look at a form of multiplexing called time division multiple access (TDMA).

ALOHA

In the early 1970s, Norman Abramson, at the University of Hawaii, devised a technique for uncoordinated users to effectively compete for a channel. The approach is called the ALOHA system; it is so named because the word ALOHA is a Hawaiian greeting without regard to whether a person is arriving or departing. The original ALOHA technique used a ground-based radio packet system, rather than satellites, but the ideas are applicable to any channel media when users are contending for their use.

The premise of ALOHA is that users are acting on a peer-to-peer basis—they all have equal access to the channel. A user station transmits whenever it has data to send. Since the channel is not allocated by any primary/secondary structure, it is possible (and probable) that users will occasionally transmit at approximately the same time. Simultaneous transmission results in the signals interfering and distorting each other as the separate signals propagate up to the satellite transponder. These "collisions" necessitate the retransmission of the damaged frames. (The term "packet" is used in place of "frame" under the ALOHA scheme.) Since the users of the satellite link know exactly what was transmitted onto the up-link channel and when it was transmitted, they only need listen to the down-link channel at a prescribed time to determine if the broadcast packet arrived without damage.

If the packet is damaged due to a collision, the stations are required to retransmit the damaged packet. In essence, the idea is to listen to the down-link channel one up-and-down delay time after the packet was sent. If the packet is destroyed, the transmitting site is required to wait a short random period and then retransmit. The randomized wait period diminishes the chances of the competing stations colliding again, since the waiting times will likely differ and result in retransmissions at different times. When traffic increases, the randomized waits can be increased to diminish the collisions.

Figure 21-2 depicts a typical ALOHA system using satellite communications. Stations A and B are transmitting packets on a shared channel. The down-link channel shows that packet 1 from station A is transmitted up and down safely; packet 2 from station B is also transmitted without error. However, the second packet from A and the first packet from B are transmitted at approximately the same time. As the transmissions of the two stations are narrow-casted up to the satellite station, the signals interfere with each other, resulting in a collision.

The satellite station is not responsible for error detection or error correction; it transmits what it receives from the up-link. On the down-link,

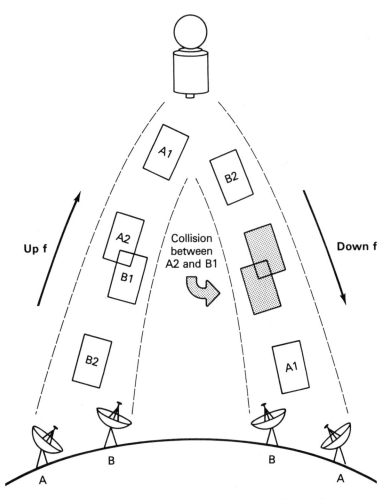

FIGURE 21-2. Random ALOHA on Satellite Links

stations A and B note that the packets have collided and, upon waiting a random period of time (usually a few milliseconds), attempt to retransmit. This approach is quite effective when the users are uncoordinated and are sending traffic in bursts, such as data from keyboard terminals.

Calculating Delay on an ALOHA Channel. We assume a packet is initially transmitted which takes t seconds and is received after Nt seconds of transmission delay. If interference occurs, the sender waits a random period (between 0 and K packet times) before retransmitting. On the average, a wait of (1 + K) t/2 seconds takes place before another retransmission.

Let us assume further that s represents channel throughput, that is, the amount of traffic successfully delivered. The value g represents total traffic, including successful and unsucccessful deliveries. Therefore, the ratio g/s represents the number of times each packet has to be retransmitted before a successful delivery occurs.

Given these assumptions, the total average delay (TAD) through an ALOHA channel is computed as [ROSN82]:

$$\text{TAD} = t/2 \, [1 + e^{2g} \, (1 + 2N) + K \, (e^{2g} - 1)]$$

Where: t = packet length in seconds; g = total traffic (bits per second); N = propagation delay in packet lengths; K = retransmission protocol delay in packet lengths; e = 2.718 (base of natural logarithms).

Figure 21-3 plots several ALOHA channel delay scenarios, with a channel rate of 50 Kbit/s and a packet length of 1000 bits [ROSN82]. The value t is 20 ms (1000/50000 = .02). Figure 21-3 reveals that little delay is encoun-

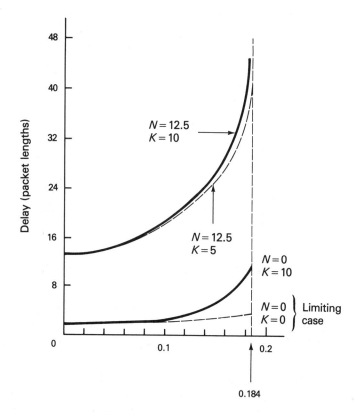

ALOHA channel throughput, S

N = Round-trip satellite delay, in packet lengths

K = Protocol retransmission delay (maximum waiting time before retransmitting a collided packet), in packet lengths

FIGURE 21-3. An ALOHA Channel Delay versus Throughput [ROSN82]

tered with a light load on the channel. As traffic increases, more collisions occur and the delay increases. The curves show the packet retransmission delay (K) increases as throughput (s) increases.

Random ALOHA experiences considerable degradation of throughput when the channel is heavily utilized. However, it should be kept in mind that what is transmitted across the channel is all end-user data. Unlike the primary/secondary polling systems, ALOHA uses no polls, selects, or negative responses to polls. Only end-user information is transmitted. Nonetheless, the pure random scheme can be improved by adapting a more efficient strategy for using the uncoordinated channel, called Slotted ALOHA.

Slotted ALOHA requires that common clocks be established at the earth stations and at the satellite. The clocks are synchronized to send traffic at specific periods. For example, the clocks may require that packets are transmitted only on 20 ms (.020 second) increments. In this example, the 20 ms increment is derived from a 50,000-bit/s channel and 1000-bit packets (1000 ÷ 50,000 = .020 second).

The 20 ms increment is referred to as the packet duration, which is the time in which the packet is transmitted on the channel. All stations are required to transmit at the beginning of a slot period. A packet cannot be transmitted if it overlaps more than one slot.

The Slotted ALOHA approach increases throughput substantially on the channel, because if packets overlap or collide, they do so completely; at most, only one slot is damaged. However, like pure Random ALOHA, the Slotted ALOHA does offer opportunities for collisions. For example, if two stations transmit in the same clock period, their packets collide. As in the pure Random ALOHA approach, the stations are required to wait a random period of time before attempting to seize a slot for retransmission.

Another refinement to Slotted ALOHA is Slotted ALOHA with Nonowner. The channel slots are combined into an ALOHA frame. The ALOHA frame must equal or exceed the up-and-down propagation delay. This relationship is defined as:

$$AFL \geqq PD$$
$$\text{or}$$
$$NSL * SLT \geqq PD$$

Where: AFL = ALOHA frame length; PD = the up-and-down propagation delay; NSL = number of slots in an ALOHA frame; and SLT = time interval of a slot.

Consequently, a 1000-bit packet lasting 20 ms would require a minimum of 12 slots to make up the ALOHA frame: 12 slots × 20 ms = 240 ms. The 240 ms period represents the minimum up-and-down propagation delay (120 ms [up] + 120 ms [down] = 240 ms).

Slotted ALOHA with Nonowner requires that a station select an empty slot in the frame. Once the user has seized the slot, it is reserved for the user for successive frames until the user relinquishes the slot. The relinquishment occurs by the station sending a protocol control code, such as EOT (end of transmission). Upon receiving an EOT, the next frame transmitted is empty for that particular slot. A user station then is allowed to contend for the slot with the next subsequent frame. The only collisions occurring on Slotted ALOHA with Nonowner are when stations pick the same slot in the 240 ms frame.

Another variation of Slotted ALOHA is Slotted ALOHA with Owner. The slots of each frame are now owned by users. The user has exclusive use of its slot within the frame as long as it has data to transmit. In the event that the user relinquishes the slot, it so indicates with an established code. The slot becomes empty and is available for any other user to seize it. Once another user has seized the slot, it has exclusive rights to the use of the slot, until the original owner seizes the slot. The rightful owner can claim the slot at any time by beginning transmissions within its designated slot in the frame. The relinquishment is required when the rightful owner transmits. Obviously, the first time the owner transmits in its slot a collision may occur. On the subsequent frame, the rightful owner retransmits. The relinquishing station then must look for another free slot or go to its own slots, if it has them. This refined approach of ALOHA is classified as a peer-to-peer priority structure, since some stations can be given priority ownership over other stations.

Time Division Multiple Access (TDMA)

COMSAT initiated work on TDMA in the mid-1960s. Since then, scores of TDMA systems have been implemented worldwide. Even though FDMA is still the prevalent technique for signalling, TDMA is used more on new systems. TDMA shares a satellite transponder by dividing access into time slots. Each earth terminal is designated a time and its transmission burst is precisely timed into the slot. Our example of TDMA is the Satellite Business System (SBS).

TDMA assigns slots as needed. However, unlike the ALOHA system, the slots are assigned by a primary station called the reference (REF). As depicted in Figure 21-4, the reference station accepts requests from the other stations, and based on the nature of the traffic and available channel capacity, the REF assigns these requests to specific frames for subsequent transmission. Every 20 frames, the reference station is assigned to each transponder of the system. SBS provides for as many as 10 active transponders per satellite.

Figure 21-4 also shows the earth station components. The major components consist of the port adapter, the satellite communications controller (SCC), a burst modem, the transmit/receive device, and an antenna.

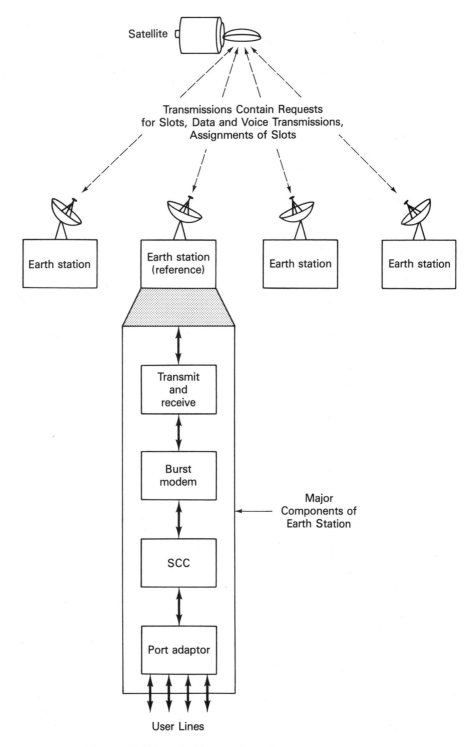

Satellite

Transmissions Contain Requests
for Slots, Data and Voice Transmissions,
Assignments of Slots

Earth station

Earth station
(reference)

Earth station

Earth station

Transmit
and
receive

Burst
modem

← Major
Components of
Earth Station

SCC

Port adaptor

User Lines

SCC: Satellite Communications Controller

FIGURE 21-4. Satellite Business Systems (SBS) TDMA

The port adapter is responsible for interfacing the user lines into the earth station. The adapter accepts voice images at a rate of 32 Kbit/s, and data at rates varying from 2.4 Kbit/s to 1.544 Mbit/s.

All digital images are passed to the satellite communications controller, which is a software-oriented unit that consolidates the functions of timing, station assignment, switching, and processing of voice and data calls. It calculates channel requirements based on the number of voice connections, the number of data ports available, and the number of queued data connection requests. It then assigns these requests to TDMA frames.

The burst modem sends out a 48 Mbit/s signal with 15 ms frames (.015 second) under the direction of the satellite controller. Thus, each transponder has the capability of operating at 48 Mbit/s (see Figure 21-5).

The transmit/receive antennas are responsible for transmitting and receiving the up-and-down channel links. SBS operates at 14 gigahertz on the up-link and 12 gigahertz on the down-link. This transmission band was chosen because it is relatively free from other satellite transmissions, and it allows the earth stations to operate relatively free from the terrestrial microwave operations of 4/6 gigahertz.

On a 15 ms frame, the reference station (REF) transmits an assignment set for all SCCs using the transponder. As mentioned earlier, this transmission is sent every 20 frames. The assignment set specifies the capacity and position of each SCC's traffic burst to the transponder. Recall that assignments are made in response to the requests received in earlier frames. The control field of the frame contains the assignments and the requests from the competing stations. The remainder of the frame consists of the traffic, which contains the traffic bursts from each SCC that was assigned a position by the reference station.

The traffic is packed in 512-bit channels consisting of a 32-bit destination address and 480 bits of data. The 480-bit data frame was chosen to

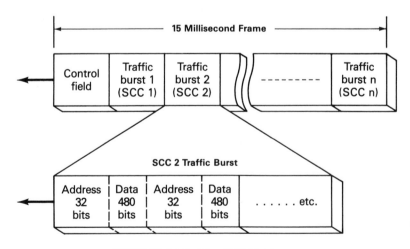

FIGURE 21-5. The TDMA Frame

accommodate the requirement for a voice transmission rate of 32 Kbit/s (480 × [1 second/.015 slot] = 32,000).

The 32 Kbit/s rate uses only a small fraction of the total 48 Mbit channel capacity. Consequently, many voice and data transmissions can be time division multiplexed (TDM) efficiently onto the high-speed 48 Kbit/s channel.

Satellite-Switched Time Division Multiple Access (SS/TDMA). SS/TDMA uses TDMA and multi-beam antennas. The antennas cover several geographical zones. A switch at the satellite connects the up-link and down-link channels by switching the configuration as necessary. SS/TDMA may also use communications channels directly between the satellites. Often, communicating ground stations are not visible by the same satellite. An intersatellite link (ISL) can be used to directly link-up two satellites [BERT87]. The combination of SS/TDMA and ISL appears very promising and the 1990s will likely see operational systems.

Satellite Occasional Use Services

Many people have heard a television program commentator warn the audience that the broadcast may be terminated before the program ends (the "Heidi" effect). The satellite providing the media has not gone out of operation; the television program producer did not buy enough channel time. Most satellite carriers market an occasional use package, designed for a broadcaster who requires only periodic use of the satellite channel. Concerts, sporting events, and political conventions are typical examples.

Occasional use service is generally provided in two segments. The space segment includes the leased satellite channel capacity. The earth segment consists of the transmit and receive facilities. Most carriers offer transportable earth stations as part of the earth segment arrangements. The mobile stations are designed for flexible, rapid employment and usually have self-contained television units. They use a relatively small 4.5 meter antenna and operate at 6/4 or 14/12 GHz.

The prices vary widely. A prime-time channel hour on a 6/4 GHz package runs from $500–$900 (U.S.). A 14/12 GHz package is even lower; a prime-time hour ranges from $300–$700 (U.S.). This charge does not include the earth segment packages.

Without question, occasional use satellite services have had a tremendous impact on our personal and professional lives.

VSAT Systems

The very small aperture terminal (VSAT) is a satellite system that offers low cost and flexibility. The earth stations are compact and use a small antenna/dish (about 6 feet or 1.8 meters). Due to the small size, they can be located directly on the user site and interface directly with user equipment, such as workstations and cluster controllers. The systems can be configured for one-way or two-way transmission, at speeds of about 120 Kbit/s. VSAT is typically used with automated teller machines (ATMs), point-of-sale (POS) devices, financial/news networks, and other inquiry-response applications.

MARITIME COMMUNICATIONS

In the past, ships at sea were equipped with high frequency (HF) radio systems, using telephony and TELEX transmission schemes. The earlier systems also relied on Morse code. While HF systems are still used (with signal reflection across the ionized layers) the majority of maritime users are utilizing satellite systems for transmission and reception of data, video, and voice.

In 1979, the International Maritime Satellite Organization (INMARSAT) was founded to foster standards and operational facilities for at-sea communications. It became operational in 1982 and now provides continuous communications services to equipped ships in all parts of the world.

The operation of INMARSAT is governed by several CCITT recommendations. In this section we discuss the operations of a maritime-ship communication system as well as the CCITT mobile data transmissions specifications.

An at-sea ship's communications process with a satellite is controlled by an earth station (obviously a misnomer in this case). The ship's antenna dish is quite small, only .9 meter in diameter. It is mounted on the superstructure of the ship, to prevent interference with the signal. In order to maintain alignment with the satellite, a stabilization system is utilized to keep the dish pointing directly to the communicating satellite.

The CCITT has developed these recommendations to govern the communications for maritime operations:

X.350   General requirements for maritime satellite service.

X.351   Packet assembly/disassembly facilities (PADs) in association with maritime services.

X.352   Internetworking public packet networks and maritime satellite systems.

X.353   Routing principles for maritime satellite systems and public data networks.

The structure for a maritime satellite service is depicted in Figure 21-6. The maritime local circuit is between the ship's DTE and the ship's earth station. The maritime satellite circuit is the satellite channel between the ship's earth station and the coastal earth station. The maritime terrestrial circuit is the circuit connecting the coastal earth station to the maritime

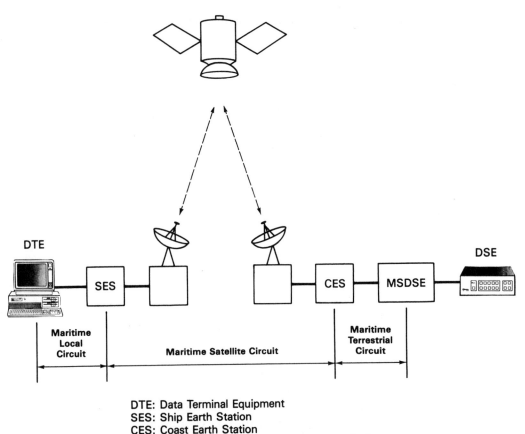

DTE: Data Terminal Equipment
SES: Ship Earth Station
CES: Coast Earth Station
MSDSE: Maritime Satellite Data Switching Exchange
DSE: Data Switching Exchange

FIGURE 21-6. Maritime Satellite Service

satellite data switching exchange (MSDSE). This exchange provides the internetworking between the satellite system and the public data network. It handles routing and call control for ships at sea. It is also responsible for managing the charging of the calls.

X.350 specifies several options for the interface between the components. For example, recommendations X.21 bis and X.22 are permitted for circuit switched public data networks, and X.25 is permitted for interfacing into packet networks. It is recommended that the interface be provided through an X.25 public data network due to the multiplicity of functions provided in this specification and its worldwide use.

Recommendation X.121 is used to address ships at sea. The format for the shipboard DTE is composed as: the DNIC plus a ship station identity (recommendation E.210/F.120) plus optional digits identifying the on-board DTE. Three DNICs have been assigned, one each to the Atlantic, Pacific, and Indian oceans. Their numbers are 1111, 1112, and 1113, respectively.

TABLE 21-1. Examples of Maritime Satellite Service Prefix and Access Codes

Code	Application
15	Radiogram service
20	Access-to-maritime PAD
24	Telex letter service
32	Medical advice
34	Person-to-person call
36	Credit card calls
38	Medical advice
39	Maritime assistance
41	Meteorological reports
42	Navigational hazards and warnings
43	Ship position reports
51	Meteorological forecasts
55	News, international
56	News, national

In addition to the X.121 identification scheme, the actual types of transmissions are identified by prefix codes. Presently, a two-digit code is used to describe the types of calls, such as telephone, TELEX, or data, and the category of calls within those transmission types. Some examples for the use of prefix codes are shown in Table 21-1.

X.351 provides the specifications for the implementation of PAD support for the maritime service. Essentially, recommendations X.3 and recommendations X.29 are used for the PAD support. The reader may wish to refer to Chapter 18 for a discussion of these specifications. Generally speaking, the PAD parameter settings are similar to the settings of X.3, but some of the parameter values do differ and the reader should refer to the specific X.351 specification if more detail is needed.

ENHANCED TELEVISION

It is beyond the scope of this book to delve into the technology of television. However, a few words are in order about some recent events that will affect all of us. These events revolve around using the analog-to-digital and compression techniques discussed earlier in this book.

An improved standard is being considered for television called multiplexed analog components (MAC). It has been used for direct broadcast satellite service. Several proposals currently are being examined in the industry, but all of them use some common features. For example, the chrominance and luminance TV signals are compressed and time division multiplexed (in contrast to the frequency division multiplex techniques of conventional television systems). The sound and data signals are inserted into the modulated video signal. The use of these compression techniques provides substantial quality at reduced bandwidth. Some systems have operated with a total data capacity of 1.6 Mbit/s, and provide 6 high-quality audio channels as well as the video signals.

Several systems are under development which will substantially improve the quality of color television. Various countries and companies have embarked upon efforts to develop specifications for these systems. They are broadly classified as follows [GAGG87]:

Enhanced television

Extended definition television (EDTV)

High-definition television (HDTV)

The efforts to enhance the current television systems relate principally to decreasing distortions due to color quadrature distortion and phase and amplitude distortions. Considerable effort is being devoted to improving the television receivers' band-pass filters to discern the colors more accurately. Many of the systems are working on techniques to reduce the interline flicker and large area flicker that occur due to the interlaced display of the alternate fields.

The International Radio Consultative Committee (CCIR) is working on a digital television standard. The standard is quite similar to the analog-to-digital conversion techniques discussed in earlier chapters of this book. The recommendation currently in favor is compatible with current TV standards with regard to the 525 lines. It calls for a sampling of the luminance signal at 13.5 MHz and the sampling of the color difference signals at 6.75 MHz. Each sample is coded into an 8-bit word. Consequently, the 8-bit word provides for up to 256 quantization levels.

The Japanese Broadcasting Company, the CBS Corporation, and other organizations are working on a completely new approach, generally called high definition television (HDTV). The CBS system uses 1050 interlaced lines with a requirement of 16 MHz of video bandwidth. Other organizations are working with similar concepts but are trying to develop proposals which require less bandwidth than the CBS system. It is quite likely that newer systems will evolve because they make sense economically. For example, electronic teleconferencing, publishing, printing, and certainly electronic cinematography are all using some form of digitized video technique.

The flexibile and economical digital technology encourages the transition to digital television. The quality of HDTV virtually ensures its use. These factors have already encouraged several manufacturers to develop digital video products for VCRs, video theater (replacing 35 mm), video conferencing, and sales promotions.

SUGGESTED READINGS

[EVAN86] provides a succinct discussion of antennas. The trade-offs of satellite TDMA and FDMA are summarized in [SHAR87] and [HEYD87]. [OLSO86] provides a good overview of satellite bands. [WATE85] is an informative description of FM radio. [ROSN82] is a valuable text on satellite and packet-based systems.

QUESTIONS

TRUE/FALSE

1. The reflection of a sky wave depends on both the ionization density and the frequency of the wave.
2. A satellite link using a half-duplex protocol benefits from short blocks of transmissions.
3. The Slotted ALOHA protocol uses statistical multiplexing schemes.
4. The color video signals of a television transmission must contain the luminance and chrominance components.
5. Match the type of radio wave to its appropriate description.

   Description

   a) Uses the ionosphere for a "reflector."
   b) Line-of-vision wave.
   c) Propagation along the earth's surface.

   Term

   1. Space wave
   2. Ground wave
   3. Sky wave

6. Satellite-based transmissions used some version of frequency division multiplexing (FDM) or time division multiplexing (TDM). Compare these two schemes and cite their advantages and disadvantages. Explain the advantages of using statistical TDM on these links.
7. Even though the Slotted ALOHA protocol is more efficient than Random ALOHA, it also has some disadvantages. From your analysis of this protocol, what do you think are its problems?
8. Explain the effect of satellite channel propagation delay on response time and throughput.
9. The sidebands of a modulated television video signal exceed the bandwidth capacity of a 6 MHz TV channel. What technique is employed to continue the signal to the prescribed bandwidth?

SELECTED ANSWERS

1. True.

2. False.

3. False. It uses a non-statistical TDM scheme.

4. True.

5.
Description	Type
a)	3
b)	1
c)	2

7. As stated in the text, each station must have a clock which is synchronized on the actual distance between the station and the satellite. These clocks must be adjusted to compensate for the slight difference of distance. Another disadvantage is that Slotted ALOHA works with a time division multiplexing slot. That is to say, the slot is fixed in length. As a consequence, if users have less data to transmit (which is often the case), then the length of the slot will waste channel capacity because some of the slot is empty.

9. Television systems employ sideband filters to suppress the lower sideband.

CHAPTER 22

Personal Computers: Data Communications and Networks

INTRODUCTION

In the past, the term "personal computer" (PC) described a small machine that was put to personal use.[1] Prior to the advent of the name, these machines were called microcomputers to connote their smallness, not particularly in size (although that as well), but in their limited computing and input/output capacity. Today, many PCs are powerful enough for rather extensive business applications.

To give the reader an idea of the progress made in computer architecture only in the past 10 years, Table 22-1 provides the author's 1975 definitions for these machines along with the characteristics of a modern, typical, state-of-the-art personal computer [BLAC87C].

It is evident that what was classified as a midi (or even a maxi, in some instances) only 10 years ago is now called a personal computer. Some of us carry the PC around as if it were a briefcase. Ten years ago, a large room was required to house the same capacity computer now contained in the briefcase.

Nonetheless, the personal computer is still considered a machine of limited capacity, especially when compared to the "large" computers of today. For instance, the IBM 3090 (Model 400) processor computes at 52.7 MIPS (millions of instructions per second), has 128 Mbytes of memory, and costs $9,000,000. Overall computing power is still a primary consideration in the purchase or acquisition of the PC. Because of these "limitations," some of the networking and communications capabilities of the PC are also limited.

---

[1]Unless noted otherwise, the term PC is used to describe any personal computer.

824

TABLE 22-1. Comparison of 1970s Computer Architecture with Typical 1988 Personal Computer

	COMPUTER ARCHITECTURE, 1975 DEFINITIONS				TYPICAL 1988 PC
	Micro	*Mini*	*Midi*	*Maxi*	
Word Size	8 bits	16 bits	24–32 bits	32–64 bits	16–32 bits
Terminals	1–4	4–32	32+	100+	6–16
CPU Throughput (IPS)*	250,000 (8 bit INST)	450,000 (16 bit INST)	1m (32 bit INST)	3m (32 bit INST)	2–4m (16 or 32 bit INST)
Memory	64 Kbytes	64–512 Kbytes	1–4 Mbytes	16 Mbytes	1–16 Mbytes
Communications	ASYNC	ASYNC/BSC	ASYNC/BSC/ SYNC	ASYNC/BSC/ SYNC	ASYNC (some SYNC)
Instruction Repertoire	8–150	70–256	256	>256	256
Power Requirements	Low	Medium	Medium	High	Low
Software	FORTRAN, BASIC, Assembler	Many, DBMS	Many, DBMS	Extensive	Extensive
Price	$7K–$10K	$10K–$100K	$70K–$180K	>$400K	$2K–$9K
Memory Cycle Time (Nsec/Word)	600–1000	500–1000	400–900	200–600	200–700

*IPS: Instructions Per Second

825

In this chapter we describe the data communications and networking characteristics of personal computers, recent progress in the PC industry, and opportunities for utilizing these machines more effectively. Due to the wide use of the IBM PC and PS (Personal System) family, the MS-DOS operating system, Novell's Netware, and the 3-Com EtherSeries, we highlight these systems in more detail.

PERSONAL COMPUTER COMMUNICATIONS CHARACTERISTICS

The communications characteristics of personal computers bear many similarities to larger mainframe computers. However, differences exist that must be considered when using the PC for networking and data communications. First, most personal computers are asynchronous. No technical reason exists why a PC cannot be synchronous, but many PC vendors have not built their communications board (port) with the wires or logic necessary for carrying the timing signals required for synchronous transmission. However, more products are entering the marketplace that provide synchronous capabilities, such as SDLC, Bisync, and even X.25.

It is possible for asynchronous PCs to communicate with synchronous systems by placing an asynchronous-to-synchronous adapter unit between the PC and its modem. The adapter may also be placed on a board. The adapter provides clocking signals to achieve clocking between the personal computer and the modem.

PC modems typically operate at 300 and 1200 bit/s, and 2400 bit/s modems are now widely used. These modems are full-duplex, dial-up asynchronous and are V.22 bis compatible. Several PC modems also operate at 9.6 Kbit/s.

Many PCs house the modem within the PC cabinet. These devices are called plug-in modems or on-board modems and can free workspace at a crowded desk and provide a portable modem for the traveler. Their principal disadvantage lies in the fact that they cannot be used by other devices.

The high-speed modems are increasing in use because of the decreased time required for a data transmission. Anyone who has sat in front of a PC waiting for the transfer of data across a slow-speed modem will attest to the slow transfer rate. For example, a 300 bit/s modem transfers a one-page document in about two minutes. In contrast, a 1200 bit/s modem transfers the same document in 30 seconds. A 2400 bit/s modem is twice as fast—it transfers the document in 15 seconds. The newer PC modems transfer a document even faster. For example, a 4800 bit/s modem transfers the same document in 7.5 seconds, and a 9.6 Kbit/s modem transfers the document in 3.75 seconds.

Many PCs today use "smart" modems that are designed with built-in intelligence to allow the PC to control many communications activities. For example, the Hayes modem uses the ASCII command characters for various communications functions (see Chapters 9 and 12).

PC TO MAINFRAME COMMUNICATIONS

In today's office, the PC is increasingly used as an ancillary tool to tie into the company's larger-scale computer system (mainframe computers). Several very good reasons exist for linking PCs to mainframes. First, the PC provides a valuable tool for distributing the workload onto less expensive machines to perform simple tasks. Generalized mainframe computing is quite expensive, so it is preferable that the large-scale computer be used primarily for complex functions requiring powerful computation capabilities. Second, the PC might need to use the processing power of the mainframe, for example to perform complex calculations such as linear regressions or involved data base manipulations. Third, the PC may wish to share the software and the data bases of the mainframe computer. Sharing is quite common in almost all offices today, where users perform certain calculations with their own PCs but go to the mainframe to obtain support for interaction with other applications and data bases.

Several options are readily available in the marketplace for connecting a PC to the mainframe. These options are depicted in Figure 22-1. They are not all-encompassing, but provide some practical examples of how PC/mainframe systems can be connected:

1. Protocol conversion software is installed in the host computer (or front-end processor, if available) (see Figure 22-1[a]). The software works with the host's operating system and telecommunications packages to allow the personal computer to communicate in its conventional asynchronous, full-duplex EIA-232 mode. The asynchronous ports are less expensive than their synchronous counterparts. Additionally, no protocol conversion board is needed for the PCs. However, each PC requires a port to the host.

2. A personal computer can be used to emulate a cluster controller (Figure 22-1[b]). The other personal computers use their conventional modes to communicate with the cluster emulator. This configuration reduces the number of ports required, since the emulator has only one coaxial cable connection to the host. However, the cluster can act as a bottleneck if it is overloaded with too many personal computers. Moreover, personal computers are quite limited in the number of ports that can be installed within the machine.

3. Many organizations opt for the configuration in Figure 22-1(c). A protocol converter board is installed in each personal computer and communicates with the cluster controller through coaxial cable or EIA-232 and the cluster's proprietary protocol. This option allows the PC to emulate a mainframe workstation. This approach is cost-

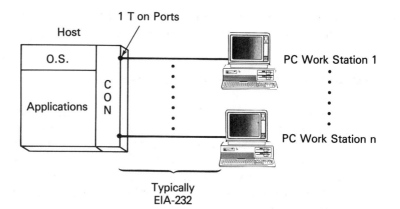

(a) Protocol Conversion Software at Host

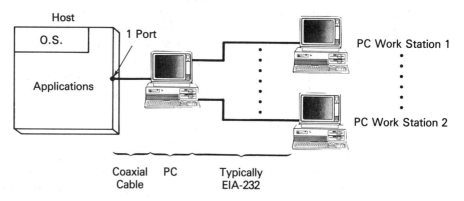

(b) Personal Computer Emulates Cluster Controller

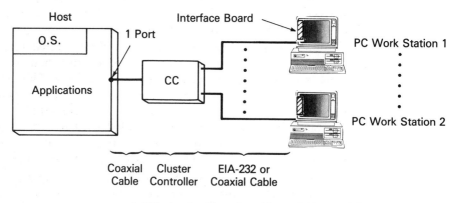

(c) Placing Interface Board in each Personal Computer

CON: Protocol Converter
OS: Host Operating System

FIGURE 22-1. Personal Computer to Mainframe Communications

effective for a few personal computer connections to the host. However, the cost of multiple PC connections will likely sway users in favor of other options.

FILE TRANSFER ON PCS

XMODEM

During the infant days of microcomputing, the field was dominated primarily by hobbyists and other individuals who wished to experiment with this interesting new machine. One of the major problems during this time was exchanging data between the computers. Ward Christiansen solved this problem in 1977 by writing a program which addressed the dual problems of (a) incompatible PC software and (b) incompatible telephone channel-oriented protocols. Christiansen based his program on the fact that the telephone line was usually the path to exchange data between computers and the PC, and at that time almost always utilized the simple 300 bit/s modem. Most of these modems use identical modulation techniques. Christiansen wrote a file-transfer program and placed it in the public domain by donating it to various user groups. Today several versions exist of the now famous program in the public domain. Two of the better known programs are MODEM7 and XMODEM. XMODEM is described next, since it is a very widely used personal computer file transfer protocol.

The data flow for XMODEM is quite simple. The transmission between the two PCs begins by the receiving computer sending a NAK control character to the transmitting site. The receiver can send the NAK as a timeout, if it does not receive data. The data blocks are exchanged one block at a time. The receiving site performs the checksum and sends back an ACK or NAK based on the previous transmission.

Like other protocols discussed in this book, personal computer protocols like XMODEM have additional features. For example, if a transmitting PC retransmits a message unsuccessfully nine times, it performs a timeout and sends the Cancel (CAN) control character. This technique is found in the N1 (retry) and T1 (timer) functions of the HDLC family. Likewise, if the sender does not hear a receiver's response, it waits a period of 10 seconds (or another specific time) before attempting another retransmission. The logic provides the ability for a receiving PC to ignore the duplicate message.

YMODEM

YMODEM is quite similar to XMODEM. It has some additional features:

- Aborting a file transfer with two consecutive ASCII Cancel (CAN) characters.
- CCITT CRC-16 error checking.

- Use of 1 Kbyte blocks (1024 bytes) instead of XMODEM's 128 bytes, and mixed modes allowed by sending STX for 1 Kbyte blocks and SOH for 128 byte blocks.
- Allows multiple files to be sent at once by the use of additional control characters.

BLAST

Another popular package for the personal computer is BLAST. This product is available for most widely sold personal computers. The BLAST protocol is more powerful than XMODEM. It uses a two-way, full-duplex procedure with the sliding-window concept discussed in Chapter 10. In addition, the error-checking technique utilizes CRC. BLAST allows data (binary) files as well as text files to be transferred to another computer.

KERMIT

Another package available for the PC is called KERMIT. KERMIT is similar to XMODEM; it provides for a simple transparent method of transferring data between personal computers. KERMIT is available on a wide variety of machines (to be summarized later). KERMIT uses a conventional block-check count in the SOH field as XMODEM does. It uses the simple sequencing techniques as well. One of its principal attributes is a type field to delineate the actual type of packet transmitted between the personal computers.

MNP

Yet another popular PC package is Microcom MNP. It is available as a point-to-point protocol and supports a wide variety of computers.

MNP is somewhat different from the other systems in that it uses a layered protocol approach very similar to that of the OSI model. At the physical layer, it uses the 8-bit asynchronous start/stop approach. The data-link level provides for error detection using a CRC 16-bit field; it also provides for continuous ARQ error correction. It provides for sliding window systems as well. It has options for half or full duplex and provides other features, such as link disconnect. In addition to these lower-level procedures, MNP provides for file-transfer capabilities similar to those of the previous systems discussed in this part. The full frame structure of MNP product is similar to the binary synchronous control protocol (BSC or Bisync), except that each character within the frame is surrounded by the asynchronous start/stop bits. The start/stop bits provide the clocking signals across the interface between the devices, which enables the PCs to utilize the conventional asynchronous board.

Our discussions thus far have focused on several rather simple and straightforward PC communications protocols. Before we examine the more complex subject of PC networking, some background information is needed on the IBM PC architecture. This information is used as a foundation for examining other aspects of PC-based communications.

THE ORIGINAL IBM PC

The original highly successful IBM PC (over 3 million sold) was designed around the 16-bit 8088 microprocessor. Today, it seems quite primitive. It was packaged with "only" 64 K of memory, and a five-slot bus; it could be equipped with 544 K of RAM!

The operating systems on the early personal computers were quite simple and performed relatively few functions. The first version of the IBM PC operating system was MS-DOS 1.0, developed by Microsoft in 1981. As PCs evolved and achieved more functionality, DOS also changed. Today, DOS 3.3 still resembles the original version, but it has undergone many major enhancements.

Notwithstanding the improvements to DOS, its original architecture limits its ability to perform some advanced functions that are now feasible on the new PCs (more on this topic later).

The introduction of MS-DOS 3.1 was a very significant step toward PC software standards. DOS 3.1 was changed to use standard interfaces (primitives) to control access between an application program and DOS. Therefore, any software written to the DOS 3.1 standards runs on any network that supports 3.1.

IBM PERSONAL SYSTEM/2 (PS/2)

In August 1981, IBM announced the IBM Personal Computer (PC). It quickly became a de facto industry standard, principally because IBM adapted an "open architecture policy." This policy allowed third-party hardware and software products to enter the marketplace based on IBM's architecture. This decision has proved to be beneficial to users, the third-party vendors, and IBM.

On April 2, 1987, IBM announced a new line of systems named IBM Personal System/2 (PS/2). The announcement and subsequent events have created significant changes in the industry. Because the PS/2 family remains the industry de facto standard, we examine the architecture and compare it to the PC XT and PC AT systems. Unless otherwise noted, the discussions focus on the mid-level models (30/60/80).

The upper-end PS/2 personal computers are based on the Intel 80386 microprocessor. (The PC XT uses the 8088 and the PC AT is based on the 80286 processor.) The 80386 runs at a clock rate of 12.5 or 16 MHz, compared to 80286 which runs at 8 or 10 MHz. The PS/2 model 80 (with the

80386) outperforms the PC AT by over 150 percent. This speed is attributed to the faster microprocessor, faster memory, and faster disk access.

Another significant change is the improved expansion capability of the PS/2. The standard features are all packaged on the System Board, which allows the expansion slots to be used for additional features and growth. Moreover, the PS/2 expansion slots have been redesigned and offer faster speeds and more options than the XT and AT computers. (These expansion slots are called the Micro Channel.) The major changes in the PS/2 family are summarized in Box 22-1.

BOX 22-1.   Major Features of IBM Personal System/2

- Some PS/2 models use faster microprocessors (80386).
- More capabilities are placed on the System Board.
- Expansion slots (Micro Channels) are more powerful.
- Bolts and screws are replaced with snaps and thumbscrews.
- Some models have paged memory systems to speed memory access.
- Extended memory support (in Protected Mode) provides up to 16 MB of memory.
- Multi-application support (in Protected Mode) allows multiple programs to execute simultaneously without interfering with each other.
- Virtual memory support (in Protected Mode) allows swapping data/programs between disk and memory. An 80386 on PS/2 allows a virtual memory address space up to 64 terabytes.
- Virtual 86 mode (with the 80386) allows the AT/XT programs to run with several of the PS/2 advanced features.
- Uses 3.5-inch diskettes.
- Multi-device arbitration allows temporary transfer of data without the use of the microprocessor or the direct memory access (DMA) chip.
- The programmable option select (POS) replaces mechanical switches with switches that are controlled by software.
- The auxiliary video connector allows graphics circuitry to be monitored and changed for other extended graphics.
- PS/2 displays are based on analog signals instead of digital signals.
- Video graphics array (VGA) chip is located on System Board, which frees an expansion slot.
- Asynchronous port speeded up to 19.2 Kbit/s.
- DIP electronic package replaced with enhanced Surface Mount Technology (SMT).

IBM OPERATING SYSTEM/2 (OS/2)

The PS/2 operating system (called OS/2) is considerably different from DOS. One of the major changes is the use of Protected Mode instead of the DOS Real Mode. It allows programs to execute without interference when more than one program is running simultaneously. It also gives an 80286 PC up to 16 MB of memory and the 80386 up to 4 GB of memory. OS/2 is part of IBM System Application Architecture (SAA) environment, the applications-level equivalent to the lower levels (communications) of SNA.

PS/2 Communications Options

The PS/2 supports a variety of feature cards (communications boards) for communications functions. The following feature cards are available:

> Dual Async Adapter/A
> 300/1200 Internal Modem/A
> System 36/38 Workstation Emulation Adapter
> 3270 Connection
> Multi-protocol Adapter/A
> PC Network Adapters (discussed later)
> Token-Ring Network Adapter/A (discussed later)

The *Dual Async Adapter/A* provides an asynchronous communications interface with external modems, dumb terminals, printers, etc. The adapter can operate at speeds of up to 19.2 Kbit/s with an ASCII/IA5 and parity checking. The adapter also works with the EIA-232 interface and uses two 9-pin male D-shell connectors. The IBM Mainframe Communications Assistant (MCA) program can be installed in the PS/2 to emulate an async device (see Figure 22-2[a]).

The *300/1200 Internal Modem/A* card is designed for an interface to a telephone line. The card uses a cable to connect to a standard telephone jack. It is the same set-up as the Dual Async Adapter/A, except that it uses a modem for signal conversion. This card is compatible with the widely used Hayes modem, which is explained in more detail in Chapter 12. This configuration is also supported by the MCA software shown in Figure 22-2(a).

The *System 36/38 Workstation Emulation Adapter* allows a personal computer to emulate an IBM 5250 Information Display System, a widely used workstation used on IBM's System 36 or System 38 computer systems (see Figure 22-2[b]). The card supports up to four independent sessions with the host. A 15-pin connector interfaces the port to a System 36/38 twin-axial cable. The interface consists of an adapter and the Workstation Emulation Program (WEP). The WEP allows the PS/2 to emulate a 5250 workstation or a 5250 printer.

PS/2

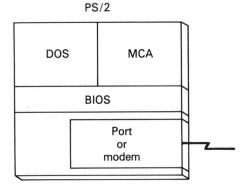

(a) Mainframe Communications Assistant (MCA)

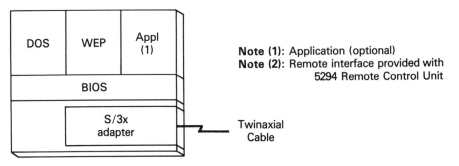

Note **(1)**: Application (optional)
Note **(2)**: Remote interface provided with
5294 Remote Control Unit

Twinaxial
Cable

(b) Work Station Emulation Program (WEP)

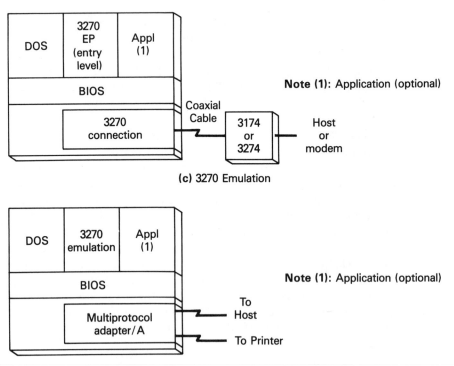

Note **(1)**: Application (optional)

(c) 3270 Emulation

Note **(1)**: Application (optional)

(d) Emulation of Printer, Control Unit and Terminal

FIGURE 22-2. Mainframe Interfaces and Emulations

The *3270 Connection Card* supports a personal computer emulation of an IBM 3278/79 terminal or an IBM 3287 printer. The personal computer communicates with the host computer via a coaxial cable. As illustrated in Figure 22-2 (c), the PS/2 is equipped with the 3270 connection and the IBM PC 3270 Emulation Program (Entry Level). An IBM 3174 or 3274 control unit is also required for this configuration. From the PS/2, the user can execute host application programs, transfer files, and use host printers and disk units.

This configuration also permits an Application Program Interface (API) to communicate with the host. The API is provided by the Emulation Program. Moreover, an application program can be executed while the Emulation Program is suspended. In effect, execution can be switched between programs.

In addition to the 3270 emulation, the PS/2 can be configured to emulate the control unit as well. This configuration is shown in Figure 22-2 (d). It consists of the multi-protocol communications adapter and the IBM PC 3270 Emulation Program (version 3.0 or higher). In this configuration, SDLC (synchronous data link control) is used to link the PS/2 with the host computer. Note that this configuration also permits the direct use of a 3278 printer.

PERSONAL COMPUTER NETWORKING

The biggest improvement in PC communications during the past few years is in PC networking. Features such as file sharing and data base lockouts are now common offerings. We examine PC networking in this section with discussions on

NETBIOS
Novell's Advanced Netware
3-Com Networks
IBM PS/2 Local Area Network Interfaces
The Macintosh PC Networking Interfaces

As discussed earlier, the 1984 release of Microsoft's MS-DOS 3.1 provided a standard for software developers to write applications to run on multiple personal computers. DOS 3.1 established conventions for file management such as file locking, record locking, and multi-user functions. Releases since DOS 3.1 (DOS 3.3) have added to the functionality of the operating system.

DOS is classified as a presentation layer protocol even though it does not perform functions normally associated with the OSI presentation layer. It is situated at this layer because it provides the applications interface to a network. In contrast, NETBIOS establishes standard applications interfaces at the session, transport, and network layers.

BOX 22-2. NETBIOS Commands

Adapter Status	provides status for local or remote adapter: Adapter identification number Results of last self-test Software version number Traffic and error statistics Resource statistics Quantity of names in the local name table Local name table
Add Group Name	adds a unique 16-character group name to the local name table
Add Name	adds a unique 16-character name to the local name table
Cancel	cancels a command (a specific NCB)
Chain Send	sends two buffers of data
Call	opens a session with another network name (called name must have a listen command outstanding)
Delete Name	deletes a name from the local name table in the adapter
Hangup	closes a session with another network name
Listen	enables a session to be established with another network name
Receive	receives data from a specified session
Receive Any	receives data from any session
Receive Broadcast	receives a message from any station that issues a Send Broadcast
Receive Datagram	receives any datagram message directed to station
Reset	resets adapter status and other resets (allows application to change NCBs and sessions)
Send	sends a buffer of data
Send Broadcast	sends a message to any station with a Receive Broadcast outstanding
Send Datagram	sends a datagram to a unique group name
Session Status	gets status of all active sessions for a network name

NETBIOS (Network Basic Input/Output System)

NETBIOS is an IBM protocol that permits peer-to-peer communications between machines without an intervening host computer. It was first provided as firmware on the IBM PC Network Adapter. Vendors that provide PC networking capabilities typically emulate NETBIOS.

To communicate with NETBIOS, an application must give the system commands in the form of a NCB (Network Control Block). The NETBIOS commands are summarized in Box 22-2.

IBM decided to place NETBIOS on the IBM PC Network Adapter. In so doing, it off-loaded the PC from low-level functions, but caused a bottleneck on the PC network adapter. Consequently, some companies have implemented systems that bypass the NETBIOS firmware on the Adapter and emulate NETBIOS [LEWI87].

NETBIOS uses a distributed approach to LAN network management. A connection to another resource requires a machine to send the relevant resource name to each machine on the network. If the name is found, a connection is made. This broadcast aspect of NETBIOS can create a considerable number of overhead messages in the network. Some LAN vendors have supplemented the NETBIOS distributed name directories with a centralized, hierarchical method. For example, Novell and 3-Com use the Xerox Network Systems (XNS), which requires interconnections to be established with specific (not broadcast) calls.

Netware from Novell

Netware (or Advanced Netware) is one of the most widely used PC-based systems in the industry. Novell has captured a substantial share of the PC LAN industry, principally with the Netware software. Due to its position in the industry, Netware is examined in this section.

Novell uses advanced Netware to overcome some of the limitations of the DOS and IBM's read only memory basis input/output system (ROMBIOS). In essence, Netware communicates directly with the hardware of the personal computer. In so doing, other vendors must supply their own disk drivers because they cannot use the DOS disk drivers. However, many tests have revealed that the Netware approach provides better throughput than do conventional systems.

3-Com Networks

Several Ethernet-type products are provided for personal computers by 3-Com. The term to describe the product line is EtherSeries. The EtherSeries provides the following capabilities:

EtherShare:	Disk Management
EtherPrint:	Print Sharer

EtherMail:	Electronic Mail
EtherMenu:	Customized Menu Lists
EtherTerm:	Terminal Emulation
EtherBackup:	Disk-to-Tape Backup
Ether3270:	3270 Emulator

The EtherSeries uses a CSMA/CD protocol. EtherShare is a file-server support package. It manages disks at the disk volume level and provides for multiple use into the files.

EtherShare provides other functions, such as a print support package called EtherPrint. The EtherSeries also provides for electronic mail support in a product called EtherMail. EtherPrint is a powerful print-serving function. It allows users to perform multiple printing tasks simultaneously without interfering with each other. The server keeps separate buffers on the disk and interleaves the various users onto the printer as they close their files. 3-Com also provides terminal emulation packages (EtherTerm and Ether3270).

3-Com's systems are flexible, easy to install, and easy to use. Interface cards are provided for all the IBM personal computers as well as the devices of other vendors such as Hewlett Packard and Texas Instruments.

PS/2 Local Area Network Interfaces

Chapter 20 introduced the subject of local area networks (LANs). This part describes the following IBM PS/2 LAN configurations and gateways:

Baseband IBM PC Network
Broadband IBM PC Network
IBM Token Ring Network

The IBM LAN systems are implemented as extensions to DOS through the IBM PC LAN program. A user can operate on a LAN through the PC LAN Program with an application program or a provided Application Program Interface (API). These two techniques can be switched as needed.

The PC LAN Program is used to configure the systems as a workstation node or a server node. The workstation node allows the personal computer to operate as a stand-alone unit on the local area network and access any shared resource. However, it does not provide resources to any other unit. The server node allows the personal computer to act as a workstation node and also offer services and resources to other network nodes. A server node is typically configured as a disk or printer server.

Baseband IBM PC Network. The IBM PC Network Baseband Adapter/A allows the personal computer to interface into a baseband network. It also provides a NETBIOS interface (and other advanced functions). The configuration also uses the Network Support Program and the PC LAN Program.

This network operates with CSMA/CD at 2 Mbit/s with baseband twisted pair technology. The latter feature is less expensive than the broadband system (discussed next). Moreover, the baseband adapters can be joined directly on the twisted pair link without additional translator units that are required in a broadband network.

The baseband network allows interconnections of up to 200 feet and a Baseband Extender is available for systems to extend the network to around 800 feet.

Broadband IBM PC Network. The IBM PC Network Adapter II/A allows the personal computer to interface into a broadband network. The IBM PC Network Protocol Driver supports the interface of the original PC Network Adapter (NETBIOS). The IBM Network Support Program supports interfaces such as the IEEE 802.2 and the APPC/PC.

The adapter must be connected to a translator unit. This unit performs frequency division multiplexing operations by transmitting and receiving signals at different frequency ranges.

The broadband configuration operates with coaxial cable and CSMA/CD. It can accommodate up to eight nodes with distances of up to 200 feet. The network can be extended to 72 nodes and 1000 feet with the addition of other components. Moreover, cable television equipment can be used to extend the capacity further.

IBM Token Ring Network. The Token Ring Network Adapter/A provides an interface for the personal computer into the IBM token ring network. The adapter supports the 4 Mbit/s interfaces with a 9-pin connector. It is designed to support larger computers as well as personal computers.

The adapter is attached to the 8228 Multi-station Access Unit (MAU), which is responsible for sending and receiving messages. It supports up to eight nodes and uses a modular jack to attach to the node. The details of the token ring network are covered in Chapter 20.

Apple Talk and EtherTalk from Macintosh

The Apple Talk network protocol is one of the industry's best sellers and is especially attractive from the standpoint of cost. Its purpose is to connect file servers and printers to PC-based workstations. As many as 32 computers and peripherals can be connected with Apple Talk.

The system uses shielded twisted pair cable. The physical level interface is a variation of EIA RS-422. The network signalling speed is 230.4 Kbit/s. Apple Talk uses a SDLC format and a CSMA/CA link level protocol (carrier-sense multiple access with collision avoidance).

The Macintosh II can also support an add-on board called EtherTalk. It is considerably faster than Apple Talk and uses a 3-Com board to connect a Mac to an Ethernet cable at 10 Mbit/s.

Due to the wide use of the Mac family of computers, several vendors are building communications interfaces for these computers. For example, Centram Systems West, Inc., offers an Apple Talk to a TCP/IP interface. The system allows Mac users to interface with other PCs or large host computers for access to files, applications, mail services, and bulletin boards.

Novell also has Macintosh network products. These offerings include software and boards that allow a Mac user to send and receive binary or text files from a mainframe host computer. The system emulates the IBM 3178, 3179, 3278, and 3279 terminals.

SUGGESTED READINGS:

[JORD83] and [DURR84] provide introductions to the IBM personal computer. [SMIT87] is a good description of the Intel 80386 microprocessor. [HOSK87] is a valuable review of the PS/2 computer. [LEWI87] provides an excellent overview of MS DOS and Netware. [ARCH86] is one of the better descriptions of major PC-based networks.

QUESTIONS

TRUE/FALSE

1. The majority of personal computer communications interfaces uses asynchronous protocols.
2. Disk server software is largely obsolete.
3. The newer personal computers support multi-processing and multi-tasking.
4. IBM adapted an open architecture policy with its 1981 PC.
5. DOS cannot be extended beyond 640 KB of address space.
6. Match the OS/2 features with the appropriate descriptions:

Description

a) Uses Protected mode to prevent one program from interfering with another.
b) Perceived availability of more memory than is really available.
c) Supports 8086 programs on the 80386.

Feature

1. Virtual memory
2. Virtual 86 mode
3. Multi-application support

7. Compare the DOS access mode and sharing mode.

8. Briefly summarize the major features of the Intel 80386 microprocessor.

9. Name at least six attributes of the PS/2 that are enhancements over the AT and XT.

10. Compare and contrast the following IBM networks:

   • Baseband PC network
   • Broadband PC network
   • Token ring network

SELECTED ANSWERS

1. True.

2. True. Most systems today use file servers.

3. False. The newer systems support multi-tasking but not multi-processing.

4. True.

5. False. However, special programs are required.

6.
	Description	Type
a)		3
b)		1
c)		2

8. The 80386 uses a 32-bit register, 32-bit data bus, and a 32-bit address bus. Its CPU, ALU and registers are located on one chip.

   80386 uses "pipelining," which does pre-fetching, pre-coding, and execution of instructions. With the 80386, the accessing of memory is pipelined. The 80386 has a provision for interleaving memory. It divides the memory into multiple banks, where sequential process memory can be alternated across different memory banks.

   The 80386 is faster than its predecessors. It operates at 12.5 or 16 MHz. It also is capable of multi-tasking operations.

CHAPTER 23

The PBX and Data Communications Networks

INTRODUCTION

In the late 1970s and early 1980s, the private branch exchange (PBX) was used predominantly as a telephone switching device for the office. Telephones were connected into the PBX, which performed the task of switching calls between offices within an organization and the trunks to the telephone central office. During this time, several PBX manufacturers decided to design PBXs to handle voice and data traffic. Through a series of gradual changes, the PBX has evolved into a powerful tool for integrated voice/data transmission and networking.

The PBX is called by several other names: private automated branch exchange (PABX) and computerized branch exchange (CBX). This chapter uses the generic term PBX to describe the device and provides a general, introductory discussion of the PBX.

One might reasonably ask, why should the PBX be used for data communications? There are several answers to this question. First, two separate technologies have been used to support communications in the office: analog technology for voice communications and digital technology for data communications. This approach has often resulted in redundant and conflicting efforts between two separate systems. The PBX provides the opportunity to integrate some of these systems (as well as the personnel) to reduce redundancy, decrease costs, and take advantage of the superior aspects of digital technology. Second, since most data communications systems use the telephone system, the PBX provides a convenient conduit to the local telephone office and the telephone network.

Third, the telephone wires are already installed in a building and provide the paths for a local area network (LAN) without the very significant problem of pulling separate wire or cable. Fourth, for several years the PBX has had the necessary architecture to provide administrative and management support in controlling a telecommunications system. Fifth, as discussed in Chapter 19, the integration of voice and data mekes good sense from many standpoints. Stince the PBX is now an integrated voice/data digital device, it becomes a valuable tool to accelerate the trend of transmitting, switching, and managing all transmissions in digital images.

EVOLUTION OF THE PBX

Like many hardware and software systems, PBXs have evolved from relatively simple devices with limited functions to powerful multifunction systems. This section provides a brief description of the evolution of the PBX.

The PBXs designed and sold in the 1970s were essentially telephone circuit-switching systems. Consequently, earlier PBXs had data capabilities "tacked" onto the systems without much forethought, which often resulted in poor performance. In these early systems, different wires were used to accommodate voice and data traffic.

The major problem hampering early PBXs stemmed from their design. Voice-only PBXs were built with the expectation of handling connections that lasted only a short period of time, which is characteristic of most voice calls in a typical office environment. However, data calls are often of much longer duration. A terminal-to-computer session often lasts several minutes, sometimes several hours. Moreover, during the time the data calls are taking place, the communications channels and other resources are used in intermittent bursts, because many communications devices (e.g., terminals operated by humans) do not use the resources continuously. However, the earlier PBXs dedicated resources to each connection. Dedicated connections require a fixed capacity through the switch during the entire connection. Therefore, the PBX wasted valuable switching and systems management capacity for extended data calls that transmitted periodic bursts of traffic.

The earlier systems also supported data interfaces through a conventional EIA-232 connection. The PBX received the data and converted them into a PBX channel format. In the late 1970s and early 1980s, PBX manufacturers began to move away from the EIA-232 connection toward a digital data interface connection. With this approach, the data bits are transmitted digitally to the PBX through a digital data interface (DDI) translation. Afterward, the data are switched by the PBX as if they were voice traffic. This approach is an improvement in that it does not require an associated telephone to set up data calls through the modem. Rather, the DDI provides direct communications with the user DTE, such as a terminal, keyboard, or CRT monitor. However, this approach requires the PBX to know it is dealing with a transmission that is different from voice traffic.

More recently, PBXs have provided an integration of voice and data across the same local twisted-wire pair. This is a significant improvement. It eliminates an additional set of wires for each user station. The internal architecture of the PBX still provides dedicated switching facilities to a voice or data communications connection. Cabling costs are substantially reduced with this approach, but the switch itself is still working in an inefficient mode.

Today, the newer PBXs have full digital switching. Digital switching is quite similar to packet switching in concept in that neither is dedicated to one particular connection. Rather, multiple users can share one physical path with the switch interleaving data or voice connections during periods of voice silence or during absences of transmission from the DTEs. In most PBXs, this concept is integrated with the digital-switching concept, which is discussed in Chapter 19.

While the earlier PBXs were relatively simple telephone circuit switches, today's PBXs are very powerful processors with provisions for least-cost routing (routing the call onto the least expensive carrier connection, such as WATS, AT&T, or MCI). The new PBXs also provide such features such as redial capabilities, call waiting, and call forwarding.

ISSUE OF VOICE/DATA INTEGRATION

The early PBX industry concentrated primarily on voice transmission and voice switching. Presently, less than 35 percent of the line cards placed in a PBX are used for data. PBXs, although moving toward full-function capabilities, are still dominated by voice connections. To integrate voice/data or not to integrate voice/data is a question that is of major concern if an organization is using PBXs developed in the early 1980s. The new PBXs are powerful enough to obviate many (but not all) voice/data integration issues.

The basic questions about PBX use for data revolve around the DTE protocols, line speeds, data formats, throughput, and response time support capabilities of the PBX. A PBX evaluation for data usage is not unlike a typical evaluation for other data communications components.

The reason cited by some people for using an all-digital PBX is to be "ready" for ISDN. This is not a very good reason. ISDN specifications are still undergoing changes. Moreover, organizations with limited data communications may not need a digital PBX.

ISSUE OF USING A PBX IN A LAN

One issue with the PBX is its use as a local area network (LAN). Without question, the issue of office automation has come to fruition because of the intelligent workstation and the personal computer revolution in the office environment. The supporters of the PBX for office automation have cited numerous advantages to using PBXs for the LAN. In contrast, LAN vendors have cited the LAN advantages and the PBX disadvantages for use in office automation.

The PBX will certainly play an important role in office automation and local area networks, if for no other reason than the fact that the PBX is well entrenched (it is a pervasive tool in offices today), and it connects to the ubiquitous telephone lines. To illustrate the presence of the PBX, Northern Telecom (the SL-1 PBX) has installations in over 40 countries and supports over 8000 users (8000 individual companies). The SL-1 supports over 3,000,000 voice-grade lines located in various offices around the world.

What are the trade-offs of using PBXs for local area networks? First, let us cite some advantages.

- As stated previously, the PBX uses the telephone lines connecting the offices to each other, as well as to the telephone company network.
- The PBX is a traffic-efficient circuit switch—its capabilities are well understood; it has been designed to be very efficient for voice traffic.
- The overall technology of the PBX is mature and well proven.
- The PBX provides long haul interfaces to communications systems around the world through the telephone system.
- The modern PBXs provide full-function integration of voice and data, thus permitting the use of voice and data transmissions in the end-user office (perhaps from a single terminal).

The critics of the PBX for use as a LAN cite the disadvantages:

- The lack of adequate data-switching capability in the PBX is still evident. (With fourth-generation systems, this is not as big a problem, but still remains.)
- Much of the architecture of the PBXs still revolves around voice technology.
- The PBX's multifunction support of the diverse world of data communications is not as extensive as equipment such as packet switches and intelligent multiplexers.
- The PBX is not fast enough to support multiple CPU-to-CPU traffic. The basic speed of a typical PBX port is 64 Kbit/s—certainly fast enough to support most traffic. However, the digital switch (PBX) must be fast enough to support the switching of all lines attached to it. It must prevent congestion, avoid blockage, and provide high throughput and low response time.

The PBX and LAN technologies are not mutually exclusive. The automated office can benefit from the use of both approaches. Indeed, the office can benefit from integrating their capabilities. The LAN and the PBX can coexist to support the automated office. The practical approach is not to choose one over the other, but to determine in what combination they can be used to support the end-user application in the best way.

THE FOURTH-GENERATION PBX

Several PBX firms now have "fourth-generation" systems, which are touted as successful blends of the functions of local area networks, PBXs, and integrated voice/data support. In this section we examine some recent PBX announcements.

There is no concise definition as to what constitutes a fourth-generation PBX. However, it is generally agreed that such a system has the following capabilities:

- The switch is all digital and integrates voice and data.
- The system provides for the use of LANs with PBXs and provides gateways to wide area networks as well.
- The PBX is modular in its design, both from the standpoint of hardware and software. The modular design provides for growth to accommodate a larger user base. In many instances, the modules (added on) can be dedicated to specific applications, such as word processing. The modular growth allows for small or large numbers of users (from 1 to 20,000 user connections) and aggregate throughput rates to 300 Kbit/s.
- The switch is nonblocking.
- The PBX supports communications with telephones and conventional terminals as well as mainframe central processing units.
- The PBX provides for a high level of security.
- The design is built to handle an evolution to the ISDN.
- The PBX supports a conventional PCM (pulse code modulation) transmission of 64 Kbit/s as well as higher TDM (time division multiplexed) speeds, such as 1.544 Mbit/s or 2.048 Mbit/s.
- Options allow a 32 Kbit/s digitized voice signal.

AT&T's System 75 and System 85

Figure 23-1 provides an example of AT&T's System 75/85 PBX family. The following options (labeled 1 to 17 in the figure) are available with the PBX:

1. One-pair wire to support conventions EIA-232, EIA-449, V.35 devices up to 64 Kbit/s using AT&T's DCP (digital communications protocol).

2. One-pair wire to support digital phones and EIA-232 asynchronous terminals, operating at a total speed of 136 Kbit/s (64 Kbit/s PCM voice; 64 Kbit/s data; 8 Kbit/s for control signalling).

3. Interface unit for IBM 327X terminal family. Converts 2.358 Mbit/s coaxial transmission to 64 Kbit/s one-pair wire.

4. Interface unit for IBM 327X cluster controller family; provides same conversion as in option 3.

5. Two-pair wire to AT&T's Dataphone digital service (DDS) at 56 Kbit/s.

6. Two-pair wire to a 1.544 Mbit/s T1 carrier interfaced to a host computer.

7. Two-pair wire to other PBXs via T1.

8. Conventional asynchronous EIA-232 ports.

9. Interface of PBX to AT&T's local area network ISN, with additional interfaces to the following.

10. Connection to either bisync (BSC) or SNA/SDLC devices.

11. Conventional interfaces to EIA-232 asynchronous devices.

12. Optic fiber connection to a remote ISN interface/concentrator, supporting IBM 327X cluster controllers with their connections to IBM hosts.

13. The same configuration as option 12, except individual 327X terminals are supported with a coax/wire pair converter (balun).

14. Wire pair connections into the Starlan local area network.

15. A coaxial cable interface into an Ethernet local area network.

16. Optic fiber connection into another ISN or AT&T 3B20 computer or a VAX computer.

17. Wire pair connections to a telephone company DDS or a DS-1 with transmission speeds up to 2.048 Mbit/s.

AT&T Information System Network ISN

American Telephone and Telegraph (AT&T) has also entered the LAN market with several offerings. One is the Information System Network (ISN). It is based on a star topology utilizing twisted-pair cable from a central controller to the attached DTEs.

Figure 23-2 illustrates the major components of ISN. The system employs three buses inside a central controller. The contention bus is dedicated to handling access to the network. The other two are the transmit bus and receive bus. The purpose of the transmit and receive buses is to provide a high-speed interface to components, such as multiplexers or computers. The two input/output modules utilize optic fibers for the transmission media. The central controller directs the traffic into and out of the system through the use of a TDMA arrangement. The DTEs are attached to ISN

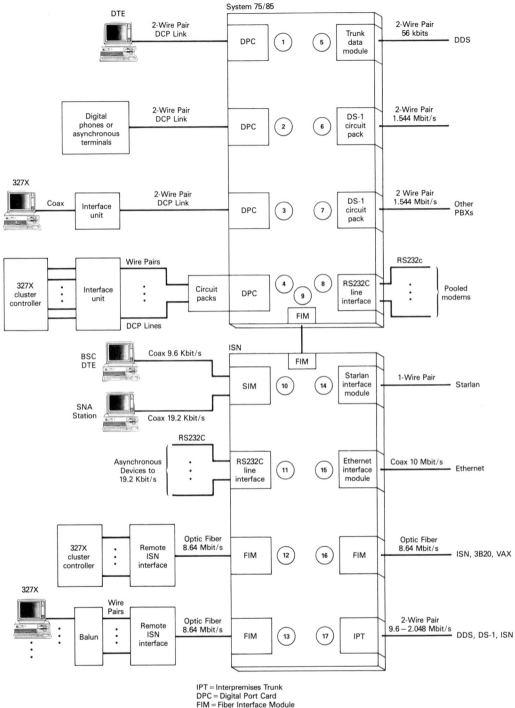

FIGURE 23-1. System 75/85 PBX and the ISN

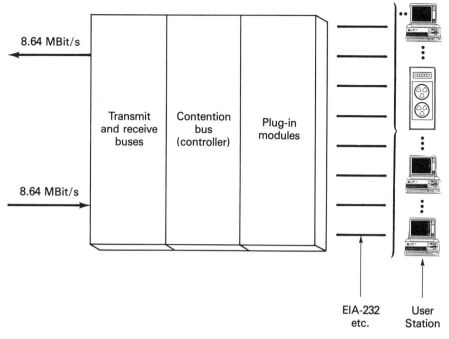

FIGURE 23-2. ISN

through conventional interfaces, such as EIA-232. The contention bus and its associated logic provide the assignment of transmission time slots to the attached DTEs. The actual allocation of the time slots depends on the priority of the request from the DTE and the amount of traffic to be handled.

The TDMA-like controller allocates 50 millisecond (0.050 second) time slots. These short data bursts interleave many packets in a short period of time. AT&T states an ISN can switch up to 48,000 of these small 180-bit packets per second. This equates to the 8.64 Mbit/s rate of all three internal systems.

End-user devices are attached through plug-in modules into the system. Up to 42 plug-in modules representing 336 local devices are supported by a central controller. However, multiple controllers can be attached to each other.

AT&T provides BSC or SDLC device attachments to its ISN. Another enhanced package supports the direct attachment of 3270-family devices. AT&T provides these features, not only for the ISN, but for its System 75 and System 85 PBXs. The support packages also allow the networking of an ISN with a System 75 or 85, interfaces into T1 and Dataphone Digital Service (DDS) offerings, and gateways to Ethernet or Starlan local networks. Moreover, the 3270 adapters allow users to replace 3270 coaxial cable with twisted-pair cable.

The ISN Collision-Free Protocol. The ISN uses a collision-free protocol to manage the transmit bus and receive bus. The contention bus is used to arbitrate the stations' use of two data buses. Let us examine this protocol in more detail.

The ISN contention bus experiences an end-to-end propagation delay of only .025 microsecond. It is designed to permit every attached device to sense every bit transmitted from other devices within one bit time. In other words, a transmitted bit is detected by all stations before another bit is transmitted. This approach allows each station to compare its transmitted bit with the bit on the channel. If they match, the station continues to transmit its 18-bit contention bit code. However, if the transmitted bit does not match the bit on the channel, it is an indication that another station of a higher priority is contending for the channel. The lower-priority station must stop sending its contention code and defer to the "winning" device. The reader may note the similarity of AT&T's approach to that of the ISDN LAN protocol discussed in Chapter 19.

To illustrate how the ISN channel protocol operates, consider a system in which stations A–F are assigned the following contention code priorities (the 18-bit code is shortened to 4 bits for brevity):

A = 1100 . . . .
B = 1000 . . . .
C = 1111 . . . .
D = 0111 . . . .
E = 0011 . . . .
F = 1011 . . . .

It is evident that station C has the highest priority followed by A, F, B, D and E in descending order. As Figure 23-3 shows, the stations transmit their contention codes onto the bus one bit at a time. They read the bus as they send each bit and drop out of the contention when they recognize a 1 bit that does not match their first transmitted 0 bit. The losing stations have their codes raised to a higher priority to increase their chances to gain access to the bus in subsequent contention rounds.

The contention bus operates at 864 Kbit/s, which is one-tenth the speed of the transmit and receive buses (8.64 Mbit/s). Therefore, the 18-bit contention code occupies the same time slot on the contention bus as the 180-bit data packet occupies on the data buses. The conclusion of a contention slot coincides with the beginning of the next transmission and reception time slots. In other words, the n − 1 contention time slot is used for the n data transmission; the n contention is used for the n + 1 data transmission time slot, and so forth. This idea is depicted in Figure 23-4.

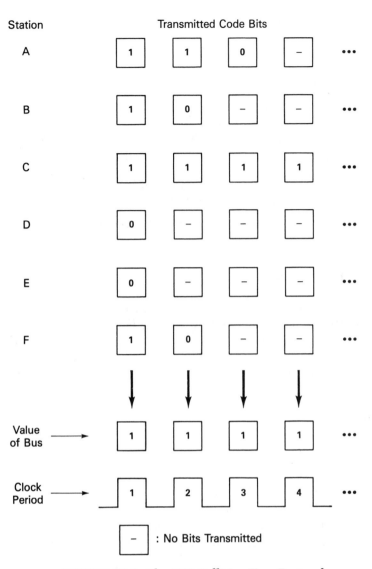

Station | Transmitted Code Bits

A   1   1   0   −   •••

B   1   0   −   −   •••

C   1   1   1   1   •••

D   0   −   −   −   •••

E   0   −   −   −   •••

F   1   0   −   −   •••

Value of Bus →   1   1   1   1   •••

Clock Period →   1   2   3   4   •••

 : No Bits Transmitted

FIGURE 23-3. The ISN Collision-Free Protocol

CONCLUSION

The modern PBXs now support a wide variety of integrated voice/data applications. The technologies of integrated services digital networks (ISDN), packet voice, LANs, and X.25 are finding their way into the architecture of the PBX. In the future, it will be difficult to discern the difference between a PBX and some other data communications components.

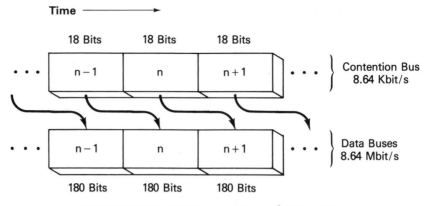

FIGURE 23-4. ISN Contention and Data Bits

SUGGESTED READINGS

The following references are useful introductory PBX tutorials: [BHUS85], [COOV85], [HEAT85] and [WILL84]. [LEUI87] describes options for PBX configurations. [JEWE85] provides a description of the so-called fourth-generation PBXs. [ISN84] provides an excellent description of the AT&T Information Systems Network (ISN).

QUESTIONS

TRUE/FALSE

1. PBXs now integrate voice and data transmissions with one twisted-wire pair cable.
2. PBXs are non-blocking switches.
3. The AT&T ISN uses a star topology.
4. List several attributes of a "fourth-generation" PBX.

SELECTED ANSWERS

1. True.
2. False. Some PBXs are blocking switches.
3. True.

CHAPTER 24

Conclusions and a Look at the Future

Many people are captivated by science fiction novels. Our imaginations can be carried away by reading the fantastic scenarios described in these books. We began this book by stating, "What was once extraordinary is now commonplace." In Chapter 1, we also made reference to some recent advances in computer communications that seem almost like science fiction. A science fiction writer could certainly pen the following (somewhat fanciful) scenario:

An individual is sitting at a workstation with a high-definition television screen. The person speaks to the workstation, and the station responds to the human in the form of a spoken voice. With spoken commands, the individual directs the station to perform tasks. For example, a spoken command could be, "Retrieve profit/loss statements for Department A for fourth quarter of 1988."

Since the user is dealing with a highly intelligent machine, the machine queries the person, "You said statements. Department A has only one profit/loss statement for the fourth quarter of 1988. Do you wish this report for all your departments or, if not, which department do you wish to see?"

The individual responds, "Department A only."

The machine analyzes this information, and determines it is not available locally. It executes several programs dynamically to determine the location of the required information. It then establishes a connection with a high-speed communications network, and retrieves the information from a remote data base—perhaps from another part of the world.

Our human also wishes to have a telephone conversation with a certain department in the company. The person says to the workstation, "Place a call to an account manager I can talk with."

The machine responds, "I assume the account manager is in Department A? By the way, you should not end a sentence with a preposition."

The user replies, "Yes, in Department A. Please turn off your grammar-check logic for this session. I'm not making a speech."

The machine places a branch around its grammar-check logic, retrieves the location of an appropriate account manager and places the telephone call. When the called individual comes on-line, his/her image appears on a window of the lifelike television screen. The two people communicate as if they were talking with each other directly.

In the meantime, the data base retrieval has arrived. However, the speaker is not interrupted. Another window on the screen provides information about the fourth quarter profit/loss. While the station user is engaged in the conversation, he/she uses a pointer on the screen to retrieve "menus" and directs the workstation to perform an analysis of the profit/loss across the industry on a similar product line. The machine then accesses other processors which build programs dynamically to retrieve and model this individual request. While the modeling analysis is being performed, the individual is still engaged in the video-telephone conversation.

During this period, the terminal user also receives an incoming call. The calling individual appears on the screen, states he is Mr. Jones, provides a password, and asks the workstation user for some confidential company information. Since this person does not look familiar, the station user speaks to the workstation, "Give me a face-pattern scan on window two. Verify the identity of this person."

The workstation then sends requests to other machines and data bases to assist in performing a pattern recognition check on the caller's face. If the caller identification is validated by a pattern scan, the workstation is so informed. It responds to the station user, "The caller is indeed Mr. Jones. Please excuse the delay, but Mr. Jones's face varies from our records of his face four months ago, and our neural computer and holography process required several different profile scans."

"What seems to be the difference?" asks the station user.

"Mr. Jones's face is larger," the machine replies.

"What is your inference from this fact?" the station user asks.

"Mr. Jones's face has gained weight," the machine replies.

If the user decides to respond to the call, two separate windows are used for the two conversations. During this time, the terminal user still has sessions ongoing with an account manager and the interactive profit/loss task.

Let us also assume the terminal operator tells the machine to create a letter. An electronic mail system is then accessed which accepts vocal input from the individual, and not only creates the complete letter but also corrects the grammar of the speaker. It allows the user to establish copy recipients, blind copy recipients, delayed and/or expedited deliveries. The machine then uses the "electronic mail system" to distribute the letter and its copies to selected recipients in the far reaches of the world. It also performs language translations, if necessary.

Technical Progress

This scenario can be extended to many other possibilities, and it is not entirely science fiction. Systems are now in place for some types of "intellectual utility." Today, single boards are being developed that provide a conventional personal computer with (a) voice, (b) data, (c) Macintosh-like graphics, and (d) ISDN access. While the "intelligence" of these systems does not remotely compare to that of our science fiction station, we have really only begun our trip into the computer/communications revolution, and systems with extraordinary capabilities will soon enter the mainstream of our lives. Just consider the progress of the last decade and the technical progress we will likely witness before the year 2000.

- Expert systems and artificial intelligence (AI) will play a dramatic role in computers and communications in the future. Currently, researchers at IBM have developed a system that recognizes 20,000 spoken words. It uses 60 million instructions and is relatively expensive. But with the use of AI, expert systems, decreasing chip costs, and faster memory processing, these speaking machines will be in the marketplace soon.
- Miniaturization will continue to reduce the cost of computing at the rate of 20–30% per year. This trend will continue for the next 10 to 15 years.
- The density of components on a chip will increase by a factor of 20 to 40. These processors will probably be 10 times faster than the existing machines.
- Video systems will utilize high-definition television technologies to provide lifelike images.
- Pattern recognition systems will be able to pick out objects such as trees, artwork, and even faces (perhaps not as discerning as our workstation).
- Many computers will be linked together to perform very complex tasks. The use of parallelism (multiple processor units working in conjunction with each other) will make feasible applications which, in the past, were too complex or required too much computing power.
- Memory chips will be available which offer storage capacity of 16 million, 64 million, and perhaps 256 million bits, as a consequence of new techniques in production lithography.

- Disks will increase their storage capacity. It is likely that the continuation of the current trend will see storage densities on the order of 300 million bytes/square inch. Currently, the storage capability is about 20 million bytes/square inch.

Technology and Future Applications

Most sensible people do not try to predict what this future technology will mean in terms of our personal and professional lives. Predictions can be made for the next few years, but technology is advancing and improving at an astounding rate. Some researchers have tried to use mathematical modeling to predict the future, but it has proved inaccurate and somewhat futile.

Nonetheless, while we can only conjecture about the future, the current environment provides many fascinating clues about computers and communications and their likely impact on our lives. A few possibilities are discussed here.

Communications Links. Without question, superconductors are going to have an enormous impact on our world. Ceramic semiconductors carry electricity with near-perfect efficiency at much higher temperatures than the conventional superconductors. It is anticipated that the use of superconductors will radically transform many of our electrically dependent systems.

Optical fibers are already capable of transmission speeds exceeding the gigabit range. Continued progress will see optical systems with speeds exceeding scores of gigabits per second. Without question, optical fiber links will change our thinking about error-prone and low-capacity communications channels.

Optical Processors. Light technology will also have an enormous impact on computing and switching. Earlier discussions in this book explained how optical fibers provide high transmission speeds and reliable transmissions. Today, scientists have demonstrated the ability to operate an optically driven processor at 20 gigabit/s. The speed is over 300% higher than the previously recorded processing speed of a digital processor.

This technology is now being applied to digital switching. The optical switch refracts rays of light to and from optical links, and the switching is controlled by another optical control signal. It is technically feasible today to switch optical waveguides by changing the switch from a transparent to a reflecting mode. Scientists believe switching speeds of less than 1 picosecond (.000000000001 second) are possible. A switch developed by General Electric operates at a rate of 20 to 30 gigabit/s and is smaller than the size of the eye of a dwarf ant.

Optical Storage. Today, personal computer-based products that use read-only optical disks for retrieving information are available. Manufacturers are now placing complete books onto a disk which can be purchased for as little as $200. This *one* disk can contain several dictionaries, thesauruses, almanacs, zip code directories, etc. With the use of software retrieval and expert systems, this information can be accessed, analyzed, sorted, modeled, and integrated into other systems. Indeed, in our science fiction scenario, we could access a word or "look up" something from *Bartlett's Familiar Quotations* by a verbal command to our workstation. We could even ask the station to provide a selection of quotations by a verbal command consisting of key words that would permit a search of the entire book (in a few seconds).

The current technology stores some two billion bits on a disk slightly over 4.7 inches. This device stores over 250,000 pages of text, and this is not considered the state of the art for the technology today. Future systems will use chips to store millions of pages of text.

This writer will risk making the prediction that magnetic rotating disk drives will go the way of the dinosaur: They must physically move, and they move too slowly.

Computing. An earlier reference was made to parallel processing. Presently, a parallel computer has been developed called the connection machine. It incorporates 65,536 processors. Each processor is rather simple, but in tandem they execute several billion instructions per second. It is one of the fastest computers ever constructed.

In addition to parallel processing, reduced instructions set computers (RISC) will reduce the time required to run applications on the computer. These machines have moved into many applications and are now available in the IBM PC accelerator card.

Artificial Intelligence (AI). The speed, capacity, and efficiency of computers and computer networks will be enhanced by "smart" software/firmware to provide services currently beyond our grasp. Our science fiction terminal is only one example.

Much of the research being conducted in AI attempts to describe how the human brain works. While very little about the brain is known, it is believed that the brain functions in a parallel mode during certain problem-solving activities. Conventional computers operate serially: on one instruction and one task at a time. To really achieve the power of computation to solve complex problems and AI operations, parallel processing is needed.

Artificial intelligence (AI) has received much attention in the last 20 years. It describes the use of a computer to "mimic" the activities of the brain. But perhaps a more useful term is "expert system." Expert systems are becoming quite sophisticated today, and they will assume an integral role in our personal and professional lives.

It is common practice today for doctors, engineers, attorneys, etc. to seek the "advice" of expert systems to solve complex problems. Communications networks are now being designed with AI techniques. The formidable tasks of capacity analysis, minimum cuts, and topology design are now performed by software that operates with heuristics. This term describes an expert system that operates by rules that are fed into the system by experts who have "programmed" their knowledge into the software. An automated expert communications designer can perform the following services:

- Establish an initial network layout (a minimum spanning tree).
- Simulate the configuration to determine (a) minimum packet delay, (b) computer loading, (c) computer performance, (d) packet switch performance, and (e) total costs.
- Simulate various reconfigurations and recompute all the factors just mentioned.
- Determine bottlenecks and "recommend" the deletion of nodes and lines.

These complex activities once required many weeks of labor by talented (and expensive) designers. An expert system that can perform these operations now costs only $200,000. It can be used repeatedly. It does not ask for a raise, and it does not resign in the middle of a project to go "across the street" to take a job with a competitor. In the future, it will be possible to purchase a PC board with just such a system on it.

The Promise of AI. Scientists working in the AI field believe certain parts of the human mind can be emulated. They also acknowledge that brain behavior is immensely complex. We take for granted trivial tasks like a three-year-old learning a new word. Yet the programming of learning capabilities into a computer, not to mention the learning of the word itself, is an extremely complicated task. Indeed, it is recognized that for a period of time a young child learns words at a rate of more than 10 per day. Perhaps the most amazing intellectual activity of the human mind is learning a language.

Speech Recognition. As discussed earlier in this chapter, machines that have a fairly large vocabulary already exist. These machines are able to "understand" several thousand words, and they even recognize the "voice print" of the person speaking. It is easy to see how such machines will transform the way many of us do our work. This writer can hardly wait for the first economical voice synthesis word processing/grammar package to come to the marketplace. An actual "talking" machine with considerable inferential capabilities will be available to the public in the near future.

We know much about how to program a computer to recognize words and form comprehensible sentences from those words. To the uninitiated, it seems a rather simple task. After all, of the some 600,000 active words in the English language, only 43 account for half the words actually spoken or written and a mere 9 words account for one-fourth of all utterances. (Can you guess what they are? And, be, have, it, of, the, to, will, you. Are you suprised that the word "I" is not one of the nine words?) Surely a computer can be programmed to recognize and create an intelligible conversation.

But it is not so simple. One of the biggest challenges is programming the computer to discern the nuances of the language. Let me cite an example from an actual experience that occurred in my youth.

After graduating from college in New Mexico and serving a tour in the Navy, I was driving across the country to report to a new job in the "east." I was young, naive, and very provincial. To me, the "east" was a foreign land. Upon nearing the environs of Washington, D.C., my old car stopped running. I walked to the nearest pay phone, searched the yellow pages for help, and placed a call to a local towing service. A man answered the phone and the conversation went something like this:

"Hello, Joe's Towing Service."

"Yes, hello. Look, can you give me a hand? I'm afoot."

Well, most of us know that giving someone a hand is to help them. Well, isn't it? It also means to applaud them, which is also helping them. But the difference between helping and applauding is quite significant as it pertains to social interactions between people.

I think Joe understood the first colloquialism, "Give me a hand," but he certainly did not understand, "I'm afoot." To my provincial ways, the term means: I have no transportation. Yet, some people and cultures (the British, for example) use the term to mean "What's going on?" as in, "What's afoot?"

Can the reader begin to imagine the challenge we face in creating a computer that thinks like a human? In our science fiction scenario, the workstation might have to ask our national origin to determine the meaning of a term in a sentence. We could pursue the discussion almost endlessly (how does the computer adjust to a "Brit" living in New Mexico?). However, let us finish this story about Joe and the towing service.

Joe did not respond to my question for a few moments. When he did respond, it was an incredulous, "You're a what?"

After repeating my statement and receiving the same reply, I became a bit vexed and said, "Look, what is the problem? I'm afoot and I need a hand."

To my bewilderment, Joe shouted back into the phone, "Mister, you are not a foot, you are an ass!" He then hung up, or in the words of the computer, went on hook.

It was readily apparent that Joe and I were not programmed to communicate with each other. Later that day, my eastern friends pointed out the "errors" in my vocabulary. Only at that time did I realize the extent of my communications problems with people from another part of this country. (After reciting this story to one of my friends, his reply was, "Imagine Joe's reaction if you had said, 'can you give me a hand? I'm afoot and I need a tow.'")

On a more serious note, computer-based spoken word recognition is becoming a practical application. It has not reached the point of understanding many of the phrases we take for granted (such as "afoot"), but the technology is progressing rapidly.

Pattern Recognition. A complete and integrated AI system must also perform pattern recognition, i.e., visually recognize and identify objects. Pattern recognition presents enormous problems. Yet, it might intuitively be considered a simple process. After all, a three-year-old child can pick out a tree in a picture. The child can distinguish a tree from a pole, or even one tree from another type of tree. A conventional computer cannot even begin to perform this simple activity.

Nonetheless, research indicates that fairly sophisticated pattern recognition systems will be a reality within a decade. Optical neural computers now exist that emulate the anatomic structure of the brain. They consist of many processors that are extensively connected and internetworked. Successive iterations through a neural computer actually provide the "logic" for the computer to select fairly complex images, such as different types of trees. With the use of AI, the neural computer is able to "train" itself, and does not need a formal, mathematical set of solutions. It only needs a set of possible solutions (a set of pictures of trees, for example).

The Limits of Technologies

One should not overestimate the ability of these upcoming technologies. Many scientists now state that we are very far from realizing the goal of building a computer capable of true intellectual activity. Yet some people continue to believe that computers possess fantastic "intellectual" qualities, and many articles appear about future machines that will "out-think" humans.

In some tasks, computers surely do out-think humans. After all, what human can think through several hundred thousand permutations of a chess game in a few seconds? But this same machine could also conclude that "Mr. Jones's face has gained weight." The conclusion is accurate, but the awkward utterance demonstrates the computer's basic social stupidity (or perhaps it has been programmed with a subtle sense of humor).

We should recognize that the human mind possesses qualities that are presently undefined. Learning and cognition are largely guided by qualities inherent in the genetic makeup of the individual. Recent studies indicate that intelligence is mainly innate and that much of our behavior is based on instinct. It should not be expected that the computer can be designed to assume instinctual qualities. Certainly the computer can fool us into believing it has intelligence, but this supposed intelligence is largely dependent upon the intelligence with which humans program the computer.

So, the sensible approach is to recognize the limits of the computer and at the same time exploit its power to increase our productivity and enhance the quality of our lives.

We have only touched the surface of the power of these machines to bring us comfort and joy. The computer (serving as the expert system) and the communications network (serving as the medium) will assume a monumental role in our future lives. Our journey with this exciting technology has only just begun.

Mathematical, Electrical, And Algebraic Notations

These symbols and terms are used in this book.

Sine:
In a right triangle, the ratio between the side opposite a given angle and the hypotenuse. Notation is $\sin \theta$

Cosine:
In a right triangle, the ratio between the side adjacent to a given angle and the hypotenuse. Notation is $\cos \theta$

Pi:
The 16th letter of the Greek alphabet is used to describe the ratio of the circumference of a circle to its diameter. The ratio is 3.141592. The notation is π

Summation:
The 18th letter of the Greek alphabet is used to denote the sum of algebraic terms. For example, $x_1 + x_2 + x_3 + x_4$ can be shown as:

$$\sum_{i=1}^{4} X_i$$

The notation is read as "The sum of all the terms x_i as i takes on the values from 1 to 4."

Wavelength:
The 11th letter in the Greek alphabet is used to denote wavelength. The notation is λ, and is pronounced lambda. Certain formulas use λ for objects other than wavelength.

Infinity:	In math, an assumed sequence that increases without bound. The notation is ∞.
Inductance:	Defined by the symbol L and measured by the basic unit called a henry, which is noted as H. H is equal to the inductance in which an electromotive force of 1 volt is produced by a current of 1 ampere per second.
Capacitance:	Defined by the symbol C and measured by the basic unit called a farad which is noted as f and is the unit of capacitance equal to the change in the number of colombs of change per volt of charge of potential.
Logarithm:	The exponent of the power to which a base number must be raised to equal a given number. The notation is:

$$\log_x Y$$

Where: x = base and Y = the number. For example:

$$100 = 10^2 \text{ is the same as } \log_{10} 100 = 2$$

Impedance:	The total opposition of a circuit to current. Expressed in ohms and noted with Z (zeta), the 6th letter of the Greek alphabet.
Factorial:	The product of all the integers of a given number x. Noted by x!
	For example: $4! = 4 * 3 * 2 * 1 = 24$
Integral sign:	Used to describe the integral of a function (a limiting value). For example, the notation:

$$\int_1^3 f(x)\, dx$$

means the definite integral of f(x) with respect to x in the internal from x = 1 to x = 3.

Square root:	A quantity of which a given quantity is the square. The notation $\sqrt{\ }$. For example $\sqrt{81} = 9$.
Exclusive Or:	A symbol noting the Boolean joining of two binary values. The rules for its use are described in Chapter 7. The notation is ⊕.

Bibliography

AHO74 Aho, A. V., Hopcroft, J. E., and Ullman, J. D. *The Design and Analysis of Computer Algorithms*. Reading, MA: Addison Wesley, 1974.

AKGU74 Akgun, M. B. "Transmission Objectives for a Subscriber Loop System Digital Voice Code." *International Symposium—Subscriber Loops and Services*. Ottawa, Canada: 1974.

AMOS79 Amos, E. Joel, Jr. "Circuit Switching: Unique Architecture and Applications." *IEEE Computer* June 1979.

ANIK86 "Aniksat: Occasional Use Services." Telesat Canada. Ottawa, Canada: 1986.

ARCH86 Archer, Roland. *The Practical Guide to Local Area Networks*. Berkeley, CA: Osborne, McGraw-Hill, Inc. 1986.

ARON77 Aronson, J. "Data Compression—A Comparison of Methods." National Bureau of Standards, PB-269296. June 1977.

ASH87 Ash, G. R. "Use of Trunk Status Map for Real-Time DNHR." ITC-11. 1987.

AT&T80 AT&T Network Planning Division. *Notes on the Network*. 1980.

AT&T81 AT&T Technical Reference Number 54016. 1981.

AT&T84 AT&T Communications. "AT&T–Telecom Canada Specification of CCITT Signalling System No. 7." Technical Publication Number 34020. July 1984.

AT&T86 AT&T Technical Publication Number 54070. "M44 Multiplexing." September 1986.

AT&T86A AT&T Technical Publication Number 54010. "X.25 Interface Specifications." May 1986.

BATE86 Bates, Richard, and Abramson, Paul. "You Can Use Phone Wire for Your Token Ring LAN." *Data Communications* November 1986.

BECK68 Beckmann, Petr. *Elementary Queuing Theory and Telephone Traffic*. ABC of the Telephone Series. Geneva, IL: 1968.

BEDE86 Bederman, Sy. "Source Routing." *Data Communications* February 1986.

BELL82 Bellamy, John. *Digital Telephony* New York, NY: John Wiley and Sons, 1982.

BELL82A Bell Laboratories. *Transmission Systems for Communications*, Number 500-036. Holmdel, NJ: 1982.

BELLND Figures 5-1 and 5-2 were extracted from several Bell Telephone company manuals: "Communicating and the Telephone," "How the Telephone Works," "Bell's Great Invention." All are available from the local Bell Operating Company office. No Date.

BERN81 Bernstein, Philip A., and Goodman, Nathan. "Concurrency Control in Distributed Data Base Systems." *ACM Computing Surveys* 13, 2 (June 1981).

BERT87 Bertossi, A., Bongiovanni, G., and Bonuccelli, M. "Time Slot Assignment in SS/TDMA Systems with Intersatellite Links." *IEEE Transactions on Communications* COM-35, 6 (June 1987).

BHUS85   Bhushan, Briij, and Opderbeck, Holger. "The Evolution of Data Switching for PBX's." *IEEE Journal* July 1985.

BLAC82   Black, Uyless D. "Data Link Controls: The Great Variety Calls for Wise and Careful Choices." *Data Communications* June 12, 1982.

BLAC86   Black, Uyless. *Physical Interfaces*. Arlington, VA: Information Engineering Educational Series, 1986.

BLAC86A   Black, Uyless. *HDLC: High Level Data Link Control*. Arlington, VA: Information Engineering Educational Series, 1986.

BLAC87   Black, Uyless. Symposium on Data Communications. London, England: October 1987.

BLAC87A   Black, Uyless. *Communications: An Introduction*. Arlington, VA: Information Engineering Educational Series, 1987.

BLAC87B   Black, Uyless. *Data Communications and Distributed Networks*. Englewood Cliffs, NJ: Prentice-Hall, Inc., 1987.

BLAC87C   Black, Uyless. *Computer Networks: Protocols, Standards and Interfaces*. Englewood Cliffs, NJ: Prentice-Hall, Inc., 1987.

BLAC88   Black, Uyless. *Physical Level Interfaces and Protocols*. Washington, DC: IEEE Computer Society Press, 1988.

BUNN85   Bunn, Christopher R. "Message Handling Systems and Their Protocols." *Open Systems Data Transfer*. Vienna, VA: Omnicom, Inc. June 1985.

BURK56   Burke, J. "The Output of a Queuing System." *Operations Research* 4 (December 1956).

BUX86   Bux, Werner, and Pitt, Daniel. "Flow Control." *Data Communications*. February 1986.

CALL83   Callon, R. "Internetwork Protocols." *Proceedings of the IEEE*. December 1983.

CAMP84   Campbell, Joe. *The RS-232 Solution*. Berkeley, CA: Sybex, Inc., 1984.

CERF78   Cerf, V., and Kristein, P. T. "Issues in Packet-Network Interconnection." *Proceedings of the IEEE*. November 1978.

CHU73   Chu, W. "Asynchronous Time-Division Multiplexing Systems." *Computer Communications Networks*. Englewood Cliffs, NJ: Prentice-Hall, Inc., 1973.

CHU84   Chu, W., ed. *Computer Communications, Vol II: System and Applications*.

Englewood Cliffs, NJ: Prentice-Hall, Inc., 1984.

CLEMND   Clement, M. A. *Transmission*. Chicago, IL: Telephony Publishing Corp., no date.

CONA80   Conard, James W. "Character-Oriented Data Link Control Protocols." *IEEE Transactions on Communications*. April 1980.

COOP81   Cooper, R. B. *Introduction to Queuing Theory*, 2nd ed. New York, NY: North Holland Press, 1981.

COOV85   Coover, Edwin R., and Kane, Michael J. "Notes from Mid-Revolution: Searching for the Perfect PBX." *Data Communications* August 1985.

COUC83   Couch, L. *Digital and Analog Communications Systems*. New York, NY: Macmillan Publishing Company, 1983.

CROC83   Crochier, R. E., and Flanagan, J. L. "Current Perspectives in Digital Speech." *IEEE Communications Magazine*. January 1983.

CRUT86   Crutchfield, J. P. "Chaos." *Scientific American* May 1986.

DAVI86   Davison, Wayne E. "Upper Layer Architecture." *Open Systems Data Transfer*. Vienna, VA: Omnicom, Inc., February 1986.

DECN82   *DECnet Digital Network Architecture*, Document Number AA-X435A-TK. Maynard, MA: Digital Equipment Corporation, May 1982.

DECN82A   *DECnet* Publication Number AA-N149A-TC Maynard, MA: Digital Equipment Corporation, May 1982.

DERF83   Derfler, F., and Stallings, W. *A Managers Guide to Local Networks*. Englewood Cliffs, NJ: Prentice-Hall/Spectrum, 1983.

DIJK59   Dijkstra, E. "A Note on Two Problems in Connection with Graphs." *Numerical Mathematics* October 1959.

DOLL78   Doll, D. R. *Data Communications: Facilities, Networks and System Design*. New York, NY: John Wiley & Sons, 1978.

DONO86   Donohoe, Douglas C., Johannessen, Grant H., and Stone, Roger E. "Realization of a Signaling System No. 7 Network for AT & T." *IEEE Journal—Selected Areas in Communications* SAC–4 (November 6, 1986)

DURR84   Durr, Michael. *Networking IBM PCs*. Indianapolis, IN: Que Corporation, 1984.

ECMA79 ECMA-61. HDLC, European Computer Manufacturers Association. August 1979.

EVAN86 Evans, Alvis J. *Antennas: Selection and Installation*. Fort Worth, TX: Tandy Corporation, 1986.

FALE87 Falek, James I., and Johnston, Mary A. "Standards Makes Cementing ISDN Subnetwork Layers." *Data Communications* October 1987.

FIEL86 Field, J. "Logical Link Control." Proceedings, *IEEE Infocom '86* April 1986.

FIPS80 "Guideline for Implementing Advanced Data Communication Control Procedures." Federal Information Processing Standards Publication 78. September 1980.

FLAN86 Flanagan, William A. *The Teleconnect Guide to T-1 Networking*. New York, NY: Telecom Library, 1986.

FLET82 Fletcher, John G. "An Arithmetic Checksum for Serial Transmission." *IEEE Transactions on Communications*, 30, 1 (January 1982).

GAGG87 Gaggioni, H. P. "The Evolution of Video Technologies." *IEEE Communications Magazine* November 1987.

GECS83 Gecsci, J. *The Architecture of Videotex Systems*. Englewood Cliffs, NJ: Prentice-Hall, Inc., 1983.

GOFT86 Gofton, Peter W. *Mastering Serial Communications*. Berkeley, CA: Sybex, Inc., 1986.

GOSI87 *U.S. Government Open Systems Interconnection Profile (GOSIP)*. Gaithersburg, MD: National Bureau of Standards, April 22, 1987.

GREE86 Green, James H. "Microcomputer Programs Can Be Adapted for Data Network Designs." *Data Communications* April 1986.

GREE87 Green, P. E., Jr., and Godard, D. N. "Prospects and Design Choices for Integrated Private Networks." *IBM Systems Journal* 26, 1 (1987).

GROB71 Grob, Bernard. *Basic Electronics*. New York, NY: McGraw-Hill, Inc., 1971.

HAMM50 Hamming, R. W. "Error Detecting and Error Correcting Codes." *Bell System Technical Journal* April 1950.

HART28 Hartley, R. V. L. "Theory of Information." *Bell System Technical Journal* 1928.

HAYE83 *Hardware Reference Manual for the IBM Personal Computer*. Norcross, GA: Hayes Microcomputer Products, Inc., 1983.

HEAT81 "Electronic Communications." Benton Harbor, MI: Heath Company, 1981.

HEAT85 Heather, John A. "Integrated PBX's: The Solution to Information Management Needs." *Telecommunications* February 1985.

HEGG85 Heggestad, H. M. "The Testbed for Evaluation of Network Routing and Control Techniques." MICOM 85. October 1985.

HELD84 Held, Gilbert. *Data Compression*. New York, NY: John Wiley & Sons, 1984.

HEYD87 Heyden, Thomas Van Der. "New Focus on TDMA in Satellite Technology." *Telephony* August 24, 1987.

HOPK79 Hopkins, G. "Multimode Communications on the MITRENET." *Proceedings, Local Area Communications Network Symposium* 1979.

HOPK80 Hopkins, G. T., and Wagner, D. E. "Multiple Access Digital Communications System." U.S. Patent 4,210,780. July 1, 1980.

HOSK87 Hoskins, Jim. *IBM Personal System/2*. New York, NY: John Wiley & Sons, 1987.

HURL87 Hurley, B. R., Seidl, C. J. R., and Sewell, W. F. "A Survey of Dynamic Routing Methods for Circuit Switched Traffic." *IEEE Communications Magazine* 25, 9 (September 1987).

IBM70 *Binary Synchronous Communications*. GA27-3004-2. IBM Corp., 1970.

IBM81 *Systems Network Architecture*. GC30-3072. IBM Corp., 1981.

IEEE83 "Special Issue on OSI." *Proceedings of the IEEE*. New York, NY: December 1983.

ISN84 "Information Systems Network." AT&T Information Systems. June 1984.

JACK57 Jackson, J. R. "Networks of Waiting Lines." *Operations Research* 5 (August 1957).

JEWE76 Jewell, G. C. "Text Compaction for Information Retrieval Systems." *IEEE SMC Newsletter*, 5, 1 (1976).

JEWE85 Jewett, Roger F. "The Fourth-Generation PBX: Beyond the Integration of Voice and Data." *Telecommunications* February 1985.

JORD83 Jordan, Larry E., and Churchill, Bruce. *Communications and Networking for the IBM PC*. Bowie, MD: Robert J. Brady Company, 1983.

JUDI87 Judice, C. N., and LeGall, D. "Telematic Services and Terminals: Are We Ready?" *IEEE Communications Magazine* 25, 7 (July 1987).

JURE81 Jurenko, John A. "All About Modems and Related Topics." Huntsville, AL: Universal Data Systems, 1981.

KASS86 Kasson, J. M. "An Advanced Voice/Data Telephone Switching System." *IBM Systems Journal* 25, 314 (1986).

KLEI86 Klein, Lloyd, ed.. *Digital Switching Systems*. Ottawa, Ontario, Canada: Bell Northern Research, 1986.

LANG86 Langley, Graham. *Telecommunications Primer*. London, England: Pittman Publishing, 1986.

LARM85 Larmouth, John. "Common Application Service Element (CASE) Standardization." *Open System Data Transfer*. Vienna, VA: Omnicom, Inc., December 1985.

LEE73 Lee, Frank L. "Telephone Theory, Principles and Practice." Geneva, IL: 1973.

LEE86 Lee, Edward H. "A BOC Explains Where the Bits Went." *Data Communications* June 1986.

LEVI87 Levin, David. "Private Branch Exchanges: The Best Time to Shop May Be Right Now." *Data Communications* August 1987.

LEWA86 Lewan, Douglas. "Elements of the FTAM Standard." *Open Systems Data Transfer*. Vienna, VA: Omnicom, Inc., October 1986.

LEWI87 Lewis, Jamie. *LAN Operating Systems Report*. Provo, UT: Novell, Inc., 1987.

LIN84 Lin, Shu, Costello, Daniel, Jr., and Miller, Michael. "Automatic-Repeat-Request Error Control Schemes." *IEEE Communications Magazine*, 22, 12 (December 1984).

LINN87 Linnell, Dennis. *SNA Concepts Design and Implementation*. McLean, VA: Gate Technology, 1987.

LIPP85 Lippman, R. "New Routing and Preemption Algorithms for Circuit-Switched Mixed Media Networks." MILCOM 85. October 1985.

LITT61 Little, J. D. C. "A Proof of the Queuing Formula L = $\lambda\omega,^n$." *Operations Research* 9, 3 (1961).

MALA88 Malamud, Carl. "Digital Systems and Architectures." A Workbook Prepared for Information Engineering Institute. Falls Church, VA: 1988.

MART72 Martin, James. *Systems Analysis for Data Transmission*. Englewood Cliffs, NJ: Prentice-Hall, Inc., 1972.

MART76 Martin, James. *Telecommunications and the Computer*. Englewood Cliffs, NJ: Prentice-Hall, Inc., 1976.

MART87 Martin, James, and Chapman, Kathleen Kavanagh. *SNA IBM's Networking Solution*. Englewood Cliffs, NJ: Prentice-Hall, Inc., 1987.

MCNA82 McNamara, John E. *Technical Aspects of Data Communication*. 2nd ed., Bedford, MA: Digital Press, 1982.

METC76 Metcalfe, R. M., and Boggs, D. R. "Ethernet: Distributed Packet Switching for Local Computer Networks." *Communications of the ACM* July 1976.

METC77 Metcalfe, R. M., Boggs, D. R., Thacker, C. P., and Lampson, B. W. "Multipoint Data Communication System with Collision Detection." U.S. Patent 4,063,220. 1977

MIER85 Mier, Edwin R. "Long Overdue, T1 Takes Off—But Where Is It Heading?" *Data Communications* June 1985.

MIER86 Mier, Edwin E. "Brewing Standards Conflict Blurs Fiber Optic's Future." *Data Communications* February 1986.

MIER86A Mier, Edwin E. "Comparing the Long-Distance Carriers." *Data Communications* August 1986.

MIER86B Mier, Edwin E. "How AT&T Plans to Conquer Voice-Data Integrations." *Data Communications* July 1986.

MILL79 Miller, James H. "Grounding." *Lee's ABC of the Telephone*. Geneva, IL: 1979.

MOTO86 "The X.25 Protocol Controller (XPC)." Motorola Technical Summary Number MC68605. Pheonix, AZ: 1986.

MOUS86 Mousseau, Kevin J. "Digital Microwave Radio: Determining First Fresnel Zone Clearances." *Telephony* March 3, 1986.

MULL85 Mullaney, John. "PBX's and LAN's: The Missing Link." *Telecommunications* February 1985.

NARE82 Narendra, K. S., and Srikantakumer, P. R. "A Learning Model for Routing in Telephone Networks." *SIAM Journal of Control and Optimization*, 20, 1 (January 1982).

NBS80 National Bureau of Standards. "Features of Internetwork Protocol." ICSJ/HCNP 80-8.

NEAL76 Neal, S. R., and Hill, D. W. "Traffic Capacity of a Probability-Engineered Trunk Group." *Bell System Technical Journal* Number 55:831-842. 1976.

NELS75 Nelson, Kenneth C. "Understanding Station Carrier." *Lee's ABC of the Telephone*. Geneva, IL: 1975.

NEWM84 Newman, Hannah. "Presentation Layer Syntaxes For Videotex." *Open Systems Data Transfer*. Vienna, VA: Omnicom, Inc., December 1984.

NOGU86 Noguchi, T., Daido, Y., and Nossek, J. A. "Modulation Techniques for Microwave Digital Radio." *IEEE Communications Magazine* 24, 10 (October 1986).

NYQU24 Nyquist, H. "Certain Factors Affecting Telegraph Speed." *Transactions A.I.E.E*, 1924.

OLSO86 Olson, M. L., Johnson, D., and Arst, P. L. "Interactive Networking with a Satellite." *Data Communications* April 1986.

OMNI85 *Open Systems Handbook*, Omnicom Information Service. Vienna, VA: February 1985.

OMNI87 *OSI Upper Layer Applications Protocols*. Vienna, VA: Omnicom, Inc., 1987.

PAPO84 Papoulis, A. *Probability, Random Variables and Stochastic Processes*, 2nd ed. New York, NY: McGraw-Hill, Inc. 1984.

PAYT85 Payton, John, and Qureshi, Shahid. "Trellis Encoding: What It Is and How It Affects Data Transmission." *Data Communications* May 1985.

PETE61 Peterson, W., and Brown, D. "Cyclic Codes for Error Detection." *Proceedings of the IRE* January 1961.

PETE78 Peterson, J. L., Bitner, J. R., and Howard, J. H. "The Selection of Optimal Tab Settings." *The Communications of the ACM*, 21, 12 (1978).

PICK83 Pickens, R. "Wideband Transmission Media I: Radio Communication." *Computer Communications*, vol I: Principles. Englewood Cliffs, NJ: Prentice-Hall, Inc., 1983.

PIER80 Pierce, John R. *An Introduction to Information Theory*. New York, NY: Dover Publications, Inc., 1980.

POUS83 Poussard, Trevor. "The X.22 Interface: An Economic Standard for Multiplexing." *Data Communications* September 1983.

REGH81 Reghbati, H. K. "An Overview of Data Compression Techniques." *IEEE Computer* April 1981.

REY83 Rey, R. F., technical ed. *Engineering and Operations in the Bell System*, 2nd ed. Murray Hill, NJ: AT & T Laboratories, 1983.

RICH85 Richwell, Gunnar. "The Remote Information Station as a Voice/Data Terminal." *Telecommunications* February 1985.

RILE76 Riley, Eugene W., and Acuna, Victor E. "Transmission Systems." *Lee's ABC of the Telephone*. Geneva, IL: 1976.

ROSN82 Rosner, Roy D. *Distributed Telecommunications Networks*. Belmont, CA: Lifetime Learning Publications, 1982.

ROUT87 Routt, Thomas J. "SNA to OSI: IBM Building Upper-Layer Gateways." *Data Communications* May 1987.

ROUT87A Routt, Thomas, J. "Distributed SNA: A Network Architecture Gets on Track." *Data Communications* February 1987.

RUBE84 Rubenstein, Polly, and Smith, Glenn. "The Async Route—Best Suited for a Microcomputer's Local Traffic." *Data Communications* October 1984.

RUBI76 Rubin, F. "Experiments in Text File Compression." *Communications of the ACM*, 19, 11 (1976).

RUFF87 Ruffalo, Daniel R. "Understanding T1 Basics: Prime Offers Picture of Networking Future." *Data Communications* March 1987.

RUTH72 Ruth, S., and Kreutzer, P. "Data Compression for Large Business Files." *Datamation*, 18, 9 (1972).

RYAN86 Ryan, Donald J. "Making Sense of Today's Image Communications Alternatives." *Data Communications* April 1987.

SATY61 Saty, T. L. *Elements of Queuing Theory*. New York, NY: McGraw-Hill, Inc. 1961

SCHL86 Schlanger, G. Gary. "An Overview of Signaling System No. 7." *IEEE Journal of Selected Areas in Communications* SAC-4, 3 (May 1986).

SCHW77 Schwartz, M. *Computer-Communication Network Design and Analysis*. Englewood Cliffs, NJ: Prentice-Hall, Inc., 1977.

SCHW80 Schwartz, M., and Stern, T. E. "Routing Techniques Used in Computer

Communications Networks." *IEEE Transactions on Communications* April 1980.

SCHW87 Schwartz, Misha. *Telecommunications Networks: Protocols, Modeling and Analysis*. Addison-Wesley Publishing Company. Reading MA: 1987.

SEYE84 Seyer, Martin D. *RS-232 Made Easy*. Englewood Cliffs, NJ: Prentice-Hall, Inc., 1984.

SHAN48 Shannon, C. "Mathematical Theory of Communication." *Bell System Technical Journal 27* (July and October 1948).

SHAR87 Sharma, Ranjana. "Satellite Network Design Parameters and Trade-Off Analysis." *Telecommunications* August 24, 1987.

SHER85 Sherman, Ken. *Data Communications: A Users Guide*. Reston, VA: Reston Publishing Company, Inc., 1985.

SIMO79 Simon, J. M., and Danet, A. "Controle des Ressources et Principes du Routage dans le Reseau Transpac." *Symposium on Flow Control in Computer Networks*. Versailles, France: February 1979.

SIMP86 X.25 Switched Virtual Interface, DC 900-0144. San Diego, CA: Simpact Associates, Inc., 1986.

SMIT87 Smith, Bud E., and Johnson, Mark T. *Programming the Intel 80386*. Glenview, IL: Scott, Foresman and Co., 1987.

SPIL77 Spilker, J. *Digital Communications by Satellite*. Englewood Cliffs, NJ: Prentice-Hall, Inc., 1977.

STAL84 Stallings, William. *Local Networks an Introduction*. London, England: Macmillan Publishing Company, 1984.

STAL85 Stallings, William. *Data and Computer Communications*. New York, NY: Macmillan Publishing Company, 1985.

STAL86 Stallings, William. "Here is One Way to Get a Close Estimate of a Data Link's Efficiency." *Data Communications* October 1986.

STAL87 Stallings, William. *Handbook of Computer-Communications Standards, vol. 2*. New York, NY: Macmillan Publishing Company, 1987.

STEW84 Stewart, B., Hawe, B., and Kriby, A. "Local Area Network Connection." *Telecommunications* April 1984.

STRO86 Strole, Norman C. "Overview: How IBM Addresses LAN Requirements with the Token Ring." *Data Communications* February 1986.

TAKA62 Takacs, L. *Introduction to the Theory of Queues*. New York, NY: Oxford University Press, 1962.

TALL87 Talley, David. *Basic Telephone Switching Systems*. Rochelle Park, NJ: Hayden Book Company, Inc., 1987.

TANE81 Tanebaum, Andrew S. *Computer Networks*. Englewood Cliffs, NJ: Prentice-Hall, Inc., 1981.

TCP83 *Transmission Control Protocol*. Military Standard, MIL-STD-1778. Washington DC: U.S. Department of Defense, November 20, 1983.

TELE86 "Telesat Report," 1, 3. Telesat Canada. Ottawa, Canada: Fall 1986.

TYDE82 Tydeman, J., Lipinski, H, Adler, R., Nyhan, M., and Zwimpter, L. *Teletext and Videotext in the United States*. New York, NY: McGraw-Hill, Inc. 1982.

VAXO86 "VAX OSI Transport Service." Document Number AA-HA89B-TE. Digital Equipment Corp., 1986.

VERI86 "The Book on ESF." San Jose, CA: The Verilink Corp., 1986.

VITE67 Viterbi, A. J. "Error Bounds for Convolutional Codes and an Asymptotically Optimum Decoding Algorithm." IEEE Transactions, Information Theory (IT)-13. April 1967.

VITE79 Viterbi, A. J., and Omura, J. K. *Principles of Digital Communication and Coding*. New York, NY: McGraw-Hill, Inc. 1979.

WATE87 Waters, Dennis P. "Surfacing: FM Radio Provides a New Alternative for Carrying Data." *Data Communications* July 1987.

WATK81 Watkins, Rick. *Data Communications Protocols*. Denton, TX: Micro Development, Inc., 1981.

WILK56 Wilkinson, R. I. "Theories for Toll Traffic Engineering in the USA." *Bell Systems Technical Journal*. Number 35:421-514. 1956.

WILL84 Williamson, John. "Office Automation: PABXs and LANs." *Telephony* September 1984.

WITT85 Wittmann, William J. "Will Your Voice/Data PABX System Meet Future Needs?" *Telecommunications* February 1985.

Index